Core Statutes on **Contract, Tort & Restitution** — Graham Stephenson

Core Statutes on **Criminal Law** — Mark James

Core Statutes on **Family Law** — Amanda Millmore

Core Statutes on **Property Law** — Peter Luther & Alan Moran

Core Statutes on **Company Law** — Gowan Ervine

Core Statutes on **Employment Law** — Rachel Horton

Core Statutes on **Commercial & Consumer Law** — Graham Stephenson

Core **EU Legislation** — Paul Drury

Core Statutes on **Conflict of Laws** — Emmanuel Maganaris

    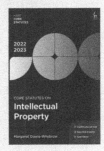

Core Statutes on **Criminal Justice & Sentencing** — Martin Wasik

Core Statutes on **Evidence** — Jonathan McGahan

Core Documents on **International Law** — Karen Hulme

Core Documents on **European & International Human Rights** — Rhona Smith

Core Statutes on **Intellectual Property** — Margaret Dowie-Whybrow

The Hart Core Statutes series has been developed to meet the needs of today's law students. Compiled by experienced lecturers, each title contains the essential materials needed at LLB level and, where applicable, on GDL/CPE courses. They are specifically designed to be easy to use under exam conditions and in the lecture hall.

https://www.bloomsbury.com/uk/series/hart-core-statutes/

# ·HART·

OXFORD · LONDON · NEW YORK · NEW DELHI · SYDNEY

HART PUBLISHING

Bloomsbury Publishing Plc

Kemp House, Chawley Park, Cumnor Hill, Oxford, OX2 9PH, UK

1385 Broadway, New York, NY 10018, USA

29 Earlsfort Terrace, Dublin 2, Ireland

HART PUBLISHING, the Hart/Stag logo, BLOOMSBURY and the Diana logo are
trademarks of Bloomsbury Publishing Plc

Previous editions published by Red Globe Press.

Copyright © Rachel Horton, 2022

Rachel Horton has asserted their right under the Copyright, Designs and Patents
Act 1988 to be identified as Author of this work.

All rights reserved. No part of this publication may be reproduced or transmitted in any form or by any means,
electronic or mechanical, including photocopying, recording, or any information storage or retrieval system,
without prior permission in writing from the publishers.

While every care has been taken to ensure the accuracy of this work, no responsibility for loss or damage
occasioned to any person acting or refraining from action as a result of any statement in it can be
accepted by the authors, editors or publishers.

All UK Government legislation and other public sector information used in the work is Crown Copyright ©.
All House of Lords and House of Commons information used in the work is Parliamentary Copyright ©.
This information is reused under the terms of the Open Government Licence v3.0 (http://www.
nationalarchives.gov.uk/doc/open-government-licence/version/3) except where otherwise stated.

A catalogue record for this book is available from the British Library.

A catalogue record for this book is available from the Library of Congress.

| ISBN: | PB: | 978-1-50996-223-5 |
| | ePDF: | 978-1-50996-225-9 |
| | ePub: | 978-1-50996-224-2 |

Typeset by Compuscript Ltd, Shannon

To find out more about our authors and books visit www.hartpublishing.co.uk.
Here you will find extracts, author information, details of forthcoming events
and the option to sign up for our newsletters.

# CONTENTS

# ALPHABETICAL LIST OF CONTENTS

# PREFACE

Dear Reader,

Thank you for buying this edition of *Core Statutes on Employment Law 2022–23*. As you know, employment law is a very fast moving and exciting area of law and there is scope to study it from several different perspectives. In compiling this collection I have selected the 'core' primary and secondary employment legislation relevant to courses in employment law, labour law and industrial relations law at both undergraduate and postgraduate levels. In recent years there has been an increase in academic attention to the role of human rights in the workplace and so this edition includes relevant sections of the Human Rights Act 1998 and European Convention on Human Rights, as well as extracts from the Modern Slavery Act 2015. It also includes sections from the European Union (Withdrawal) Act 2018. I hope it will be a useful source for anyone who needs quick-and-easy access to up-to-date employment legislation. As an unannotated collection of legislation, it will be appropriate for students who are permitted to take statutes into their exams. Good luck with your studies and I hope you enjoy employment law as much as I do!

In this edition the law is generally stated as at June 2022.

*Rachel Horton*
*June 2022*

# STATUTES

## TRADE UNION AND LABOUR RELATIONS (CONSOLIDATION) ACT 1992
### (1992, c. 52)

*Meaning of 'trade union'*

**1 Meaning of 'trade union'**

In this Act a 'trade union' means an organisation (whether temporary or permanent)—

    (a) which consists wholly or mainly of workers of one or more descriptions and whose principal purposes include the regulation of relations between workers of that description or those descriptions and employers or employers' associations; or

    (b) which consists wholly or mainly of—

        (i) constituent or affiliated organisations which fulfil the conditions in paragraph (a) (or themselves consist wholly or mainly of constituent or affiliated organisations which fulfil those conditions), or

        (ii) representatives of such constituent or affiliated organisations,

and whose principal purposes include the regulation of relations between workers and employers or between workers and employers' associations, or the regulation of relations between its constituent or affiliated organisations.

*The list of trade unions*

**2 The list of trade unions**

(1) The Certification Officer shall keep a list of trade unions containing the names of—

    (a) the organisations whose names were, immediately before the commencement of this Act, duly entered in the list of trade unions kept by him under section 8 of the Trade Union and Labour Relations Act 1974, and

    (b) the names of the organisations entitled to have their names entered in the list in accordance with this Part.

(2) The Certification Officer shall keep copies of the list of trade unions, as for the time being in force, available for public inspection at all reasonable hours free of charge.

(3) A copy of the list shall be included in his annual report.

(4) The fact that the name of an organisation is included in the list of trade unions is evidence (in Scotland, sufficient evidence) that the organisation is a trade union.

(5) On the application of an organisation whose name is included in the list, the Certification Officer shall issue it with a certificate to that effect.

(6) A document purporting to be such a certificate is evidence (in Scotland, sufficient evidence) that the name of the organisation is entered in the list.

**3 Application to have name entered in the list**

(1) An organisation of workers, whenever formed, whose name is not entered in the list of trade unions may apply to the Certification Officer to have its name entered in the list.

(2) The application shall be made in such form and manner as the Certification Officer may require and shall be accompanied by—

    (a) a copy of the rules of the organisation,

    (b) a list of its officers,

    (c) the address of its head or main office, and

    (d) the name under which it is or is to be known,

and by the prescribed fee.

(3) If the Certification Officer is satisfied—
  (a) that the organisation is a trade union,
  (b) that subsection (2) has been complied with, and
  (c) that entry of the name in the list is not prohibited by subsection (4),
  he shall enter the name of the organisation in the list of trade unions.

(4) The Certification Officer shall not enter the name of an organisation in the list of trade unions if the name is the same as that under which another organisation—
  (a) was on 30 September 1971 registered as a trade union under the Trade Union Acts 1871 to 1964,
  (b) was at any time registered as a trade union or employers' association under the Industrial Relations Act 1971, or
  (c) is for the time being entered in the list of trade unions or in the list of employers' associations kept under Part II of this Act,
  or if the name is one so nearly resembling any such name as to be likely to deceive the public.

## 4 Removal of name from the list

(1) If it appears to the Certification Officer, on application made to him or otherwise, that an organisation whose name is entered in the list of trade unions is not a trade union, he may remove its name from the list.

(2) He shall not do so without giving the organisation notice of his intention and considering any representations made to him by the organisation within such period (of not less than 28 days beginning with the date of the notice) as may be specified in the notice.

(3) The Certification Officer shall remove the name of an organisation from the list of trade unions if—
  (a) he is requested by the organisation to do so, or
  (b) he is satisfied that the organisation has ceased to exist.

*Certification as independent trade union*

## 5 Meaning of 'independent trade union'

In this Act an 'independent trade union' means a trade union which—
  (a) is not under the domination or control of an employer or group of employers or of one or more employers' associations, and
  (b) is not liable to interference by an employer or any such group or association (arising out of the provision of financial or material support or by any other means whatsoever) tending towards such control;
and references to 'independence', in relation to a trade union, shall be construed accordingly.

## 6 Application for certificate of independence

(1) A trade union whose name is entered on the list of trade unions may apply to the Certification Officer for a certificate that it is independent.
  The application shall be made in such form and manner as the Certification Officer may require and shall be accompanied by the prescribed fee.

(2) The Certification Officer shall maintain a record showing details of all applications made to him under this section and shall keep it available for public inspection (free of charge) at all reasonable hours.

(3) If an application is made by a trade union whose name is not entered on the list of trade unions, the Certification Officer shall refuse a certificate of independence and shall enter that refusal on the record.

(4) In any other case, he shall not come to a decision on the application before the end of the period of one month after it has been entered on the record; and before coming to his decision he shall make such enquiries as he thinks fit and shall take into account any relevant information submitted to him by any person.

(5) He shall then decide whether the applicant trade union is independent and shall enter his decision and the date of his decision on the record.

(6) If he decides that the trade union is independent he shall issue a certificate accordingly; and if he decides that it is not, he shall give reasons for his decision.

## 7    Withdrawal or cancellation of certificate

(1)   The Certification Officer may withdraw a trade union's certificate of independence if he is of the opinion that the union is no longer independent.

(2)   Where he proposes to do so he shall notify the trade union and enter notice of the proposal in the record.

(3)   He shall not come to a decision on the proposal before the end of the period of one month after notice of it was entered on the record; and before coming to his decision he shall make such enquiries as he thinks fit and shall take into account any relevant information submitted to him by any person.

(4)   He shall then decide whether the trade union is independent and shall enter his decision and the date of his decision on the record.

(5)   He shall confirm or withdraw the certificate accordingly; and if he decides to withdraw it, he shall give reasons for his decision.

(6)   Where the name of an organisation is removed from the list of trade unions, the Certification Officer shall cancel any certificate of independence in force in respect of that organisation by entering on the record the fact that the organisation's name has been removed from that list and that the certificate is accordingly cancelled.

## 8    Conclusive effect of Certification Officer's decision

(1)   A certificate of independence which is in force is conclusive evidence for all purposes that a trade union is independent; and a refusal, withdrawal or cancellation of a certificate of independence, entered on the record, is conclusive evidence for all purposes that a trade union is not independent.

(2)   A document purporting to be a certificate of independence and to be signed by the Certification Officer, or by a person authorised to act on his behalf, shall be taken to be such a certificate unless the contrary is proved.

(3)   A document purporting to be a certified copy of an entry on the record and to be signed by the Certification Officer, or by a person authorised to act on his behalf, shall be taken to be a true copy of such an entry unless the contrary is proved.

(4)   If in any proceedings before a court, the Employment Appeal Tribunal, the Central Arbitration Committee, ACAS or an employment tribunal a question arises whether a trade union is independent and there is no certificate of independence in force and no refusal, withdrawal or cancellation of a certificate recorded in relation to that trade union—

(a)    that question shall not be decided in those proceedings, and

(b)    the proceedings shall instead be stayed or sisted until a certificate of independence has been issued or refused by the Certification Officer.

(5)   The body before whom the proceedings are stayed or sisted may refer the question of the independence of the trade union to the Certification Officer who shall proceed in accordance with section 6 as on an application by that trade union.

*Supplementary*

## 9    Appeal against decision of Certification Officer

(1)   An organisation aggrieved by the refusal of the Certification Officer to enter its name in the list of trade unions, or by a decision of his to remove its name from the list, may appeal to the Employment Appeal Tribunal.

(2)   A trade union aggrieved by the refusal of the Certification Officer to issue it with a certificate of independence, or by a decision of his to withdraw its certificate, may appeal to the Employment Appeal Tribunal.

(3)   If on appeal the Tribunal is satisfied that the organisation's name should be or remain entered in the list or, as the case may be, that the certificate should be issued or should not be withdrawn, it shall declare that fact and give directions to the Certification Officer accordingly.

(4)   The rights of appeal conferred by this section extend to any question of fact or law arising in the proceedings before, or arising from the decision of, the Certification Officer.

CHAPTER II
STATUS AND PROPERTY OF TRADE UNIONS

*General*

## 10   Quasi-corporate status of trade unions

(1)   A trade union is not a body corporate but—

   (a)   it is capable of making contracts;

   (b)   it is capable of suing and being sued in its own name, whether in proceedings relating to property or founded on contract or tort or any other cause of action; and

   (c)   proceedings for an offence alleged to have been committed by it or on its behalf may be brought against it in its own name.

(2)   A trade union shall not be treated as if it were a body corporate except to the extent authorised by the provisions of this Part.

(3)   A trade union shall not be registered—

   (a)   as a company under the Companies Act 1985; or

   (b)   under the Friendly Societies Act 1974 or Cooperative and Community Benefit Societies Act 2014;

and any such registration of a trade union (whenever effected) is void.

## 11   Exclusion of common law rules as to restraint of trade

(1)   The purposes of a trade union are not, by reason only that they are in restraint of trade, unlawful so as—

   (a)   to make any member of the trade union liable to criminal proceedings for conspiracy or otherwise, or

   (b)   to make any agreement or trust void or voidable.

(2)   No rule of a trade union is unlawful or unenforceable by reason only that it is in restraint of trade.

*Property of trade union*

## 12   Property to be vested in trustees

(1)   All property belonging to a trade union shall be vested in trustees in trust for it.

(2)   A judgment, order or award made in proceedings of any description brought against a trade union is enforceable, by way of execution, diligence, punishment for contempt or otherwise, against any property held in trust for it to the same extent and in the same manner as if it were a body corporate.

(3)   Subsection (2) has effect subject to section 23 (restriction on enforcement of awards against certain property).

## 13   Vesting of property in new trustees

(1)   The provisions of this section apply in relation to the appointment or discharge of trustees in whom any property is vested in trust for a trade union whose name is entered in the list of trade unions.

(2)   In the following sections as they apply to such trustees references to a deed shall be construed as references to an instrument in writing—

   (a)   section 39 of the Trustee Act 1925 and section 38 of the Trustee Act (Northern Ireland) 1958 (retirement of trustee without a new appointment), and

   (b)   section 40 of the Trustee Act 1925 and section 39 of the Trustee Act (Northern Ireland) 1958 (vesting of trust property in new or continuing trustees).

(3)   Where such a trustee is appointed or discharged by a resolution taken by or on behalf of the union, the written record of the resolution shall be treated for the purposes of those sections as an instrument in writing appointing or discharging the trustee.

(4)   In section 40 of the Trustee Act 1925 and section 39 of the Trustee Act (Northern Ireland) 1958 as they apply to such trustees, paragraphs (a) and (c) of subsection (4) (which exclude certain property from the section) shall be omitted.

## 15   Prohibition on use of funds to indemnify unlawful conduct

(1)   It is unlawful for property of a trade union to be applied in or towards—

     (a)   the payment for an individual of a penalty which has been or may be imposed on him for an offence or for contempt of court,

     (b)   the securing of any such payment, or

     (c)   the provision of anything for indemnifying an individual in respect of such a penalty.

(2)   Where any property of a trade union is so applied for the benefit of an individual on whom a penalty has been or may be imposed, then—

     (a)   in the case of a payment, an amount equal to the payment is recoverable by the union from him, and

     (b)   in any other case, he is liable to account to the union for the value of the property applied.

(3)   If a trade union fails to bring or continue proceedings which it is entitled to bring by virtue of subsection (2), a member of the union who claims that the failure is unreasonable may apply to the court on that ground for an order authorising him to bring or continue the proceedings on the union's behalf and at the union's expense.

(4)   In this section 'penalty', in relation to an offence, includes an order to pay compensation and an order for the forfeiture of any property; and references to the imposition of a penalty for an offence shall be construed accordingly.

(5)   The Secretary of State may by order designate offences in relation to which the provisions of this section do not apply.

Any such order shall be made by statutory instrument which shall be subject to annulment in pursuance of a resolution of either House of Parliament.

(6)   This section does not affect—

     (a)   any other enactment, any rule of law or any provision of the rules of a trade union which makes it unlawful for the property of a trade union to be applied in a particular way; or

     (b)   any other remedy available to a trade union, the trustees of its property or any of its members in respect of an unlawful application of the union's property.

(7)   In this section 'member', in relation to a trade union consisting wholly or partly of, or representatives of, constituent or affiliated organisations, includes a member of any of the constituent or affiliated organisations.

## 16   Remedy against trustees for unlawful use of union property

(1)   A member of a trade union who claims that the trustees of the union's property—

     (a)   have so carried out their functions, or are proposing so to carry out their functions, as to cause or permit an unlawful application of the union's property, or

     (b)   have complied, or are proposing to comply, with an unlawful direction which has been or may be given, or purportedly given, to them under the rules of the union,

may apply to the court for an order under this section.

(2)   In a case relating to property which has already been unlawfully applied, or to an unlawful direction that has already been complied with, an application under this section may be made only by a person who was a member of the union at the time when the property was applied or, as the case may be, the direction complied with.

(3)   Where the court is satisfied that the claim is well-founded, it shall make such order as it considers appropriate.

The court may in particular—

     (a)   require the trustees (if necessary, on behalf of the union) to take all such steps as may be specified in the order for protecting or recovering the property of the union;

     (b)   appoint a receiver of, or in Scotland a judicial factor on, the property of the union;

     (c)   remove one or more of the trustees.

(4)   Where the court makes an order under this section in a case in which—

     (a)   property of the union has been applied in contravention of an order of any court, or in compliance with a direction given in contravention of such an order, or

     (b)   the trustees were proposing to apply property in contravention of such an order or to comply with any such direction, the court shall by its order remove all the trustees except any trustee who satisfies the court that there is a good reason for allowing him to remain a trustee.

(5) Without prejudice to any other power of the court, the court may on an application for an order under this section grant such interlocutory relief (in Scotland, such interim order) as it considers appropriate.

(6) This section does not affect any other remedy available in respect of a breach of trust by the trustees of a trade union's property.

(7) In this section 'member', in relation to a trade union consisting wholly or partly of, or of representatives of, constituent or affiliated organisations, includes a member of any of the constituent or affiliated organisations.

*Liability of trade unions in proceedings in tort*

## 20 Liability of trade union in certain proceedings in tort

(1) Where proceedings in tort are brought against a trade union—
  (a) on the ground that an act—
    (i) induces another person to break a contract or interferes or induces another person to interfere with its performance, or
    (ii) consists in threatening that a contract (whether one to which the union is a party or not) will be broken or its performance interfered with, or that the union will induce another person to break a contract or interfere with its performance, or
  (b) in respect of an agreement or combination by two or more persons to do or to procure the doing of an act which, if it were done without any such agreement or combination, would be actionable in tort on such a ground,

then, for the purpose of determining in those proceedings whether the union is liable in respect of the act in question, that act shall be taken to have been done by the union if, but only if, it is to be taken to have been authorised or endorsed by the trade union in accordance with the following provisions.

(2) An act shall be taken to have been authorised or endorsed by a trade union if it was done, or was authorised or endorsed—
  (a) by any person empowered by the rules to do, authorise or endorse acts of the kind in question, or
  (b) by the principal executive committee or the president or general secretary, or (c) by any other committee of the union or any other official of the union (whether employed by it or not).

(3) For the purposes of paragraph (c) of subsection (2)—
  (a) any group of persons constituted in accordance with the rules of the union is a committee of the union; and
  (b) an act shall be taken to have been done, authorised or endorsed by an official if it was done, authorised or endorsed by, or by any member of, any group of persons of which he was at the material time a member, the purposes of which included organising or co-ordinating industrial action.

(4) The provisions of paragraphs (b) and (c) of subsection (2) apply notwithstanding anything in the rules of the union, or in any contract or rule of law, but subject to the provisions of section 21 (repudiation by union of certain acts).

(5) Where for the purposes of any proceedings an act is by virtue of this section taken to have been done by a trade union, nothing in this section shall affect the liability of any other person, in those or any other proceedings, in respect of that act.

(6) In proceedings arising out of an act which is by virtue of this section taken to have been done by a trade union, the power of the court to grant an injunction or interdict includes power to require the union to take such steps as the court considers appropriate for ensuring—
  (a) that there is no, or no further, inducement of persons to take part or to continue to take part in industrial action, and
  (b) that no person engages in any conduct after the granting of the injunction or interdict by virtue of having been induced before it was granted to take part or to continue to take part in industrial action.

The provisions of subsections (2) to (4) above apply in relation to proceedings for failure to comply with any such injunction or interdict as they apply in relation to the original proceedings.

(7)   In this section 'rules', in relation to a trade union, means the written rules of the union and any other written provision forming part of the contract between a member and the other members.

## 21     Repudiation by union of certain acts

(1)   An act shall not be taken to have been authorised or endorsed by a trade union by virtue only of paragraph (c) of section 20(2) if it was repudiated by the executive, president or general secretary as soon as reasonably practicable after coming to the knowledge of any of them.

(2)   Where an act is repudiated—

(a)   written notice of the repudiation must be given to the committee or official in question, without delay, and

(b)   the union must do its best to give individual written notice of the fact and date of repudiation, without delay—

(i)   to every member of the union who the union has reason to believe is taking part, or might otherwise take part, in industrial action as a result of the act, and

(ii)   to the employer of every such member.

(3)   The notice given to members in accordance with paragraph (b)(i) of subsection (2) must contain the following statement—

'Your union has repudiated the call (or calls) for industrial action to which this notice relates and will give no support to unofficial industrial action taken in response to it (or them). If you are dismissed while taking unofficial industrial action, you will have no right to complain of unfair dismissal.'

(4)   If subsection (2) or (3) is not complied with, the repudiation shall be treated as ineffective.

(5)   An act shall not be treated as repudiated if at any time after the union concerned purported to repudiate it the executive, president or general secretary has behaved in a manner which is inconsistent with the purported repudiation.

(6)   The executive, president or general secretary shall be treated as so behaving if, on a request made to any of them within three months of the purported repudiation by a person who—

(a)   is a party to a commercial contract whose performance has been or may be interfered with as a result of the act in question, and

(b)   has not been given written notice by the union of the repudiation, it is not forthwith confirmed in writing that the act has been repudiated.

(7)   In this section 'commercial contract' means any contract other than—

(a)   a contract of employment, or

(b)   any other contract under which a person agrees personally to do work or perform services for another.

## 22     Limit on damages awarded against trade unions in actions in tort

(1)   This section applies to any proceedings in tort brought against a trade union, except—

(a)   proceedings for personal injury as a result of negligence, nuisance or breach of duty;

(b)   proceedings for breach of duty in connection with the ownership, occupation, possession, control or use of property;

(c)   proceedings brought by virtue of Part I of the Consumer Protection Act 1987 (product liability).

(2)   In any proceedings in tort to which this section applies the amount which may be awarded against the union by way of damages shall not exceed the following limit—

| Number of members of union | Maximum award of damages |
|---|---|
| Less than 5,000 | £10,000 |
| 5,000 or more but less than 25,000 | £50,000 |
| 25,000 or more but less than 100,000 | £125,000 |
| 100,000 or more | £250,000 |

...

(5) In this section—

'breach of duty' means breach of a duty imposed by any rule of law or by or under any enactment;

'personal injury' includes any disease and any impairment of a person's physical or mental condition; and

'property' means any property, whether real or personal (or in Scotland, heritable or moveable).

*Restriction on enforcement against certain property*

## 23 Restriction on enforcement of awards against certain property

(1) Where in any proceedings an amount is awarded by way of damages, costs or expenses—

    (a) against a trade union,

    (b) against trustees in whom property is vested in trust for a trade union, in their capacity as such (and otherwise than in respect of a breach of trust on their part), or

    (c) against members or officials of a trade union on behalf of themselves and all of the members of the union,

no part of that amount is recoverable by enforcement against any protected property.

(2) The following is protected property—

    (a) property belonging to the trustees otherwise than in their capacity as such;

    (b) property belonging to any member of the union otherwise than jointly or in common with the other members;

    (c) property belonging to an official of the union who is neither a member nor a trustee;

    (d) property comprised in the union's political fund where that fund—

        (i) is subject to rules of the union which prevent property which is or has been comprised in the fund from being used for financing strikes or other industrial action, and

        (ii) was so subject at the time when the act in respect of which the proceedings are brought was done;

    (e) property comprised in a separate fund maintained in accordance with the rules of the union for the purpose only of providing provident benefits.

(3) For this purpose 'provident benefits' includes—

    (a) any payment expressly authorised by the rules of the union which is made—

        (i) to a member during sickness or incapacity from personal injury or while out of work, or

        (ii) to an aged member by way of superannuation, or

        (iii) to a member who has met with an accident or has lost his tools by fire or theft;

    (b) a payment in discharge or aid of funeral expenses on the death of a member or the wife of a member or as provision for the children of a deceased member.

## CHAPTER III
## TRADE UNION ADMINISTRATION

*Register of members' names and addresses*

## 24 Duty to maintain register of members' names and addresses

(1) A trade union shall compile and maintain a register of the names and addresses of its members, and shall secure, so far as is reasonably practicable, that the entries in the register are accurate and are kept up-to-date.

(2) The register may be kept by means of a computer.

(3) A trade union shall—

    (a) allow any member, upon reasonable notice, to ascertain from the register, free of charge and at any reasonable time, whether there is an entry on it relating to him; and

    (b) if requested to do so by any member, supply him as soon as reasonably practicable, either free of charge or on payment of a reasonable fee, with a copy of any entry on the register relating to him.

(4)    ...

(5)    For the purposes of this section a member's address means either his home address or another address which he has requested the union in writing to treat as his postal address.

(6)    The remedy for failure to comply with the requirements of this section is by way of application under section 25 (to the Certification Officer) or section 26 (to the court); see also the powers of the Certification Officer under section 24B to make a declaration and an enforcement order.

## 24ZA Duty to provide membership audit certificate

(1)    A trade union required to maintain a register of the names and addresses of its members by section 24 must send to the Certification Officer a membership audit certificate in relation to each reporting period.

(2)    In this section and in sections 24ZB to 24ZF, a 'reporting period' means a period in relation to which the union is required by section 32 to send an annual return to the Certification Officer.

(3)    The union must send the membership audit certificate in relation to a reporting period to the Certification Officer at the same time as it sends to the Officer its annual return under section 32 in relation to that period.

(4)    In the case of a trade union required by section 24ZB to appoint an assurer in relation to a reporting period, the 'membership audit certificate' in relation to that period is the certificate which the assurer is required to provide to the union in relation to that period pursuant to that appointment.

(5)    In any other case, the 'membership audit certificate' in relation to a reporting period is a certificate which—
    (a)    must be signed by an officer of the trade union who is authorised to sign on its behalf,
    (b)    must state the officer's name, and
    (c)    must state whether, to the best of the officer's knowledge and belief, the union has complied with its duties under section 24(1) throughout the reporting period.

(6)    A trade union must, at a person's request, supply the person with a copy of its most recent membership audit certificate either free of charge or on payment of a reasonable charge.

(7)    The Certification Officer must at all reasonable hours keep available for public inspection, either free of charge or on payment of a reasonable charge, copies of all membership audit certificates sent to the Officer under this section.

## 24ZB Duty to appoint an assurer

(1)    A trade union required to maintain a register of the names and addresses of its members by section 24 must, in relation to each reporting period, appoint a qualified independent person to be an assurer in relation to that period.

(2)    There is incorporated in the assurer's appointment a duty which the assurer owes to the trade union—
    (a)    to provide to the union a membership audit certificate in relation to the reporting period which accords with the requirements of section 24ZD, and
    (b)    to carry out such enquiries as the assurer considers necessary to enable the assurer to provide that certificate.

(3)    A person is a 'qualified independent person' if—
    (a)    the person either satisfies such conditions as may be specified for the purposes of this section by order of the Secretary of State or is specified by name in such an order, and
    (b)    the trade union has no grounds for believing that—
        (i)    the person will carry out an assurer's functions otherwise than competently, or
        (ii)    the person's independence in relation to the union might reasonably be called into question.

(4)    None of the following may act as an assurer—
    (a)    an officer or employee of the trade union or of any of its branches or sections;
    (b)    a person who is a partner of, or in the employment of, or who employs, such an officer or employee.

(5)   This section does not apply to a trade union in relation to a reporting period if the number of its members at the end of the preceding reporting period did not exceed 10,000.

(6)   Any order under this section is to be made by statutory instrument and is to be subject to annulment in pursuance of a resolution of either House of Parliament.

## 24ZC  Appointment and removal of an assurer

(1)   The rules of every trade union to which section 24ZB applies must contain provision for the appointment and removal of an assurer.

But the following provisions have effect notwithstanding anything in the rules.

(2)   An assurer must not be removed from office except by resolution passed at a general meeting of the members of the union or of delegates of its members.

(3)   A person duly appointed as an assurer in relation to a reporting period must be reappointed as assurer in relation to the following reporting period, unless—

  (a)   a resolution has been passed at a general meeting of the trade union appointing somebody else instead or providing expressly that the person is not to be re-appointed,

  (b)   the person has given notice to the union in writing of the person's unwillingness to be re-appointed,

  (c)   the person is not qualified for the appointment in accordance with section 24ZB, or

  (d)   the person has ceased to act as assurer by reason of incapacity.

(4)   But a person need not automatically be re-appointed where—

  (a)   the person is retiring,

  (b)   notice has been given of an intended resolution to appoint somebody else instead, and

  (c)   that resolution cannot be proceeded with at the meeting because of the death or incapacity of the proposed replacement.

## 24ZD  Requirements of assurer's membership audit certificate

(1)   For the purposes of section 24ZB(2)(a) the requirements of a membership audit certificate in relation to a reporting period provided by an assurer are as follows.

(2)   The certificate must state the name of, and be signed by, the assurer.

(3)   The certificate must state—

  (a)   whether, in the assurer's opinion, the trade union's system for compiling and maintaining the register of the names and addresses of its members was satisfactory for the purposes of complying with the union's duties under section 24(1) throughout the reporting period, and

  (b)   whether, in the assurer's opinion, the assurer has obtained the information and explanations which the assurer considers necessary for the performance of the assurer's functions.

(4)   If the certificate states that—

  (a)   in the assurer's opinion, the trade union's system for compiling and maintaining the register was not satisfactory for the purposes of complying with the union's duties under section 24(1) throughout the reporting period, or

  (b)   in the assurer's opinion, the assurer has failed to obtain the information and explanations which the assurer considers necessary for the performance of the assurer's functions,

  the certificate must state the assurer's reasons for making that statement.

(5)   In the case of a failure to obtain information or explanations as described in subsection (4)(b), the certificate must also—

  (a)   provide a description of the information or explanations requested or required which have not been obtained, and

  (b)   state whether the assurer required that information or those explanations from the union's officers, or officers of any of its branches or sections, under section 24ZE.

(6)   The reference in subsection (2) to signature by the assurer is, where that office is held by a body corporate or partnership, to signature in the name of the body corporate or partnership by an individual authorised to sign on its behalf.

**24ZE  Rights of assurer**

(1)  An assurer appointed by a trade union under section 24ZB—

(a)  has a right of access at all reasonable times to the register of the names and addresses of the union's members and to all other documents which the assurer considers may be relevant to whether the union has complied with any of the requirements of section 24(1), and

(b)  is entitled to require from the union's officers, or the officers of any of its branches or sections, such information and explanations as the assurer considers necessary for the performance of the assurer's functions.

(2)  In subsection (1) references to documents include information recorded in any form.

**24ZF  Duty to inform the Certification Officer**

If an assurer provides a membership audit certificate in relation to a reporting period to a trade union which states that, in the assurer's opinion—

(a)  the union's system for compiling and maintaining the register was not satisfactory for the purposes of complying with the union's duties under section 24(1) throughout that period, or

(b)  the assurer has failed to obtain the information and explanations which the assurer considers necessary for the performance of the assurer's functions,

the assurer must send a copy of the certificate to the Certification Officer as soon as is reasonably practicable after it is provided to the union.

**24ZG  Duty of confidentiality**

(1)  The duty of confidentiality as respects the register is incorporated in an assurer's appointment by a trade union under section 24ZB.

(2)  The duty of confidentiality as respects the register is a duty which the assurer owes to the union—

(a)  not to disclose any name or address in the register of the names and addresses of the union's members except in permitted circumstances, and

(b)  to take all reasonable steps to secure that there is no disclosure of any such name or address by another person except in permitted circumstances.

(3)  The circumstances in which disclosure of a member's name or address is permitted are—

(a)  where the member consents,

(b)  where it is required or requested by the Certification Officer for the purposes of the discharge of any of the Officer's functions,

(c)  where it is required for the purposes of the discharge of any of the functions of an inspector appointed by the Officer,

(d)  where it is required for the purposes of the discharge of any of the functions of the assurer, or

(e)  where it is required for the purposes of the investigation of crime or criminal proceedings.

**24A  Securing confidentiality of register during ballots**

(1)  This section applies in relation to a ballot of the members of a trade union on—

(a)  an election under Chapter IV for a position to which that Chapter applies,

(b)  a political resolution under Chapter VI, and

(c)  a resolution to approve an instrument of amalgamation or transfer under Chapter VII.

(2)  Where this section applies in relation to a ballot the trade union shall impose the duty of confidentiality in relation to the register of members' names and addresses on the scrutineer appointed by the union for the purposes of the ballot and on any person appointed by the union as the independent person for the purposes of the ballot.

(3)  The duty of confidentiality in the context of a scrutineer or independent person in relation to the register of members' names and addresses is, when imposed on a scrutineer or on an independent person, a duty—

(a)  not to disclose any name or address in the register except in permitted circumstances; and

(b)  to take all reasonable steps to secure that there is no disclosure of any such name or address by any other person except in permitted circumstances;

and any reference in this Act to 'the duty of confidentiality' is a reference to the duty prescribed in this subsection.

(4)  The circumstances in which disclosure of a member's name and address is permitted are—

(a)  where the member consents;

(b)  where it is required or requested by the Certification Officer for the purposes of the discharge of any of his functions or it is required for the purposes of the discharge of any of the functions of an inspector appointed by him;

(c)  where it is required for the purposes of the discharge of any of the functions of the scrutineer or independent person, as the case may be, under the terms of his appointment;

(d)  where it is required for the purposes of the investigation of crime or of criminal proceedings.

(5)  Any provision of this Part which incorporates the duty of confidentiality as respects the register into the appointment of a scrutineer or an independent person has the effect of imposing that duty on the scrutineer or independent person as a duty owed by him to the trade union.

(6)  The remedy for failure to comply with the requirements of this section is by way of application under section 25 (to the Certification Officer) or section 26 (to the court).

## 24B    Enforcement of sections 24 to 24ZC by Certification Officer

(1)  Where the Certification Officer is satisfied that a trade union has failed to comply with any of the requirements of section 24, 24ZA, 24ZB or 24ZC (duties etc. relating to the register of members), the Officer may make a declaration to that effect.

(2)  Before making such a declaration, the Certification Officer—

(a)  may make such enquiries as the Officer thinks fit,

(b)  must give the union an opportunity to make written representations, and

(c)  may give the union an opportunity to make oral representations.

(3)  If the Certification Officer makes a declaration it must specify the provisions with which the union has failed to comply.

(4)  Where the Certification Officer makes a declaration and is satisfied—

(a)  that steps have been taken by the union with a view to remedying the declared failure or securing that a failure of the same or any similar kind does not occur in future, or

(b)  that the union has agreed to take such steps,

the Officer must specify those steps in the declaration.

(5)  Where a declaration is made, the Certification Officer must give reasons in writing for making the declaration.

(6)  Where a declaration is made, the Certification Officer must also make an enforcement order unless the Officer considers that to do so would be inappropriate.

(7)  An 'enforcement order' is an order imposing on the union one or both of the following requirements—

(a)  to take such steps to remedy the declared failure, within such period, as may be specified in the order;

(b)  to abstain from such acts as may be so specified with a view to securing that a failure of the same or a similar kind does not occur in future.

(8)  Where, having given the union an opportunity to make written representations under subsection (2)(b), the Certification Officer determines not to make a declaration under subsection (1), the Officer must give the union notice in writing of that determination.

(9)  Where the Certification Officer requests a person to provide information to the Officer in connection with enquiries under this section, the Officer must specify the date by which that information is to be provided.

(10)  Where the information is not provided by the specified date, the Certification Officer must proceed with determining whether to make a declaration under subsection (1) unless the Officer considers that it would be inappropriate to do so.

(11)  A declaration made by the Certification Officer under this section may be relied on as if it were a declaration made by the court.

(12) An enforcement order made by the Certification Officer under this section may be enforced by the Officer in the same way as an order of the court.

(13) Where an enforcement order has been made, a person who is a member of the union and was a member at the time it was made is entitled to enforce obedience to the order as if the order had been made on an application by that person.

## 25     Remedy for failure: application to Certification Officer

(1)     A member of a trade union who claims that the union has failed to comply with any of the requirements of section 24 or 24A (duties with respect to register of members' names and addresses) may apply to the Certification Officer for a declaration to that effect.

(2)     On an application being made to him, the Certification Officer shall—

    (a)     make such enquiries as he thinks fit, and

    (b)     give the applicant and the trade union an opportunity to be heard, and may make or refuse the declaration asked for.

(3)     If he makes a declaration he shall specify in it the provisions with which the trade union has failed to comply.

(4)     Where he makes a declaration and is satisfied that steps have been taken by the union with a view to remedying the declared failure, or securing that a failure of the same or any similar kind does not occur in future, or that the union has agreed to take such steps, he shall specify those steps in the declaration.

(5)     Whether he makes or refuses a declaration, he shall give reasons for his decision in writing; and the reasons may be accompanied by written observations on any matter arising from, or connected with, the proceedings.

(5A) Where the Certification Officer makes a declaration he shall also, unless he considers that to do so would be inappropriate, make an enforcement order, that is, an order imposing on the union one or both of the following requirements—

    (a)     to take such steps to remedy the declared failure, within such period, as may be specified in the order;

    (b)     to abstain from such acts as may be so specified with a view to securing that a failure of the same or a similar kind does not occur in future.

(5B) Where an enforcement order has been made, any person who is a member of the union and was a member at the time it was made is entitled to enforce obedience to the order as if he had made the application on which the order was made.

(6)     In exercising his functions under this section the Certification Officer shall ensure that, so far as is reasonably practicable, an application made to him is determined within six months of being made.

(6A) For the purposes of subsection (6) the circumstances in which it is not reasonably practicable to determine an application within that time frame may include, in particular, where delay is caused by the exercise of the powers under paragraph 2 or 3 of Schedule A3 (powers to require production of documents etc. and to appoint inspectors).

(7)     Where he requests a person to furnish information to him in connection with enquiries made by him under this section, he shall specify the date by which that information is to be furnished and, unless he considers that it would be inappropriate to do so, shall proceed with his determination of the application notwithstanding that the information has not been furnished to him by the specified date.

(8)     The Certification Officer shall not entertain an application for a declaration as respects an alleged failure to comply with the requirements of section 24A in relation to a ballot to which that section applies unless the application is made before the end of the period of one year beginning with the last day on which votes could be cast in the ballot.

(9)     A declaration made by the Certification Officer under this section may be relied on as if it were a declaration made by the court.

(10) An enforcement order made by the Certification Officer under this section may be enforced (by the Certification Officer, the applicant or a person mentioned in subsection (5B)) in the same way as an order of the court.

(11) the following paragraphs have effect in a person applies under section 26 in relation to an alleged failure—
    (a)   that person may not apply under this section in relation to that failure;
    (b)   on an application by a different person under this section in relation to that failure, the Certification Officer shall have due regard to any declaration, order, observations or reasons made or given by the court regarding that failure and brought to the Certification Officer's notice.

## 26    Remedy for failure: application to court

(1)   A member of a trade union who claims that the union has failed to comply with any of the requirements of section 24 or 24A (duties with respect to register of members' names and addresses) may apply to the court for a declaration to that effect.

(2)   …

(3)   If the court makes a declaration it shall specify in it the provisions with which the trade union has failed to comply.

(4)   Where the court makes a declaration it shall also, unless it considers that to do so would be inappropriate, make an enforcement order, that is, an order imposing on the union one or both of the following requirements—
    (a)   to take such steps to remedy the declared failure, within such period, as may be specified in the order;
    (b)   to abstain from such acts as may be so specified with a view to securing that a failure of the same or a similar kind does not occur in future.

(5)   Where an enforcement order has been made, any person who is a member of the union and was a member at the time it was made, is entitled to enforce obedience to the order as if he had made the application on which the order was made.

(6)   Without prejudice to any other power of the court, the court may on an application under this section grant such interlocutory relief (in Scotland, such interim order) as it considers appropriate.

(7)   The court shall not entertain an application for a declaration as respects an alleged failure to comply with the requirements of section 24A in relation to a ballot to which that section applies unless the application is made before the end of the period of one year beginning with the last day on which votes could be cast in the ballot.

(8)   The following paragraphs have effect if a person applies under section 25 in relation to an alleged failure—
    (a)   that person may not apply under this section in relation to that failure;
    (b)   on an application by a different person under this section in relation to that failure, the court shall have due regard to any declaration, order, observations or reasons made or given by the Certification Officer regarding that failure and brought to the court's notice.

(9)   Where a person applies under this section in relation to an alleged failure and the Certification Officer has made a declaration regarding that failure under section 24B, the court must have due regard to the declaration and any order, observations or reasons made or given by the Officer under that section regarding that failure and brought to the court's notice.

*Duty to supply copy of rules*

## 27    Duty to supply copy of rules

A trade union shall at the request of any person supply him with a copy of its rules either free of charge or on payment of a reasonable charge.

CHAPTER IV
ELECTIONS FOR CERTAIN POSITIONS

*Duty to hold elections*

## 46    Duty to hold elections for certain positions

(1)   A trade union shall secure—
    (a)   that every person who holds a position in the union to which this Chapter applies does so by virtue of having been elected to it at an election satisfying the requirements of this Chapter, and

    (b)    that no person continues to hold such a position for more than five years without being re-elected at such an election.

(2)    The positions to which this Chapter applies (subject as mentioned below) are—
    (a)    member of the executive,
    (b)    any position by virtue of which a person is a member of the executive,
    (c)    president, and
    (d)    general secretary;
and the requirements referred to above are those set out in sections 47 to 52 below.

(3)    In this Chapter 'member of the executive' includes any person who, under the rules or practice of the union, may attend and speak at some or all of the meetings of the executive, otherwise than for the purpose of providing the committee with factual information or with technical or professional advice with respect to matters taken into account by the executive in carrying out its functions.

(4)    This Chapter does not apply to the position of president or general secretary if the holder of that position—
    (a)    is not, in respect of that position, either a voting member of the executive or an employee of the union,
    (b)    holds that position for a period which under the rules of the union cannot end more than 13 months after he took it up, and
    (c)    has not held either position at any time in the period of twelve months ending with the day before he took up that position.

(5)    A 'voting member of the executive' means a person entitled in his own right to attend meetings of the executive and to vote on matters on which votes are taken by the executive (whether or not he is entitled to attend all such meetings or to vote on all such matters or in all circumstances).

(6)    The provisions of this Chapter apply notwithstanding anything in the rules or practice of the union; and the terms and conditions on which a person is employed by the union shall be disregarded in so far as they would prevent the union from complying with the provisions of this Chapter.

*Requirements to be satisfied with respect to elections*

## 47    Candidates

(1)    No member of the trade union shall be unreasonably excluded from standing as a candidate.

(2)    No candidate shall be required, directly or indirectly, to be a member of a political party.

(3)    A member of a trade union shall not be taken to be unreasonably excluded from standing as a candidate if he is excluded on the ground that he belongs to a class of which all the members are excluded by the rules of the union.
But a rule which provides for such a class to be determined by reference to whom the union chooses to exclude shall be disregarded.

## 48    Election addresses

(1)    The trade union shall—
    (a)    provide every candidate with an opportunity of preparing an election address in his own words and of submitting it to the union to be distributed to the persons accorded entitlement to vote in the election; and
    (b)    secure that, so far as reasonably practicable, copies of every election address submitted to it in time are distributed to each of those persons by post along with the voting papers for the election.

(2)    The trade union may determine the time by which an election address must be submitted to it for distribution; but the time so determined must not be earlier than the latest time at which a person may become a candidate in the election.

(3)    The trade union may provide that election addresses submitted to it for distribution—
    (a)    must not exceed such length, not being less than one hundred words, as may be determined by the union, and
    (b)    may, as regards photographs and other matter not in words, incorporate only such matter as the union may determine.

(4)   The trade union shall secure that no modification of an election address submitted to it is made by any person in any copy of the address to be distributed except—
  (a)   at the request or with the consent of the candidate, or (b) where the modification is necessarily incidental to the method adopted for producing that copy.

(5)   The trade union shall secure that the same method of producing copies is applied in the same way to every election address submitted and, so far as reasonably practicable, that no such facility or information as would enable a candidate to gain any benefit from—
  (a)   the method by which copies of the election addresses are produced, or
  (b)   the modifications which are necessarily incidental to that method, is provided to any candidate without being provided equally to all the others.

(6)   The trade union shall, so far as reasonably practicable, secure that the same facilities and restrictions with respect to the preparation, submission, length or modification of an election address, and with respect to the incorporation of photographs or other matter not in words, are provided or applied equally to each of the candidates.

(7)   The arrangements made by the trade union for the production of the copies to be so distributed must be such as to secure that none of the candidates is required to bear any of the expense of producing the copies.

(8)   No-one other than the candidate himself shall incur any civil or criminal liability in respect of the publication of a candidate's election address or of any copy required to be made for the purposes of this section.

## 49   Appointment of independent scrutineer

(1)   The trade union shall, before the election is held, appoint a qualified independent person ("the scrutineer") to carry out—
  (a)   the functions in relation to the election which are required under this section to be contained in his appointment; and
  (b)   such additional functions in relation to the election as may be specified in his appointment.

(2)   A person is a qualified independent person in relation to an election if—
  (a)   he satisfies such conditions as may be specified for the purposes of this section by order of the Secretary of State or is himself so specified; and
  (b)   the trade union has no grounds for believing either that he will carry out any functions conferred on him in relation to the election otherwise than competently or that his independence in relation to the union, or in relation to the election, might reasonably be called into question.
  An order under paragraph (a) shall be made by statutory instrument which shall be subject to annulment in pursuance of a resolution of either House of Parliament.

(3)   The scrutineer's appointment shall require him—
  (a)   to be the person who supervises the production of the voting papers and (unless he is appointed under section 51A to undertake the distribution of the voting papers) their distribution and to whom the voting papers are returned by those voting;
  (aa)  to—
      (i)    inspect the register of names and addresses of the members of the trade union, or
      (ii)   examine the copy of the register as at the relevant date which is supplied to him in accordance with subsection (5A)(a),
      whenever it appears to him appropriate to do so and, in particular, when the conditions specified in subsection (3A) are satisfied;
  (b)   to take such steps as appear to him to be appropriate for the purpose of enabling him to make his report (see section 52);
  (c)   to make his report to the trade union as soon as reasonably practicable after the last date for the return of voting papers; and
  (d)   to retain custody of all voting papers returned for the purposes of the election and the copy of the register supplied to him in accordance with subsection (5A)(a)—
      (i)    until the end of the period of one year beginning with the announcement by the union of the result of the election; and

    (ii)    if within that period an application is made under section 54 (complaint of failure to comply with election requirements), until the Certification Officer or the court authorises him to dispose of the papers or copy.

...

## 50    Entitlement to vote

(1)    Subject to the provisions of this section, entitlement to vote shall be accorded equally to all members of the trade union.

(2)    The rules of the union may exclude entitlement to vote in the case of all members belonging to one of the following classes, or to a class falling within one of the following—

    (a)    members who are not in employment;

    (b)    members who are in arrears in respect of any subscription or contribution due to the union;

    (c)    members who are apprentices, trainees or students or new members of the union.

(3)    The rules of the union may restrict entitlement to vote to members who fall within—

    (a)    a class determined by reference to a trade or occupation,

    (b)    a class determined by reference to a geographical area, or

    (c)    a class which is by virtue of the rules of the union treated as a separate section within the union,

or to members who fall within a class determined by reference to any combination of the factors mentioned in paragraphs (a), (b) and (c).

The reference in paragraph (c) to a section of a trade union includes a part of the union which is itself a trade union.

(4)    Entitlement may not be restricted in accordance with subsection (3) if the effect is that any member of the union is denied entitlement to vote at all elections held for the purposes of this Chapter otherwise than by virtue of belonging to a class excluded in accordance with subsection (2).

## 51    Voting

(1)    The method of voting must be by the marking of a voting paper by the person voting.

(2)    Each voting paper must—

    (a)    state the name of the independent scrutineer and clearly specify the address to which, and the date by which, it is to be returned,

    (b)    be given one of a series of consecutive whole numbers every one of which is used in giving a different number in that series to each voting paper printed or otherwise produced for the purposes of the election, and

    (c)    be marked with its number.

(3)    Every person who is entitled to vote at the election must—

    (a)    be allowed to vote without interference from, or constraint imposed by, the union or any of its members, officials or employees, and

    (b)    so far as is reasonably practicable, be enabled to do so without incurring any direct cost to himself.

(4)    So far as is reasonably practicable, every person who is entitled to vote at the election must—

    (a)    have sent to him by post, at his home address or another address which he has requested the trade union in writing to treat as his postal address, a voting paper which either lists the candidates at the election or is accompanied by a separate list of those candidates; and

    (b)    be given a convenient opportunity to vote by post.

(5)    The ballot shall be conducted so as to secure that—

    (a)    so far as is reasonably practicable, those voting do so in secret, and

    (b)    the votes given at the election are fairly and accurately counted.

For the purposes of paragraph (b) an inaccuracy in counting shall be disregarded if it is accidental and on a scale which could not affect the result of the election.

(6)    The ballot shall be so conducted as to secure that the result of the election is determined solely by counting the number of votes cast directly for each candidate.

(7)   Nothing in subsection (6) shall be taken to prevent the system of voting used for the election being the single transferable vote, that is, a vote capable of being given so as to indicate the voter's order of preference for the candidates and of being transferred to the next choice—
   (a)   when it is not required to give a prior choice the necessary quota of votes, or
   (b)   when, owing to the deficiency in the number of votes given for a prior choice, that choice is eliminated from the list of candidates.

## 51A   Counting of votes etc. by independent person

(1)   The trade union shall ensure that—
   (a)   the storage and distribution of the voting papers for the purposes of the election, and
   (b)   the counting of the votes cast in the election,
   are undertaken by one or more independent persons appointed by the union.
(2)   A person is an independent person in relation to an election if—
   (a)   he is the scrutineer, or
   (b)   he is a person other than the scrutineer and the trade union has no grounds for believing either that he will carry out any functions conferred on him in relation to the election otherwise than competently or that his independence in relation to the union, or in relation to the election, might reasonably be called into question.
(3)   An appointment under this section shall require the person appointed to carry out his functions so as to minimise the risk of any contravention of requirements imposed by or under any enactment or the occurrence of any unfairness or malpractice.
(4)   The duty of confidentiality as respects the register is incorporated in an appointment under this section.
(5)   Where the person appointed to undertake the counting of votes is not the scrutineer, his appointment shall require him to send the voting papers back to the scrutineer as soon as reasonably practicable after the counting has been completed.
(6)   The trade union—
   (a)   shall ensure that nothing in the terms of an appointment under this section is such as to make it reasonable for any person to call into question the independence of the person appointed in relation to the union,
   (b)   shall ensure that a person appointed under this section duly carries out his functions and that there is no interference with his carrying out of those functions which would make it reasonable for any person to call into question the independence of the person appointed in relation to the union, and
   (c)   shall comply with all reasonable requests made by a person appointed under this section for the purposes of, or in connection with, the carrying out of his functions.

## 52   Scrutineer's report

(1)   The scrutineer's report on the election shall state—
   (a)   the number of voting papers distributed for the purposes of the election,
   (b)   the number of voting papers returned to the scrutineer,
   (c)   the number of valid votes cast in the election for each candidate,
   (d)   the number of spoiled or otherwise invalid voting papers returned, and
   (e)   the name of the person (or of each of the persons) appointed under section 51A or, if no person was so appointed, that fact.
(2)   The report shall also state whether the scrutineer is satisfied—
   (a)   that there are no reasonable grounds for believing that there was any contravention of a requirement imposed by or under any enactment in relation to the election,
   (b)   that the arrangements made (whether by him or any other person) with respect to the production, storage, distribution, return or other handling of the voting papers used in the election, and the arrangements for the counting of the votes, included all such security arrangements as were reasonably practicable for the purpose of minimising the risk that any unfairness or malpractice might occur, and

    (c)   that he has been able to carry out his functions without such interference as would make it reasonable for any person to call his independence in relation to the union into question;

and if he is not satisfied as to any of those matters, the report shall give particulars of his reasons for not being satisfied as to that matter.

...

## 53    Uncontested elections

Nothing in this Chapter shall be taken to require a ballot to be held at an uncontested election.

*Remedy for failure to comply with requirements*

## 54    Remedy for failure to comply with requirements: general

(1)   A person alleging a failure on the part of a trade union to comply with any of the requirements of this Chapter may apply for—

    (a)   a declaration under section 55 (by the Certification Officer), or

    (b)   a declaration under section 56 (by the court);

but the Certification Officer may also exercise the powers under section 55 where no application is made.

(2)   An application for a declaration under section 55 or 56 may be made only—

    (a)   by a person who is a member of the trade union (provided, where the election has been held, he was also a member at the time when it was held), or

    (b)   by a person who is or was a candidate at the election;

and the references in those sections to a person having a sufficient interest are to such a person.

(3)   [Where an election has been held, no application under those sections with respect to that election] may be made after the end of the period of one year beginning with the day on which the union announced the result of the election.

**Notes:**

Sub-s (1): substituted by the Trade Union Act 2016, s 17(3), Sch 2, para 2(1), (2). Date in force: to be appointed.

Sub-s (2): words 'An application under those sections may be made—' in italics repealed and subsequent words in square brackets substituted by the Trade Union Act 2016, s 17(3), Sch 2, para 2(1), (3). Date in force: to be appointed.

## 55    Application to Certification Officer

(1)   Where the Certification Officer is satisfied that a trade union has failed to comply with any of the requirements of this Chapter, either—

    (a)   on an application by a person having a sufficient interest (see section 54(2)), or

    (b)   without any such application having been made,

the Officer may make a declaration to that effect.

(2)   Before deciding the matter the Certification Officer—

    (a)   may make such enquiries as the Officer thinks fit,

    (b)   must give the union and the applicant (if any) an opportunity to make written representations, and

    (c)   may give the union and the applicant (if any) an opportunity to make oral representations.

(3)   If he makes a declaration he shall specify in it the provisions with which the trade union has failed to comply.

(4)   Where he makes a declaration and is satisfied that steps have been taken by the union with a view to remedying the declared failure, or securing that a failure of the same or any similar kind does not occur in future, or that the union has agreed to take such steps, he shall specify those steps in the declaration.

(5)   Whether he makes or refuses a declaration, he shall give reasons for his decision in writing; and the reasons may be accompanied by written observations on any matter arising from, or connected with, the proceedings.

(5A) Where the Certification Officer makes a declaration he shall also, unless he considers that to do so would be inappropriate, make an enforcement order, that is, an order imposing on the union one or more of the following requirements—

    (a)    to secure the holding of an election in accordance with the order;

    (b)    to take such other steps to remedy the declared failure as may be specified in the order;

    (c)    to abstain from such acts as may be so specified with a view to securing that a failure of the same or a similar kind does not occur in future.

The Certification Officer shall in an order imposing any such requirement as is mentioned in paragraph (a) or (b) specify the period within which the union is to comply with the requirements of the order.

(5B) Where the Certification Officer makes an order requiring the union to hold a fresh election, he shall (unless he considers that it would be inappropriate to do so in the particular circumstances of the case) require the election to be conducted in accordance with the requirements of this Chapter and such other provisions as may be made by the order.

(5C) Where an enforcement order has been made—

    (a)    any person who is a member of the union and was a member at the time the order was made, or

    (b)    any person who is or was a candidate in the election in question,

is entitled to enforce obedience to the order as if he had made an application under this section.

(6)    In exercising his functions under this section the Certification Officer shall ensure that, so far as is reasonably practicable, an application made to him is determined within six months of being made.

(7)    Where he requests a person to furnish information to him in connection with enquiries made by him under this section, he shall specify the date by which that information is to be furnished and, unless he considers that it would be inappropriate to do so, shall proceed with his determination *of the application* notwithstanding that the information has not been furnished to him by the specified date.

(8)    A declaration made by the Certification Officer under this section may be relied on as if it were a declaration made by the court.

(9)    An enforcement order made by the Certification Officer under this section may be enforced (by the Certification Officer, the applicant or a person mentioned in subsection (5C)) in the same way as an order of the court.

(10)    The following paragraphs have effect if a person applies under section 56 in relation to an alleged failure—

    (a)    that person may not apply under this section in relation to that failure;

    (b)    on an application by a different person under this section in relation to that failure, the Certification Officer shall have due regard to any declaration, order, observations or reasons made or given by the court regarding that failure and brought to the Certification Officer's notice.

**Notes:**

Section heading: words 'Application to' in italics repealed and subsequent words in square brackets substituted by the Trade Union Act 2016, s 17(3), Sch 2, para 3(1), (2). Date in force: to be appointed.

Sub-ss (1), (2): substituted by the Trade Union Act 2016, s 17(3), Sch 2, para 3(1), (3). Date in force: to be appointed.

Sub-s (5C): words 'the application on which the order was made' in italics repealed and subsequent words in square brackets substituted by the Trade Union Act 2016, s 17(3), Sch 2, para 3(1), (4). Date in force: to be appointed.

Sub-s (7): words 'of the application' in italics repealed by the Trade Union Act 2016, s 17(3), Sch 2, para 3(1), (5). Date in force: to be appointed.

Sub-s (9): words from '(by the Certification' to 'in subsection (5C))' in square brackets inserted by the Trade Union Act 2016, s 19(4). Date in force: to be appointed.

## 56    Application to court

(1)    A person having a sufficient interest (see section 54(2)) who claims that a trade union has failed to comply with any of the requirements of this Chapter may apply to the court for a declaration to that effect.

(2)    ...

(3)    If the court makes the declaration asked for, it shall specify in the declaration the provisions with which the trade union has failed to comply.

(4)    Where the court makes a declaration it shall also, unless it considers that to do so would be inappropriate, make an enforcement order, that is, an order imposing on the union one or more of the following requirements —

    (a)    to secure the holding of an election in accordance with the order;

    (b)    to take such other steps to remedy the declared failure as may be specified in the order;

    (c)    to abstain from such acts as may be so specified with a view to securing that a failure of the same or a similar kind does not occur in future.

The court shall in an order imposing any such requirement as is mentioned in paragraph (a) or (b) specify the period within which the union is to comply with the requirements of the order.

(5)    Where the court makes an order requiring the union to hold a fresh election, the court shall (unless it considers that it would be inappropriate to do so in the particular circumstances of the case) require the election to be conducted in accordance with the requirements of this Chapter and such other provisions as may be made by the order.

(6)    Where an enforcement order has been made —

    (a)    any person who is a member of the union and was a member at the time the order was made, or

    (b)    any person who is or was a candidate in the election in question,

is entitled to enforce obedience to the order as if he had made the application on which the order was made.

(7)    Without prejudice to any other power of the court, the court may on an application under this section grant such interlocutory relief (in Scotland, such interim order) as it considers appropriate.

(8)    The following paragraphs have effect if a person applies under section 55 in relation to an alleged failure —

    (a)    that person may not apply under this section in relation to that failure;

    (b)    on an application by a different person under this section in relation to that failure, the court shall have due regard to any declaration, order, observations or reasons made or given by the Certification Officer regarding that failure and brought to the court's notice.

## 56A  Appeals from Certification Officer

An appeal lies to the Employment Appeal Tribunal on any question of law arising [on any question arising] in proceedings before or arising from any decision of the Certification Officer under section 55.

CHAPTER V
RIGHTS OF TRADE UNION MEMBERS

*Right to a ballot before industrial action*

## 62  Right to a ballot before industrial action

(1)    A member of a trade union who claims that members of the union, including himself, are likely to be or have been induced by the union to take part or to continue to take part in industrial action which does not have the support of a ballot may apply to the court for an order under this section.

In this section 'the relevant time' means the time when the application is made.

(2)    For this purpose the question whether industrial action is regarded as having the support of a ballot shall be determined in accordance with section 226(2).

Any reference in this subsection to a requirement of a provision which is disapplied or modified by section 232 has effect subject to that section.

(3)    Where on an application under this section the court is satisfied that the claim is well-founded, it shall make such order as it considers appropriate for requiring the union to take steps for ensuring —

    (a)    that there is no, or no further, inducement of members of the union to take part or to continue to take part in the industrial action to which the application relates, and

(b)    that no member engages in conduct after the making of the order by virtue of having been induced before the making of the order to take part or continue to take part in the action.

(4)    Without prejudice to any other power of the court, the court may on an application under this section grant such interlocutory relief (in Scotland, such interim order) as it considers appropriate.

(5)    For the purposes of this section an act shall be taken to be done by a trade union if it is authorised or endorsed by the union; and the provisions of section 20(2) to (4) apply for the purpose of determining whether an act is to be taken to be so authorised or endorsed. Those provisions also apply in relation to proceedings for failure to comply with an order under this section as they apply in relation to the original proceedings.

(6)    In this section—
'inducement' includes an inducement which is or would be ineffective, whether because of the member's unwillingness to be influenced by it or for any other reason; and 'industrial action' means a strike or other industrial action by persons employed under contracts of employment.

(7)    Where a person holds any office or employment under the Crown on terms which do not constitute a contract of employment between that person and the Crown, those terms shall nevertheless be deemed to constitute such a contract for the purposes of this section.

(8)    References in this section to a contract of employment include any contract under which one person personally does work or performs services for another; and related expressions shall be construed accordingly.

(9)    Nothing in this section shall be construed as requiring a trade union to hold separate ballots for the purposes of this section and sections 226 to 234 (requirement of ballot before action by trade union).

*Right not to be denied access to the courts*

## 63    Right not to be denied access to the courts

(1)    This section applies where a matter is under the rules of a trade union required or allowed to be submitted for determination or conciliation in accordance with the rules of the union, but a provision of the rules purporting to provide for that to be a person's only remedy has no effect (or would have no effect if there were one).

(2)    Notwithstanding anything in the rules of the union or in the practice of any court, if a member or former member of the union begins proceedings in a court with respect to a matter to which this section applies, then if—
(a)    he has previously made a valid application to the union for the matter to be submitted for determination or conciliation in accordance with the union's rules, and
(b)    the court proceedings are begun after the end of the period of six months beginning with the day on which the union received the application,
the rules requiring or allowing the matter to be so submitted, and the fact that any relevant steps remain to be taken under the rules, shall be regarded for all purposes as irrelevant to any question whether the court proceedings should be dismissed, stayed or sisted, or adjourned.

(3)    An application shall be deemed to be valid for the purposes of subsection (2)(a) unless the union informed the applicant, before the end of the period of 28 days beginning with the date on which the union received the application, of the respects in which the application contravened the requirements of the rules.

(4)    If the court is satisfied that any delay in the taking of relevant steps under the rules is attributable to unreasonable conduct of the person who commenced the proceedings, it may treat the period specified in subsection (2)(b) as extended by such further period as it considers appropriate.

(5)    In this section—
(a)    references to the rules of a trade union include any arbitration or other agreement entered into in pursuance of a requirement imposed by or under the rules; and
(b)    references to the relevant steps under the rules, in relation to any matter, include any steps falling to be taken in accordance with the rules for the purposes of or in connection with the determination or conciliation of the matter, or any appeal, review or reconsideration of any determination or award.

(6)    This section does not affect any enactment or rule of law by virtue of which a court would apart from this section disregard any such rules of a trade union or any such fact as is mentioned in subsection (2).

*Right not to be unjustifiably disciplined*

## 64    Right not to be unjustifiably disciplined

(1)    An individual who is or has been a member of a trade union has the right not to be unjustifiably disciplined by the union.

(2)    For this purpose an individual is 'disciplined' by a trade union if a determination is made, or purportedly made, under the rules of the union or by an official of the union or a number of persons including an official that—

(a)    he should be expelled from the union or a branch or section of the union,

(b)    he should pay a sum to the union, to a branch or section of the union or to any other person;

(c)    sums tendered by him in respect of an obligation to pay subscriptions or other sums to the union, or to a branch or section of the union, should be treated as unpaid or paid for a different purpose,

(d)    he should be deprived to any extent of, or of access to, any benefits, services or facilities which would otherwise be provided or made available to him by virtue of his membership of the union, or a branch or section of the union,

(e)    another trade union, or a branch or section of it, should be encouraged or advised not to accept him as a member, or

(f)    he should be subjected to some other detriment;

and whether an individual is 'unjustifiably disciplined' shall be determined in accordance with section 65.

(3)    Where a determination made in infringement of an individual's right under this section requires the payment of a sum or the performance of an obligation, no person is entitled in any proceedings to rely on that determination for the purpose of recovering the sum or enforcing the obligation.

(4)    Subject to that, the remedies for infringement of the right conferred by this section are as provided by sections 66 and 67, and not otherwise.

(5)    The right not to be unjustifiably disciplined is in addition to (and not in substitution for) any right which exists apart from this section; and, subject to section 66(4), nothing in this section or sections 65 to 67 affects any remedy for infringement of any such right.

## 65    Meaning of "unjustifiably disciplined"

(1)    An individual is unjustifiably disciplined by a trade union if the actual or supposed conduct which constitutes the reason, or one of the reasons, for disciplining him is—

(a)    conduct to which this section applies, or

(b)    something which is believed by the union to amount to such conduct;

but subject to subsection (6) (cases of bad faith in relation to assertion of wrongdoing).

(2)    This section applies to conduct which consists in—

(a)    failing to participate in or support a strike or other industrial action (whether by members of the union or by others), or indicating opposition to or a lack of support for such action;

(b)    failing to contravene, for a purpose connected with such a strike or other industrial action, a requirement imposed on him by or under a contract of employment;

(c)    asserting (whether by bringing proceedings or otherwise) that the union, any official or representative of it or a trustee of its property has contravened, or is proposing to contravene, a requirement which is, or is thought to be, imposed by or under the rules of the union or any other agreement or by or under any enactment (whenever passed) or any rule of law;

(d)    encouraging or assisting a person—

(i)    to perform an obligation imposed on him by a contract of employment, or

(ii)    to make or attempt to vindicate any such assertion as is mentioned in paragraph (c);

(e)    contravening a requirement imposed by or in consequence of a determination which infringes the individual's or another individual's right not to be unjustifiably disciplined;

(f)  failing to agree, or withdrawing agreement, to the making from his wages (in accordance with arrangements between his employer and the union) of deductions representing payments to the union in respect of his membership,

(g)  resigning or proposing to resign from the union or from another union, becoming or proposing to become a member of another union, refusing to become a member of another union, or being a member of another union,

(h)  working with, or proposing to work with, individuals who are not members of the union or who are or are not members of another union,

(i)  working for, or proposing to work for, an employer who employs or who has employed individuals who are not members of the union or who are or are not members of another union, or

(j)  requiring the union to do an act which the union is, by any provision of this Act, required to do on the requisition of a member.

(3)  This section applies to conduct which involves the Certification Officer being consulted or asked to provide advice or assistance with respect to any matter whatever, or which involves any person being consulted or asked to provide advice or assistance with respect to a matter which forms, or might form, the subject-matter of any such assertion as is mentioned in subsection (2)(c) above.

(4)  This section also applies to conduct which consists in proposing to engage in, or doing anything preparatory or incidental to, conduct falling within subsection (2) or (3).

(5)  This section does not apply to an act, omission or statement comprised in conduct falling within subsection (2), (3) or (4) above if it is shown that the act, omission or statement is one in respect of which individuals would be disciplined by the union irrespective of whether their acts, omissions or statements were in connection with conduct within subsection (2) or (3) above.

(6)  An individual is not unjustifiably disciplined if it is shown—

(a)  that the reason for disciplining him, or one of them, is that he made such an assertion as is mentioned in subsection (2)(c), or encouraged or assisted another person to make or attempt to vindicate such an assertion,

(b)  that the assertion was false, and

(c)  that he made the assertion, or encouraged or assisted another person to make or attempt to vindicate it, in the belief that it was false or otherwise in bad faith,

and that there was no other reason for disciplining him or that the only other reasons were reasons in respect of which he does not fall to be treated as unjustifiably disciplined.

(7)  In this section—

"conduct" includes statements, acts and omissions;

"contract of employment", in relation to an individual, includes any agreement between that individual and a person for whom he works or normally works,

"employer" includes such a person and related expressions shall be construed accordingly;

"representative", in relation to a union, means a person acting or purporting to act—

(a)  in his capacity as a member of the union, or

(b)  on the instructions or advice of a person acting or purporting to act in that capacity or in the capacity of an official of the union.

"require" (on the part of an individual) includes request or apply for, and "requisition" shall be construed accordingly; and

"wages" shall be construed in accordance with the definitions of "contract of employment", "employer" and related expressions.

(8)  Where a person holds any office or employment under the Crown on terms which do not constitute a contract of employment between him and the Crown, those terms shall nevertheless be deemed to constitute such a contract for the purposes of this section.

## 66  Complaint of infringement of right

(1)  An individual who claims that he has been unjustifiably disciplined by a trade union may present a complaint against the union to an employment tribunal.

(2)  The tribunal shall not entertain such a complaint unless it is presented—

(a)   before the end of the period of three months beginning with the date of the making of the determination claimed to infringe the right, or

(b)   where the tribunal is satisfied—

   (i)    that it was not reasonably practicable for the complaint to be presented before the end of that period, or

   (ii)   that any delay in making the complaint is wholly or partly attributable to a reasonable attempt to appeal against the determination or to have it reconsidered or reviewed,

within such further period as the tribunal considers reasonable.

(2A) Section 292A (extension of time limits to facilitate conciliation before institution of proceedings) applies for the purposes of subsection (2)(a).

(3)   Where the tribunal finds the complaint well-founded, it shall make a declaration to that effect.

(4)   Where a complaint relating to an expulsion which is presented under this section is declared to be well-founded, no complaint in respect of the expulsion shall be presented or proceeded with under section 174 (right not to be excluded or expelled from trade union).

## 67   Further remedies for infringement of right

(1)   An individual whose complaint under section 66 has been declared to be well-founded may make an application to an employment tribunal for one or both of the following—

(a)   an award of compensation to be paid to him by the union;

(b)   an order that the union pay him an amount equal to any sum which he has paid in pursuance of any such determination as is mentioned in section 64(2)(b).

(2)   ...

(3)   An application under this section shall not be entertained if made before the end of the period of four weeks beginning with the date of the declaration or after the end of the period of six months beginning with that date.

(4)   ...

(5)   The amount of compensation awarded shall, subject to the following provisions, be such as the employment tribunal considers just and equitable in all the circumstances.

(6)   In determining the amount of compensation to be awarded, the same rule shall be applied concerning the duty of a person to mitigate his loss as applies to damages recoverable under the common law in England and Wales or Scotland.

(7)   Where the employment tribunal finds that the infringement complained of was to any extent caused or contributed to by the action of the applicant, it shall reduce the amount of the compensation by such proportion as it considers just and equitable having regard to that finding.

(8)   The amount of compensation calculated in accordance with subsections (5) to (7) shall not exceed the aggregate of—

(a)   an amount equal to 30 times the limit for the time being imposed by section 227(1)(a) of the Employment Rights Act 1996 (maximum amount of a week's pay for basic award in unfair dismissal cases), and

(b)   an amount equal to the limit for the time being imposed by section 124(1) of that Act (maximum compensatory award in such cases) ...

(8A) If on the date on which the application was made—

(a)   the determination infringing the applicant's right not to be unjustifiably disciplined has not been revoked, or

(b)   the union has failed to take all the steps necessary for securing the reversal of anything done for the purpose of giving effect to the determination,

the amount of compensation shall be not less than the amount for the time being specified in section 176(6A).

(9)   ...

*Right not to suffer deduction of unauthorised union subscriptions*

## 68   Right not to suffer deduction of unauthorised union subscriptions

(1)   Where arrangements ('subscription deduction arrangements') exist between the employer of a worker and a trade union relating to the making from workers' wages of

deductions representing payments to the union in respect of the workers' membership of the union ('subscription deductions'), the employer shall ensure that no subscription deduction is made from wages payable to the worker on any day unless—

   (a)   the worker has authorised in writing the making from his wages of subscription deductions; and

   (b)   the worker has not withdrawn the authorisation.

(2)   A worker withdraws an authorisation given for the purposes of subsection (1), in relation to a subscription deduction which falls to be made from wages payable to him on any day, if a written notice withdrawing the authorisation has been received by the employer in time for it to be reasonably practicable for the employer to secure that no such deduction is made.

(3)   A worker's authorisation of the making of subscription deductions from his wages shall not give rise to any obligation on the part of the employer to the worker to maintain or continue to maintain subscription deduction arrangements.

(4)   In this section and section 68A, 'employer', 'wages' and 'worker' have the same meanings as in the Employment Rights Act 1996.

## 68A   Complaint of infringement of rights

(1)   A worker may present a complaint to an employment tribunal that his employer has made a deduction from his wages in contravention of section 68—

   (a)   within the period of three months beginning with the date of the payment of the wages from which the deduction, or (if the complaint relates to more than one deduction) the last of the deductions, was made, or

   (b)   where the tribunal is satisfied that it was not reasonably practicable for the complaint to be presented within that period, within such further period as the tribunal considers reasonable.

(1A) Section 292A (extension of time limits to facilitate conciliation before institution of proceedings) applies for the purposes of subsection (1)(a).

(2)   Where a tribunal finds that a complaint under this section is well-founded, it shall make a declaration to that effect and shall order the employer to pay to the worker the whole amount of the deduction, less any such part of the amount as has already been paid to the worker by the employer.

(3)   Where the making of a deduction from the wages of a worker both contravenes section 68(1) and involves one or more of the contraventions specified in subsection (4) of this section, the aggregate amount which may be ordered by an employment tribunal or court (whether on the same occasion or on different occasions) to be paid in respect of the contraventions shall not exceed the amount, or (where different amounts may be ordered to be paid in respect of different contraventions) the greatest amount, which may be ordered to be paid in respect of any one of them.

(4)   The contraventions referred to in subsection (3) are—

   (a)   a contravention of the requirement not to make a deduction without having given the particulars required by section 8 (itemised pay statements) or 9(1) (standing statements of fixed deductions) of the Employment Rights Act 1996,

   (b)   a contravention of section 13 of that Act (requirement not to make unauthorised deductions), and

   (c)   a contravention of section 86(1) or 90(1) of this Act (requirements not to make deductions of political fund contributions in certain circumstances).

*Right to terminate membership of union*

## 69   Right to terminate membership of union

In every contract of membership of a trade union, whether made before or after the passing of this Act, a term conferring a right on the member, on giving reasonable notice and complying with any reasonable conditions, to terminate his membership of the union shall be implied.

*Supplementary*

## 70    Membership of constituent or affiliated organisation

In this Chapter 'member', in relation to a trade union consisting wholly or partly of, or of representatives of, constituent or affiliated organisations, includes a member of any of the constituent or affiliated organisations.

CHAPTER VII

A BREACH OF RULES

## 108A  Right to apply to Certification Officer

(1)   A person who claims that there has been a breach or threatened breach of the rules of a trade union relating to any of the matters mentioned in subsection (2) may apply to the Certification Officer for a declaration to that effect, subject to subsections (3) to (7).

(2)   The matters are—

    (a)   the appointment or election of a person to, or the removal of a person from, any office;

    (b)   disciplinary proceedings by the union (including expulsion);

    (c)   the balloting of members on any issue other than industrial action;

    (d)   the constitution or proceedings of any executive committee or of any decision-making meeting;

    (e)   such other matters as may be specified in an order made by the Secretary of State.

(3)   The applicant must be a member of the union, or have been one at the time of the alleged breach or threatened breach.

(4)   A person may not apply under subsection (1) in relation to a claim if he is entitled to apply under section 80 in relation to the claim.

(5)   No application may be made regarding—

    (a)   the dismissal of an employee of the union;

    (b)   disciplinary proceedings against an employee of the union.

(6)   An application must be made—

    (a)   within the period of six months starting with the day on which the breach or threatened breach is alleged to have taken place, or

    (b)   if within that period any internal complaints procedure of the union is invoked to resolve the claim, within the period of six months starting with the earlier of the days specified in subsection (7).

(7)   Those days are—

    (a)   the day on which the procedure is concluded, and (b) the last day of the period of one year beginning with the day on which the procedure is invoked.

(8)   The reference in subsection (1) to the rules of a union includes references to the rules of any branch or section of the union.

(9)   In subsection (2)(c) 'industrial action' means a strike or other industrial action by persons employed under contracts of employment.

(10)  For the purposes of subsection (2)(d) a committee is an executive committee if—

    (a)   it is a committee of the union concerned and has power to make executive decisions on behalf of the union or on behalf of a constituent body,

    (b)   it is a committee of a major constituent body and has power to make executive decisions on behalf of that body, or

    (c)   it is a sub-committee of a committee falling within paragraph (a) or (b).

(11)  For the purposes of subsection (2)(d) a decision-making meeting is—

    (a)   a meeting of members of the union concerned (or the representatives of such members) which has power to make a decision on any matter which, under the rules of the union, is final as regards the union or which, under the rules of the union or a constituent body, is final as regards that body, or

    (b)   a meeting of members of a major constituent body (or the representatives of such members) which has power to make a decision on any matter which, under the rules of the union or the body, is final as regards that body.

(12) For the purposes of subsections (10) and (11), in relation to the trade union concerned—
    (a)    a constituent body is any body which forms part of the union, including a branch, group, section or region;
    (b)    a major constituent body is such a body which has more than 1,000 members.

(13) Any order under subsection (2)(e) shall be made by statutory instrument; and no such order shall be made unless a draft of it has been laid before and approved by resolution of each House of Parliament.

(14) If a person applies to the Certification Officer under this section in relation to an alleged breach or threatened breach he may not apply to the court in relation to the breach or threatened breach; but nothing in this subsection shall prevent such a person from exercising any right to appeal against or challenge the Certification Officer's decision on the application to him.

(15) If—
    (a)    a person applies to the court in relation to an alleged breach or threatened breach, and
    (b)    the breach or threatened breach is one in relation to which he could have made an application to the Certification Officer under this section,
he may not apply to the Certification Officer under this section in relation to the breach or threatened breach.

## 108B  Declarations and orders

(1) The Certification Officer may refuse to accept an application under section 108A unless he is satisfied that the applicant has taken all reasonable steps to resolve the claim by the use of any internal complaints procedure of the union.

(2) If he accepts an application under section 108A the Certification Officer—
    (a)    shall make such enquiries as he thinks fit,
    (b)    shall give the applicant and the union an opportunity to be heard,
    (c)    shall ensure that, so far as is reasonably practicable, the application is determined within six months of being made,
    (d)    may make or refuse the declaration asked for, and
    (e)    shall, whether he makes or refuses the declaration, give reasons for his decision in writing.

(3) Where the Certification Officer makes a declaration he shall also, unless he considers that to do so would be inappropriate, make an enforcement order, that is, an order imposing on the union one or both of the following requirements—
    (a)    to take such steps to remedy the breach, or withdraw the threat of a breach, as may be specified in the order;
    (b)    to abstain from such acts as may be so specified with a view to securing that a breach or threat of the same or a similar kind does not occur in future.

(4) The Certification Officer shall in an order imposing any such requirement as is mentioned in subsection (3)(a) specify the period within which the union is to comply with the requirement.

(5) Where the Certification Officer requests a person to furnish information to him in connection with enquiries made by him under this section, he shall specify the date by which that information is to be furnished and, unless he considers that it would be inappropriate to do so, shall proceed with his determination of the application notwithstanding that the information has not been furnished to him by the specified date.

(6) A declaration made by the Certification Officer under this section may be relied on as if it were a declaration made by the court.

(7) Where an enforcement order has been made, any person who is a member of the union and was a member at the time it was made is entitled to enforce obedience to the order as if he had made the application on which the order was made.

(8) An enforcement order made by the Certification Officer under this section may be enforced by the Certificate Officer, the applicant or a person mentioned in the same way as an order of the court.

(9) An order under section 108A(2)(e) may provide that, in relation to an application under section 108A with regard to a prescribed matter, the preceding provisions of this section shall apply with such omissions or modifications as may be specified in the order; and a prescribed matter is such matter specified under section 108A(2)(e) as is prescribed under this subsection.

## 108C  Appeals from Certification Officer

An appeal lies to the Employment Appeal Tribunal on any question arising in proceedings before or arising from any decision of the Certification Officer under this Chapter.

**Note:** Words 'on any question of law arising' in italics repealed and subsequent words in square brackets substituted by the Trade Union Act 2016, s 21(e). Date in force: to be appointed.

### CHAPTER IX
### MISCELLANEOUS AND GENERAL PROVISIONS

*Exceptions and adaptations for certain bodies*

## 118  Federated trade unions

(1)  In this section a 'federated trade union' means a trade union which consists wholly or mainly of constituent or affiliated organisations, or representatives of such organisations, as described in paragraph (b) of the definition of 'trade union' in section 1.

(2)  The provisions of this Part apply to federated trade unions subject to the following exceptions and adaptations.

(3)  For the purposes of section 22 (limit on amount of damages) as it applies to a federated trade union, the members of such of its constituent or affiliated organisations as have their head or main office in Great Britain shall be treated as members of the union.

(4)  The following provisions of Chapter III (trade union administration) do not apply to a federated trade union which consists wholly or mainly of representatives of constituent or affiliated organisations—

    (a)    section 27 (duty to supply copy of rules),

    (b)    section 28 (duty to keep accounting records),

    (c)    sections 32 to 37 (annual return, statement for members, accounts and audit),

    (ca)   sections 37A to 37E (investigation of financial affairs), and

    (d)    sections 38 to 42 (members' superannuation schemes).

(4A)  In the case of a federated trade union which, by virtue of subsection (4), is not required to send an annual return to the Certification Officer under section 32, section 24ZA (duty to provide membership audit certificate) applies as if section 32 does apply to the union.

(5)  Sections 29 to 31 (right of member to access to accounting records) do not apply to a federated trade union which has no members other than constituent or affiliated organisations or representatives of such organisations.

(6)  Sections 24 to 26 (register of members' names and addresses) and Chapter IV (elections for certain trade union positions) do not apply to a federated trade union—

    (a)    if it has no individual members other than representatives of constituent or affiliated organisations, or

    (b)    if its individual members (other than such representatives) are all merchant seamen and a majority of them are ordinarily resident outside the United Kingdom. For this purpose 'merchant seaman' means a person whose employment, or the greater part of it, is carried out on board sea-going ships.

(7)  The provisions of Chapter VI (application of funds for political objects) apply to a trade union which is in whole or part an association or combination of other unions as if the individual members of the component unions were members of that union and not of the component unions.

But nothing in that Chapter prevents a component union from collecting contributions on behalf of the association or combination from such of its members as are contributions to the political fund of the association or combination.

(8)  In the application of section 116A to a federated trade union, subsection (2) of that section shall be omitted.

*Interpretation*

## 119  Expressions relating to trade unions

In this Act, in relation to a trade union—

'agent' means a banker or solicitor of, or any person employed as an auditor by, the union or any branch or section of the union;

'branch or section', except where the context otherwise requires, includes a branch or section which is itself a trade union;

'executive' means the principal committee of the union exercising executive functions, by whatever name it is called;

'financial affairs' means affairs of the union relating to any fund which is applicable for the purposes of the union (including any fund of a branch or section of the union which is so applicable);

'general secretary' means the official of the union who holds the office of general secretary or, where there is no such office, holds an office which is equivalent, or (except in section 14(4)) the nearest equivalent, to that of general secretary;

'officer' includes—

(a)     any member of the governing body of the union, and

(b)     any trustee of any fund applicable for the purposes of the union;

'official' means—

(a)     an officer of the union or of a branch or section of the union, or

(b)     a person elected or appointed in accordance with the rules of the union to be a representative of its members or of some of them,

and includes a person so elected or appointed who is an employee of the same employer as the members or one or more of the members whom he is to represent;

'president' means the official of the union who holds the office of president or, where there is no such office, who holds an office which is equivalent, or (except in section 14(4) or Chapter IV) the nearest equivalent, to that of president; and

'rules', except where the context otherwise requires, includes the rules of any branch or section of the union.

## PART II
## EMPLOYERS' ASSOCIATIONS

### Introductory

## 122   Meaning of 'employers' association'

(1)   In this Act an 'employers' association' means an organisation (whether temporary or permanent)—

(a)     which consists wholly or mainly of employers or individual owners of undertakings of one or more descriptions and whose principal purposes include the regulation of relations between employers of that description or those descriptions and workers or trade unions; or

(b)     which consists wholly or mainly of—

(i)     constituent or affiliated organisations which fulfil the conditions in paragraph (a) (or themselves consist wholly or mainly of constituent or affiliated organisations which fulfil those conditions), or

(ii)     representatives of such constituent or affiliated organisations,

and whose principal purposes include the regulation of relations between employers and workers or between employers and trade unions, or the regulation of relations between its constituent or affiliated organisations.

(2)   References in this Act to employers' associations include combinations of employers and employers' associations.

## PART III
## RIGHTS IN RELATION TO UNION MEMBERSHIP AND ACTIVITIES

### Access to employment

## 137   Refusal of employment on grounds related to union membership

(1)   It is unlawful to refuse a person employment—

(a)     because he is, or is not, a member of a trade union, or

(b)     because he is unwilling to accept a requirement—

(i)     to take steps to become or cease to be, or to remain or not to become, a member of a trade union, or

(ii)     to make payments or suffer deductions in the event of his not being a member of a trade union.

(2)   A person who is thus unlawfully refused employment has a right of complaint to an employment tribunal.

(3)   Where an advertisement is published which indicates, or might reasonably be understood as indicating—

    (a)   that employment to which the advertisement relates is open only to a person who is, or is not, a member of a trade union, or

    (b)   that any such requirement as is mentioned in subsection (1)(b) will be imposed in relation to employment to which the advertisement relates,

a person who does not satisfy that condition or, as the case may be, is unwilling to accept that requirement, and who seeks and is refused employment to which the advertisement relates, shall be conclusively presumed to have been refused employment for that reason.

(4)   Where there is an arrangement or practice under which employment is offered only to persons put forward or approved by a trade union, and the trade union puts forward or approves only persons who are members of the union, a person who is not a member of the union and who is refused employment in pursuance of the arrangement or practice shall be taken to have been refused employment because he is not a member of the trade union.

(5)   A person shall be taken to be refused employment if he seeks employment of any description with a person and that person—

    (a)   refuses or deliberately omits to entertain and process his application or enquiry, or

    (b)   causes him to withdraw or cease to pursue his application or enquiry, or

    (c)   refuses or deliberately omits to offer him employment of that description, or

    (d)   makes him an offer of such employment the terms of which are such as no reasonable employer who wished to fill the post would offer and which is not accepted, or

    (e)   makes him an offer of such employment but withdraws it or causes him not to accept it.

(6)   Where a person is offered employment on terms which include a requirement that he is, or is not, a member of a trade union, or any such requirement as is mentioned in subsection (1)(b), and he does not accept the offer because he does not satisfy or, as the case may be, is unwilling to accept the requirement, he shall be treated as having been refused employment for that reason.

(7)   Where a person may not be considered for appointment or election to an office in a trade union unless he is a member of the union, or of a particular branch or section of the union or of one of a number of particular branches or sections of the union, nothing in this section applies to anything done for the purpose of securing compliance with that condition although as holder of the office he would be employed by the union.

For this purpose an 'office' means any position—

    (a)   by virtue of which the holder is an official of the union, or

    (b)   to which Chapter IV of Part I applies (duty to hold elections).

(8)   The provisions of this section apply in relation to an employment agency acting, or purporting to act, on behalf of an employer as in relation to an employer.

## 138   Refusal of service of employment agency on grounds related to union membership

(1)   It is unlawful for an employment agency to refuse a person any of its services—

    (a)   because he is, or is not, a member of a trade union, or

    (b)   because he is unwilling to accept a requirement to take steps to become or cease to be, or to remain or not to become, a member of a trade union.

(2)   A person who is thus unlawfully refused any service of an employment agency has a right of complaint to an employment tribunal.

(2A) Section 12A of the Employment Tribunals Act 1996 (financial penalties) applies in relation to a complaint under this section as it applies in relation to a claim involving an employer and a worker (reading references to an employer as references to the employment agency and references to a worker as references to the complainant).

(3)   Where an advertisement is published which indicates, or might reasonably be understood as indicating—

    (a)    that any service of an employment agency is available only to a person who is, or is not, a member of a trade union, or

    (b)    that any such requirement as is mentioned in subsection (1)(b) will be imposed in relation to a service to which the advertisement relates,

a person who does not satisfy that condition or, as the case may be, is unwilling to accept that requirement, and who seeks to avail himself of and is refused that service, shall be conclusively presumed to have been refused it for that reason.

(4)    A person shall be taken to be refused a service if he seeks to avail himself of it and the agency—

    (a)    refuses or deliberately omits to make the service available to him, or

    (b)    causes him not to avail himself of the service or to cease to avail himself of it, or

    (c)    does not provide the same service, on the same terms, as is provided to others.

(5)    Where a person is offered a service on terms which include a requirement that he is, or is not, a member of a trade union, or any such requirement as is mentioned in subsection (1)(b), and he does not accept the offer because he does not satisfy or, as the case may be, is unwilling to accept that requirement, he shall be treated as having been refused the service for that reason.

## 139   Time limit for proceedings

(1)    An employment tribunal shall not consider a complaint under section 137 or 138 unless it is presented to the tribunal—

    (a)    before the end of the period of three months beginning with the date of the conduct to which the complaint relates, or

    (b)    where the tribunal is satisfied that it was not reasonably practicable for the complaint to be presented before the end of that period, within such further period as the tribunal considers reasonable.

(2)    The date of the conduct to which a complaint under section 137 relates shall be taken to be—

    (a)    in the case of an actual refusal, the date of the refusal;

    (b)    in the case of a deliberate omission—

        (i)    to entertain and process the complainant's application or enquiry, or

        (ii)   to offer employment,

the end of the period within which it was reasonable to except the employer to act;

    (c)    in the case of conduct causing the complainant to withdraw or cease to pursue his application or enquiry, the date of that conduct;

    (d)    in a case where an offer was made but withdrawn, the date when it was withdrawn;

    (e)    in any other case where an offer was made but not accepted, the date on which it was made.

(3)    The date of the conduct to which a complaint under section 138 relates shall be taken to be—

    (a)    in the case of an actual refusal, the date of the refusal;

    (b)    in the case of a deliberate omission to make a service available, the end of the period within which it was reasonable to expect the employment agency to act;

    (c)    in the case of conduct causing the complainant not to avail himself of a service or to cease to avail himself of it, the date of that conduct;

    (d)    in the case of failure to provide the same service, on the same terms, as is provided to others, the date or last date on which the service in fact provided was provided.

(4)    Section 292A (extension of time limits to facilitate conciliation before institution of proceedings) applies for the purposes of subsection (1)(a).

## 140   Remedies

(1)    Where the employment tribunal finds that a complaint under section 137 or 138 is well-founded, it shall make a declaration to that effect and may make such of the following as it considers just and equitable—

    (a)    an order requiring the respondent to pay compensation to the complainant of such amount as the tribunal may determine;

    (b)    a recommendation that the respondent take within a specified period action appearing to the tribunal to be practicable for the purpose of obviating or reducing the adverse effect on the complainant of any conduct to which the complaint relates.

(2)    Compensation shall be assessed on the same basis as damages for breach of statutory duty and may include compensation for injury to feelings.

(3)    If the respondent fails without reasonable justification to comply with a recommendation to take action, the tribunal may increase its award of compensation or, if it has not made such an award, make one.

(4)    The total amount of compensation shall not exceed the limit for the time being imposed by section 124(1) of the Employment Rights Act 1996 (limit on compensation for unfair dismissal).

## 141    Complaint against employer and employment agency

(1)    Where a person has a right of complaint against a prospective employer and against an employment agency arising out of the same facts, he may present a complaint against either of them or against them jointly.

(2)    If a complaint is brought against one only, he or the complainant may request the tribunal to join or sist the other as a party to the proceedings.

The request shall be granted if it is made before the hearing of the complaint begins, but may be refused if it is made after that time; and no such request may be made after the tribunal has made its decision as to whether the complaint is well-founded.

(3)    Where a complaint is brought against an employer and an employment agency jointly, or where it is brought against one and the other is joined or sisted as a party to the proceedings, and the tribunal—

    (a)    finds that the complaint is well-founded as against the employer and the agency, and

    (b)    makes an award of compensation,

it may order that the compensation shall be paid by the one or the other, or partly by one and partly by the other, as the tribunal may consider just and equitable in the circumstances.

## 142    Awards against third parties

(1)    If in proceedings on a complaint under section 137 or 138 either the complainant or the respondent claims that the respondent was induced to act in the manner complained of by pressure which a trade union or other person exercised on him by calling, organising, procuring or financing a strike or other industrial action, or by threatening to do so, the complainant or the respondent may request the employment tribunal to direct that the person who he claims exercised the pressure be joined or sisted as a party to the proceedings.

(2)    The request shall be granted if it is made before the hearing of the complaint begins, but may be refused if it is made after that time; and no such request may be made after the tribunal has made its decision as to whether the complaint is well-founded.

(3)    Where a person has been so joined or sisted as a party to the proceedings and the tribunal—

    (a)    finds that the complaint is well-founded,

    (b)    makes an award of compensation, and

    (c)    also finds that the claim in subsection (1) above is well-founded,

it may order that the compensation shall be paid by the person joined instead of by the respondent, or partly by that person and partly by the respondent, as the tribunal may consider just and equitable in the circumstances.

(4)    Where by virtue of section 141 (complaint against employer and employment agency) there is more than one respondent, the above provisions apply to either or both of them.

## 143 Interpretation and other supplementary provisions

(1) In sections 137 to 143—

'advertisement' includes every form of advertisement or notice, whether to the public or not, and references to publishing an advertisement shall be construed accordingly;

'employment' means employment under a contract of employment, and related expressions shall be construed accordingly; and

'employment agency' means a person who, for profit or not, provides services for the purpose of finding employment for workers or supplying employers with workers, but subject to subsection (2) below.

(2) For the purposes of sections 137 to 143 as they apply to employment agencies—

    (a) services other than those mentioned in the definition of 'employment agency' above shall be disregarded, and

    (b) a trade union shall not be regarded as an employment agency by reason of services provided by it only for, or in relation to, its members.

(3) References in sections 137 to 143 to being or not being a member of a trade union are to being or not being a member of any trade union, of a particular trade union or of one of a number of particular trade unions.

Any such reference includes a reference to being or not being a member of a particular branch or section of a trade union or of one of a number of particular branches or sections of a trade union.

(4) The remedy of a person for conduct which is unlawful by virtue of section 137 or 138 is by way of a complaint to an employment tribunal in accordance with this Part, and not otherwise.

No other legal liability arises by reason that conduct is unlawful by virtue of either of those sections.

*Detriment*

## 146 Detriment on grounds related to union membership or activities

(1) A worker has the right not to be subjected to any detriment as an individual by any act, or any deliberate failure to act, by his employer if the act or failure takes place for the sole or main purpose of—

    (a) preventing or deterring him from being or seeking to become a member of an independent trade union, or penalising him for doing so,

    (b) preventing or deterring him from taking part in the activities of an independent trade union at an appropriate time, or penalising him for doing so,

    (ba) preventing or deterring him from making use of trade union services at an appropriate time, or penalising him for doing so, or

    (c) compelling him to be or become a member of any trade union or of a particular trade union or of one of a number of particular trade unions.

(2) In subsection (1) 'an appropriate time' means—

    (a) a time outside the worker's working hours, or

    (b) a time within his working hours at which, in accordance with arrangements agreed with or consent given by his employer, it is permissible for him to take part in the activities of a trade union or (as the case may be) make use of trade union services;

and for this purpose 'working hours', in relation to a worker, means any time when, in accordance with his contract of employment (or other contract personally to do work or perform services), he is required to be at work.

(2A) In this section—

    (a) 'trade union services' means services made available to the worker by an independent trade union by virtue of his membership of the union, and

    (b) references to a worker's 'making use' of trade union services include his consenting to the raising of a matter on his behalf by an independent trade union of which he is a member.

(2B) If an independent trade union of which a worker is a member raises a matter on his behalf (with or without his consent), penalising the worker for that is to be treated as penalising him as mentioned in subsection (1)(ba).

(2C) A worker also has the right not to be subjected to any detriment as an individual by any act, or any deliberate failure to act, by his employer if the act or failure takes place because of the worker's failure to accept an offer made in contravention of section 145A or 145B.

(2D) For the purposes of subsection (2C), not conferring a benefit that, if the offer had been accepted by the worker, would have been conferred on him under the resulting agreement shall be taken to be subjecting him to a detriment as an individual (and to be a deliberate failure to act).

(3) A worker also has the right not to be subjected to any detriment as an individual by any act, or any deliberate failure to act, by his employer if the act or failure takes place for the sole or main purpose of enforcing a requirement (whether or not imposed by a contract of employment or in writing) that, in the event of his not being a member of any trade union or of a particular trade union or of one of a number of particular trade unions, he must make one or more payments.

(4) For the purposes of subsection (3) any deduction made by an employer from the remuneration payable to a worker in respect of his employment shall, if it is attributable to his not being a member of any trade union or of a particular trade union or of one of a number of particular trade unions, be treated as a detriment to which he has been subjected as an individual by an act of his employer taking place for the sole or main purpose of enforcing a requirement of a kind mentioned in that subsection.

(5) A worker or former worker may present a complaint to an employment tribunal on the ground that he has been subjected to a detriment by his employer in contravention of this section.

(5A) This section does not apply where—
  (a)   the worker is an employee; and
  (b)   the detriment in question amounts to dismissal.

## 147   Time limit for proceedings

(1) An employment tribunal shall not consider a complaint under section 146 unless it is presented—
  (a)   before the end of the period of three months beginning with the date of the act or failure to which the complaint relates or, where that act or failure is part of a series of similar acts or failures (or both) the last of them, or
  (b)   where the tribunal is satisfied that it was not reasonably practicable for the complaint to be presented before the end of that period, within such further period as it considers reasonable.

(2) For the purposes of subsection (1)—
  (a)   where an act extends over a period, the reference to the date of the act is a reference to the last day of that period;
  (b)   a failure to act shall be treated as done when it was decided on.

(3) For the purposes of subsection (2), in the absence of evidence establishing the contrary an employer shall be taken to decide on a failure to act—
  (a)   when he does an act inconsistent with doing the failed act, or (b) if he has done no such inconsistent act, when the period expires within which he might reasonably have been expected to do the failed act if it was to be done.

(4) Section 292A (extension of time limits to facilitate conciliation before institution of proceedings) applies for the purposes of subsection (1)(a).

## 148   Consideration of complaint

(1) On a complaint under section 146 it shall be for the employer to show the purpose for which he acted or failed to act.

(2) In determining any question whether the employer acted or failed to act, or the purpose for which he did so, no account shall be taken of any pressure which was exercised on him by calling, organising, procuring or financing a strike or other industrial action, or by threatening to do so; and that question shall be determined as if no such pressure had been exercised.

(3) In determining what was the purpose for which the employer acted or failed to act in a case where—
  (a)   there is evidence that the employer's purpose was to further a change in his relationship with all or any class of his employees, and
  (b)   there is also evidence that his purpose was one falling within section 146,

the tribunal shall regard the purpose mentioned in paragraph (a) (and not the purpose mentioned in paragraph (b)) as the purpose for which the employer acted or failed to act, unless it considers that no reasonable employer would act or fail to act in the way concerned having regard to the purpose mentioned in paragraph (a).

(4) Where the tribunal determines that—
  (a) the complainant has been subjected to a detriment by an act or deliberate failure to act by his employer, and
  (b) the act or failure took place in consequence of a previous act or deliberate failure to act by the employer,
  paragraph (a) of subsection (3) is satisfied if the purpose mentioned in that paragraph was the purpose of the previous act or failure.

(5) In subsection (3) 'class', in relation to an employer and his employees, means those employed at a particular place of work, those employees of a particular grade, category or description or those of a particular grade, category or description employed at a particular place of work.

## 149  Remedies

(1) Where the employment tribunal finds that a complaint under section 146 is well-founded, it shall make a declaration to that effect and may make an award of compensation to be paid by the employer to the complainant in respect of the act or failure complained of.

(2) The amount of the compensation awarded shall be such as the tribunal considers just and equitable in all the circumstances having regard to the infringement complained of and to any loss sustained by the complainant which is attributable to the act or failure which infringed his right.

(3) The loss shall be taken to include—
  (a) any expenses reasonably incurred by the complainant in consequence of the act or failure complained of, and
  (b) loss of any benefit which he might reasonably be expected to have had but for that act or failure.

(4) In ascertaining the loss, the tribunal shall apply the same rule concerning the duty of a person to mitigate his loss as applies to damages recoverable under the common law of England and Wales or Scotland.

(5) In determining the amount of compensation to be awarded no account shall be taken of any pressure which was exercised on the employer by calling, organising, procuring or financing a strike or other industrial action, or by threatening to do so; and that question shall be determined as if no such pressure had been exercised.

(6) Where the tribunal finds that the act or failure complained of was to any extent caused or contributed to by action of the complainant, it shall reduce the amount of the compensation by such proportion as it considers just and equitable having regard to that finding.

## 150  Awards against third parties

(1) If in proceedings on a complaint under section 146—
  (a) the complaint is made on the ground that the complainant has been subjected to detriment by an act or failure by his employer taking place for the purpose of compelling him to be or become a member of any trade union or of a particular trade union or of one of a number of particular trade unions, and
  (b) either the complainant or the employer claims in proceedings before the tribunal that the employer was induced to act or fail to act in the way complained of by pressure which a trade union or other person exercised on him by calling, organising, procuring or financing a strike or other industrial action, or by threatening to do so,
  the complainant or the employer may request the tribunal to direct that the person who he claims exercised the pressure be joined or sisted as a party to the proceedings.

(2) The request shall be granted if it is made before the hearing of the complaint begins, but may be refused if it is made after that time; and no such request may be made after the tribunal has made a declaration that the complaint is well-founded.

(3)  Where a person has been so joined or sisted as a party to proceedings and the tribunal—

   (a)   makes an award of compensation, and

   (b)   finds that the claim mentioned in subsection (1)(b) is well-founded,

   it may order that the compensation shall be paid by the person joined instead of by the employer, or partly by that person and partly by the employer, as the tribunal may consider just and equitable in the circumstances.

## 151    Interpretation and other supplementary provisions

(1)  References in sections 146 to 150 to being, becoming or ceasing to remain a member of a trade union include references to being, becoming or ceasing to remain a member of a particular branch or section of that union and to being, becoming or ceasing to remain a member of one of a number of particular branches or sections of that union; and references to taking part in the activities of a trade union shall be similarly construed.

(2)  The remedy of an employee for infringement of the right conferred on him by section 146 is by way of a complaint to an employment tribunal in accordance with this Part, and not otherwise.

*Dismissal of employees*

## 152    Dismissal of employee on grounds related to union membership or activities

(1)  For purposes of Part X of the Employment Rights Act 1996 (unfair dismissal) the dismissal of an employee shall be regarded as unfair if the reason for it (or, if more than one, the principal reason) was that the employee—

   (a)   was, or proposed to become, a member of an independent trade union,

   (b)   had taken part, or proposed to take part, in the activities of an independent trade union at an appropriate time,

   (ba)  had made use, or proposed to make use, of trade union services at an appropriate time,

   (bb)  had failed to accept an offer made in contravention of section 145A or 145B, or

   (c)   was not a member of any trade union, or of a particular trade union, or of one of a number of particular trade unions, or had refused, or proposed to refuse, to become or remain a member.

(2)  In subsection (1) 'an appropriate time' means—

   (a)   a time outside the employee's working hours, or

   (b)   a time within his working hours at which, in accordance with arrangements agreed with or consent given by his employer, it is permissible for him to take part in the activities of a trade union or (as the case may be) make use of trade union services;

   and for this purpose 'working hours', in relation to an employee, means any time when, in accordance with his contract of employment, he is required to be at work.

(2A) In this section—

   (a)   'trade union services' means services made available to the employee by an independent trade union by virtue of his membership of the union, and

   (b)   references to an employee's 'making use' of trade union services include his consenting to the raising of a matter on his behalf by an independent trade union of which he is a member.

(2B) Where the reason or one of the reasons for the dismissal was that an independent trade union (with or without the employee's consent) raised a matter on behalf of the employee as one of its members, the reason shall be treated as falling within subsection (1)(ba).

(3)  Where the reason, or one of the reasons, for the dismissal was—

   (a)   the employee's refusal, or proposed refusal, to comply with a requirement (whether or not imposed by his contract of employment or in writing) that, in the event of his not being a member of any trade union, or of a particular trade union, or of one of a number of particular trade unions, he must make one or more payments, or

(b)    his objection, or proposed objection, (however expressed) to the operation of a provision (whether or not forming part of his contract of employment or in writing) under which, in the event mentioned in paragraph (a), his employer is entitled to deduct one or more sums from the remuneration payable to him in respect of his employment,

the reason shall be treated as falling within subsection (1)(c).

(4)    References in this section to being, becoming or ceasing to remain a member of a trade union include references to being, becoming or ceasing to remain a member of a particular branch or section of that union or of one of a number of particular branches or sections of that trade union …

(5)    References in this section—
(a)    to taking part in the activities of a trade union, and
(b)    to services made available by a trade union by virtue of membership of the union, shall be construed in accordance with subsection (4).

## 153    Selection for redundancy on grounds related to union membership or activities

Where the reason or principal reason for the dismissal of an employee was that he was redundant, but it is shown—
(a)    that the circumstances constituting the redundancy applied equally to one or more other employees in the same undertaking who held positions similar to that held by him and who have not been dismissed by the employer, and
(b)    that the reason (or, if more than one, the principal reason) why he was selected for dismissal was one of those specified in section 152(1),

the dismissal shall be regarded as unfair for the purposes of Part X of the Employment Rights Act 1996 (unfair dismissal).

## 154    Disapplication of qualifying period and upper age limit for unfair dismissal

Sections 108(1) and 109(1) of the Employment Rights Act 1996 (qualifying period and upper age limit for unfair dismissal protection) do not apply to a dismissal which by virtue of section 152 or 153 is regarded as unfair for the purposes of Part 10 of that Act.

## 155    Matters to be disregarded in assessing contributory fault

(1)    Where an employment tribunal makes an award of compensation for unfair dismissal in a case where the dismissal is unfair by virtue of section 152 or 153, the tribunal shall disregard, in considering whether it would be just and equitable to reduce, or further reduce, the amount of any part of the award, any such conduct or action of the complainant as is specified below.

(2)    Conduct or action of the complainant shall be disregarded in so far as it constitutes a breach or proposed breach of a requirement—
(a)    to be or become a member of any trade union or of a particular trade union or of one of a number of particular trade unions,
(b)    to cease to be, or refrain from becoming, a member of any trade union or of a particular trade union or of one of a number of particular trade unions, or
(c)    not to take part in the activities of any trade union or of a particular trade union or of one of a number of particular trade unions.

For the purposes of this subsection a requirement means a requirement imposed on the complainant by or under an arrangement or contract of employment or other agreement.

(3)    Conduct or action of the complainant shall be disregarded in so far as it constitutes a refusal, or proposed refusal, to comply with a requirement of a kind mentioned in section 152(3)(a) (payments in lieu of membership) or an objection, or proposed objection, (however expressed) to the operation of a provision of a kind mentioned in section 152(3)(b) (deductions in lieu of membership).

## 156    Minimum basic award

(1)    Where a dismissal is unfair by virtue of section 152(1) or 153, the amount of the basic award of compensation, before any reduction is made under section 122 of the Employment Rights Act 1996 shall be not less than £6,959.

(2) But where the dismissal is unfair by virtue of section 153, subsection (2) of that section (reduction for contributory fault) applies in relation to so much of the basic award as is payable because of subsection (1) above.

## 160  Awards against third parties

(1) If in proceedings before an employment tribunal on a complaint of unfair dismissal either the employer or the complainant claims—

    (a) that the employer was induced to dismiss the complainant by pressure which a trade union or other person exercised on the employer by calling, organising, procuring or financing a strike or other industrial action, or by threatening to do so, and

    (b) that the pressure was exercised because the complainant was not a member of any trade union or of a particular trade union or of one of a number of particular trade unions,

the employer or the complainant may request the tribunal to direct that the person who he claims exercised the pressure be joined or sisted as a party to the proceedings.

(2) The request shall be granted if it is made before the hearing of the complaint begins, but may be refused after that time; and no such request may be made after the tribunal has made an award of compensation for unfair dismissal or an order for reinstatement or re-engagement.

(3) Where a person has been so joined or sisted as a party to the proceedings and the tribunal—

    (a) makes an award of compensation for unfair dismissal, and

    (b) finds that the claim mentioned in subsection (1) is well-founded,

the tribunal may order that the compensation shall be paid by that person instead of the employer, or partly by that person and partly by the employer, as the tribunal may consider just and equitable.

## 161  Application for interim relief

(1) An employee who presents a complaint of unfair dismissal alleging that the dismissal is unfair by virtue of section 152 may apply to the tribunal for interim relief.

(2) The tribunal shall not entertain an application for interim relief unless it is presented to the tribunal before the end of the period of seven days immediately following the effective date of termination (whether before, on or after that date).

(3) In a case where the employee relies on section 152(1)(a) or (b) the tribunal shall not entertain an application for interim relief unless before the end of that period there is also so presented a certificate in writing signed by an authorised official of the independent trade union of which the employee was or proposed to become a member stating—

    (a) that on the date of the dismissal the employee was or proposed to become a member of the union, and

    (b) that there appear to be reasonable grounds for supposing that the reason for his dismissal (or, if more than one, the principal reason) was one alleged in the complaint.

(4) An 'authorised official' means an official of the trade union authorised by it to act for the purposes of this section.

(5) A document purporting to be an authorisation of an official by a trade union to act for the purposes of this section and to be signed on behalf of the union shall be taken to be such an authorisation unless the contrary is proved; and a document purporting to be a certificate signed by such an official shall be taken to be signed by him unless the contrary is proved.

(6) For the purposes of subsection (3) the date of dismissal shall be taken to be—

    (a) where the employee's contract of employment was terminated by notice (whether given by his employer or by him), the date on which the employer's notice was given, and

    (b) in any other case, the effective date of termination.

## 162    Application to be promptly determined

(1)    An employment tribunal shall determine an application for interim relief as soon as practicable after receiving the application and, where appropriate, the requisite certificate.

(2)    The tribunal shall give to the employer, not later than seven days before the hearing, a copy of the application and of any certificate, together with notice of the date, time and place of the hearing.

(3)    If a request under section 160 (awards against third parties) is made three days or more before the date of the hearing, the tribunal shall also give to the person to whom the request relates, as soon as reasonably practicable, a copy of the application and of any certificate, together with notice of the date, time and place of the hearing.

(4)    The tribunal shall not exercise any power it has of postponing the hearing of an application for interim relief except where it is satisfied that special circumstances exist which justify it in doing so.

## 163    Procedure on hearing of application and making of order

(1)    If on hearing an application for interim relief it appears to the tribunal that it is likely that on determining the complaint to which the application relates that it will find that, by virtue of section 152, the complainant has been unfairly dismissed, the following provisions apply.

(2)    The tribunal shall announce its findings and explain to both parties (if present) what powers the tribunal may exercise on the application and in what circumstances it will exercise them, and shall ask the employer (if present) whether he is willing, pending the determination or settlement of the complaint—

(a)    to reinstate the employee, that is to say, to treat him in all respects as if he had not been dismissed, or

(b)    if not, to re-engage him in another job on terms and conditions not less favourable than those which would have been applicable to him if he had not been dismissed.

(3)    For this purpose 'terms and conditions not less favourable than those which would have been applicable to him if he had not been dismissed' means as regards seniority, pension rights and other similar rights that the period prior to the dismissal shall be regarded as continuous with his employment following the dismissal.

(4)    If the employer states that he is willing to reinstate the employee, the tribunal shall make an order to that effect.

(5)    If the employer states that he is willing to re-engage the employee in another job, and specifies the terms and conditions on which he is willing to do so, the tribunal shall ask the employee whether he is willing to accept the job on those terms and conditions; and—

(a)    if the employee is willing to accept the job on those terms and conditions, the tribunal shall make an order to that effect, and

(b)    if he is not, then, if the tribunal is of the opinion that the refusal is reasonable, the tribunal shall make an order for the continuation of his contract of employment, and otherwise the tribunal shall make no order.

(6)    If on the hearing of an application for interim relief the employer fails to attend before the tribunal, or states that he is unwilling either to reinstate the employee or re-engage him as mentioned in subsection (2), the tribunal shall make an order for the continuation of the employee's contract of employment.

## 164    Order for continuation of contract of employment

(1)    An order under section 163 for the continuation of a contract of employment is an order that the contract of employment continue in force—

(a)    for the purposes of pay or any other benefit derived from the employment, seniority, pension rights and other similar matters, and

(b)    for the purpose of determining for any purpose the period for which the employee has been continuously employed,

from the date of its termination (whether before or after the making of the order) until the determination or settlement of the complaint.

(2)   Where the tribunal makes such an order it shall specify in the order the amount which is to be paid by the employer to the employee by way of pay in respect of each normal pay period, or part of any such period, falling between the date of dismissal and the determination or settlement of the complaint.

(3)   Subject as follows, the amount so specified shall be that which the employee could reasonably have been expected to earn during that period, or part, and shall be paid—

(a)   in the case of payment for any such period falling wholly or partly after the making of the order, on the normal pay day for that period, and

(b)   in the case of a payment for any past period, within such time as may be specified in the order.

(4)   If an amount is payable in respect only of part of a normal pay period, the amount shall be calculated by reference to the whole period and reduced proportionately.

(5)   Any payment made to an employee by an employer under his contract of employment, or by way of damages for breach of that contract, in respect of a normal pay period or part of any such period shall go towards discharging the employer's liability in respect of that period under subsection (2); and conversely any payment under that subsection in respect of a period shall go towards discharging any liability of the employer under, or in respect of the breach of, the contract of employment in respect of that period.

(6)   If an employee, on or after being dismissed by his employer, receives a lump sum which, or part of which, is in lieu of wages but is not referable to any normal pay period, the tribunal shall take the payment into account in determining the amount of pay to be payable in pursuance of any such order.

(7)   For the purposes of this section the amount which an employee could reasonably have been expected to earn, his normal pay period and the normal pay day for each such period shall be determined as if he had not been dismissed.

## 165   Application for variation or revocation of order

(1)   At any time between the making of an order under section 163 and the determination or settlement of the complaint, the employer or the employee may apply to an employment tribunal for the revocation or variation of the order on the ground of a relevant change of circumstances since the making of the order.

(2)   Sections 161 to 163 apply in relation to such an application as in relation to an original application for interim relief, except that—

(a)   no certificate need be presented to the tribunal under section 161(3), and

(b)   in the case of an application by the employer, section 162(2) (service of copy of application and notice of hearing) has effect with the substitution of a reference to the employee for the reference to the employer.

## 166   Consequences of failure to comply with order

(1)   If on the application of an employee an employment tribunal is satisfied that the employer has not complied with the terms of an order for the reinstatement or re-engagement of the employee under section 163(4) or (5), the tribunal shall—

(a)   make an order for the continuation of the employee's contract of employment, and (b) order the employer to pay the employee such compensation as the tribunal considers just and equitable in all the circumstances having regard—

(i)    to the infringement of the employee's right to be reinstated or re-engaged in pursuance of the order, and

(ii)   to any loss suffered by the employee in consequence of the noncompliance.

(2)   Section 164 applies to an order under subsection (1)(a) as in relation to an order under section 163.

(3)   If on the application of an employee an employment tribunal is satisfied that the employer has not complied with the terms of an order for the continuation of a contract of employment, the following provisions apply.

(4)   If the non-compliance consists of a failure to pay an amount by way of pay specified in the order, the tribunal shall determine the amount owed by the employer on the date of the determination.

If on that date the tribunal also determines the employee's complaint that he has been unfairly dismissed, it shall specify that amount separately from any other sum awarded to the employee.

(5)    In any other case, the tribunal shall order the employer to pay the employee such compensation as the tribunal considers just and equitable in all the circumstances having regard to any loss suffered by the employee in consequence of the noncompliance.

## 167    Interpretation and other supplementary provisions

(1)    Part X of the Employment Rights Act 1996 (unfair dismissal) has effect subject to the provisions of sections 152 to 166 above.

(2)    Those sections shall be construed as one with that Part; and in those sections–
'complaint of unfair dismissal' means a complaint under section 111 of the Employment Rights Act 1996;
'award of compensation for unfair dismissal' means an award of compensation for unfair dismissal under section 112(4) or 117(3)(a) of that Act; and
'order for reinstatement or re-engagement' means an order for reinstatement or re-engagement under section 113 of that Act.

(3)    Nothing in those sections shall be construed as conferring a right to complain of unfair dismissal from employment of a description to which that Part does not otherwise apply.

*Time off for trade union duties and activities*

## 168    Time off for carrying out trade union duties

(1)    An employer shall permit an employee of his who is an official of an independent trade union recognised by the employer to take time off during his working hours for the purpose of carrying out any duties of his, as such an official, concerned with—
   (a)    negotiations with the employer related to or connected with matters falling within section 178(2) (collective bargaining) in relation to which the trade union is recognised by the employer, or
   (b)    the performance on behalf of employees of the employer of functions related to or connected with matters falling within that provision which the employer has agreed may be so performed by the trade union, or
   (c)    receipt of information from the employer and consultation by the employer under section 188 (redundancies) or under the Transfer of Undertakings (Protection of Employment) Regulations 2006, or
   (d)    negotiations with a view to entering into an agreement under regulation 9 of the Transfer of Undertakings (Protection of Employment) Regulations 2006 that applies to employees of the employer, or
   (e)    the performance on behalf of employees of the employer of functions related to or connected with the making of an agreement under that regulation.

(2)    He shall also permit such an employee to take time off during his working hours for the purpose of undergoing training in aspects of industrial relations—
   (a)    relevant to the carrying out of such duties as are mentioned in subsection (1), and
   (b)    approved by the Trades Union Congress or by the independent trade union of which he is an official.

(3)    The amount of time off which an employee is to be permitted to take under this section and the purposes for which, the occasions on which and any conditions subject to which time off may be so taken are those that are reasonable in all the circumstances having regard to any relevant provisions of a Code of Practice issued by ACAS.

(4)    An employee may present a complaint to an employment tribunal that his employer has failed to permit him to take time off as required by this section.

## 168A  Time off for union learning representatives

(1)    An employer shall permit an employee of his who is—
   (a)    a member of an independent trade union recognised by the employer, and
   (b)    a learning representative of the trade union,
   to take time off during his working hours for any of the following purposes.

(2)  The purposes are—
  (a)  carrying on any of the following activities in relation to qualifying members of the trade union—
      (i)    analysing learning or training needs,
      (ii)   providing information and advice about learning or training matters,
      (iii)  arranging learning or training, and
      (iv)   promoting the value of learning or training,
  (b)  consulting the employer about carrying on any such activities in relation to such members of the trade union,
  (c)  preparing for any of the things mentioned in paragraphs (a) and (b).
(3)  Subsection (1) only applies if—
  (a)  the trade union has given the employer notice in writing that the employee is a learning representative of the trade union, and
  (b)  the training condition is met in relation to him.
(4)  The training condition is met if—
  (a)  the employee has undergone sufficient training to enable him to carry on the activities mentioned in subsection (2), and the trade union has given the employer notice in writing of that fact,
  (b)  the trade union has in the last six months given the employer notice in writing that the employee will be undergoing such training, or
  (c)  within six months of the trade union giving the employer notice in writing that the employee will be undergoing such training, the employee has done so, and the trade union has given the employer notice of that fact.
(5)  Only one notice under subsection (4)(b) may be given in respect of any one employee.
(6)  References in subsection (4) to sufficient training to carry out the activities mentioned in subsection (2) are to training that is sufficient for those purposes having regard to any relevant provision of a Code of Practice issued by ACAS or the Secretary of State.
(7)  If an employer is required to permit an employee to take time off under subsection (1), he shall also permit the employee to take time off during his working hours for the following purposes—
  (a)  undergoing training which is relevant to his functions as a learning representative, and
  (b)  where the trade union has in the last six months given the employer notice under subsection (4)(b) in relation to the employee, undergoing such training as is mentioned in subsection (4)(a).
(8)  The amount of time off which an employee is to be permitted to take under this section and the purposes for which, the occasions on which and any conditions subject to which time off may be so taken are those that are reasonable in all the circumstances having regard to any relevant provision of a Code of Practice issued by ACAS or the Secretary of State.
(9)  An employee may present a complaint to an employment tribunal that his employer has failed to permit him to take time off as required by this section.
(10)  In subsection (2)(a), the reference to qualifying members of the trade union is to members of the trade union—
  (a)  who are employees of the employer of a description in respect of which the union is recognised by the employer, and
  (b)  in relation to whom it is the function of the union learning representative to act as such.
(11)  For the purposes of this section, a person is a learning representative of a trade union if he is appointed or elected as such in accordance with its rules.

## 169  Payment for time off under section 168

(1)  An employer who permits an employee to take time off under section 168 or 168A shall pay him for the time taken off pursuant to the permission.
(2)  Where the employee's remuneration for the work he would ordinarily have been doing during that time does not vary with the amount of work done, he shall be paid as if he had worked at that work for the whole of that time.

(3)   Where the employee's remuneration for the work he would ordinarily have been doing during that time varies with the amount of work done, he shall be paid an amount calculated by reference to the average hourly earnings for that work.

The average hourly earnings shall be those of the employee concerned or, if no fair estimate can be made of those earnings, the average hourly earnings for work of that description of persons in comparable employment with the same employer or, if there are no such persons, a figure of average hourly earnings which is reasonable in the circumstances.

(4)   A right to be paid an amount under this section does not affect any right of an employee in relation to remuneration under his contract of employment, but—

(a)   any contractual remuneration paid to an employee in respect of a period of time off to which this section applies shall go towards discharging any liability of the employer under this section in respect of that period, and

(b)   any payment under this section in respect of a period shall go towards discharging any liability of the employer to pay contractual remuneration in respect of that period.

(5)   An employee may present a complaint to an employment tribunal that his employer has failed to pay him in accordance with this section.

## 170   Time off for trade union activities

(1)   An employer shall permit an employee of his who is a member of an independent trade union recognised by the employer in respect of that description of employee to take time off during his working hours for the purpose of taking part in—

(a)   any activities of the union, and

(b)   any activities in relation to which the employee is acting as a representative of the union.

(2)   The right conferred by subsection (1) does not extend to activities which themselves consist of industrial action, whether or not in contemplation or furtherance of a trade dispute.

(2A)   The right conferred by subsection (1) does not extend to time off for the purpose of acting as, or having access to services provided by, a learning representative of a trade union.

(2B)   An employer shall permit an employee of his who is a member of an independent trade union recognised by the employer in respect of that description of employee to take time off during his working hours for the purpose of having access to services provided by a person in his capacity as a learning representative of the trade union.

(2C)   Subsection (2B) only applies if the learning representative would be entitled to time off under subsection (1) of section 168A for the purpose of carrying on in relation to the employee activities of the kind mentioned in subsection (2) of that section.

(3)   The amount of time off which an employee is to be permitted to take under this section and the purposes for which, the occasions on which and any conditions subject to which time off may be so taken are those that are reasonable in all the circumstances having regard to any relevant provisions of a Code of Practice issued by ACAS.

(4)   An employee may present a complaint to an employment tribunal that his employer has failed to permit him to take time off as required by this section.

(5)   For the purposes of this section—

(a)   a person is a learning representative of a trade union if he is appointed or elected as such in accordance with its rules, and

(b)   a person who is a learning representative of a trade union acts as such if he carries on the activities mentioned in section 168A(2) in that capacity.

## 171   Time limit for proceedings

(1)   An [employment tribunal] shall not consider a complaint under section 168, [168A,] 169 or 170 unless it is presented to the tribunal—

(a)   within three months of the date when the failure occurred, or

(b)   where the tribunal is satisfied that it was not reasonably practicable for the complaint to be presented within that period, within such further period as the tribunal considers reasonable.

(2)   Section 292A (extension of time limits to facilitate conciliation before institution of proceedings) applies for the purposes of subsection (1)(a).

## 172  Remedies

(1)  Where the tribunal finds a complaint under section 168, 168A or 170 is well-founded, it shall make a declaration to that effect and may make an award of compensation to be paid by the employer to the employee.

(2)  The amount of the compensation shall be such as the tribunal considers just and equitable in all the circumstances having regard to the employer's default in failing to permit time off to be taken by the employee and to any loss sustained by the employee which is attributable to the matters complained of.

(3)  Where on a complaint under section 169 the tribunal finds that the employer has failed to pay the employee in accordance with that section, it shall order him to pay the amount which it finds to be due.

## 172A  Publication requirements in relation to facility time

(1)  A Minister of the Crown may by regulations made by statutory instrument require relevant public sector employers to publish any information within subsection (3).

(2)  An employer is a relevant public sector employer if the employer—
  (a)  is a public authority specified, or of a description specified, in the regulations, and
  (b)  has at least one employee who is a relevant union official.

(2A)  But regulations under subsection (1) may not specify—
  (a)  a devolved Welsh authority, or
  (b)  a description of public authority that applies to a devolved Welsh authority.

(3)  The information that is within this subsection is information relating to facility time for relevant union officials including, in particular—
  (a)  how many of an employer's employees are relevant union officials, or relevant union officials within specified categories;
  (b)  the total amount spent by an employer in a specified period on paying relevant union officials for facility time, or for specified categories of facility time;
  (c)  the percentage of an employer's total pay bill for a specified period spent on paying relevant union officials for facility time, or for specified categories of facility time;
  (d)  the percentage of the aggregate amount of facility time taken by an employer's relevant union officials in a specified period that was attributable to specified categories of duties or activities;
  (e)  information relating to facilities provided by an employer for use by relevant union officials in connection with facility time.

(4)  In subsection (3) 'specified' means specified in the regulations.

(5)  The regulations may make provision—
  (a)  as to the times or intervals at which the information is to be published;
  (b)  as to the form in which the information is to be published.

(6)  The regulations may make different provision for different employers or different categories of employer.

(7)  In this section a 'relevant union official' means—
  (a)  a trade union official;
  (b)  a learning representative of a trade union, within the meaning given by section 168A(11);
  (c)  a safety representative appointed under regulations made under section 2(4) of the Health and Safety at Work etc. Act 1974.

(8)  In this section 'facility time' means time off taken by a relevant union official that is permitted by the official's employer under—
  (a)  section 168, section 168A or section 170(1)(b);
  (b)  section 10(6) of the Employment Relations Act 1999;
  (c)  regulations made under section 2(4) of the Health and Safety at Work etc. Act 1974.

(9)  The regulations may provide, in relation to a body or other person that is not a public authority but has functions of a public nature and is funded wholly or mainly from public funds, that the body or other person is to be treated as a public authority for the purposes of subsection (2).

(10)  The regulations may make provision specifying the person or other entity that is to be treated for the purposes of this section as the employer of a relevant union official who is employed by the Crown.

   (11) The regulations may—
- (a) deem a category of persons holding an office or employment under the Crown (or two or more such categories taken together) to be an entity for the purposes of provision made under subsection (10);
- (b) make different provision under subsection (10) for different categories of persons holding an office or employment under the Crown.

   (12) No regulations containing provision made by virtue of subsection (9) shall be made unless a draft of the statutory instrument containing them has been laid before Parliament and approved by a resolution of each House.

   (13) Regulations under this section to which subsection (12) does not apply shall be subject to annulment in pursuance of a resolution of either House of Parliament.

## 173 Interpretation and other supplementary provisions

   (1) For the purposes of sections 168, 168A and 170 the working hours of an employee shall be taken to be any time when in accordance with his contract of employment he is required to be at work.

   (2) The remedy of an employee for infringement of the rights conferred on him by section 168, 168A, 169 or 170 is by way of complaint to an employment tribunal in accordance with this Part, and not otherwise.

   (3) The Secretary of State may by order made by statutory instrument amend section 168A for the purpose of changing the purposes for which an employee may take time off under that section.

   (4) No order may be made under subsection (3) unless a draft of the order has been laid before and approved by resolution of each House of Parliament.

*Right to membership of trade union*

## 174 Right not to be excluded or expelled from union

   (1) An individual shall not be excluded or expelled from a trade union unless the exclusion or expulsion is permitted by this section.

   (2) The exclusion or expulsion of an individual from a trade union is permitted by this section if (and only if)—
- (a) he does not satisfy, or no longer satisfies, an enforceable membership requirement contained in the rules of the union,
- (b) he does not qualify, or no longer qualifies, for membership of the union by reason of the union operating only in a particular part or particular parts of Great Britain,
- (c) in the case of a union whose purpose is the regulation of relations between its members and one particular employer or a number of particular employers who are associated, he is not, or is no longer, employed by that employer or one of those employers, or
- (d) the exclusion or expulsion is entirely attributable to conduct of his (other than excluded conduct) and the conduct to which it is wholly or mainly attributable is not protected conduct.

   (3) A requirement in relation to membership of a union is 'enforceable' for the purposes of subsection (2)(a) if it restricts membership solely by reference to one or more of the following criteria—
- (a) employment in a specified trade, industry or profession,
- (b) occupational description (including grade, level or category of appointment), and
- (c) possession of specified trade, industrial or professional qualifications or work experience.

   (4) For the purposes of subsection (2)(d) 'excluded conduct', in relation to an individual, means—
- (a) conduct which consists in his being or ceasing to be, or having been or ceased to be, a member of another trade union,
- (b) conduct which consists in his being or ceasing to be, or having been or ceased to be, employed by a particular employer or at a particular place, or
- (c) conduct to which section 65 (conduct for which an individual may not be disciplined by a union) applies or would apply if the references in that section to

the trade union which is relevant for the purposes of that section were references to any trade union.

(4A) For the purposes of subsection (2)(d) 'protected conduct' is conduct which consists in the individual's being or ceasing to be, or having been or ceased to be, a member of a political party.

(4B) Conduct which consists of activities undertaken by an individual as a member of a political party is not conduct falling within subsection (4A).

(4C) Conduct which consists in an individual's being or having been a member of a political party is not conduct falling within subsection (4A) if membership of that political party is contrary to—

(a)   a rule of the trade union, or

(b)   an objective of the trade union.

(4D) For the purposes of subsection (4C)(b) in the case of conduct consisting in an individual's being a member of a political party, an objective is to be disregarded—

(a)   in relation to an exclusion, if it is not reasonably practicable for the objective to be ascertained by a person working in the same trade, industry or profession as the individual;

(b)   in relation to an expulsion, if it is not reasonably practicable for the objective to be ascertained by a member of the union.

(4E) For the purposes of subsection (4C)(b) in the case of conduct consisting in an individual's having been a member of a political party, an objective is to be disregarded—

(a)   in relation to an exclusion, if at the time of the conduct it was not reasonably practicable for the objective to be ascertained by a person working in the same trade, industry or profession as the individual;

(b)   in relation to an expulsion, if at the time of the conduct it was not reasonably practicable for the objective to be ascertained by a member of the union.

(4F) Where the exclusion or expulsion of an individual from a trade union is wholly or mainly attributable to conduct which consists of an individual's being or having been a member of a political party but which by virtue of subsection (4C) is not conduct falling within subsection (4A), the exclusion or expulsion is not permitted by virtue of subsection (2)(d) if any one or more of the conditions in subsection (4G) apply.

(4G) Those conditions are—

(a)   the decision to exclude or expel is taken otherwise than in accordance with the union's rules;

(b)   the decision to exclude or expel is taken unfairly;

(c)   the individual would lose his livelihood or suffer other exceptional hardship by reason of not being, or ceasing to be, a member of the union.

(4H) For the purposes of subsection (4G)(b) a decision to exclude or expel an individual is taken unfairly if (and only if)—

(a)   before the decision is taken the individual is not given—

(i)    notice of the proposal to exclude or expel him and the reasons for that proposal, and

(ii)   a fair opportunity to make representations in respect of that proposal, or

(b)   representations made by the individual in respect of that proposal are not considered fairly.

(5)   An individual who claims that he has been excluded or expelled from a trade union in contravention of this section may present a complaint to an employment tribunal.

## 175   Time limit for proceedings

(1)   An [employment tribunal] shall not entertain a complaint under section 174 unless it is presented—

(a)   before the end of the period of six months beginning with the date of the exclusion or expulsion, or

(b)   where the tribunal is satisfied that it was not reasonably practicable for the complaint to be presented before the end of that period, within such further period as the tribunal considers reasonable.

(2)   Section 292A (extension of time limits to facilitate conciliation before institution of proceedings) applies for the purposes of subsection (1)(a).

## 176    Remedies

(1)   Where the employment tribunal finds a complaint under section 174 is well-founded, it shall make a declaration to that effect.

(1A) If a tribunal makes a declaration under subsection (1) and it appears to the tribunal that the exclusion or expulsion was mainly attributable to conduct falling within section 174(4A) it shall make a declaration to that effect.

(1B) If a tribunal makes a declaration under subsection (1A) and it appears to the tribunal that the other conduct to which the exclusion or expulsion was attributable consisted wholly or mainly of conduct of the complainant which was contrary to—
   (a)   a rule of the union, or
   (b)   an objective of the union,
   it shall make a declaration to that effect.

(1C) For the purposes of subsection (1B), it is immaterial whether the complainant was a member of the union at the time of the conduct contrary to the rule or objective.

(1D) A declaration by virtue of subsection (1B)(b) shall not be made unless the union shows that, at the time of the conduct of the complainant which was contrary to the objective in question, it was reasonably practicable for that objective to be ascertained—
   (a)   if the complainant was not at that time a member of the union, by a person working in the same trade, industry or profession as the complainant, and
   (b)   if he was at that time a member of the union, by a member of the union.

(2)   An individual whose complaint has been declared to be well-founded may make an application to an employment tribunal for an award of compensation to be paid to him by the union.

...

(3)   The application shall not be entertained if made—
   (a)   before the end of the period of four weeks beginning with the date of the declaration under subsection (1), or
   (b)   after the end of the period of six months beginning with that date.

(4)   The amount of compensation awarded shall, subject to the following provisions, be such as the employment tribunal considers just and equitable in all the circumstances.

(5)   Where the employment tribunal finds that the exclusion or expulsion complained of was to any extent caused or contributed to by the action of the applicant, it shall reduce the amount of the compensation by such proportion as it considers just and equitable having regard to that finding.

(6)   The amount of compensation calculated in accordance with subsections (4) and (5) shall not exceed the aggregate of—
   (a)   an amount equal to thirty times the limit for the time being imposed by section 227(1)(a) of the Employment Rights Act 1996 (maximum amount of a week's pay for basic award in unfair dismissal cases), and
   (b)   an amount equal to the limit for the time being imposed by section 124(1) of that Act (maximum compensatory award in such cases);

...

(6A) If on the date on which the application was made the applicant had not been admitted or re-admitted to the union, the award shall not be less than £10,628.

(6B) Subsection (6A) does not apply in a case where the tribunal which made the declaration under subsection (1) also made declarations under subsections (1A) and (1B).

(7), (8) ...

## 177    Interpretation and other supplementary provisions

(1)   For the purposes of section 174—
   (a)   'trade union' does not include an organisation falling within paragraph (b) of section 1,
   (b)   'conduct' includes statements, acts and omissions, and
   (c)   'employment' includes any relationship whereby an individual personally does work or performs services for another person (related expressions being construed accordingly).

(2)   For the purposes of sections 174 to 176—
   (a)   if an individual's application for membership of a trade union is neither granted nor rejected before the end of the period within which it might reasonably have been expected to be granted if it was to be granted, he shall be treated as having been excluded from the union on the last day of that period, and

    (b)    an individual who under the rules of a trade union ceases to be a member of the union on the happening of an event specified in the rules shall be treated as having been expelled from the union.

(3)    The remedy of an individual for infringement of the rights conferred by section 174 is by way of a complaint to an employment tribunal in accordance with that section, sections 175 and 176 and this section, and not otherwise.

(4)    Where a complaint relating to an expulsion which is presented under section 174 is declared to be well-founded, no complaint in respect of the expulsion shall be presented or proceeded with under section 66 (complaint of infringement of right not to be unjustifiably disciplined).

(5)    The rights conferred by section 174 are in addition to, and not in substitution for, any right which exists apart from that section; and, subject to subsection (4), nothing in that section, section 175 or 176 or this section affects any remedy for infringement of any such right.

## PART IV
## INDUSTRIAL RELATIONS

## CHAPTER I
## COLLECTIVE BARGAINING

*Introductory*

## 178   Collective agreements and collective bargaining

(1)    In this Act 'collective agreement' means any agreement or arrangement made by or on behalf of one or more trade unions and one or more employers or employers' associations and relating to one or more of the matters specified below; and 'collective bargaining' means negotiations relating to or connected with one or more of those matters.

(2)    The matters referred to above are—

    (a)    terms and conditions of employment, or the physical conditions in which any workers are required to work;

    (b)    engagement or non-engagement, or termination or suspension of employment or the duties of employment, of one or more workers;

    (c)    allocation of work or the duties of employment between workers or groups of workers;

    (d)    matters of discipline;

    (e)    a worker's membership or non-membership of a trade union;

    (f)    facilities for officials of trade unions; and

    (g)    machinery for negotiation or consultation, and other procedures, relating to any of the above matters, including the recognition by employers or employers' associations of the right of a trade union to represent workers in such negotiation or consultation or in the carrying out of such procedures.

(3)    In this Act 'recognition', in relation to a trade union, means the recognition of the union by an employer, or two or more associated employers, to any extent, for the purpose of collective bargaining; and 'recognised' and other related expressions shall be construed accordingly.

*Enforceability of collective agreements*

## 179   Whether agreement intended to be a legally enforceable contract

(1)    A collective agreement shall be conclusively presumed not to have been intended by the parties to be a legally enforceable contract unless the agreement—

    (a)    is in writing, and

    (b)    contains a provision which (however expressed) states that the parties intend that the agreement shall be a legally enforceable contract.

(2)    A collective agreement which does satisfy those conditions shall be conclusively presumed to have been intended by the parties to be a legally enforceable contract.

(3) If a collective agreement is in writing and contains a provision which (however expressed) states that the parties intend that one or more parts of the agreement specified in that provision, but not the whole of the agreement, shall be a legally enforceable contract, then—
  (a) the specified part or parts shall be conclusively presumed to have been intended by the parties to be a legally enforceable contract, and
  (b) the remainder of the agreement shall be conclusively presumed not to have been intended by the parties to be such a contract.
(4) A part of a collective agreement which by virtue of subsection (3)(b) is not a legally enforceable contract may be referred to for the purpose of interpreting a part of the agreement which is such a contract.

## 180 Effect of provisions restricting right to take industrial action

(1) Any terms of a collective agreement which prohibit or restrict the right of workers to engage in a strike or other industrial action, or have the effect of prohibiting or restricting that right, shall not form part of any contract between a worker and the person for whom he works unless the following conditions are met.
(2) The conditions are that the collective agreement—
  (a) is in writing,
  (b) contains a provision expressly stating that those terms shall or may be incorporated in such a contract,
  (c) is reasonably accessible at his place of work to the worker to whom it applies and is available for him to consult during working hours, and
  (d) is one where each trade union which is a party to the agreement is an independent trade union;
  and that the contract with the worker expressly or impliedly incorporates those terms in the contract.
(3) The above provisions have effect notwithstanding anything in section 179 and notwithstanding any provision to the contrary in any agreement (including a collective agreement or a contract with any worker).

*Disclosure of information for purposes of collective bargaining*

## 181 General duty of employers to disclose information

(1) An employer who recognises an independent trade union shall, for the purposes of all stages of collective bargaining about matters, and in relation to descriptions of workers, in respect of which the union is recognised by him, disclose to representatives of the union, on request, the information required by this section.
  In this section and sections 182 to 185 'representative', in relation to a trade union, means an official or other person authorised by the union to carry on such collective bargaining.
(2) The information to be disclosed is all information relating to the employer's undertaking, including information relating to use of agency workers in that undertaking, which is in his possession, or that of an associated employer, and is information—
  (a) without which the trade union representatives would be to a material extent impeded in carrying on collective bargaining with him, and
  (b) which it would be in accordance with good industrial relations practice that he should disclose to them for the purposes of collective bargaining.
(3) A request by trade union representatives for information under this section shall, if the employer so requests, be in writing or be confirmed in writing.
(4) In determining what would be in accordance with good industrial relations practice, regard shall be had to the relevant provisions of any Code of Practice issued by ACAS, but not so as to exclude any other evidence of what that practice is.
(5) Information which an employer is required by virtue of this section to disclose to trade union representatives shall, if they so request, be disclosed or confirmed in writing.

## 182 Restrictions on general duty

(1) An employer is not required by section 181 to disclose information—
  (a) the disclosure of which would be against the interests of national security, or

(b) which he could not disclose without contravening a prohibition imposed by or under an enactment, or

(c) which has been communicated to him in confidence, or which he has otherwise obtained in consequence of the confidence reposed in him by another person, or

(d) which relates specifically to an individual (unless that individual has consented to its being disclosed), or

(e) the disclosure of which would cause substantial injury to his undertaking for reasons other than its effect on collective bargaining, or

(f) obtained by him for the purpose of bringing, prosecuting or defending any legal proceedings.

In formulating the provisions of any Code of Practice relating to the disclosure of information, ACAS shall have regard to the provisions of this subsection.

(2) In the performance of his duty under section 181 an employer is not required—

(a) to produce, or allow inspection of, any document (other than a document prepared for the purpose of conveying or confirming the information) or to make a copy of or extracts from any document, or

(b) to compile or assemble any information where the compilation or assembly would involve an amount of work or expenditure out of reasonable proportion to the value of the information in the conduct of collective bargaining.

## 183 Complaint of failure to disclose information

(1) A trade union may present a complaint to the Central Arbitration Committee that an employer has failed—

(a) to disclose to representatives of the union information which he was required to disclose to them by section 181, or

(b) to confirm such information in writing in accordance with that section.

The complaint must be in writing and in such form as the Committee may require.

(2) If on receipt of a complaint the Committee is of the opinion that it is reasonably likely to be settled by conciliation, it shall refer the complaint to ACAS and shall notify the trade union and employer accordingly, whereupon ACAS shall seek to promote a settlement of the matter.

If a complaint so referred is not settled or withdrawn and ACAS is of the opinion that further attempts at conciliation are unlikely to result in a settlement, it shall inform the Committee of its opinion.

(3) If the complaint is not referred to ACAS or, if it is so referred, on ACAS informing the Committee of its opinion that further attempts at conciliation are unlikely to result in a settlement, the Committee shall proceed to hear and determine the complaint and shall make a declaration stating whether it finds the complaint well-founded, wholly or in part, and stating the reasons for its findings.

(4) On the hearing of a complaint any person who the Committee considers has a proper interest in the complaint is entitled to be heard by the Committee, but a failure to accord a hearing to a person other than the trade union and employer directly concerned does not affect the validity of any decision of the Committee in those proceedings.

(5) If the Committee finds the complaint wholly or partly well-founded, the declaration shall specify—

(a) the information in respect of which the Committee finds that the complaint is well-founded,

(b) the date (or, if more than one, the earliest date) on which the employer refused or failed to disclose or, as the case may be, to confirm in writing, any of the information in question, and

(c) a period (not being less than one week from the date of the declaration) within which the employer ought to disclose that information, or, as the case may be, to confirm it in writing.

(6) On a hearing of a complaint under this section a certificate signed by or on behalf of a Minister of the Crown and certifying that a particular request for information could not be complied with except by disclosing information the disclosure of which would have been against the interests of national security shall be conclusive evidence of that fact. A document which purports to be such a certificate shall be taken to be such a certificate unless the contrary is proved.

## 184  Further complaint of failure to comply with declaration

(1)  After the expiration of the period specified in a declaration under section 183(5)(c) the trade union may present a further complaint to the Central Arbitration Committee that the employer has failed to disclose or, as the case may be, to confirm in writing to representatives of the union information specified in the declaration. The complaint must be in writing and in such form as the Committee may require.

(2)  On receipt of a further complaint the Committee shall proceed to hear and determine the complaint and shall make a declaration stating whether they find the complaint well-founded, wholly or in part, and stating the reasons for their finding.

(3)  On the hearing of a further complaint any person who the Committee consider has a proper interest in that complaint shall be entitled to be heard by the Committee, but a failure to accord a hearing to a person other than the trade union and employer directly concerned shall not affect the validity of any decision of the Committee in those proceedings.

(4)  If the Committee find the further complaint wholly or partly well-founded the declaration shall specify the information in respect of which the Committee find that that complaint is well-founded.

## 185  Determination of claim and award

(1)  On or after presenting a further complaint under section 184 the trade union may present to the Central Arbitration Committee a claim, in writing, in respect of one or more descriptions of employees (but not workers who are not employees) specified in the claim that their contracts should include the terms and conditions specified in the claim.

(2)  The right to present a claim expires if the employer discloses or, as the case may be, confirms in writing, to representatives of the trade union the information specified in the declaration under section 183(5) or 184(4); and a claim presented shall be treated as withdrawn if the employer does so before the Committee make an award on the claim.

(3)  If the Committee find, or have found, the further complaint wholly or partly well-founded, they may, after hearing the parties, make an award that in respect of any description of employees specified in the claim the employer shall, from a specified date, observe either—
    (a)  the terms and conditions specified in the claim; or
    (b)  other terms and conditions which the Committee consider appropriate.
    The date specified may be earlier than that on which the award is made but not earlier than the date specified in accordance with section 183(5)(b) in the declaration made by the Committee on the original complaint.

(4)  An award shall be made only in respect of a description of employees, and shall comprise only terms and conditions relating to matters in respect of which the trade union making the claim is recognised by the employer.

(5)  Terms and conditions which by an award under this section an employer is required to observe in respect of an employee have effect as part of the employee's contract of employment as from the date specified in the award, except in so far as they are superseded or varied—
    (a)  by a subsequent award under this section,
    (b)  by a collective agreement between the employer and the union for the time being representing that employee, or
    (c)  by express or implied agreement between the employee and the employer so far as that agreement effects an improvement in terms and conditions having effect by virtue of the award.

(6)  Where—
    (a)  by virtue of any enactment, other than one contained in this section, providing for minimum remuneration or terms and conditions, a contract of employment is to have effect as modified by an award, order or other instrument under that enactment, and
    (b)  by virtue of an award under this section any terms and conditions are to have effect as part of that contract,

that contract shall have effect in accordance with that award, order or other instrument or in accordance with the award under this section, whichever is the more favourable, in respect of any terms and conditions of that contract, to the employee.

(7)  No award may be made under this section in respect of terms and conditions of employment which are fixed by virtue of any enactment.

*Prohibition of union recognition requirements*

## 186  Recognition requirement in contract for goods or services void

A term or condition of a contract for the supply of goods or services is void in so far as it purports to require a party to the contract—

    (a)  to recognise one or more trade unions (whether or not named in the contract) for the purpose of negotiating on behalf of workers, or any class of worker, employed by him, or

    (b)  to negotiate or consult with, or with an official of, one or more trade unions (whether or not so named).

## 187  Refusal to deal on grounds of union exclusion prohibited

(1)  A person shall not refuse to deal with a supplier or prospective supplier of goods or services if the ground or one of the grounds for his action is that the person against whom it is taken does not, or is not likely to—

    (a)  recognise one or more trade unions for the purpose of negotiating on behalf of workers, or any class of worker, employed by him, or

    (b)  negotiate or consult with, or with an official of, one or more trade unions.

(2)  A person refuses to deal with a person if—

    (a)  where he maintains (in whatever form) a list of approved suppliers of goods or services, or of persons from whom tenders for the supply of goods or services may be invited, he fails to include the name of that person in that list; or

    (b)  in relation to a proposed contract for the supply of goods or services—

        (i)  he excludes that person from the group of persons from whom tenders for the supply of the goods or services are invited, or

        (ii)  he fails to permit that person to submit such a tender, or

        (iii)  he otherwise determines not to enter into a contract with that person for the supply of the goods or services; or

    (c)  he terminates a contract with that person for the supply of goods or services.

(3)  The obligation to comply with this section is a duty owed to the person with whom there is a refusal to deal and to any other person who may be adversely affected by its contravention; and a breach of the duty is actionable accordingly (subject to the defences and other incidents applying to actions for breach of statutory duty).

CHAPTER II
PROCEDURE FOR HANDLING REDUNDANCIES

*Duty of employer to consult representatives*

## 188  Duty of employer to consult representatives

(1)  Where an employer is proposing to dismiss as redundant 20 or more employees at one establishment within a period of 90 days or less, the employer shall consult about the dismissals all the persons who are appropriate representatives of any of the employees who may be affected by the proposed dismissals or may be affected by measures taken in connection with those dismissals.

(1A)  The consultation shall begin in good time and in any event—

    (a)  where the employer is proposing to dismiss 100 or more employees as mentioned in subsection (1), at least 45 days, and

    (b)  otherwise, at least 30 days,

before the first of the dismissals takes effect.

(1B)  For the purposes of this section the appropriate representatives of any affected employees are—

    (a)  if the employees are of a description in respect of which an independent trade union is recognised by their employer, representatives of the trade union, or

     (b)   in any other case, whichever of the following employee representatives the employer chooses—

         (i)   employee representatives appointed or elected by the affected employees otherwise than for the purposes of this section, who (having regard to the purposes for and the method by which they were appointed or elected) have authority from those employees to receive information and to be consulted about the proposed dismissals on their behalf;

        (ii)   employee representatives elected by the affected employees, for the purposes of this section, in an election satisfying the requirements of section 188A(1).

(2)   The consultation shall include consultation about ways of—

     (a)   avoiding the dismissals,

     (b)   reducing the numbers of employees to be dismissed, and

     (c)   mitigating the consequences of the dismissals,

and shall be undertaken by the employer with a view to reaching agreement with the appropriate representatives.

(3)   In determining how many employees an employer is proposing to dismiss as redundant no account shall be taken of employees in respect of whose proposed dismissals consultation has already begun.

(4)   For the purposes of the consultation the employer shall disclose in writing to the appropriate representatives—

     (a)   the reasons for his proposals,

     (b)   the numbers and descriptions of employees whom it is proposed to dismiss as redundant,

     (c)   the total number of employees of any such description employed by the employer at the establishment in question,

     (d)   the proposed method of selecting the employees who may be dismissed,

     (e)   the proposed method of carrying out the dismissals, with due regard to any agreed procedure, including the period over which the dismissals are to take effect,

     (f)   the proposed method of calculating the amount of any redundancy payments to be made (otherwise than in compliance with an obligation imposed by or by virtue of any enactment) to employees who may be dismissed,

     (g)   the number of agency workers working temporarily for and under the supervision and direction of the employer,

     (h)   the parts of the employer's undertaking in which those agency workers are working, and

     (i)   the type of work those agency workers are carrying out.

(5)   That information shall be given to each of the appropriate representatives by being delivered to them or sent by post to an address notified by them to the employer, or (in the case of representatives of a trade union) sent by post to the union at the address of its head or main office.

(5A) The employer shall allow the appropriate representatives access to the affected employees and shall afford to those representatives such accommodation and other facilities as may be appropriate.

(6)   ...

(7)   If in any case there are special circumstances which render it not reasonably practicable for the employer to comply with a requirement of subsection (1A), (2) or (4), the employer shall take all such steps towards compliance with that requirement as are reasonably practicable in those circumstances.

Where the decision leading to the proposed dismissals is that of a person controlling the employer (directly or indirectly), a failure on the part of that person to provide information to the employer shall not constitute special circumstances rendering it not reasonably practicable for the employer to comply with such a requirement.

(7A) Where—

     (a)   the employer has invited any of the affected employees to elect employee representatives, and

     (b)   the invitation was issued long enough before the time when the consultation is required by subsection (1A)(a) or (b) to begin to allow them to elect representatives by that time, the employer shall be treated as complying with the requirements of this section in relation to those employees if he complies with those requirements as soon as is reasonably practicable after the election of the representatives.

(7B) If, after the employer has invited affected employees to elect representatives, the affected employees fail to do so within a reasonable time, he shall give to each affected employee the information set out in subsection (4).

(8)  This section does not confer any rights on a trade union, a representative or an employee except as provided by sections 189 to 192 below.

## 188A Election of employee representatives

(1)  The requirements for the election of employee representatives under section 188(1B)(b)(ii) are that—

   (a)  the employer shall make such arrangements as are reasonably practical to ensure that the election is fair;

   (b)  the employer shall determine the number of representatives to be elected so that there are sufficient representatives to represent the interests of all the affected employees having regard to the number and classes of those employees;

   (c)  the employer shall determine whether the affected employees should be represented either by representatives of all the affected employees or by representatives of particular classes of those employees;

   (d)  before the election the employer shall determine the term of office as employee representatives so that it is of sufficient length to enable information to be given and consultations under section 188 to be completed;

   (e)  the candidates for election as employee representatives are affected employees on the date of the election;

   (f)  no affected employee is unreasonably excluded from standing for election;

   (g)  all affected employees on the date of the election are entitled to vote for employee representatives;

   (h)  the employees entitled to vote may vote for as many candidates as there are representatives to be elected to represent them or, if there are to be representatives for particular classes of employees, may vote for as many candidates as there are representatives to be elected to represent their particular class of employee;

   (i)  the election is conducted so as to secure that—

      (i)  so far as is reasonably practicable, those voting do so in secret, and

      (ii)  the votes given at the election are accurately counted.

(2)  Where, after an election of employee representatives satisfying the requirements of subsection (1) has been held, one of those elected ceases to act as an employee representative and any of those employees are no longer represented, they shall elect another representative by an election satisfying the requirements of subsection (1)(a), (e), (f) and (i).

## 189 Complaint and protective award

(1)  Where an employer has failed to comply with a requirement of section 188 or section 188A, a complaint may be presented to an employment tribunal on that ground—

   (a)  in the case of a failure relating to the election of employee representatives, by any of the affected employees or by any of the employees who have been dismissed as redundant;

   (b)  in the case of any other failure relating to employee representatives, by any of the employee representatives to whom the failure related,

   (c)  in the case of failure relating to representatives of a trade union, by the trade union, and

   (d)  in any other case, by any of the affected employees or by any of the employees who have been dismissed as redundant.

(1A) If on a complaint under subsection (1) a question arises as to whether or not any employee representative was an appropriate representative for the purposes of section 188, it shall be for the employer to show that the employee representative had the authority to represent the affected employees.

(1B) On a complaint under subsection (1)(a) it shall be for the employer to show that the requirements in section 188A have been satisfied.

(2) If the tribunal finds the complaint well-founded it shall make a declaration to that effect and may also make a protective award.

(3) A protective award is an award in respect of one or more descriptions of employees—

    (a) who has been dismissed as redundant, or whom it is proposed to dismiss as redundant, and

    (b) in respect of whose dismissal or proposed dismissal the employer has failed to comply with a requirement of section 188,

ordering the employer to pay remuneration for the protected period.

(4) The protected period—

    (a) begins with the date on which the first of the dismissals to which the complaint relates takes effect, or the date of the award, whichever is the earlier, and

    (b) is of such length as the tribunal determines to be just and equitable in all the circumstances having regard to the seriousness of the employer's default in complying with any requirement of section 188;

but shall not exceed 90 days.

(5) An employment tribunal shall not consider a complaint under this section unless it is presented to the tribunal—

    (a) before the date on which the last of the dismissals to which the complaint relates takes effect, or

    (b) during the period of three months beginning with that date, or

    (c) where the tribunal is satisfied that it was not reasonably practicable for the complaint to be presented within the period of three months, within such further period as it considers reasonable.

(5A) Where the complaint concerns a failure to comply with a requirement of section 188 [or 188A], section 292A (extension of time limits to facilitate conciliation before institution of proceedings) applies for the purposes of subsection (5)(b).

(6) If on a complaint under this section a question arises—

    (a) whether there were special circumstances which rendered it not reasonably practicable for the employer to comply with any requirement of section 188, or

    (b) whether he took all such steps towards compliance with that requirement as were reasonably practicable in those circumstances,

it is for the employer to show that there were and that he did.

## 190  Entitlement under protective award

(1) Where an employment tribunal has made a protective award, every employee of a description to which the award relates is entitled, subject to the following provisions and to section 191, to be paid remuneration by his employer for the protected period.

(2) The rate of remuneration payable is a week's pay for each week of the period; and remuneration in respect of a period less than one week shall be calculated by reducing proportionately the amount of a week's pay.

(3) ...

(4) An employee is not entitled to remuneration under a protective award in respect of a period during which he is employed by the employer unless he would be entitled to be paid by the employer in respect of that period—

    (a) by virtue of his contract of employment, or

    (b) by virtue of sections 87 to 91 of the Employment Rights Act 1996 (rights of employee in period of notice),

if that period fell within the period of notice required to be given by section 86(1) of that Act.

(5) Chapter II of Part XIV of the Employment Rights Act 1996 applies with respect to the calculation of a week's pay for the purposes of this section.

The calculation date for the purposes of that Chapter is the date on which the protective award was made or, in the case of an employee who was dismissed before the date on which the protective award was made, the date which by virtue of section 226(5) is the calculation date for the purpose of computing the amount of a redundancy payment in relation to that dismissal (whether or not the employee concerned is entitled to any such payment).

(6)    If an employee of a description to which a protective award relates dies during the protected period, the award has effect in his case as if the protected period ended on his death.

## 191   Termination of employment during protected period

(1)    Where the employee is employed by the employer during the protected period and—

    (a)    he is fairly dismissed by his employer otherwise than as redundant, or

    (b)    he unreasonably terminates the contract of employment,

then, subject to the following provisions, he is not entitled to remuneration under the protective award in respect of any period during which but for that dismissal or termination he would have been employed.

(2)    If an employer makes an employee an offer (whether in writing or not and whether before or after the ending of his employment under the previous contract) to renew his contract of employment, or to re-engage him under a new contract, so that the renewal or re-engagement would take effect before or during the protected period, and either—

    (a)    the provisions of the contract as renewed, or of the new contract, as to the capacity and place in which he would be employed, and as to the other terms and conditions of his employment, would not differ from the corresponding provisions of the previous contract, or

    (b)    the offer constitutes an offer of suitable employment in relation to the employee,

the following subsections have effect.

(3)    If the employee unreasonably refuses the offer, he is not entitled to remuneration under the protective award in respect of a period during which but for that refusal he would have been employed.

(4)    If the employee's contract of employment is renewed, or he is re-engaged under a new contract of employment, in pursuance of such an offer as is referred to in subsection (2)(b), there shall be a trial period in relation to the contract as renewed, or the new contract (whether or not there has been a previous trial period under this section).

(5)    The trial period begins with the ending of his employment under the previous contract and ends with the expiration of the period of four weeks beginning with the date on which he starts work under the contract as renewed, or the new contract, or such longer period as may be agreed in accordance with subsection (6) for the purpose of retraining the employee for employment under that contract.

(6)    Any such agreement—

    (a)    shall be made between the employer and the employee or his representative before the employee starts work under the contract as renewed or, as the case may be, the new contract,

    (b)    shall be in writing,

    (c)    shall specify the date of the end of the trial period, and

    (d)    shall specify the terms and conditions of employment which will apply in the employee's case after the end of that period.

(7)    If during the trial period—

    (a)    the employee, for whatever reason, terminates the contract, or gives notice to terminate it and the contract is thereafter, in consequence, terminated, or

    (b)    the employer, for a reason connected with or arising out of the change to the renewed, or new, employment, terminates the contract, or gives notice to terminate it and the contract is thereafter, in consequence, terminated,

the employee remains entitled under the protective award unless, in a case falling within paragraph (a), he acted unreasonably in terminating or giving notice to terminate the contract.

## 192   Complaint by employee to employment tribunal

(1)    An employee may present a complaint to an employment tribunal on the ground that he is an employee of a description to which a protective award relates and that his employer has failed, wholly or in part, to pay him remuneration under the award.

(2)    An employment tribunal shall not entertain a complaint under this section unless it is presented to the tribunal—

(a)     before the end of the period of three months beginning with the day (or, if the complaint relates to more than one day, the last of the days) in respect of which the complaint is made of failure to pay remuneration, or

(b)     where the tribunal is satisfied that it was not reasonably practicable for the complaint to be presented within the period of three months, within such further period as it may consider reasonable.

(2A) Section 292A (extension of time limits to facilitate conciliation before institution of proceedings) applies for the purposes of subsection (2)(a).

(3)     Where the tribunal finds a complaint under this section well-founded it shall order the employer to pay the complainant the amount of remuneration which it finds is due to him.

(4)     The remedy of an employee for infringement of his right to remuneration under a protective award is by way of complaint under this section, and not otherwise.

### *Duty of employer to notify Secretary of State*

## 193     Duty of employer to notify Secretary of State of certain redundancies

(1)     An employer proposing to dismiss as redundant 100 or more employees at one establishment within a period of 90 days or less shall notify the Secretary of State, in writing, of his proposal—

(a)     before giving notice to terminate an employee's contract of employment in respect of any of those dismissals, and

(b)     at least [45 days] before the first of those dismissals takes effect.

(2)     An employer proposing to dismiss as redundant [20] or more employees at one establishment within [such a period] shall notify the Secretary of State, in writing, of his proposal—

(a)     before giving notice to terminate an employee's contract of employment in respect of any of those dismissals, and

(b)     at least 30 days before the first of those dismissals takes effect.

(3)     In determining how many employees an employer is proposing to dismiss as redundant within the period mentioned in subsection (1) or (2), no account shall be taken of employees in respect of whose proposed dismissal notice has already been given to the Secretary of State.

(4)     A notice under this section shall—

(a)     be given to the Secretary of State by delivery to him or by sending it by post to him, at such address as the Secretary of State may direct in relation to the establishment where the employees proposed to be dismissed are employed,

(b)     where there are representatives to be consulted under section 188, identify them and state the date when consultation with them under that section began, and

(c)     be in such form and contain such particulars, in addition to those required by paragraph (b), as the Secretary of State may direct.

(5)     After receiving a notice under this section from an employer the Secretary of State may by written notice require the employer to give him such further information as may be specified in the notice.

(6)     Where there are representatives to be consulted under section 188 the employer shall give to each of them a copy of any notice given under subsection (1) or (2).

The copy shall be delivered to them or sent by post to an address notified by them to the employer, or (in the case of representatives of a trade union) sent by post to the union at the address of its head or main office.

(7)     If in any case there are special circumstances rendering it not reasonably practicable for the employer to comply with any of the requirements of subsections (1) to (6), he shall take all such steps towards compliance with that requirement as are reasonably practicable in the circumstances.

Where the decision leading to the proposed dismissals is that of a person controlling the employer (directly or indirectly), a failure on the part of that person to provide information to the employer shall not constitute special circumstances rendering it not reasonably practicable for the employer to comply with any of those requirements.

*Supplementary provisions*

## 195 Construction of references to dismissal as redundant etc.

(1) In this Chapter references to dismissal as redundant are references to dismissal for a reason not related to the individual concerned or for a number of reasons all of which are not so related.

(2) For the purposes of any proceedings under this Chapter, where an employee is or is proposed to be dismissed it shall be presumed, unless the contrary is proved, that he is or is proposed to be dismissed as redundant.

## 196 Construction of references to representatives

(1) For the purposes of this Chapter persons are employee representatives if—

(a) they have been elected by employees for the specific purpose of being consulted by their employer about dismissals proposed by him, or

(b) having been elected or appointed by employees (whether before or after dismissals have been proposed by their employer) otherwise than for that specific purpose, it is appropriate (having regard to the purposes for which they were elected) for the employer to consult them about dismissals proposed by him,

and (in either case) they are employed by the employer at the time when they are elected or appointed.

(2) References in this Chapter to representatives of a trade union, in relation to an employer, are to officials or other persons authorised by the trade union to carry on collective bargaining with the employer.

(3) References in this Chapter to affected employees are to employees who may be affected by the proposed dismissals or who may be affected by measures taken in connection with such dismissals.

## 198 Power to adapt provisions in case of collective agreement

(1) This section applies where there is in force a collective agreement which establishes—

(a) arrangements for providing alternative employment for employees to whom the agreement relates if they are dismissed as redundant by an employer to whom it relates, or

(b) arrangements for handling the dismissal of employees as redundant.

(2) On the application of all the parties to the agreement the Secretary of State may, if he is satisfied having regard to the provisions of the agreement that the arrangements are on the whole at least as favourable to those employees as the foregoing provisions of this Chapter, by order made by statutory instrument adapt, modify or exclude any of those provisions both in their application to all or any of those employees and in their application to any other employees of any such employer.

(3) The Secretary of State shall not make such an order unless the agreement—

(a) provides for procedures to be followed (whether by arbitration or otherwise) in cases where an employee to whom the agreement relates claims that any employer or other person to whom it relates has not complied with the provisions of the agreement, and

(b) provides that those procedures include a right to arbitration or adjudication by an independent referee or body in cases where (by reason of an equality of votes or otherwise) a decision cannot otherwise be reached,

or indicates that any such employee may present a complaint to an employment tribunal that any such employer or other person has not complied with those provisions.

(4) An order under this section may confer on an employment tribunal to whom a complaint is presented as mentioned in subsection (3) such powers and duties as the Secretary of State considers appropriate.

(5) An order under this section may be varied or revoked by a subsequent order thereunder either in pursuance of an application made by all or any of the parties to the agreement in question or without any such application.

CHAPTER III
CODES OF PRACTICE

*Codes of Practice issued by ACAS*

## 198A   Employees being transferred to the employer from another undertaking

(1) This section applies where the following conditions are met—
    (a) there is to be, or is likely to be, a relevant transfer,
    (b) the transferee is proposing to dismiss as redundant 20 or more employees at one establishment within a period of 90 days or less, and
    (c) the individuals who work for the transferor and who are to be (or are likely to be) transferred to the transferee's employment under the transfer ('transferring individuals') include one or more individuals who may be affected by the proposed dismissals or by measures taken in connection with the proposed dismissals.

(2) Where this section applies, the transferee may elect to consult, or to start to consult, representatives of affected transferring individuals about the proposed dismissals before the transfer takes place ('pre-transfer consultation').

(3) Any such election—
    (a) may be made only if the transferor agrees to it, and
    (b) must be made by way of written notice to the transferor.

(4) If the transferee elects to carry out pre-transfer consultation—
    (a) sections 188 to 198 apply from the time of the election (and continue to apply after the transfer) as if the transferee were already the transferring individuals' employer and as if any transferring individuals who may be affected by the proposed dismissals were already employed at the establishment mentioned in subsection (1)(b) (but this is subject to section 198B), and
    (b) the transferor may provide information or other assistance to the transferee to help the transferee meet the requirements of this Chapter.

(5) A transferee who elects to carry out pre-transfer consultation may cancel that election at any time by written notice to the transferor.

(6) If the transferee cancels an election to carry out pre-transfer consultation—
    (a) sections 188 to 198 no longer apply as mentioned in subsection (4)(a),
    (b) anything done under those sections has no effect so far as it was done in reliance on the election,
    (c) if the transferee notified an appropriate representative, a transferring individual or the Secretary of State of the election or the proposed dismissals, the transferee must notify him or her of the cancellation as soon as reasonably practicable, and
    (d) the transferee may not make another election under subsection (2) in relation to the proposed dismissals.

(7) For the purposes of this section and section 198B—
'affected transferring individual' means a transferring individual who may be affected by the proposed dismissals or who may be affected by measures taken in connection with the proposed dismissals;
'pre-transfer consultation' has the meaning given in subsection (2);
'relevant transfer' means—
    (a) a relevant transfer under the Transfer of Undertakings (Protection of Employment) Regulations 2006,
    (b) anything else regarded, by virtue of an enactment, as a relevant transfer for the purposes of those Regulations, or
    (c) where an enactment provides a power to make provision which is the same as or similar to those Regulations, any other novation of a contract of employment effected in the exercise of that power,
and 'transferor' and 'transferee' are to be construed accordingly;
'transferring individual' has the meaning given in subsection (1)(c).

## 198B  Section 198A: supplementary

(1)  Where section 198A applies and the transferee elects to carry out pre-transfer consultation (and has not cancelled the election), the application under section 198A(4)(a) of sections 188 to 198 is (both before and after the transfer) subject to the following modifications—

   (a)   for section 188(1B)(a) substitute—

       '(a)   for transferring individuals of a description in respect of which an independent trade union is recognised by the transferor, representatives of that trade union,

       (aa)  for employees, other than transferring individuals, of a description in respect of which an independent trade union is recognised by the transferee, representatives of that trade union, or';

   (b)   in section 188(5), for 'the employer' substitute 'the transferor or transferee';

   (c)   in section 188(5A), for 'shall allow the appropriate representatives access to the affected employees and shall afford to those representatives such accommodation and other facilities as may be appropriate' substitute 'shall ensure that the appropriate representatives are allowed access to the affected transferring individuals and that such accommodation and other facilities as may be appropriate are afforded to those representatives';

   (d)   in section 188(7), at the end insert—
       'A failure on the part of the transferor to provide information or other assistance to the transferee does not constitute special circumstances rendering it not reasonably practicable for the transferee to comply with such a requirement.';

   (e)   where an employment tribunal makes a protective award under section 189 ordering the transferee to pay remuneration for a protected period in respect of a transferring individual, then, so far as the protected period falls before the relevant transfer, the individual's employer before the transfer is to be treated as the employer for the purpose of determining under sections 190(2) to (6) and 191 the period (if any) in respect of which, and the rate at which, the individual is entitled to be paid remuneration by the transferee under section 190(1);

   (f)   in section 189, at the end insert—
       '(7)   If on a complaint under this section a question arises whether the transferor agreed to an election or the transferee gave notice of an election as required under section 198A(3), it is for the transferee to show that the agreement or notice was given as required.';

   (g)   in section 192, at the end insert—
       '(5)   If on a complaint under this section a question arises whether the transferor agreed to an election or the transferee gave notice of an election as required under section 198A(3), it is for the transferee to show that the agreement or notice was given as required.';

   (h)   in section 193(6), for 'the employer' the second time it appears substitute 'the transferor or transferee';

   (i)   in section 193(7), at the end insert—
       'A failure on the part of the transferor to provide information or other assistance to the transferee does not constitute special circumstances rendering it not reasonably practicable for the transferee to comply with any of those requirements.';

   (j)   in section 196(1), in the closing words, for 'employed by the employer' substitute 'employed by the transferor or transferee';

   (k)   for section 196(2) substitute—
       '(2)   References in this Chapter to representatives of a trade union are to officials or other persons authorised by the trade union to carry on collective bargaining with the transferee.'.

(2)  Where section 198A applies and the transferee elects to carry out pre-transfer consultation (and has not cancelled the election), both before and after the transfer section 168(1)(c) applies as follows in relation to an official of an independent trade union who, as such an official, is an affected transferring individual's appropriate representative under section 188(1B)(a)—

    (a)  in relation to the official's duties as such a representative, the reference in the opening words of section 168(1) to an independent trade union being recognised by the employer is to be read as a reference to an independent trade union being recognised by the transferor;

    (b)  the references in section 168(1)(c) to the employer in relation to section 188 are to be read as references to the transferee.

## 199  Issue of Codes of Practice by ACAS

(1)  ACAS may issue Codes of Practice containing such practical guidance as it thinks fit for the purpose of promoting the improvement of industrial relations or for purposes connected with trade union learning representatives.

...

*Codes of Practice issued by the Secretary of State*

## 203  Issue of Codes of Practice by the Secretary of State

(1)  The Secretary of State may issue Codes of Practice containing such practical guidance as he thinks fit for the purpose or for purposes connected with trade union learning representatives—

    (a)  of promoting the improvement of industrial relations, or (b) of promoting what appear to him to be desirable practices in relation to the conduct by trade unions of ballots and elections.

...

*Supplementary provisions*

## 207  Effect of failure to comply with Code

(1)  A failure on the part of any person to observe any provision of a Code of Practice issued under this Chapter shall not of itself render him liable to any proceedings.

(2)  In any proceedings before an employment tribunal or the Central Arbitration Committee any Code of Practice issued under this Chapter by ACAS shall be admissible in evidence, and any provision of the Code which appears to the tribunal or Committee to be relevant to any question arising in the proceedings shall be taken into account in determining that question.

(3)  In any proceedings before a court or employment tribunal or the Central Arbitration Committee any Code of Practice issued under this Chapter by the Secretary of State shall be admissible in evidence, and any provision of the Code which appears to the court, tribunal or Committee to be relevant to any question arising in the proceedings shall be taken into account in determining that question.

## 207A  Effect of failure to comply with Code: adjustment of awards

(1)  This section applies to proceedings before an employment tribunal relating to a claim by an employee under any of the jurisdictions listed in Schedule A2.

(2)  If, in the case of proceedings to which this section applies, it appears to the employment tribunal that—

    (a)  the claim to which the proceedings relate concerns a matter to which a relevant Code of Practice applies,

    (b)  the employer has failed to comply with that Code in relation to that matter, and

    (c)  that failure was unreasonable,

the employment tribunal may, if it considers it just and equitable in all the circumstances to do so, increase any award it makes to the employee by no more than 25%.

(3)  If, in the case of proceedings to which this section applies, it appears to the employment tribunal that—

    (a)  the claim to which the proceedings relate concerns a matter to which a relevant Code of Practice applies,

    (b)  the employee has failed to comply with that Code in relation to that matter, and

    (c)  that failure was unreasonable,

the employment tribunal may, if it considers it just and equitable in all the circumstances to do so, reduce any award it makes to the employee by no more than 25%.

(4)  In subsections (2) and (3), 'relevant Code of Practice' means a Code of Practice issued under this Chapter which relates exclusively or primarily to procedure for the resolution of disputes.

(5) Where an award falls to be adjusted under this section and under section 38 of the Employment Act 2002, the adjustment under this section shall be made before the adjustment under that section.

(6) The Secretary of State may by order amend Schedule A2 for the purpose of—

    (a) adding a jurisdiction to the list in that Schedule, or

    (b) removing a jurisdiction from that list.

(7) The power of the Secretary of State to make an order under subsection (6) includes power to make such incidental, supplementary, consequential or transitional provision as the Secretary of State thinks fit.

(8) An order under subsection (6) shall be made by statutory instrument.

(9) No order shall be made under subsection (6) unless a draft of the statutory instrument containing it has been laid before Parliament and approved by a resolution of each House.

## CHAPTER IV
## GENERAL

### Functions of ACAS

## 209 General duty to promote improvement of industrial relations

It is the general duty of ACAS to promote the improvement of industrial relations.

## 210 Conciliation

(1) Where a trade dispute exists or is apprehended ACAS may, at the request of one or more parties to the dispute or otherwise, offer the parties to the dispute its assistance with a view to bringing about a settlement.

(2) The assistance may be by way of conciliation or by other means, and may include the appointment of a person other than an officer or servant of ACAS to offer assistance to the parties to the dispute with a view to bringing about a settlement.

(3) In exercising its functions under this section ACAS shall have regard to the desirability of encouraging the parties to a dispute to use any appropriate agreed procedures for negotiation or the settlement of disputes.

## 210A Information required by ACAS for purposes of settling recognition disputes

(1) This section applies where ACAS is exercising its functions under section 210 with a view to bringing about a settlement of a recognition dispute.

(2) The parties to the recognition dispute may jointly request ACAS or a person nominated by ACAS to do either or both of the following—

    (a) hold a ballot of the workers involved in the dispute;

    (b) ascertain the union membership of the workers involved in the dispute.

(3) In the following provisions of this section references to ACAS include references to a person nominated by ACAS; and anything done by such a person under this section shall be regarded as done in the exercise of the functions of ACAS mentioned in subsection (1).

(4) At any time after ACAS has received a request under subsection (2), it may require any party to the recognition dispute—

    (a) to supply ACAS with specified information concerning the workers involved in the dispute, and

    (b) to do so within such period as it may specify.

(5) ACAS may impose a requirement under subsection (4) only if it considers that it is necessary to do so—

    (a) for the exercise of the functions mentioned in subsection (1); and

    (b) in order to enable or assist it to comply with the request.

(6) The recipient of a requirement under this section must, within the specified period, supply ACAS with such of the specified information as is in the recipient's possession.

(7) A request under subsection (2) may be withdrawn by any party to the recognition dispute at any time and, if it is withdrawn, ACAS shall take no further steps to hold the ballot or to ascertain the union membership of the workers involved in the dispute.

(8) If a party to a recognition dispute fails to comply with subsection (6), ACAS shall take no further steps to hold the ballot or to ascertain the union membership of the workers involved in the dispute.

(9) Nothing in this section requires ACAS to comply with a request under subsection (2).

(10) In this section—

'party', in relation to a recognition dispute, means each of the employers, employers' associations and trade unions involved in the dispute;

'a recognition dispute' means a trade dispute between employers and workers which is connected wholly or partly with the recognition by employers or employers' associations of the right of a trade union to represent workers in negotiations, consultations or other procedures relating to any of the matters mentioned in paragraphs (a) to (f) of section 218(1);

'specified' means specified in a requirement under this section; and

'workers' has the meaning given in section 218(5).

## 211    Conciliation officers

(1) ACAS shall designate some of its officers to perform the functions of conciliation officers under any enactment (whenever passed) relating to matters which are or could be the subject to proceedings before an employment tribunal.

(2) References in any such enactment to a conciliation officer are to an officer designated under this section.

## 212    Arbitration

(1) Where a trade dispute exists or is apprehended ACAS may, at the request of one or more of the parties to the dispute and with the consent of all the parties to the dispute, refer all or any of the matters to which the dispute relates for settlement to the arbitration of—

   (a) one or more persons appointed by ACAS for that purpose (not being officers or employees of ACAS), or

   (b) the Central Arbitration Committee.

(2) In exercising its functions under this section ACAS shall consider the likelihood of the dispute being settled by conciliation.

(3) Where there exist appropriate agreed procedures for negotiation or the settlement of disputes, ACAS shall not refer a matter for settlement to arbitration under this section unless—

   (a) those procedures have been used and have failed to result in a settlement, or

   (b) there is, in ACAS's opinion a special reason which justifies arbitration under this section as an alternative to those procedures.

(4) Where a matter is referred to arbitration under subsection (1)(a)—

   (a) if more than one arbitrator or arbiter is appointed, ACAS shall appoint one of them to act as chairman; and

   (b) the award may be published if ACAS so decides and all the parties consent.

(5) Part I of the Arbitration Act 1996 (general provisions as to arbitration) does not apply to an arbitration under this section.

## 212B    Dismissal procedures agreements

ACAS may, in accordance with any dismissal procedures agreement (within the meaning of the Employment Rights Act 1996), refer any matter to the arbitration of a person appointed by ACAS for the purpose (not being an officer or employee of ACAS).

## 213    Advice

(1) ACAS may, on request or otherwise, give employers, employers' associations, workers and trade unions such advice as it thinks appropriate on matters concerned with or affecting or likely to affect industrial relations.

(2) ACAS may also publish general advice on matters concerned with or affecting or likely to affect industrial relations.

## 214    Inquiry

(1) ACAS may, if it thinks fit, inquire into any question relating to industrial relations generally or to industrial relations in any particular industry or in any particular undertaking or part of an undertaking.

(2)   The findings of an inquiry under this section, together with any advice given by ACAS in connection with those findings, may be published by ACAS if—

   (a)   it appears to ACAS that publication is desirable for the improvement of industrial relations, either generally or in relation to the specific question inquired into, and

   (b)   after sending a draft of the findings to all parties appearing to be concerned and taking account of their views, it thinks fit.

*Courts of inquiry*

## 215   Inquiry and report by court of inquiry

(1)   Where a trade dispute exists or is apprehended, the Secretary of State may inquire into the causes and circumstances of the dispute, and, if he thinks fit, appoint a court of inquiry and refer to it any matters appearing to him to be connected with or relevant to the dispute.

(2)   The court shall inquire into the matters referred to it and report on them to the Secretary of State; and it may make interim reports if it thinks fit.

(3)   Any report of the court, and any minority report, shall be laid before both Houses of Parliament as soon as possible.

(4)   The Secretary of State may, before or after the report has been laid before Parliament, publish or cause to be published from time to time, in such manner as he thinks fit, any information obtained or conclusions arrived at by the court as the result or in the course of its inquiry.

(5)   No report or publication made or authorised by the court or the Secretary of State shall include any information obtained by the court of inquiry in the course of its inquiry—

   (a)   as to any trade union, or

   (b)   as to any individual business (whether carried on by a person, firm, or company), which is not available otherwise than through evidence given at the inquiry, except with the consent of the secretary of the trade union or of the person, firm, or company in question. Nor shall any individual member of the court or any person concerned in the inquiry disclose such information without such consent.

(6)   The Secretary of State shall from time to time present to Parliament a report of his proceedings under this section.

*Supplementary provisions*

## 218   Meaning of 'trade dispute' in Part IV

(1)   In this Part 'trade dispute' means a dispute between employers and workers, or between workers and workers, which is connected with one or more of the following matters—

   (a)   terms and conditions of employment, or the physical conditions in which any workers are required to work;

   (b)   engagement or non-engagement, or termination or suspension of employment or the duties of employment, of one or more workers;

   (c)   allocation of work or the duties of employment as between workers or groups of workers;

   (d)   matters of discipline;

   (e)   the membership or non-membership of a trade union on the part of a worker;

   (f)   facilities for officials of trade unions; and

   (g)   machinery for negotiation or consultation, and other procedures, relating to any of the foregoing matters, including the recognition by employers or employers' associations of the right of a trade union to represent workers in any such negotiation or consultation or in the carrying out of such procedures.

(2)   A dispute between a Minister of the Crown and any workers shall, notwithstanding that he is not the employer of those workers, be treated for the purposes of this Part as a dispute between an employer and those workers if the dispute relates—

   (a)   to matters which have been referred for consideration by a joint body on which, by virtue of any provision made by or under any enactment, that minister is represented, or

   (b)   to matters which cannot be settled without that Minister exercising a power conferred on him by or under an enactment.

(3) There is a trade dispute for the purpose of this Part even though it relates to matters occurring outside Great Britain.

(4) A dispute to which a trade union or employer's association is a party shall be treated for the purposes of this Part as a dispute to which workers or, as the case may be, employers are parties.

(5) In this section—

'employment' includes any relationship whereby one person personally does work or performs services for another; and

'worker', in relation to a dispute to which an employer is a party, includes any worker even if not employed by that employer.

## PART V
## INDUSTRIAL ACTION

### *Protection of acts in contemplation or furtherance of trade dispute*

## 219 Protection from certain tort liabilities

(1) An act done by a person in contemplation or furtherance of a trade dispute is not actionable in tort on the ground only—

 (a) that it induces another person to break a contract or interferes or induces another person to interfere with its performance, or

 (b) that it consists in his threatening that a contract (whether one to which he is a party or not) will be broken or its performance interfered with, or that he will induce another person to break a contract or interfere with its performance.

(2) An agreement or combination by two or more persons to do or procure the doing of an act in contemplation or furtherance of a trade dispute is not actionable in tort if the act is one which if done without any such agreement or combination would not be actionable in tort.

(3) Nothing in subsections (1) and (2) prevents an act done in the course of picketing from being actionable in tort unless—

 (a) it is done in the course of attendance declared lawful by section 220 (peaceful picketing), and

 (b) in the case of picketing to which section 220A applies, the requirements in that section (union supervision of picketing) are complied with.

(4) Subsections (1) and (2) have effect subject to sections 222 to 225 (action excluded from protection) and to sections 226 (requirement of ballot before action by trade union) and 234A (requirement of notice to employer of industrial action); and in those sections 'not protected' means excluded from the protection afforded by this section or, where the expression is used with reference to a particular person, excluded from that protection as respects that person.

## 220 Peaceful picketing

(1) It is lawful for a person in contemplation or furtherance of a trade dispute to attend—

 (a) at or near his own place of work, or

 (b) if he is an official of a trade union, at or near the place of work of a member of the union whom he is accompanying and whom he represents,

for the purpose only of peacefully obtaining or communicating information, or peacefully persuading any person to work or abstain from working.

(2) If a person works or normally works—

 (a) otherwise than at any one place, or

 (b) at a place the location of which is such that attendance there for a purpose mentioned in subsection (1) is impracticable, his place of work for the purposes of that subsection shall be any premises of his employer from which he works or from which his work is administered.

(3) In the case of a worker not in employment where—

 (a) his last employment was terminated in connection with a trade dispute, or

 (b) the termination of his employment was one of the circumstances giving rise to a trade dispute, in relation to that dispute his former place of work shall be treated for the purposes of subsection (1) as being his place of work.

(4)    A person who is an official of a trade union by virtue only of having been elected or appointed to be a representative of some of the members of the union shall be regarded for the purposes of subsection (1) as representing only those members; but otherwise an official of a union shall be regarded for those purposes as representing all its members.

## 220A  Union supervision of picketing

(1)    Section 220 does not make lawful any picketing that a trade union organises, or encourages its members to take part in, unless the requirements in subsections (2) to (8) are complied with.

(2)    The union must appoint a person to supervise the picketing.

(3)    That person ('the picket supervisor') must be an official or other member of the union who is familiar with any provisions of a Code of Practice issued under section 203 that deal with picketing.

(4)    The union or picket supervisor must take reasonable steps to tell the police—
   (a)    the picket supervisor's name;
   (b)    where the picketing will be taking place;
   (c)    how to contact the picket supervisor.

(5)    The union must provide the picket supervisor with a letter stating that the picketing is approved by the union.

(6)    If an individual who is, or is acting on behalf of, the employer asks the picket supervisor for sight of the approval letter, the picket supervisor must show it to that individual as soon as reasonably practicable.

(7)    While the picketing is taking place, the picket supervisor must—
   (a)    be present where it is taking place, or
   (b)    be readily contactable by the union and the police, and able to attend at short notice.

(8)    While present where the picketing is taking place, the picket supervisor must wear something that readily identifies the picket supervisor as such.

(9)    In this section—
   'approval letter' means the letter referred to in subsection (5);
   'employer' means the employer to which the trade dispute relates;
   'picketing' means attendance at or near a place of work, in contemplation or furtherance of a trade dispute, for the purpose of—
   (a)    obtaining or communicating information, or
   (b)    persuading any person to work or abstain from working.

(10)   In relation to picketing that two or more unions organise or encourage members to take part in—
   (a)    in subsection (2) 'the union' means any one of those unions, and
   (b)    other references in this section to 'the union' are to that union.

## 221  Restrictions on grant of injunctions and interdicts

(1)    Where—
   (a)    an application for an injunction or interdict is made to a court in the absence of the party against whom it is sought or any representative of his, and
   (b)    he claims, or in the opinion of the court would be likely to claim, that he acted in contemplation or furtherance of a trade dispute,
   the court shall not grant the injunction or interdict unless satisfied that all steps which in the circumstances were reasonable have been taken with a view to securing that notice of the application and an opportunity of being heard with respect to the application have been given to him.

(2)    Where—
   (a)    an application for an interlocutory injunction is made to a court pending the trial of an action, and
   (b)    the party against whom it is sought claims that he acted in contemplation or furtherance of a trade dispute,
   the court shall, in exercising its discretion whether or not to grant the injunction, have regard to the likelihood of that party's succeeding at the trial of the action in establishing any matter which would afford a defence to the action under section 219 (protection from certain tort liabilities) or section 220 (peaceful picketing).
   This subsection does not extend to Scotland.

*Action excluded from protection*

## 222  Action to enforce trade union membership

(1)  An act is not protected if the reason, or one of the reasons, for which it is done is the fact or belief that a particular employer—

    (a)  is employing, has employed or might employ a person who is not a member of a trade union, or

    (b)  is failing, has failed or might fail to discriminate against such a person.

(2)  For the purposes of subsection (1)(b) an employer discriminates against a person if, but only if, he ensures that his conduct in relation to—

    (a)  persons, or persons of any description, employed by him, or who apply to be, or are, considered by him for employment, or

    (b)  the provision of employment for such persons,

is different, in some or all cases, according to whether or not they are members of a trade union, and is more favourable to those who are.

(3)  An act is not protected if it constitutes, or is one of a number of acts which together constitute, an inducement or attempted inducement of a person—

    (a)  to incorporate in a contract to which that person is a party, or a proposed contract to which he intends to be a party, a term or condition which is or would be void by virtue of section 144 (union membership requirement in contract for goods or services), or

    (b)  to contravene section 145 (refusal to deal with person on grounds relating to union membership).

(4)  References in this section to an employer employing a person are to a person acting in the capacity of the person for whom a worker works or normally works.

(5)  References in this section to not being a member of a trade union are to not being a member of any trade union, of a particular trade union or of one of a number of particular trade unions.

Any such reference includes a reference to not being a member of a particular branch or section of a trade union or of one of a number of particular branches or sections of a trade union.

## 223  Action taken because of dismissal for taking unofficial action

An act is not protected if the reason, or one of the reasons, for doing it is the fact or belief that an employer has dismissed one or more employees in circumstances such that by virtue of section 237 (dismissal in connection with unofficial action) they have no right to complain of unfair dismissal.

## 224  Secondary action

(1)  An act is not protected if one of the facts relied on for the purpose of establishing liability is that there has been secondary action which is not lawful picketing.

(2)  There is secondary action in relation to a trade dispute when, and only when, a person—

    (a)  induces another to break a contract of employment or interferes or induces another to interfere with its performance, or

    (b)  threatens that a contract of employment under which he or another is employed will be broken or its performance interfered with, or that he will induce another to break a contract of employment or to interfere with its performance,

and the employer under the contract of employment is not the employer party to the dispute.

(3)  Lawful picketing means acts done in the course of such attendance as is declared lawful by section 220 (peaceful picketing)—

    (a)  by a worker employed (or, in the case of a worker not in employment, last employed)

by the employer party to the dispute, or

    (b)  by a trade union official whose attendance is lawful by virtue of subsection (1)(b) of that section.

(4)  For the purposes of this section an employer shall not be treated as party to a dispute between another employer and workers of that employer; and where more than one

employer is in dispute with his workers, the dispute between each employer and his workers shall be treated as a separate dispute.

In this subsection 'worker' has the same meaning as in section 244 (meaning of 'trade dispute').

(5)   An act in contemplation or furtherance of a trade dispute which is primary action in relation to that dispute may not be relied on as secondary action in relation to another trade dispute.

Primary action means such action as is mentioned in paragraph (a) or (b) of subsection (2) where the employer under the contract of employment is the employer party to the dispute.

(6)   In this section 'contract of employment' includes any contract under which one person personally does work or performs services for another, and related expressions shall be construed accordingly.

## 225   Pressure to impose union recognition requirement

(1)   An act is not protected if it constitutes, or is one of a number of acts which together constitute, an inducement or attempted inducement of a person—

(a)   to incorporate in a contract to which that person is a party, or a proposed contract to which he intends to be a party, a term or condition which is or would be void by virtue of section 186 (recognition requirement in contract for goods or services), or

(b)   to contravene section 187 (refusal to deal with person on grounds of union exclusion).

(2)   An act is not protected if—

(a)   it interferes with the supply (whether or not under a contract) of goods or services, or can reasonably be expected to have that effect, and

(b)   one of the facts relied upon for the purpose of establishing liability is that a person has—

(i)   induced another to break a contract of employment or interfered or induced another to interfere with its performance, or

(ii)   threatened that a contract of employment under which he or another is employed will be broken or its performance interfered with, or that he will induce another to break a contract of employment or to interfere with its performance, and

(c)   the reason, or one of the reasons, for doing the act is the fact or belief that the supplier (not being the employer under the contract of employment mentioned in paragraph (b)) does not, or might not—

(i)   recognise one or more trade unions for the purpose of negotiating on behalf of workers, or any class of worker, employed by him, or

(ii)   negotiate or consult with, or with an official of, one or more trade unions.

*Requirement of ballot before action by trade union*

## 226   Requirement of ballot before action by trade union

(1)   An act done by a trade union to induce a person to take part, or continue to take part, in industrial action

(a)   is not protected unless the industrial action has the support of a ballot, and

(b)   where section 226A falls to be complied with in relation to the person's employer, is not protected as respects the employer unless the trade union has complied with section 226A in relation to him.

In this section 'the relevant time', in relation to an act by a trade union to induce a person to take part, or continue to take part, in industrial action, means the time at which proceedings are commenced in respect of the act.

(2)   Industrial action shall be regarded as having the support of a ballot only if—

(a)   the union has held a ballot in respect of the action—

(i)   in relation to which the requirements of section 226B so far as applicable before and during the holding of the ballot were satisfied,

(ii)   in relation to which the requirements of sections 227 to 231 were satisfied,

...

(iia)   in which at least 50% of those who were entitled to vote in the ballot did so, and (iii)　in which [the required number of persons (see subsections (2A) to (2C)) answered 'Yes' to the question applicable in accordance with section 229(2) to industrial action of the kind to which the act of inducement relates;

   (b)　such of the requirements of the following sections as have fallen to be satisfied at the relevant time have been satisfied, namely —

     (i)　section 226B so far as applicable after the holding of the ballot, and

     (ii)　section 231B; …

  (bb)　section 232A does not prevent the industrial action from being regarded as having the support of the ballot; and

   (c)　the requirements of section 233 (calling of industrial action with support of ballot) are satisfied.

Any reference in this subsection to a requirement of a provision which is disapplied or modified by section 232 has effect subject to that section.

(2A)　In all cases, the required number of persons for the purposes of subsection (2)(a)(iii) is the majority voting in the ballot.

(2B)　There is an additional requirement where the majority of those who were entitled to vote in the ballot are at the relevant time normally engaged in the provision of important public services, unless at that time the union reasonably believes this not to be the case.

(2C)　The additional requirement is that at least 40% of those who were entitled to vote in the ballot answered 'Yes' to the question.

(2D)　In subsection (2B) 'important public services' has the meaning given by regulations made by statutory instrument by the Secretary of State.

(2E)　Regulations under subsection (2D) may specify only services that fall within any of the following categories —

   (a)　health services;

(2EA)　But regulations under subsection (2D) may not specify services provided by a devolved Welsh authority.

   (b)　education of those aged under 17;

   (c)　fire services;

   (d)　transport services;

   (e)　decommissioning of nuclear installations and management of radioactive waste and spent fuel;

   (f)　border security.

(2F)　No regulations shall be made under subsection (2D) unless a draft of them has been laid before Parliament and approved by a resolution of each House of Parliament.

(3)　Where separate workplace ballots are held by virtue of section 228(1) —

   (a)　industrial action shall be regarded as having the support of a ballot if the conditions specified in subsection (2) are satisfied, and

   (b)　the trade union shall be taken to have complied with the requirements relating to a ballot imposed by section 226A if those requirements are complied with,

in relation to the ballot for the place of work of the person induced to take part, or continue to take part, in the industrial action.

(3A)　If the requirements of section 231A fall to be satisfied in relation to an employer, as respects that employer industrial action shall not be regarded as having the support of a ballot unless those requirements are satisfied in relation to that employer.

(4)　For the purposes of this section an inducement, in relation to a person, includes an inducement which is or would be ineffective, whether because of his unwillingness to be influenced by it or for any other reason.

## 226A　Notice of ballot and sample voting paper for employers

(1)　The trade union must take such steps as are reasonably necessary to ensure that —

   (a)　not later than the seventh day before the opening day of the ballot, the notice specified in subsection (2), and

   (b)　not later than the third day before the opening day of the ballot, the sample voting paper specified in subsection (2F),

is received by every person who it is reasonable for the union to believe (at the latest time when steps could be taken to comply with paragraph (a)) will be the employer of persons who will be entitled to vote in the ballot.

(2)   The notice referred to in paragraph (a) of subsection (1) is a notice in writing—
   (a)   stating that the union intends to hold the ballot,
   (b)   specifying the date which the union reasonably believes will be the opening day of the ballot, and
   (c)   containing—
      (i)    the lists mentioned in subsection (2A) and the figures mentioned in subsection (2B), together with an explanation of how those figures were arrived at, or
      (ii)   where some or all of the employees concerned are employees from whose wages the employer makes deductions representing payments to the union, either those lists and figures and that explanation or the information mentioned in subsection (2C)

(2A) The lists are—
   (a)   a list of the categories of employee to which the employees concerned belong, and
   (b)   a list of the workplaces at which the employees concerned work.

(2B) The figures are—
   (a)   the total number of employees concerned,
   (b)   the number of the employees concerned in each of the categories in the list mentioned in subsection (2A)(a), and
   (c)   the number of the employees concerned who work at each workplace in the list mentioned in subsection (2A)(b).

(2C) The information referred to in subsection (2)(c)(ii) is such information as will enable the employer readily to deduce—
   (a)   the total number of employees concerned,
   (b)   the categories of employee to which the employees concerned belong and the number of the employees concerned in each of those categories, and
   (c)   the workplaces at which the employees concerned work and the number of them who work at each of those workplaces.

(2D) The lists and figures supplied under this section, or the information mentioned in subsection (2C) that is so supplied, must be as accurate as is reasonably practicable in the light of the information in the possession of the union at the time when it complies with subsection (1)(a).

(2E) For the purposes of subsection (2D) information is in the possession of the union if it is held, for union purposes—
   (a)   in a document, whether in electronic form or any other form, and
   (b)   in the possession or under the control of an officer or employee of the union.

(2F) The sample voting paper referred to in paragraph (b) of subsection (1) is—
   (a)   a sample of the form of voting paper which is to be sent to the employees concerned, or
   (b)   where the employees concerned are not all to be sent the same form of voting paper, a sample of each form of voting paper which is to be sent to any of them.

(2G) Nothing in this section requires a union to supply an employer with the names of the employees concerned.

(2H) In this section references to the 'employees concerned' are references to those employees of the employer in question who the union reasonably believes will be entitled to vote in the ballot.

(2I) For the purposes of this section, the workplace at which an employee works is—
   (a)   in relation to an employee who works at or from a single set of premises, those premises, and
   (b)   in relation to any other employee, the premises with which his employment has the closest connection.

(3)–(3B) …

(4)   In this section references to the opening day of the ballot are references to the first day when a voting paper is sent to any person entitled to vote in the ballot.

(5)   This section, in its application to a ballot in which merchant seamen to whom section 230(2A) applies are entitled to vote, shall have effect with the substitution in subsection (2F), for references to the voting paper which is to be sent to the employees, of references to the voting paper which is to be sent or otherwise provided to them.

## 226B  Appointment of scrutineer

(1)  The trade union shall, before the ballot in respect of the industrial action is held, appoint a qualified person ('the scrutineer') whose terms of appointment shall require him to carry out in relation to the ballot the functions of—

   (a)  taking such steps as appear to him to be appropriate for the purpose of enabling him to make a report to the trade union (see section 231B); and

   (b)  making the report as soon as reasonably practicable after the date of the ballot and, in any event, not later than the end of the period of four weeks beginning with that date.

(2)  A person is a qualified person in relation to a ballot if—

   (a)  he satisfies such conditions as may be specified for the purposes of this section by order of the Secretary of State or is himself so specified; and

   (b)  the trade union has no grounds for believing either that he will carry out the functions conferred on him under subsection (1) otherwise than competently or that his independence in relation to the union, or in relation to the ballot, might reasonably be called into question.

   An order under paragraph (a) shall be made by statutory instrument which shall be subject to annulment in pursuance of a resolution of either House of Parliament.

(3)  The trade union shall ensure that the scrutineer duly carries out the functions conferred on him under subsection (1) and that there is no interference with the carrying out of those functions from the union or any of its members, officials or employees.

(4)  The trade union shall comply with all reasonable requests made by the scrutineer for the purposes of, or in connection with, the carrying out of those functions.

## 226C  Exclusion for small ballots

Nothing in section 226B, section 229(1A)(a) or section 231B shall impose a requirement on a trade union unless—

   (a)  the number of members entitled to vote in the ballot, or

   (b)  where separate workplace ballots are held in accordance with section 228(1), the aggregate of the number of members entitled to vote in each of them,

exceeds 50.

## 227  Entitlement to vote in ballot

(1)  Entitlement to vote in the ballot must be accorded equally to all the members of the trade union who it is reasonable at the time of the ballot for the union to believe will be induced by the union to take part or, as the case may be, to continue to take part in the industrial action in question, and to no others.

(2)  ...

## 228  Separate workplace ballots

(1)  Subject to subsection (2), this section applies if the members entitled to vote in a ballot by virtue of section 227 do not all have the same workplace.

(2)  This section does not apply if the union reasonably believes that all those members have the same workplace.

(3)  Subject to section 228A, a separate ballot shall be held for each workplace; and entitlement to vote in each ballot shall be accorded equally to, and restricted to, members of the union who—

   (a)  are entitled to vote by virtue of section 227, and

   (b)  have that workplace.

(4)  In this section and section 228A 'workplace' in relation to a person who is employed means—

   (a)  if the person works at or from a single set of premises, those premises, and

   (b)  in any other case, the premises with which the person's employment has the closest connection.

## 228A  Separate workplaces: single and aggregate ballots

(1)  Where section 228(3) would require separate ballots to be held for each workplace, a ballot may be held in place of some or all of the separate ballots if one of subsections (2) to (4) is satisfied in relation to it.

(2)   This subsection is satisfied in relation to a ballot if the workplace of each member entitled to vote in the ballot is the workplace of at least one member of the union who is affected by the dispute.

(3)   This subsection is satisfied in relation to a ballot if entitlement to vote is accorded to, and limited to, all the members of the union who—

  (a)   according to the union's reasonable belief have an occupation of a particular kind or have any of a number of particular kinds of occupation, and

  (b)   are employed by a particular employer, or by any of a number of particular employers, with whom the union is in dispute.

(4)   This subsection is satisfied in relation to a ballot if entitlement to vote is accorded to, and limited to, all the members of the union who are employed by a particular employer, or by any of a number of particular employers, with whom the union is in dispute.

(5)   For the purposes of subsection (2) the following are members of the union affected by a dispute—

  (a)   if the dispute relates (wholly or partly) to a decision which the union reasonably believes the employer has made or will make concerning a matter specified in subsection (1)(a), (b) or (c) of section 244 (meaning of 'trade dispute'), members whom the decision directly affects,

  (b)   if the dispute relates (wholly or partly) to a matter specified in subsection (1)(d) of that section, members whom the matter directly affects,

  (c)   if the dispute relates (wholly or partly) to a matter specified in subsection (2)(e) of that section, persons whose membership or non-membership is in dispute,

  (d)   if the dispute relates (wholly or partly) to a matter specified in subsection (1)(f) of that section, officials of the union who have used or would use the facilities concerned in the dispute.

## 229   Voting paper

(1)   The method of voting in a ballot must be by the marking of a voting paper by the person voting.

(1A)  Each voting paper must—

  (a)   state the name of the independent scrutineer,

  (b)   clearly specify the address to which, and the date by which, it is to be returned,

  (c)   be given one of a series of consecutive whole numbers every one of which is used in giving a different number in that series to each voting paper printed or otherwise produced for the purposes of the ballot, and

  (d)   be marked with its number.

This subsection, in its application to a ballot in which merchant seamen to whom section 230(2A) applies are entitled to vote, shall have effect with the substitution, for the reference to the address to which the voting paper is to be returned, of a reference to the ship to which the seamen belong.

(2)   The voting paper must contain at least one of the following questions—

  (a)   a question (however framed) which requires the person answering it to say, by answering 'Yes' or 'No', whether he is prepared to take part or, as the case may be, to continue to take part in a strike;

  (b)   a question (however framed) which requires the person answering it to say, by answering 'Yes' or 'No', whether he is prepared to take part or, as the case may be, to continue to take part in industrial action short of a strike.

(2A)  For the purposes of subsection (2) an overtime ban and a call-out ban constitute industrial action short of a strike.

(2B)  The voting paper must include a summary of the matter or matters in issue in the trade dispute to which the proposed industrial action relates.

(2C)  Where the voting paper contains a question about taking part in industrial action short of a strike, the type or types of industrial action must be specified (either in the question itself or elsewhere on the voting paper).

(2D)  The voting paper must indicate the period or periods within which the industrial action or, as the case may be, each type of industrial action is expected to take place.

(3)   The voting paper must specify who, in the event of a vote in favour of industrial action, is authorised for the purposes of section 233 to call upon members to take part or continue to take part in the industrial action.

The person or description of persons so specified need not be authorised under the rules of the union but must be within section 20(2) (persons for whose acts the union is taken to be responsible).

(4)   The following statement must (without being qualified or commented upon by anything else on the voting paper) appear on every voting paper—

'If you take part in a strike or other industrial action, you may be in breach of your contract of employment. However, if you are dismissed for taking part in strike or other industrial action which is called officially and is otherwise lawful, the dismissal will be unfair if it takes place fewer than twelve weeks after you started taking part in the action, and depending on the circumstances may be unfair if it takes place later.'

## 230   Conduct of ballot

(1)   Every person who is entitled to vote in the ballot must—
    (a)   be allowed to vote without interference from, or constraint imposed by, the union or any of its members, officials or employees, and
    (b)   so far as is reasonably practicable, be enabled to do so without incurring any direct cost to himself.

(2)   Except as regards persons falling within subsection (2A), so far as is reasonably practicable, every person who is entitled to vote in the ballot must—
    (a)   have a young paper sent to him by post at his home address or any other address which he has requested the trade union in writing to treat as his postal address; and
    (b)   be given a convenient opportunity to vote by post.

(2A) Subsection (2B) applies to a merchant seaman if the trade union reasonably believes that—
    (a)   he will be employed in a ship either at sea or at a place outside Great Britain at some time in the period during which votes may be cast, and
    (b)   it will be convenient for him to receive a voting paper and to vote while on the ship or while at a place where the ship is rather than in accordance with subsection (2).

(2B) Where this subsection applies to a merchant seaman he shall, if it is reasonably practicable—
    (a)   have a voting paper made available to him while on the ship or while at a place where the ship is, and
    (b)   be given an opportunity to vote while on the ship or while at a place where the ship is.

(2C) In subsections (2A) and (2B) 'merchant seaman' means a person whose employment, or the greater part of it, is carried out on board sea-going ships.

(3)   ...

(4)   A ballot shall be conducted so as to secure that—
    (a)   so far as is reasonably practicable, those voting do so in secret, and
    (b)   the votes given in the ballot are fairly and accurately counted.

For the purposes of paragraph (b) an inaccuracy in counting shall be disregarded if it is accidental and on a scale which could not affect the result of the ballot.

## 231   Information as to result of ballot

As soon as is reasonably practicable after the holding of the ballot, the trade union shall take such steps as are reasonably necessary to ensure that all persons entitled to vote in the ballot are told—
    (a)   the number of individuals who were entitled to vote in the ballot,
    (b)   the number of votes cast in the ballot,
    (c)   the number of individuals answering 'Yes' to the question, or as the case may be, to each question,
    (d)   the number of individuals answering 'No' to the question, or as the case may be, to each question,

(e)   the number of spoiled or otherwise invalid voting papers returned,

(f)   whether or not the number of votes cast in the ballot is at least 50% of the number of individuals who were entitled to vote in the ballot, and

(g)   where section 226(2B) applies, whether or not the number of individuals answering 'Yes' to the question (or each question) is at least 40% of the number of individuals who were entitled to vote in the ballot.

## 231A  Employers to be informed of ballot result

(1)   As soon as reasonably practicable after the holding of the ballot, the trade union shall take such steps as are reasonably necessary to ensure that every relevant employer is informed of the matters mentioned in section 231.

(2)   In subsection (1) 'relevant employer' means a person who it is reasonable for the trade union to believe (at the time when the steps are taken) was at the time of the ballot the employer of any persons entitled to vote.

## 231B  Scrutineer's report

(1)   The scrutineer's report on the ballot shall state whether the scrutineer is satisfied—

(a)   that there are no reasonable grounds for believing that there was any contravention of a requirement imposed by or under any enactment in relation to the ballot,

(b)   that the arrangements made with respect to the production, storage, distribution, return or other handling of the voting papers used in the ballot, and the arrangements for the counting of the votes, included all such security arrangements as were reasonably practicable for the purpose of minimising the risk that any unfairness or malpractice might occur, and

(c)   that he has been able to carry out the functions conferred on him under section 226B(1) without any interference from the trade union or any of its members, officials or employees;

and if he is not satisfied as to any of those matters, the report shall give particulars of his reason for not being satisfied as to that matter.

(2)   If at any time within six months from the date of the ballot—

(a)   any person entitled to vote in the ballot, or

(b)   the employer of any such person,

requests a copy of the scrutineer's report, the trade union must, as soon as practicable, provide him with one either free of charge or on payment of such reasonable fee as may be specified by the trade union.

## 232A  Inducement of member denied entitlement to vote

Industrial action shall not be regarded as having the support of a ballot if the following conditions apply in the case of any person—

(a)   he was a member of the trade union at the time when the ballot was held,

(b)   it was reasonable at that time for the trade union to believe he would be induced to take part or, as the case may be, to continue to take part in the industrial action,

(c)   he was not accorded entitlement to vote in the ballot, and

(d)   he was induced by the trade union to take part or, as the case may be, to continue to take part in the industrial action.

## 232B  Small accidental failures to be disregarded

(1)   If—

(a)   in relation to a ballot there is a failure (or there are failures) to comply with a provision mentioned in subsection (2) or with more than one of those provisions, and

(b)   the failure is accidental and on a scale which is unlikely to affect the result of the ballot or, as the case may be, the failures are accidental and taken together are on a scale which is unlikely to affect the result of the ballot,

the failure (or failures) shall be disregarded for all purposes (including, in particular, those of section 232A(c)).

(2)   The provisions are section 227(1), section 230(2) and section 230(2B).

## 233    Calling of industrial action with support of ballot

(1)    Industrial action shall be regarded as having the support of a ballot only if—

    (a)    it is called by a person specified or of a description specified in the voting paper for the ballot in accordance with section 229(3), and

    (b)    there was no call by the trade union to take part or continue to take part in industrial action to which the ballot relates, or any authorisation or endorsement by the union of any such industrial action, before the date of the ballot.

(4)    For the purposes of this section a call shall be taken to have been made by a trade union if it was authorised or endorsed by the union; and the provisions of section 20(2) to (4) apply for the purpose of determining whether a call, or industrial action, is to be taken to have been so authorised or endorsed.

## 234    Period after which ballot ceases to be effective

(1)    Industrial action that is regarded as having the support of a ballot shall cease to be so regarded at the end of the period, beginning with the date of the ballot—

    (a)    of six months, or

    (b)    of such longer duration not exceeding nine months as is agreed between the union and the members' employer.

(1A)    Subsection (1) has effect—

    (a)    without prejudice to the possibility of the industrial action getting the support of a fresh ballot; and

    (b)    subject to the following provisions.

(2)    Where for the whole or part of that period the calling or organising of industrial action is prohibited—

    (a)    by virtue of a court order which subsequently lapses or is discharged, recalled or set aside, or

    (b)    by virtue of an undertaking given to a court by any person from which he is subsequently released or by which he ceases to be bound,

the trade union may apply to the court for an order that the period during which the prohibition had effect shall not count towards the period referred to in subsection (1).

(3)    The application must be made forthwith upon the prohibition ceasing to have effect—

    (a)    to the court by virtue of whose decision it ceases to have effect, or

    (b)    where an order lapses or an undertaking ceases to bind without any such decision, to the court by which the order was made or to which the undertaking was given;

(4)    The court shall not make an order if it appears to the court—

    (a)    that the result of the ballot no longer represents the views of the union members concerned, or

    (b)    that an event is likely to occur as a result of which those members would vote against industrial action if another ballot were to be held.

(5)    No appeal lies from the decision of the court to make or refuse an order under this section.

(6)    The period between the making of an application under this section and its determination does not count towards the period referred to in subsection (1).

*Requirement on trade union to give notice of industrial action*

## 234A    Notice to employers of industrial action

(1)    An act done by a trade union to induce a person to take part, or continue to take part, in industrial action is not protected as respects his employer unless the union has taken or takes such steps as are reasonably necessary to ensure that the employer receives within the appropriate period a relevant notice covering the act.

(2)    Subsection (1) imposes a requirement in the case of an employer only if it is reasonable for the union to believe, at the latest time when steps could be taken to ensure that he receives such a notice, that he is the employer of persons who will be or have been induced to take part, or continue to take part, in the industrial action.

(3)    For the purposes of this section a relevant notice is a notice in writing which—

    (a)    contains—

        (i)    the lists mentioned in subsection (3A) and the figures mentioned in subsection (3B), together with an explanation of how those figures were arrived at, or

        (ii)    where some or all of the affected employees are employees from whose wages the employer makes deductions representing payments to the union, either those lists and figures and that explanation or the information mentioned in subsection (3C), and

    (b)    states whether industrial action is intended to be continuous or discontinuous and specifies—

        (i)    where it is to be continuous, the intended date for any of the affected employees to begin to take part in the action,

        (ii)    where it is to be discontinuous, the intended dates for any of the affected employees to take part in the action.

(3A) The lists referred to in subsection (3)(a) are—

    (a)    a list of the categories of employee to which the affected employees belong, an

    (b)    a list of the workplaces at which the affected employees work.

(3B) The figures referred to in subsection (3)(a) are—

    (a)    the total number of the affected employees,

    (b)    the number of the affected employees in each of the categories in the list mentioned in subsection (3A)(a), and

    (c)    the number of the affected employees who work at each workplace in the list mentioned in subsection (3A)(b).

(3C) The information referred to in subsection (3)(a)(ii) is such information as will enable the employer readily to deduce—

    (a)    the total number of the affected employees,

    (b)    the categories of employee to which the affected employees belong and the number of the affected employees in each of those categories, and

    (c)    the workplaces at which the affected employees work and the number of them who work at each of those workplaces.

(3D) The lists and figures supplied under this section, or the information mentioned in subsection (3C) that is so supplied, must be as accurate as is reasonably practicable in the light of the information in the possession of the union at the time when it complies with subsection (1).

(3E) For the purposes of subsection (3D) information is in the possession of the union if it is held, for union purposes—

    (a)    in a document, whether in electronic form or any other form, and

    (b)    in the possession or under the control of an officer or employee of the union.

(3F) Nothing in this section requires a union to supply an employer with the names of the affected employees.

(4)    For the purposes of subsection (1) the appropriate period is the period—

    (a)    beginning with the day when the union satisfies the requirement of section 231A in relation to the ballot in respect of the industrial action, and

    (b)    ending with the 14th day before the starting date, or the seventh day before that date if the union and the employer so agree.

In paragraph (b) 'starting date' means the day, or the first of the days, specified in the relevant notice.

(5)    For the purposes of subsection (1) a relevant notice covers an act done by the union if the person induced falls within a notified category of employee and the workplace at which he works is a notified workplace and—

    (a)    where he is induced to take part or continue to take part in industrial action which the union intends to be continuous, if—

        (i)    the notice states that the union intends the industrial action to be continuous, and

        (ii)    there is no participation by him in the industrial action before the date specified in the notice in consequence of any inducement by the union not covered by a relevant notice; and

    (b)    where he is induced to take part or continue to take part in industrial action which the union intends to be discontinuous, if there is no participation by him in the industrial action on a day not so specified in consequence of any inducement by the union not covered by a relevant notice.

(5B) In subsection (5)—

    (a)    a 'notified category of employee' means—

        (i)    a category of employee that is listed in the notice, or

        (ii)    where the notice contains the information mentioned in subsection (3C), a category of employee that the employer (at the time he receives the notice) can readily deduce from the notice is a category of employee to which some or all of the affected employees belong, and

    (b)    a 'notified workplace' means—

        (i)    a workplace that is listed in the notice, or

        (ii)    where the notice contains the information mentioned in subsection (3C), a workplace that the employer (at the time he receives the notice) can readily deduce from the notice is the workplace at which some or all of the affected employees work.

(5C) In this section references to the 'affected employees' are references to those employees of the employer who the union reasonably believes will be induced by the union, or have been so induced, to take part or continue to take part in the industrial action.

(5D) For the purposes of this section, the workplace at which an employee works is—

    (a)    in relation to an employee who works at or from a single set of premises, those premises, and

    (b)    in relation to any other employee, the premises with which his employment has the closest connection.

(6)    For the purposes of this section—

    (a)    a union intends industrial action to be discontinuous if it intends it to take place only on some days on which there is an opportunity to take the action, and

    (b)    a union intends industrial action to be continuous if it intends it to be not so restricted.

(7)    Subject to subsections (7A) and (7B), where—

    (a)    continuous industrial action which has been authorised or endorsed by a union ceases to be so authorised or endorsed, and

    (b)    the industrial action has at a later date again been authorised or endorsed by the union (whether as continuous or discontinuous action),

no relevant notice covering acts done to induce persons to take part in the earlier action shall operate to cover acts done to induce persons to take part in the action authorised or endorsed at the later date and this section shall apply in relation to an act to induce a person to take part, or continue to take part, in the industrial action after that date as if the references in subsection (3)(b)(i) to the industrial action were to the industrial action taking place after that date.

(7A) Subsection (7) shall not apply where industrial action ceases to be authorised or endorsed in order to enable the union to comply with a court order or an undertaking given to a court.

(7B) Subsection (7) shall not apply where—

    (a)    a union agrees with an employer, before industrial action ceases to be authorised or endorsed, that it will cease to be authorised or endorsed with effect from a date specified in the agreement ('the suspension date') and that it may again be authorised or endorsed with effect from a date not earlier than a date specified in the agreement ('the resumption date'),

    (b)    the action ceases to be authorised or endorsed with effect from the suspension date, and

    (c)    the action is again authorised or endorsed with effect from a date which is not earlier than the resumption date or such later date as may be agreed between the union and the employer.

(8)    The requirement imposed on a trade union by subsection (1) shall be treated as having been complied with if the steps were taken by other relevant persons or committees whose acts were authorised or endorsed by the union and references to the belief or intention of the union in subsection (2) or, as the case may be, subsections (3), (5), (5C) and (6) shall be construed as references to the belief or the intention of the person or committee taking the steps.

(9)    The provisions of section 20(2) to (4) apply for the purpose of determining for the purposes of subsection (1) who are relevant persons or committees and whether the trade union is to be taken to have authorised or endorsed the steps the person or

committee took and for the purposes of subsections (7) to (7B) whether the trade union is to be taken to have authorised or endorsed the industrial action.

## 235 Construction of references to contract of employment

In sections 226 to 234A (requirement of ballot before action by trade union) references to a contract of employment include any contract under which one person personally does work or performs services for another; and 'employer' and other related expressions shall be construed accordingly.

*Industrial action affecting supply of goods or services to an individual*

## 235A Industrial action affecting supply of goods or services to an individual

(1) Where an individual claims that—

(a) any trade union or other person has done, or is likely to do, an unlawful act to induce any person to take part, or to continue to take part, in industrial action, and

(b) an effect, or a likely effect, of the industrial action is or will be to—

(i) prevent or delay the supply of goods or services, or

(ii) reduce the quality of goods or services supplied,

to the individual making the claim,

he may apply to the High Court or the Court of Session for an order under this section.

(2) For the purposes of this section an act to induce any person to take part, or to continue to take part, in industrial action is unlawful—

(a) if it is actionable in tort by any one or more persons, or

(b) (where it is or would be the act of a trade union) if it could form the basis of an application by a member under section 62.

(3) In determining whether an individual may make an application under this section it is immaterial whether or not the individual is entitled to be supplied with the goods or services in question.

(4) Where on an application under this section the court is satisfied that the claim is well-founded, it shall make such order as it considers appropriate for requiring the person by whom the act of inducement has been, or is likely to be, done to take steps for ensuring—

(a) that no, or no further, act is done by him to induce any persons to take part or to continue to take part in the industrial action, and

(b) that no person engages in conduct after the making of the order by virtue of having been induced by him before the making of the order to take part or continue to take part in the industrial action.

(5) Without prejudice to any other power of the court, the court may on an application under this section grant such interlocutory relief (in Scotland, such interim order) as it considers appropriate.

(6) For the purposes of this section an act of inducement shall be taken to be done by a trade union if it is authorised or endorsed by the union; and the provisions of section 20(2) to (4) apply for the purposes of determining whether such an act is to be taken to be so authorised or endorsed.

Those provisions also apply in relation to proceedings for failure to comply with an order under this section as they apply in relation to the original proceedings.

*No compulsion to work*

## 236 No compulsion to work

No court shall, whether by way of—

(a) an order for specific performance or specific implement of a contract of employment, or

(b) an injunction or interdict restraining a breach or threatened breach of such a contract,

compel an employee to do any work or attend at any place for the doing of any work.

*Loss of unfair dismissal protection*

## 237 Dismissal of those taking part in unofficial industrial action

(1) An employee has no right to complain of unfair dismissal if at the time of dismissal he was taking part in an unofficial strike or other unofficial industrial action.

(1A) Subsection (1) does not apply to the dismissal of the employee if it is shown that the reason (or, if more than one, the principal reason) for the dismissal or, in a redundancy case, for selecting the employee for dismissal was one of those specified in or under —

    (a) section 98B, 99, 100, 101A(d), 103, 103A, 104C, 104D or 104E of the Employment Rights Act 1996 (dismissal in jury service, family, health and safety, working time, employee representative, protected disclosure, flexible working, pension scheme membership and study and training cases),

    (b) section 104 of that Act in its application in relation to time off under section 57A of that Act (dependants);

In this subsection 'redundancy case' has the meaning given in section 105(9) of that Act; and a reference to a specified reason for dismissal includes a reference to specified circumstances of dismissal.

(2) A strike or other industrial action is unofficial in relation to an employee unless —

    (a) he is a member of a trade union and the action is authorised or endorsed by that union, or

    (b) he is not a member of a trade union but there are among those taking part in the industrial action members of a trade union by which the action has been authorised or endorsed.

Provided that, a strike or other industrial action shall not be regarded as unofficial if none of those taking part in it are members of a trade union.

(3) The provisions of section 20(2) apply for the purpose of determining whether industrial action is to be taken to have been authorised or endorsed by a trade union.

(4) The question whether industrial action is to be so taken in any case shall be determined by reference to the facts as at the time of dismissal.

Provided that, where an act is repudiated as mentioned in section 21, industrial action shall not thereby be treated as unofficial before the end of the next working day after the day on which the repudiation takes place.

(5) In this section the 'time of dismissal' means —

    (a) where the employee's contract of employment is terminated by notice, when the notice is given,

    (b) where the employee's contract of employment is terminated without notice, when the termination takes effect, and

    (c) where the employee is employed under a contract for a fixed term which expires without being renewed under the same contract, when that term expires;

and a 'working day' means any day which is not a Saturday or Sunday, Christmas Day, Good Friday or a bank holiday under the Banking and Financial Dealings Act 1971.

(6) For the purposes of this section membership of a trade union for purposes unconnected with the employment in question shall be disregarded; but an employee who was a member of a trade union when he began to take part in industrial action shall continue to be treated as a member for the purpose of determining whether that action is unofficial in relation to him or another notwithstanding that he may in fact have ceased to be a member.

## 238 Dismissals in connection with other industrial action

(1) This section applies in relation to an employee who has a right to complain of unfair dismissal (the 'complainant') and who claims to have been unfairly dismissed, where at the date of the dismissal —

    (a) the employer was conducting or instituting a lock-out, or

    (b) the complainant was taking part in a strike or other industrial action.

(2) In such a case an employment tribunal shall not determine whether the dismissal was fair or unfair unless it is shown —

    (a) that one or more relevant employees of the same employer have not been dismissed, or

    (b) that a relevant employee has before the expiry of the period of three months beginning with the date of his dismissal been offered re-engagement and that the complainant has not been offered re-engagement.

(2A) Subsection (2) does not apply to the dismissal of the employee if it is shown that the reason (or, if more than one, the principal reason) for the dismissal or, in a redundancy case, for selecting the employee for dismissal was one of those specified in or under—

   (a)    section 98B, 99, 100, 101A(d), 103, 104C or 104D of the Employment Rights Act 1996 (dismissal in jury service, family, health and safety, working time, employee representative, flexible working, pension scheme membership and study and training cases),

   (b)    section 104 of that Act in its application in relation to time off under section 57A of that Act (dependants).

   In this subsection 'redundancy case' has the meaning given in section 105(9) of that Act; and a reference to a specified reason for dismissal includes a reference to specified circumstances of dismissal.

(2B) Subsection (2) does not apply in relation to an employee who is regarded as unfairly dismissed by virtue of section 238A below.

(3)    For this purpose 'relevant employees' means—

   (a)    in relation to a lock-out, employees who were directly interested in the dispute in contemplation or furtherance of which the lock-out occurred, and

   (b)    in relation to a strike or other industrial action, those employees at the establishment of the employer at or from which the complainant works who at the date of his dismissal were taking part in the action.

   Nothing in section 237 (dismissal of those taking part in unofficial industrial action) affects the question who are relevant employees for the purposes of this section.

(4)    An offer of re-engagement means an offer (made either by the original employer or by a successor of that employer or an associated employer) to re-engage an employee, either in the job which he held immediately before the date of dismissal or in a different job which would be reasonably suitable in his case.

(5)    In this section 'date of dismissal' means—

   (a)    where the employee's contract of employment was terminated by notice, the date on which the employer's notice was given, and

   (b)    in any other case, the effective date of termination.

## 238A  Participation in official industrial action

(1)    For the purposes of this section an employee takes protected industrial action if he commits an act which, or a series of acts each of which, he is induced to commit by an act which by virtue of section 219 is not actionable in tort.

(2)    An employee who is dismissed shall be regarded for the purposes of Part X of the Employment Rights Act 1996 (unfair dismissal) as unfairly dismissed if—

   (a)    the reason (or, if more than one, the principal reason) for the dismissal is that the employee took protected industrial action, and

   (b)    subsection (3), (4) or (5) applies to the dismissal.

(3)    This subsection applies to a dismissal if the date of the dismissal is within the protected period.

(4)    This subsection applies to a dismissal if—

   (a)    the date of the dismissal is after the end of that period, and

   (b)    the employee had stopped taking protected industrial action before the end of that period.

(5)    This subsection applies to a dismissal if—

   (a)    the date of the dismissal is after the end of that period, (b) the employee had not stopped taking protected industrial action before the end of that period, and

   (b)    the employer had not taken such procedural steps as would have been reasonable for the purposes of resolving the dispute to which the protected industrial action relates.

(6)    In determining whether an employer has taken those steps regard shall be had, in particular, to—

   (a)    whether the employer or a union had complied with procedures established by any applicable collective or other agreement;

   (b)    whether the employer or a union offered or agreed to commence or resume negotiations after the start of the protected industrial action;

   (c)    whether the employer or a union unreasonably refused, after the start of the protected industrial action, a request that conciliation services be used;

    (d)    whether the employer or a union unreasonably refused, after the start of the protected industrial action, a request that mediation services be used in relation to procedures to be adopted for the purposes of resolving the dispute;

    (e)    where there was agreement to use either of the services mentioned in paragraphs (a) and (d), the matters specified in section 238B.

(7) In determining whether an employer has taken those steps no regard shall be had to the merits of the dispute.

(7A) For the purposes of this section 'the protected period', in relation to the dismissal of an employee, is the sum of the basic period and any extension period in relation to that employee.

(7B) The basic period is twelve weeks beginning with the first day of protected industrial action.

(7C) An extension period in relation to an employee is a period equal to the number of days falling on or after the first day of protected industrial action (but before the protected period ends) during the whole or any part of which the employee is locked out by his employer.

(7D) In subsections (7B) and (7C), the 'first day of protected industrial action' means the day on which the employee starts to take protected industrial action (even if on that day he is locked out by his employer).

(8) For the purposes of this section no account shall be taken of the repudiation of any act by a trade union as mentioned in section 21 in relation to anything which occurs before the end of the next working day (within the meaning of section 237) after the day on which the repudiation takes place.

(9) In this section 'date of dismissal' has the meaning given by section 238(5).

## 238B Conciliation and mediation: supplementary provisions

(1) The matters referred to in subsection (6)(e) of section 238A are those specified in subsections (2) to (5); and references in this section to 'the service provider' are to any person who provided a service mentioned in subsection (6)(c) or (d) of that section.

(2) The first matter is: whether, at meetings arranged by the service provider, the employer or, as the case may be, a union was represented by an appropriate person.

(3) The second matter is: whether the employer or a union, so far as requested to do so, co-operated in the making of arrangements for meetings to be held with the service provider.

(4) The third matter is: whether the employer or a union fulfilled any commitment given by it during the provision of the service to take particular action.

(5) The fourth matter is: whether, at meetings arranged by the service provider between the parties making use of the service, the representatives of the employer or a union answered any reasonable question put to them concerning the matter subject to conciliation or mediation.

(6) For the purposes of subsection (2) an 'appropriate person' is—

    (a)    in relation to the employer—

        (i)    a person with the authority to settle the matter subject to conciliation or mediation on behalf of the employer, or

        (ii)    a person authorised by a person of that type to make recommendations to him with regard to the settlement of that matter, and

    (b)    in relation to a union, a person who is responsible for handling on the union's behalf the matter subject to conciliation or mediation.

(7) For the purposes of subsection (4) regard may be had to any timetable which was agreed for the taking of the action in question or, if no timetable was agreed, to how long it was before the action was taken.

(8) In any proceedings in which regard must be had to the matters referred to in section 238A(6)(e)—

    (a)    notes taken by or on behalf of the service provider shall not be admissible in evidence;

    (b)    the service provider must refuse to give evidence as to anything communicated to him in connection with the performance of his functions as a conciliator or mediator if, in his opinion, to give the evidence would involve his making a damaging disclosure; and

(c)   the service provider may refuse to give evidence as to whether, for the purposes of subsection (5), a particular question was or was not a reasonable one.

(9)   For the purposes of subsection (8)(b) a 'damaging disclosure' is—

(a)   a disclosure of information which is commercially sensitive, or

(b)   a disclosure of information that has not previously been disclosed which relates to a position taken by a party using the conciliation or mediation service on the settlement of the matter subject to conciliation or mediation,

to which the person who communicated the information to the service provider has not consented.

## 239  Supplementary provisions relating to unfair dismissal

(1)   Sections 237 to 238A (loss of unfair dismissal protection in connection with industrial action) shall be construed as one with Part X of the Employment Rights Act 1996 (unfair dismissal); but sections 108 and 109 of that Act (qualifying period and age limit) shall not apply in relation to section 238A of this Act.

(2)   In relation to a complaint to which section 238 or 238A applies, section 111(2) of that Act (time limit for complaint) does not apply, but an employment tribunal shall not consider the complaint unless it is presented to the tribunal—

(a)   before the end of the period of six months beginning with the date of the complainant's dismissal (as defined by section 238(5)), or

(b)   where the tribunal is satisfied that it was not reasonably practicable for the complaint to be presented before the end of that period, within such further period as the tribunal considers reasonable.

(3)   Where it is shown that the condition referred to in section 238(2)(b) is fulfilled (discriminatory re-engagement), the references in—

(a)   sections 98 to 106 of the Employment Rights Act 1996, and

(b)   sections 152 and 153 of this Act,

to the reason or principal reason for which the complainant was dismissed shall be read as references to the reason or principal reason he has not been offered re-engagement.

(4)   In relation to a complaint under section 111 of the 1996 Act (unfair dismissal: complaint to employment tribunal) that a dismissal was unfair by virtue of section 238A of this Act—

(a)   no order shall be made under section 113 of the 1996 Act (reinstatement or re-engagement) until after the conclusion of protected industrial action by any employee in relation to the relevant dispute,

(b)   regulations under section 7 of the Employment Tribunals Act 1996 may make provision about the adjournment and renewal of applications (including provision requiring adjournment in specified circumstances), and

(c)   regulations under section 9 of that Act may require a pre-hearing review to be carried out in specified circumstances.

*Supplementary*

## 244  Meaning of 'trade dispute' in Part V

(1)   In this Part a 'trade dispute' means a dispute between workers and their employer which relates wholly or mainly to one or more of the following—

(a)   terms and conditions of employment, or the physical conditions in which any workers are required to work;

(b)   engagement or non-engagement, or termination or suspension of employment or the duties of employment, of one or more workers;

(c)   allocation of work or the duties of employment between workers or groups of workers;

(d)   matters of discipline;

(e)   a worker's membership or non-membership of a trade union;

(f)   facilities for officials of trade unions; and

(g)   machinery for negotiation or consultation, and other procedures, relating to any of the above matters, including the recognition by employers or employers' associations of the right of a trade union to represent workers in such negotiation or consultation or in the carrying out of such procedures.

(2)   A dispute between a Minister of the Crown and any workers shall, notwithstanding that he is not the employer of those workers, be treated as a dispute between those workers and their employer if the dispute relates to matters which—

   (a)   have been referred for consideration by a joint body on which, by virtue of provision made by or under any enactment, he is represented, or

   (b)   cannot be settled without him exercising a power conferred on him by or under an enactment.

(3)   There is a trade dispute even though it relates to matters occurring outside the United Kingdom, so long as the person or persons whose actions in the United Kingdom are said to be in contemplation or furtherance of a trade dispute relating to matters occurring outside the United Kingdom are likely to be affected in respect of one or more of the matters specified in subsection (1) by the outcome of the dispute.

(4)   An act, threat or demand done or made by one person or organisation against another which, if restricted, would have led to a trade dispute with that other, shall be treated as being done or made in contemplation of a trade dispute with that other, notwithstanding that because that other submits to the act or threat or accedes to the demand no dispute arises.

(5)   In this section—

'employment' includes any relationship whereby one person personally does work or performs services for another; and

'worker', in relation to a dispute with an employer, means—

   (a)   a worker employed by that employer; or

   (b)   a person who has ceased to be so employed if his employment was terminated in connection with the dispute or if the termination of his employment was one of the circumstances giving rise to the dispute.

## 246   Minor definitions

In this Part—

'date of the ballot' means, in the case of a ballot in which votes may be cast on more than one day, the last of those days;

'strike' means any concerted stoppage of work;

'working hours', in relation to a person, means any time when under his contract of employment, or other contract personally to do work or perform services, he is required to be at work.

PART VI

ADMINISTRATIVE PROVISIONS

*ACAS*

## 247   ACAS

(1)   There shall continue to be a body called the Advisory, Conciliation and Arbitration Service (referred to in this Act as 'ACAS').

(2)   ACAS is a body corporate of which the corporators are the members of its Council.

(3)   Its functions, and those of its officers and servants, shall be performed on behalf of the Crown, but not so as to make it subject to directions of any kind from any Minister of the Crown as to the manner in which it is to exercise its functions under any enactment.

(4)   For the purposes of civil proceedings arising out of those functions the Crown Proceedings Act 1947 applies to ACAS as if it were a government department and the Crown Suits (Scotland) Act 1857 applies to it as if it were a public department.

...

*The Certification Officer*

## 254   The Certification Officer

(1)   There shall continue to be an officer called the Certification Officer.

(2)   The Certification Officer shall be appointed by the Secretary of State after consultation with ACAS.

(3)    The Certification Officer may appoint one or more assistant certification officers and shall appoint an assistant certification officer for Scotland.

(4)    The Certification Officer may delegate to an assistant certification officer such functions as he thinks appropriate, and in particular may delegate to the assistant certification officer for Scotland such functions as he thinks appropriate in relation to organisations whose principal office is in Scotland.

References to the Certification Officer in enactments relating to his functions shall be construed accordingly.

(5)    ACAS shall provide for the Certification Officer the requisite staff (from among the officers and servants of ACAS) and the requisite accommodation, equipment and other facilities.

(5A)    ACAS shall pay to the Certification Officer such sums as he may require for the performance of any of his functions.

## 256    Procedure before the Certification Officer

(1)    Except in relation to matters as to which express provision is made by or under an enactment, the Certification Officer may regulate the procedure to be followed—
    (a)    on any application or complaint made to him, or
    (b)    where his approval is sought with respect to any matter, or
    (c)    determining whether to make a declaration order under section 24B, 32ZC, 45C, 55, 72A, 80, 82 or 103 or under paragraph 5 of Schedule A3.

(2)    He shall in particular make provision about the disclosure, and restriction of the disclosure, of the identity of an individual who has made or is proposing to make any such application or complaint.

(2A)    Provision under subsection (2) shall be such that if the application or complaint relates to a trade union—
    (a)    the individual's identity is disclosed to the union unless the Certification Officer thinks the circumstances are such that it should not be so disclosed;
    (b)    the individual's identity is disclosed to such other persons (if any) as the Certification Officer thinks fit.

...

*Central Arbitration Committee*

## 259    The Central Arbitration Committee

(1)    There shall continue to be a body called the Central Arbitration Committee.

(2)    The functions of the Committee shall be performed on behalf of the Crown, but not so as to make it subject to directions of any kind from any Minister of the Crown as to the manner in which it is to exercise its functions.

(3)    ACAS shall provide for the Committee the requisite staff (from among the officers and servants of ACAS) and the requisite accommodation, equipment and other facilities.

PART VII
MISCELLANEOUS AND GENERAL

*Interpretation*

## 295    Meaning of 'employee' and related expressions

(1)    In this Act—
    'contract of employment' means a contract of service or of apprenticeship,
    'employee' means an individual who has entered into or works under (or, where the employment has ceased, worked under) a contract of employment, and
    'employer', in relation to an employee, means the person by whom the employee is (or, where the employment has ceased, was) employed.

(2)    Subsection (1) has effect subject to section 235 and other provisions conferring a wider meaning on 'contract of employment', or related expressions.

## 296    Meaning of 'worker' and related expressions

(1)    In this Act 'worker' means an individual who works, or normally works or seeks to work—
    (a)    under a contract of employment, or

      (b)    under any other contract whereby he undertakes to do or perform personally any work or services for another party to the contract who is not a professional client of his, or

      (c)    in employment under or for the purposes of a government department (otherwise than as a member of the naval, military or air forces of the Crown) in so far as such employment does not fall within paragraph (a) or (b) above.

(2)    In this Act 'employer', in relation to a worker, means a person for whom one or more workers work, or have worked or normally work or seek to work.

(3)    This section shall have effect subject to sections 68(4), 145F(3) and 151(1B).

## 297   Associated employers

For the purposes of this Act any two employers shall be treated as associated if—

      (a)    one is a company of which the other (directly or indirectly) has control, or

      (b)    both are companies of which a third person (directly or indirectly) has control;

and 'associated employer' shall be construed accordingly.

# EMPLOYMENT RIGHTS ACT 1996
## (1996, c. 18)

PART I

EMPLOYMENT PARTICULARS

*Right to statements of employment particulars*

## 1   Statement of initial employment particulars

(1)    Where a worker begins employment with an employer, the employer shall give to the worker a written statement of particulars of employment

(2)    Subject to sections 2(2) to (4)—

      (a)    the particulars required by subsections (3) and (4) must be included in a single document; and

      (b)    the statement must be given not later than the beginning of the employment.

(3)    The statement shall contain particulars of—

      (a)    the names of the employer and worker,

      (b)    the date when the employment began, and

      (c)    in the case of a statement given to an employee, the date on which the employee's period of continuous employment began (taking into account any employment with a previous employer which counts towards that period).

(4)    The statement shall also contain particulars, as at a specified date not more than seven days before the statement (or the instalment of a statement given under section 2(4) containing them) is given, of—

      (a)    the scale or rate of remuneration or the method of calculating remuneration,

      (b)    the intervals at which remuneration is paid (that is, weekly, monthly or other specified intervals),

      (d)    any terms and conditions relating to hours of work including any terms and conditions relating to—

            (i)    normal working hours,

            (ii)    the days of the week the worker is required to work, and

            (iii)    whether or not such hours or days may be variable, and if they may be how they vary or how that variation is to be determined.

      (f)    any terms and conditions relating to any of the following—

            (i)    entitlement to holidays, including public holidays, and holiday pay (the particulars given being sufficient to enable the worker's entitlement, including any entitlement to accrued holiday pay on the termination of employment, to be precisely calculated),

            (ii)    incapacity for work due to sickness or injury, including any provision for sick pay,

           (iia)    any other paid leave, and

            (v)    pensions and pension schemes,

(da)  any other benefits provided by the employer that do not fall within another paragraph of this subsection,

(i)  the length of notice which the worker is obliged to give and entitled to receive to terminate his contract of employment or other worker's contract,

(j)  the title of the job which the worker is employed to do or a brief description of the work for which he is employed,

(k)  where the employment is not intended to be permanent, the period for which it is expected to continue or, if it is for a fixed term, the date when it is to end,

(ga)  any probationary period, including any conditions and its duration,

(n)  either the place of work or, where the worker is required or permitted to work at various places, an indication of that and of the address of the employer,

(j)  any collective agreements which directly affect the terms and conditions of the employment including, where the employer is not a party, the persons by whom they were made,

(k)  where the worker is required to work outside the United Kingdom for a period of more than one month—

    (i)  the period for which he is to work outside the United Kingdom,

    (ii)  the currency in which remuneration is to be paid while he is working outside the United Kingdom,

    (iii)  any additional remuneration payable to him, and any benefits to be provided to or in respect of him, by reason of his being required to work outside the United Kingdom, and

    (iv)  any terms and conditions relating to his return to the United Kingdom.

(l)  any training entitlement provided by the employer,

(m)  any part of that training entitlement which the employer requires the worker to complete, and

(n)  any other training which the employer requires the worker to complete and which the employer will not bear the cost of.

(7)  Subsection (4)(d)(iii) does not apply to a worker of a body or authority if—

(a)  the worker's pension rights depend on the terms of a pension scheme established under any provision contained in or having effect under any Act, and

(b)  any such provision requires the body or authority to give to a new worker information concerning the worker's pension rights or the determination of questions affecting those rights.

## 2 Statement of initial particulars: supplementary

(1)  If, in the case of a statement under section 1, there are no particulars to be entered under any of the heads of paragraph (d) or (k) of subsection (4) of that section, or under any of the other paragraphs of subsection (3) or (4) of that section, that fact shall be stated.

(2)  A statement under section 1 may refer the worker for particulars of any of the matters specified in subsection (4)(d)(ii) to (iii) and (l) of that section to the provisions of some other document which is reasonably accessible to the worker.

(9)  A statement under section 1 may refer the worker for particulars of either of the matters specified in subsection (4)(e) of that section to the law or to the provisions of any collective agreement directly affecting the terms and conditions of the employment which is reasonably accessible to the worker.

(12)  A statement, insofar as it relates to the particulars required by section1(4)(d)(iii), (j) and (l) and the note required by section 3—

(a)  may be given in instalments; and

(b)  must be given not later than two months after the beginning of the employment, even where the employment ends before that date.

(14)  Where before the end of the period of two months after the beginning of a worker's employment the worker is to begin to work outside the United Kingdom for a period of more than one month, any insertion of a statement given under subsection (4) shall be given to him not later than the time when he leaves the United Kingdom in order to begin so to work.

## 3　Note about disciplinary procedures and pensions

(1) A statement under section 1 shall include a note—

   (a)　specifying any disciplinary rules applicable to the worker or referring the employee to the provisions of a document specifying such rules which is reasonably accessible to the worker,

   (aa)　specifying any procedure applicable to the taking of disciplinary decisions relating to the worker, or to a decision to dismiss the worker, or referring the worker to the provisions of a document specifying such a procedure which is reasonably accessible to the worker,

   (b)　specifying (by description or otherwise)—

      (i)　a person to whom the worker can apply if dissatisfied with any disciplinary decision relating to him or any decision to dismiss him, and

      (ii)　a person to whom the worker can apply for the purpose of seeking redress of any grievance relating to his employment,

   and the manner in which any such application should be made, and

   (c)　where there are further steps consequent on any such application, explaining those steps or referring to the provisions of a document explaining them which is reasonably accessible to the worker.

(2) Subsection (1) does not apply to rules, disciplinary decisions, decisions to dismiss, grievances or procedures relating to health or safety at work.

(3), (4), (5) …

## 4　Statement of changes

(1) If, after the material date, there is a change in any of the matters particulars of which are required by sections 1 to 3 to be included or referred to in a statement under section 1, the employer shall give to the worker a written statement containing particulars of the change.

(2) For the purposes of subsection (1)—

   (a)　in relation to a matter particulars of which are included or referred to in a statement given under section 1, the material date is the date to which the statement relates,

   (b)　in relation to a matter particulars of which—

      (i)　are included or referred to in an instalment of a statement given under section 2(4),

   the material date is the date to which the instalment relates, and

   (c)　in relation to any other matter, the material date is the date by which a statement under section 1 is required to be given.

(3) A statement under subsection (1) shall be given at the earliest opportunity and, in any event, not later than—

   (a)　one month after the change in question, or

   (b)　where that change results from the worker being required to work outside the United Kingdom for a period of more than one month, the time when he leaves the United Kingdom in order to begin so to work, if that is earlier.

(4) A statement under subsection (1) may refer the worker to the provisions of some other document which is reasonably accessible to the worker for a change in any of the matters specified in sections 1(4)(d)(ii) and (iii) and 3(1)(a) and (c).

(5) A statement under subsection (1) may refer the worker for a change in either of the matters specified in section 1(4)(e) to the law or to the provisions of any collective agreement directly affecting the terms and conditions of the employment which is reasonably accessible to the worker.

(6) Where, after an employer has given to a worker a statement under section 1, either—

   (a)　the name of the employer (whether an individual or a body corporate or partnership) is changed without any change in the identity of the employer, or

   (b)　in the case of a statement given to an employee, the identity of the employer is changed in circumstances in which the continuity of the employee's period of employment is not broken,

   and subsection (7) applies in relation to the change, the person who is the employer immediately after the change is not required to give to the worker a statement under section 1; but the change shall be treated as a change falling within subsection (1) of this section.

(7) This subsection applies in relation to a change if it does not involve any change in any of the matters (other than the names of the parties) particulars of which are required by sections 1 to 3 to be included or referred to in the statement under section 1.

(8) A statement under subsection (1) which informs an employee of a change such as is referred to in subsection (6)(b) shall specify the date on which the employee's period of continuous employment began.

## 5 Exclusion from rights to statements

(1) Sections 1 to 4 apply to a worker who at any time comes or ceases to come within the exceptions from those sections provided by section 199, and under section 209, as if his employment with his employer terminated or began at that time.

(2) The fact that section 1 is directed by subsection (1) to apply to a worker as if his employment began on his ceasing to come within the exceptions referred to in that subsection does not affect the obligation under section 1(3)(b) to specify the date on which his employment actually began.

## 6 Reasonably accessible document or collective agreement

In sections 2 to 4 references to a document or collective agreement which is reasonably accessible to a worker are references to a document or collective agreement which—

(a) the worker has reasonable opportunities of reading in the course of his employment, or

(b) is made reasonably accessible to the worker in some other way.

## 7 Power to require particulars of further matters

The Secretary of State may by order provide that section 1 shall have effect as if particulars of such further matters as may be specified in the order were included in the particulars required by that section; and, for that purpose, the order may include such provisions amending that section as appear to the Secretary of State to be expedient.

## 7A Use of alternative documents to give particulars

(1) Subsections (2) and (3) apply where—

(a) an employer gives a worker a document in writing in the form of a contract of employment or other worker's contract or letter of engagement,

(b) the document contains information which, were the document in the form of a statement under section 1, would meet the employer's obligation under that section in relation to the matters mentioned in that section save for the particulars specified in section 2(4), and

(e) the document is given not later than the beginning of the employment.

(2) The employer's duty under section 1 in relation to any matter shall be treated as met if the document given to the worker contains information which, were the document in the form of a statement under that section, would meet the employer's obligation under that section in relation to that matter.

(3) The employer's duty under section 3 shall be treated as met if the document given to the worker contains information which, were the document in the form of a statement under section 1 and the information included in the form of a note, would meet the employer's obligation under section 3.

(4) For the purposes of this section a document to which subsection (1)(a) applies shall be treated, in relation to information in respect of any of the matters mentioned in section 1(4), as specifying the date on which the document is given to the worker as the date as at which the information applies.

(5) Where subsection (2) applies in relation to any matter, the date on which the document by virtue of which that subsection applies is given to the worker shall be the material date in relation to that matter for the purposes of section 4(1).

(6) Where subsection (3) applies, the date on which the document by virtue of which that subsection applies is given to the worker shall be the material date for the purposes of section 4(1) in relation to the matters of which particulars are required to be given under section 3.

(7) The reference in section 4(6) to an employer having given a statement under section 1 shall be treated as including his having given a document by virtue of which his duty to give such a statement is treated as met.

**7B   Giving of alternative documents before start of employment**

A document in the form of a contract of employment or other worker's contract or letter of engagement given by an employer to a worker before the beginning of the worker's employment with the employer shall, when the employment begins, be treated for the purposes of section 7A as having been given at that time.

*Right to itemised pay statement*

**8   Itemised pay statement**

(1)   A worker has the right to be given by his employer, at or before the time at which any payment of wages or salary is made to him, a written itemised pay statement.

(2)   The statement shall contain particulars of—

    (a)   the gross amount of the wages or salary,

    (b)   the amounts of any variable, and (subject to section 9) any fixed, deductions from that gross amount and the purposes for which they are made,

    (c)   the net amount of wages or salary payable,

    (d)   where different parts of the net amount are paid in different ways, the amount and method of payment of each part-payment, and

    (e)   where the amount of wages or salary varies by reference to time worked, the total number of hours worked in respect of the variable amount of wages or salary either as—

        (i)   a single aggregate figure, or

        (ii)   separate figures for different types of work or different rates of pay.

**9   Standing statement of fixed deductions**

(1)   A pay statement given in accordance with section 8 need not contain separate particulars of a fixed deduction if—

    (a)   it contains instead an aggregate amount of fixed deductions, including that deduction, and

    (b)   the employer has given to the worker, at or before the time at which the pay statement is given, a standing statement of fixed deductions which satisfies subsection (2).

(2)   A standing statement of fixed deductions satisfies this subsection if—

    (a)   it is in writing,

    (b)   it contains, in relation to each deduction comprised in the aggregate amount of deductions, particulars of—

        (i)   the amount of the deduction,

        (ii)   the intervals at which the deduction is to be made, and

        (iii)   the purpose for which it is made, and

    (c)   it is (in accordance with subsection (5)) effective at the date on which the pay statement is given.

(3)   A standing statement of fixed deductions may be amended, whether by—

    (a)   addition of a new deduction,

    (b)   a change in the particulars, or

    (c)   cancellation of an existing deduction,

by notice in writing, containing particulars of the amendment, given by the employer to the worker.

(4)   An employer who has given to a worker a standing statement of fixed deductions shall—

    (a)   within the period of twelve months beginning with the date on which the first standing statement was given, and

    (b)   at intervals of not more than twelve months afterwards,

re-issue it in a consolidated form incorporating any amendments notified in accordance with subsection (3).

(5)   For the purposes of subsection (2)(c) a standing statement of fixed deductions—

    (a)   becomes effective on the date on which it is given to the worker, and

    (b)   ceases to be effective at the end of the period of twelve months beginning with that date or, where it is re-issued in accordance with subsection (4), with the end of the period of twelve months beginning with the date of the last re-issue.

*Enforcement*

## 11 References to employment tribunals

(1) Where an employer does not give a worker a statement as required by section 1, 4 or 8 (either because the employer gives the worker no statement or because the statement the employer gives does not comply with what is required), the worker may require a reference to be made to an employment tribunal to determine what particulars ought to have been included or referred to in a statement so as to comply with the requirements of the section concerned.

(2) Where—

    (a) a statement purporting to be a statement under section 1 or 4, or a pay statement or a standing statement of fixed deductions purporting to comply with section 8 or 9 has been given to a worker, and

    (b) a question arises as to the particulars which ought to have been included or referred to in the statement so as to comply with the requirements of this Part,

either the employer or the worker may require the question to be referred to and determined by an employment tribunal.

(3) For the purposes of this section—

    (a) ...

    (b) a question as to the particulars which ought to have been included in a pay statement or standing statement of fixed deductions does not include a question solely as to the accuracy of an amount stated in any such particulars.

(4) An employment tribunal shall not consider a reference under this section in a case where the employment to which the reference relates has ceased unless an application requiring the reference to be made was made—

    (a) before the end of the period of three months beginning with the date on which the employment ceased, or

    (b) within such further period as the tribunal considers reasonable in a case where it is satisfied that it was not reasonably practicable for the application to be made before the end of that period of three months.

(6) Section 207B (extension of time limits to facilitate conciliation before institution of proceedings) also applies for the purposes of subsection (4)(a).

## 12 Determination of references

(1) Where, on a reference under section 11(1), an employment tribunal determines particulars as being those which ought to have been included or referred to in a statement given under section 1 or 4, the employer shall be deemed to have given to the worker a statement in which those particulars were included, or referred to, as specified in the decision of the tribunal.

(2) On determining a reference under section 11(2) relating to a statement purporting to be a statement under section 1 or 4, an employment tribunal may—

    (a) confirm the particulars as included or referred to in the statement given by the employer,

    (b) amend those particulars, or

    (c) substitute other particulars for them,

as the tribunal may determine to be appropriate; and the statement shall be deemed to have been given by the employer to the worker in accordance with the decision of the tribunal.

(3) Where on a reference under section 11 an employment tribunal finds—

    (a) that an employer has failed to give a worker any pay statement in accordance with section 8, or

    (b) that a pay statement or standing statement of fixed deductions does not, in relation to a deduction, contain the particulars required to be included in that statement by that section or section 9,

the tribunal shall make a declaration to that effect.

(4) Where on a reference in the case of which subsection (3) applies the tribunal further finds that any unnotified deductions have been made from the pay of the worker during the period of thirteen weeks immediately preceding the date of the application for the reference (whether or not the deductions were made in breach of the contract of employment), the tribunal may order the employer to pay the worker a sum not exceeding the aggregate of the unnotified deductions so made.

(5)     For the purposes of subsection (4) a deduction is an unnotified deduction if it is made without the employer giving the worker, in any pay statement or standing statement of fixed deductions, the particulars of the deduction required by section 8 or 9.

PART II
PROTECTION OF WAGES

*Deductions by employer*

## 13      Right not to suffer unauthorised deductions

(1)     An employer shall not make a deduction from wages of a worker employed by him unless—

(a)     the deduction is required or authorised to be made by virtue of a statutory provision or a relevant provision of the worker's contract, or

(b)     the worker has previously signified in writing his agreement or consent to the making of the deduction.

(2)     In this section 'relevant provision', in relation to a worker's contract, means a provision of the contract comprised—

(a)     in one or more written terms of the contract of which the employer has given the worker a copy on an occasion prior to the employer making the deduction in question, or

(b)     in one or more terms of the contract (whether express or implied and, if express, whether oral or in writing) the existence and effect, or combined effect, of which in relation to the worker the employer has notified to the worker in writing on such an occasion.

(3)     Where the total amount of wages paid on any occasion by an employer to a worker employed by him is less than the total amount of the wages properly payable by him to the worker on that occasion (after deductions), the amount of the deficiency shall be treated for the purposes of this Part as a deduction made by the employer from the worker's wages on that occasion.

(4)     Subsection (3) does not apply in so far as the deficiency is attributable to an error of any description on the part of the employer affecting the computation by him of the gross amount of the wages properly payable by him to the worker on that occasion.

(5)     For the purposes of this section a relevant provision of a worker's contract having effect by virtue of a variation of the contract does not operate to authorise the making of a deduction on account of any conduct of the worker, or any other event occurring, before the variation took effect.

(6)     For the purposes of this section an agreement or consent signified by a worker does not operate to authorise the making of a deduction on account of any conduct of the worker, or any other event occurring, before the agreement or consent was signified.

(7)     This section does not affect any other statutory provision by virtue of which a sum payable to a worker by his employer but not constituting 'wages' within the meaning of this Part is not to be subject to a deduction at the instance of the employer.

## 14      Excepted deductions

(1)     Section 13 does not apply to a deduction from a worker's wages made by his employer where the purpose of the deduction is the reimbursement of the employer in respect of—

(a)     an overpayment of wages, or

(b)     an overpayment in respect of expenses incurred by the worker in carrying out his employment,

made (for any reason) by the employer to the worker.

(2)     Section 13 does not apply to a deduction from a worker's wages made by his employer in consequence of any disciplinary proceedings if those proceedings were held by virtue of a statutory provision.

(3)     Section 13 does not apply to a deduction from a worker's wages made by his employer in pursuance of a requirement imposed on the employer by a statutory provision to deduct and pay over to a public authority amounts determined by that authority as being due to it from the worker if the deduction is made in accordance with the relevant determination of that authority.

(4) Section 13 does not apply to a deduction from a worker's wages made by his employer in pursuance of any arrangements which have been established—

    (a) in accordance with a relevant provision of his contract to the inclusion of which in the contract the worker has signified his agreement or consent in writing, or

    (b) otherwise with the prior agreement or consent of the worker signified in writing, and under which the employer is to deduct and pay over to a third person amounts notified to the employer by that person as being due to him from the worker, if the deduction is made in accordance with the relevant notification by that person.

(5) Section 13 does not apply to a deduction from a worker's wages made by his employer where the worker has taken part in a strike or other industrial action and the deduction is made by the employer on account of the worker's having taken part in that strike or other action.

(6) Section 13 does not apply to a deduction from a worker's wages made by his employer with his prior agreement or consent signified in writing where the purpose of the deduction is the satisfaction (whether wholly or in part) of an order of a court or tribunal requiring the payment of an amount by the worker to the employer.

*Payments to employer*

## 15 Right not to have to make payments to employer

(1) An employer shall not receive a payment from a worker employed by him unless—

    (a) the payment is required or authorised to be made by virtue of a statutory provision or a relevant provision of the worker's contract, or

    (b) the worker has previously signified in writing his agreement or consent to the making of the payment.

(2) In this section 'relevant provision', in relation to a worker's contract, means a provision of the contract comprised—

    (a) in one or more written terms of the contract of which the employer has given the worker a copy on an occasion prior to the employer receiving the payment in question, or

    (b) in one or more terms of the contract (whether express or implied and, if express, whether oral or in writing) the existence and effect, or combined effect, of which in relation to the worker the employer has notified to the worker in writing on such an occasion.

(3) For the purposes of this section a relevant provision of a worker's contract having effect by virtue of a variation of the contract does not operate to authorise the receipt of a payment on account of any conduct of the worker, or any other event occurring, before the variation took effect.

(4) For the purposes of this section an agreement or consent signified by a worker does not operate to authorise the receipt of a payment on account of any conduct of the worker, or any other event occurring, before the agreement or consent was signified.

(5) Any reference in this Part to an employer receiving a payment from a worker employed by him is a reference to his receiving such a payment in his capacity as the worker's employer.

## 16 Excepted payments

(1) Section 15 does not apply to a payment received from a worker by his employer where the purpose of the payment is the reimbursement of the employer in respect of—

    (a) an overpayment of wages, or

    (b) an overpayment in respect of expenses incurred by the worker in carrying out his employment,

made (for any reason) by the employer to the worker.

(2) Section 15 does not apply to a payment received from a worker by his employer in consequence of any disciplinary proceedings if those proceedings were held by virtue of a statutory provision.

(3) Section 15 does not apply to a payment received from a worker by his employer where the worker has taken part in a strike or other industrial action and the payment has been required by the employer on account of the worker's having taken part in that strike or other action.

(4) Section 15 does not apply to a payment received from a worker by his employer where the purpose of the payment is the satisfaction (whether wholly or in part) of an order of a court or tribunal requiring the payment of an amount by the worker to the employer.

*Enforcement*

## 23    Complaints to employment tribunals

(1)   A worker may present a complaint to an employment tribunal—

  (a)   that his employer has made a deduction from his wages in contravention of section 13 (including a deduction made in contravention of that section as it applies by virtue of section 18(2)),

  (b)   that his employer has received from him a payment in contravention of section 15 (including a payment received in contravention of that section as it applies by virtue of section 20(1)),

  (c)   that his employer has recovered from his wages by means of one or more deductions falling within section 18(1) an amount or aggregate amount exceeding the limit applying to the deduction or deductions under that provision, or

  (d)   that his employer has received from him in pursuance of one or more demands for payment made (in accordance with section 20) on a particular pay day, a payment or payments of an amount or aggregate amount exceeding the limit applying to the demand or demands under section 21(1).

(2)   Subject to subsection (4), an employment tribunal shall not consider a complaint under this section unless it is presented before the end of the period of three months beginning with—

  (a)   in the case of a complaint relating to a deduction by the employer, the date of payment of the wages from which the deduction was made, or

  (b)   in the case of a complaint relating to a payment received by the employer, the date when the payment was received.

(3)   Where a complaint is brought under this section in respect of—

  (a)   a series of deductions or payments, or

  (b)   a number of payments falling within subsection (1)(d) and made in pursuance of demands for payment subject to the same limit under section 21(1) but received by the employer on different dates,

  the references in subsection (2) to the deduction or payment are to the last deduction or payment in the series or to the last of the payments so received.

(3A)  Section 207B (extension of time limits to facilitate conciliation before institution of proceedings) applies for the purposes of subsection (2).

(4)   Where the employment tribunal is satisfied that it was not reasonably practicable for a complaint under this section to be presented before the end of the relevant period of three months, the tribunal may consider the complaint if it is presented within such further period as the tribunal considers reasonable.

(4A)  An employment tribunal is not (despite subsections (3) and (4)) to consider so much of a complaint brought under this section as relates to a deduction where the date of payment of the wages from which the deduction was made was before the period of two years ending with the date of presentation of the complaint.

(4B)  Subsection (4A) does not apply so far as a complaint relates to a deduction from wages that are of a kind mentioned in section 27(1)(b) to (j).

(5)   No complaint shall be presented under this section in respect of any deduction made in contravention of section 86 of the Trade Union and Labour Relations (Consolidation) Act 1992 (deduction of political fund contribution where certificate of exemption or objection has been given).

## 24    Determination of complaints

(1)   Where a tribunal finds a complaint under section 23 well-founded, it shall make a declaration to that effect and shall order the employer—

  (a)   in the case of a complaint under section 23(1)(a), to pay to the worker the amount of any deduction made in contravention of section 13,

  (b)   in the case of a complaint under section 23(1)(b), to repay to the worker the amount of any payment received in contravention of section 15,

  (c)   in the case of a complaint under section 23(1)(c), to pay to the worker any amount recovered from him in excess of the limit mentioned in that provision, and

  (d)   in the case of a complaint under section 23(1)(d), to repay to the worker any amount received from him in excess of the limit mentioned in that provision.

(2)    Where a tribunal makes a declaration under subsection (1), it may order the employer to pay to the worker (in addition to any amount ordered to be paid under that subsection) such amount as the tribunal considers appropriate in all the circumstances to compensate the worker for any financial loss sustained by him which is attributable to the matter complained of.

## 25    Determinations: supplementary

(1)    Where, in the case of any complaint under section 23(1)(a), a tribunal finds that, although neither of the conditions set out in section 13(1)(a) and (b) was satisfied with respect to the whole amount of the deduction, one of those conditions was satisfied with respect to any lesser amount, the amount of the deduction shall for the purposes of section 24(a) be treated as reduced by the amount with respect to which that condition was satisfied.

(2)    Where, in the case of any complaint under section 23(1)(b), a tribunal finds that, although neither of the conditions set out in section 15(1)(a) and (b) was satisfied with respect to the whole amount of the payment, one of those conditions was satisfied with respect to any lesser amount, the amount of the payment shall for the purposes of section 24(b) be treated as reduced by the amount with respect to which that condition was satisfied.

(3)    An employer shall not under section 24 be ordered by a tribunal to pay or repay to a worker any amount in respect of a deduction or payment, or in respect of any combination of deductions or payments, in so far as it appears to the tribunal that he has already paid or repaid any such amount to the worker.

(4)    Where a tribunal has under section 24 ordered an employer to pay or repay to a worker any amount in respect of a particular deduction or payment falling within section 23(1)(a) to (d), the amount which the employer is entitled to recover (by whatever means) in respect of the matter in relation to which the deduction or payment was originally made or received shall be treated as reduced by that amount.

(5)    Where a tribunal has under section 24 ordered an employer to pay or repay to a worker any amount in respect of any combination of deductions or payments falling within section 23(1)(c) or (d), the aggregate amount which the employer is entitled to recover (by whatever means) in respect of the cash shortages or stock deficiencies in relation to which the deductions or payments were originally made or required to be made shall be treated as reduced by that amount.

## 26    Complaints and other remedies

Section 23 does not affect the jurisdiction of an employment tribunal to consider a reference under section 11 in relation to any deduction from the wages of a worker; but the aggregate of any amounts ordered by an employment tribunal to be paid under section 12(4) and under section 24 (whether on the same or different occasions) in respect of a particular deduction shall not exceed the amount of the deduction.

*Supplementary*

## 27    Meaning of 'wages' etc.

(1)    In this Part 'wages', in relation to a worker, means any sums payable to the worker in connection with his employment, including—

    (a)    any fee, bonus, commission, holiday pay or other emolument referable to his employment, whether payable under his contract or otherwise,

    (b)    statutory sick pay under Part XI of the Social Security Contributions and Benefits Act 1992,

    (c)    statutory maternity pay under Part XII of that Act,

    (ca)    statutory paternity pay under Part 12ZA of that Act,

    (cb)    statutory adoption pay under Part 12ZB of that Act,

    (cc)    statutory shared parental pay under Part 12ZC of that Act,

    (cd)    statutory parental bereavement pay under Part 127D of that Act,

    (d)    a guarantee payment (under section 28 of this Act),

    (e)    any payment for time off under Part VI of this Act or section 169 of the Trade Union and Labour Relations (Consolidation) Act 1992 (payment for time off for carrying out trade union duties etc.),

    (f)    remuneration on suspension on medical grounds under section 64 of this Act and remuneration on suspension on maternity grounds under section 68 of this Act, (fa)    remuneration on ending the supply of an agency worker on maternity grounds under section 68C of this Act,

(g)    any sum payable in pursuance of an order for reinstatement or re-engagement under section 113 of this Act,

(h)    any sum payable in pursuance of an order for the continuation of a contract of employment under section 130 of this Act or section 164 of the Trade Union and Labour Relations (Consolidation) Act l992, and

(i)    remuneration under a protective award under section 189 of that Act, but excluding any payments within subsection (2).

(2)    Those payments are—

(a)    any payment by way of an advance under an agreement for a loan or by way of an advance of wages (but without prejudice to the application of section 13 to any deduction made from the worker's wages in respect of any such advance),

(b)    any payment in respect of expenses incurred by the worker in carrying out his employment,

(c)    any payment by way of a pension, allowance or gratuity in connection with the worker's retirement or as compensation for loss of office,

(d)    any payment referable to the worker's redundancy, and

(e)    any payment to the worker otherwise than in his capacity as a worker.

(3)    Where any payment in the nature of a non-contractual bonus is (for any reason) made to a worker by his employer, the amount of the payment shall for the purposes of this Part—

(a)    be treated as wages of the worker, and

(b)    be treated as payable to him as such on the day on which the payment is made.

(4)    In this Part 'gross amount', in relation to any wages payable to a worker, means the total amount of those wages before deductions of whatever nature.

(5)    For the purposes of this Part any monetary value attaching to any payment or benefit in kind furnished to a worker by his employer shall not be treated as wages of the worker except in the case of any voucher, stamp or similar document which is—

(a)    of a fixed value expressed in monetary terms, and

(b)    capable of being exchanged (whether on its own or together with other vouchers, stamps or documents, and whether immediately or only after a time) for money, goods or services (or for any combination of two or more of those things).

PART IIA
ZERO HOURS WORKERS

## 27A  Exclusivity terms unenforceable in zero hours contracts

(1)    In this section 'zero hours contract' means a contract of employment or other worker's contract under which—

(a)    the undertaking to do or perform work or services is an undertaking to do so conditionally on the employer making work or services available to the worker, and

(b)    there is no certainty that any such work or services will be made available to the worker.

(2)    For this purpose, an employer makes work or services available to a worker if the employer requests or requires the worker to do the work or perform the services.

(3)    Any provision of a zero hours contract which—

(a)    prohibits the worker from doing work or performing services under another contract or under any other arrangement, or

(b)    prohibits the worker from doing so without the employer's consent, is unenforceable against the worker.

(4)    Subsection (3) is to be disregarded for the purposes of determining any question whether a contract is a contract of employment or other worker's contract.

## 27B  Power to make further provision in relation to zero hours workers

(1)    The Secretary of State may by regulations make provision for the purpose of securing that zero hours workers, or any description of zero hours workers, are not restricted by any provision or purported provision of their contracts or arrangements with their employers from doing any work otherwise than under those contracts or arrangements.

(2)   In this section, 'zero hours workers' means—
    (a)   employees or other workers who work under zero hours contracts;
    (b)   individuals who work under non-contractual zero hours arrangements;
    (c)   individuals who work under worker's contracts of a kind specified by the regulations.

(3)   The worker's contracts which may be specified by virtue of subsection (2)(c) are those in relation to which the Secretary of State considers it appropriate for provision made by the regulations to apply, having regard, in particular, to provision made by the worker's contracts as to income, rate of pay or working hours.

(4)   In this section 'non-contractual zero hours arrangement' means an arrangement other than a worker's contract under which—
    (a)   an employer and an individual agree terms on which the individual will do any work where the employer makes it available to the individual and the individual agrees to do it, but
    (b)   the employer is not required to make any work available to the individual, nor the individual required to accept it,
and in this section 'employer', in relation to a non-contractual zero hours arrangement, is to be read accordingly.

(5)   Provision that may be made by regulations under subsection (1) includes provision for—
    (a)   modifying—
        (i)    zero hours contracts;
        (ii)   non-contractual zero hours arrangements;
        (iii)  other worker's contracts;
    (b)   imposing financial penalties on employers;
    (c)   requiring employers to pay compensation to zero hours workers;
    (d)   conferring jurisdiction on employment tribunals;
    (e)   conferring rights on zero hours workers.

(6)   Provision that may be made by virtue of subsection (5)(a) may, in particular, include provision for exclusivity terms in prescribed categories of worker's contracts to be unenforceable, in cases in which section 27A does not apply.
For this purpose an exclusivity term is any term by virtue of which a worker is restricted from doing any work otherwise than under the worker's contract.

(7)   Regulations under this section may—
    (a)   make different provision for different purposes;
    (b)   make provision subject to exceptions.

(8)   For the purposes of this section—
    (a)   'zero hours contract' has the same meaning as in section 27A;
    (b)   an employer makes work available to an individual if the employer requests or requires the individual to do it;
    (c)   references to work and doing work include references to services and performing them.

(9)   Nothing in this section is to be taken to affect any worker's contract except so far as any regulations made under this section expressly apply in relation to it.

PART III
GUARANTEE PAYMENTS

## 28   Right to guarantee payment

(1)   Where throughout a day during any part of which an employee would normally be required to work in accordance with his contract of employment the employee is not provided with work by his employer by reason of—
    (a)   a diminution in the requirements of the employer's business for work of the kind which the employee is employed to do, or
    (b)   any other occurrence affecting the normal working of the employer's business in relation to work of the kind which the employee is employed to do,
the employee is entitled to be paid by his employer an amount in respect of that day.

(2)   In this Act a payment to which an employee is entitled under subsection (1) is referred to as a guarantee payment.

(3) In this Part—
    (a)    a day falling within subsection (1) is referred to as a 'workless day', and
    (b)    'workless period' has a corresponding meaning.
(4) In this Part 'day' means the period of twenty-four hours from midnight to midnight.
(5) Where a period of employment begun on any day extends, or would normally extend, over midnight into the following day—
    (a)    if the employment before midnight is, or would normally be, of longer duration than that after midnight, the period of employment shall be treated as falling wholly on the first day, and
    (b)    in any other case, the period of employment shall be treated as falling wholly on the second day.

## 29  Exclusions from right to guarantee payment

(1) An employee is not entitled to a guarantee payment unless he has been continuously employed for a period of not less than one month ending with the day before that in respect of which the guarantee payment is claimed.
(2) …
(3) An employee is not entitled to a guarantee payment in respect of a workless day if the failure to provide him with work for that day occurs in consequence of a strike, lock-out or other industrial action involving any employee of his employer or of an associated employer.
(4) An employee is not entitled to a guarantee payment in respect of a workless day if—
    (a)    his employer has offered to provide alternative work for that day which is suitable in all the circumstances (whether or not it is work which the employee is under his contract employed to perform), and
    (b)    the employee has unreasonably refused that offer.
(5) An employee is not entitled to a guarantee payment if he does not comply with reasonable requirements imposed by his employer with a view to ensuring that his services are available.

## 30  Calculation of guarantee payment

(1) Subject to section 31, the amount of a guarantee payment payable to an employee in respect of any day is the sum produced by multiplying the number of normal working hours on the day by the guaranteed hourly rate; and, accordingly, no guarantee payment is payable to an employee in whose case there are no normal working hours on the day in question.
(2) The guaranteed hourly rate, in relation to an employee, is the amount of one week's pay divided by the number of normal working hours in a week for that employee when employed under the contract of employment in force on the day in respect of which the guarantee payment is payable.
(3) But where the number of normal working hours differs from week to week or over a longer period, the amount of one week's pay shall be divided instead by—
    (a)    the average number of normal working hours calculated by dividing by twelve the total number of the employee's normal working hours during the period of twelve weeks ending with the last complete week before the day in respect of which the guarantee payment is payable, or
    (b)    where the employee has not been employed for a sufficient period to enable the calculation to be made under paragraph (a), a number which fairly represents the number of normal working hours in a week having regard to such of the considerations specified in subsection (4) as are appropriate in the circumstances.
(4) The considerations referred to in subsection (3)(b) are—
    (a)    the average number of normal working hours in a week which the employee could expect in accordance with the terms of his contract, and
    (b)    the average number of normal working hours of other employees engaged in relevant comparable employment with the same employer.
(5) If in any case an employee's contract has been varied, or a new contract has been entered into, in connection with a period of short-time working, subsections (2) and (3) have effect as if for the references to the day in respect of which the guarantee payment is payable there were substituted references to the last day on which the original contract was in force.

## 31    Limits on amount of and entitlement to guarantee payment

(1)    The amount of a guarantee payment payable to an employee in respect of any day shall not exceed £31.00.

(2)    An employee is not entitled to guarantee payments in respect of more than the specified number of days in any period of three months.

(3)    The specified number of days for the purposes of subsection (2) is the number of days, not exceeding five, on which the employee normally works in a week under the contract of employment in force on the day in respect of which the guarantee payment is claimed.

(4)    But where that number of days varies from week to week or over a longer period, the specified number of days is instead—

    (a)    the average number of such days, not exceeding five, calculated by dividing by twelve the total number of such days during the period of twelve weeks ending with the last complete week before the day in respect of which the guarantee payment is claimed, and rounding up the resulting figure to the next whole number, or

    (b)    where the employee has not been employed for a sufficient period to enable the calculation to be made under paragraph (a), a number which fairly represents the number of the employee's normal working days in a week, not exceeding five, having regard to such of the considerations specified in subsection (5) as are appropriate in the circumstances.

(5)    The considerations referred to in subsection (4)(b) are—

    (a)    the average number of normal working days in a week which the employee could expect in accordance with the terms of his contract, and

    (b)    the average number of such days of other employees engaged in relevant comparable employment with the same employer.

(6)    If in any case an employee's contract has been varied, or a new contract has been entered into, in connection with a period of short-time working, subsections (3) and (4) have effect as if for the references to the day in respect of which the guarantee payment is claimed there were substituted references to the last day on which the original contract was in force.

(7)    The Secretary of State may by order vary—

    (a)    the length of the period specified in subsection (2);

    (b)    a limit specified in subsection (3) or (4).

## 32    Contractual remuneration

(1)    A right to a guarantee payment does not affect any right of an employee in relation to remuneration under his contract of employment ('contractual remuneration').

(2)    Any contractual remuneration paid to an employee in respect of a workless day goes towards discharging any liability of the employer to pay a guarantee payment in respect of that day; and, conversely, any guarantee payment paid in respect of a day goes towards discharging any liability of the employer to pay contractual remuneration in respect of that day.

(3)    For the purposes of subsection (2), contractual remuneration shall be treated as paid in respect of a workless day—

    (a)    where it is expressed to be calculated or payable by reference to that day or any part of that day, to the extent that it is so expressed, and

    (b)    in any other case, to the extent that it represents guaranteed remuneration, rather than remuneration for work actually done, and is referable to that day when apportioned rateably between that day and any other workless period falling within the period in respect of which the remuneration is paid.

## 34    Complaints to employment tribunals

(1)    An employee may present a complaint to an employment tribunal that his employer has failed to pay the whole or any part of a guarantee payment to which the employee is entitled.

(2)    An employment tribunal shall not consider a complaint relating to a guarantee payment in respect of any day unless the complaint is presented to the tribunal—

    (a)    before the end of the period of three months beginning with that day, or

(b)    within such further period as the tribunal considers reasonable in a case where it is satisfied that it was not reasonably practicable for the complaint to be presented before the end of that period of three months.

(2A)  Section 207B (extension of time limits to facilitate conciliation before institution of proceedings) applies for the purposes of subsection (2)(a).

(3)    Where an employment tribunal finds a complaint under this section well-founded, the tribunal shall order the employer to pay to the employee the amount of guarantee payment which it finds is due to him.

## PART IV
## SUNDAY WORKING FOR SHOP AND BETTING WORKERS

### *Protected shop workers and betting workers*

### 36    Protected shop workers and betting workers

(1)    Subject to subsection (5), a shop worker or betting worker is to be regarded as 'protected' for the purposes of any provision of this Act if (and only if) subsection (2) or (3) applies to him.

(2)    This subsection applies to a shop worker or betting worker if—
   (a)    on the day before the relevant commencement date he was employed as a shop worker or a betting worker but not to work only on Sunday,
   (b)    he has been continuously employed during the period beginning with that day and ending with the day which, in relation to the provision concerned, is the appropriate date, and
   (c)    throughout that period, or throughout every part of it during which his relations with his employer were governed by a contract of employment, he was a shop worker or a betting worker.

(3)    This subsection applies to any shop worker or betting worker whose contract of employment is such that under it he—
   (a)    is not, and may not be, required to work on Sunday, and
   (b)    could not be so required even if the provisions of this Part were disregarded.

(4)    Where on the day before the relevant commencement date an employee's relations with his employer had ceased to be governed by a contract of employment, he shall be regarded as satisfying subsection (2)(a) if—
   (a)    that day fell in a week which counts as a period of employment with that employer under section 212(2) or (3) or under regulations under section 219, and
   (b)    on the last day before the relevant commencement date on which his relations with his employer were governed by a contract of employment, the employee was employed as a shop worker or a betting worker but not to work only on Sunday.

(5)    A shop worker is not a protected shop worker, and a betting worker is not a protected betting worker, if—
   (a)    he has given his employer an opting-in notice on or after the relevant commencement date, and
   (b)    after giving the notice, he has expressly agreed with his employer to do shop work, or betting work, on Sunday or on a particular Sunday.

(6)    In this Act 'opting-in notice', in relation to a shop worker or a betting worker, means written notice, signed and dated by the shop worker or betting worker, in which the shop worker or betting worker expressly states that he wishes to work on Sunday or that he does not object to Sunday working.

(7)    In this Act 'the relevant commencement date' means—
   (a)    in relation to a shop worker, 26th August 1994, and
   (b)    in relation to a betting worker, 3rd January 1995.

### 37    Contractual requirements relating to Sunday work

(1)    Any contract of employment under which a shop worker or betting worker who satisfies section 36(2)(a) was employed on the day before the relevant commencement date is unenforceable to the extent that it—

    (a)   requires the shop worker to do shop work, or the betting worker to do betting work, on Sunday on or after that date, or

    (b)   requires the employer to provide the shop worker with shop work, or the betting worker with betting work, on Sunday on or after that date.

(2)   Subject to subsection (3), any agreement entered into after the relevant commencement date between a protected shop worker, or a protected betting worker, and his employer is unenforceable to the extent that it—

    (a)   requires the shop worker to do shop work, or the betting worker to do betting work, on Sunday, or

    (b)   requires the employer to provide the shop worker with shop work, or the betting worker with betting work, on Sunday.

(3)   Where, after giving an opting-in notice, a protected shop worker or a protected betting worker expressly agrees with his employer to do shop work or betting work on Sunday or on a particular Sunday (and so ceases to be protected), his contract of employment shall be taken to be varied to the extent necessary to give effect to the terms of the agreement.

(4)   ...

(5)   For the purposes of section 36(2)(b), the appropriate date—

    (a)   in relation to subsections (2) and (3) of this section, is the day on which the agreement is entered into, and

    (b)   ...

## 38   Contracts with guaranteed hours

(1)   This section applies where—

    (a)   under the contract of employment under which a shop worker or betting worker who satisfies section 36(2)(a) was employed on the day before the relevant commencement date, the employer is, or may be, required to provide him with shop work, or betting work, for a specified number of hours each week,

    (b)   under the contract the shop worker or betting worker was, or might have been, required to work on Sunday before that date, and

    (c)   the shop worker has done shop work, or the betting worker betting work, on Sunday in that employment (whether or not before that day) but has, on or after that date, ceased to do so.

(2)   So long as the shop worker remains a protected shop worker, or the betting worker remains a protected betting worker, the contract shall not be regarded as requiring the employer to provide him with shop work, or betting work, on weekdays in excess of the hours normally worked by the shop worker or betting worker on weekdays before he ceased to do shop work, or betting work, on Sunday.

(3)   For the purposes of section 36(2)(b), the appropriate date in relation to this section is any time in relation to which the contract is to be enforced.

## 39   Reduction of pay etc.

(1)   This section applies where—

    (a)   under the contract of employment under which a shop worker or betting worker who satisfies section 36(2)(a) was employed on the day before the relevant commencement date, the shop worker or betting worker was, or might have been, required to work on Sunday before the relevant commencement date,

    (b)   the shop worker has done shop work, or the betting worker has done betting work, on Sunday in that employment (whether or not before that date) but has, on or after that date, ceased to do so, and

    (c)   it is not apparent from the contract what part of the remuneration payable, or of any other benefit accruing, to the shop worker or betting worker was intended to be attributable to shop work, or betting work, on Sunday.

(2)   So long as the shop worker remains a protected shop worker, or the betting worker remains a protected betting worker, the contract shall be regarded as enabling the employer to reduce the amount of remuneration paid, or the extent of the other benefit provided, to the shop worker or betting worker in respect of any period by the relevant proportion.

(3)   In subsection (2) 'the relevant proportion' means the proportion which the hours of shop work, or betting work, which (apart from this Part) the shop worker, or betting worker, could have been required to do on Sunday in the period ('the contractual Sunday hours') bears to the aggregate of those hours and the hours of work actually done by the shop worker, or betting worker, in the period.

(4)   Where, under the contract of employment, the hours of work actually done on weekdays in any period would be taken into account in determining the contractual Sunday hours, they shall be taken into account in determining the contractual Sunday hours for the purposes of subsection (3).

(5)   For the purposes of section 36(2)(b), the appropriate date in relation to this section is the end of the period in respect of which the remuneration is paid or the benefit accrues.

*Opting-out of Sunday work*

## 40    Notice of objection to Sunday working

(1)   A shop worker or betting worker to whom this section applies may at any time give his employer written notice, signed and dated by the shop worker or betting worker, to the effect that he objects to Sunday working.

(2)   In this Act 'opting-out notice' means a notice given under subsection (1) by a shop worker or betting worker to whom this section applies.

(3)   This section applies to any shop worker or betting worker who under his contract of employment—
(a)   is or may be required to work on Sunday (whether or not as a result of previously giving an opting-in notice), but
(b)   is not employed to work only on Sunday.

## 41    Opted-out shop workers and betting workers

(1)   Subject to subsection (2), a shop worker or betting worker is to be regarded as 'opted-out' for the purposes of any provision of this Act if (and only if)—
(a)   he has given his employer an opting-out notice,
(b)   he has been continuously employed during the period beginning with the day on which the notice was given and ending with the day which, in relation to the provision concerned, is the appropriate date, and
(c)   throughout that period, or throughout every part of it during which his relations with his employer were governed by a contract of employment, he was a shop worker or a betting worker.

(2)   A shop worker is not an opted-out shop worker, and a betting worker is not an opted-out betting worker, if—
(a)   after giving the opting-out notice concerned, he has given his employer an opting-in notice, and
(b)   after giving the opting-in notice, he has expressly agreed with his employer to do shop work, or betting work, on Sunday or on a particular Sunday.

(3)   In this Act 'notice period', in relation to an opted-out shop worker or an opted-out betting worker, means—
(a)   in the case of an opted-out shop worker who does shop work in or about a large shop, the period of one month beginning with the day on which the opting-out notice concerned was given;
(b)   in any other case, the period of three months beginning with that day.
This subsection is subject to sections 41D(2) and 42(2).

## 41A   Notice of objection by shop workers to working additional hours on Sunday

(1)   A shop worker may at any time give to his or her employer a written notice, signed and dated by the shop worker, to the effect that he or she objects to doing shop work for additional hours on Sunday.

(2)   In this Part—
'additional hours' means any number of hours of shop work that a shop worker is (or could be) required to work under a contract of employment on Sunday that are (or would be) in excess of the shop worker's normal Sunday working hours;
'objection notice' means a notice given under subsection (1).

(3)    The 'normal Sunday working hours' of a shop worker are to be calculated in accordance with regulations.

(4)    Regulations under this section may provide—

(a)    for the calculation to be determined (for example) by reference to the average number of hours that the shop worker has worked on Sundays during a period specified or described in the regulations;

(b)    for a calculation of the kind mentioned in paragraph (a) to be varied in special cases;

(c)    for the right to give an objection notice not to be exercisable in special cases (and subsection (1) is subject to provision made by virtue of this paragraph).

(5)    Provision under subsection (4)(b) or (c) may, in particular, include provision—

(a)    about how the calculation of normal Sunday working hours is to be made in the case of a shop worker who has not been employed for a sufficient period of time to enable a calculation to be made as otherwise provided for in the regulations;

(b)    for the right to give an objection notice not to be exercisable by such a shop worker until he or she has completed a period of employment specified or described in the regulations.

(6)    But regulations under this section may not include provision preventing a shop worker who has been continuously employed under a contract of employment for a period of one year or more from giving to the employer an objection notice.

(7)    Regulations under this section may make different provision for different purposes.

## 41B    Explanatory statement: persons who become shop workers

(1)    This section applies where a person becomes a shop worker who, under a contract of employment, is or may be required to do shop work on Sundays.

(2)    The employer must give to the shop worker a written statement informing the shop worker of the following rights—

(a)    the right to object to working on Sundays by giving the employer an opting-out notice (if section 40 applies to the shop worker);

(b)    the right to object to doing shop work for additional hours on Sundays by giving the employer an objection notice.

(3)    The statement must be given before the end of the period of two months beginning with the day on which the person becomes a shop worker as mentioned in subsection (1).

(4)    An employer does not fail to comply with subsections (2) and (3) in a case where, before the end of the period referred to in subsection (3), the shop worker has given to the employer an opting-out notice (and that notice has not been withdrawn).

(5)    A statement under this section must comply with such requirements as to form and content as regulations may provide.

(6)    Regulations under this section may make different provision for different purposes.

## 41C    Explanatory statement: shop workers at commencement date

(1)    This section applies where—

(a)    under a contract of employment a shop worker is or may be required to do shop work on Sundays, and

(b)    the shop worker was employed under that contract on the day before the commencement date.

(2)    The shop worker's employer must give to the shop worker a written statement informing the shop worker of the rights mentioned in section 41B(2).

(3)    The statement must be given before the end of the period of two months beginning with the commencement date.

(4)    An employer does not fail to comply with subsections (2) and (3) in a case where, before the end of the period referred to in subsection (3), the shop worker has given to the employer an opting-out notice (and that notice has not been withdrawn).

(5)    A statement under this section must comply with such requirements as to form and content as regulations may provide.

(6)    Regulations under this section may make different provision for different purposes.

(7)    In this section 'commencement date' means the date appointed by regulations under section 44 of the Enterprise Act 2016 for the coming into force of section 33 of, and Schedule 5 to, that Act.

**41D    Failure to give explanatory statement under section 41B or 41C**

(1)    This section applies if an employer fails to give to a shop worker a written statement in accordance with—

    (a)    section 41B(2) and (3), or

    (b)    section 41C(2) and (3).

(2)    If the shop worker gives to the employer an opting-out notice, the notice period under section 41(3) that applies in relation to the shop worker is varied as follows—

    (a)    if the notice period under that provision would have been one month, it becomes 7 days instead;

    (b)    if the notice period under that provision would have been three months, it becomes one month instead.

(3)    If the shop worker gives to the employer an objection notice, the relevant period under section 43ZA(2) that applies in relation to the shop worker is varied as follows—

    (a)    if the relevant period under that provision would have been one month, it becomes 7 days instead;

    (b)    if the relevant period under that provision would have been three months, it becomes one month instead.

**42    Explanatory statement: betting workers**

(1)    Where a person becomes a shop worker or betting worker to whom section 40 applies, his employer shall, before the end of the period of two months beginning with the day on which that person becomes such a worker, give him a written statement in the prescribed form.

(2)    If—

    (a)    an employer fails to comply with subsection (1) in relation to any shop worker or betting worker, and

    (b)    the betting worker, on giving the employer an opting-out notice, becomes an opted-out betting worker,

section 41(3) has effect in relation to the betting worker with the substitution for 'three months' of 'one month'.

(3)    An employer shall not be regarded as failing to comply with subsection (1) in any case where, before the end of the period referred to in that subsection, the betting worker has given him an opting-out notice.

**43    Contractual requirements relating to Sunday work: opting out notices**

(1)    Where a shop worker or betting worker gives his employer an opting-out notice, the contract of employment under which he was employed immediately before he gave that notice becomes unenforceable to the extent that it—

    (a)    requires the shop worker to do shop work, or the betting worker to do betting work, on Sunday after the end of the notice period, or

    (b)    requires the employer to provide the shop worker with shop work, or the betting worker with betting work, on Sunday after the end of that period.

(2)    Subject to subsection (3), any agreement entered into between an opted-out shop worker, or an opted-out betting worker, and his employer is unenforceable to the extent that it—

    (a)    requires the shop worker to do shop work, or the betting worker to do betting work, on Sunday after the end of the notice period, or

    (b)    requires the employer to provide the shop worker with shop work, or the betting worker with betting work, on Sunday after the end of that period.

(3)    Where, after giving an opting-in notice, an opted-out shop worker or an opted-out betting worker expressly agrees with his employer to do shop work or betting work on Sunday or on a particular Sunday (and so ceases to be opted-out), his contract of employment shall be taken to be varied to the extent necessary to give effect to the terms of the agreement.

(4)    …

(5)    For the purposes of section 41(1)(b), the appropriate date—

    (a)    in relation to subsections (2) and (3) of this section, is the day on which the agreement is entered into,

    (b)    …

PART IVA
PROTECTED DISCLOSURES

## 43ZA Contractual requirements relating to working additional hours on Sundays: objection notices

(1)   Where a shop worker gives to his or her employer an objection notice, any agreement entered into between the shop worker and the employer becomes unenforceable to the extent that—

  (a)   it requires the shop worker to do shop work for additional hours on Sunday after the end of the relevant period, or

  (b)   it requires the employer to provide the shop worker with shop work for additional hours on Sunday after the end of that period.

(2)   The 'relevant period' is—

  (a)   in the case of a shop worker who is or may be required to do shop work in or about a large shop, the period of one month beginning with the day on which the objection notice is given;

  (b)   in any other case, the period of three months beginning with that day.

  This subsection is subject to section 41D(3).

(3)   A shop worker who has given an objection notice may revoke the notice by giving a further written notice to the employer.

(4)   Where—

  (a)   a shop worker gives to the employer a notice under subsection (3), and

  (b)   after giving the notice the shop worker expressly agrees with the employer to do shop work for additional hours on Sunday (whether on Sundays generally or on a particular Sunday),

  the contract of employment between the shop worker and the employer is to be taken to be varied to the extent necessary to give effect to the terms of the agreement.

(5)   The reference in subsection (1) to any agreement—

  (a)   includes the contract of employment under which the shop worker is employed immediately before giving the objection notice;

  (b)   includes an agreement of a kind mentioned in subsection (4), or a contract of employment as taken to be varied under that subsection, only if an objection notice is given in relation to the working of additional hours under that agreement or contract as varied.

## 43ZB Interpretation

(1)   In this Part—

  'additional hours' has the meaning given in section 41A(2);

  'large shop' means a shop which has a relevant floor area exceeding 280 square metres;

  'objection notice' has the meaning given in section 41A(2);

  'regulations' means regulations made by the Secretary of State.

(2)   In the definition of 'large shop' in subsection (1)—

  (a)   'shop' means any premises where there is carried on a trade or business consisting wholly or mainly of the sale of goods;

  (b)   'relevant floor area' means the internal floor area of so much of the large shop in question as consists of or is comprised in a building.

(3)   For the purposes of subsection (2), any part of the shop which is not used for the serving of customers in connection with the sale or display of goods is to be disregarded.

(4)   The references in subsections (2) and (3) to the sale of goods does not include—

  (a)   the sale of meals, refreshments or alcohol (within the meaning of the Licensing Act 2003 or, in relation to Scotland, the Licensing (Scotland) Act 2005 (asp 16)) for consumption on the premises on which they are sold, or

  (b)   the sale of meals or refreshments prepared to order for immediate consumption off those premises.

## 43A Meaning of 'protected disclosure'

In this Act a 'protected disclosure' means a qualifying disclosure (as defined by section 43B) which is made by a worker in accordance with any of sections 43C to 43H.

**43B    Disclosures qualifying for protection**

(1)   In this Part a 'qualifying disclosure' means any disclosure of information which, in the reasonable belief of the worker making the disclosure, is made in the public interest and tends to show one or more of the following—

    (a)   that a criminal offence has been committed, is being committed or is likely to be committed,

    (b)   that a person has failed, is failing or is likely to fail to comply with any legal obligation to which he is subject,

    (c)   that a miscarriage of justice has occurred, is occurring or is likely to occur,

    (d)   that the health or safety of any individual has been, is being or is likely to be endangered,

    (e)   that the environment has been, is being or is likely to be damaged, or

    (f)   that information tending to show any matter falling within any one of the preceding paragraphs has been, is being or is likely to be deliberately concealed.

(2)   For the purposes of subsection (1), it is immaterial whether the relevant failure occurred, occurs or would occur in the United Kingdom or elsewhere, and whether the law applying to it is that of the United Kingdom or of any other country or territory.

(3)   A disclosure of information is not a qualifying disclosure if the person making the disclosure commits an offence by making it.

(4)   A disclosure of information in respect of which a claim to legal professional privilege (or, in Scotland, to confidentiality as between client and professional legal adviser) could be maintained in legal proceedings is not a qualifying disclosure if it is made by a person to whom the information had been disclosed in the course of obtaining legal advice.

(5)   In this Part 'the relevant failure', in relation to a qualifying disclosure, means the matter falling within paragraphs (a) to (f) of subsection (1).

**43C    Disclosure to employer or other responsible person**

(1)   A qualifying disclosure is made in accordance with this section if the worker makes the disclosure—

    (a)   to his employer, or

    (b)   where the worker reasonably believes that the relevant failure relates solely or mainly to—

       (i)   the conduct of a person other than his employer, or

       (ii)   any other matter for which a person other than his employer has legal responsibility,

to that other person.

(2)   A worker who, in accordance with a procedure whose use by him is authorised by his employer, makes a qualifying disclosure to a person other than his employer, is to be treated for the purposes of this Part as making the qualifying disclosure to his employer.

**43D    Disclosure to legal adviser**

A qualifying disclosure is made in accordance with this section if it is made in the course of obtaining legal advice.

**43E    Disclosure to Minister of the Crown**

A qualifying disclosure is made in accordance with this section if—

    (a)   the worker's employer is—

       (i)   an individual appointed under any enactment (including any enactment comprised in, or in an instrument made under, an Act of the Scottish Parliament) by a Minister of the Crown or a member of the Scottish Executive, or

       (ii)   a body any of whose members are so appointed, and

    (b)   the disclosure is made to a Minister of the Crown or a member of the Scottish Executive.

**43F    Disclosure to prescribed person**

(1)   A qualifying disclosure is made in accordance with this section if the worker—

    (a)   makes the disclosure to a person prescribed by an order made by the Secretary of State for the purposes of this section, and

    (b)   reasonably believes—
        (i)   that the relevant failure falls within any description of matters in respect of which that person is so prescribed, and
       (ii)   that the information disclosed, and any allegation contained in it, are substantially true.

(2)   An order prescribing persons for the purposes of this section may specify persons or descriptions of persons and shall specify the descriptions of matters in respect of which each person, or persons of each description, is or are prescribed.

## 43FA   Prescribed persons: duty to report on disclosures of information

(1)   The Secretary of State may make regulations requiring a person prescribed for the purposes of section 43F to produce an annual report on disclosures of information made to the person by workers.

(2)   The regulations must set out the matters that are to be covered in a report, but must not require a report to provide detail that would enable either of the following to be identified—
    (a)   a worker who has made a disclosure;
    (b)   an employer or other person in respect of whom a disclosure has been made.

(3)   The regulations must make provision about the publication of a report, and such provision may include (but is not limited to) any of the following requirements—
    (a)   to send the report to the Secretary of State for laying before Parliament;
    (b)   to include the report in another report or in information required to be published by the prescribed person;
    (c)   to publish the report on a website.

(4)   The regulations may make provision about the time period within which a report must be produced and published.

(5)   Regulations under subsections (2) to (4) may make different provision for different prescribed persons.

## 43G   Disclosure in other cases

(1)   A qualifying disclosure is made in accordance with this section if—
    (a)   ...
    (b)   the worker reasonably believes that the information disclosed, and any allegation contained in it, are substantially true,
    (c)   he does not make the disclosure for purposes of personal gain,
    (d)   any of the conditions in subsection (2) is met, and
    (e)   in all the circumstances of the case, it is reasonable for him to make the disclosure.

(2)   The conditions referred to in subsection (1)(d) are—
    (a)   that, at the time he makes the disclosure, the worker reasonably believes that he will be subjected to a detriment by his employer if he makes a disclosure to his employer or in accordance with section 43F,
    (b)   that, in a case where no person is prescribed for the purposes of section 43F in relation to the relevant failure, the worker reasonably believes that it is likely that evidence relating to the relevant failure will be concealed or destroyed if he makes a disclosure to his employer, or
    (c)   that the worker has previously made a disclosure of substantially the same information—
        (i)   to his employer, or
       (ii)   in accordance with section 43F.

(3)   In determining for the purposes of subsection (1)(e) whether it is reasonable for the worker to make the disclosure, regard shall be had, in particular, to—
    (a)   the identity of the person to whom the disclosure is made,
    (b)   the seriousness of the relevant failure,
    (c)   whether the relevant failure is continuing or is likely to occur in the future,
    (d)   whether the disclosure is made in breach of a duty of confidentiality owed by the employer to any other person,
    (e)   in a case falling within subsection (2)(c)(i) or (ii), any action which the employer or the person to whom the previous disclosure in accordance with section 43F

was made has taken or might reasonably be expected to have taken as a result of the previous disclosure, and

(f)    in a case falling within subsection (2)(c)(i), whether in making the disclosure to the employer the worker complied with any procedure whose use by him was authorised by the employer.

(4)    For the purposes of this section a subsequent disclosure may be regarded as a disclosure of substantially the same information as that disclosed by a previous disclosure as mentioned in subsection (2)(c) even though the subsequent disclosure extends to information about action taken or not taken by any person as a result of the previous disclosure.

### 43H  Disclosure of exceptionally serious failure

(1)    A qualifying disclosure is made in accordance with this section if—

(a)    ...

(b)    the worker reasonably believes that the information disclosed, and any allegation contained in it, are substantially true,

(c)    he does not make the disclosure for purposes of personal gain,

(d)    the relevant failure is of an exceptionally serious nature, and

(e)    in all the circumstances of the case, it is reasonable for him to make the disclosure.

(2)    In determining for the purposes of subsection (1)(e) whether it is reasonable for the worker to make the disclosure, regard shall be had, in particular, to the identity of the person to whom the disclosure is made.

### 43J  Contractual duties of confidentiality

(1)    Any provision in an agreement to which this section applies is void in so far as it purports to preclude the worker from making a protected disclosure.

(2)    This section applies to any agreement between a worker and his employer (whether a worker's contract or not), including an agreement to refrain from instituting or continuing any proceedings under this Act or any proceedings for breach of contract.

### 43K  Extension of meaning of 'worker' etc. for Part IVA

(1)    For the purposes of this Part 'worker' includes an individual who is not a worker as defined by section 230(3) but who—

(a)    works or worked for a person in circumstances in which—

    (i)    he is or was introduced or supplied to do that work by a third person, and

    (ii)    the terms on which he is or was engaged to do the work are or were in practice substantially determined not by him but by the person for whom he works or worked, by the third person or by both of them,

(b)    contracts or contracted with a person, for the purposes of that person's business, for the execution of work to be done in a place not under the control or management of that person and would fall within section 230(3)(b) if for 'personally' in that provision there were substituted '(whether personally or otherwise)',

(ba)    works or worked as a person performing services under a contract entered into by him with a Primary Care Trust under section 83(2), 84, 92, 100, 107, 115(4), 117 or 134 of, or Schedule 12 to, the National Health Service Act 2006 or with a Local Health Board under section 41(2)(b), 42, 50, 57, 64 or 92 of, or Schedule 7 to, the National Health Service (Wales) Act 2006,

(bb)    works or worked as a person performing services under a contract entered into by him with a Health Board under section 17J or 17Q of the National Health Service (Scotland) Act 1978,

(c)    works or worked as a person providing services in accordance with arrangements made—

    (i)    by a Primary Care Trust or Health Authority under section 126 of the National Health Service Act 2006, or Local Health Board under section 71 or 80 of the National Health Service (Wales) Act 2006, or

    (ii)    by a Health Board under section 2C, 17AA, 17C, 25, 26 or 27 of the National Health Service (Scotland) Act 1978, (ca) ...

(cb) is or was provided with work experience provided pursuant to a course of education or training approved by, or under arrangements with, the Nursing and Midwifery Council in accordance with article 15(6)(a) of the Nursing and Midwifery Order 2001 (SI 2002/253), or

(d) is or was provided with work experience provided pursuant to a training course or programme or with training for employment (or with both) otherwise than—

    (i) under a contract of employment, or

    (ii) by an educational establishment on a course run by that establishment;

and any reference to a worker's contract, to employment or to a worker being 'employed' shall be construed accordingly.

(2) For the purposes of this Part 'employer' includes—

(a) in relation to a worker falling within paragraph (a) of subsection (1), the person who substantially determines or determined the terms on which he is or was engaged,

(aa) in relation to a worker falling within paragraph (ba) of that subsection, the Primary Care Trust or Local Health Board referred to in that paragraph,

(ab) in relation to a worker falling within paragraph (bb) of that subsection, the Health Board referred to in that paragraph,

(b) in relation to a worker falling within paragraph (c) of that subsection, the authority or board referred to in that paragraph, and

(c) in relation to a worker falling within paragraph (d) of that subsection, the person providing the work experience or training.

(3) In this section 'educational establishment' includes any university, college, school or other educational establishment.

(4) The Secretary of State may by order make amendments to this section as to what individuals count as 'workers' for the purposes of this Part (despite not being within the definition in section 230(3)).

(5) An order under subsection (4) may not make an amendment that has the effect of removing a category of individual unless the Secretary of State is satisfied that there are no longer any individuals in that category.

## 43L  Other interpretative provisions

(1) In this Part—

'qualifying disclosure' has the meaning given by section 43B;

'the relevant failure', in relation to a qualifying disclosure, has the meaning given by section 43B(5).

(2) In determining for the purposes of this Part whether a person makes a disclosure for purposes of personal gain, there shall be disregarded any reward payable by or under any enactment.

(3) Any reference in this Part to the disclosure of information shall have effect, in relation to any case where the person receiving the information is already aware of it, as a reference to bringing the information to his attention.

PART V

PROTECTION FROM SUFFERING DETRIMENT IN EMPLOYMENT

*Rights not to suffer detriment*

## 43M  Jury service

(1) An employee has the right not to be subjected to any detriment by any act, or any deliberate failure to act, by his employer on the ground that the employee—

(a) has been summoned under the Juries Act 1974, the Coroners Act 1988, the Court of Session Act 1988 or the Criminal Procedure (Scotland) Act 1995 to attend for service as a juror, or

(b) has been absent from work because he attended at any place in pursuance of being so summoned.

(2) This section does not apply where the detriment in question amounts to dismissal within the meaning of Part 10.

(3) For the purposes of this section, an employee is not to be regarded as having been subjected to a detriment by a failure to pay remuneration in respect of a relevant period unless under his contract of employment he is entitled to be paid that remuneration.

(4) In subsection (3) 'a relevant period' means any period during which the employee is absent from work because of his attendance at any place in pursuance of being summoned as mentioned in subsection (1)(a).

## 44 Health and safety cases

(1) An employee has the right not to be subjected to any detriment by any act, or any deliberate failure to act, by his employer done on the ground that—

 (a) having been designated by the employer to carry out activities in connection with preventing or reducing risks to health and safety at work, the employee carried out (or proposed to carry out) any such activities,

 (b) being a representative of workers on matters of health and safety at work or member of a safety committee—

  (i) in accordance with arrangements established under or by virtue of any enactment, or

  (ii) by reason of being acknowledged as such by the employer,

 the employee performed (or proposed to perform) any functions as such a representative or a member of such a committee,

 (ba) the employee took part (or proposed to take part) in consultation with the employer pursuant to the Health and Safety (Consultation with Employees) Regulations 1996 or in an election of representatives of employee safety within the meaning of those Regulations (whether as a candidate or otherwise),

 (c) being an employee at a place where—

  (i) there was no such representative or safety committee, or

  (ii) there was such a representative or safety committee but it was not reasonably practicable for the employee to raise the matter by those means,

 he brought to his employer's attention, by reasonable means, circumstances connected with his work which he reasonably believed were harmful or potentially harmful to health or safety,

(1A) A worker has the right not to be subjected to any detriment by any act, or any deliberate failure to act, by his or her employer done on the ground that—

 (a) in circumstances of danger which the worker reasonably believed to be serious and imminent and which he or she could not reasonably have been expected to avert, he or she left (or proposed to leave) or (while the danger persisted) refused to return to his or her place of work or any dangerous part of his or her place of work, or

 (b) in circumstances of danger which the worker reasonably believed to be serious and imminent, he or she took (or proposed to take) appropriate steps to protect himself or herself or other persons from the danger.

(2) For the purposes of subsection (1A)(b) whether steps which a worker took (or proposed to take) were appropriate is to be judged by reference to all the circumstances including, in particular, his knowledge and the facilities and advice available to him at the time.

(3) A worker is not to be regarded as having been subjected to any detriment on the ground specified in subsection (1A)(b) if the employer shows that it was (or would have been) so negligent for the worker to take the steps which he took (or proposed to take) that a reasonable employer might have treated him as the employer did.

(4) This section does not apply where the worker is an employee and the detriment in question amounts to dismissal (within the meaning of Part X).

## 45 Sunday working for shop and betting workers

(1) An employee who is—

 (a) a protected shop worker or an opted-out shop worker, or

 (b) a protected betting worker or an opted-out betting worker,

 has the right not to be subjected to any detriment by any act, or any deliberate failure to act, by his employer done on the ground that the employee refused (or proposed to refuse) to do shop work, or betting work, on Sunday or on a particular Sunday.

(2) Subsection (1) does not apply to anything done in relation to an opted-out shop worker or an opted-out betting worker on the ground that he refused (or proposed to refuse) to do shop work, or betting work, on any Sunday or Sundays falling before the end of the notice period.

(3) An employee who is a shop worker or a betting worker has the right not to be subjected to any detriment by any act, or any deliberate failure to act, by his employer done on the ground that the employee gave (or proposed to give) an opting-out notice to his employer.

(4) Subsections (1) and (3) do not apply where the detriment in question amounts to dismissal (within the meaning of Part X).

(5) For the purposes of this section a shop worker or betting worker who does not work on Sunday or on a particular Sunday is not to be regarded as having been subjected to any detriment by—

(a) a failure to pay remuneration in respect of shop work, or betting work, on a Sunday which he has not done,

(b) a failure to provide him with any other benefit, where that failure results from the application (in relation to a Sunday on which the employee has not done shop work, or betting work) of a contractual term under which the extent of that benefit varies according to the number of hours worked by the employee or the remuneration of the employee, or

(c) a failure to provide him with any work, remuneration or other benefit which by virtue of section 38 or 39 the employer is not obliged to provide.

(6) Where an employer offers to pay a sum specified in the offer to any one or more employees—

(a) who are protected shop workers or opted-out shop workers or protected betting workers or opted-out betting workers, or

(b) who under their contracts of employment are not obliged to do shop work, or betting work, on Sunday,

if they agree to do shop work, or betting work, on Sunday or on a particular Sunday subsections (7) and (8) apply.

(7) An employee to whom the offer is not made is not to be regarded for the purposes of this section as having been subjected to any detriment by any failure to make the offer to him or to pay him the sum specified in the offer.

(8) An employee who does not accept the offer is not to be regarded for the purposes of this section as having been subjected to any detriment by any failure to pay him the sum specified in the offer.

(9) For the purposes of section 36(2)(b) or 41(1)(b), the appropriate date in relation to this section is the date of the act or failure to act.

(10) For the purposes of subsection (9)—

(a) where an act extends over a period, the 'date of the act' means the first day of that period, and

(b) a deliberate failure to act shall be treated as done when it was decided on; and, in the absence of evidence establishing the contrary, an employer shall be taken to decide on a failure to act when he does an act inconsistent with doing the failed act or, if he has done no such inconsistent act, when the period expires within which he might reasonably have been expected to do the failed act if it was to be done.

## 45ZA Sunday working for shop workers: additional hours

(1) Subsection (2) applies where a shop worker has given an objection notice to his or her employer and the notice has not been withdrawn.

(2) The shop worker has the right not to be subjected to any detriment by any act, or any deliberate failure to act, by the employer done on the ground that the shop worker refused (or proposed to refuse) to do shop work for additional hours on Sunday or on a particular Sunday.

(3) Subsection (2) does not apply to anything done on the ground that the shop worker refused (or proposed to refuse) to do shop work for additional hours on any Sunday or Sundays falling before the end of the relevant period.

(4) A shop worker has the right not to be subjected to any detriment by any act, or any deliberate failure to act, by his or her employer on the ground that the shop worker gave (or proposed to give) an objection notice to the employer.

(5)  Subsections (2) and (4) do not apply where the detriment in question amounts to dismissal (within the meaning of Part 10).

(6)  For the purposes of this section, a shop worker who does not do shop work for additional hours on Sunday or on a particular Sunday is not to be regarded as having been subjected to any detriment by—

   (a)  a failure to pay remuneration in respect of doing shop work for additional hours on Sunday which the shop worker has not done, or

   (b)  a failure to provide any other benefit where the failure results from the application (in relation to a Sunday on which the shop worker has not done shop work for additional hours) of a contractual term under which the extent of the benefit varies according to the number of hours worked by, or the remuneration paid to, the shop worker.

(7)  Subsections (8) and (9) apply where—

   (a)  an employer offers to pay a sum specified in the offer to a shop worker if he or she agrees to do shop work for additional hours on Sunday or on a particular Sunday, and

   (b)  the shop worker—

      (i)  has given an objection notice to the employer that has not been withdrawn, or

      (ii)  is not obliged under a contract of employment to do shop work for additional hours on Sunday.

(8)  A shop worker to whom the offer is not made is not to be regarded for the purposes of this section as having been subjected to any detriment by any failure—

   (a)  to make the offer to the shop worker, or

   (b)  to pay the shop worker the sum specified in the offer.

(9)  A shop worker who does not accept the offer is not to be regarded for the purposes of this section as having been subjected to any detriment by any failure to pay the shop worker the sum specified in the offer.

(10)  In this section—

   'additional hours' and 'objection notice' have the meanings given by section 41A(2);

   'relevant period' means the period determined by section 43ZA(2) (but subject to section 41D(3)).

## 45A  Working time cases

(1)  A worker has the right not to be subjected to any detriment by any act, or any deliberate failure to act, by his employer done on the ground that the worker—

   (a)  refused (or proposed to refuse) to comply with a requirement which the employer imposed (or proposed to impose) in contravention of the Working Time Regulations 1998,

   (b)  refused (or proposed to refuse) to forgo a right conferred on him by those Regulations,

   (c)  failed to sign a workforce agreement for the purposes of those Regulations, or to enter into, or agree to vary or extend, any other agreement with his employer which is provided for in those Regulations,

   (d)  being—

      (i)  a representative of members of the workforce for the purposes of Schedule 1 to those Regulations, or

      (ii)  a candidate in an election in which any person elected will, on being elected, be such a representative,

      performed (or proposed to perform) any functions or activities as such a representative or candidate,

   (e)  brought proceedings against the employer to enforce a right conferred on him by those Regulations, or

   (f)  alleged that the employer had infringed such a right.

(2)  It is immaterial for the purposes of subsection (1)(e) or (f)—

   (a)  whether or not the worker has the right, or

   (b)  whether or not the right has been infringed,

   but, for those provisions to apply, the claim to the right and that it has been infringed must be made in good faith.

(3) It is sufficient for subsection (1)(f) to apply that the worker, without specifying the right, made it reasonably clear to the employer what the right claimed to have been infringed was.

(4) This section does not apply where a worker is an employee and the detriment in question amounts to dismissal within the meaning of Part X.

(5) A reference in this section to the Working Time Regulations 1998 includes a reference to—

    (a) the Merchant Shipping (Working Time: Inland Waterways) Regulations 2003;

    (b) the Fishing Vessels (Working Time: Sea-fishermen) Regulations 2004;

    (c) the Cross-border Railway Services (Working Time) Regulations 2008;

    (d) the Merchant Shipping (Maritime Labour Convention) (Hours of Work) Regulations 2018.

## 46 Trustees of occupational pension schemes

(1) An employee has the right not to be subjected to any detriment by any act, or any deliberate failure to act, by his employer done on the ground that, being a trustee of a relevant occupational pension scheme which relates to his employment, the employee performed (or proposed to perform) any functions as such a trustee.

(2) This section does not apply where the detriment in question amounts to dismissal (within the meaning of Part X).

(2A) This section applies to an employee who is a director of a company which is a trustee of a relevant occupational pension scheme as it applies to an employee who is a trustee of such a scheme (references to such a trustee being read for this purpose as references to such a director).

(3) In this section 'relevant occupational pension scheme' means an occupational pension scheme (as defined in section 1 of the Pension Schemes Act 1993) established under a trust.

## 47 Employee representatives

(1) An employee has the right not to be subjected to any detriment by any act, or any deliberate failure to act, by his employer done on the ground that, being—

    (a) an employee representative for the purposes of Chapter II of Part IV of the Trade Union and Labour Relations (Consolidation) Act 1992 (redundancies) or Regulations 9, 13 and 15 of the Transfer of Undertakings (Protection of Employment) Regulations 2006, or

    (b) a candidate in an election in which any person elected will, on being elected, be such an employee representative,

he performed (or proposed to perform) any functions or activities as such an employee representative or candidate.

(1A) An employee has the right not to be subjected to any detriment by any act, or by any deliberate failure to act, by his employer done on the ground of his participation in an election of employee representatives for the purposes of Chapter II of Part IV of the Trade Union and Labour Relations (Consolidation) Act 1992 (redundancies) or Regulations 9, 13 and 15 of the Transfer of Undertakings (Protection of Employment) Regulations 2006.

(2) This section does not apply where the detriment in question amounts to a dismissal (within the meaning of Part X).

## 47A Employees exercising right to time off work for study or training

(1) An employee has the right not to be subjected to any detriment by any act, or any deliberate failure to act, by his employer or the principal (within the meaning of section 63A(3)) done on the ground that, being a person entitled to—

    (a) time off under section 63A(1) or (3), and

    (b) remuneration under section 63B(1) in respect of that time taken off,

the employee exercised (or proposed to exercise) that right or received (or sought to receive) such remuneration.

(2) This section does not apply where the detriment in question amounts to dismissal (within the meaning of Part X).

## 47B Protected disclosures

(1) A worker has the right not to be subjected to any detriment by any act, or any deliberate failure to act, by his employer done on the ground that the worker has made a protected disclosure.

(1A) A worker ('W') has the right not to be subjected to any detriment by any act, or any deliberate failure to act, done—

    (a) by another worker of W's employer in the course of that other worker's employment, or

    (b) by an agent of W's employer with the employer's authority, on the ground that W has made a protected disclosure.

(1B) Where a worker is subjected to detriment by anything done as mentioned in subsection (1A), that thing is treated as also done by the worker's employer.

(1C) For the purposes of subsection (1B), it is immaterial whether the thing is done with the knowledge or approval of the worker's employer.

(1D) In proceedings against W's employer in respect of anything alleged to have been done as mentioned in subsection (1A)(a), it is a defence for the employer to show that the employer took all reasonable steps to prevent the other worker—

    (a) from doing that thing, or

    (b) from doing anything of that description.

(1E) A worker or agent of W's employer is not liable by reason of subsection (1A) for doing something that subjects W to detriment if—

    (a) the worker or agent does that thing in reliance on a statement by the employer that doing it does not contravene this Act, and

    (b) it is reasonable for the worker or agent to rely on the statement.

But this does not prevent the employer from being liable by reason of subsection (1B).

(2) This section does not apply where—

    (a) the worker is an employee, and

    (b) the detriment in question amounts to dismissal (within the meaning of Part X).

(3) For the purposes of this section, and of sections 48 and 49 so far as relating to this section, 'worker', 'worker's contract', 'employment' and 'employer' have the extended meaning given by section 43K.

## 47C Leave for family and domestic reasons

(1) An employee has the right not to be subjected to any detriment by any act, or any deliberate failure to act, by his employer done for a prescribed reason.

(2) A prescribed reason is one which is prescribed by regulations made by the Secretary of State and which relates to—

    (a) pregnancy, childbirth or maternity,

    (aa) time off under section 57ZE,

    (ab) time off under section 57ZJ or 57ZL,

    (b) ordinary, compulsory or additional maternity leave,

    (ba) ordinary or additional adoption leave,

    (bb) shared parental leave,

    (c) parental leave,

    (ca) paternity leave,

    (cb) parental bereavement leave, or

    (d) time off under section 57A.

(3) A reason prescribed under this section in relation to parental leave may relate to action which an employee takes, agrees to take or refuses to take under or in respect of a collective or workforce agreement.

(4) Regulations under this section may make different provision for different cases or circumstances.

(5) An agency worker has the right not to be subjected to any detriment by any act, or any deliberate failure to act, by the temporary work agency or the hirer done on the ground that—

    (a) being a person entitled to—

        (i) time off under section 57ZA, and

        (ii) remuneration under section 57ZB in respect of that time off,

the agency worker exercised (or proposed to exercise) that right or received (or sought to receive) that remuneration,

      (b)    being a person entitled to time off under section 57ZG, the agency worker exercised (or proposed to exercise) that right,

      (c)    being a person entitled to—

          (i)    time off under section 57ZN, and

          (ii)    remuneration under section 57ZO in respect of that time off,

the agency worker exercised (or proposed to exercise) that right or received (or sought to receive) that remuneration, or

      (d)    being a person entitled to time off under section 57ZP, the agency worker exercised (or proposed to exercise) that right.

(6)    Subsection (5) does not apply where the agency worker is an employee.

(7)    In this section the following have the same meaning as in the Agency Workers Regulations 2010 (SI 2010/93)—

'agency worker';

'hirer';

'temporary work agency'.

## 47D  Tax credits

(1)    An employee has the right not to be subjected to any detriment by any act, or any deliberate failure to act, by his employer, done on the ground that—

      (a)    any action was taken, or was proposed to be taken, by or on behalf of the employee with a view to enforcing, or otherwise securing the benefit of, a right conferred on the employee by regulations under section 25 of the Tax Credits Act 2002,

      (b)    a penalty was imposed on the employer, or proceedings for a penalty were brought against him, under that Act, as a result of action taken by or on behalf of the employee for the purpose of enforcing, or otherwise securing the benefit of, such a right, or

      (c)    the employee is entitled, or will or may be entitled, to working tax credit.

(2)    It is immaterial for the purposes of subsection (1)(a) or (b)—

      (a)    whether or not the employee has the right, or

      (b)    whether or not the right has been infringed,

but, for those provisions to apply, the claim to the right and (if applicable) the claim that it has been infringed must be made in good faith.

(3)    Subsections (1) and (2) apply to a person who is not an employee within the meaning of this Act but who is an employee within the meaning of section 25 of the Tax Credits Act 2002, with references to his employer in those subsections (and sections 48(2) and (4) and 49(1)) being construed in accordance with that section.

(4)    Subsections (1) and (2) do not apply to an employee if the detriment in question amounts to dismissal (within the meaning of Part 10).

## 47E  Flexible working

(1)    An employee has the right not to be subjected to any detriment by any act, or any deliberate failure to act, by his employer done on the ground that the employee—

      (a)    made (or proposed to make) an application under section 80F,

      (b)    ...

      (c)    brought proceedings against the employer under section 80H, or

      (d)    alleged the existence of any circumstance which would constitute a ground for bringing such proceedings.

(2)    This section does not apply where the detriment in question amounts to dismissal within the meaning of Part 10.

## 47F  Study and training

(1)    An employee has the right not to be subjected to any detriment by any act, or any deliberate failure to act, by the employee's employer done on the ground that the employee—

      (a)    made (or proposed to make) a section 63D application,

      (b)    exercised (or proposed to exercise) a right conferred on the employee under section 63F,

      (c)    brought proceedings against the employer under section 63I, or

      (d)    alleged the existence of any circumstance which would constitute a ground for bringing such proceedings.

(2) This section does not apply if the detriment in question amounts to dismissal within the meaning of Part 10.

## 47G Employee shareholder status

(1) An employee has the right not to be subjected to a detriment by any act, or any deliberate failure to act, by the employee's employer done on the ground that the employee refused to accept an offer by the employer for the employee to become an employee shareholder (within the meaning of section 205A).

(2) This section does not apply if the detriment in question amounts to dismissal within the meaning of Part 10.

*Enforcement*

## 48 Complaints to employment tribunals

(1) An employee may present a complaint to an employment tribunal that he has been subjected to a detriment in contravention of section 43M, 44(1), 45, 46, 47, 47A, 47C(1) or 47E.

(1XA) A worker may present a complaint to an employment tribunal that the worker has been subjected to a detriment in contravention of section 44(1A).

(1YA) A shop worker may present a complaint to an employment tribunal that he or she has been subjected to a detriment in contravention of section 45ZA.

(1ZA) A worker may present a complaint to an employment tribunal that he has been subjected to a detriment in contravention of section 45A.

(1A) A worker may present a complaint to an employment tribunal that he has been subjected to a detriment in contravention of section 47B.

(1AA) An agency worker may present a complaint to an employment tribunal that the agency worker has been subjected to a detriment in contravention of section 47C(5) by the temporary work agency or the hirer.

(1B) A person may present a complaint to an employment tribunal that he has been subjected to a detriment in contravention of section 47D.

(2) On a complaint under subsection (1), (1XA), (1ZA), (1A) or (1B) it is for the employer to show the ground on which any act, or deliberate failure to act, was done.

(2A) On a complaint under subsection (1AA) it is for the temporary work agency or (as the case may be) the hirer to show the ground on which any act, or deliberate failure to act, was done.

(3) An employment tribunal shall not consider a complaint under this section unless it is presented—
(a) before the end of the period of three months beginning with the date of the act or failure to act to which the complaint relates or, where that act or failure is part of a series of similar acts or failures, the last of them, or
(b) within such further period as the tribunal considers reasonable in a case where it is satisfied that it was not reasonably practicable for the complaint to be presented before the end of that period of three months.

(4) For the purposes of subsection (3)—
(a) where an act extends over a period, the 'date of the act' means the last day of that period, and
(b) a deliberate failure to act shall be treated as done when it was decided on;
and, in the absence of evidence establishing the contrary, an employer, a temporary work agency or a hirer shall be taken to decide on a failure to act when he does an act inconsistent with doing the failed act or, if he has done no such inconsistent act, when the period expires within which he might reasonably have been expected to do the failed act if it was to be done.

(4A) Section 207B (extension of time limits to facilitate conciliation before institution of proceedings) applies for the purposes of subsection (3)(a).

(5) In this section and section 49 any reference to the employer includes—
(a) where a person complains that he has been subjected to a detriment in contravention of section 47A, the principal (within the meaning of section 63A(3)).
(b) in the case of proceedings against a worker or agent under section 47B(1A), the worker or agent.

(6)   In this section and section 49 the following have the same meaning as in the Agency Workers Regulations 2010 (SI 2010/93) —
'agency worker';
'hirer';
'temporary work agency'.

## 49   Remedies

(1)   Where an employment tribunal finds a complaint under section 48(1), (1XA), (1ZA), (1A) or (1B) well-founded, the tribunal —
(a)   shall make a declaration to that effect, and
(b)   may make an award of compensation to be paid by the employer to the complainant in respect of the act or failure to act to which the complaint relates.

(1A)   Where an employment tribunal finds a complaint under section 48(1AA) well-founded, the tribunal —
(a)   shall make a declaration to that effect, and
(b)   may make an award of compensation to be paid by the temporary work agency or (as the case may be) the hirer to the complainant in respect of the act or failure to act to which the complaint relates.

(2)   Subject to subsections (5ZA), (5A) and (6) the amount of the compensation awarded shall be such as the tribunal considers just and equitable in all the circumstances having regard to —
(a)   the infringement to which the complaint relates, and
(b)   any loss which is attributable to the act, or failure to act, which infringed the complainant's right.

(3)   The loss shall be taken to include —
(a)   any expenses reasonably incurred by the complainant in consequence of the act, or failure to act, to which the complaint relates, and
(b)   loss of any benefit which he might reasonably be expected to have had but for that act or failure to act.

(4)   In ascertaining the loss the tribunal shall apply the same rule concerning the duty of a person to mitigate his loss as applies to damages recoverable under the common law of England and Wales or (as the case may be) Scotland.

(5)   Where the tribunal finds that the act, or failure to act, to which the complaint relates was to any extent caused or contributed to by action of the complainant, it shall reduce the amount of the compensation by such proportion as it considers just and equitable having regard to that finding.

(5ZA)   Where —
(a)   the complaint is made under section 48(1XA),
(b)   the detriment to which the worker is subjected is the termination of his or her contract, and
(c)   that contract is not a contract of employment,
any compensation must not exceed the compensation that would be payable under Chapter II of Part X if the worker had been an employee and had been dismissed for the reason specified in section 100.

(5A)   Where —
(a)   the complaint is made under section 48(1ZA),
(b)   the detriment to which the worker is subjected is the termination of his worker's contract, and
(c)   that contract is not a contract of employment,
any compensation must not exceed the compensation that would be payable under Chapter II of Part X if the worker had been an employee and had been dismissed for the reason specified in section 101A.

(6)   Where —
(a)   the complaint is made under section 48(1A), (b) the detriment to which the worker is subjected is the termination of his worker's contract, and
(b)   that contract is not a contract of employment,
any compensation must not exceed the compensation that would be payable under Chapter II of Part X if the worker had been an employee and had been dismissed for the reason specified in section 103A.

(6A)   Where —
(a)   the complaint is made under section 48(1A), and

(b)    it appears to the tribunal that the protected disclosure was not made in good faith, the tribunal may, if it considers it just and equitable in all the circumstances to do so, reduce any award it makes to the worker by no more than 25%.

...

## PART VA
### PROTECTION FOR APPLICANTS FOR EMPLOYMENT ETC. IN THE HEALTH SERVICE

**49B    Regulations prohibiting discrimination because of protected disclosure**

(1)    The Secretary of State may make regulations prohibiting an NHS employer from discriminating against an applicant because it appears to the NHS employer that the applicant has made a protected disclosure.

(2)    An 'applicant', in relation to an NHS employer, means an individual who applies to the NHS employer for—

     (a)    a contract of employment,

     (b)    a contract to do work personally, or

     (c)    appointment to an office or post.

(3)    For the purposes of subsection (1), an NHS employer discriminates against an applicant if the NHS employer refuses the applicant's application or in some other way treats the applicant less favourably than it treats or would treat other applicants in relation to the same contract, office or post.

(4)    Regulations under this section may, in particular—

     (a)    make provision as to circumstances in which discrimination by a worker or agent of an NHS employer is to be treated, for the purposes of the regulations, as discrimination by the NHS employer;

     (b)    confer jurisdiction (including exclusive jurisdiction) on employment tribunals or the Employment Appeal Tribunal;

     (c)    make provision for or about the grant or enforcement of specified remedies by a court or tribunal;

     (d)    make provision for the making of awards of compensation calculated in accordance with the regulations;

     (e)    make different provision for different cases or circumstances;

     (f)    make incidental or consequential provision, including incidental or consequential provision amending—

         (i)    an Act of Parliament (including this Act),

         (ii)    an Act of the Scottish Parliament,

         (iii)    a Measure or Act of the National Assembly for Wales, or

         (iv)    an instrument made under an Act or Measure within any of sub-paragraphs (i) to (iii).

(5)    Subsection (4)(f) does not affect the application of section 236(5) to the power conferred by this section.

(6)    'NHS employer' means an NHS public body prescribed by regulations under this section.

(7)    'NHS public body' means—

     (a)    the National Health Service Commissioning Board;

     (b)    a clinical commissioning group;

     (c)    a Special Health Authority;

     (d)    an NHS trust;

     (e)    an NHS foundation trust;

     (f)    the Care Quality Commission;

     (g)    Health Education England;

     (h)    the Health Research Authority;

     (i)    the Health and Social Care Information Centre;

     (j)    the National Institute for Health and Care Excellence;

     (k)    Monitor;

     (l)    a Local Health Board established under section 11 of the National Health Service (Wales) Act 2006;

     (m)    the Common Services Agency for the Scottish Health Service;

     (n)    Healthcare Improvement Scotland;

(o)     a Health Board constituted under section 2 of the National Health Service (Scotland) Act 1978;

(p)     a Special Health Board constituted under that section.

(8)    The Secretary of State must consult the Welsh Ministers before making regulations prescribing any of the following NHS public bodies for the purposes of the definition of 'NHS employer'—

(a)     a Special Health Authority established under section 22 of the National Health Service (Wales) Act 2006;

(b)     an NHS trust established under section 18 of that Act;

(c)     a Local Health Board established under section 11 of that Act.

(9)    The Secretary of State must consult the Scottish Ministers before making regulations prescribing an NHS public body within any of paragraphs (m) to (p) of subsection (7) for the purposes of the definition of 'NHS employer'.

(10)   For the purposes of subsection (4)(a)—

(a)     'worker' has the extended meaning given by section 43K, and

(b)     a person is a worker of an NHS employer if the NHS employer is an employer in relation to the person within the extended meaning given by that section.

PART VI
TIME OFF WORK

*Public duties*

## 50 Rights to time off for public duties

(1)    An employer shall permit an employee of his who is—

(a)     a justice of the peace, or

(b)     an independent prison monitor appointed in accordance with section 7B(2) of the Prisons (Scotland) Act 1989,

to take time off during the employee's working hours for the purpose of performing any of the duties of the office.

(2)    An employer shall permit an employee of his who is a member of—

(a)     a local authority,

(b)     a statutory tribunal,

(c)     ...

(ca)    ...

(d)     an independent monitoring board for a prison or a prison visiting committee,

(e)     a relevant health body,

(f)     a relevant education body,

(g)     the Environment Agency or the Scottish Environment Protection Agency,

(h)     Scottish Water...,

(i)     a panel of lay observers appointed in accordance with section 81(1)(b) of the Criminal Justice Act 1991,

(j)     a Visiting Committee appointed in accordance with section 152(1) of the Immigration and Asylum Act 1999, or

(k)     a Visiting Committee appointed by the Secretary of State for a short-term holding facility (within the meaning given by section 147 of the Immigration and Asylum Act 1999).

to take time off during the employee's working hours for the purposes specified in subsection (3).

(3)    The purposes referred to in subsection (2) are—

(a)     attendance at a meeting of the body or any of its committees or sub-committees, and

(b)     the doing of any other thing approved by the body, or anything of a class so approved, for the purpose of the discharge of the functions of the body or of any of its committees or sub-committees, and

(c)     in the case of a local authority which are operating executive arrangements—

(i)      attendance at a meeting of the executive of that local authority or committee of that executive; and

(ii)     the doing of any other thing, by an individual member of that executive, for the purposes of the discharge of any function which is to any extent the responsibility of that executive.

(4)   The amount of time off which an employee is to be permitted to take under this section, and the occasions on which and any conditions subject to which time off may be so taken, are those that are reasonable in all the circumstances having regard, in particular, to—

(a)   how much time off is required for the performance of the duties of the office or as a member of the body in question, and how much time off is required for the performance of the particular duty,

(b)   how much time off the employee has already been permitted under this section or sections 168 and 170 of the Trade Union and Labour Relations (Consolidation) Act 1992 (time off for trade union duties and activities), and

(c)   the circumstances of the employer's business and the effect of the employee's absence on the running of that business.

...

## 51   Complaints to employment tribunals

(1)   An employee may present a complaint to an employment tribunal that his employer has failed to permit him to take time off as required by section 50.

(2)   An employment tribunal shall not consider a complaint under this section that an employer has failed to permit an employee to take time off unless it is presented—

(a)   before the end of the period of three months beginning with the date on which the failure occurred, or

(b)   within such further period as the tribunal considers reasonable in a case where it is satisfied that it was not reasonably practicable for the complaint to be presented before the end of that period of three months.

(2A)  Section 207B (extension of time limits to facilitate conciliation before institution of proceedings) applies for the purposes of subsection (2)(a).

(3)   Where an employment tribunal finds a complaint under this section well-founded, the tribunal—

(a)   shall make a declaration to that effect, and

(b)   may make an award of compensation to be paid by the employer to the employee.

(4)   The amount of the compensation shall be such as the tribunal considers just and equitable in all the circumstances having regard to—

(a)   the employer's default in failing to permit time off to be taken by the employee, and

(b)   any loss sustained by the employee which is attributable to the matters to which the complaint relates.

*Looking for work and making arrangements for training*

## 52   Right to time off to look for work or arrange training

(1)   An employee who is given notice of dismissal by reason of redundancy is entitled to be permitted by his employer to take reasonable time off during the employee's working hours before the end of his notice in order to—

(a)   look for new employment, or

(b)   make arrangements for training for future employment.

(2)   An employee is not entitled to take time off under this section unless, on whichever is the later of—

(a)   the date on which the notice is due to expire, and

(b)   the date on which it would expire were it the notice required to be given by section 86(1),

he will have been (or would have been) continuously employed for a period of two years or more.

(3)   For the purposes of this section the working hours of an employee shall be taken to be any time when, in accordance with his contract of employment, the employee is required to be at work.

## 53   Right to remuneration for time off under section 52

(1)   An employee who is permitted to take time off under section 52 is entitled to be paid remuneration by his employer for the period of absence at the appropriate hourly rate.

(2)   The appropriate hourly rate, in relation to an employee, is the amount of one week's pay divided by the number of normal working hours in a week for that employee when employed under the contract of employment in force on the day when the notice of dismissal was given.

(3)    But where the number of normal working hours differs from week to week or over a longer period, the amount of one week's pay shall be divided instead by the average number of normal working hours calculated by dividing by twelve the total number of the employee's normal working hours during the period of twelve weeks ending with the last complete week before the day on which the notice was given.

(4)    If an employer unreasonably refuses to permit an employee to take time off from work as required by section 52, the employee is entitled to be paid an amount equal to the remuneration to which he would have been entitled under subsection (1) if he had been permitted to take the time off.

(5)    The amount of an employer's liability to pay remuneration under subsection (1) shall not exceed, in respect of the notice period of any employee, forty per cent. of a week's pay of that employee.

(6)    A right to any amount under subsection (1) or (4) does not affect any right of an employee in relation to remuneration under his contract of employment ('contractual remuneration').

(7)    Any contractual remuneration paid to an employee in respect of a period of time off under section 52 goes towards discharging any liability of the employer to pay remuneration under subsection (1) in respect of that period; and, conversely, any payment of remuneration under subsection (1) in respect of a period goes towards discharging any liability of the employer to pay contractual remuneration in respect of that period.

## 54    Complaints to employment tribunals

(1)    An employee may present a complaint to an employment tribunal that his employer—
    (a)    has unreasonably refused to permit him to take time off as required by section 52, or
    (b)    has failed to pay the whole or any part of any amount to which the employee is entitled under section 53(1) or (4).

(2)    An employment tribunal shall not consider a complaint under this section unless it is presented—
    (a)    before the end of the period of three months beginning with the date on which it is alleged that the time off should have been permitted, or
    (b)    within such further period as the tribunal considers reasonable in a case where it is satisfied that it was not reasonably practicable for the complaint to be presented before the end of that period of three months.

(3)    Where an employment tribunal finds a complaint under this section well-founded, the tribunal shall—
    (a)    make a declaration to that effect, and
    (b)    order the employer to pay to the employee the amount which it finds due to him.

(4)    The amount which may be ordered by a tribunal to be paid by an employer under subsection (3) (or, where the employer is liable to pay remuneration under section 53, the aggregate of that amount and the amount of that liability) shall not exceed, in respect of the notice period of any employee, forty per cent. of a week's pay of that employee.

*Ante-natal care*

## 55    Right to time off for ante-natal care

(1)    An employee who—
    (a)    is pregnant, and
    (b)    has, on the advice of a registered medical practitioner, registered midwife or registered nurse, made an appointment to attend at any place for the purpose of receiving ante-natal care,
is entitled to be permitted by her employer to take time off during the employee's working hours in order to enable her to keep the appointment.

(2)    An employee is not entitled to take time off under this section to keep an appointment unless, if her employer requests her to do so, she produces for his inspection—
    (a)    a certificate from a registered medical practitioner, registered midwife or registered nurse stating that the employee is pregnant, and
    (b)    an appointment card or some other document showing that the appointment has been made.

(3)  Subsection (2) does not apply where the employee's appointment is the first appointment during her pregnancy for which she seeks permission to take time off in accordance with subsection (1).

(4)  For the purposes of this section the working hours of an employee shall be taken to be any time when, in accordance with her contract of employment, the employee is required to be at work.

...

## 56      Right to remuneration for time off under section 55

(1)  An employee who is permitted to take time off under section 55 is entitled to be paid remuneration by her employer for the period of absence at the appropriate hourly rate.

(2)  The appropriate hourly rate, in relation to an employee, is the amount of one week's pay divided by the number of normal working hours in a week for that employee when employed under the contract of employment in force on the day when the time off is taken.

(3)  But where the number of normal working hours differs from week to week or over a longer period, the amount of one week's pay shall be divided instead by—

(a)  the average number of normal working hours calculated by dividing by twelve the total number of the employee's normal working hours during the period of twelve weeks ending with the last complete week before the day on which the time off is taken, or

(b)  where the employee has not been employed for a sufficient period to enable the calculation to be made under paragraph (a), a number which fairly represents the number of normal working hours in a week having regard to such of the considerations specified in subsection (4) as are appropriate in the circumstances.

(4)  The considerations referred to in subsection (3)(b) are—

(a)  the average number of normal working hours in a week which the employee could expect in accordance with the terms of her contract, and

(b)  the average number of normal working hours of other employees engaged in relevant comparable employment with the same employer.

(5)  A right to any amount under subsection (1) does not affect any right of an employee in relation to remuneration under her contract of employment ('contractual remuneration').

(6)  Any contractual remuneration paid to an employee in respect of a period of time off under section 55 goes towards discharging any liability of the employer to pay remuneration under subsection (1) in respect of that period; and, conversely, any payment of remuneration under subsection (1) in respect of a period goes towards discharging any liability of the employer to pay contractual remuneration in respect of that period.

## 57      Complaints to employment tribunals

(1)  An employee may present a complaint to an employment tribunal that her employer—

(a)  has unreasonably refused to permit her to take time off as required by section 55, or

(b)  has failed to pay the whole or any part of any amount to which the employee is entitled under section 56.

(2)  An employment tribunal shall not consider a complaint under this section unless it is presented—

(a)  before the end of the period of three months beginning with the date of the appointment concerned, or

(b)  within such further period as the tribunal considers reasonable in a case where it is satisfied that it was not reasonably practicable for the complaint to be presented before the end of that period of three months.

(2A) Section 207B (extension of time limits to facilitate conciliation before institution of proceedings) applies for the purposes of subsection (2)(a).

(3)  Where an employment tribunal finds a complaint under this section well-founded, the tribunal shall make a declaration to that effect.

(4)  If the complaint is that the employer has unreasonably refused to permit the employee to take time off, the tribunal shall also order the employer to pay to the employee an amount that is twice the amount of the remuneration to which she would have been entitled under section 56 if the employer had not refused.

(5)  If the complaint is that the employer has failed to pay the employee the whole or part of any amount to which she is entitled under section 56, the tribunal shall also order the employer to pay to the employee the amount which it finds due to her.

*Ante-natal care: agency workers*

## 57ZA  Right to time off for ante-natal care (agency workers)

(1)   An agency worker who —
  (a)   is pregnant, and
  (b)   has, on the advice of a registered medical practitioner, registered midwife or registered nurse, made an appointment to attend at any place for the purpose of receiving ante-natal care,
  is entitled to be permitted, by the temporary work agency and the hirer, to take time off during the agency worker's working hours in order to enable her to keep the appointment.
(2)   An agency worker is not entitled to be permitted by either of those persons to take time off under this section to keep an appointment unless, if that person requests her to do so, she produces for that person's inspection —
  (a)   a certificate from a registered medical practitioner, registered midwife or registered nurse stating that the agency worker is pregnant, and
  (b)   an appointment card or some other document showing that the appointment has been made.
(3)   Subsection (2) does not apply where the agency worker's appointment is the first appointment during her pregnancy for which she seeks permission to take time off in accordance with subsection (1).
(4)   For the purposes of this section the working hours of an agency worker shall be taken to be any time when, in accordance with the terms under which the agency worker works temporarily for and under the supervision and direction of the hirer, the agency worker is required to be at work.
(5)   In this section references to a registered nurse have the same meaning as in section 55.

## 57ZB  Right to remuneration for time off under section 57ZA

(1)   An agency worker who is permitted to take time off under section 57ZA is entitled to be paid remuneration by the temporary work agency for the period of absence at the appropriate hourly rate.
(2)   The appropriate hourly rate, in relation to an agency worker, is the amount of one week's pay divided by the number of normal working hours in a week for that agency worker in accordance with the terms under which the agency worker works temporarily for and under the supervision and direction of the hirer that are in force on the day when the time off is taken.
(3)   But where the number of normal working hours during the assignment differs from week to week or over a longer period, the amount of one week's pay shall be divided instead by the average number of normal working hours calculated by dividing by twelve the total number of the agency worker's normal working hours during the period of twelve weeks ending with the last complete week before the day on which the time off is taken.
(4)   A right to any amount under subsection (1) does not affect any right of an agency worker in relation to remuneration under her contract with the temporary work agency ('contractual remuneration').
(5)   Any contractual remuneration paid to an agency worker in respect of a period of time off under section 57ZA goes towards discharging any liability of the temporary work agency to pay remuneration under subsection (1) in respect of that period; and, conversely, any payment of remuneration under subsection (1) in respect of a period goes towards discharging any liability of the temporary work agency to pay contractual remuneration in respect of that period.

## 57ZC  Complaint to employment tribunal: agency workers

(1)   An agency worker may present a complaint to an employment tribunal that the temporary work agency —
  (a)   has unreasonably refused to permit her to take time off as required by section 57ZA, or
  (b)   has failed to pay the whole or any part of any amount to which she is entitled under section 57ZB.
(2)   An agency worker may present a complaint to an employment tribunal that the hirer has unreasonably refused to permit her to take time off as required by section 57ZA.

(3) An employment tribunal shall not consider a complaint under subsection (1) or (2) unless it is presented—

(a) before the end of the period of three months beginning with the date of the appointment concerned, or

(b) within such further period as the tribunal considers reasonable in a case where it is satisfied that it was not reasonably practicable for the complaint to be presented before the end of that period of three months.

(3A) Section 207B (extension of time limits to facilitate conciliation before institution of proceedings) applies for the purposes of subsection (3)(a).

(4) Where an employment tribunal finds a complaint under this section well-founded, the tribunal shall make a declaration to that effect.

(5) If the complaint is that the temporary work agency or hirer has unreasonably refused to permit the agency worker to take time off, the tribunal shall also order payment to the agency worker of an amount that is twice the amount of the remuneration to which she would have been entitled under section 57ZB if she had not been refused the time off.

(6) Where the tribunal orders payment under subsection (5), the amount payable by each party shall be such as may be found by the tribunal to be just and equitable having regard to the extent of each respondent's responsibility for the infringement to which the complaint relates.

(7) If the complaint is that the temporary work agency has failed to pay the agency worker the whole or part of any amount to which she is entitled under section 57ZB, the tribunal shall also order the temporary work agency to pay to the agency worker the amount which it finds due to her.

## 57ZD Agency workers: supplementary

(1) Without prejudice to any other duties of the hirer or temporary work agency under any enactment or rule of law sections 57ZA to 57ZC do not apply where the agency worker—

(a) has not completed the qualifying period, or

(b) is no longer entitled to the rights conferred by regulation 5 of the Agency Workers Regulations 2010 pursuant to regulation 8(a) or (b) of those Regulations.

(2) Nothing in those sections imposes a duty on the hirer or temporary work agency beyond the original intended duration, or likely duration of the assignment, whichever is the longer.

(3) Those sections do not apply where sections 55 to 57 apply.

(4) In this section and sections 57ZA to 57ZC the following have the same meaning as in the Agency Workers Regulations 2010—

'agency worker';

'assignment';

'hirer';

'qualifying period';

'temporary work agency'.

*Accompanying to ante-natal appointments*

## 57ZE Right to time off to accompany to ante-natal appointment

(1) An employee who has a qualifying relationship with a pregnant woman or her expected child is entitled to be permitted by his or her employer to take time off during the employee's working hours in order that he or she may accompany the woman when she attends by appointment at any place for the purpose of receiving ante-natal care.

(2) In relation to any particular pregnancy, an employee is not entitled to take time off for the purpose specified in subsection (1) on more than two occasions.

(3) On each of those occasions, the maximum time off during working hours to which the employee is entitled is six and a half hours.

(4) An employee is not entitled to take time off for the purpose specified in subsection (1) unless the appointment is made on the advice of a registered medical practitioner, registered midwife or registered nurse.

(5) Where the employer requests the employee to give the employer a declaration signed by the employee, the employee is not entitled to take time off for the purpose specified in subsection (1) unless the employee gives that declaration (which may be given in electronic form).

(6) The employee must state in the declaration—
  (a) that the employee has a qualifying relationship with a pregnant woman or her expected child,
  (b) that the employee's purpose in taking time off is the purpose specified in subsection (1),
  (c) that the appointment in question is made on the advice of a registered medical practitioner, registered midwife or registered nurse, and
  (d) the date and time of the appointment.
(7) A person has a qualifying relationship with a pregnant woman or her expected child if—
  (a) the person is the husband or civil partner of the pregnant woman,
  (b) the person, being of a different sex or the same sex, lives with the woman in an enduring family relationship but is not a relative of the woman,
  (c) the person is the father of the expected child,
  (d) the person is a parent of the expected child by virtue of section 42 or 43 of the Human Fertilisation and Embryology Act 2008,
  (e) the person is a potential applicant for a parental order under section 54 of the Human Fertilisation and Embryology Act 2008 in respect of the expected child, or
  (f) the person is a potential applicant for a parental order under section 54A of the Human Fertilisation and Embryology Act 2008 in respect of the expected child.

...

## 57ZF Complaint to employment tribunal

(1) An employee may present a complaint to an employment tribunal that his or her employer has unreasonably refused to let him or her take time off as required by section 57ZE.
(2) An employment tribunal may not consider a complaint under this section unless it is presented—
  (a) before the end of the period of three months beginning with the day of the appointment in question, or
  (b) within such further period as the tribunal considers reasonable in a case where it is satisfied that it was not reasonably practicable for the complaint to be presented before the end of that period of three months.
(3) Section 207B applies for the purposes of subsection (2)(a).
(4) Where an employment tribunal finds a complaint under subsection (1) well-founded, it—
  (a) must make a declaration to that effect, and
  (b) must order the employer to pay to the employee an amount determined in accordance with subsection (5).
(5) The amount payable to the employee is—

$$A \times B \times 2$$

where—
  a A is the appropriate hourly rate for the employee, and
  b B is the number of working hours for which the employee would have been entitled under section 57ZE to be absent if the time off had not been refused.
(6) The appropriate hourly rate, in relation to an employee, is the amount of one week's pay divided by the number of normal working hours in a week for that employee when employed under the contract of employment in force on the day when the time off would have been taken.
(7) But where the number of normal working hours differs from week to week or over a longer period, the amount of one week's pay shall be divided instead by—
  (a) the average number of normal working hours calculated by dividing by twelve the total number of the employee's normal working hours during the period of twelve weeks ending with the last complete week before the day on which the time off would have been taken, or
  (b) where the employee has not been employed for a sufficient period to enable the calculation to be made under paragraph (a), a number which fairly

represents the number of normal working hours in a week having regard to such of the considerations specified in subsection (8) as are appropriate in the circumstances.

(8) The considerations referred to in subsection (7)(b) are—

 (a) the average number of normal working hours in a week which the employee could expect in accordance with the terms of the employee's contract, and

 (b) the average number of normal working hours of other employees engaged in relevant comparable employment with the same employer.

*Accompanying to ante-natal appointments: agency workers*

## 57ZG Right to time off to accompany to ante-natal appointment: agency workers

(1) An agency worker who has a qualifying relationship with a pregnant woman or her expected child is entitled to be permitted, by the temporary work agency and the hirer, to take time off during the agency worker's working hours in order that he or she may accompany the woman when she attends by appointment at any place for the purpose of receiving ante-natal care.

(2) In relation to any particular pregnancy, an agency worker is not entitled to take time off for the purpose specified in subsection (1) on more than two occasions.

(3) On each of those occasions, the maximum time off during working hours to which the agency worker is entitled is six and a half hours.

(4) An agency worker is not entitled to take time off for the purpose specified in subsection (1) unless the appointment is made on the advice of a registered medical practitioner, registered midwife or registered nurse.

(5) Where the temporary work agency or the hirer requests the agency worker to give that person a declaration signed by the agency worker, the agency worker is not entitled to take time off for the purpose specified in subsection (1) unless the agency worker gives that declaration (which may be given in electronic form).

(6) The agency worker must state in the declaration—

 (a) that the agency worker has a qualifying relationship with a pregnant woman or her expected child,

 (b) that the agency worker's purpose in taking time off is the purpose specified in subsection (1),

 (c) that the appointment in question is made on the advice of a registered medical practitioner, registered midwife or registered nurse, and

 (d) the date and time of the appointment.

(7) A person has a qualifying relationship with a pregnant woman or her expected child if—

 (a) the person is the husband or civil partner of the pregnant woman,

 (b) the person, being of a different sex or the same sex, lives with the woman in an enduring family relationship but is not a relative of the woman,

 (c) the person is the father of the expected child,

 (d) the person is a parent of the expected child by virtue of section 42 or 43 of the Human Fertilisation and Embryology Act 2008,

 (e) the person is a potential applicant for a parental order under section 54 of the Human Fertilisation and Embryology Act 2008 in respect of the expected child, or

 (f) the person is a potential applicant for a parental order under section 54A of the Human Fertilisation and Embryology Act 2008 in respect of the expected child.

...

(12) For the purposes of this section the working hours of an agency worker are to be taken to be any time when, in accordance with the terms under which the agency worker works temporarily for and under the supervision and direction of the hirer, the agency worker is required to be at work.

## 57ZH Complaint to employment tribunal: agency workers

(1) An agency worker may present a complaint to an employment tribunal that the temporary work agency has unreasonably refused to let him or her take time off as required by section 57ZG.

(2) An agency worker may present a complaint to an employment tribunal that the hirer has unreasonably refused to let him or her take time off as required by section 57ZG.

(3) An employment tribunal may not consider a complaint under subsection (1) or (2) unless it is presented—

    (a) before the end of the period of three months beginning with the day of the appointment in question, or

    (b) within such further period as the tribunal considers reasonable in a case where it is satisfied that it was not reasonably practicable for the complaint to be presented before the end of that period of three months.

(4) Section 207B applies for the purposes of subsection (3)(a).

(5) Where an employment tribunal finds a complaint under subsection (1) or (2) well-founded, it—

    (a) must make a declaration to that effect, and

    (b) must order the payment to the agency worker of an amount determined in accordance with subsection (7).

(6) Where the tribunal orders that payment under subsection (5) be made by the temporary work agency and the hirer, the proportion of that amount payable by each respondent is to be such as may be found by the tribunal to be just and equitable having regard to the extent of each respondent's responsibility for the infringement to which the complaint relates.

(7) The amount payable to the agency worker is—

$$A \times B \times 2$$

where—

    a    A is the appropriate hourly rate for the agency worker, and

    b    B is the number of working hours for which the agency worker would have been entitled under section 57ZG to be absent if the time off had not been refused.

(8) The appropriate hourly rate, in relation to an agency worker, is the amount of one week's pay divided by the number of normal working hours in a week for that agency worker in accordance with the terms under which the agency worker works temporarily for and under the supervision and direction of the hirer that are in force on the day when the time off would have been taken.

(9) But where the number of normal working hours during the assignment differs from week to week or over a longer period, the amount of one week's pay shall be divided instead by the average number of normal working hours calculated by dividing by twelve the total number of the agency worker's normal working hours during the period of twelve weeks ending with the last complete week before the day on which the time off would have been taken.

## 57ZI Agency workers: supplementary

(1) Without prejudice to any other duties of the hirer or temporary work agency under any enactment or rule of law, sections 57ZG and 57ZH do not apply where the agency worker—

    (a) has not completed the qualifying period, or

    (b) pursuant to regulation 8(a) or (b) of the Agency Workers Regulations 2010 (S.I. 2010/93), is no longer entitled to the rights conferred by regulation 5 of those Regulations.

(2) Nothing in sections 57ZG and 57ZH imposes a duty on the hirer or temporary work agency beyond the original intended duration, or likely duration, of the assignment, whichever is the longer.

(3) Sections 57ZG and 57ZH do not apply where sections 57ZE and 57ZF apply.

(4) In this section and sections 57ZG and 57ZH the following have the same meaning as in the Agency Workers Regulations 2010—

'agency worker';

'assignment';

'hirer';

'qualifying period';

'temporary work agency'.

*Dependants*

## 57A　Time off for dependants

(1)　An employee is entitled to be permitted by his employer to take a reasonable amount of time off during the employee's working hours in order to take action which is necessary—

    (a)　to provide assistance on an occasion when a dependant falls ill, gives birth or is injured or assaulted,

    (b)　to make arrangements for the provision of care for a dependant who is ill or injured,

    (c)　in consequence of the death of a dependant,

    (d)　because of the unexpected disruption or termination of arrangements for the care of a dependant, or

    (e)　to deal with an incident which involves a child of the employee and which occurs unexpectedly in a period during which an educational establishment which the child attends is responsible for him.

(2)　Subsection (1) does not apply unless the employee—

    (a)　tells his employer the reason for his absence as soon as reasonably practicable, and

    (b)　except where paragraph (a) cannot be complied with until after the employee has returned to work, tells his employer for how long he expects to be absent.

(3)　Subject to subsections (4) and (5), for the purposes of this section 'dependant' means, in relation to an employee—

    (a)　a spouse or civil partner,

    (b)　a child,

    (c)　a parent,

    (d)　a person who lives in the same household as the employee, otherwise than by reason of being his employee, tenant, lodger or boarder.

(4)　For the purposes of subsection (1)(a) or (b) 'dependant' includes, in addition to the persons mentioned in subsection (3), any person who reasonably relies on the employee—

    (a)　for assistance on an occasion when the person falls ill or is injured or assaulted, or

    (b)　to make arrangements for the provision of care in the event of illness or injury.

(5)　For the purposes of subsection (1)(d) 'dependant' includes, in addition to the persons mentioned in subsection (3), any person who reasonably relies on the employee to make arrangements for the provision of care.

(6)　A reference in this section to illness or injury includes a reference to mental illness or injury.

## 57B　Complaint to employment tribunal

(1)　An employee may present a complaint to an employment tribunal that his employer has unreasonably refused to permit him to take time off as required by section 57A.

(2)　An employment tribunal shall not consider a complaint under this section unless it is presented—

    (a)　before the end of the period of three months beginning with the date when the refusal occurred, or

    (b)　within such further period as the tribunal considers reasonable in a case where it is satisfied that it was not reasonably practicable for the complaint to be presented before the end of that period of three months.

(2A) Section 207B (extension of time limits to facilitate conciliation before institution of proceedings) applies for the purposes of subsection (2)(a).

(3)　Where an employment tribunal finds a complaint under subsection (1) well-founded, it—

    (a)　shall make a declaration to that effect, and

    (b)　may make an award of compensation to be paid by the employer to the employee.

(4)　the amount of compensation shall be such as the tribunal considers just and equitable in all the circumstances having regard to—

    (a)　the employer's default in refusing to permit time off to be taken by the employee, and

(b)    any loss sustained by the employee which is attributable to the matters complained of.

*Occupational pension scheme trustees*

## 58    Right to time off for pension scheme trustees

(1)    The employer in relation to a relevant occupational pension scheme shall permit an employee of his who is a trustee of the scheme to take time off during the employee's working hours for the purpose of—

    (a)    performing any of his duties as such a trustee, or

    (b)    undergoing training relevant to the performance of those duties.

(2)    The amount of time off which an employee is to be permitted to take under this section and the purposes for which, the occasions on which and any conditions subject to which time off may be so taken are those that are reasonable in all the circumstances having regard, in particular, to—

    (a)    how much time off is required for the performance of the duties of a trustee of the scheme and the undergoing of relevant training, and how much time off is required for performing the particular duty or for undergoing the particular training, and

    (b)    the circumstances of the employer's business and the effect of the employee's absence on the running of that business.

(2A)  This section applies to an employee who is a director of a company which is a trustee of a relevant occupational pension scheme as it applies to an employee who is a trustee of such a scheme (references to such a trustee being read for this purpose as references to such a director).

(3)    In this section—

    (a)    'relevant occupational pension scheme' means an occupational pension scheme (as defined in section 1 of the Pension Schemes Act 1993) established under a trust, and

    (b)    references to the employer, in relation to such a scheme, are to an employer of persons in the description of employment to which the scheme relates, and

    (c)    reference to training are to training on the employer's premises or elsewhere.

(4)    For the purposes of this section the working hours of an employee shall be taken to be any time when, in accordance with his contract of employment, the employee is required to be at work.

## 59    Right to payment for time off under section 58

(1)    An employer who permits an employee to take time off under section 58 shall pay him for the time taken off pursuant to the permission.

(2)    Where the employee's remuneration for the work he would ordinarily have been doing during that time does not vary with the amount of work done, he must be paid as if he had worked at that work for the whole of that time.

(3)    Where the employee's remuneration for the work he would ordinarily have been doing during that time varies with the amount of work done, he must be paid an amount calculated by reference to the average hourly earnings for that work.

(4)    The average hourly earnings mentioned in subsection (3) are—

    (a)    those of the employee concerned, or

    (b)    if no fair estimate can be made of those earnings, the average hourly earnings for work of that description of persons in comparable employment with the same employer or, if there are no such persons, a figure of average hourly earnings which is reasonable in the circumstances.

(5)    A right to be paid an amount under subsection (1) does not affect any right of an employee in relation to remuneration under his contract of employment ('contractual remuneration').

(6)    Any contractual remuneration paid to an employee in respect of a period of time off under section 58 goes towards discharging any liability of the employer under subsection (1) in respect of that period; and, conversely, any payment under subsection (1) in respect of a period goes towards discharging any liability of the employer to pay contractual remuneration in respect of that period.

## 60     Complaints to employment tribunals

(1)    An employee may present a complaint to an employment tribunal that his employer—

    (a)    has failed to permit him to take time off as required by section 58, or

    (b)    has failed to pay him in accordance with section 59.

(2)    An employment tribunal shall not consider a complaint under this section unless it is presented—

    (a)    before the end of the period of three months beginning with the date when the failure occurred, or

    (b)    within such further period as the tribunal considers reasonable in a case where it is satisfied that it was not reasonably practicable for the complaint to be presented before the end of that period of three months.

(3)    Where an employment tribunal finds a complaint under subsection (1)(a) well-founded, the tribunal—

    (a)    shall make a declaration to that effect, and

    (b)    may make an award of compensation to be paid by the employer to the employee.

(4)    The amount of the compensation shall be such as the tribunal considers just and equitable in all the circumstances having regard to—

    (a)    the employer's default in failing to permit time off to be taken by the employee, and

    (b)    any loss sustained by the employee which is attributable to the matters complained of.

(5)    Where on a complaint under subsection (1)(b) an employment tribunal finds that an employer has failed to pay an employee in accordance with section 59, it shall order the employer to pay the amount which it finds to be due.

*Employee representatives*

## 61     Right to time off for employee representatives

(1)    An employee who is—

    (a)    an employee representative for the purposes of Chapter II of Part IV of the Trade Union and Labour Relations (Consolidation) Act 1992 (redundancies) or Regulations 9, 13 and 15 of the Transfer of Undertakings (Protection of Employment) Regulations 2006, or

    (b)    a candidate in an election in which any person elected will, on being elected, be such an employee representative,

is entitled to be permitted by his employer to take reasonable time off during the employee's working hours in order to perform his functions as such an employee representative or candidate or in order to undergo training to perform such functions.

(2)    For the purposes of this section the working hours of an employee shall be taken to be any time when, in accordance with his contract of employment, the employee is required to be at work.

## 62     Right to remuneration for time off under section 61

(1)    An employee who is permitted to take time off under section 61 is entitled to be paid remuneration by his employer for the time taken off at the appropriate hourly rate.

(2)    The appropriate hourly rate, in relation to an employee, is the amount of one week's pay divided by the number of normal working hours in a week for that employee when employed under the contract of employment in force on the day when the time off is taken.

(3)    But where the number of normal working hours differs from week to week or over a longer period, the amount of one week's pay shall be divided instead by—

    (a)    the average number of normal working hours calculated by dividing by twelve the total number of the employee's normal working hours during the period of twelve weeks ending with the last complete week before the day on which the time off is taken, or

    (b)    where the employee has not been employed for a sufficient period to enable the calculation to be made under paragraph (a), a number which fairly represents the number of normal working hours in a week having regard to such of the considerations specified in subsection (4) as are appropriate in the circumstances.

(4) The considerations referred to in subsection (3)(b) are—

  (a) the average number of normal working hours in a week which the employee could expect in accordance with the terms of his contract, and

  (b) the average number of normal working hours of other employees engaged in relevant comparable employment with the same employer.

(5) A right to any amount under subsection (1) does not affect any right of an employee in relation to remuneration under his contract of employment ('contractual remuneration').

(6) Any contractual remuneration paid to an employee in respect of a period of time off under section 61 goes towards discharging any liability of the employer to pay remuneration under subsection (1) in respect of that period; and, conversely, any payment of remuneration under subsection (1) in respect of a period goes towards discharging any liability of the employer to pay contractual remuneration in respect of that period.

## 63   Complaints to employment tribunals

(1) An employee may present a complaint to an employment tribunal that his employer—

  (a) has unreasonably refused to permit him to take time off as required by section 61, or

  (b) has failed to pay the whole or any part of any amount to which the employee is entitled under section 62.

(2) An employment tribunal shall not consider a complaint under this section unless it is presented—

  (a) before the end of the period of three months beginning with the day on which the time off was taken or on which it is alleged the time off should have been permitted, or

  (b) within such further period as the tribunal considers reasonable in a case where it is satisfied that it was not reasonably practicable for the complaint to be presented before the end of that period of three months.

(2A) Section 207B (extension of time limits to facilitate conciliation before institution of proceedings) applies for the purposes of subsection (2)(a).

(3) Where an employment tribunal finds a complaint under this section well-founded, the tribunal shall make a declaration to that effect.

(4) If the complaint is that the employer has unreasonably refused to permit the employee to take time off, the tribunal shall also order the employer to pay to the employee an amount equal to the remuneration to which he would have been entitled under section 62 if the employer had not refused.

(5) If the complaint is that the employer has failed to pay the employee the whole or part of any amount to which he is entitled under section 62, the tribunal shall also order the employer to pay to the employee the amount which it finds due to him.

## 63A   Right to time off for young person in Wales or Scotland

(1) An employee who—

  (a) is aged 16 or 17,

  (b) is not receiving full-time secondary or further education, and

  (c) has not attained such standard of achievement as is prescribed by regulations made by the Secretary of State,

is entitled to be permitted by his employer to take time off during the employee's working hours in order to undertake study or training leading to a relevant qualification.

  ...

(3) An employee who—

  (a) satisfies the requirements of paragraphs (a) to (c) of subsection (1), and

  (b) is for the time being supplied by his employer to another person ('the principal') to perform work in accordance with a contract made between the employer and the principal, is entitled to be permitted by the principal to take time off during the employee's working hours in order to undertake study or training leading to a relevant qualification.

(4)    Where an employee—

    (a)    is aged 18,

    (b)    is undertaking study or training leading to a relevant qualification, and

    (c)    began such study or training before attaining that age,

subsections (1) and (3) shall apply to the employee, in relation to that study or training, as if 'or 18' were inserted at the end of subsection (1)(a).

(5)    The amount of time off which an employee is to be permitted to take under this section, and the occasions on which and any conditions subject to which time off may be so taken, are those that are reasonable in all the circumstances having regard, in particular, to—

    (a)    the requirements of the employee's study or training, and

    (b)    the circumstances of the business of the employer or the principal and the effect of the employee's time off on the running of that business.

...

(7)    References in this section to study or training are references to study or training on the premises of the employer or (as the case may be) principal or elsewhere.

(8)    For the purposes of this section the working hours of an employee shall be taken to be any time when, in accordance with his contract of employment, the employee is required to be at work.

## 63B    Right to remuneration for time off under section 63A

(1)    An employee who is permitted to take time off under section 63A is entitled to be paid remuneration by his employer for the time taken off at the appropriate hourly rate.

(2)    The appropriate hourly rate, in relation to an employee, is the amount of one week's pay divided by the number of normal working hours in a week for that employee when employed under the contract of employment in force on the day when the time off is taken.

(3)    But where the number of normal working hours differs from week to week or over a longer period, the amount of one week's pay shall be divided instead by—

    (a)    the average number of normal working hours calculated by dividing by twelve the total number of the employee's working hours during the period of twelve weeks ending with the last complete week before the day on which the time off is taken, or

    (b)    where the employee has not been employed for a sufficient period to enable the calculation to be made under paragraph (a), a number which fairly represents the number of normal working hours in a week having regard to such of the considerations specified in subsection (4) as are appropriate in the circumstances.

(4)    The considerations referred to in subsection (3)(b) are—

    (a)    the average number of normal working hours in a week which the employee could expect in accordance with the terms of his contract, and

    (b)    the average number of normal working hours of other employees engaged in relevant comparable employment with the same employer.

(5)    A right to any amount under subsection (1) does not affect any right of an employee in relation to remuneration under his contract of employment ('contractual remuneration').

(6)    Any contractual remuneration paid to an employee in respect of a period of time off under section 63A goes towards discharging any liability of the employer to pay remuneration under subsection (1) in respect of that period; and, conversely, any payment of remuneration under subsection (1) in respect of a period goes towards discharging any liability of the employer to pay contractual remuneration in respect of that period.

## 63C    Complaints to employment tribunals

(1)    An employee may present a complaint to an employment tribunal that—

    (a)    his employer, or the principal referred to in subsection (3) of section 63A, has unreasonably refused to permit him to take time off as required by that section, or

    (b)    his employer has failed to pay the whole or any part of any amount to which the employee is entitled under section 63B.

(2) An employment tribunal shall not consider a complaint under this section unless it is presented—

    (a) before the end of the period of three months beginning with the day on which the time off was taken or on which it is alleged the time off should have been permitted, or

    (b) within such further period as the tribunal considers reasonable in a case where it is satisfied that it was not reasonably practicable for the complaint to be presented before the end of that period of three months.

(2A) Section 207B (extension of time limits to facilitate conciliation before institution of proceedings) applies for the purposes of subsection (2)(a).

(3) Where an employment tribunal finds a complaint under this section well-founded, the tribunal shall make a declaration to that effect.

(4) If the complaint is that the employer or the principal has unreasonably refused to permit the employee to take time off, the tribunal shall also order the employer or the principal, as the case may be, to pay to the employee an amount equal to the remuneration to which he would have been entitled under section 63B if the employer or the principal had not refused.

(5) If the complaint is that the employer has failed to pay the employee the whole or part of any amount to which he is entitled under section 63B, the tribunal shall also order the employer to pay to the employee the amount which it finds due to him.

## 63D Statutory right to make request in relation to study or training

(1) A qualifying employee may make an application under this section to his or her employer.

(2) An application under this section (a 'section 63D application') is an application that meets—

    (a) the conditions in subsections (3) to (5), and

    (b) any further conditions specified by the Secretary of State in regulations.

(3) The application must be made for the purpose of enabling the employee to undertake study or training (or both) within subsection (4).

(4) Study or training is within this subsection if its purpose is to improve—

    (a) the employee's effectiveness in the employer's business, and

    (b) the performance of the employer's business.

(5) The application must state that it is an application under this section.

(6) An employee is a qualifying employee for the purposes of this section if the employee—

    (a) satisfies any conditions about duration of employment specified by the Secretary of State in regulations, and

    (b) is not a person within subsection (7).

(7) The following persons are within this subsection—

    (a) a person of compulsory school age (or, in Scotland, school age);

    (b) a person to whom Part 1 of the Education and Skills Act 2008 (duty to participate in education or training for 16 and 17 year olds) applies;

    (c) a person who, by virtue of section 29 of that Act, is treated as a person to whom that Part applies for the purposes specified in that section (extension for person reaching 18);

    (d) a person to whom section 63A of this Act (right to time off for young person for study or training) applies;

    (e) an agency worker;

    (f) a person of a description specified by the Secretary of State in regulations.

(8) Nothing in this Part prevents an employee and an employer from making any other arrangements in relation to study or training.

(9) In this section—

'agency worker' means a worker supplied by a person (the 'agent') to do work for another person (the 'principal') under a contract or other arrangement between the agent and principal;

'compulsory school age' has the meaning given in section 8 of the Education Act 1996; 'school age' has the meaning given in section 31 of the Education (Scotland) Act 1980.

PART VII
SUSPENSION FROM WORK

*Suspension on medical grounds*

**64    Right to remuneration on suspension on medical grounds**

(1)    An employee who is suspended from work by his employer on medical grounds is entitled to be paid by his employer remuneration while he is so suspended for a period not exceeding twenty-six weeks.

(2)    For the purposes of this Part an employee is suspended from work on medical grounds if he is suspended from work in consequence of—

(a)    a requirement imposed by or under a provision of an enactment or of an instrument made under an enactment, or

(b)    a recommendation in a provision of a code of practice issued or approved under section 16 of the Health and Safety at Work etc. Act 1974,

and the provision is for the time being specified in subsection (3).

(3)    The provisions referred to in subsection (2) are—

Regulation 16 of the Control of Lead at Work Regulations 1980,

Regulation 25 of the Ionising Radiations Regulations 2017, and

Regulation 11 of the Control of Substances Hazardous to Health Regulations 1988.

(4)    The Secretary of State may by order add provisions to or remove provisions from the list of provisions specified in subsection (3).

(5)    For the purposes of this Part an employee shall be regarded as suspended from work on medical grounds only if and for so long as he—

(a)    continues to be employed by his employer, but

(b)    is not provided with work or does not perform the work he normally performed before the suspension.

**65    Exclusions from right to remuneration**

(1)    An employee is not entitled to remuneration under section 64 unless he has been continuously employed for a period of not less than one month ending with the day before that on which the suspension begins.

(2)    ...

(3)    An employee is not entitled to remuneration under section 64 in respect of any period during which he is incapable of work by reason of disease or bodily or mental disablement.

(4)    An employee is not entitled to remuneration under section 64 in respect of any period if—

(a)    his employer has offered to provide him with suitable alternative work during the period (whether or not it is work which the employee is under his contract, or was under the contract in force before the suspension, employed to perform) and the employee has unreasonably refused to perform that work, or

(b)    he does not comply with reasonable requirements imposed by his employer with a view to ensuring that his services are available.

*Suspension on maternity grounds*

**66    Meaning of suspension on maternity grounds**

(1)    For the purposes of this Part an employee is suspended from work on maternity grounds if, in consequence of any relevant requirement or relevant recommendation, she is suspended from work by her employer on the ground that she is pregnant, has recently given birth or is breastfeeding a child.

(2)    In subsection (1)—

'relevant requirement' means a requirement imposed by or under a specified provision of an enactment or of an instrument made under an enactment, and

'relevant recommendation' means a recommendation in a specified provision of a code of practice issued or approved under section 16 of the Health and Safety at Work etc. Act 1974;

and in this subsection 'specified provision' means a provision for the time being specified in an order made by the Secretary of State under this subsection.

(3) For the purposes of this Part an employee shall be regarded as suspended from work on maternity grounds only if and for so long as she—

    (a) continues to be employed by her employer, but

    (b) is not provided with work or (disregarding alternative work for the purposes of section 67) does not perform the work she normally performed before the suspension.

## 67 Right to offer of alternative work

(1) Where an employer has available suitable alternative work for an employee, the employee has a right to be offered to be provided with the alternative work before being suspended from work on maternity grounds.

(2) For alternative work to be suitable for an employee for the purposes of this section—

    (a) the work must be of a kind which is both suitable in relation to her and appropriate for her to do in the circumstances, and

    (b) the terms and conditions applicable to her for performing the work, if they differ from the corresponding terms and conditions applicable to her for performing the work she normally performs under her contract of employment, must not be substantially less favourable to her than those corresponding terms and conditions.

## 68 Right to remuneration

(1) An employee who is suspended from work on maternity grounds is entitled to be paid remuneration by her employer while she is so suspended.

(2) An employee is not entitled to remuneration under this section in respect of any period if—

    (a) her employer has offered to provide her during the period with work which is suitable alternative work for her for the purposes of section 67, and

    (b) the employee has unreasonably refused to perform that work.

*Ending the supply of an agency worker on maternity grounds*

## 68A Meaning of ending the supply of an agency worker on maternity grounds

(1) For the purposes of this Part the supply of an agency worker to a hirer is ended on maternity grounds if, in consequence of action taken pursuant to a provision listed in subsection (2), the supply of the agency worker to the hirer is ended on the ground that she is pregnant, has recently given birth or is breastfeeding a child.

(2) The provisions are—

    (a) regulations 8(3) or 9(2) of the Merchant Shipping and Fishing Vessels (Health and Safety at Work) Regulations 1997;

    (b) regulation 16A(2) or 17A of the Management of Health and Safety at Work Regulations 1999; or

    (c) regulation 20 of the Conduct of Employment Agencies and Employment Businesses Regulations 2003.

## 68B Right to offer of alternative work

(1) Where the supply of an agency worker to a hirer is ended on maternity grounds and the temporary work agency has available suitable alternative work, the agency worker has a right to be offered to be proposed for such alternative work.

(2) For alternative work to be suitable for an agency worker for the purposes of this section—

    (a) the work must be of a kind which is both suitable in relation to her and appropriate for her to do in the circumstances, and

    (b) the terms and conditions applicable to her whilst performing the work, if they differ from the corresponding terms and conditions which would have applied to her but for the fact that the supply of the agency worker to the hirer was ended on maternity grounds, must not be substantially less favourable to her than those corresponding terms and conditions.

(3) Subsection (1) does not apply—

(a) where the agency worker has confirmed in writing that she no longer requires the work-finding services of the temporary work agency, or

(b) beyond the original intended duration, or likely duration, whichever is the longer, of the assignment which ended when the supply of the agency worker to the hirer was ended on maternity grounds.

## 68C    Right to remuneration

(1) Where the supply of an agency worker to a hirer is ended on maternity grounds, that agency worker is entitled to be paid remuneration by the temporary work agency.

(2) An agency worker is not entitled to remuneration under this section in respect of any period if—

(a) the temporary work agency has—

(i) offered to propose the agency worker to a hirer that has alternative work available which is suitable alternative work for her for the purposes of section 68B, or

(ii) proposed the agency worker to a hirer that has such suitable alternative work available, and that hirer has agreed to the supply of that agency worker, and

(b) the agency worker has unreasonably refused that offer or to perform that work.

(3) Nothing in this section imposes a duty on the temporary work agency to pay remuneration beyond the original intended duration, or likely duration, whichever is the longer, of the assignment which ended when the supply of the agency worker to the hirer was ended on maternity grounds.

## 68D    Agency workers: supplementary

(1) Without prejudice to any other duties of the hirer or temporary work agency under any enactment or rule of law sections 68A, 68B and 68C do not apply where the agency worker—

(a) has not completed the qualifying period, or

(b) is no longer entitled to the rights conferred by regulation 5 of the Agency Workers Regulations 2010 pursuant to regulation 8(a) or (b) of those Regulations.

(2) Nothing in those sections imposes a duty on the hirer or temporary work agency beyond the original intended duration, or likely duration of the assignment, whichever is the longer.

(3) Those sections do not apply where sections 66 to 68 apply.

(4) In this section and sections 68A to 68C the following have the same meaning as in the Agency Workers Regulations 2010—

'agency worker';

'assignment';

'hirer';

'qualifying period';

'temporary work agency'.

*General*

## 69    Calculation of remuneration

(1) The amount of remuneration payable by an employer to an employee under section 64 or 68 is a week's pay in respect of each week of the period of suspension; and if in any week remuneration is payable in respect of only part of that week the amount of a week's pay shall be reduced proportionately.

(2) A right to remuneration under section 64 or 68 does not affect any right of an employee in relation to remuneration under the employee's contract of employment ('contractual remuneration').

(3) Any contractual remuneration paid by an employer to an employee in respect of any period goes towards discharging the employer's liability under section 64 or 68 in

respect of that period; and, conversely, any payment of remuneration in discharge of an employer's liability under section 64 or 68 in respect of any period goes towards discharging any obligation of the employer to pay contractual remuneration in respect of that period.

## 69A Calculation of remuneration (agency workers)

(1) The amount of remuneration payable by a temporary work agency to an agency worker under section 68C is a week's pay in respect of each week for which remuneration is payable in accordance with section 68C; and if in any week remuneration is payable in respect of only part of that week the amount of a week's pay shall be reduced proportionately.

(2) A right to remuneration under section 68C does not affect any right of the agency worker in relation to remuneration under the contract with the temporary work agency ('contractual remuneration').

(3) Any contractual remuneration paid by the temporary work agency to an agency worker in respect of any period goes towards discharging the temporary work agency's liability under section 68C in respect of that period; and, conversely, any payment of remuneration in discharge of a temporary work agency's liability under section 68C in respect of any period goes towards discharging any obligation of the temporary work agency to pay contractual remuneration in respect of that period.

(4) For the purposes of subsection (1), a week's pay is the weekly amount that would have been payable to the agency worker for performing the work, according to the terms of the contract with the temporary work agency, but for the fact that the supply of the agency worker to the hirer was ended on maternity grounds.

(5) Expressions used in this section and sections 68A to 68C have the same meaning as in those sections (see section 68D).

## 70 Complaints to employment tribunals

(1) An employee may present a complaint to an employment tribunal that his or her employer has failed to pay the whole or any part of remuneration to which the employee is entitled under section 64 or 68.

(2) An employment tribunal shall not consider a complaint under subsection (1) relating to remuneration in respect of any day unless it is presented—
  (a) before the end of the period of three months beginning with that day, or (b) within such further period as the tribunal considers reasonable in a case where it is satisfied that it was not reasonably practicable for the complaint to be presented within that period of three months.

(3) Where an employment tribunal finds a complaint under subsection (1) well-founded, the tribunal shall order the employer to pay the employee the amount of remuneration which it finds is due to him or her.

(4) An employee may present a complaint to an employment tribunal that in contravention of section 67 her employer has failed to offer to provide her with work.

(5) An employment tribunal shall not consider a complaint under subsection (4) unless it is presented—
  (a) before the end of the period of three months beginning with the first day of the suspension, or
  (b) within such further period as the tribunal considers reasonable in a case where it is satisfied that it was not reasonably practicable for the complaint to be presented within that period of three months.

(6) Where an employment tribunal finds a complaint under subsection (4) well-founded, the tribunal may make an award of compensation to be paid by the employer to the employee.

(7) The amount of the compensation shall be such as the tribunal considers just and equitable in all the circumstances having regard to—
  (a) the infringement of the employee's right under section 67 by the failure on the part of the employer to which the complaint relates, and
  (b) any loss sustained by the employee which is attributable to that failure.

**70A    Complaints to employment tribunals: agency workers**

(1)    An agency worker may present a complaint to an employment tribunal that the temporary work agency has failed to pay the whole or any part of remuneration to which the agency worker is entitled under section 68C.

(2)    An employment tribunal shall not consider a complaint under subsection (1) relating to remuneration in respect of any day unless it is presented—

    (a)    before the end of the period of three months beginning with the day on which the supply of the agency worker to a hirer was ended on maternity grounds, or

    (b)    within such further period as the tribunal considers reasonable in a case where it is satisfied that it was not reasonably practicable for the complaint to be presented within that period of three months.

(3)    Where an employment tribunal finds a complaint under subsection (1) well-founded, the tribunal shall order the temporary work agency to pay the agency worker the amount of remuneration which it finds is due to her.

(4)    An agency worker may present a complaint to an employment tribunal that in contravention of section 68B the temporary work agency has failed to offer to propose the agency worker to a hirer that has suitable alternative work available.

(5)    An employment tribunal shall not consider a complaint under subsection (4) unless it is presented—

    (a)    before the end of the period of three months beginning with the day on which the supply of the agency worker to a hirer was ended on maternity grounds, or

    (b)    within such further period as the tribunal considers reasonable in a case where it is satisfied that it was not reasonably practicable for the complaint to be presented within that period of three months.

(6)    Where an employment tribunal finds a complaint under subsection (4) well-founded, the tribunal shall order the temporary work agency to pay the agency worker the amount of compensation which it finds is due to her.

(7)    The amount of the compensation shall be such as the tribunal considers just and equitable in all the circumstances having regard to—

    (a)    the infringement of the agency worker's right under section 68B by the failure on the part of the temporary work agency to which the complaint relates, and

    (b)    any loss sustained by the agency worker which is attributable to that failure.

(7A)  Section 207B (extension of time limits to facilitate conciliation before institution of proceedings) applies for the purposes of subsections (2)(a) and (5)(a).

(8)    Expressions used in this section and sections 68A to 68C have the same meaning as in those sections (see section 68D).

PART VIII
GENERAL RIGHT TO MATERNITY LEAVE

CHAPTER I
MATERNITY LEAVE

**71    Ordinary maternity leave**

(1)    An employee may, provided that she satisfies any conditions which may be prescribed, be absent from work at any time during an ordinary maternity leave period.

(2)    An ordinary maternity leave period is a period calculated in accordance with regulations made by the Secretary of State.

(3)    Regulations under subsection (2)—

    (a)    shall secure that no ordinary maternity leave period is less than 18 weeks;

    (b)    may allow an employee to choose, subject to any prescribed restrictions, the date on which an ordinary maternity leave period starts;

    (ba)   may allow an employee to bring forward the date on which an ordinary maternity leave period ends, subject to prescribed restrictions and subject to satisfying prescribed conditions;

    (bb)   may allow an employee in prescribed circumstances to revoke, or to be treated as revoking, the bringing forward of that date;

      (c)    may specify circumstances in which an employee may work for her employer during an ordinary maternity leave period without bringing that period to an end.

(3A)   Provision under subsection (3)(ba) is to secure that an employee may bring forward the date on which an ordinary maternity leave period ends only if the employee or another person has taken, or is taking, prescribed steps as regards leave under section 75E or statutory shared parental pay in respect of the child.

(4)    Subject to section 74, an employee who exercises her right under subsection (1)—

      (a)    is entitled for such purposes and to such extent as may be prescribed to the benefit of the terms and conditions of employment which would have applied if she had not been absent,

      (b)    is bound for such purposes and to such extent as may be prescribed by any obligations arising under those terms and conditions (except in so far as they are inconsistent with subsection (1)), and

      (c)    is entitled to return from leave to the job of a prescribed kind.

(5)    In subsection (4)(a) 'terms and conditions of employment'—

      (a)    includes matters connected with an employee's employment whether or not they arise under her contract of employment, but

      (b)    does not include terms and conditions about remuneration.

(6)    The Secretary of State may make regulations specifying matters which are, or are not, to be treated as remuneration for the purposes of this section.

(7)    The Secretary of State may make regulations making provision, in relation to the right to return under subsection (4)(c) above, about—

      (a)    seniority, pension rights and similar rights;

      (b)    terms and conditions of employment on return.

## 72   Compulsory maternity leave

(1)    An employer shall not permit an employee who satisfies prescribed conditions to work during a compulsory maternity leave period.

(2)    A compulsory maternity leave period is a period calculated in accordance with regulations made by the Secretary of State.

(3)    Regulations under subsection (2) shall secure—

      (a)    that no compulsory leave period is less than two weeks, and

      (b)    that every compulsory maternity leave period falls within an ordinary maternity leave period.

(4)    Subject to subsection (5), any provision of or made under the Health and Safety at Work etc. Act 1974 shall apply in relation to the prohibition under subsection (1) as if it were imposed by regulations under section 15 of that Act.

(5)    Section 33(1)(c) of the 1974 Act shall not apply in relation to the prohibition under subsection (1); and an employer who contravenes that subsection shall be—

      (a)    guilty of an offence, and

      (b)    liable on summary conviction to a fine not exceeding level 2 on the standard scale.

## 73   Additional maternity leave

(1)    An employee who satisfies prescribed conditions may be absent from work at any time during an additional maternity leave period.

(2)    An additional maternity leave period is a period calculated in accordance with regulations made by the Secretary of State.

(3)    Regulations under subsection (2)—

      (a)    may allow an employee to bring forward the date on which an additional maternity leave period ends, subject to prescribed restrictions and subject to satisfying prescribed conditions;

     (aa)   may allow an employee in prescribed circumstances to revoke, or to be treated as revoking, the bringing forward of that date;

      (b)    may specify circumstances in which an employee may work for her employer during an additional maternity leave period without bringing the period to an end.

(3A) Provision under subsection (3)(a) is to secure that an employee may bring forward the date on which an additional maternity leave period ends only if the employee or another person has taken, or is taking, prescribed steps as regards leave under section 75E or statutory shared parental pay in respect of the child.

(4) Subject to section 74, an employee who exercises her right under subsection (1)—

 (a) is entitled, for such purposes and to such extent as may be prescribed, to the benefit of the terms and conditions of employment which would have applied if she had not been absent,

 (b) is bound, for such purposes and to such extent as may be prescribed, by obligations arising under those terms and conditions (except in so far as they are inconsistent with subsection (1)), and

 (c) is entitled to return from leave to a job of a prescribed kind.

(5) In subsection (4)(a) 'terms and conditions of employment'—

 (a) includes matters connected with an employee's employment whether or not they arise under her contract of employment, but

 (b) does not include terms and conditions about remuneration.

(5A) In subsection (4)(c), the reference to return from leave includes, where appropriate, a reference to a continuous period of absence attributable partly to additional maternity leave and partly to ordinary maternity leave.

…

## CHAPTER II
## PARENTAL LEAVE

## 80 Complaint to employment tribunal

(1) An employee may present a complaint to an employment tribunal that his employer—

 (a) has unreasonably postponed a period of parental leave requested by the employee, or

 (b) has prevented or attempted to prevent the employee from taking parental leave.

(2) An employment tribunal shall not consider a complaint under this section unless it is presented—

 (a) before the end of the period of three months beginning with the date (or last date) of the matters complained of, or

 (b) within such further period as the tribunal considers reasonable in a case where it is satisfied that it was not reasonably practicable for the complaint to be presented before the end of that period of three months.

(2A) Section 207B (extension of time limits to facilitate conciliation before institution of proceedings) applies for the purposes of subsection (2)(a).

(3) Where an employment tribunal finds a complaint under this section well-founded it—

 (a) shall make a declaration to that effect, and

 (b) may make an award of compensation to be paid by the employer to the employee.

(4) The amount of compensation shall be such as the tribunal considers just and equitable in all the circumstances having regard to—

 (a) the employer's behaviour, and

 (b) any loss sustained by the employee which is attributable to the matters complained of.

## CHAPTER III
## PATERNITY LEAVE

## 80A Entitlement to paternity leave: birth

(1) The Secretary of State shall make regulations entitling an employee who satisfies specified conditions—

 (a) as to duration of employment,

 (b) as to relationship with a newborn, or expected, child, and

 (c) as to relationship with the child's mother,

to be absent from work on leave under this section for the purpose of caring for the child or supporting the mother.

(2) The regulations shall include provision for determining—

    (a) the extent of an employee's entitlement to leave under this section in respect of a child;

    (b) when leave under this section may be taken.

(3) Provision under subsection (2)(a) shall secure that where an employee is entitled to leave under this section in respect of a child he is entitled to at least two weeks' leave.

(4) Provision under subsection (2)(b) shall secure that leave under this section must be taken before the end of a period of at least 56 days beginning with the date of the child's birth.

(4A) Provision under subsection (2)(b) must secure that, once an employee takes leave under section 75E in respect of a child, the employee may not take leave under this section in respect of the child.

(5) Regulations under subsection (1) may—

    (a) specify things which are, or are not, to be taken as done for the purpose of caring for a child or supporting the child's mother;

    (b) make provision excluding the right to be absent on leave under this section in respect of a child where more than one child is born as a result of the same pregnancy;

    (c) make provision about how leave under this section may be taken.

(6) Where more than one child is born as a result of the same pregnancy, the reference in subsection (4) to the date of the child's birth shall be read as a reference to the date of birth of the first child born as a result of the pregnancy.

(7) In this section—

'newborn child' includes a child stillborn after twenty-four weeks of pregnancy;

'week' means any period of seven days.

## 80B Entitlement to paternity leave: adoption

(1) The Secretary of State shall make regulations entitling an employee who satisfies specified conditions—

    (a) as to duration of employment,

    (b) as to relationship with a child placed, or expected to be placed, for adoption under the law of any part of the United Kingdom, and

    (c) as to relationship with a person with whom the child is, or is expected to be, so placed for adoption,

to be absent from work on leave under this section for the purpose of caring for the child or supporting the person by reference to whom he satisfies the condition under paragraph (c).

(2) The regulations shall include provision for determining—

    (a) the extent of an employee's entitlement to leave under this section in respect of a child;

    (b) when leave under this section may be taken.

(3) Provision under subsection (2)(a) shall secure that where an employee is entitled to leave under this section in respect of a child he is entitled to at least two weeks' leave.

(4) Provision under subsection (2)(b) shall secure that leave under this section must be taken before the end of a period of at least 56 days beginning with the date of the child's placement for adoption.

(4A) Provision under subsection (2)(b) must secure that, once an employee takes leave under section 75G in respect of a child, the employee may not take leave under this section in respect of the child.

(5) Regulations under subsection (1) may—

    (a) specify things which are, or are not, to be taken as done for the purpose of caring for a child or supporting a person with whom a child is placed for adoption;

    (aa) make provision excluding the right to be absent on leave under this section in the case of an employee who, by virtue of provision under subsection (6A), has already exercised a right to be absent on leave under this section in connection with the same child;

     (b)    make provision excluding the right to be absent on leave under this section in the case of an employee who exercises a right to be absent from work on adoption leave;

     (ba)   make provision excluding the right to be absent on leave under this section in the case of an employee who has exercised a right to take time off under section 57ZJ;

     (c)    make provision excluding the right to be absent on leave under this section in respect of a child where more than one child is placed for adoption as part of the same arrangement;

     (d)    make provision about how leave under this section may be taken.

(6)    Where more than one child is placed for adoption as part of the same arrangement, the reference in subsection (4) to the date of the child's placement shall be read as a reference to the date of placement of the first child to be placed as part of the arrangement.

(6A)  Regulations under subsection (1) shall include provision for leave in respect of a child placed, or expected to be placed—

     (a)    under section 22C of the Children Act 1989 by a local authority in England, or

     (b)    under section 81 of the Social Services and Well-being (Wales) Act 2014 by a local authority in Wales,

with a local authority foster parent who has been approved as a prospective adopter.

(6B)  This section has effect in relation to regulations made by virtue of subsection (6A) as if—

     (a)    references to being placed for adoption were references to being placed under section 22C of the Children Act 1989, or section 81 of the Social Services and Well-being (Wales) Act 2014 with a local authority foster parent who has been approved as a prospective adopter;

     (b)    references to placement for adoption were references to placement under section 22C of the Children Act 1989, or section 81 of the Social Services and Well-being (Wales) Act 2014 with such a person;

     (c)    paragraph (aa) of subsection (5) were omitted.

(7)    In this section, 'week' means any period of seven days.

(8)    The Secretary of State may by regulations provide for this section to have effect in relation to cases which involve adoption, but not the placement of a child for adoption under the law of any part of the United Kingdom, with such modifications as the regulations may prescribe.

(9)    The Secretary of State may by regulations provide for this section to have effect in relation to cases which involve an employee who has applied, or intends to apply, with another person for a parental order under section 54 of the Human Fertilisation and Embryology Act 2008 and a child who is, or will be, the subject of the order, with such modifications as the regulations may prescribe.

## 80C   Rights during and after paternity leave

(1)    Regulations under section 80A [...] shall provide—

     (a)    that an employee who is absent on leave under that section is entitled, for such purposes and to such extent as the regulations may prescribe, to the benefit of the terms and conditions of employment which would have applied if he had not been absent;

     (b)    that an employee who is absent on leave under that section is bound, for such purposes and to such extent as the regulations may prescribe, by obligations arising under those terms and conditions (except in so far as they are inconsistent with subsection (1) of that section), and

     (c)    that an employee who is absent on leave under that section is entitled to return from leave to a job of a kind prescribed by regulations, subject to section 80D(1).

(2)    The reference in subsection (1)(c) to absence on leave under section 80A [...] includes, where appropriate, a reference to a continuous period of absence attributable partly to leave under that section and partly to any one or more of the following—

     (za)   ...

     (a)    maternity leave,

     (b)    adoption leave, ...

     (ba)   shared parental leave,

(bb)    parental bereavement leave, and
    (c)    parental leave.
(3)    Subsection (1) shall apply to regulations under section 80B […] as it applies to regulations under section 80A. ...
(4)    In the application of subsection (1)(c) to regulations under section 80B […], the reference to absence on leave under that section includes, where appropriate, a reference to a continuous period of absence attributable partly to leave under that section and partly to any one or more of the following—
    (za)    ...
    (a)    maternity leave,
    (b)    adoption leave,
    (ba)    shared parental leave,
    (bb)    parental bereavement leave,
    (c)    parental leave, and
    (d)    leave under section 80A […].
(5)    In subsection (1)(a), 'terms and conditions of employment'—
    (a)    includes matters connected with an employee's employment whether or not they arise under his contract of employment, but
    (b)    does not include terms and conditions about remuneration.
(6)    Regulations under section 80A or 80B may specify matters which are, or are not, to be treated as remuneration for the purposes of this section.
(7)    Regulations under section 80A or 80B may make provision, in relation to the right to return mentioned in subsection (1)(c), about—
    (a)    seniority, pension rights and similar rights;
    (b)    terms and conditions of employment on return.

CHAPTER 4
PARENTAL BEREAVEMENT LEAVE

## 80EA  Parental bereavement leave

(1)    The Secretary of State must make regulations entitling an employee who is a bereaved parent to be absent from work on leave under this section.
(2)    For the purposes of subsection (1) an employee is a 'bereaved parent' if the employee satisfies conditions specified in the regulations as to relationship with a child who has died.
(3)    The conditions specified under subsection (2) may be framed, in whole or in part, by reference to the employee's care of the child before the child's death.
(4)    The regulations must include provision for determining—
    (a)    the extent of an employee's entitlement to leave under this section in respect of a child;
    (b)    when leave under this section may be taken.
(5)    Provision under subsection (4)(a) must secure that where an employee is entitled to leave under this section in respect of a child the employee is entitled to at least two weeks' leave.
(6)    Provision under subsection (4)(b) must secure that leave under this section must be taken before the end of a period of at least 56 days beginning with the date of the child's death.
(7)    The regulations must secure that where a person is eligible under subsection (1) as the result of the death of more than one child, the person is entitled to leave in respect of each child.
(8)    The regulations may make provision about how leave under this section is to be taken.
(9)    In this section—
    •    'child' means a person under the age of 18 (see also section 80EE for the application of this Chapter in relation to stillbirths);
    •    'week' means any period of seven days.

## 80EB  Rights during and after bereavement leave

(1)    Regulations under section 80EA must provide—
    (a)    that an employee who is absent on leave under that section is entitled, for such purposes and to such extent as the regulations may prescribe, to the benefit of

the terms and conditions of employment which would have applied but for the absence,

(b) that an employee who is absent on leave under that section is bound, for such purposes and to such extent as the regulations may prescribe, by obligations arising under those terms and conditions (except in so far as they are inconsistent with subsection (1) of that section), and

(c) that an employee who is absent on leave under that section is entitled to return from leave to a job of a kind prescribed by regulations, subject to section 80EC(1).

(2) The reference in subsection (1)(c) to absence on leave under section 80EA includes, where appropriate, a reference to a continuous period of absence attributable partly to leave under that section and partly to any one or more of the following—

(a) maternity leave,

(b) paternity leave,

(c) adoption leave,

(d) shared parental leave, and

(e) parental leave.

(3) In subsection (1)(a), 'terms and conditions of employment'—

(a) includes matters connected with an employee's employment whether or not they arise under the contract of employment, but

(b) does not include terms and conditions about remuneration.

(4) Regulations under section 80EA may specify matters which are, or are not, to be treated as remuneration for the purposes of this section.

(5) Regulations under section 80EA may make provision, in relation to the right to return mentioned in subsection (1)(c), about—

(a) seniority, pension rights and similar rights;

(b) terms and conditions of employment on return.

## PART 8A
## FLEXIBLE WORKING

**80F  Statutory right to request contract variation**

(1) A qualifying employee may apply to his employer for a change in his terms and conditions of employment if—

(a) the change relates to—

(i) the hours he is required to work,

(ii) the times when he is required to work,

(iii) where, as between his home and a place of business of his employer, he is required to work, or

(iv) such other aspect of his terms and conditions of employment as the Secretary of State may specify by regulations...

(b) ... .

(2) An application under this section must—

(a) state that it is such an application,

(b) specify the change applied for and the date on which it is proposed the change should become effective, [and]

(c) explain what effect, if any, the employee thinks making the change applied for would have on his employer and how, in his opinion, any such effect might be dealt with...

(d) ... .

(3) ...

(4) If an employee has made an application under this section, he may not make a further application under this section to the same employer before the end of the period of twelve months beginning with the date on which the previous application was made.

(5) The Secretary of State may by regulations make provision about—

(a) the form of applications under this section, and

(b) when such an application is to be taken as made.

(6) ...

(7) ...

(8) For the purposes of this section, an employee is—

(a)    a qualifying employee if he—

    (i)    satisfies such conditions as to duration of employment as the Secretary of State may specify by regulations, and

    (ii)    is not an agency worker (other than an agency worker who is returning to work from a period of parental leave under regulations under section 76);

(b)    an agency worker if he is supplied by a person ('the agent') to do work for another ('the principal') under a contract or other arrangement made between the agent and the principal.

(9)    Regulations under this section may make different provision for different cases.

(10)    ...

## 80G    Employer's duties in relation to application under section 80F

(1)    An employer to whom an application under section 80F is made—

    (a)    shall deal with the application in a reasonable manner,

    (aa)    shall notify the employee of the decision on the application within the decision period, and

    (b)    shall only refuse the application because he considers that one or more of the following grounds applies—

        (i)    the burden of additional costs,

        (ii)    detrimental effect on ability to meet customer demand,

        (iii)    inability to re-organise work among existing staff,

        (iv)    inability to recruit additional staff,

        (v)    detrimental impact on quality,

        (vi)    detrimental impact on performance,

        (vii)    insufficiency of work during the periods the employee proposes to work,

        (viii)    planned structural changes, and

        (ix)    such other grounds as the Secretary of State may specify by regulations.

(1A)    If an employer allows an employee to appeal a decision to reject an application, the reference in subsection (1)(aa) to the decision on the application is a reference to—

    (a)    the decision on the appeal, or

    (b)    if more than one appeal is allowed, the decision on the final appeal.

(1B)    For the purposes of subsection (1)(aa) the decision period applicable to an employee's application under section 80F is—

    (a)    the period of three months beginning with the date on which the application is made, or

    (b)    such longer period as may be agreed by the employer and the employee.

(1C)    An agreement to extend the decision period in a particular case may be made—

    (a)    before it ends, or

    (b)    with retrospective effect, before the end of a period of three months beginning with the day after that on which the decision period that is being extended came to an end.

(1D)    An application under section 80F is to be treated as having been withdrawn by the employee if—

    (a)    the employee without good reason has failed to attend both the first meeting arranged by the employer to discuss the application and the next meeting arranged for that purpose, or

    (b)    where the employer allows the employee to appeal a decision to reject an application or to make a further appeal, the employee without good reason has failed to attend both the first meeting arranged by the employer to discuss the appeal and the next meeting arranged for that purpose,

and the employer has notified the employee that the employer has decided to treat that conduct of the employee as a withdrawal of the application.

(2)    ...

(3)    ...

(4)    ...

## 80H    Complaints to employment tribunals

(1)    An employee who makes an application under section 80F may present a complaint to an employment tribunal—

       (a)     that his employer has failed in relation to the application to comply with section 80G(1), ...

       (b)     that a decision by his employer to reject the application was based on incorrect facts, or

       (c)     that the employer's notification under section 80G(1D) was given in circumstances that did not satisfy one of the requirements in section 80G(1D)(a) and (b).

(2)    No complaint [under subsection (1)(a) or (b)] may be made in respect of an application which has been disposed of by agreement or withdrawn.

(3)    In the case of an application which has not been disposed of by agreement or withdrawn, no complaint under subsection (1)(a) or (b) may be made until—

       (a)     the employer notifies the employee of the employer's decision on the application, or

       (b)     if the decision period applicable to the application (see section 80G(1B)) comes to an end without the employer notifying the employee of the employer's decision on the application, the end of the decision period.

(3A)  If an employer allows an employee to appeal a decision to reject an application, a reference in other subsections of this section to the decision on the application is a reference to the decision on the appeal or, if more than one appeal is allowed, the decision on the final appeal.

(3B)  If an agreement to extend the decision period is made as described in section 80G(1C)(b), subsection (3)(b) is to be treated as not allowing a complaint until the end of the extended period.

(3C)  A complaint under subsection (1)(c) may be made as soon as the notification under section 80G(1D) complained of is given to the employee.

(4)    ...

(5)    An employment tribunal shall not consider a complaint under this section unless it is presented—

       (a)     before the end of the period of three months beginning with the relevant date, or

       (b)     within such further period as the tribunal considers reasonable in a case where it is satisfied that it was not reasonably practicable for the complaint to be presented before the end of that period of three months.

(6)    In subsection (5)(a), the reference to the relevant date is a reference to the first date on which the employee may make a complaint under subsection (1)(a), (b) or (c), as the case may be.

(7)    Section 207B (extension of time limits to facilitate conciliation before institution of proceedings) applies for the purposes of subsection (5)(a).

## 80I   Remedies

(1)    Where an employment tribunal finds a complaint under section 80H well-founded it shall make a declaration to that effect and may—

       (a)     make an order for reconsideration of the application, and

       (b)     make an award of compensation to be paid by the employer to the employee.

(2)    The amount of compensation shall be such amount, not exceeding the permitted maximum, as the tribunal considers just and equitable in all the circumstances.

(3)    For the purposes of subsection (2), the permitted maximum is such number of weeks' pay as the Secretary of State may specify by regulations.

(4)    Where an employment tribunal makes an order under subsection (1)(a), section 80G shall apply as if the application had been made on the date of the order.

PART IX

TERMINATION OF EMPLOYMENT

*Minimum period of notice*

## 86   Rights of employer and employee to minimum notice

(1)    The notice required to be given by an employer to terminate the contract of employment of a person who has been continuously employed for one month or more—

       (a)     is not less than one week's notice if his period of continuous employment is less than two years,

    (b)   is not less than one week's notice for each year of continuous employment if his period of continuous employment is two years or more but less than twelve years, and

    (c)   is not less than twelve weeks' notice if his period of continuous employment is twelve years or more.

(2)   The notice required to be given by an employee who has been continuously employed for one month or more to terminate his contract of employment is not less than one week.

(3)   Any provision for shorter notice in any contract of employment with a person who has been continuously employed for one month or more has effect subject to subsections (1) and (2); but this section does not prevent either party from waiving his right to notice on any occasion or from accepting a payment in lieu of notice.

(4)   Any contract of employment of a person who has been continuously employed for three months or more which is a contract for a term certain of one month or less shall have effect as if it were for an indefinite period; and, accordingly, subsections (1) and (2) apply to the contract.

(5)   ...

(6)   This section does not affect any right of either party to a contract of employment to treat the contract as terminable without notice by reason of the conduct of the other party.

## 87   Rights of employee in period of notice

(1)   If an employer gives notice to terminate the contract of employment of a person who has been continuously employed for one month or more, the provisions of sections 88 to 91 have effect as respects the liability of the employer for the period of notice required by section 86(1).

(2)   If an employee who has been continuously employed for one month or more gives notice to terminate his contract of employment, the provisions of sections 88 to 91 have effect as respects the liability of the employer for the period of notice required by section 86(2).

(3)   In sections 88 to 91 'period of notice' means—

    (a)   where notice is given by an employer, the period of notice required by section 86(1), and

    (b)   where notice is given by an employee, the period of notice required by section 86(2).

(4)   This section does not apply in relation to a notice given by the employer or the employee if the notice to be given by the employer to terminate the contract must be at least one week more than the notice required by section 86(1).

## 88   Employments with normal working hours

(1)   If an employee has normal working hours under the contract of employment in force during the period of notice and during any part of those normal working hours—

    (a)   the employee is ready and willing to work but no work is provided for him by his employer,

    (b)   the employee is incapable of work because of sickness or injury,

    (c)   the employee is absent from work wholly or partly because of pregnancy or childbirth or on adoption leave, shared parental leave, parental bereavement leave, parental leave or paternity leave, or

    (d)   the employee is absent from work in accordance with the terms of his employment relating to holidays,

the employer is liable to pay the employee for the part of normal working hours covered by any of paragraphs (a), (b), (c) and (d) a sum not less than the amount of remuneration for that part of normal working hours calculated at the average hourly rate of remuneration produced by dividing a week's pay by the number of normal working hours.

(2)   Any payments made to the employee by his employer in respect of the relevant part of the period of notice (whether by way of sick pay, statutory sick pay, maternity pay, statutory maternity pay, paternity pay, statutory paternity pay, adoption pay,

statutory adoption pay, shared parental pay, statutory shared parental pay, parental bereavement pay, statutory parental bereavement pay, holiday pay or otherwise) go towards meeting the employer's liability under this section.

(3)    Where notice was given by the employee, the employer's liability under this section does not arise unless and until the employee leaves the service of the employer in pursuance of the notice.

## 89    Employments without normal working hours

(1)    If an employee does not have normal working hours under the contract of employment in force in the period of notice, the employer is liable to pay the employee for each week of the period of notice a sum not less than a week's pay.

(2)    The employer's liability under this section is conditional on the employee being ready and willing to do work of a reasonable nature and amount to earn a week's pay.

(3)    Subsection (2) does not apply—

(a)    in respect of any period during which the employee is incapable of work because of sickness or injury,

(b)    in respect of any period during which the employee is absent from work wholly or partly because of pregnancy or childbirth or on adoption leave, shared parental leave, parental bereavement leave, parental leave or paternity leave, or

(c)    in respect of any period during which the employee is absent from work in accordance with the terms of his employment relating to holidays.

(4)    Any payment made to an employee by his employer in respect of a period within subsection (3) (whether by way of sick pay, statutory sick pay, maternity pay, statutory maternity pay, paternity pay, statutory paternity pay, adoption pay, statutory adoption pay, shared parental pay, statutory shared parental pay, parental bereavement pay, statutory parental bereavement pay, holiday pay or otherwise) shall be taken into account for the purposes of this section as if it were remuneration paid by the employer in respect of that period.

(5)    Where notice was given by the employee, the employer's liability under this section does not arise unless and until the employee leaves the service of the employer in pursuance of the notice.

## 90    Short-term incapacity benefit, contributory employment and support allowance and industrial injury benefit

(1)    This section has effect where the arrangements in force relating to the employment are such that—

(a)    payments by way of sick pay are made by the employer to employees to whom the arrangements apply, in cases where any such employees are incapable of work because of sickness or injury, and

(b)    in calculating any payment so made to any such employee an amount representing, or treated as representing, short-term incapacity benefit, contributory employment and support allowance or industrial injury benefit is taken into account, whether by way of deduction or by way of calculating the payment as a supplement to that amount.

(2)    If—

(a)    during any part of the period of notice the employee is incapable of work because of sickness or injury,

(b)    one or more payments by way of sick pay are made to him by the employer in respect of that part of the period of notice, and

(c)    in calculating any such payment such an amount as is referred to in paragraph (b) of subsection (1) is taken into account as mentioned in that paragraph,

for the purposes of section 88 or 89 the amount so taken into account shall be treated as having been paid by the employer to the employee by way of sick pay in respect of that part of that period, and shall go towards meeting the liability of the employer under that section accordingly.

## 91    Supplementary

(1)    An employer is not liable under section 88 or 89 to make any payment in respect of a period during which an employee is absent from work with the leave of the employer

granted at the request of the employee, including any period of time off taken in accordance with—

(a)     Part VI of this Act, or

(b)     section 168 or 170 of the Trade Union and Labour Relations (Consolidation) Act 1992 (trade union duties and activities).

(2)     No payment is due under section 88 or 89 in consequence of a notice to terminate a contract given by an employee if, after the notice is given and on or before the termination of the contract, the employee takes part in a strike of employees of the employer.

(3)     If, during the period of notice, the employer breaks the contract of employment, payments received under section 88 or 89 in respect of the part of the period after the breach go towards mitigating the damages recoverable by the employee for loss of earnings in that part of the period of notice.

(4)     If, during the period of notice, the employee breaks the contract and the employer rightfully treats the breach as terminating the contract, no payment is due to the employee under section 88 or 89 in respect of the part of the period falling after the termination of the contract.

(5)     If an employer fails to give the notice required by section 86, the rights conferred by sections 87 to 90 and this section shall be taken into account in assessing his liability for breach of the contract.

(6)     Sections 86 to 90 and this section apply in relation to a contract all or any of the terms of which are terms which take effect by virtue of any provision contained in or having effect under an Act (whether public or local) as in relation to any other contract; and the reference in this subsection to an Act includes, subject to any express provision to the contrary, an Act passed after this Act.

*Written statement of reasons for dismissal*

## 92     Right to written statement of reasons for dismissal

(1)     An employee is entitled to be provided by his employer with a written statement giving particulars of the reasons for the employee's dismissal—

(a)     if the employee is given by the employer notice of termination of his contract of employment,

(b)     if the employee's contract of employment is terminated by the employer without notice, or

(c)     if the employee is employed under a limited-term contract and the contract terminates by virtue of the limiting event without being renewed under the same contract.

(2)     Subject to subsections (4) and (4A), an employee is entitled to a written statement under this section only if he makes a request for one; and a statement shall be provided within fourteen days of such a request.

(3)     Subject to subsections (4) and (4A), an employee is not entitled to a written statement under this section unless on the effective date of termination he has been, or will have been, continuously employed for a period of not less than two years ending with that date.

(4)     An employee is entitled to a written statement under this section without having to request it and irrespective of whether she has been continuously employed for any period if she is dismissed—

(a)     at any time while she is pregnant, or

(b)     after childbirth in circumstances in which her ordinary or additional maternity leave period ends by reason of the dismissal.

(4A)   An employee who is dismissed while absent from work during an ordinary or additional adoption leave period is entitled to a written statement under this section without having to request it and irrespective of whether he has been continuously employed for any period if he is dismissed in circumstances in which that period ends by reason of the dismissal.

(5)     A written statement under this section is admissible in evidence in any proceedings.

(6) Subject to subsection (7), in this section 'the effective date of termination'—

    (a) in relation to an employee whose contract of employment is terminated by notice, means the date on which the notice expires,

    (b) in relation to an employee whose contract of employment is terminated without notice, means the date on which the termination takes effect, and

    (c) in relation to an employee who is employed under a limited-term contract which terminates by virtue of the limiting event without being renewed under the same contract, means the date on which the termination takes effect.

(7) Where—

    (a) the contract of employment is terminated by the employer, and

    (b) the notice required by section 86 to be given by an employer would, if duly given on the material date, expire on a date later than the effective date of termination (as defined by subsection (6)),

the later date is the effective date of termination.

(8) In subsection (7)(b) 'the material date' means—

    (a) the date when notice of termination was given by the employer, or

    (b) where no notice was given, the date when the contract of employment was terminated by the employer.

## 93 Complaints to employment tribunal

(1) A complaint may be presented to an employment tribunal by an employee on the ground that—

    (a) the employer unreasonably failed to provide a written statement under section 92, or

    (b) the particulars of reasons given in purported compliance with that section are inadequate or untrue.

(2) Where an employment tribunal finds a complaint under this section well-founded, the tribunal—

    (a) may make a declaration as to what it finds the employer's reasons were for dismissing the employee, and

    (b) shall make an award that the employer pay to the employee a sum equal to the amount of two weeks' pay.

(3) An employment tribunal shall not consider a complaint under this section relating to the reasons for a dismissal unless it is presented to the tribunal at such a time that the tribunal would, in accordance with section 111, consider a complaint of unfair dismissal in respect of that dismissal presented at the same time.

PART X
UNFAIR DISMISSAL

CHAPTER I
RIGHT NOT TO BE UNFAIRLY DISMISSED

*The right*

## 94 The right

(1) An employee has the right not to be unfairly dismissed by his employer.

(2) Subsection (1) has effect subject to the following provisions of this Part (in particular sections 108 to 110) and to the provisions of the Trade Union and Labour Relations (Consolidation) Act 1992 (in particular sections 237 to 239).

*Dismissal*

## 95 Circumstances in which an employee is dismissed

(1) For the purposes of this Part an employee is dismissed by his employer if (and, subject to subsection (2) only if)—

    (a) the contract under which he is employed is terminated by the employer (whether with or without notice),

(b)     he is employed under a limited term contract and that contract terminates by virtue of the limiting event without being renewed under the same contract, or

(c)     the employee terminates the contract under which he is employed (with or without notice) in circumstances in which he is entitled to terminate it without notice by reason of the employer's conduct.

(2)     An employee shall be taken to be dismissed by his employer for the purposes of this Part if—

(a)     the employer gives notice to the employee to terminate his contract of employment, and

(b)     at a time within the period of that notice the employee gives notice to the employer to terminate the contract of employment on a date earlier than the date on which the employer's notice is due to expire;

and the reason for the dismissal is to be taken to be the reason for which the employer's notice is given.

## 97     Effective date of termination

(1)     Subject to the following provisions of this section, in this Part 'the effective date of termination'—

(a)     in relation to an employee whose contract of employment is terminated by notice, whether given by his employer or by the employee, means the date on which the notice expires,

(b)     in relation to an employee whose contract of employment is terminated without notice, means the date on which the termination takes effect, and

(c)     in relation to an employee who is employed under a limited term contract which terminates by virtue of the limiting event without being renewed under the same contract, means the date on which the termination takes effect.

(2)     Where—

(a)     the contract of employment is terminated by the employer, and

(b)     the notice required by section 86 to be given by an employer would, if duly given on the material date, expire on a date later than the effective date of termination (as defined by subsection (1)),

for the purposes of sections 108(1), 119(1) and 227(3) the later date is the effective date of termination.

(3)     In subsection (2)(b) 'the material date' means—

(a)     the date when notice of termination was given by the employer, or

(b)     where no notice was given, the date when the contract of employment was terminated by the employer.

(4)     Where—

(a)     the contract of employment is terminated by the employee,

(b)     the material date does not fall during a period of notice given by the employer to terminate that contract, and

(c)     had the contract been terminated not by the employee but by notice given on the material date by the employer, that notice would have been required by section 86 to expire on a date later than the effective date of termination (as defined by subsection (1)),

for the purposes of sections 108(1), 119(1) and 227(3) the later date is the effective date of termination.

(5)     In subsection (4) 'the material date' means—

(a)     the date when notice of termination was given by the employee, or

(b)     where no notice was given, the date when the contract of employment was terminated by the employee.

(6)     ...

*Fairness*

## 98     General

(1)     In determining for the purposes of this Part whether the dismissal of an employee is fair or unfair, it is for the employer to show—

     (a)     the reason (or, if more than one, the principal reason) for the dismissal, and

     (b)     that it is either a reason falling within subsection (2) or some other substantial reason of a kind such as to justify the dismissal of an employee holding the position which the employee held.

(2)    A reason falls within this subsection if it—

     (a)     relates to the capability or qualifications of the employee for performing work of the kind which he was employed by the employer to do,

     (b)     relates to the conduct of the employee,

     (ba)    ...

     (c)     is that the employee was redundant, or

     (d)     is that the employee could not continue to work in the position which he held without contravention (either on his part or on that of his employer) of a duty or restriction imposed by or under an enactment.

(2A)  ...

(3)    In subsection (2)(a)—

     (a)     'capability', in relation to an employee, means his capability assessed by reference to skill, aptitude, health or any other physical or mental quality, and

     (b)     'qualifications', in relation to an employee, means any degree, diploma or other academic, technical or professional qualification relevant to the position which he held.

(3A)  ...

(4)    Where the employer has fulfilled the requirements of subsection (1), the determination of the question whether the dismissal is fair or unfair (having regard to the reason shown by the employer)—

     (a)     depends on whether in the circumstances (including the size and administrative resources of the employer's undertaking) the employer acted reasonably or unreasonably in treating it as a sufficient reason for dismissing the employee, and

     (b)     shall be determined in accordance with equity and the substantial merits of the case.

(5)    ...

(6)    Subsection (4) is subject to—

     (a)     sections 98A to 107 of this Act, and

     (b)     sections 152, 153, 238 and 238A of the Trade Union and Labour Relations (Consolidation) Act 1992 (dismissal on ground of trade union membership or activities or in connection with industrial action).

*Other dismissals*

## 99   Leave for family reasons

(1)    An employee who is dismissed shall be regarded for the purposes of this Part as unfairly dismissed if—

     (a)     the reason or principal reason for the dismissal is of a prescribed kind, or

     (b)     the dismissal takes place in prescribed circumstances.

(2)    In this section 'prescribed' means prescribed by regulations made by the Secretary of State.

(3)    A reason or set of circumstances prescribed under this section must relate to—

     (a)     pregnancy, childbirth or maternity,

     (aa)    time off under section 57ZE,

     (ab)    time off under section 57ZJ or 57ZL,

     (b)     ordinary, compulsory or additional maternity leave,

     (ba)    ordinary or additional adoption leave,

     (bb)    shared parental leave,

     (c)     parental leave,

     (ca)    paternity leave,

     (cb)    parental bereavement leave, or

     (d)     time off under section 57A;

and it may also relate to redundancy or other factors.

(4)   A reason or set of circumstances prescribed under subsection (1) satisfies subsection (3)(c) or (d) if it relates to action which an employee—

    (a)   takes

    (b)   agrees to take, or

    (c)   refuses to take, under or in respect of a collective or workforce agreement which deals with parental leave.

(5)   Regulations under this section may—

    (a)   make different provision for different cases or circumstances;

    (b)   apply any enactment, in such circumstances as may be specified, in relation to persons regarded as unfairly dismissed by reason of this section.

## 100   Health and safety cases

(1)   An employee who is dismissed shall be regarded for the purposes of this Part as unfairly dismissed if the reason (or, if more than one, the principal reason) for the dismissal is that—

    (a)   having been designated by the employer to carry out activities in connection with preventing or reducing risks to health and safety at work, the employee carried out (or proposed to carry out) any such activities,

    (b)   being a representative of workers on matters of health and safety at work or member of a safety committee—

        (i)   in accordance with arrangements established under or by virtue of any enactment, or

        (ii)   by reason of being acknowledged as such by the employer,

    the employee performed (or proposed to perform) any functions as such a representative or a member of such a committee,

    (ba)   the employee took part (or proposed to take part) in consultation with the employer pursuant to the Health and Safety (Consultation with Employees) Regulations 1996 or in an election of representatives of employee safety within the meaning of those Regulations (whether as a candidate or otherwise),

    (c)   being an employee at a place where—

        (i)   there was no such representative or safety committee, or

        (ii)   there was such a representative or safety committee but it was not reasonably practicable for the employee to raise the matter by those means,

    he brought to his employer's attention, by reasonable means, circumstances connected with his work which he reasonably believed were harmful or potentially harmful to health or safety,

    (d)   in circumstances of danger which the employee reasonably believed to be serious and imminent and which he could not reasonably have been expected to avert, he left (or proposed to leave) or (while the danger persisted) refused to return to his place of work or any dangerous part of his place of work, or

    (e)   in circumstances of danger which the employee reasonably believed to be serious and imminent, he took (or proposed to take) appropriate steps to protect himself or other persons from the danger.

(2)   For the purposes of subsection (1)(e) whether steps which an employee took (or proposed to take) were appropriate is to be judged by reference to all the circumstances including, in particular, his knowledge and the facilities and advice available to him at the time.

(3)   Where the reason (or, if more than one, the principal reason) for the dismissal of an employee is that specified in subsection (1)(e), he shall not be regarded as unfairly dismissed if the employer shows that it was (or would have been) so negligent for the employee to take the steps which he took (or proposed to take) that a reasonable employer might have dismissed him for taking (or proposing to take) them.

## 101   Shop workers and betting workers who refuse Sunday work

(1)   Where an employee who is—

    (a)   a protected shop worker or an opted-out shop worker, or

    (b)   a protected betting worker or an opted-out betting worker, is dismissed, he shall be regarded for the purposes of this Part as unfairly dismissed if the reason (or, if more than one, the principal reason) for the dismissal is that he refused (or proposed to refuse) to do shop work, or betting work, on Sunday or on a particular Sunday.

(2) Subsection (1) does not apply in relation to an opted-out shop worker or an opted-out betting worker where the reason (or principal reason) for the dismissal is that he refused (or proposed to refuse) to do shop work, or betting work, on any Sunday or Sundays falling before the end of the notice period.

(3) A shop worker or betting worker who is dismissed shall be regarded for the purposes of this Part as unfairly dismissed if the reason (or, if more than one, the principal reason) for the dismissal is that the shop worker or betting worker gave (or proposed to give) an opting-out notice to the employer.

(4) For the purposes of section 36(2)(b) or 41(1)(b), the appropriate date in relation to this section is the effective date of termination.

## 101ZA  Shop workers who refuse to work additional hours on Sunday

(1) Subsection (2) applies where a shop worker has given an objection notice that has not been withdrawn and he or she is dismissed.

(2) The shop worker is to be regarded for the purposes of this Part as unfairly dismissed if the reason (or the principal reason) for the dismissal is that he or she refused, or proposed to refuse, to do shop work for additional hours on Sunday or on a particular Sunday.

(3) Subsection (2) does not apply where the reason (or principal reason) for the dismissal is that the shop worker refused (or proposed to refuse) to do shop work for additional hours on any Sunday or Sundays falling before the end of the relevant period.

(4) A shop worker who is dismissed is to be regarded for the purposes of this Part as unfairly dismissed if the reason (or principal reason) for the dismissal is that the worker gave (or proposed to give) an objection notice to the employer.

(5) In this section—
'additional hours' and 'objection notice' have the meanings given by section 41A(2);
'relevant period' means the period determined by section 43ZA(2) (but subject to section 41D(3)).

## 101A  Working time cases

(1) An employee who is dismissed shall be regarded for the purposes of this Part as unfairly dismissed if the reason (or, if more than one, the principal reason) for the dismissal is that the employee—

(a) refused (or proposed to refuse) to comply with a requirement which the employer imposed (or proposed to impose) in contravention of the Working Time Regulations 1998,

(b) refused (or proposed to refuse) to forgo a right conferred on him by those Regulations,

(c) failed to sign a workforce agreement for the purposes of those Regulations, or to enter into, or agree to vary or extend, any other agreement with his employer which is provided for in those Regulations, or

(d) being—
(i) a representative of members of the workforce for the purposes of Schedule 1 to those Regulations, or
(ii) a candidate in an election in which any person elected will, on being elected, be such a representative,
performed (or proposed to perform) any functions or activities as such a representative or candidate.

…

## 102  Trustees of occupational pension schemes

(1) An employee who is dismissed shall be regarded for the purposes of this Part as unfairly dismissed if the reason (or, if more than one, the principal reason) for the dismissal is that, being a trustee of a relevant occupational pension scheme which

relates to his employment, the employee performed (or proposed to perform) any functions as such a trustee.

(1A) This section applies to an employee who is a director of a company which is a trustee of a relevant occupational pension scheme as it applies to an employee who is a trustee of such a scheme (references to such a trustee being read for this purpose as references to such a director).

(2) In this section 'relevant occupational pension scheme' means an occupational pension scheme (as defined in section 1 of the Pension Schemes Act 1993) established under a trust.

## 103 Employee representatives

(1) An employee who is dismissed shall be regarded for the purposes of this Part as unfairly dismissed if the reason (or, if more than one, the principal reason) for the dismissal is that the employee, being—

    (a) an employee representative for the purposes of Chapter II of Part IV of the Trade Union and Labour Relations (Consolidation) Act 1992 (redundancies) or Regulations 9, 13 and 15 of the Transfer of Undertakings (Protection of Employment) Regulations 2006, or

    (b) a candidate in an election in which any person elected will, on being elected, be such an employee representative,

performed (or proposed to perform) any functions or activities as such an employee representative or candidate.

(2) An employee who is dismissed shall be regarded for the purposes of this Part as unfairly dismissed if the reason (or, if more than one, the principal reason) for the dismissal is that the employee took part in an election of employee representatives for the purposes of Chapter II of Part IV of the Trade Union and Labour Relations (Consolidation) Act 1992 (redundancies) or Regulations 9, 13 and 15 of the Transfer of Undertakings (Protection of Employment) Regulations 2006.

## 103A Protected disclosure

An employee who is dismissed shall be regarded for the purposes of this Part as unfairly dismissed if the reason (or, if more than one, the principal reason) for the dismissal is that the employee made a protected disclosure.

## 104 Assertion of statutory right

(1) An employee who is dismissed shall be regarded for the purposes of this Part as unfairly dismissed if the reason (or, if more than one, the principal reason) for the dismissal is that the employee—

    (a) brought proceedings against the employer to enforce a right of his which is a relevant statutory right, or

    (b) alleged that the employer had infringed a right of his which is a relevant statutory right.

(2) It is immaterial for the purposes of subsection (1)—

    (a) whether or not the employee has the right, or

    (b) whether or not the right has been infringed;

but, for that subsection to apply, the claim to the right and that it has been infringed must be made in good faith.

(3) It is sufficient for subsection (1) to apply that the employee, without specifying the right, made it reasonably clear to the employer what the right claimed to have been infringed was.

(4) The following are relevant statutory rights for the purposes of this section—

    (a) any right conferred by this Act for which the remedy for its infringement is by way of a complaint or reference to an employment tribunal,

    (b) the right conferred by section 86 of this Act,

    (c) the rights conferred by sections 68, 86, 145A, 145B, 146, 168, 168A, 169 and 170 of the Trade Union and Labour Relations (Consolidation) Act 1992 (deductions from pay, union activities and time off),

    (d) the rights conferred by the Working Time Regulations 1998, the Merchant Shipping (Maritime Labour Convention) (Hours of Work) Regulations 2018, the Merchant Shipping (Working Time: Inland Waterway) Regulations 2003, the Fishing Vessels (Working Time: Sea-fisherman) Regulations 2004 or the Cross-border Railway Services (Working Time) Regulations 2008, and

    (e)    the rights conferred by the Transfer of Undertakings (Protection of Employment) Regulations 2006.

(5)    In this section any reference to an employer includes, where the right in question is conferred by section 63A, the principal (within the meaning of section 63A(3)).

## 104A  The national minimum wage

(1)    An employee who is dismissed shall be regarded for the purposes of this Part as unfairly dismissed if the reason (or, if more than one, the principal reason) for the dismissal is that—

    (a)    any action was taken, or was proposed to be taken, by or on behalf of the employee with a view to enforcing, or otherwise securing the benefit of, a right of the employee's to which this section applies; or

    (b)    the employer was prosecuted for an offence under section 31 of the National Minimum Wage Act 1998 as a result of action taken by or on behalf of the employee for the purpose of enforcing, or otherwise securing the benefit of, a right of the employee's to which this section applies; or

    (c)    the employee qualifies, or will or might qualify, for the national minimum wage or for a particular rate of national minimum wage.

(2)    It is immaterial for the purposes of paragraph (a) or (b) of subsection (1) above—

    (a)    whether or not the employee has the right, or

    (b)    whether or not the right has been infringed,

but, for that subsection to apply, the claim to the right and, if applicable, the claim that it has been infringed must be made in good faith.

(3)    The following are the rights to which this section applies—

    (a)    any right conferred by, or by virtue of, any provision of the National Minimum Wage Act 1998 for which the remedy for its infringement is by way of a complaint to an employment tribunal; and

    (b)    any right conferred by section 17 of the National Minimum Wage Act 1998 (worker receiving less than national minimum wage entitled to additional remuneration).

## 104C  Flexible working

An employee who is dismissed shall be regarded for the purposes of this Part as unfairly dismissed if the reason (or, if more than one, the principal reason) for the dismissal is that the employee—

    (a)    made (or proposed to make) an application under section 80F,

    (b)    ...

    (c)    brought proceedings against the employer under section 80H, or

    (d)    alleged the existence of any circumstance which would constitute a ground for bringing such proceedings.

## 104F  Blacklists

(1)    An employee who is dismissed shall be regarded for the purposes of this Part as unfairly dismissed if the reason (or, if more than one, the principal reason) for the dismissal relates to a prohibited list, and either—

    (a)    the employer contravenes regulation 3 of the 2010 Regulations in relation to that prohibited list, or

    (b)    the employer—

        (i)    relies on information supplied by a person who contravenes that regulation in relation to that list, and

        (ii)    knows or ought reasonably to know that the information relied on is supplied in contravention of that regulation.

(2)    If there are facts from which the tribunal could conclude, in the absence of any other explanation, that the employer—

    (a)    contravened regulation 3 of the 2010 Regulations, or

    (b)    relied on information supplied in contravention of that regulation, the tribunal must find that such a contravention or reliance on information occurred, unless the employer shows that it did not.

(3)   In this section—

'the 2010 Regulations' means the Employment Relations Act 1999 (Blacklists) Regulations 2010, and

'prohibited list' has the meaning given in those Regulations (see regulation 3(2)).

## 104G  Employee shareholder status

An employee who is dismissed is to be regarded for the purposes of this Part as unfairly dismissed if the reason (or, if more than one, the principal reason) for the dismissal is that the employee refused to accept an offer by the employer for the employee to become an employee shareholder (within the meaning of section 205A).

## 105  Redundancy

(1)   An employee who is dismissed shall be regarded for the purposes of this Part as unfairly dismissed if—

(a)   the reason (or, if more than one, the principal reason) for the dismissal is that the employee was redundant,

(b)   it is shown that the circumstances constituting the redundancy applied equally to one or more other employees in the same undertaking who held positions similar to that held by the employee and who have not been dismissed by the employer, and

(c)   it is shown that any of subsections (2A) to (7N) applies.

(2)   ...

(2A)  This subsection applies if the reason (or, if more than one, the principal reason) for which the employee was selected for dismissal was one of those specified in subsection (1) of section 98B (unless the case is one to which subsection (2) of that section applies).

(3)   This subsection applies if the reason (or, if more than one, the principal reason) for which the employee was selected for dismissal was one of those specified in subsection (1) of section 100 (read with subsections (2) and (3) of that section).

(4)   This subsection applies if either—

(a)   the employee was a protected shop worker or an opted-out shop worker, or a protected betting worker or an opted-out betting worker, and the reason (or, if more than one, the principal reason) for which the employee was selected for dismissal was that specified in subsection (1) of section 101 (read with subsection (2) of that section), or

(b)   the employee was a shop worker or a betting worker and the reason (or, if more than one, the principal reason) for which the employee was selected for dismissal was that specified in subsection (3) of that section.

(4A)  This subsection applies if the reason (or, if more than one, the principal reason) for which the employee was selected for dismissal was one of those specified in section 101A.

(5)   This subsection applies if the reason (or, if more than one, the principal reason) for which the employee was selected for dismissal was that specified in section 102(1).

(6)   This subsection applies if the reason (or, if more than one, the principal reason) for which the employee was selected for dismissal was that specified in section 103.

(6A)  This subsection applies if the reason (or, if more than one, the principal reason) for which the employee was selected for dismissal was that specified in section 103A.

(7)   This subsection applies if the reason (or, if more than one, the principal reason) for which the employee was selected for dismissal was one of those specified in subsection (1) of section 104 (read with subsections (2) and (3) of that section).

(7A)  This subsection applies if the reason (or, if more than one, the principal reason) for which the employee was selected for dismissal was one of those specified in subsection (1) of section 104A (read with subsection (2) of that section).

(7B) This subsection applies if the reason (or, if more than one, the principal reason) for which the employee was selected for dismissal was one of those specified in subsection (1) of section 104B (read with subsection (2) of that section).

(7BA) This subsection applies if the reason (or, if more than one, the principal reason) for which the employee was selected for dismissal was one of those specified in section 104C.

(7C) This subsection applies if—

    (a)    the reason (or, if more than one, the principal reason) for which the employee was selected for dismissal was the reason mentioned in section 238A(2) of the Trade Union and Labour Relations (Consolidation) Act 1992 (participation in official industrial action), and

    (b)    subsection (3), (4) or (5) of that section applies to the dismissal.

(7D) This subsection applies if the reason (or, if more than one, the principal reason) for which the employee was selected for dismissal was one specified in paragraph (3) or (6) of regulation 28 of the Transnational Information and Consultation of Employees Regulations 1999 (read with paragraphs (4) and (7) of that regulation).

(7E) This subsection applies if the reason (or, if more than one, the principal reason) for which the employee was selected for dismissal was one specified in paragraph (3) of regulation 7 of the Part-time Workers (Prevention of Less Favourable Treatment) Regulations 2000 (unless the case is one to which paragraph (4) of that regulation applies).

(7F) This subsection applies if the reason (or, if more than one, the principal reason) for which the employee was selected for dismissal was one specified in paragraph (3) of regulation 6 of the Fixed-term Employees (Prevention of Less Favourable Treatment) Regulations 2002 (unless the case is one to which paragraph (4) of that regulation applies).

(7G) This subsection applies if the reason (or, if more than one, the principal reason) for which the employee was selected for dismissal was one specified in paragraph (3) or (6) of regulation 42 of the European Public Limited-Liability Company Regulations 2004 (read with paragraphs (4) and (7) of that regulation).

(7H) This subsection applies if the reason (or, if more than one, the principal reason) for which the employee was selected for dismissal was one specified in paragraph (3) or (6) of regulation 30 of the Information and Consultation of Employees Regulations 2004 (read with paragraphs (4) and (7) of that regulation).

(7I) This subsection applies if the reason (or, if more than one, the principal reason) for which the employee was selected for dismissal was one specified in paragraph 5(3) or (5) of the Schedule to the Occupational and Personal Pension Schemes (Consultation by Employers and Miscellaneous Amendment) Regulations 2006 (read with paragraph 5(6) of that Schedule).

(7IA) …

(7J) This subsection applies if the reason (or, if more than one, the principal reason) for which the employee was selected for dismissal was one specified in paragraph (3) or (6) of regulation 31 of the European Cooperative Society (Involvement of Employees) Regulations 2006 (read with paragraphs (4) and (7) of that regulation).

(7K) …

(7L) This subsection applies if the reason (or, if more than one, the principal reason) for which the employee was selected for dismissal was one specified in paragraph (3) or (6) of regulation 29 of the European Public Limited-Liability Company (Employee Involvement) (Great Britain) Regulations 2009 (SI 2009/2401) (read with paragraphs (4) and (7) of that regulation).

(7M) This subsection applies if—

    (a)    the reason (or, if more than one, the principal reason) for which the employee was selected for dismissal was the one specified in the opening words of section 104F(1), and

    (b)    the condition in paragraph (a) or (b) of that subsection was met.

(7N) This subsection applies if the reason (or, if more than one, the principal reason) for which the employee was selected for dismissal was one specified in paragraph (3) of regulation 17 of the Agency Workers Regulations 2010 (unless the case is one to which paragraph (4) of that regulation applies).

(8)   For the purposes of section 36(2)(b) or 41(1)(b), the appropriate date in relation to this section is the effective date of termination.

(9)   In this Part 'redundancy case' means a case where paragraphs (a) and (b) of subsection (1) of this section are satisfied.

## 106   Replacements

(1)   Where this section applies to an employee he shall be regarded for the purposes of section 98(1)(b) as having been dismissed for a substantial reason of a kind such as to justify the dismissal of an employee holding the position which the employee held.

(2)   This section applies to an employee where—

    (a)   on engaging him the employer informs him in writing that his employment will be terminated on the resumption of work by another employee who is, or will be, absent wholly or partly because of pregnancy or childbirth, or on adoption leave or shared parental leave, and

    (b)   the employer dismisses him in order to make it possible to give work to the other employee.

(3)   This section also applies to an employee where—

    (a)   on engaging him the employer informs him in writing that his employment will be terminated on the end of a suspension of another employee from work on medical grounds or maternity grounds (within the meaning of Part VII), and

    (b)   the employer dismisses him in order to make it possible to allow the resumption of work by the other employee.

(4)   Subsection (1) does not affect the operation of section 98(4) in a case to which this section applies.

## 107   Pressure on employer to dismiss unfairly

(1)   This section applies where there falls to be determined for the purposes of this Part a question—

    (a)   as to the reason, or principal reason, for which an employee was dismissed,

    (b)   whether the reason or principal reason for which an employee was dismissed was a reason fulfilling the requirement of section 98(1)(b), or

    (c)   whether an employer acted reasonably in treating the reason or principal reason for which an employee was dismissed as a sufficient reason for dismissing him.

(2)   In determining the question no account shall be taken of any pressure which by calling, organising, procuring or financing a strike or other industrial action, or threatening to do so, was exercised on the employer to dismiss the employee; and the question shall be determined as if no such pressure had been exercised.

*Exclusion of right*

## 108   Qualifying period of employment

(1)   Section 94 does not apply to the dismissal of an employee unless he has been continuously employed for a period of not less than two years ending with the effective date of termination.

(2)   If an employee is dismissed by reason of any such requirement or recommendation as is referred to in section 64(2), subsection (1) has effect in relation to that dismissal as if for the words 'two years' there were substituted the words 'one month'.

    ...

(4)   Subsection (1) does not apply if the reason (or, if more than one, the principal reason) for the dismissal is, or relates to, the employee's political opinions or affiliation.

(5)   Subsection (1) does not apply if the reason (or, if more than one, the principal reason) for the dismissal is, or is connected with, the employee's membership of a reserve force (as defined in section 374 of the Armed Forces Act 2006).

## 110   Dismissal procedures agreements

(1)   Where a dismissal procedures agreement is designated by an order under subsection (3) which is for the time being in force—

   (a)   the provisions of that agreement relating to dismissal shall have effect in substitution for any rights under section 94, and

   (b)   accordingly, section 94 does not apply to the dismissal of an employee from any employment if it is employment to which, and he is an employee to whom, those provisions of the agreement apply.

(2)   But if the agreement includes provision that it does not apply to dismissals of particular descriptions, subsection (1) does not apply in relation to a dismissal of any such description.

(3)   An order designating a dismissal procedures agreement may be made by the Secretary of State, on an application being made to him jointly by all the parties to the agreement, if he is satisfied that—

   (a)   every trade union which is a party to the agreement is an independent trade union,

   (b)   the agreement provides for procedures to be followed in cases where an employee claims that he has been, or is in the course of being, unfairly dismissed,

   (c)   those procedures are available without discrimination to all employees falling within any description to which the agreement applies,

   (d)   the remedies provided by the agreement in respect of unfair dismissal are on the whole as beneficial as (but not necessarily identical with) those provided in respect of unfair dismissal by this Part,

   (e)   the agreement includes provision either for arbitration in every case or for—

      (i)   arbitration where (by reason of equality of votes or for any other reason) a decision under the agreement cannot otherwise be reached, and

      (ii)   a right to submit to arbitration any question of law arising out of such a decision, and

   (f)   the provisions of the agreement are such that it can be determined with reasonable certainty whether or not a particular employee is one to whom the agreement applies.

(3A) The Secretary of State may by order amend subsection (3) so as to add to the conditions specified in that subsection such conditions as he may specify in the order.

(4)   If at any time when an order under subsection (3) is in force in relation to a dismissal procedures agreement the Secretary of State is satisfied, whether on an application made to him by any of the parties to the agreement or otherwise, either—

   (a)   that it is the desire of all the parties to the agreement that the order should be revoked, or

   (b)   that the agreement no longer satisfies all the conditions specified in subsection (3), the Secretary of State shall revoke the order by an order under this subsection.

(5)   The transitional provisions which may be made in an order under subsection (4) include, in particular, provisions directing—

   (a)   that an employee—

      (i)   shall not be excluded from his right under section 94 where the effective date of termination falls within a transitional period which ends with the date on which the order takes effect and which is specified in the order, and

      (ii)   shall have an extended time for presenting a complaint under section 111 in respect of a dismissal where the effective date of termination falls within that period, and

   (b)   that, where the effective date of termination falls within such a transitional period, an employment tribunal shall, in determining any complaint of unfair dismissal presented by an employee to whom the dismissal procedures agreement applies, have regard to such considerations as are specified in the order (in addition to those specified in this Part and section 10(4) and (5) of the Employment Tribunals Act 1996).

(6) Where an award is made under a designated dismissal procedures agreement—
  (a) in England and Wales it may be enforced, by leave of the county court, in the same manner as a judgment of the court to the same effect and, where leave is given, judgment may be entered in terms of the award, and
  (b) in Scotland it may be recorded for execution in the Books of Council and Session and shall be enforceable accordingly.

## CHAPTER II
## REMEDIES FOR UNFAIR DISMISSAL

*Introductory*

## 111 Complaints to employment tribunal

(1) A complaint may be presented to an employment tribunal against an employer by any person that he was unfairly dismissed by the employer.
(2) Subject to the following provisions of this section, an employment tribunal shall not consider a complaint under this section unless it is presented to the tribunal—
  (a) before the end of the period of three months beginning with the effective date of termination, or
  (b) within such further period as the tribunal considers reasonable in a case where it is satisfied that it was not reasonably practicable for the complaint to be presented before the end of that period of three months.
(3) Where a dismissal is with notice, an employment tribunal shall consider a complaint under this section if it is presented after the notice is given but before the effective date of termination.
(4) In relation to a complaint which is presented as mentioned in subsection (3), the provisions of this Act, so far as they relate to unfair dismissal, have effect as if—
  (a) references to a complaint by a person that he was unfairly dismissed by his employer included references to a complaint by a person that his employer has given him notice in such circumstances that he will be unfairly dismissed when the notice expires,
  (b) references to reinstatement included references to the withdrawal of the notice by the employer,
  (c) references to the effective date of termination included references to the date which would be the effective date of termination on the expiry of the notice, and
  (d) references to an employee ceasing to be employed included references to an employee having been given notice of dismissal.
(5) Where the dismissal is alleged to be unfair by virtue of section 104F (blacklists)—
  (a) subsection (2)(b) does not apply, and
  (b) an employment tribunal may consider a complaint that is otherwise out of time if, in all the circumstances of the case, it considers that it is just and equitable to do so.

## 111A Confidentiality of negotiations before termination of employment

(1) Evidence of pre-termination negotiations is inadmissible in any proceedings on a complaint under section 111.
This is subject to subsections (3) to (5).
(2) In subsection (1) 'pre-termination negotiations' means any offer made or discussions held, before the termination of the employment in question, with a view to it being terminated on terms agreed between the employer and the employee.
(3) Subsection (1) does not apply where, according to the complainant's case, the circumstances are such that a provision (whenever made) contained in, or made under, this or any other Act requires the complainant to be regarded for the purposes of this Part as unfairly dismissed.
(4) In relation to anything said or done which in the tribunal's opinion was improper, or was connected with improper behaviour, subsection (1) applies only to the extent that the tribunal considers just.
(5) Subsection (1) does not affect the admissibility, on any question as to costs or expenses, of evidence relating to an offer made on the basis that the right to refer to it on any such question is reserved.

## 112 The remedies: orders and compensation

(1) This section applies where, on a complaint under section 111, an employment tribunal finds that the grounds of the complaint are well-founded.

(2) The tribunal shall—

    (a) explain to the complainant what orders may be made under section 113 and in what circumstances they may be made, and

    (b) ask him whether he wishes the tribunal to make such an order.

(3) If the complainant expresses such a wish, the tribunal may make an order under section 113.

(4) If no order is made under section 113, the tribunal shall make an award of compensation for unfair dismissal (calculated in accordance with sections 118 to 126) to be paid by the employer to the employee.

(5), (6) ...

*Orders for reinstatement or re-engagement*

## 113 The orders

An order under this section may be—

    (a) an order for reinstatement (in accordance with section 114), or

    (b) an order for re-engagement (in accordance with section 115),

as the tribunal may decide.

## 114 Order for reinstatement

(1) An order for reinstatement is an order that the employer shall treat the complainant in all respects as if he had not been dismissed.

(2) On making an order for reinstatement the tribunal shall specify—

    (a) any amount payable by the employer in respect of any benefit which the complainant might reasonably be expected to have had but for the dismissal (including arrears of pay) for the period between the date of termination of employment and the date of reinstatement,

    (b) any rights and privileges (including seniority and pension rights) which must be restored to the employee, and

    (c) the date by which the order must be complied with.

(3) If the complainant would have benefited from an improvement in his terms and conditions of employment had he not been dismissed, an order for reinstatement shall require him to be treated as if he had benefited from that improvement from the date on which he would have done so but for being dismissed.

(4) In calculating for the purposes of subsection (2)(a) any amount payable by the employer, the tribunal shall take into account, so as to reduce the employer's liability, any sums received by the complainant in respect of the period between the date of termination of employment and the date of reinstatement by way of—

    (a) wages in lieu of notice or ex gratia payments paid by the employer, or

    (b) remuneration paid in respect of employment with another employer,

and such other benefits as the tribunal thinks appropriate in the circumstances.

(5) ...

## 115 Order for re-engagement

(1) An order for re-engagement is an order, on such terms as the tribunal may decide, that the complainant be engaged by the employer, or by a successor of the employer or by an associated employer, in employment comparable to that from which he was dismissed or other suitable employment.

(2) On making an order for re-engagement the tribunal shall specify the terms on which re-engagement is to take place, including—

    (a) the identity of the employer,

    (b) the nature of the employment

    (c) the remuneration for the employment,

    (d) any amount payable by the employer in respect of any benefit which the complainant might reasonably be expected to have had but for the dismissal (including arrears of pay) for the period between the date of termination of employment and the date of re-engagement,

(e)    any rights and privileges (including seniority and pension rights) which must be restored to the employee, and

(f)    the date by which the order must be complied with.

(3)    In calculating for the purposes of subsection (2)(d) any amount payable by the employer, the tribunal shall take into account, so as to reduce the employer's liability, any sums received by the complainant in respect of the period between the date of termination of employment and the date of re-engagement by way of—

(a)    wages in lieu of notice or ex gratia payments paid by the employer, or

(b)    remuneration paid in respect of employment with another employer,

and such other benefits as the tribunal thinks appropriate in the circumstances.

(4)    ...

## 116    Choice of order and its terms

(1)    In exercising its discretion under section 113 the tribunal shall first consider whether to make an order for reinstatement and in so doing shall take into account—

(a)    whether the complainant wishes to be reinstated,

(b)    whether it is practicable for the employer to comply with an order for reinstatement, and

(c)    where the complainant caused or contributed to some extent to the dismissal, whether it would be just to order his reinstatement.

(2)    If the tribunal decides not to make an order for reinstatement it shall then consider whether to make an order for re-engagement and, if so, on what terms.

(3)    In so doing the tribunal shall take into account—

(a)    any wish expressed by the complainant as to the nature of the order to be made,

(b)    whether it is practicable for the employer (or a successor or an associated employer)

to comply with an order for re-engagement, and

(c)    where the complainant caused or contributed to some extent to the dismissal, whether it would be just to order his re-engagement and (if so) on what terms.

(4)    Except in a case where the tribunal takes into account contributory fault under subsection (3)(c) it shall, if it orders re-engagement, do so on terms which are, so far as is reasonably practicable, as favourable as an order for reinstatement.

(5)    Where in any case an employer has engaged a permanent replacement for a dismissed employee, the tribunal shall not take that fact into account in determining, for the purposes of subsection (1)(b) or (3)(b), whether it is practicable to comply with an order for reinstatement or re-engagement.

(6)    Subsection (5) does not apply where the employer shows—

(a)    that it was not practicable for him to arrange for the dismissed employee's work to be done without engaging a permanent replacement, or

(b)    that—

(i)    he engaged the replacement after the lapse of a reasonable period, without having heard from the dismissed employee that he wished to be reinstated or re-engaged, and

(ii)    when the employer engaged the replacement it was no longer reasonable for him to arrange for the dismissed employee's work to be done except by a permanent replacement.

## 117    Enforcement of order and compensation

(1)    An employment tribunal shall make an award of compensation, to be paid by the employer to the employee, if—

(a)    an order under section 113 is made and the complainant is reinstated or re-engaged, but

(b)    the terms of the order are not fully complied with.

(2)    Subject to section 124, the amount of the compensation shall be such as the tribunal thinks fit having regard to the loss sustained by the complainant in consequence of the failure to comply fully with the terms of the order.

(2A)   There shall be deducted from any award under subsection (1) the amount of any award made under section 112(5) at the time of the order under section 113.

(3)  Subject to subsections (1) and (2), if an order under section 113 is made but the complainant is not reinstated or re-engaged in accordance with the order, the tribunal shall make—

    (a)  an award of compensation for unfair dismissal (calculated in accordance with sections 118 to 126), and

    (b)  except where this paragraph does not apply, an additional award of compensation of an amount not less than twenty-six nor more than fifty-two weeks' pay,

to be paid by the employer to the employee.

(4)  Subsection (3)(b) does not apply where—

    (a)  the employer satisfies the tribunal that it was not practicable to comply with the order,

    (b)  ...

(5), (6) ...

(7)  Where in any case an employer has engaged a permanent replacement for a dismissed employee, the tribunal shall not take that fact into account in determining for the purposes of subsection (4)(a) whether it was practicable to comply with the order for reinstatement or re-engagement unless the employer shows that it was not practicable for him to arrange for the dismissed employee's work to be done without engaging a permanent replacement.

(8)  Where in any case an employment tribunal finds that the complainant has unreasonably prevented an order under section 113 from being complied with, in making an award of compensation for unfair dismissal it shall take that conduct into account as a failure on the part of the complainant to mitigate his loss.

*Compensation*

## 118  General

(1)  Where a tribunal makes an award of compensation for unfair dismissal under section 112(4) or 117(3)(a) the award shall consist of—

    (a)  a basic award (calculated in accordance with sections 119 to 122 and 126), and

    (b)  a compensatory award (calculated in accordance with sections 123, 124, 124A and 126).

(2)–(4) ...

## 119  Basic award

(1)  Subject to the provisions of this section, sections 120 to 122 and section 126, the amount of the basic award shall be calculated by—

    (a)  determining the period, ending with the effective date of termination, during which the employee has been continuously employed,

    (b)  reckoning backwards from the end of that period the number of years of employment falling within that period, and

    (c)  allowing the appropriate amount for each of those years of employment.

(2)  In subsection (1)(c) 'the appropriate amount' means—

    (a)  one and a half weeks' pay for a year of employment in which the employee was not below the age of forty-one,

    (b)  one week's pay for a year of employment (not within paragraph (a)) in which he was not below the age of twenty-two, and

    (c)  half a week's pay for a year of employment not within paragraph (a) or (b).

(3)  Where twenty years of employment have been reckoned under subsection (1), no account shall be taken under that subsection of any year of employment earlier than those twenty years.

(4)  ...

(6)  ...

## 120  Basic award: minimum in certain cases

(1)  The amount of the basic award (before any reduction under section 122) shall not be less than £6,959 where the reason (or, if more than one, the principal reason)—

    (a)  in a redundancy case, for selecting the employee for dismissal, or

    (b)  otherwise, for the dismissal,

is one of those specified in section 100(1)(a) and (b), 101A(d), 102(1) or 103.

(1A), (1B) ...

(1C) Where an employee is regarded as unfairly dismissed by virtue of section 104F (blacklists) (whether or not the dismissal is unfair or regarded as unfair for any other reason), the amount of the basic award of compensation (before any reduction is made under section 122) shall not be less than £5,000.

(2)    ...

## 121    Basic award of two weeks' pay in certain cases

The amount of the basic award shall be two weeks' pay where the tribunal finds that the reason (or, where there is more than one, the principal reason) for the dismissal of the employee is that he was redundant and the employee—

(a)    by virtue of section 138 is not regarded as dismissed for the purposes of Part XI, or

(b)    by virtue of section 141 is not, or (if he were otherwise entitled) would not be, entitled to a redundancy payment.

## 122    Basic award: reductions

(1)    Where the tribunal finds that the complainant has unreasonably refused an offer by the employer which (if accepted) would have the effect of reinstating the complainant in his employment in all respects as if he had not been dismissed, the tribunal shall reduce or further reduce the amount of the basic award to such extent as it considers just and equitable having regard to that finding.

(2)    Where the tribunal considers that any conduct of the complainant before the dismissal (or, where the dismissal was with notice, before the notice was given) was such that it would be just and equitable to reduce or further reduce the amount of the basic award to any extent, the tribunal shall reduce or further reduce that amount accordingly.

(3)    Subsection (2) does not apply in a redundancy case unless the reason for selecting the employee for dismissal was one of those specified in section 100(1)(a) and (b), 101A(d), 102(1) or 103; and in such a case subsection (2) applies only to so much of the basic award as is payable because of section 120.

(3A) Where the complainant has been awarded any amount in respect of the dismissal under a designated dismissal procedures agreement, the tribunal shall reduce or further reduce the amount of the basic award to such extent as it considers just and equitable having regard to that award.

(4)    The amount of the basic award shall be reduced or further reduced by the amount of—

(a)    any redundancy payment awarded by the tribunal under Part XI in respect of the same dismissal, or

(b)    any payment made by the employer to the employee on the ground that the dismissal was by reason of redundancy (whether in pursuance of Part XI or otherwise).

(5)    Where a dismissal is regarded as unfair by virtue of section 104F (blacklists), the amount of the basic award shall be reduced or further reduced by the amount of any basic award in respect of the same dismissal under section 156 of the Trade Union and Labour Relations (Consolidation) Act 1992 (minimum basic award in case of dismissal on grounds related to trade union membership or activities).

## 123    Compensatory award

(1)    Subject to the provisions of this section and sections 124, 124A and 126, the amount of the compensatory award shall be such amount as the tribunal considers just and equitable in all the circumstances having regard to the loss sustained by the complainant in consequence of the dismissal in so far as that loss is attributable to action taken by the employer.

(2)    The loss referred to in subsection (1) shall be taken to include—

(a)    any expenses reasonably incurred by the complainant in consequence of the dismissal, and

(b)    subject to subsection (3), loss of any benefit which he might reasonably be expected to have had but for the dismissal.

(3)    The loss referred to in subsection (1) shall be taken to include in respect of any loss of—

(a)    any entitlement or potential entitlement to a payment on account of dismissal by reason of redundancy (whether in pursuance of Part XI or otherwise), or

(b)    any expectation of such a payment,

only the loss referable to the amount (if any) by which the amount of that payment would have exceeded the amount of a basic award (apart from any reduction under section 122) in respect of the same dismissal.

(4)     In ascertaining the loss referred to in subsection (1) the tribunal shall apply the same rule concerning the duty of a person to mitigate his loss as applies to damages recoverable under the common law of England and Wales or (as the case may be) Scotland.

(5)     In determining, for the purposes of subsection (1), how far any loss sustained by the complainant was attributable to action taken by the employer, no account shall be taken of any pressure which by—

(a)     calling, organising, procuring or financing a strike or other industrial action, or

(b)     threatening to do so,

was exercised on the employer to dismiss the employee; and that question shall be determined as if no such pressure had been exercised.

(6)     Where the tribunal finds that the dismissal was to any extent caused or contributed to by any action of the complainant, it shall reduce the amount of the compensatory award by such proportion as it considers just and equitable having regard to that finding.

(6A) Where—

(a)     the reason (or principal reason) for the dismissal is that the complainant made a protected disclosure, and

(b)     it appears to the tribunal that the disclosure was not made in good faith,

the tribunal may, if it considers it just and equitable in all the circumstances to do so, reduce any award it makes to the complainant by no more than 25%.

(7)     If the amount of any payment made by the employer to the employee on the ground that the dismissal was by reason of redundancy (whether in pursuance of Part XI or otherwise) exceeds the amount of the basic award which would be payable but for section 122(4), that excess goes to reduce the amount of the compensatory award.

(8)     Where the amount of the compensatory award falls to be calculated for the purposes of an award under section 117(3)(a), there shall be deducted from the compensatory award any award made under section 112(5) at the time of the order under section 113.

## 124    Limit of compensatory award etc.

(1)     The amount of—

(a)     any compensation awarded to a person under section 117(1) and (2), or

(b)     a compensatory award to a person calculated in accordance with section 123, shall not exceed the amount specified in subsection (1ZA).

(1ZA) The amount specified in this subsection is the lower of—

(a)     £93,878 and

(b)     52 multiplied by a week's pay of the person concerned.

(1A) Subsection (1) shall not apply to compensation awarded, or a compensatory award made, to a person in a case where he is regarded as unfairly dismissed by virtue of section 100, 103A, 105(3) or 105(6A).

(2)     ...

(3)     In the case of compensation awarded to a person under section 117(1) and (2), the limit imposed by this section may be exceeded to the extent necessary to enable the award fully to reflect the amount specified as payable under section 114(2)(a) or section 115(2)(d).

(4)     Where—

(a)     a compensatory award is an award under paragraph (a) of subsection (3) of section 117, and

(b)     an additional award falls to be made under paragraph (b) of that subsection,

the limit imposed by this section on the compensatory award may be exceeded to the extent necessary to enable the aggregate of the compensatory and additional awards fully to reflect the amount specified as payable under section 114(2)(a) or section 115(2)(d).

(5)     The limit imposed by this section applies to the amount which the employment tribunal would, apart from this section, award in respect of the subject matter of the complaint after taking into account—

(a)     any payment made by the respondent to the complainant in respect of that matter, and

(b)     any reduction in the amount of the award required by any enactment or rule of law.

### 124A  Adjustments under the Employment Act 2002

Where an award of compensation for unfair dismissal falls to be—

    (a)    reduced or increased under section 207A of the Trade Union and Labour Relations (Consolidation) Act 1992 (effect of failure to comply with Code: adjustment of awards), or

    (b)    increased under section 38 of that Act (failure to give statement of employment particulars),

the adjustment shall be in the amount awarded under section 118(1)(b) and shall be applied immediately before any reduction under section 123(6) or (7).

### 126  Acts which are both unfair dismissal and discrimination

(1)    This section applies where compensation falls to be awarded in respect of any act both under—

    (a)    the provisions of this Act relating to unfair dismissal, and

    (b)    the Equality Act 2010.

(2)    An employment tribunal shall not award compensation under either of those Acts or Regulations in respect of any loss or other matter which is or has been taken into account under the other by the tribunal (or another employment tribunal) in awarding compensation on the same or another complaint in respect of that act.

*Interim relief*

### 128  Interim relief pending determination of complaint

(1)    An employee who presents a complaint to an employment tribunal that he has been unfairly dismissed and—

    (a)    that the reason (or if more than one the principal reason) for the dismissal is one of those specified in—

        (i)    section 100(1)(a) and (b), 101A(d), 102(1), 103 or 103A, or

        (ii)    paragraph 161(2) of Schedule A1 to the Trade Union and Labour Relations (Consolidation) Act 1992, or

    (b)    that the reason (or, if more than one, the principal reason) for which the employee was selected for dismissal was the one specified in the opening words of section 104F(1) and the condition in paragraph (a) or (b) of that subsection was met,

may apply to the tribunal for interim relief.

(2)    The tribunal shall not entertain an application for interim relief unless it is presented to the tribunal before the end of the period of seven days immediately following the effective date of termination (whether before, on or after that date).

(3)    The tribunal shall determine the application for interim relief as soon as practicable after receiving the application.

(4)    The tribunal shall give to the employer not later than seven days before the date of the hearing a copy of the application together with notice of the date, time and place of the hearing.

(5)    The tribunal shall not exercise any power it has of postponing the hearing of an application for interim relief except where it is satisfied that special circumstances exist which justify it in doing so.

### 129  Procedure on hearing of application and making of order

(1)    This section applies where, on hearing an employee's application for interim relief, it appears to the tribunal that it is likely that on determining the complaint to which the application relates the tribunal will find—

    (a)    that the reason (or if more than one the principal reason) for the dismissal is one of those specified in—

        (i)    section 100(1)(a) and (b), 101A(d), 102(1), 103 or 103A, or

        (ii)    paragraph 161(2) of Schedule A1 to the Trade Union and Labour Relations (Consolidation) Act 1992, or

    (b)    that the reason (or, if more than one, the principal reason) for which the employee was selected for dismissal was the one specified in the opening words of section 104F(1) and the condition in paragraph (a) or (b) of that subsection was met.

(2)    The tribunal shall announce its findings and explain to both parties (if present)—

    (a)    what powers the tribunal may exercise on the application, and

    (b)    in what circumstances it will exercise them.

(3)   The tribunal shall ask the employer (if present) whether he is willing, pending the determination or settlement of the complaint—

(a)   to reinstate the employee (that is, to treat him in all respects as if he had not been dismissed), or

(b)   if not, to re-engage him in another job on terms and conditions not less favourable than those which would have been applicable to him if he had not been dismissed.

(4)   For the purposes of subsection (3)(b) 'terms and conditions not less favourable than those which would have been applicable to him if he had not been dismissed' means, as regards seniority, pension rights and other similar rights, that the period prior to the dismissal should be regarded as continuous with his employment following the dismissal.

(5)   If the employer states that he is willing to reinstate the employee, the tribunal shall make an order to that effect.

(6)   If the employer—

(a)   states that he is willing to re-engage the employee in another job, and

(b)   specifies the terms and conditions on which he is willing to do so,

the tribunal shall ask the employee whether he is willing to accept the job on those terms and conditions.

(7)   If the employee is willing to accept the job on those terms and conditions, the tribunal shall make an order to that effect.

(8)   If the employee is not willing to accept the job on those terms and conditions—

(a)   where the tribunal is of the opinion that the refusal is reasonable, the tribunal shall make an order for the continuation of his contract of employment, and

(b)   otherwise, the tribunal shall make no order.

(9)   If on the hearing of an application for interim relief the employer—

(a)   fails to attend before the tribunal, or

(b)   states that he is unwilling either to reinstate or re-engage the employee as mentioned in subsection (3),

the tribunal shall make an order for the continuation of the employee's contract of employment.

## 130   Order for continuation of contract of employment

(1)   An order under section 129 for the continuation of a contract of employment is an order that the contract of employment continue in force—

(a)   for the purposes of pay or any other benefit derived from the employment, seniority, pension rights and other similar matters, and

(b)   for the purposes of determining for any purpose the period for which the employee has been continuously employed,

from the date of its termination (whether before or after the making of the order) until the determination or settlement of the complaint.

(2)   Where the tribunal makes such an order it shall specify in the order the amount which is to be paid by the employer to the employee by way of pay in respect of each normal pay period, or part of any such period, falling between the date of dismissal and the determination or settlement of the complaint.

(3)   Subject to the following provisions, the amount so specified shall be that which the employee could reasonably have been expected to earn during that period, or part, and shall be paid—

(a)   in the case of a payment for any such period falling wholly or partly after the making of the order, on the normal pay day for that period, and

(b)   in the case of a payment for any past period, within such time as may be specified in the order.

(4)   If an amount is payable in respect only of part of a normal pay period, the amount shall be calculated by reference to the whole period and reduced proportionately.

(5)   Any payment made to an employee by an employer under his contract of employment, or by way of damages for breach of that contract, in respect of a normal pay period, or part of any such period, goes towards discharging the employer's liability in respect of that period under subsection (2); and, conversely, any payment under that subsection in respect of a period goes towards discharging any liability of the employer under, or in respect of breach of, the contract of employment in respect of that period.

(6) If an employee, on or after being dismissed by his employer, receives a lump sum which, or part of which, is in lieu of wages but is not referable to any normal pay period, the tribunal shall take the payment into account in determining the amount of pay to be payable in pursuance of any such order.

(7) For the purposes of this section, the amount which an employee could reasonably have been expected to earn, his normal pay period and the normal pay day for each such period shall be determined as if he had not been dismissed.

## 131 Application for variation or revocation of order

(1) At any time between—
   (a) the making of an order under section 129, and
   (b) the determination or settlement of the complaint,
   the employer or the employee may apply to an employment tribunal for the revocation or variation of the order on the ground of a relevant change of circumstances since the making of the order.

(2) Sections 128 and 129 apply in relation to such an application as in relation to an original application for interim relief except that, in the case of an application by the employer, section 128(4) has effect with the substitution of a reference to the employee for the reference to the employer.

## 132 Consequence of failure to comply with order

(1) If, on the application of an employee, an employment tribunal is satisfied that the employer has not complied with the terms of an order for the reinstatement or re-engagement of the employee under section 129(5) or (7), the tribunal shall—
   (a) make an order for the continuation of the employee's contract of employment, and
   (b) order the employer to pay compensation to the employee.

(2) Compensation under subsection (1)(b) shall be of such amount as the tribunal considers just and equitable in all the circumstances having regard—
   (a) to the infringement of the employee's right to be reinstated or re-engaged in pursuance of the order, and
   (b) to any loss suffered by the employee in consequence of the non-compliance.

(3) Section 130 applies to an order under subsection (1)(a) as in relation to an order under section 129.

(4) If on the application of an employee an employment tribunal is satisfied that the employer has not complied with the terms of an order for the continuation of a contract of employment subsection (5) or (6) applies.

(5) Where the non-compliance consists of a failure to pay an amount by way of pay specified in the order—
   (a) the tribunal shall determine the amount owed by the employer on the date of the determination, and
   (b) if on that date the tribunal also determines the employee's complaint that he has been unfairly dismissed, it shall specify that amount separately from any other sum awarded to the employee.

(6) In any other case, the tribunal shall order the employer to pay the employee such compensation as the tribunal considers just and equitable in all the circumstances having regard to any loss suffered by the employee in consequence of the noncompliance.

CHAPTER III
SUPPLEMENTARY

## 133 Death of employer or employee

(1) Where—
   (a) an employer has given notice to an employee to terminate his contract of employment, and
   (b) before that termination the employee or the employer dies,
   this Part applies as if the contract had been duly terminated by the employer by notice expiring on the date of the death.

(2) Where—

    (a)    an employee's contract of employment has been terminated,

    (b)    by virtue of subsection (2) or (4) of section 97 a date later than the effective date of termination as defined in subsection (1) of that section is to be treated for certain purposes as the effective date of termination, and

    (c)    the employer or the employee dies before that date,

subsection (2) or (4) of section 97 applies as if the notice referred to in that subsection as required by section 86 expired on the date of the death.

(3) Where an employee has died, sections 113 to 116 do not apply; and, accordingly, if the employment tribunal finds that the grounds of the complaint are well-founded, the case shall be treated as falling within section 112(4) as a case in which no order is made under section 113.

(4) Subsection (3) does not prejudice an order for reinstatement or re-engagement made before the employee's death.

(5) Where an order for reinstatement or re-engagement has been made and the employee dies before the order is complied with—

    (a)    if the employer has before the death refused to reinstate or re-engage the employee in accordance with the order, subsections (3) to (6) of section 117 apply, and an award shall be made under subsection (3)(b) of that section, unless the employer satisfies the tribunal that it was not practicable at the time of the refusal to comply with the order, and

    (b)    if there has been no such refusal, subsections (1) and (2) of that section apply if the employer fails to comply with any ancillary terms of the order which remain capable of fulfilment after the employee's death as they would apply to such a failure to comply fully with the terms of an order where the employee had been reinstated or re-engaged.

PART XI
REDUNDANCY PAYMENTS ETC.

CHAPTER I
RIGHT TO REDUNDANCY PAYMENT

## 135   The right

(1) An employer shall pay a redundancy payment to any employee of his if the employee—

    (a)    is dismissed by the employer by reason of redundancy, or

    (b)    is eligible for a redundancy payment by reason of being laid off or kept on short-time.

(2) Subsection (1) has effect subject to the following provisions of this Part (including, in particular, sections 140 to 144, 149 to 152, 155 to 161 and 164).

CHAPTER II
RIGHT ON DISMISSAL BY REASON OF REDUNDANCY

*Dismissal by reason of redundancy*

## 136   Circumstances in which an employee is dismissed

(1) Subject to the provisions of this section and sections 137 and 138, for the purposes of this Part an employee is dismissed by his employer if (and only if)—

    (a)    the contract under which he is employed by the employer is terminated by the employer (whether with or without notice),

    (b)    he is employed under a limited term contract and that contract terminates by virtue of the limiting event without being renewed under the same contract, or

    (c)    the employee terminates the contract under which he is employed (with or without notice) in circumstances in which he is entitled to terminate it without notice by reason of the employer's conduct.

(2)    Subsection (1)(c) does not apply if the employee terminates the contract without notice in circumstances in which he is entitled to do so by reason of a lock-out by the employer.

(3)    An employee shall be taken to be dismissed by his employer for the purposes of this Part if—

   (a)    the employer gives notice to the employee to terminate his contract of employment, and

   (b)    at a time within the obligatory period of notice the employee gives notice in writing to the employer to terminate the contract of employment on a date earlier than the date on which the employer's notice is due to expire.

(4)    In this Part the 'obligatory period of notice', in relation to notice given by an employer to terminate an employee's contract of employment, means—

   (a)    the actual period of the notice in a case where the period beginning at the time when the notice is given and ending at the time when it expires is equal to the minimum period which (by virtue of any enactment or otherwise) is required to be given by the employer to terminate the contract of employment, and

   (b)    the period which—

      (i)    is equal to the minimum period referred to in paragraph (a), and

      (ii)    ends at the time when the notice expires,

   in any other case.

(5)    Where in accordance with any enactment or rule of law—

   (a)    an act on the part of an employer, or

   (b)    an event affecting an employer (including, in the case of an individual, his death), operates to terminate a contract under which an employee is employed by him, the act or event shall be taken for the purposes of this Part to be a termination of the contract by the employer.

## 138    No dismissal in cases of renewal of contract or re-engagement

(1)    Where—

   (a)    an employee's contract of employment is renewed, or he is re-engaged under a new contract of employment in pursuance of an offer (whether in writing or not) made before the end of his employment under the previous contract, and

   (b)    the renewal or re-engagement takes effect either immediately on, or after an interval of not more than four weeks after, the end of that employment, the employee shall not be regarded for the purposes of this Part as dismissed by his employer by reason of the ending of his employment under the previous contract.

(2)    Subsection (1) does not apply if—

   (a)    the provisions of the contract as renewed, or of the new contract, as to—

      (i)    the capacity and place in which the employee is employed, and

      (ii)    the other terms and conditions of his employment,

   differ (wholly or in part) from the corresponding provisions of the previous contract, and

   (b)    during the period specified in subsection (3)—

      (i)    the employee (for whatever reason) terminates the renewed or new contract, or gives notice to terminate it and it is in consequence terminated, or

      (ii)    the employer, for a reason connected with or arising out of any difference between the renewed or new contract and the previous contract, terminates the renewed or new contract, or gives notice to terminate it and it is in consequence terminated.

(3)    The period referred to in subsection (2)(b) is the period—

   (a)    beginning at the end of the employee's employment under the previous contract, and

   (b)    ending with—

      (i)    the period of four weeks beginning with the date on which the employee starts work under the renewed or new contract, or

      (ii)    such longer period as may be agreed in accordance with subsection (6) for the purpose of retraining the employee for employment under that contract;

and is in this Part referred to as the 'trial period'.

(4) Where subsection (2) applies, for the purposes of this Part—

    (a) the employee shall be regarded as dismissed on the date on which his employment under the previous contract (or, if there has been more than one trial period, the original contract) ended, and

    (b) the reason for the dismissal shall be taken to be the reason for which the employee was then dismissed, or would have been dismissed had the offer (or original offer) of renewed or new employment not been made, or the reason which resulted in that offer being made.

(5) Subsection (2) does not apply if the employee's contract of employment is again renewed, or he is again re-engaged under a new contract of employment, in circumstances such that subsection (1) again applies.

(6) For the purposes of subsection (3)(b)(ii) a period of retraining is agreed in accordance with this subsection only if the agreement—

    (a) is made between the employer and the employee or his representative before the employee starts work under the contract as renewed, or the new contract,

    (b) is in writing,

    (c) specifies the date on which the period of retraining ends, and

    (d) specifies the terms and conditions of employment which will apply in the employee's case after the end of that period.

## 139  Redundancy

(1) For the purposes of this Act an employee who is dismissed shall be taken to be dismissed by reason of redundancy if the dismissal is wholly or mainly attributable to—

    (a) the fact that his employer has ceased or intends to cease—

        (i) to carry on the business for the purposes of which the employee was employed by him, or

        (ii) to carry on that business in the place where the employee was so employed, or

    (b) the fact that the requirements of that business—

        (i) for employees to carry out work of a particular kind, or

        (ii) for employees to carry out work of a particular kind in the place where the employee was employed by the employer,

    have ceased or diminished or are expected to cease or diminish.

(2) For the purposes of subsection (1) the business of the employer together with the business or businesses of his associated employers shall be treated as one (unless either of the conditions specified in paragraphs (a) and (b) of that subsection would be satisfied without so treating them).

(3) For the purposes of subsection (1) the activities carried on by a local authority with respect to the schools maintained by it, and the activities carried on by the governing bodies of those schools, shall be treated as one business (unless either of the conditions specified in paragraphs (a) and (b) of that subsection would be satisfied without so treating them).

(4) Where—

    (a) the contract under which a person is employed is treated by section 136(5) as terminated by his employer by reason of an act or event, and

    (b) the employee's contract is not renewed and he is not re-engaged under a new contract of employment,

    he shall be taken for the purposes of this Act to be dismissed by reason of redundancy if the circumstances in which his contract is not renewed, and he is not re-engaged, are wholly or mainly attributable to either of the facts stated in paragraphs (a) and (b) of subsection (1).

(5) In its application to a case within subsection (4), paragraph (a)(i) of subsection (1) has effect as if the reference in that subsection to the employer included a reference to any person to whom, in consequence of the act or event, power to dispose of the business has passed.

(6) In subsection (1) 'cease' and 'diminish' mean cease and diminish either permanently or temporarily and for whatever reason.

(7) In subsection (3) 'local authority' has the meaning given by section 57G(1) of the Education Act 1996.

*Exclusions*

## 140 Summary dismissal

(1) Subject to subsections (2) and (3), an employee is not entitled to a redundancy payment by reason of dismissal where his employer, being entitled to terminate his contract of employment without notice by reason of the employee's conduct, terminates it either—

    (a) without notice,

    (b) by giving shorter notice than that which, in the absence of conduct entitling the employer to terminate the contract without notice, the employer would be required to give to terminate the contract, or

    (c) by giving notice which includes, or is accompanied by, a statement in writing that the employer would, by reason of the employee's conduct, be entitled to terminate the contract without notice.

(2) Where an employee who—

    (a) has been given notice by his employer to terminate his contract of employment, or (b) has given notice to his employer under section 148(1) indicating his intention to claim a redundancy payment in respect of lay-off or short-time,

takes part in a strike at any relevant time in circumstances which entitle the employer to treat the contract of employment as terminable without notice, subsection (1) does not apply if the employer terminates the contract by reason of his taking part in the strike.

(3) Where the contract of employment of an employee who—

    (a) has been given notice by his employer to terminate his contract of employment, or

    (b) has given notice to his employer under section 148(1) indicating his intention to claim a redundancy payment in respect of lay-off or short-time,

is terminated as mentioned in subsection (1) at any relevant time otherwise than by reason of his taking part in a strike, an employment tribunal may determine that the employer is liable to make an appropriate payment to the employee if on a reference to the tribunal it appears to the tribunal, in the circumstances of the case, to be just and equitable that the employee should receive it.

(4) In subsection (3) 'appropriate payment' means—

    (a) the whole of the redundancy payment to which the employee would have been entitled apart from subsection (1), or

    (b) such part of that redundancy payment as the tribunal thinks fit.

(5) In this section 'relevant time'—

    (a) in the case of an employee who has been given notice by his employer to terminate his contract of employment, means any time within the obligatory period of notice, and

    (b) in the case of an employee who has given notice to his employer under section 148(1), means any time after the service of the notice.

## 141 Renewal of contract or re-engagement

(1) This section applies where an offer (whether in writing or not) is made to an employee before the end of his employment—

    (a) to renew his contract of employment, or

    (b) to re-engage him under a new contract of employment,

with renewal or re-engagement to take effect either immediately on, or after an interval of not more than four weeks after, the end of his employment.

(2) Where subsection (3) is satisfied, the employee is not entitled to a redundancy payment if he unreasonably refuses the offer.

(3) This subsection is satisfied where—

    (a) the provisions of the contract as renewed, or of the new contract, as to—

        (i) the capacity and place in which the employee would be employed, and

        (ii) the other terms and conditions of his employment,

    would not differ from the corresponding provisions of the previous contract, or

(b)  those provisions of the contract as renewed, or of the new contract, would differ from the corresponding provisions of the previous contract but the offer constitutes an offer of suitable employment in relation to the employee.

(4)  The employee is not entitled to a redundancy payment if—

  (a)  his contract of employment is renewed, or he is re-engaged under a new contract of employment, in pursuance of the offer,

  (b)  the provisions of the contract as renewed or new contract as to the capacity or place in which he is employed or the other terms and conditions of his employment differ (wholly or in part) from the corresponding provisions of the previous contract,

  (c)  the employment is suitable in relation to him, and

  (d)  during the trial period he unreasonably terminates the contract, or unreasonably gives notice to terminate it and it is in consequence terminated.

## 142  Employee anticipating expiry of employer's notice

(1)  Subject to subsection (3), an employee is not entitled to a redundancy payment where—

  (a)  he is taken to be dismissed by virtue of section 136(3) by reason of giving to his employer notice terminating his contract of employment on a date earlier than the date on which notice by the employer terminating the contract is due to expire,

  (b)  before the employee's notice is due to expire, the employer gives him a notice such as is specified in subsection (2), and

  (c)  the employee does not comply with the requirements of that notice.

(2)  The employer's notice referred to in subsection (1)(b) is a notice in writing—

  (a)  requiring the employee to withdraw his notice terminating the contract of employment and to continue in employment until the date on which the employer's notice terminating the contract expires, and

  (b)  stating that, unless he does so, the employer will contest any liability to pay to him a redundancy payment in respect of the termination of his contract of employment.

(3)  An employment tribunal may determine that the employer is liable to make an appropriate payment to the employee if on a reference to the tribunal it appears to the tribunal, having regard to—

  (a)  the reasons for which the employee seeks to leave the employment, and

  (b)  the reasons for which the employer requires him to continue in it,

  to be just and equitable that the employee should receive the payment.

(4)  In subsection (3) 'appropriate payment' means—

  (a)  the whole of the redundancy payment to which the employee would have been entitled apart from subsection (1), or

  (b)  such part of that redundancy payment as the tribunal thinks fit.

## 143  Strike during currency of employer's notice

(1)  This section applies where—

  (a)  an employer has given notice to an employee to terminate his contract of employment ('notice of termination'),

  (b)  after the notice is given the employee begins to take part in a strike of employees of the employer, and

  (c)  the employer serves on the employee a notice of extension.

(2)  A notice of extension is a notice in writing which—

  (a)  requests the employee to agree to extend the contract of employment beyond the time of expiry by a period comprising as many available days as the number of working days lost by striking ('the proposed period of extension'),

  (b)  indicates the reasons for which the employer makes that request, and (c) states that the employer will contest any liability to pay the employee a redundancy payment in respect of the dismissal effected by the notice of termination unless either—

    (i)  the employee complies with the request, or

       (ii)    the employer is satisfied that, in consequence of sickness or injury or otherwise, the employee is unable to comply with it or that (even though he is able to comply with it) it is reasonable in the circumstances for him not to do so.

(3)    Subject to subsections (4) and (5), if the employee does not comply with the request contained in the notice of extension, he is not entitled to a redundancy payment by reason of the dismissal effected by the notice of termination.

(4)    Subsection (3) does not apply if the employer agrees to pay a redundancy payment to the employee in respect of the dismissal effected by the notice of termination even though he has not complied with the request contained in the notice of extension.

(5)    An employment tribunal may determine that the employer is liable to make an appropriate payment to the employee if on a reference to the tribunal it appears to the tribunal that—

    (a)    the employee has not complied with the request contained in the notice of extension and the employer has not agreed to pay a redundancy payment in respect of the dismissal effected by the notice of termination, but

    (b)    either the employee was unable to comply with the request or it was reasonable in the circumstances for him not to comply with it.

(6)    In subsection (5) 'appropriate payment' means—

    (a)    the whole of the redundancy payment to which the employee would have been entitled apart from subsection (3), or

    (b)    such part of that redundancy payment as the tribunal thinks fit.

(7)    If the employee—

    (a)    complies with the request contained in the notice of extension, or

    (b)    does not comply with it but attends at his proper or usual place of work and is ready and willing to work on one or more (but not all) of the available days within the proposed period of extension,

the notice of termination has effect, and shall be deemed at all material times to have had effect, as if the period specified in it had been appropriately extended; and sections 87 to 91 accordingly apply as if the period of notice required by section 86 were extended to a corresponding extent.

(8)    In subsection (7) 'appropriately extended' means—

    (a)    in a case within paragraph (a) of that subsection, extended beyond the time of expiry by an additional period equal to the proposed period of extension, and

    (b)    in a case within paragraph (b) of that subsection, extended beyond the time of expiry up to the end of the day (or last of the days) on which he attends at his proper or usual place of work and is ready and willing to work.

## 144    Provisions supplementary to section 143

(1)    For the purposes of section 143 an employee complies with the request contained in a notice of extension if, but only if, on each available day within the proposed period of extension, he—

    (a)    attends at his proper or usual place of work, and

    (b)    is ready and willing to work,

whether or not he has signified his agreement to the request in any other way.

(2)    The reference in section 143(2) to the number of working days lost by striking is a reference to the number of working days in the period—

    (a)    beginning with the date of service of the notice of termination, and

    (b)    ending with the time of expiry, which are days on which the employee in question takes part in a strike of employees of his employer.

(3)    In section 143 and this section—

'available day', in relation to an employee, means a working day beginning at or after the time of expiry which is a day on which he is not taking part in a strike of employees of the employer,

'available day within the proposed period of extension' means an available day which begins before the end of the proposed period of extension,

'time of expiry', in relation to a notice of termination, means the time at which the notice would expire apart from section 143, and

'working day', in relation to an employee, means a day on which, in accordance with his contract of employment, he is normally required to work.

(4)    Neither the service of a notice of extension nor any extension by virtue of section 143(7) of the period specified in a notice of termination affects—

   (a)    any right either of the employer or of the employee to terminate the contract of employment (whether before, at or after the time of expiry) by a further notice or without notice, or

   (b)    the operation of this Part in relation to any such termination of the contract of employment.

*Supplementary*

## 145    The relevant date

(1)    For the purposes of the provisions of this Act relating to redundancy payments 'the relevant date' in relation to the dismissal of an employee has the meaning given by this section.

(2)    Subject to the following provisions of this section, 'the relevant date'—

   (a)    in relation to an employee whose contract of employment is terminated by notice, whether given by his employer or by the employee, means the date on which the notice expires,

   (b)    in relation to an employee whose contract of employment is terminated without notice, means the date on which the termination takes effect, and

   (c)    in relation to an employee who is employed under a limited term contract which terminates by virtue of the limiting event without being renewed under the same contract, means the date on which the termination takes effect.

(3)    Where the employee is taken to be dismissed by virtue of section 136(3) the 'relevant date' means the date on which the employee's notice to terminate his contract of employment expires.

(4)    Where the employee is regarded by virtue of section 138(4) as having been dismissed on the date on which his employment under an earlier contract ended, 'the relevant date' means—

   (a)    for the purposes of section 164(1), the date which is the relevant date as defined by subsection (2) in relation to the renewed or new contract or, where there has been more than one trial period, the last such contract, and

   (b)    for the purposes of any other provision, the date which is the relevant date as defined by subsection (2) in relation to the previous contract or, where there has been more than one such trial period, the original contract.

(5)    Where—

   (a)    the contract of employment is terminated by the employer, and

   (b)    the notice required by section 86 to be given by an employer would, if duly given on the material date, expire on a date later than the relevant date (as defined by the previous provisions of this section),

   for the purposes of sections 155, 162(1) and 227(3) the later date is the relevant date.

(6)    In subsection (5)(b) 'the material date' means—

   (a)    the date when notice of termination was given by the employer, or

   (b)    where no notice was given, the date when the contract of employment was terminated by the employer.

(7)    ...

## 146    Provisions supplementing sections 138 and 141

(1)    In sections 138 and 141—

   (a)    references to re-engagement are to re-engagement by the employer or an associated employer, and

   (b)    references to an offer are to an offer made by the employer or an associated employer.

(2)    For the purposes of the application of section 138(1) or 141(1) to a contract under which the employment ends on a Friday, Saturday or Sunday—

   (a)    the renewal or re-engagement shall be treated as taking effect immediately on the ending of the employment under the previous contract if it takes effect on or before the next Monday after that Friday, Saturday or Sunday, and

   (b)    the interval of four weeks to which those provisions refer shall be calculated as if the employment had ended on that next Monday.

(3)    ...

CHAPTER III
RIGHT BY REASON OF LAY-OFF OR SHORT-TIME

*Lay-off and short-time*

### 147  Meaning of 'lay-off' and 'short-time'

(1)  For the purposes of this Part an employee shall be taken to be laid off for a week if—

    (a)  he is employed under a contract on terms and conditions such that his remuneration under the contract depends on his being provided by the employer with work of the kind which he is employed to do, but

    (b)  he is not entitled to any remuneration under the contract in respect of the week because the employer does not provide such work for him.

(2)  For the purposes of this Part an employee shall be taken to be kept on short-time for a week if by reason of a diminution in the work provided for the employee by his employer (being work of a kind which under his contract the employee is employed to do) the employee's remuneration for the week is less than half a week's pay.

### 148  Eligibility by reason of lay-off or short-time

(1)  Subject to the following provisions of this Part, for the purposes of this Part an employee is eligible for a redundancy payment by reason of being laid off or kept on short-time if—

    (a)  he gives notice in writing to his employer indicating (in whatever terms) his intention to claim a redundancy payment in respect of lay-off or short-time (referred to in this Part as 'notice of intention to claim'), and

    (b)  before the service of the notice he has been laid off or kept on short-time in circumstances in which subsection (2) applies.

(2)  This subsection applies if the employee has been laid off or kept on short-time—

    (a)  for four or more consecutive weeks of which the last before the service of the notice ended on, or not more than four weeks before, the date of service of the notice, or

    (b)  for a series of six or more weeks (of which not more than three were consecutive) within a period of thirteen weeks, where the last week of the series before the service of the notice ended on, or not more than four weeks before, the date of service of the notice.

*Exclusions*

### 149  Counter-notices

Where an employee gives to his employer notice of intention to claim but—

    (a)  the employer gives to the employee, within seven days after the service of that notice, notice in writing (referred to in this Part as a 'counter-notice') that he will contest any liability to pay to the employee a redundancy payment in pursuance of the employee's notice, and

    (b)  the employer does not withdraw the counter-notice by a subsequent notice in writing,

the employee is not entitled to a redundancy payment in pursuance of his notice of intention to claim except in accordance with a decision of an employment tribunal.

### 150  Resignation

(1)  An employee is not entitled to a redundancy payment by reason of being laid off or kept on short-time unless he terminates his contract of employment by giving such period of notice as is required for the purposes of this section before the end of the relevant period.

(2)  The period of notice required for the purposes of this section—

    (a)  where the employee is required by his contract of employment to give more than one week's notice to terminate the contract, is the minimum period which he is required to give, and

    (b)  otherwise, is one week.

(3)  In subsection (1) 'the relevant period'—

    (a)    if the employer does not give a counter-notice within seven days after the service of the notice of intention to claim, is three weeks after the end of those seven days,

    (b)    if the employer gives a counter-notice within that period of seven days but withdraws it by a subsequent notice in writing, is three weeks after the service of the notice of withdrawal, and

    (c)    if—

        (i)    the employer gives a counter-notice within that period of seven days, and does not so withdraw it, and

        (ii)    a question as to the right of the employee to a redundancy payment in pursuance of the notice of intention to claim is referred to an employment tribunal,

    is three weeks after the tribunal has notified to the employee its decision on that reference.

(4)    For the purposes of subsection (3)(c) no account shall be taken of—

    (a)    any appeal against the decision of the tribunal, or

    (b)    any proceedings or decision in consequence of any such appeal.

## 151    Dismissal

(1)    An employee is not entitled to a redundancy payment by reason of being laid off or kept on short-time if he is dismissed by his employer.

(2)    Subsection (1) does not prejudice any right of the employee to a redundancy payment in respect of the dismissal.

## 152    Likelihood of full employment

(1)    An employee is not entitled to a redundancy payment in pursuance of a notice of intention to claim if—

    (a)    on the date of service of the notice it was reasonably to be expected that the employee (if he continued to be employed by the same employer) would, not later than four weeks after that date, enter on a period of employment of not less than thirteen weeks during which he would not be laid off or kept on short-time for any week, and

    (b)    the employer gives a counter-notice to the employee within seven days after the service of the notice of intention to claim.

(2)    Subsection (1) does not apply where the employee—

    (a)    continues or has continued, during the next four weeks after the date of service of the notice of intention to claim, to be employed by the same employer, and

    (b)    is or has been laid off or kept on short-time for each of those weeks.

*Supplementary*

## 153    The relevant date

For the purposes of the provisions of this Act relating to redundancy payments 'the relevant date' in relation to a notice of intention to claim or a right to a redundancy payment in pursuance of such a notice—

    (a)    in a case falling within paragraph (a) of subsection (2) of section 148, means the date on which the last of the four or more consecutive weeks before the service of the notice came to an end, and

    (b)    in a case falling within paragraph (b) of that subsection, means the date on which the last of the series of six or more weeks before the service of the notice came to an end.

## 154    Provisions supplementing sections 148 and 152

For the purposes of sections 148(2) and 152(2)—

    (a)    it is immaterial whether a series of weeks consists wholly of weeks for which the employee is laid off or wholly of weeks for which he is kept on short-time or partly of the one and partly of the other, and

    (b)    no account shall be taken of any week for which an employee is laid off or kept on short-time where the lay-off or short-time is wholly or mainly attributable to a strike or a lock-out (whether or not in the trade or industry in which the employee is employed and whether in Great Britain or elsewhere).

## CHAPTER IV
## GENERAL EXCLUSIONS FROM RIGHT

### 155   Qualifying period of employment

An employee does not have any right to a redundancy payment unless he has been continuously employed for a period of not less than two years ending with the relevant date.

## CHAPTER V
## OTHER PROVISIONS ABOUT REDUNDANCY PAYMENTS

### 162   Amount of a redundancy payment

(1)   The amount of a redundancy payment shall be calculated by—
   (a)   determining the period, ending with the relevant date, during which the employee has been continuously employed,
   (b)   reckoning backwards from the end of that period the number of years of employment falling within that period, and
   (c)   allowing the appropriate amount for each of those years of employment.

(2)   In subsection (1)(c) 'the appropriate amount' means—
   (a)   one and a half weeks' pay for a year of employment in which the employee was not below the age of forty-one,
   (b)   one week's pay for a year of employment (not within paragraph (a)) in which he was not below the age of twenty-two, and
   (c)   half a week's pay for each year of employment not within paragraph (a) or (b).

(3)   Where twenty years of employment have been reckoned under subsection (1), no account shall be taken under that subsection of any year of employment earlier than those twenty years.

(4), (5) …

(6)   Subsections (1) to (3) apply for the purposes of any provision of this Part by virtue of which an employment tribunal may determine that an employer is liable to pay to an employee—
   (a)   the whole of the redundancy payment to which the employee would have had a right apart from some other provision, or
   (b)   such part of the redundancy payment to which the employee would have had a right apart from some other provision as the tribunal thinks fit,
   as if any reference to the amount of a redundancy payment were to the amount of the redundancy payment to which the employee would have been entitled apart from that other provision.

(7), (8) …

### 163   References to employment tribunals

(1)   Any question arising under this Part as to—
   (a)   the right of an employee to a redundancy payment, or
   (b)   the amount of a redundancy payment,
   shall be referred to and determined by an employment tribunal.

(2)   For the purposes of any such reference, an employee who has been dismissed by his employer shall, unless the contrary is proved, be presumed to have been so dismissed by reason of redundancy.

(3)   Any question whether an employee will become entitled to a redundancy payment if he is not dismissed by his employer and he terminates his contract of employment as mentioned in section 150(1) shall for the purposes of this Part be taken to be a question as to the right of the employee to a redundancy payment.

(4)   Where an order under section 157 is in force in respect of an agreement, this section has effect in relation to any question arising under the agreement as to the right of an employee to a payment on the termination of his employment, or as to the amount of such a payment, as if the payment were a redundancy payment and the question arose under this Part.

(5)   Where a tribunal determines under subsection (1) that an employee has a right to a redundancy payment it may order the employer to pay to the worker such amount as the tribunal considers appropriate in all the circumstances to compensate the worker

for any financial loss sustained by him which is attributable to the non-payment of the redundancy payment.

## 164    Claims for redundancy payment

(1)    An employee does not have any right to a redundancy payment unless, before the end of the period of six months beginning with the relevant date—

(a)    the payment has been agreed and paid,

(b)    the employee has made a claim for the payment by notice in writing given to the employer,

(c)    a question as to the employee's right to, or the amount of, the payment has been referred to an employment tribunal, or

(d)    a complaint relating to his dismissal has been presented by the employee under section 111.

(2)    An employee is not deprived of his right to a redundancy payment by subsection (1) if, during the period of six months immediately following the period mentioned in that subsection, the employee—

(a)    makes a claim for the payment by notice in writing given to the employer,

(b)    refers to an employment tribunal a question as to his right to, or the amount of, the payment, or

(c)    presents a complaint relating to his dismissal under section 111,

and it appears to the tribunal to be just and equitable that the employee should receive a redundancy payment.

(3)    In determining under subsection (2) whether it is just and equitable that an employee should receive a redundancy payment an employment tribunal shall have regard to—

(a)    the reason shown by the employee for his failure to take any such step as is referred to in subsection (2) within the period mentioned in subsection (1), and

(b)    all the other relevant circumstances

(4)    …

(5)    Section 207B (extension of time limits to facilitate conciliation before institution of proceedings) applies for the purposes of subsections (1)(c) and (2).

## 165    Written particulars of redundancy payment

(1)    On making any redundancy payment, otherwise than in pursuance of a decision of a tribunal which specifies the amount of the payment to be made, the employer shall give to the employee a written statement indicating how the amount of the payment has been calculated.

(2)    An employer who without reasonable excuse fails to comply with subsection (1) is guilty of an offence and liable on summary conviction to a fine not exceeding level 1 on the standard scale.

(3)    If an employer fails to comply with the requirements of subsection (1), the employee may by notice in writing to the employer require him to give to the employee a written statement complying with those requirements within such period (not being less than one week beginning with the day on which the notice is given) as may be specified in the notice.

(4)    An employer who without reasonable excuse fails to comply with a notice under subsection is guilty of an offence and liable on summary conviction to a fine not exceeding level 3 on the standard scale.

CHAPTER VI
PAYMENTS BY SECRETARY OF STATE

## 166    Applications for payments

(1)    Where an employee claims that his employer is liable to pay to him an employer's payment and either—

(a)    that the employee has taken all reasonable steps, other than legal proceedings, to recover the payment from the employer and the employer has refused or failed to pay it, or has paid part of it and has refused or failed to pay the balance, or

(b) that the employer is insolvent and the whole or part of the payment remains unpaid, the employee may apply to the Secretary of State for a payment under this section.

(2) In this Part 'employer's payment', in relation to an employee, means—

(a) a redundancy payment which his employer is liable to pay to him under this Part,

(aa) a payment which his employer is liable to make to him under an agreement to refrain from instituting or continuing proceedings for a contravention or alleged contravention of section 135 which has effect by virtue of section 203(2)(e) or (f), or

(b) a payment which his employer is, under an agreement in respect of which an order is in force under section 157, liable to make to him on the termination of his contract of employment.

(3) In relation to any case where (in accordance with any provision of this Part) an employment tribunal determines that an employer is liable to pay part (but not the whole) of a redundancy payment the reference in subsection (2)(a) to a redundancy payment is to the part of the redundancy payment.

(4) In subsection (1)(a) 'legal proceedings'—

(a) does not include any proceedings before an employment tribunal, but

(b) includes any proceedings to enforce a decision or award of an employment tribunal.

(5) An employer is insolvent for the purposes of subsection (1)(b)—

(a) where the employer is an individual, if (but only if) subsection (6), (8ZA) or (8A) is satisfied,

(b) where the employer is a company, if (but only if) subsection (7), (8ZA) or (8A) is satisfied,

(c) where the employer is a limited liability partnership, if (but only if) subsection (8), (8ZA) or (8A) is satisfied, and

(d) where the employer is not any of the above, if (but only if) subsection (8ZA) or (8A) is satisfied.

(6) This subsection is satisfied in the case of an employer who is an individual—

(a) in England and Wales if—

(i) he has been made bankrupt or has made a composition or arrangement with his creditors, or

(ii) he has died and his estate falls to be administered in accordance with an order under section 421 of the Insolvency Act 1986, and

(b) in Scotland if—

(i) sequestration of his estate has been awarded or he has executed a trust deed for his creditors or has entered into a composition contract, or

(ii) he has died and a judicial factor appointed under section 11A of the Judicial Factors (Scotland) Act 1889 is required by that section to divide his insolvent estate among his creditors.

(7) This subsection is satisfied in the case of an employer which is a company—

(a) if a winding up order has been made, or a resolution for voluntary winding up has been passed, with respect to the company,

(aa) if the company is in administration for the purposes of the Insolvency Act 1986,

(b) if a receiver or (in England and Wales only) a manager of the company's undertaking has been duly appointed, or (in England and Wales only) possession has been taken, by or on behalf of the holders of any debentures secured by a floating charge, of any property of the company comprised in or subject to the charge, or

(c) if a voluntary arrangement proposed in the case of the company for the purposes of Part I of the Insolvency Act 1986 has been approved under that Part of that Act.

(8) This subsection is satisfied in the case of an employer which is a limited liability partnership—

(a) if a winding-up order, an administration order or a determination for a voluntary winding-up has been made with respect to the limited liability partnership,

(b) if a receiver or (in England and Wales only) a manager of the undertaking of the limited liability partnership has been duly appointed, or (in England and

Wales only) possession has been taken, by or on behalf of the holders of any debentures secured by a floating charge, of any property of the limited liability partnership comprised in or subject to the charge, or

(c)    if a voluntary arrangement proposed in the case of the limited liability partnership for the purpose of Part I of the Insolvency Act 1986 has been approved under that Part of that Act.

(8ZA) This subsection is satisfied in the case of an employer if—

(a)    the employer is a legal person,

(b)    a request has been made for the first opening of collective proceedings—

    (i)    based on the insolvency of the employer, as provided for under the law of any part of the United Kingdom, and

    (ii)    involving the partial or total divestment of the employer's assets and the appointment of a liquidator or a person performing a similar task, and

(c)    any of the following has decided to open the proceedings—

    (i)    a court,

    (ii)    a meeting of creditors, or

    (iii)    the creditors by a decision procedure.

(8A) This subsection is satisfied in the case of an employer if—

(a)    a request has been made for the first opening of collective proceedings—

    (i)    based on the insolvency of the employer, as provided for under the laws, regulations and administrative provisions of a member State, and

    (ii)    involving the partial or total divestment of the employer's assets and the appointment of a liquidator or a person performing a similar task, and

(b)    the competent authority has—

    (i)    decided to open the proceedings, or

    (ii)    established that the employer's undertaking or business has been definitively closed down and the available assets of the employer are insufficient to warrant the opening of the proceedings.

(8B) For the purposes of this section—

(a)    'liquidator or person performing a similar task' includes the official receiver or an administrator, trustee in bankruptcy, judicial factor, supervisor of a voluntary arrangement, or person performing a similar task,

(b)    'competent authority' includes—

    (i)    a court,

    (ii)    a meeting of creditors,

    (iii)    a creditors' committee,

    (iv)    the creditors by a decision procedure, and

    (v)    an authority of a member State empowered to open insolvency proceedings, to confirm the opening of such proceedings or to take decisions in the course of such proceedings.

(8C) An employee may apply under this section only if he or she worked or habitually worked in Great Britain in that employment to which the application relates.

(9)    In this section—

(a)    references to a company are to be read as including references to a charitable incorporated organisation, and

(b)    any reference to the Insolvency Act 1986 in relation to a company is to be read as including a reference to that Act as it applies to charitable incorporated organisations.

## 167    Making of payments

(1)    Where, on an application under section 166 by an employee in relation to an employer's payment, the Secretary of State is satisfied that the requirements specified in subsection

(2)    are met, he shall pay to the employee out of the National Insurance Fund a sum calculated in accordance with section 168 but reduced by so much (if any) of the employer's payment as has already been paid.

(3)    The requirements referred to in subsection (1) are—

(a)    that the employee is entitled to the employer's payment, and

(b)    that one of the conditions specified in paragraphs (a) and (b) of subsection (1) of section 166 is fulfilled, and, in a case where the employer's payment is a payment such as is mentioned in subsection (2)(b) of that section, that the employee's right to the payment arises by virtue of a period of continuous employment (computed in accordance with the provisions of the agreement in question) which is not less than two years.

(4) Where under this section the Secretary of State pays a sum to an employee in respect of an employer's payment—

    (a) all rights and remedies of the employee with respect to the employer's payment, or (if the Secretary of State has paid only part of it) all the rights and remedies of the employee with respect to that part of the employer's payment, are transferred to and vest in the Secretary of State, and

    (b) any decision of an employment tribunal requiring the employer's payment to be paid to the employee has effect as if it required that payment, or that part of it which the Secretary of State has paid, to be paid to the Secretary of State.

(5) Any money recovered by the Secretary of State by virtue of subsection (3) shall be paid into the National Insurance Fund.

## 168 Amount of payments

(1) The sum payable to an employee by the Secretary of State under section 167—

    (a) where the employer's payment to which the employee's application under section 166 relates is a redundancy payment or a part of a redundancy payment, is a sum equal to the amount of the redundancy payment or part,

    (aa) where the employer's payment to which the employee's application under section 166 relates is a payment which his employer is liable to make to him under an agreement having effect by virtue of section 203(2)(e) or (f), is a sum equal to the amount of the employer's payment or of any redundancy payment which the employer would have been liable to pay to the employee but for the agreement, whichever is less, and

    (b) where the employer's payment to which the employee's application under section 166 relates is a payment which the employer is liable to make under an agreement in respect of which an order is in force under section 157, is a sum equal to the amount of the employer's payment or of the relevant redundancy payment, whichever is less.

(2) The reference in subsection (1)(b) to the amount of the relevant redundancy payment is to the amount of the redundancy payment which the employer would have been liable to pay to the employee on the assumptions specified in subsection (3).

(3) The assumptions referred to in subsection (2) are that—

    (a) the order in force in respect of the agreement had not been made,

    (b) the circumstances in which the employer's payment is payable had been such that the employer was liable to pay a redundancy payment to the employee in those circumstances,

    (c) the relevant date, in relation to any such redundancy payment, had been the date on which the termination of the employee's contract of employment is treated as having taken effect for the purposes of the agreement, and

    (d) in so far as the provisions of the agreement relating to the circumstances in which the continuity of an employee's period of employment is to be treated as broken, and the weeks which are to count in computing a period of employment, are inconsistent with the provisions of Chapter I of Part XIV, the provisions of the agreement were substituted for those provisions.

## 169 Information relating to applications for payments

(1) Where an employee makes an application to the Secretary of State under section 166, the Secretary of State may, by notice in writing given to the employer, require the employer—

    (a) to provide the Secretary of State with such information, and

    (b) to produce for examination on behalf of the Secretary of State documents in his custody or under his control of such description,

as the Secretary of State may reasonably require for the purpose of determining whether the application is well-founded.

(2) Where a person on whom a notice is served under subsection (1) fails without reasonable excuse to comply with a requirement imposed by the notice, he is guilty

of an offence and liable on summary conviction to a fine not exceeding level 3 on the standard scale.

(3)　A person is guilty of an offence if—

    (a)　in providing any information required by a notice under subsection (1), he makes a statement which he knows to be false in a material particular or recklessly makes a statement which is false in a material particular, or

    (b)　he produces for examination in accordance with a notice under subsection (1) a document which to his knowledge has been wilfully falsified.

(4)　A person guilty of an offence under subsection (3) is liable—

    (a)　on summary conviction, to a fine not exceeding the statutory maximum or to imprisonment for a term not exceeding three months, or to both, or

    (b)　on conviction on indictment, to a fine or to imprisonment for a term not exceeding two years, or to both.

## 170　References to employment tribunals

(1)　Where on an application made to the Secretary of State for a payment under section 166 it is claimed that an employer is liable to pay an employer's payment, there shall be referred to an employment tribunal—

    (a)　any question as to the liability of the employer to pay the employer's payment, and

    (b)　any question as to the amount of the sum payable in accordance with section 168.

(2)　For the purposes of any reference under this section an employee who has been dismissed by his employer shall, unless the contrary is proved, be presumed to have been so dismissed by reason of redundancy.

PART XII

INSOLVENCY OF EMPLOYERS

## 182　Employee's rights on insolvency of employer

If, on an application made to him in writing by an employee, the Secretary of State is satisfied that—

    (a)　the employee's employer has become insolvent,

    (b)　the employee's employment has been terminated, and

    (c)　on the appropriate date the employee was entitled to be paid the whole or part of any debt to which this Part applies,

the Secretary of State shall, subject to section 186, pay the employee out of the National Insurance Fund the amount to which, in the opinion of the Secretary of State, the employee is entitled in respect of the debt.

## 183　Insolvency

(1)　An employer has become insolvent for the purposes of this Part—

    (a)　where the employer is an individual, if (but only if) subsection (2), (4ZA) or (4A) is satisfied,

    (b)　where the employer is a company, if (but only if) subsection (3), (4ZA) or (4A) is satisfied,

    (c)　where the employer is a limited liability partnership if (but only if) subsection (4), (4ZA) or (4A) is satisfied; and

    (d)　where the employer is not any of the above, if (but only if) subsection (4ZA) or (4A) is satisfied.

(2)　This subsection is satisfied in the case of an employer who is an individual—

    (a)　in England and Wales if—

        (i)　he has been made bankrupt or has made a composition or arrangement with his creditors, or

        (ii)　he has died and his estate falls to be administered in accordance with an order under section 421 of the Insolvency Act 1986, and

    (b)　in Scotland if—

        (i)　sequestration of his estate has been awarded or he has executed a trust deed for his creditors or has entered into a composition contract, or

        (ii)　he has died and a judicial factor appointed under section 11A of the Judicial Factors (Scotland) Act 1889 is required by that section to divide his insolvent estate among his creditors.

(3)   This subsection is satisfied in the case of an employer which is a company—
   (a)    if a winding up order has been made, or a resolution for voluntary winding up has been passed, with respect to the company,
   (aa)   if the company is in administration for the purposes of the Insolvency Act 1986,
   (b)    if a receiver or (in England and Wales only) a manager of the company's undertaking has been duly appointed, or (in England and Wales only) possession has been taken, by or on behalf of the holders of any debentures secured by a floating charge, of any property of the company comprised in or subject to the charge, or
   (c)    if a voluntary arrangement proposed in the case of the company for the purposes of Part I of the Insolvency Act 1986 has been approved under that Part of that Act.

(4)   This subsection is satisfied in the case of an employer which is a limited liability partnership—
   (a)    if a winding-up order, an administration order or a determination for a voluntary winding-up has been made with respect to the limited liability partnership,
   (b)    if a receiver or (in England and Wales only) a manager of the undertaking of the limited liability partnership has been duly appointed, or (in England and Wales only) possession has been taken, by or on behalf of the holders of any debentures secured by a floating charge, of any property of the limited liability partnership comprised in or subject to the charge, or
   (c)    if a voluntary arrangement proposed in the case of the limited liability partnership for the purposes of Part I of the Insolvency Act 1986 has been approved under that Part of that Act.

(4ZA) This subsection is satisfied in the case of an employer if—
   (a)    the employer is a legal person,
   (b)    a request has been made for the first opening of collective proceedings—
       (i)    based on the insolvency of the employer, as provided for under the law of any part of the United Kingdom, and
       (ii)   involving the partial or total divestment of the employer's assets and the appointment of a liquidator or a person performing a similar task, and
   (c)    any of the following has decided to open the proceedings—
       (i)    a court,
       (ii)   a meeting of creditors, or
       (iii)  the creditors by a decision procedure.

(4A)  This subsection is satisfied in the case of an employer if—
   (a)    a request has been made for the first opening of collective proceedings—
       (i)    based on the insolvency of the employer, as provided for under the laws, regulations and administrative provisions of a member State, and
       (ii)   involving the partial or total divestment of the employer's assets and the appointment of a liquidator or a person performing a similar task, and
   (b)    the competent authority has—
       (i)    decided to open the proceedings, or
       (ii)   established that the employer's undertaking or business has been definitively closed down and the available assets of the employer are insufficient to warrant the opening of the proceedings.

(4B)  For the purposes of this section—
   (a)    'liquidator or person performing a similar task' includes the official receiver or an administrator, trustee in bankruptcy, judicial factor, supervisor of a voluntary arrangement, or person performing a similar task,
   (b)    'competent authority' includes—
       (i)    a court,
       (ii)   a meeting of creditors,
       (iii)  a creditors' committee,
       (iv)   the creditors by a decision procedure, and
       (v)    an authority of a member State empowered to open insolvency proceedings, to confirm the opening of such proceedings or to take decisions in the course of such proceedings.

(4C)  An employee may apply under section 182 (employee's rights on insolvency of employer) only if he or she worked or habitually worked in England, Wales or Scotland in that employment to which the application relates.

(5)    In this section—
    (a)    references to a company are to be read as including references to a charitable incorporated organisation, and
    (b)    any reference to the Insolvency Act 1986 in relation to a company is to be read as including a reference to that Act as it applies to charitable incorporated organisations.

## 184    Debts to which Part applies

(1)    This Part applies to the following debts—
    (a)    any arrears of pay in respect of one or more (but not more than eight) weeks,
    (b)    any amount which the employer is liable to pay the employee for the period of notice required by section 86(1) or (2) or for any failure of the employer to give the period of notice required by section 86(1),
    (c)    any holiday pay—
        (i)    in respect of a period or periods of holiday not exceeding six weeks in all, and
        (ii)    to which the employee became entitled during the twelve months ending with the appropriate date,
    (d)    any basic award of compensation for unfair dismissal or so much of an award under a designated dismissal procedures agreement as does not exceed any basic award of compensation for unfair dismissal to which the employee would be entitled but for the agreement, and
    (e)    any reasonable sum by way of reimbursement of the whole or part of any fee or premium paid by an apprentice or articled clerk.
(2)    For the purposes of subsection (1)(a) the following amounts shall be treated as arrears of pay—
    (a)    a guarantee payment,
    (b)    any payment for time off under Part VI of this Act or section 169 of the Trade Union and Labour Relations (Consolidation) Act 1992 (payment for time off for carrying out trade union duties etc.),
    (c)    remuneration on suspension on medical grounds under section 64 of this Act and remuneration on suspension on maternity grounds under section 68 of this Act, and
    (d)    remuneration under a protective award under section 189 of the Trade Union and Labour Relations (Consolidation) Act 1992.
(3)    In subsection (1)(c) 'holiday pay', in relation to an employee, means—
    (a)    pay in respect of a holiday actually taken by the employee, or
    (b)    any accrued holiday pay which, under the employee's contract of employment, would in the ordinary course have become payable to him in respect of the period of a holiday if his employment with the employer had continued until he became entitled to a holiday.
(4)    A sum shall be taken to be reasonable for the purposes of subsection (1)(e) in a case where a trustee in bankruptcy, or (in Scotland) a [trustee or interim trustee in the sequestration of an estate under the Bankruptcy (Scotland) Act 2016], or liquidator has been or is required to be
    (a)    as respects England and Wales, if it is admitted to be reasonable by the trustee in bankruptcy or liquidator under section 348 of the Insolvency Act 1986 (effect of bankruptcy on apprenticeships etc.), whether as originally enacted or as applied to the winding up of a company by rules under section 411 of that Act, and
    (b)    as respects Scotland, if it is accepted by the trustee or liquidator for the purposes of the sequestration or winding up.

## 185    The appropriate date

In this Part 'the appropriate date'—
    (a)    in relation to arrears of pay (not being remuneration under a protective award made under section 189 of the Trade Union and Labour Relations (Consolidation) Act 1992 and to holiday pay, means the date on which the employer became insolvent,
    (b)    in relation to a basic award of compensation for unfair dismissal and to remuneration under a protective award so made, means whichever is the latest of—
        (i)    the date on which the employer became insolvent,

        (ii)    the date of the termination of the employee's employment, and

        (iii)   the date on which the award was made, and

(c)    in relation to any other debt to which this Part applies, means whichever is the latter of—

        (i)    the date on which the employer became insolvent, and

        (ii)   the date of the termination of the employee's employment.

## 186   Limit on amount payable under section 182

(1)   The total amount payable to an employee in respect of any debt to which this Part applies, where the amount of the debt is referable to a period of time, shall not exceed—

    (a)    £571 in respect of any one week, or

    (b)    in respect of a shorter period, an amount bearing the same proportion to £571 as that shorter period bears to a week.

(2)   ...

## 188   Complaints to employment tribunals

(1)   A person who has applied for a payment under section 182 may present a complaint to an employment tribunal—

    (a)    that the Secretary of State has failed to make any such payment, or

    (b)    that any such payment made by him is less than the amount which should have been paid.

(2)   An employment tribunal shall not consider a complaint under subsection (1) unless it is presented—

    (a)    before the end of the period of three months beginning with the date on which the decision of the Secretary of State on the application was communicated to the applicant, or

    (b)    within such further period as the tribunal considers reasonable in a case where it is not reasonably practicable for the complaint to be presented before the end of that period of three months.

(3)   Where an employment tribunal finds that the Secretary of State ought to make a payment under section 182, the tribunal shall—

    (a)    make a declaration to that effect, and

    (b)    declare the amount of any such payment which it finds the Secretary of State ought to make.

## 189   Transfer to Secretary of State of rights and remedies

(1)   Where, in pursuance of section 182, the Secretary of State makes a payment to an employee in respect of a debt to which this Part applies—

    (a)    on the making of the payment any rights and remedies of the employee in respect of the debt (or, if the Secretary of State has paid only part of it, in respect of that part) become rights and remedies of the Secretary of State, and

    (b)    any decision of an employment tribunal requiring an employer to pay that debt to the employee has the effect that the debt (or the part of it which the Secretary of State has paid) is to be paid to the Secretary of State.

(2)   Where a debt (or any part of a debt) in respect of which the Secretary of State has made a payment in pursuance of section 182 constitutes—

    (a)    a preferential debt within the meaning of the Insolvency Act 1986 for the purposes of any provision of that Act (including any such provision as applied by any order made under that Act) or any provision of the Companies Act 2006, or

    (b)    a preferred debt within the meaning of the Bankruptcy (Scotland) Act 2016 for the purposes of any provision of that Act (including any such provision as applied by section 11A of the Judicial Factors (Scotland) Act 1889),

the rights which become rights of the Secretary of State in accordance with subsection (1) include any right arising under any such provision by reason of the status of the debt (or that part of it) as a preferential or preferred debt.

(3)   In computing for the purposes of any provision mentioned in subsection (2)(a) or (b) the aggregate amount payable in priority to other creditors of the employer in respect of—

    (a)    any claim of the Secretary of State to be paid in priority to other creditors of the employer by virtue of subsection (2), and

(b)    any claim by the employee to be so paid made in his own right, any claim of the Secretary of State to be so paid by virtue of subsection (2) shall be treated as if it were a claim of the employee.

(4)    ...

## PART XIII
## MISCELLANEOUS

### CHAPTER I
### PARTICULAR TYPES OF EMPLOYMENT

### CHAPTER II
### OTHER MISCELLANEOUS MATTERS

*Contracting out etc. and remedies*

## 203    Restrictions on contracting out

(1)    Any provision in an agreement (whether a contract of employment or not) is void in so far as it purports—

(a)    to exclude or limit the operation of any provision of this Act, or

(b)    to preclude a person from bringing any proceedings under this Act before an employment tribunal.

(2)    Subsection (1)—

(a)    does not apply to any provision in a collective agreement excluding rights under section 28 if an order under section 35 is for the time being in force in respect of it,

(b)    does not apply to any provision in a dismissal procedures agreement excluding the right under section 94 if that provision is not to have effect unless an order under section 110 is for the time being in force in respect of it,

(c)    does not apply to any provision in an agreement if an order under section 157 is for the time being in force in respect of it,

(d)    ...

(e)    does not apply to any agreement to refrain from instituting or continuing proceedings where a conciliation officer has taken action under section 18 of the Employment Tribunals Act 1996, and

(f)    does not apply to any agreement to refrain from instituting or continuing any proceedings within the following provisions of section 18(1) of the Employment Tribunals Act 1996 (cases where conciliation available)—

(i)    paragraph (b) (proceedings under this Act),

(ii)    paragraph (l) (proceedings arising out of the Part-time Workers (Prevention of Less Favourable Treatment) Regulations 2000),

(iii)    paragraph (m) (proceedings arising out of the Fixed-term Employees (Prevention of Less Favourable Treatment) Regulations 2002),

if the conditions regulating settlement agreements under this Act are satisfied in relation to the agreement.

(3)    For the purposes of subsection (2)(f) the conditions regulating compromise agreements under this Act are that—

(a)    the agreement must be in writing,

(b)    the agreement must relate to the particular proceedings,

(c)    the employee or worker must have received advice from a relevant independent adviser as to the terms and effect of the proposed agreement and, in particular, its effect on his ability to pursue his rights before an employment tribunal,

(d)    there must be in force, when the adviser gives the advice, a contract of insurance, or an indemnity provided for members of a profession or professional body covering the risk of a claim by the employee or worker in respect of loss arising in consequence of the advice,

(e)    the agreement must identify the adviser, and

(f)    the agreement must state that the conditions regulating settlement agreements under this Act are satisfied.

(3A) A person is a relevant independent adviser for the purposes of subsection (3)(c)—

   (a)    if he is a qualified lawyer,

   (b)    if he is an officer, official, employee or member of an independent trade union who has been certified in writing by the trade union as competent to give advice and as authorised to do so on behalf of the trade union,

   (c)    if he works at an advice centre (whether as an employee or a volunteer) and has been certified in writing by the centre as competent to give advice and as authorised to do so on behalf of the centre, or

   (d)    if he is a person of a description specified in an order made by the Secretary of State.

(3B) But a person is not a relevant independent adviser for the purposes of subsection (3)(c) in relation to the employee or worker—

   (a)    if he is, is employed by or is acting in the matter for the employer or an associated employer,

   (b)    in the case of a person within subsection (3A)(b) or (c), if the trade union or advice centre is the employer or an associated employer,

   (c)    in the case of a person within subsection (3A)(c), if the employee or worker makes a payment for the advice received from him, or

   (d)    in the case of a person of a description specified in an order under subsection (3A)(d), if any condition specified in the order in relation to the giving of advice by persons of that description is not satisfied.

(4)    In subsection (3A)(a) 'qualified lawyer' means—

   (a)    as respects England and Wales, a person who, for the purposes of the Legal Services Act 2007, is an authorised person in relation to an activity which constitutes the exercise of a right of audience or the conduct of litigation (within the meaning of that Act), and

   (b)    as respects Scotland, an advocate (whether in practice as such or employed to give legal advice), or a solicitor who holds a practising certificate.

(5)    An agreement under which the parties agree to submit a dispute to arbitration—

   (a)    shall be regarded for the purposes of subsection (2)(e) and (f) as being an agreement to refrain from instituting or continuing proceedings if—

      (i)    the dispute is covered by a scheme having effect by virtue of an order under section 212A of the Trade Union and Labour Relations (Consolidation) Act 1992, and

      (ii)    the agreement is to submit it to arbitration in accordance with the scheme, but

   (b)    shall be regarded as neither being nor including such an agreement in any other case.

## 204   Law governing employment

(1)    For the purposes of this Act it is immaterial whether the law which (apart from this Act) governs any person's employment is the law of the United Kingdom, or of a part of the United Kingdom, or not.

(2)    ...

## 205   Remedy for infringement of certain rights

(1)    The remedy of an employee for infringement of any of the rights conferred by section 8, Part III, Parts V to VIII, section 92, Part X and Part XII is, where provision is made for a complaint or the reference of a question to an employment tribunal, by way of such a complaint or reference and not otherwise.

(1YA) In relation to the right conferred by section 44(1A), the reference in subsection (1) to an employee has effect as a reference to a worker.

(1A) In relation to the right conferred by section 47B, the reference in subsection (1) to an employee has effect as a reference to a worker.

(1ZA) In relation to the right conferred by section 45A, the reference in subsection (1) to an employee has effect as a reference to a worker.

(2)    The remedy of a worker in respect of any contravention of section 13, 15, 18(1) or 21(1) is by way of a complaint under section 23 and not otherwise.

PART XIV
INTERPRETATION

CHAPTER I
CONTINUOUS EMPLOYMENT

## 210   Introductory

(1) References in any provision of this Act to a period of continuous employment are (unless provision is expressly made to the contrary) to a period computed in accordance with this Chapter.

(2) In any provision of this Act which refers to a period of continuous employment expressed in months or years—
   (a) a month means a calendar month, and
   (b) a year means a year of twelve calendar months.

(3) In computing an employee's period of continuous employment for the purposes of any provision of this Act, any question—
   (a) whether the employee's employment is of a kind counting towards a period of continuous employment, or
   (b) whether periods (consecutive or otherwise) are to be treated as forming a single period of continuous employment,
   shall be determined week by week; but where it is necessary to compute the length of an employee's period of employment it shall be computed in months and years of twelve months in accordance with section 211.

(4) Subject to sections 215 to 217, a week which does not count in computing the length of a period of continuous employment breaks continuity of employment.

(5) A person's employment during any period shall, unless the contrary is shown, be presumed to have been continuous.

## 211   Period of continuous employment

(1) An employee's period of continuous employment for the purposes of any provision of this Act—
   (a) (subject to subsections (2) and (3)) begins with the day on which the employee starts work, and
   (b) ends with the day by reference to which the length of the employee's period of continuous employment is to be ascertained for the purposes of the provision.

(2) ...

(3) If an employee's period of continuous employment includes one or more periods which (by virtue of section 215, 216 or 217) while not counting in computing the length of the period do not break continuity of employment, the beginning of the period shall be treated as postponed by the number of days falling within that intervening period, or the aggregate number of days falling within those periods, calculated in accordance with the section in question.

## 212   Weeks counting in computing period

(1) Any week during the whole or part of which an employee's relations with his employer are governed by a contract of employment counts in computing the employee's period of employment.

(2) ...

(3) Subject to subsection (4), any week (not within subsection (1)) during the whole or part of which an employee is—
   (a) incapable of work in consequence of sickness or injury,
   (b) absent from work on account of a temporary cessation of work, or
   (c) absent from work in circumstances such that, by arrangement or custom, he is regarded as continuing in the employment of his employer for any purpose,
   (d) ...

(4) Not more than twenty-six weeks count under subsection (3)(a) between any periods falling under subsection (1).

## 213    Intervals in employment

(1)    Where in the case of an employee a date later than the date which would be the effective date of termination by virtue of subsection (1) of section 97 is treated for certain purposes as the effective date of termination by virtue of subsection (2) or (4) of that section, the period of the interval between the two dates counts as a period of employment in ascertaining for the purposes of section 108(1) or 119(1) the period for which the employee has been continuously employed.

(2)    Where an employee is by virtue of section 138(1) regarded for the purposes of Part XI as not having been dismissed by reason of a renewal or re-engagement taking effect after an interval, the period of the interval counts as a period of employment in ascertaining for the purposes of section 155 or 162(1) the period for which the employee has been continuously employed (except so far as it is to be disregarded under section 214 or 215).

(3)    Where in the case of an employee a date later than the date which would be the relevant date by virtue of subsections (2) to (4) of section 145 is treated for certain purposes as the relevant date by virtue of subsection (5) of that section, the period of the interval between the two dates counts as a period of employment in ascertaining for the purposes of section 155 or 162(1) the period for which the employee has been continuously employed (except so far as it is to be disregarded under section 214 or 215).

## 214    Special provisions for redundancy payments

(1)    This section applies where a period of continuous employment has to be determined in relation to an employee for the purposes of the application of section 155 or 162(1).

(2)    The continuity of a period of employment is broken where—

(a)    a redundancy payment has previously been paid to the employee (whether in respect of dismissal or in respect of lay-off or short-time), and

(b)    the contract of employment under which the employee was employed was renewed (whether by the same or another employer) or the employee was re-engaged under a new contract of employment (whether by the same or another employer).

(3)    The continuity of a period of employment is also broken where—

(a)    a payment has been made to the employee (whether in respect of the termination of his employment or lay-off or short-time) in accordance with a scheme under section 1 of the Superannuation Act 1972 or arrangements falling within section 177(3), and

(b)    he commenced new, or renewed, employment.

(4)    The date on which the person's continuity of employment is broken by virtue of this section—

(a)    if the employment was under a contract of employment, is the date which was the relevant date in relation to the payment mentioned in subsection (2)(a) or (3)(a), and

(b)    if the employment was otherwise than under a contract of employment, is the date which would have been the relevant date in relation to the payment mentioned in subsection (2)(a) or (3)(a) had the employment been under a contract of employment.

(5)    For the purposes of this section a redundancy payment shall be treated as having been paid if—

(a)    the whole of the payment has been paid to the employee by the employer,

(b)    a tribunal has determined liability and found that the employer must pay part (but not all) of the redundancy payment and the employer has paid that part, or

(c)    the Secretary of State has paid a sum to the employee in respect of the redundancy payment under section 167.

## 215    Employment abroad etc.

(1)    This Chapter applies to a period of employment—

(a)    (subject to the following provisions of this section) even where during the period the employee was engaged in work wholly or mainly outside Great Britain, and

(b)    even where the employee was excluded by or under this Act from any right conferred by this Act.

(2)    For the purposes of sections 155 and 162(1) a week of employment does not count in computing a period of employment if the employee—

(a) was employed outside Great Britain during the whole or part of the week, and

(b) was not during that week an employed earner for the purposes of the Social Security Contributions and Benefits Act 1992 in respect of whom a secondary Class 1 contribution was payable under that Act (whether or not the contribution was in fact paid).

(3) Where by virtue of subsection (2) a week of employment does not count in computing a period of employment, the continuity of the period is not broken by reason only that the week does not count in computing the period; and the number of days which, for the purposes of section 211(3), fall within the intervening period is seven for each week within this subsection.

(4) Any question arising under subsection (2) whether—

(a) a person was an employed earner for the purposes of the Social Security Contributions and Benefits Act 1992, or

(b) if so, whether a secondary Class 1 contribution was payable in respect of him under that Act,

shall be determined by an officer of the Commissioners of the Inland Revenue.

(5) Part II of the Social Security Contributions (Transfer of Functions, etc.) Act 1999 (decisions and appeals) shall apply in relation to the determination of any issue by the Inland Revenue under subsection (4) as if it were a decision falling within section 8(1) of that Act.

(6) Subsection (2) does not apply in relation to a person who is—

(a) employed as a master or seaman in a British ship, and

(b) ordinarily resident in Great Britain.

## 216   Industrial disputes

(1) A week does not count under section 212 if during the week, or any part of the week, the employee takes part in a strike.

(2) The continuity of an employee's period of employment is not broken by a week which does not count under this Chapter (whether or not by virtue only of subsection (1)) if during the week, or any part of the week, the employee takes part in a strike; and the number of days which, for the purposes of section 211(3), fall within the intervening period is the number of days between the last working day before the strike and the day on which work was resumed.

(3) The continuity of an employee's period of employment is not broken by a week if during the week, or any part of the week, the employee is absent from work because of a lock-out by the employer; and the number of days which, for the purposes of section 211(3), fall within the intervening period is the number of days between the last working day before the lock-out and the day on which work was resumed.

## 218   Change of employer

(1) Subject to the provisions of this section, this Chapter relates only to employment by the one employer.

(2) If a trade or business, or an undertaking (whether or not established by or under an Act), is transferred from one person to another—

(a) the period of employment of an employee in the trade or business or undertaking at the time of the transfer counts as a period of employment with the transferee, and

(b) the transfer does not break the continuity of the period of employment.

(3) If by or under an Act (whether public or local and whether passed before or after this Act) a contract of employment between any body corporate and an employee is modified and some other body corporate is substituted as the employer—

(a) the employee's period of employment at the time when the modification takes effect counts as a period of employment with the second body corporate, and

(b) the change of employer does not break the continuity of the period of employment.

(4) If on the death of an employer the employee is taken into the employment of the personal representatives or trustees of the deceased—

(a) the employee's period of employment at the time of the death counts as a period of employment with the employer's personal representatives or trustees, and

(b) the death does not break the continuity of the period of employment.

(5) If there is a change in the partners, personal representatives or trustees who employ any person—

    (a) the employee's period of employment at the time of the change counts as a period of employment with the partners, personal representatives or trustees after the change, and

    (b) the change does not break the continuity of the period of employment.

(6) If an employee of an employer is taken into the employment of another employer who, at the time when the employee enters the second employer's employment, is an associated employer of the first employer—

    (a) the employee's period of employment at that time counts as a period of employment with the second employer, and

    (b) the change of employer does not break the continuity of the period of employment.

...

## CHAPTER II
## A WEEK'S PAY

## 227 Maximum amount

(1) For the purpose of calculating—

    (zza) an award of compensation under section 63J(1)(b),

    (za) an award of compensation under section 80I(1)(b),

    (a) a basic award of compensation for unfair dismissal,

    (b) an additional award of compensation for unfair dismissal,

    (ba) an award under section 112(5), or

    (c) a redundancy payment,

the amount of a week's pay shall not exceed £571.

## CHAPTER III
## OTHER INTERPRETATION PROVISIONS

## 230 Employees, workers etc.

(1) In this Act 'employee' means an individual who has entered into or works under (or, where the employment has ceased, worked under) a contract of employment.

(2) In this Act 'contract of employment' means a contract of service or apprenticeship, whether express or implied, and (if it is express) whether oral or in writing.

(3) In this Act 'worker' (except in the phrases 'shop worker' and 'betting worker') means an individual who has entered into or works under (or, where the employment has ceased, worked under)—

    (a) a contract of employment, or

    (b) any other contract, whether express or implied and (if it is express) whether oral or in writing, whereby the individual undertakes to do or perform personally any work or services for another party to the contract whose status is not by virtue of the contract that of a client or customer of any profession or business undertaking carried on by the individual;

and any reference to a worker's contract shall be construed accordingly.

(4) In this Act 'employer', in relation to an employee or a worker, means the person by whom the employee or worker is (or, where the employment has ceased, was) employed.

(5) In this Act 'employment'—

    (a) in relation to an employee, means (except for the purposes of section 171) employment under a contract of employment, and

    (b) in relation to a worker, means employment under his contract; and 'employed' shall be construed accordingly.

(6) This section has effect subject to sections 43K, 47B(3) and 49B(10); and for the purposes of Part XIII so far as relating to Part IVA or section 47B, 'worker', 'worker's contract' and, in relation to a worker, 'employer', 'employment' and 'employed' have the extended meaning given by section 43K.

(7) This section has effect subject to section 75K(3) and (5).

## 231  Associated employer

For the purposes of this Act any two employers shall be treated as associated if—

(a)     one is a company of which the other (directly or indirectly) has control, or

(b)     both are companies of which a third person (directly or indirectly) has control;

and 'associated employer' shall be construed accordingly.

## 232  Shop workers

(1)   In this Act 'shop worker' means an employee who, under his contract of employment, is or may be required to do shop work.

(2)   In this Act 'shop work' means work in or about a shop on a day on which the shop is open for the serving of customers.

(3)   Subject to subsection (4), in this Act 'shop' includes any premises where any retail trade or business is carried on.

(4)   Where premises are used mainly for purposes other than those of retail trade or business and would not (apart from subsection (3)) be regarded as a shop, only such part of the premises as—

(a)     is used wholly or mainly for the purposes of retail trade or business, or

(b)     is used both for the purposes of retail trade or business and for the purposes of wholesale trade and is used wholly or mainly for those two purposes considered together,

is to be regarded as a shop for the purposes of this Act.

(5)   In subsection (4)(b) 'wholesale trade' means the sale of goods for use or resale in the course of a business or the hire of goods for use in the course of a business.

(6)   In this section 'retail trade or business' includes—

(a)     the business of a barber or hairdresser,

(b)     the business of hiring goods otherwise than for use in the course of a trade or business, and

(c)     retail sales by auction,

but does not include catering business or the sale at theatres and places of amusement of programmes, catalogues and similar items.

(7)   In subsection (6) 'catering business' means—

(a)     the sale of meals, refreshments or intoxicating liquor alcohol (in Scotland, alcoholic liquor) for consumption on the premises on which they are sold, or

(b)     the sale of meals or refreshments prepared to order for immediate consumption off the premises;

and in paragraph (a) 'intoxicating liquor' has the same meaning as in the Licensing Act 1964 'alcohol' has the same meaning as in the Licensing Act 2003 and 'alcoholic liquor' the same meaning as in the Licensing (Scotland) Act 1976.

(8)   In this Act—

'notice period', in relation to an opted-out shop worker, has the meaning given by section 41(3),

'opted-out', in relation to a shop worker, shall be construed in accordance with section 41(1) and (2),

'opting-in notice', in relation to a shop worker, has the meaning given by section 36(6),

'opting-out notice', in relation to a shop worker, has the meaning given by section 40(2), and

'protected', in relation to a shop worker, shall be construed in accordance with section 36(1) to (5).

## 235  Other definitions

(1)   In this Act, except in so far as the context otherwise requires—

'act' and 'action' each includes omission and references to doing an act or taking action shall be construed accordingly,

'basic award of compensation for unfair dismissal' shall be construed in accordance with section 118,

'business' includes a trade or profession and includes any activity carried on by a body of persons (whether corporate or unincorporated),

'childbirth' means the birth of a living child or the birth of a child whether living or dead after twenty-four weeks of pregnancy, 'collective agreement' has the meaning given by section 178(1) and (2) of the Trade Union and Labour Relations (Consolidation) Act 1992,

'conciliation officer' means an officer designated by the Advisory, Conciliation and Arbitration Service under section 211 of that Act,

'dismissal procedures agreement' means an agreement in writing with respect to procedures relating to dismissal made by or on behalf of one or more independent trade unions and one or more employers or employers' associations,

'employers' association' has the same meaning as in the Trade Union and Labour Relations (Consolidation) Act 1992,

'expected week of childbirth' means the week, beginning with midnight between Saturday and Sunday, in which it is expected that childbirth will occur,

'guarantee payment' has the meaning given by section 28,

'independent trade union' means a trade union which—

    (a)   is not under the domination or control of an employer or a group of employers or of one or more employers' associations, and

    (b)   is not liable to interference by an employer or any such group or association (arising out of the provision of financial or material support or by any other means whatever) tending towards such control,

'job', in relation to an employee, means the nature of the work which he is employed to do in accordance with his contract and the capacity and place in which he is so employed, 'ordinary or additional paternity leave' means leave under any of sections 80A to 80BB, 'position', in relation to an employee, means the following matters taken as a whole—

    (a)   his status as an employee,

    (b)   the nature of his work, and

    (c)   his terms and conditions of employment,

'parental bereavement leave' means leave under section 80EA,

'protected disclosure' has the meaning given by section 43A,

'redundancy payment' has the meaning given by Part XI,

'relevant date' has the meaning given by sections 145 and 153,

'renewal' includes extension, and any reference to renewing a contract or a fixed term shall be construed accordingly,

'statutory provision' means a provision, whether of a general or a special nature, contained in, or in any document made or issued under, any Act, whether of a general or special nature,

'successor', in relation to the employer of an employee, means (subject to subsection (2)) a person who in consequence of a change occurring (whether by virtue of a sale or other disposition or by operation of law) in the ownership of the undertaking, or of the part of the undertaking, for the purposes of which the employee was employed, has become the owner of the undertaking or part,

'trade union' has the meaning given by section 1 of the Trade Union and Labour Relations (Consolidation) Act 1992,

'week'—

    (a)   in Chapter I of this Part means a week ending with Saturday, and

    (b)   otherwise, except in sections 80A, 80B, 80EA and 86, means, in relation to an employee whose remuneration is calculated weekly by a week ending with a day other than Saturday, a week ending with that other day and, in relation to any other employee, a week ending with Saturday.

(2)   The definition of 'successor' in subsection (1) has effect (subject to the necessary modifications) in relation to a case where—

    (a)   the person by whom an undertaking or part of an undertaking is owned immediately before a change is one of the persons by whom (whether as partners, trustees or otherwise) it is owned immediately after the change, or

    (b)   the persons by whom an undertaking or part of an undertaking is owned immediately before a change (whether as partners, trustees or otherwise) include the persons by whom, or include one or more of the persons by whom, it is owned immediately after the change,

as it has effect where the previous owner and the new owner are wholly different persons.

(2A) For the purposes of this Act a contract of employment is a 'limited-term contract' if—

> (a)    the employment under the contract is not intended to be permanent, and
>
> (b)    provision is accordingly made in the contract for it to terminate by virtue of a limiting event.

(2B)   In this Act, 'limiting event', in relation to a contract of employment means—

> (a)    in the case of a contract for a fixed-term, the expiry of the term,
>
> (b)    in the case of a contract made in contemplation of the performance of a specific task, the performance of the task, and
>
> (c)    in the case of a contract which provides for its termination on the occurrence of an event (or the failure of an event to occur), the occurrence of the event (or the failure of the event to occur).

(3)    References in this Act to redundancy, dismissal by reason of redundancy and similar expressions shall be construed in accordance with section 139.

(4)    In sections 136(2), 154 and 216(3) and paragraph 14 of Schedule 2 'lock-out' means—

> (a)    the closing of a place of employment,
>
> (b)    the suspension of work, or
>
> (c)    the refusal by an employer to continue to employ any number of persons employed by him in consequence of a dispute,

done with a view to compelling persons employed by the employer, or to aid another employer in compelling persons employed by him, to accept terms or conditions of or affecting employment.

(5)    In sections 91(2), 140(2) and (3), 143(1), 144(2) and (3), 154 and 216(1) and (2) and paragraph 14 of Schedule 2 'strike' means—

> (a)    the cessation of work by a body of employed persons acting in combination, or
>
> (b)    a concerted refusal, or a refusal under a common understanding, of any number of employed persons to continue to work for an employer in consequence of a dispute,

done as a means of compelling their employer or any employed person or body of employed persons, or to aid other employees in compelling their employer or any employed person or body of employed persons, to accept or not to accept terms or conditions of or affecting employment.

# NATIONAL MINIMUM WAGE ACT 1998
## (1998, c. 39)

*Entitlement to the national minimum wage*

## 1    Workers to be paid at least the national minimum wage

(1)    A person who qualifies for the national minimum wage shall be remunerated by his employer in respect of his work in any pay reference period at a rate which is not less than the national minimum wage.

(2)    A person qualifies for the national minimum wage if he is an individual who—

> (a)    is a worker;
>
> (b)    is working, or ordinarily works, in the United Kingdom under his contract; and
>
> (c)    has ceased to be of compulsory school age.

(3)    The national minimum wage shall be such single hourly rate as the Secretary of State may from time to time prescribe.

(4)    For the purposes of this Act a 'pay reference period' is such period as the Secretary of State may prescribe for the purpose.

(5)    Subsections (1) to (4) above are subject to the following provisions of this Act.

*Regulations relating to the national minimum wage*

## 2    Determination of hourly rate of remuneration

(1)    The Secretary of State may by regulations make provision for determining what is the hourly rate at which a person is to be regarded for the purposes of this Act as remunerated by his employer in respect of his work in any pay reference period.

(2)    The regulations may make provision for determining the hourly rate in cases where—

> (a)    the remuneration, to the extent that it is at a periodic rate, is at a single rate;
>
> (b)    the remuneration is, in whole or in part, at different rates applicable at different times or in different circumstances;

(c)    the remuneration is, in whole or in part, otherwise than at a periodic rate or rates;

(d)    the remuneration consists, in whole or in part, of benefits in kind.

(3)    The regulations may make provision with respect to—

    (a)    circumstances in which, times at which, or the time for which, a person is to be treated as, or as not, working, and the extent to which a person is to be so treated;

    (b)    the treatment of periods of paid or unpaid absence from, or lack of, work and of remuneration in respect of such periods.

(4)    The provision that may be made by virtue of paragraph (a) of subsection (3) above includes provision for or in connection with—

    (a)    treating a person as, or as not, working for a maximum or minimum time, or for a proportion of the time, in any period;

    (b)    determining any matter to which that paragraph relates by reference to the terms of an agreement.

(5)    The regulations may make provision with respect to—

    (a)    what is to be treated as, or as not, forming part of a person's remuneration, and the extent to which it is to be so treated;

    (b)    the valuation of benefits in kind;

    (c)    the treatment of deductions from earnings;

    (d)    the treatment of any charges or expenses which a person is required to bear.

(6)    The regulations may make provision with respect to—

    (a)    the attribution to a period, or the apportionment between two or more periods, of the whole or any part of any remuneration or work, whether or not the remuneration is received or the work is done within the period or periods in question;

    (b)    the aggregation of the whole or any part of the remuneration for different periods;

    (c)    the time at which remuneration is to be treated as received or accruing.

(7)    Subsections (2) to (6) above are without prejudice to the generality of subsection (1) above.

(8)    No provision shall be made under this section which treats the same circumstances differently in relation to—

    (a)    different areas;

    (b)    different sectors of employment;

    (c)    undertakings of different sizes;

    (d)    persons of different ages; or

    (e)    persons of different occupations.

## 3    Exclusion of, and modifications for, certain classes of person

(1)    This section applies to persons who have not attained the age of 26.

(1A)  This section also applies to persons who have attained the age of 26 who are—

    (a)    within the first six months after the commencement of their employment with an employer by whom they have not previously been employed;

    (b)    participating in a scheme under which shelter is provided in return for work;

    (c)    participating in a scheme designed to provide training, work experience or temporary work;

    (d)    participating in a scheme to assist in the seeking or obtaining of work;

    (e)    undertaking a course of higher education requiring attendance for a period of work experience; or

    (f)    undertaking a course of further education requiring attendance for a period of work experience.

(2)    The Secretary of State may by regulations make provision in relation to any of the persons to whom this section applies—

    (a)    preventing them being persons who qualify for the national minimum wage; or

    (b)    prescribing an hourly rate for the national minimum wage other than the single hourly rate for the time being prescribed under section 1(3) above.

(3)    No provision shall be made under subsection (2) above which treats persons differently in relation to—

    (a)    different areas;

    (b)    different sectors of employment;

    (c)    undertakings of different sizes; or

    (d)    different occupations.

(4)	If any description of persons who have attained the age of 26 is added by regulations under section 4 below to the descriptions of person to whom this section applies, no provision shall be made under subsection (2) above which treats persons of that description differently in relation to different ages over 26.

## 4	Power to add to the persons to whom section 3 applies

(1)	The Secretary of State may by regulations amend section 3 above by adding descriptions of persons who have attained the age of 26 to the descriptions of person to whom that section applies.

(2)	No amendment shall be made under subsection (1) above which treats persons differently in relation to—
   (a)	different areas;
   (b)	different sectors of employment;
   (c)	undertakings of different sizes;
   (d)	different ages over 26; or
   (e)	different occupations.

*The Low Pay Commission*

## 5	The first regulations: referral to the Low Pay Commission

(1)	Before making the first regulations under section 1(3) or (4) or 2 above, the Secretary of State shall refer the matters specified in subsection (2) below to the Low Pay Commission for their consideration.

(2)	Those matters are—
   (a)	what single hourly rate should be prescribed under section 1(3) above as the national minimum wage;
   (b)	what period or periods should be prescribed under section 1(4) above;
   (c)	what method or methods should be used for determining under section 2 above the hourly rate at which a person is to be regarded as remunerated for the purposes of this Act;
   (d)	whether any, and if so what, provision should be made under section 3 above; and
   (e)	whether any, and if so what, descriptions of person should be added to the descriptions of person to whom section 3 above applies and what provision should be made under that section in relation to persons of those descriptions.

(3)	Where matters are referred to the Low Pay Commission under subsection (1) above, the Commission shall, after considering those matters, make a report to the Prime Minister and the Secretary of State which shall contain the Commission's recommendations about each of those matters.

(4)	If, following the report of the Low Pay Commission under subsection (3) above, the Secretary of State decides—
   (a)	not to make any regulations implementing the Commission's recommendations, or
   (b)	to make regulations implementing only some of the Commission's recommendations, or
   (c)	to prescribe under section 1(3) above a single hourly rate which is different from the rate recommended by the Commission, or
   (d)	to make regulations which in some other respect differ from the recommendations of the Commission, or
   (e)	to make regulations which do not relate to a recommendation of the Commission, the Secretary of State shall lay a report before each House of Parliament containing a statement of the reasons for the decision.

(5)	If the Low Pay Commission fail to make their report under subsection (3) above within the time allowed for doing so under section 7 below, any power of the Secretary of State to make regulations under this Act shall be exercisable as if subsection (1) above had not been enacted.

## 6    Referral of matters to the Low Pay Commission at any time

(1)   The Secretary of State may at any time refer to the Low Pay Commission such matters relating to this Act as the Secretary of State thinks fit.

(2)   Where matters are referred to the Low Pay Commission under subsection (1) above, the Commission shall, after considering those matters, make a report to the Prime Minister and the Secretary of State which shall contain the Commission's recommendations about each of those matters.

(3)   If on a referral under this section—

(a)   the Secretary of State seeks the opinion of the Low Pay Commission on a matter falling within section 5(2) above,

(b)   the Commission's report under subsection (2) above contains recommendations in relation to that matter, and

(c)   implementation of any of those recommendations involves the exercise of any power to make regulations under sections 1 to 4 above,

subsection (4) of section 5 above shall apply in relation to the report, so far as relating to the recommendations falling within paragraph (c) above, as it applies in relation to a report under subsection (3) of that section.

(4)   If on a referral under this section—

(a)   the Secretary of State seeks the opinion of the Low Pay Commission on any matter falling within section 5(2) above, but

(b)   the Commission fail to make their report under subsection (2) above within the time allowed under section 7 below,

the Secretary of State may make regulations under sections 1 to 4 above as if the opinion of the Commission had not been sought in relation to that matter.

## 7    Referrals to, and reports of, the Low Pay Commission: supplementary

(1)   This section applies where matters are referred to the Low Pay Commission under section 5 or 6 above.

(2)   The Secretary of State may by notice require the Low Pay Commission to make their report within such time as may be specified in the notice.

(3)   The time allowed to the Low Pay Commission for making their report may from time to time be extended by further notice given to them by the Secretary of State.

(4)   Before arriving at the recommendations to be included in their report, the Low Pay Commission shall consult—

(a)   such organisations representative of employers as they think fit;

(b)   such organisations representative of workers as they think fit; and

(c)   if they think fit, any other body or person.

(5)   In considering what recommendations to include in their report, the Low Pay Commission—

(a)   shall have regard to the effect of this Act on the economy of the United Kingdom as a whole and on competitiveness; and

(b)   shall take into account any additional factors which the Secretary of State specifies in referring the matters to them.

(6)   The report of the Low Pay Commission must—

(a)   identify the members of the Commission making the report;

(b)   explain the procedures adopted in respect of consultation, the taking of evidence and the receiving of representations;

(c)   set out the reasons for their recommendations; and

(d)   if the Secretary of State has specified any additional factor to be taken into account under subsection (5)(b) above, state that they have taken that factor into account in making their recommendations.

(7)   The Secretary of State shall—

(a)   lay a copy of any report of the Low Pay Commission before each House of Parliament; and

(b)   arrange for the report to be published.

(8)   In this section—

'recommendations' means the recommendations required to be contained in a report under section 5(3) or 6(2) above, as the case may be;

'report' means the report which the Low Pay Commission are required to make under section 5(3) or 6(2) above, as the case may be, on the matters referred to them as mentioned in subsection (1) above.

*Records*

## 9    Duty of employers to keep records

For the purposes of this Act, the Secretary of State may by regulations make provision requiring employers—

(a)    to keep, in such form and manner as may be prescribed, such records as may be prescribed; and

(b)    to preserve those records for such period as may be prescribed.

## 10   Worker's right of access to records

(1)    A worker may, in accordance with the following provisions of this section,—

(a)    require his employer to produce any relevant records; and

(b)    inspect and examine those records and copy any part of them.

(2)    The rights conferred by subsection (1) above are exercisable only if the worker believes on reasonable grounds that he is or may be being, or has or may have been, remunerated for any pay reference period by his employer at a rate which is less than the national minimum wage.

(3)    The rights conferred by subsection (1) above are exercisable only for the purpose of establishing whether or not the worker is being, or has been, remunerated for any pay reference period by his employer at a rate which is less than the national minimum wage.

(4)    The rights conferred by subsection (1) above are exercisable—

(a)    by the worker alone; or

(b)    by the worker accompanied by such other person as the worker may think fit.

(5)    The rights conferred by subsection (1) above are exercisable only if the worker gives notice (a 'production notice') to his employer requesting the production of any relevant records relating to such period as may be described in the notice.

(6)    If the worker intends to exercise the right conferred by subsection (4)(b) above, the production notice must contain a statement of that intention.

(7)    Where a production notice is given, the employer shall give the worker reasonable notice of the place and time at which the relevant records will be produced.

(8)    The place at which the relevant records are produced must be—

(a)    the worker's place of work; or

(b)    any other place at which it is reasonable, in all the circumstances, for the worker to attend to inspect the relevant records; or

(c)    such other place as may be agreed between the worker and the employer.

(9)    The relevant records must be produced—

(a)    before the end of the period of fourteen days following the date of receipt of the production notice; or

(b)    at such later time as may be agreed during that period between the worker and the employer.

(10)   In this section—

'records' means records which the worker's employer is required to keep and, at the time of receipt of the production notice, preserve in accordance with section 9 above;

'relevant records' means such parts of, or such extracts from, any records as are relevant to establishing whether or not the worker has, for any pay reference period to which the records relate, been remunerated by the employer at a rate which is at least equal to the national minimum wage.

## 11   Failure of employer to allow access to records

(1)    A complaint may be presented to an employment tribunal by a worker on the ground that the employer—

(a)    failed to produce some or all of the relevant records in accordance with subsections and (9) of section 10 above; or

(b)    failed to allow the worker to exercise some or all of the rights conferred by subsection (1)(b) or (4)(b) of that section.

(2) Where an employment tribunal finds a complaint under this section well-founded, the tribunal shall—

(a) make a declaration to that effect; and

(b) make an award that the employer pay to the worker a sum equal to 80 times the hourly amount of the national minimum wage (as in force when the award is made).

(3) An employment tribunal shall not consider a complaint under this section unless it is presented to the tribunal before the expiry of the period of three months following—

(a) the end of the period of fourteen days mentioned in paragraph (a) of subsection (9) of section 10 above; or

(b) in a case where a later day was agreed under paragraph (b) of that subsection, that later day.

(4) Where the employment tribunal is satisfied that it was not reasonably practicable for a complaint under this section to be presented before the expiry of the period of three months mentioned in subsection (3) above, the tribunal may consider the complaint if it is presented within such further period as the tribunal considers reasonable.

(4A) Where the complaint is presented to an employment tribunal in England and Wales or Scotland, section 11A applies for the purposes of subsection (3).

(5) Expressions used in this section and in section 10 above have the same meaning in this section as they have in that section.

## 12 Employer to provide worker with national minimum wage statement

(1) Regulations may make provision for the purpose of conferring on a worker the right to be given by his employer, at or before the time at which any payment of remuneration is made to the worker, a written statement.

(2) The regulations may make provision with respect to the contents of any such statement and may, in particular, require it to contain—

(a) prescribed information relating to this Act or any regulations under it; or

(b) prescribed information for the purpose of assisting the worker to determine whether he has been remunerated at a rate at least equal to the national minimum wage during the period to which the payment of remuneration relates.

(3) Any statement required to be given under this section to a worker by his employer may, if the worker is an employee, be included in the written itemised pay statement required to be given to him by his employer under section 8 of the Employment Rights Act 1996 or Article 40 of the Employment Rights (Northern Ireland) Order 1996, as the case may be.

(4) The regulations may make provision for the purpose of applying—

(a) sections 11 and 12 of the Employment Rights Act 1996 (references to employment tribunals and determination of references), or

(b) in relation to Northern Ireland, Articles 43 and 44 of the Employment Rights (Northern Ireland) Order 1996 (references to industrial tribunals and determination of references),

in relation to a worker and any such statement as is mentioned in subsection (1) above as they apply in relation to an employee and a statement required to be given to him by his employer under section 8 of that Act or Article 40 of that Order, as the case may be.

### Enforcement

## 17 Non-compliance: worker entitled to additional remuneration

(1) If a worker who qualifies for the national minimum wage is remunerated for any pay reference period by his employer at a rate which is less than the national minimum wage, the worker shall at any time ('the time of determination') be taken to be entitled under his contract to be paid, as additional remuneration in respect of that period, whichever is the higher of—

(a) the amount described in subsection (2) below, and

(b) the amount described in subsection (4) below.

(2) The amount referred to in subsection (1)(a) above is the difference between—

(a) the relevant remuneration received by the worker for the pay reference period; and

(b) the relevant remuneration which the worker would have received for that period had he been remunerated by the employer at a rate equal to the national minimum wage.

(3) In subsection (2) above, 'relevant remuneration' means remuneration which falls to be brought into account for the purposes of regulations under section 2 above.

(4) The amount referred to in subsection (1)(b) above is the amount determined by the formula—

(A/R1) x R2S

where—

A is the amount described in subsection (2) above,

R1 is the rate of national minimum wage which was payable in respect of the worker during the pay reference period, and

R2 is the rate of national minimum wage which would have been payable in respect of the worker during that period had the rate payable in respect of him during that period been determined by reference to regulations under section 1 and 3 above in force at the time of determination.

(5) Subsection (1) above ceases to apply to a worker in relation to any pay reference period when he is at any time paid the additional remuneration for that period to which he is at that time entitled under that subsection.

(6) Where any additional remuneration is paid to the worker under this section in relation to the pay reference period but subsection (1) above has not ceased to apply in relation to him, the amounts described in subsections (2) and (4) above shall be regarded as reduced by the amount of that remuneration.

## 18    Enforcement in the case of special classes of worker

(1) If the persons who are the worker and the employer for the purposes of section 17 above would not (apart from this section) fall to be regarded as the worker and the employer for the purposes of—

(a) Part II of the Employment Rights Act 1996 (protection of wages), or

(b) in relation to Northern Ireland, Part IV of the Employment Rights (Northern Ireland) Order 1996,

they shall be so regarded for the purposes of the application of that Part in relation to the entitlement conferred by that section.

(2) In the application by virtue of subsection (1) above of—

(a) Part II of the Employment Rights Act 1996, or

(b) Part IV of the Employment Rights (Northern Ireland) Order 1996,

in a case where there is or was, for the purposes of that Part, no worker's contract between the persons who are the worker and the employer for the purposes of section 17 above, it shall be assumed that there is or, as the case may be, was such a contract.

(3) For the purpose of enabling the amount described as additional remuneration in subsection (1) of section 17 above to be recovered in civil proceedings on a claim in contract in a case where in fact there is or was no worker's contract between the persons who are the worker and the employer for the purposes of that section, it shall be assumed for the purpose of any civil proceedings, so far as relating to that amount, that there is or, as the case may be, was such a contract.

## 19    Notices of underpayment: arrears

(1) Subsection (2) below applies where an officer acting for the purposes of this Act is of the opinion that, on any day ('the relevant day'), a sum was due under section 17 above for any one or more pay reference periods ending before the relevant day to a worker who at any time qualified for the national minimum wage.

(2) Where this subsection applies, the officer may, subject to this section, serve a notice requiring the employer to pay to the worker, within the 28-day period, the sum due to the worker under section 17 above for any one or more of the pay reference periods referred to in subsection (1) above.

(3) In this Act, 'notice of underpayment' means a notice under this section.

(4) A notice of underpayment must specify, for each worker to whom it relates—

(a) the relevant day in relation to that worker;

(b) the pay reference period or periods in respect of which the employer is required to pay a sum to the worker as specified in subsection (2) above;

(c) the amount described in section 17(2) above in relation to the worker in respect of each such period;

    (d)    the amount described in section 17(4) above in relation to the worker in respect of each of such period;

    (e)    the sum due under section 17 above to the worker for each such period.

(5)    Where a notice of underpayment relates to more than one worker, the notice may identify the workers by name or by description.

(6)    The reference in subsection (1) above to a pay reference period includes (subject to subsection (7) below) a pay reference period ending before the coming into force of this section.

(7)    A notice of underpayment may not relate to a pay reference period ending more than six years before the date of service of the notice.

(8)    In this section and sections 19A to 19C below 'the 28-day period' means the period of 28 days beginning with the date of service of the notice of underpayment.

## 19A    Notices of underpayment: financial penalty

(1)    A notice of underpayment must, subject to this section, require the employer to pay a financial penalty specified in the notice to the Secretary of State within the 28-day period.

(2)    The Secretary of State may by directions specify circumstances in which a notice of underpayment is not to impose a requirement to pay a financial penalty.

(3)    Directions under subsection (2) may be amended or revoked by further such directions.

(4)    The amount of any financial penalty is, subject as follows, to be the total of the amounts for all workers to whom the notice relates calculated in accordance with subsections (5) to (5B).

(5)    The amount for each worker to whom the notice relates is the relevant percentage of the amount specified under section 19(4)(c) in respect of each pay reference period specified under section 19(4)(b).

(5A)    In subsection (5), 'the relevant percentage', in relation to any pay reference period, means 200%.

(5B)    If the amount as calculated under subsection (5) for any worker would be more than £20,000, the amount for the worker taken into account in calculating the financial penalty is to be £20,000.

(6)    If a financial penalty as calculated under subsection (4) above would be less than £100, the financial penalty specified in the notice shall be that amount.

(7)    ...

(8)    The Secretary of State may by regulations—

    (a)    amend subsection (5A) above so as to substitute a different percentage for the percentage at any time specified there;

    (b)    amend subsection (5B) or (6) above so as to substitute a different amount for the amount at any time specified there.

(9)    A notice of underpayment must, in addition to specifying the amount of any financial penalty, state how that amount was calculated.

(10)    In a case where a notice of underpayment imposes a requirement to pay a financial penalty, if the employer on whom the notice is served, within the period of 14 days beginning with the day on which the notice was served—

    (a)    pays the amount required under section 19(2) above, and

    (b)    pays at least half the financial penalty,

    he shall be regarded as having paid the financial penalty.

(11)    A financial penalty paid to the Secretary of State pursuant to this section shall be paid by the Secretary of State into the Consolidated Fund.

## 19B    Suspension of financial penalty

(1)    This section applies in any case where it appears to the officer serving a notice of underpayment which imposes a requirement to pay a financial penalty that—

    (a)    relevant proceedings have been instituted; or

    (b)    relevant proceedings may be instituted.

(2)    In this section 'relevant proceedings' means proceedings against the employer for an offence under section 31(1) below in relation to a failure to remunerate any worker to whom the notice relates for any pay reference period specified under section 19(4)(b) above in relation to that worker.

(3) The notice of underpayment may contain provision suspending the requirement to pay the financial penalty payable under the notice until a notice terminating the suspension is served on the employer.

(4) An officer acting for the purposes of this Act may serve on the employer a notice terminating the suspension ('a penalty activation notice') if it appears to the officer—

    (a) in a case referred to in subsection (1)(a) above, that relevant proceedings have concluded without the employer having been convicted of an offence under section 31(1) below, or

    (b) in a case referred to in subsection (1)(b) above—

        (i) that relevant proceedings will not be instituted; or

        (ii) that relevant proceedings have been concluded without the employer having been convicted of an offence under section 31(1) below.

(5) Where a penalty activation notice is served, the requirement to pay the financial penalty has effect as if the notice of underpayment had been served on the day on which the penalty activation notice was served.

(6) An officer acting for the purposes of this Act must serve on the employer a notice withdrawing the requirement to pay the financial penalty if it appears to the officer that, pursuant to relevant proceedings, the employer has been convicted of an offence under section 31(1) below.

## 19C   Notices of underpayment: appeals

(1) A person on whom a notice of underpayment is served may in accordance with this section appeal against any one or more of the following—

    (a) the decision to serve the notice;

    (b) any requirement imposed by the notice to pay a sum to a worker;

    (c) any requirement imposed by the notice to pay a financial penalty.

(2) An appeal under this section lies to an employment tribunal.

(3) An appeal under this section must be made before the end of the 28-day period.

(4) An appeal under subsection (1)(a) above must be made on the ground that no sum was due under section 17 above to any worker to whom the notice relates on the day specified under section 19(4)(a) above in relation to him in respect of any pay reference period specified under section 19(4)(b) above in relation to him.

(5) An appeal under subsection (1)(b) above in relation to a worker must be made on either or both of the following grounds—

    (a) that, on the day specified under section 19(4)(a) above in relation to the worker, no sum was due to the worker under section 17 above in respect of any pay reference period specified under section 19(4)(b) above in relation to him;

    (b) that the amount specified in the notice as the sum due to the worker is incorrect.

(6) An appeal under subsection (1)(c) above must be made on either or both of the following grounds—

    (a) that the notice was served in circumstances specified in a direction under section 19A(2) above, or

    (b) that the amount of the financial penalty specified in the notice of underpayment has been incorrectly calculated (whether because the notice is incorrect in some of the particulars which affect that calculation or for some other reason).

(7) Where the employment tribunal allows an appeal under subsection (1)(a) above, it must rescind the notice.

(8) Where, in a case where subsection (7) above does not apply, the employment tribunal allows an appeal under subsection (1)(b) or (c) above—

    (a) the employment tribunal must rectify the notice, and

    (b) the notice of underpayment shall have effect as rectified from the date of the employment tribunal's determination.

## 19D   Non-compliance with notice of underpayment: recovery of arrears

(1) If a requirement to pay a sum to a worker contained in a notice of underpayment is not complied with in whole or in part, an officer acting for the purposes of this Act may, on behalf of any worker to whom the requirement relates—

    (a) present a complaint under section 23(1)(a) of the Employment Rights Act 1996 (deductions from worker's wages in contravention of section 13 of that Act) to an employment tribunal in respect of any sums due to the worker by virtue of section 17 above; or

(b)    in relation to Northern Ireland, present a complaint under Article 55(1)(a) of the Employment Rights (Northern Ireland) Order 1996 (deductions from worker's wages in contravention of Article 45 of that Order) to an industrial tribunal in respect of any sums due to the worker by virtue of section 17 above; or

(c)    commence other civil proceedings for the recovery, on a claim in contract, of any sums due to the worker by virtue of section 17 above.

(2)    The powers conferred by subsection (1) above for the recovery of sums due from an employer to a worker shall not be in derogation of any right which the worker may have to recover such sums by civil proceedings.

### 19E    Non-compliance with notice of underpayment: recovery of penalty

A financial penalty payable under a notice of underpayment—

(a)    in England and Wales, is recoverable, if a county court so orders, under section 85 of the County Courts Act 1984 or otherwise as if it were payable under an order of that court;

(b)    in Scotland, may be enforced in the same manner as an extract registered decree arbitral bearing a warrant for execution issued by the sheriff court of any sheriffdom in Scotland;

(c)    in Northern Ireland, is recoverable, if the county court so orders, as if it were payable under an order of that court.

### 19F    Withdrawal of notice of underpayment

(1)    Where a notice of underpayment has been served (and not already withdrawn or rescinded) and it appears to an officer acting for the purposes of this Act that the notice incorrectly includes or omits any requirement or is incorrect in any particular, the officer may withdraw it by serving notice of the withdrawal on the employer.

(2)    Where a notice of underpayment is withdrawn and no replacement notice of underpayment is served in accordance with section 19G below—

(a)    any sum paid by or recovered from the employer by way of financial penalty payable under the notice must be repaid to him with interest at the appropriate rate running from the date when the sum was paid or recovered;

(b)    any appeal against the notice must be dismissed;

(c)    after the withdrawal no complaint may be presented or other civil proceedings commenced by virtue of section 19D above in reliance on any non-compliance with the notice before it was withdrawn;

(d)    any complaint or proceedings so commenced before the withdrawal may be proceeded with despite the withdrawal.

(3)    In a case where subsection (2) above applies, the notice of withdrawal must indicate the effect of that subsection (but a failure to do so does not make the withdrawal ineffective).

(4)    In subsection (2)(a) above, 'the appropriate rate' means the rate that, on the date the sum was paid or recovered, was specified in section 17 of the Judgments Act 1838.

### 19G    Replacement notice of underpayment

(1)    Where an officer acting for the purposes of this Act serves a notice of withdrawal under section 19F above and is of the opinion referred to in section 19(1) above in relation to any worker specified in the notice which is being withdrawn ('the original notice'), he may at the same time serve another notice under section 19 above ('the replacement notice').

(2)    The replacement notice may not relate to any worker to whom the original notice did not relate.

(3)    If the replacement notice contravenes subsection (2) above, that fact shall be an additional ground of appeal for the purposes of section 19C above.

(4)    The replacement notice may relate to a pay reference period ending after the date of service of the original notice.

(5)    Section 19(7) above applies in relation to the replacement notice as if the reference to six years before the date of service of the notice were a reference to six years before the date of service of the original notice.

(6) The replacement notice must—
    (a)   indicate the differences between it and the original notice that it is reasonable for the officer to consider are material; and
    (b)   indicate the effect of section 19H below.
(7) Failure to comply with subsection (6) above does not make the replacement notice ineffective.
(8) Where a replacement notice is withdrawn under section 19F above, no further replacement notice may be served under subsection (1) above pursuant to the withdrawal.
(9) Nothing in this section affects any power that arises apart from this section to serve a notice of underpayment in relation to any worker.

## 19H    Effect of replacement notice of underpayment

(1) This section applies where a notice of underpayment is withdrawn under section 19F above and a replacement notice is served in accordance with section 19G above.
(2) If an appeal has been made under section 19C above against the original notice and the appeal has not been withdrawn or finally determined before the time when that notice is withdrawn—
    (a)   that appeal ('the earlier appeal') shall have effect after that time as if it were against the replacement notice; and
    (b)   the employer may exercise his right of appeal under section 19C above against the replacement notice only if he withdraws the earlier appeal.
(3) After the withdrawal no complaint may be presented or other civil proceedings commenced by virtue of section 19D above in reliance on any non-compliance with the notice before it was withdrawn; but any complaint or proceedings so commenced before the withdrawal may be proceeded with despite the withdrawal.
(4) If a sum was paid by or recovered from the employer by way of financial penalty under the original notice—
    (a)   an amount equal to that sum (or, if more than one, the total of those sums) shall be treated as having been paid in respect of the replacement notice; and
    (b)   any amount by which that sum (or total) exceeds the amount payable under the replacement notice must be repaid to the employer with interest at the appropriate rate running from the date when the sum (or, if more than one, the first of them) was paid or recovered.
(5) In subsection (4)(b) above 'the appropriate rate' means the rate that, on the date mentioned in that provision, was specified in section 17 of the Judgments Act 1838.

*Rights not to suffer unfair dismissal or other detriment*

## 23    The right not to suffer detriment

(1) A worker has the right not to be subjected to any detriment by any act. or any deliberate failure to act by his employer, cone on the ground that—
    (a)   any action was taken, or was proposed to be taken, by or on behalf of the worker with a view to enforcing, or otherwise securing the benefit of, a right of the worker's to which this section applies; or
    (b)   the employer was prosecuted for an offence under section 31 below as a result of action taken by or on behalf of the worker for the purpose of enforcing, or otherwise securing the benefit of, a right of the worker's to which this section applies; or
    (c)   the worker qualifies, or will or might qualify, for the national minimum wage or for a particular rate of national minimum wage.
(2) It is immaterial for the purposes of paragraph (a) or (b) of subsection (1) above—
    (a)   whether or not the worker has the right, or
    (b)   whether or not the right has been infringed,
but, for that subsection to apply, the claim to the right and, if applicable, the claim that it has been infringed must be made in good faith.
(3) The following are the rights to which this section applies—
    (a)   any right conferred by, or by virtue of, any provision of this Act for which the remedy for its infringement is by way of a complaint to an employment tribunal; and

(b)    any right conferred by section 17 above.

(4)    This section does not apply where the detriment in question amounts to dismissal within the meaning of—

(a)    Part X of the Employment Rights Act 1996 (unfair dismissal), or

(b)    Part XI of the Employment Rights (Northern Ireland) Order 1996 (corresponding provision for Northern Ireland),

except where in relation to Northern Ireland the person in question is dismissed in circumstances in which, by virtue of Article 240 of that Order (fixed term contracts), Part XI does not apply to the dismissal.

## 24    Enforcement of the right

(1)    A worker may present a complaint to an employment tribunal that he has been subjected to a detriment in contravention of section 23 above.

(2)    Subject to the following provisions of this section, the provisions of—

(a)    sections 48(2) to (4) and 49 of the Employment Rights Act 1996 (complaints to employment tribunals and remedies), or

(b)    in relation to Northern Ireland, Articles 71(2) to (4) and 72 of the Employment Rights (Northern Ireland) Order 1996 (complaints to industrial tribunals and remedies),

shall apply in relation to a complaint under this section as they apply in relation to a complaint under section 48 of that Act or Article 71 of that Order (as the case may be), but taking references in those provisions to the employer as references to the employer within the meaning of section 23(1) above.

(3)    Where—

(a)    the detriment to which the worker is subjected is the termination of his worker's contract, but

(b)    that contract is not a contract of employment,

any compensation awarded under section 49 of the Employment Rights Act 1996 or Article 72 of the Employment Rights (Northern Ireland) Order 1996 by virtue of subsection (2) above must not exceed the limit specified in subsection (4) below.

(4)    The limit mentioned in subsection (3) above is the total of—

(a)    the sum which would he the basic award for unfair dismissal, calculated in accordance with section 119 of the Employment Rights Act 1996 or Article 153 of the Employment Rights (Northern Ireland) Order 1996 (as the case may be), if the worker had been an employee and the contract terminated had been a contract of employment; and

(b)    the sum for the time being specified in section 124(1) of that Act or Article 158(1) of that Order (as the case may be) which is the limit for a compensatory award to a person calculated in accordance with section 123 of that Act or Article 157 of that Order (as the case may be).

(5)    Where the worker has been working under arrangements which do not fall to be regarded as a worker's contract for the purposes of—

(a)    the Employment Rights Act 1996, or

(b)    in relation to Northern Ireland, the Employment Rights (Northern Ireland) Order 1996,

he shall be treated for the purposes of subsections (3) and (4) above as if any arrangements under which he has been working constituted a worker's contract falling within section 230(3)(b) of that Act or Article 3(3)(b) of that Order (as the case may be).

## 28    Reversal of burden of proof

(1)    Where in any civil proceedings any question arises as to whether an individual qualifies or qualified at any time for the national minimum wage, it shall be presumed that the individual qualifies or, as the case may be, qualified at that time for the national minimum wage unless the contrary is established.

(2)    Where—

(a)    a complaint is made—

(i)    to an employment tribunal under section 23(1)(a) of the Employment Rights Act 1996 (unauthorised deductions from wages), or

       (ii)    to an industrial tribunal under Article 55(1)(a) of the Employment Rights (Northern Ireland) Order 1996, and

(b)    the complaint relates in whole or in part to the deduction of the amount described as additional remuneration in section 17(1) above,

it shall be presumed for the purposes of the complaint, so far as relating to the deduction of that amount, that the worker in question was remunerated at a rate less than the national minimum wage unless the contrary is established.

(3)    Where in any civil proceedings a person seeks to recover on a claim in contract the amount described as additional remuneration in section 17(1) above, it shall be presumed for the purposes of the proceedings, so far as relating to that amount, that the worker in question was remunerated at a rate less than the national minimum wage unless the contrary is established.

*Offences*

## 31    Offences

(1)    If the employer of a worker who qualifies for the national minimum wage refuses or wilfully neglects to remunerate the worker for any pay reference period at a rate which is at least equal to the national minimum wage, that employer is guilty of an offence.

…

*Special classes of person*

## 34    Agency workers who are not otherwise 'workers'

(1)    This section applies in any case where an individual ('the agency worker')—

(a)    is supplied by a person ('the agent') to do work for another ('the principal') under a contract or other arrangements made between the agent and the principal; but

(b)    is not, as respects that work, a worker, because of the absence of a worker's contract between the individual and the agent or the principal; and

(c)    is not a party to a contract under which he undertakes to do the work for another party to the contract whose status is, by virtue of the contract, that of a client or customer of any profession or business undertaking carried on by the individual.

(2)    In a case where this section applies, the other provisions of this Act shall have effect as if there were a worker's contract for the doing of the work by the agency worker made between the agency worker and—

(a)    whichever of the agent and the principal is responsible for paying the agency worker in respect of the work; or

(b)    if neither the agent nor the principal is so responsible, whichever of them pays the agency worker in respect of the work.

## 35    Home workers who are not otherwise 'workers'

(1)    In determining for the purposes of this Act whether a home worker is or is not a worker, section 54(3)(b) below shall have effect as if for the word 'personally' there were substituted '(whether personally or otherwise)'.

(2)    In this section 'home worker' means an individual who contracts with a person, for the purposes of that person's business, for the execution of work to be done in a place not under the control or management of that person.

*Extensions*

## 41    Power to apply Act to individuals who are not otherwise 'workers'

The Secretary of State may by regulations make provision for this Act to apply, with or without modifications, as if—

(a)    any individual of a prescribed description who would not otherwise be a worker for the purposes of this Act were a worker for those purposes;

(b)    there were in the case of any such individual a worker's contract of a prescribed description under which the individual works; and

(c)    a person of a prescribed description were the employer under that contract.

*Supplementary*

### 54    Meaning of 'worker', 'employee' etc.

(1)    In this Act 'employee' means an individual who has entered into or works under (or, where the employment has ceased, worked under) a contract of employment.

(2)    In this Act 'contract of employment' means a contract of service or apprenticeship, whether express or implied, and (if it is express) whether oral or in writing.

(3)    In this Act 'worker' (except in the phrases 'agency worker' and 'home worker') means an individual who has entered into or works under (or, where the employment has ceased, worked under)—

(a)    a contract of employment; or

(b)    any other contract, whether express or implied and (if it is express) whether oral or in writing, whereby the individual undertakes to do or perform personally any work or services for another party to the contract whose status is not by virtue of the contract that of a client or customer of any profession or business undertaking carried on by the individual;

and any reference to a worker's contract shall be construed accordingly.

(4)    In this Act 'employer', in relation to an employee or a worker, means the person by whom the employee or worker is (or, where the employment has ceased, was) employed.

(5)    In this Act 'employment'—

(a)    in relation to an employee, means employment under a contract of employment; and

(b)    in relation to a worker, means employment under his contract;

and 'employed' shall be construed accordingly.

## HUMAN RIGHTS ACT 1998
## (1998, c. 42)

### 1    The Convention Rights

(1)    In this Act 'the Convention rights' means the rights and fundamental freedoms set out in—

(a)    Articles 2 to 12 and 14 of the Convention,

(b)    Articles 1 to 3 of the First Protocol, and

(c)    Article 1 of the Thirteenth Protocol,

as read with Articles 16 to 18 of the Convention.

(2)    Those Articles are to have effect for the purposes of this Act subject to any designated derogation or reservation (as to which see sections 14 and 15).

(3)    The Articles are set out in Schedule 1.

...

### 2    Interpretation of Convention rights

(1)    A court or tribunal determining a question which has arisen in connection with a Convention right must take into account any—

(a)    judgment, decision, declaration or advisory opinion of the European Court of Human Rights,

(b)    opinion of the Commission given in a report adopted under Article 31 of the Convention,

(c)    decision of the Commission in connection with Article 26 or 27(2) of the Convention, or

(d)    decision of the Committee of Ministers taken under Article 46 of the Convention, whenever made or given, so far as, in the opinion of the court or tribunal, it is relevant to the proceedings in which that question has arisen.

...

### 3    Interpretation of legislation

(1)    So far as it is possible to do so, primary legislation and subordinate legislation must be read and given effect in a way which is compatible with the Convention rights.

(2)   This section—
    (a)   applies to primary legislation and subordinate legislation whenever enacted;
    (b)   does not affect the validity, continuing operation or enforcement of any incompatible primary legislation; and
    (c)   does not affect the validity, continuing operation or enforcement of any incompatible subordinate legislation if (disregarding any possibility of revocation) primary legislation prevents removal of the incompatibility.

## 4   Declaration of incompatibility

(1)   Subsection (2) applies in any proceedings in which a court determines whether a provision of primary legislation is compatible with a Convention right.

(2)   If the court is satisfied that the provision is incompatible with a Convention right, it may make a declaration of that incompatibility.

(3)   Subsection (4) applies in any proceedings in which a court determines whether a provision of subordinate legislation, made in the exercise of a power conferred by primary legislation, is compatible with a Convention right.

(4)   If the court is satisfied—
    (a)   that the provision is incompatible with a Convention right, and
    (b)   that (disregarding any possibility of revocation) the primary legislation concerned prevents removal of the incompatibility,
    it may make a declaration of that incompatibility.

(5)   In this section 'court' means—
    (a)   the Supreme Court;
    (b)   the Judicial Committee of the Privy Council;
    (c)   the Court Martial Appeal Court;
    (d)   in Scotland, the High Court of Justiciary sitting otherwise than as a trial court or the Court of Session;
    (e)   in England and Wales or Northern Ireland, the High Court or the Court of Appeal.
    (f)   the Court of Protection, in any matter being dealt with by the President of the Family Division, the Chancellor of the High Court or a puisne judge of the High Court.

(6)   A declaration under this section ('a declaration of incompatibility')—
    (a)   does not affect the validity, continuing operation or enforcement of the provision in respect of which it is given; and
    (b)   is not binding on the parties to the proceedings in which it is made.

SCHEDULE 1
THE ARTICLES

PART I
THE CONVENTION RIGHTS AND FREEDOMS

## Article 4   Prohibition of slavery and forced labour

1    No one shall be held in slavery or servitude.

2    No one shall be required to perform forced or compulsory labour.

3    For the purpose of this Article the term 'forced or compulsory labour' shall not include:
    (a)   any work required to be done in the ordinary course of detention imposed according to the provisions of Article 5 of this Convention or during conditional release from such detention;
    (b)   any service of a military character or, in case of conscientious objectors in countries where they are recognised, service exacted instead of compulsory military service;
    (c)   any service exacted in case of an emergency or calamity threatening the life or well-being of the community;
    (d)   any work or service which forms part of normal civic obligations.

## Article 6    Right to a fair trial

1    In the determination of his civil rights and obligations or of any criminal charge against him, everyone is entitled to a fair and public hearing within a reasonable time by an independent and impartial tribunal established by law. Judgment shall be pronounced publicly but the press and public may be excluded from all or part of the trial in the interest of morals, public order or national security in a democratic society, where the interests of juveniles or the protection of the private life of the parties so require, or to the extent strictly necessary in the opinion of the court in special circumstances where publicity would prejudice the interests of justice.

...

## Article 8    Right to respect for private and family life

1    Everyone has the right to respect for his private and family life, his home and his correspondence.

2    There shall be no interference by a public authority with the exercise of this right except such as is in accordance with the law and is necessary in a democratic society in the interests of national security, public safety or the economic well-being of the country, for the prevention of disorder or crime, for the protection of health or morals, or for the protection of the rights and freedoms of others.

## Article 9    Freedom of thought, conscience and religion

1    Everyone has the right to freedom of thought, conscience and religion; this right includes freedom to change his religion or belief and freedom, either alone or in community with others and in public or private, to manifest his religion or belief, in worship, teaching, practice and observance.

2    Freedom to manifest one's religion or beliefs shall be subject only to such limitations as are prescribed by law and are necessary in a democratic society in the interests of public safety, for the protection of public order, health or morals, or for the protection of the rights and freedoms of others.

## Article 10    Freedom of expression

1    Everyone has the right to freedom of expression. This right shall include freedom to hold opinions and to receive and impart information and ideas without interference by public authority and regardless of frontiers. This Article shall not prevent States from requiring the licensing of broadcasting, television or cinema enterprises.

2    The exercise of these freedoms, since it carries with it duties and responsibilities, may be subject to such formalities, conditions, restrictions or penalties as are prescribed by law and are necessary in a democratic society, in the interests of national security, territorial integrity or public safety, for the prevention of disorder or crime, for the protection of health or morals, for the protection of the reputation or rights of others, for preventing the disclosure of information received in confidence, or for maintaining the authority and impartiality of the judiciary.

## Article 11    Freedom of assembly and association

1    Everyone has the right to freedom of peaceful assembly and to freedom of association with others, including the right to form and to join trade unions for the protection of his interests.

2    No restrictions shall be placed on the exercise of these rights other than such as are prescribed by law and are necessary in a democratic society in the interests of national security or public safety, for the prevention of disorder or crime, for the protection of health or morals or for the protection of the rights and freedoms of others. This Article shall not prevent the imposition of lawful restrictions on the exercise of these rights by members of the armed forces, of the police or of the administration of the State.

## Article 14    Prohibition of discrimination

The enjoyment of the rights and freedoms set forth in this Convention shall be secured without discrimination on any ground such as sex, race, colour, language, religion, political or other opinion, national or social origin, association with a national minority, property, birth or other status.

## EMPLOYMENT RELATIONS ACT 1999
## (1999, c. 26)

*Disciplinary and grievance hearings*

**10    Right to be accompanied**

(1)   This section applies where a worker—
   (a)   is required or invited by his employer to attend a disciplinary or grievance hearing, and
   (b)   reasonably requests to be accompanied at the hearing.

(2A)  Where this section applies, the employer must permit the worker to be accompanied at the hearing by one companion who—
   (a)   is chosen by the worker; and
   (b)   is within subsection (3).

(2B)  The employer must permit the worker's companion to—
   (a)   address the hearing in order to do any or all of the following—
      (i)    put the worker's case;
      (ii)   sum up that case;
      (iii)  respond on the worker's behalf to any view expressed at the hearing;
   (b)   confer with the worker during the hearing.

(2C)  Subsection (2B) does not require the employer to permit the worker's companion to—
   (a)   answer questions on behalf of the worker;
   (b)   address the hearing if the worker indicates at it that he does not wish his companion to do so; or
   (c)   use the powers conferred by that subsection in a way that prevents the employer from explaining his case or prevents any other person at the hearing from making his contribution to it.

(3)   A person is within this subsection if he is—
   (a)   employed by a trade union of which he is an official within the meaning of section 1 and 119 of the Trade Union and Labour Relations (Consolidation) Act 1992,
   (b)   an official of a trade union (within that meaning) whom the union has reasonably certified in writing as having experience of, or as having received training in, acting as a worker's companion at disciplinary or grievance hearings, or
   (c)   another of the employer's workers.

(4)   If—
   (a)   a worker has a right under this section to be accompanied at a hearing,
   (b)   his chosen companion will not be available at the time proposed for the hearing by the employer, and
   (c)   the worker proposes an alternative time which satisfies subsection (5),
   the employer must postpone the hearing to the time proposed by the worker.

(5)   An alternative time must—
   (a)   be reasonable, and
   (b)   fall before the end of the period of five working days beginning with the first working day after the day proposed by the employer.

(6)   An employer shall permit a worker to take time off during working hours for the purpose of accompanying another of the employer's workers in accordance with a request under subsection (1)(b).

(7)   Sections 168(3) and (4), 169 and 171 to 173 of the Trade Union and Labour Relations (Consolidation) Act 1992 (time off for carrying out trade union duties) shall apply in relation to subsection (6) above as they apply in relation to section 168(1) of that Act.

**11    Complaint to employment tribunal**

(1)   A worker may present a complaint to an employment tribunal that his employer has failed, or threatened to fail, to comply with section 10(2A), (2B) or (4).

(2)   A tribunal shall not consider a complaint under this section in relation to a failure or threat unless the complaint is presented—
   (a)   before the end of the period of three months beginning with the date of the failure or threat, or

(b)    within such further period as the tribunal considers reasonable in a case where it is satisfied that it was not reasonably practicable for the complaint to be presented before the end of that period of three months.

(3)    Where a tribunal finds that a complaint under this section is well-founded it shall order the employer to pay compensation to the worker of an amount not exceeding two weeks' pay.

(4)    Chapter II of Part XIV of the Employment Rights Act 1996 (calculation of a week's pay) shall apply for the purposes of subsection (3); and in applying that Chapter the calculation date shall be taken to be—

(a)    in the case of a claim which is made in the course of a claim for unfair dismissal, the date on which the employer's notice of dismissal was given or, if there was no notice, the effective date of termination, and

(b)    in any other case, the date on which the relevant hearing took place (or was to have taken place).

(5), (6) ...

## 12    Detriment and dismissal

(1)    A worker has the right not to be subjected to any detriment by any act, or any deliberate failure to act, by his employer done on the ground that he—

(a)    exercised or sought to exercise the right under section 10(2A), (2B) or (4), or

(b)    accompanied or sought to accompany another worker (whether of the same employer or not) pursuant to a request under that section.

(2)    Section 48 of the Employment Rights Act 1996 shall apply in relation to contraventions of subsection (1) above as it applies in relation to contraventions of certain sections of that Act.

(3)    A worker who is dismissed shall be regarded for the purposes of Part X of the Employment Rights Act 1996 as unfairly dismissed if the reason (or, if more than one, the principal reason) for the dismissal is that he—

(a)    exercised or sought to exercise the right under section 10(2) or (4), or

(b)    accompanied or sought to accompany another worker (whether of the same employer or not) pursuant to a request under that section.

(4)    Sections 108 and 109 of that Act (qualifying period of employment and upper age limit) shall not apply in relation to subsection (3) above.

(5)    Sections 128 to 132 of that Act (interim relief) shall apply in relation to dismissal for the reason specified in subsection (3)(a) or (b) above as they apply in relation to dismissal for a reason specified in section 128(1)(b) of that Act.

(6)    In the application of Chapter II of Part X of that Act in relation to subsection (3) above, a reference to an employee shall be taken as a reference to a worker.

(7)    References in this section to a worker having accompanied or sought to accompany another worker include references to his having exercised or sought to exercise any of the powers conferred by section 10(2A) or (2B).

## 13    Interpretation

(1)    In sections 10 to 12 and this section 'worker' means an individual who is—

(a)    a worker within the meaning of section 230(3) of the Employment Rights Act 1996,

(b)    an agency worker,

(c)    a home worker,

(d)    a person in Crown employment within the meaning of section 191 of that Act, other than a member of the naval, military, air or reserve forces of the Crown, or

(e)    employed as a relevant member of the House of Lords staff or the House of Commons staff within the meaning of section 194(6) or 195(5) of that Act.

(2)    In subsection (1) 'agency worker' means an individual who—

(a)    is supplied by a person ('the agent') to do work for another ('the principal') by arrangement between the agent and the principal,

(b)    is not a party to a worker's contract, within the meaning of section 230(3) of that Act, relating to that work, and

(c)    is not a party to a contract relating to that work under which he undertakes to do the work for another party to the contract whose status is, by virtue of the contract, that of a client or customer of any professional or business undertaking carried on by the individual;

and, for the purposes of sections 10 to 12, both the agent and the principal are employers of an agency worker.

(3)   In subsection (1) 'home worker' means an individual who—

    (a)   contracts with a person, for the purposes of the person's business, for the execution of work to be done in a place not under the person's control or management, and

    (b)   is not a party to a contract relating to that work under which the work is to be executed for another party to the contract whose status is, by virtue of the contract, that of a client or customer of any professional or business undertaking carried on by the individual;

and, for the purposes of sections 10 to 12, the person mentioned in paragraph (a) is the home worker's employer.

(4)   For the purposes of section 10 a disciplinary hearing is a hearing which could result in—

    (a)   the administration of a formal warning to a worker by his employer,

    (b)   the taking of some other action in respect of a worker by his employer, or

    (c)   the confirmation of a warning issued or some other action taken.

(5)   For the purposes of section 10 a grievance hearing is a hearing which concerns the performance of a duty by an employer in relation to a worker.

(6)   For the purposes of section 10(5)(b) in its application to a part of Great Britain a working day is a day other than—

    (a)   a Saturday or a Sunday,

    (b)   Christmas Day or Good Friday, or

    (c)   a day which is a bank holiday under the Banking and Financial Dealings Act 1971 in that part of Great Britain.

## 14   Contracting out and conciliation

Sections 10 to 13 of this Act shall be treated as provisions of Part V of the Employment Rights Act 1996 for the purposes of—

    (a)   section 203(1), (2)(e) and (f), (3) and (4) of that Act (restrictions on contracting out), and

    (b)   section 18(1)(b) of the Employment Tribunals Act 1996 (conciliation).

## 15   National security employees

Sections 10 to 13 of this Act shall not apply in relation to a person employed for the purposes of—

    (a)   the Security Service,

    (b)   the Secret Intelligence Service, or

    (c)   the Government Communications Headquarters.

*Other rights of individuals*

## 23   Power to confer rights on individuals

(1)   This section applies to any right conferred on an individual against an employer (however defined) under or by virtue of any of the following—

    (a)   the Trade Union and Labour Relations (Consolidation) Act 1992;

    (b)   the Employment Rights Act 1996;

    (ba)  the Employment Act 2002;

    (c)   this Act;

    (d)   any instrument made under section 2(2) of the European Communities Act 1972.

(2)   The Secretary of State may by order make provision which has the effect of conferring any such right on individuals who are of a specified description.

(3)   The reference in subsection (2) to individuals includes a reference to individuals expressly excluded from exercising the right.

(4)   An order under this section may—

    (a)   provide that individuals are to be treated as parties to workers' contracts or contracts of employment;

(b)    make provision as to who are to be regarded as the employers of individuals;

(c)    make provision which has the effect of modifying the operation of any right as conferred on individuals by the order;

(d)    include such consequential, incidental or supplementary provisions as the Secretary of State thinks fit.

...

# EQUALITY ACT 2006
## (2006, c. 3)

PART 1

THE COMMISSION FOR EQUALITY AND HUMAN RIGHTS

*The Commission*

## 3    General duty

The Commission shall exercise its functions under this Part with a view to encouraging and supporting the development of a society in which—

(a)    people's ability to achieve their potential is not limited by prejudice or discrimination,

(b)    there is respect for and protection of each individual's human rights,

(c)    there is respect for the dignity and worth of each individual,

(d)    each individual has an equal opportunity to participate in society, and

(e)    there is mutual respect between groups based on understanding and valuing of diversity and on shared respect for equality and human rights.

## 4    Strategic plan

(1)    The Commission shall prepare a plan showing—

(a)    activities or classes of activity to be undertaken by the Commission in pursuance of its functions under this Act,

(b)    an expected timetable for each activity or class, and

(c)    priorities for different activities or classes, or principles to be applied in determining priorities.

(2)    The Commission shall review the plan—

(a)    at least once during the period of three years beginning with its completion,

(b)    at least once during each period of three years beginning with the completion of a review, and

(c)    at such other times as the Commission thinks appropriate.

(3)    If the Commission thinks it appropriate as a result of a review, the Commission shall revise the plan.

(4)    The Commission shall send the plan and each revision to the Minister, who shall lay a copy before Parliament.

(5)    The Commission shall publish the plan and each revision.

## 5    Strategic plan: consultation

Before preparing or reviewing a plan in accordance with section 4 the Commission shall—

(a)    consult such persons having knowledge or experience relevant to the Commission's functions as the Commission thinks appropriate,

(b)    consult such other persons as the Commission thinks appropriate,

(c)    issue a general invitation to make representations, in a manner likely in the Commission's opinion to bring the invitation to the attention of as large a class of persons who may wish to make representations as is reasonably practicable, and

(d)    take account of any representations made.

*Duties*

## 8    Equality and diversity

(1)  The Commission shall, by exercising the powers conferred by this Part—
    (a)  promote understanding of the importance of equality and diversity,
    (b)  encourage good practice in relation to equality and diversity,
    (c)  promote equality of opportunity,
    (d)  promote awareness and understanding of rights under the Equality Act 2010,
    (e)  enforce the Equality Act 2010,
    (f)  work towards the elimination of unlawful discrimination, and
    (g)  work towards the elimination of unlawful harassment.

(2)  In subsection (1)—
    'diversity' means the fact that individuals are different,
    'equality' means equality between individuals, and
    'unlawful' is to be construed in accordance with section 34.

(3)  In promoting equality of opportunity between disabled persons and others, the Commission may, in particular, promote the favourable treatment of disabled persons.

(4)  In this Part 'disabled person' means a person who—
    (a)  is a disabled person within the meaning of the Equality Act 2010, or
    (b)  has been a disabled person within that meaning (whether or not at a time when that Act had effect).

## 9    Human rights

(1)  The Commission shall, by exercising the powers conferred by this Part—
    (a)  promote understanding of the importance of human rights,
    (b)  encourage good practice in relation to human rights,
    (c)  promote awareness, understanding and protection of human rights, and
    (d)  encourage public authorities to comply with section 6 of the Human Rights Act 1998 (compliance with Convention rights).

(2)  In this Part 'human rights' means—
    (a)  the Convention rights within the meaning given by section 1 of the Human Rights Act 1998, and
    (b)  other human rights.

(3)  In determining what action to take in pursuance of this section the Commission shall have particular regard to the importance of exercising the powers conferred by this Part in relation to the Convention rights.

(4)  In fulfilling a duty under section 8 or 10 the Commission shall take account of any relevant human rights.

(5)  A reference in this Part (including this section) to human rights does not exclude any matter by reason only of its being a matter to which section 8 or 10 relates.

## 10   Groups

(1)  The Commission shall, by exercising the powers conferred by this Part—
    (a)  promote understanding of the importance of good relations—
        (i)   between members of different groups, and
        (ii)  between members of groups and others,
    (b)  encourage good practice in relation to relations—
        (i)   between members of different groups, and
        (ii)  between members of groups and others,
    (c)  work towards the elimination of prejudice against, hatred of and hostility towards members of groups, and
    (d)  work towards enabling members of groups to participate in society.

(2)  In this Part 'group' means a group or class of persons who share a common attribute in respect of any of the following matters—
    (a)  age,
    (b)  disability,
    (c)  gender,
    (d)  proposed, commenced or completed reassignment of gender (within the meaning given by section 82(1) of the Sex Discrimination Act 1975),
    (e)  race,

      (f)    religion or belief, and

      (g)    sexual orientation.

(3)    For the purposes of this Part a reference to a group (as defined in subsection (2)) includes a reference to a smaller group or smaller class, within a group, of persons who share a common attribute (in addition to the attribute by reference to which the group is defined) in respect of any of the matters specified in subsection (2)(a) to (g).

(4)    In determining what action to take in pursuance of this section the Commission shall have particular regard to the importance of exercising the powers conferred by this Part in relation to groups defined by reference to race, religion or belief.

(5)    The Commission may, in taking action in pursuance of subsection (1) in respect of groups defined by reference to disability and others, promote or encourage the favourable treatment of disabled persons.

(6)    The Minister may by order amend the list in subsection (2) so as to—

      (a)    add an entry, or

      (b)    vary an entry.

(7)    This section is without prejudice to the generality of section 8.

## 11    Monitoring the law

(1)    The Commission shall monitor the effectiveness of the equality and human rights enactments.

(2)    The Commission may—

      (a)    advise central government about the effectiveness of any of the equality and human rights enactments;

      (b)    recommend to central government the amendment, repeal, consolidation (with or without amendments) or replication (with or without amendments) of any of the equality and human rights enactments;

      (c)    advise central or devolved government about the effect of an enactment (including an enactment in or under an Act of the Scottish Parliament);

      (d)    advise central or devolved government about the likely effect of a proposed change of law.

(3)    In this section—

      (a)    'central government' means Her Majesty's Government,

      (b)    'devolved government' means—

          (i)    the Scottish Ministers, and

          (ii)    the Welsh Ministers, the First Minister for Wales and the Counsel General to the Welsh Assembly Government, and

      (c)    a reference to the equality enactments shall be treated as including a reference to any provision of this Act.

## 12    Monitoring progress

(1)    The Commission shall from time to time identify—

      (a)    changes in society that have occurred or are expected to occur and are relevant to the aim specified in section 3,

      (b)    results at which to aim for the purpose of encouraging and supporting the development of the society described in section 3 ('outcomes'), and

      (c)    factors by reference to which progress towards those results may be measured ('indicators').

(2)    In identifying outcomes and indicators the Commission shall—

      (a)    consult such persons having knowledge or experience relevant to the Commission's functions as the Commission thinks appropriate,

      (b)    consult such other persons as the Commission thinks appropriate,

      (c)    issue a general invitation to make representations, in a manner likely in the Commission's opinion to bring the invitation to the attention of as large a class of persons who may wish to make representations as is reasonably practicable, and

      (d)    take account of any representations made.

(3)    The Commission shall from time to time monitor progress towards each identified outcome by reference to any relevant identified indicator.

(4)    The Commission shall publish a report on progress towards the identified outcomes by reference to the identified indicators—

   (a) within the period of three years beginning with the date on which this section comes into force, and

   (b) within each period of three years beginning with the date on which a report is published under this subsection.

 (5) The Commission shall send each report to the Minister, who shall lay a copy before Parliament.

## 13 Information, advice, etc.

 (1) In pursuance of its duties under sections 8 and 9 the Commission may—

   (a) publish or otherwise disseminate ideas or information;

   (b) undertake research;

   (c) provide education or training;

   (d) give advice or guidance (whether about the effect or operation of an enactment or otherwise);

   (e) arrange for a person to do anything within paragraphs (a) to (d);

   (f) act jointly with, co-operate with or assist a person doing anything within paragraphs (a) to (d).

 (2) The reference to giving advice in subsection (1)(d) does not include a reference to preparing, or assisting in the preparation of, a document to be used for the purpose of legal proceedings.

## 14 Codes of practice

 (1) The Commission may issue a code of practice in connection with any matter addressed by the Equality Act 2010.

 (2) A code of practice under subsection (1) shall contain provision designed—

   (a) to ensure or facilitate compliance with the Equality Act 2010 or an enactment made under that Act, or

   (b) to promote equality of opportunity.

 (3) The Commission may issue a code of practice giving practical guidance to landlords and tenants in England or Wales about—

   (a) circumstances in which a tenant requires the consent of his landlord to make a relevant improvement, within the meaning section 190(7) of the Equality Act 2010 (improvements), to a dwelling house,

   (b) reasonableness in relation to that consent, and

   (c) the application in relation to relevant improvements (within that meaning) to dwelling houses of

    (i) section 19(2) of the Landlord and Tenant Act 1927 (consent to improvements),

    (ii) sections 81 to 85 of the Housing Act 1980 (tenant's improvements),

    (iii) sections 97 to 99 of the Housing Act 1985 (tenant's improvements), and

    (iv) section 190 of the Equality Act 2010.

 (4) The Commission may issue a code of practice giving practical guidance to landlords and tenants of houses (within the meaning of the Housing (Scotland) Act 2006) in Scotland about—

   (a) circumstances in which the tenant requires the consent of the landlord to carry out work in relation to the house for the purpose of making the house suitable for the accommodation, welfare or employment of any disabled person who occupies, or intends to occupy, the house as a sole or main residence,

   (b) circumstances in which it is unreasonable to withhold that consent,

   (c) circumstances in which any condition imposed on the granting of that consent is unreasonable, and

   (d) the application in relation to such work of—

    (i) sections 28 to 31 and 34(6) of the Housing (Scotland) Act 2001, and

    (ii) sections 52, 53 and 64(6) of the Housing (Scotland) Act 2006.

 (5) The Commission shall comply with a direction of the Secretary of State to issue a code under this section in connection with a specified matter if—

   (a) the matter is not a matter addressed by the Equality Act 2010, but

   (b) the Secretary of State expects to add it by order under section 15(6).

 (6) Before issuing a code under this section the Commission shall—

(a) publish proposals, and

(b) consult such persons as it thinks appropriate.

(7) Before issuing a code under this section the Commission shall submit a draft to the Secretary of State, who shall—

    (a) if he approves the draft—

        (i) notify the Commission, and

        (ii) lay a copy before Parliament, or

    (b) otherwise, give the Commission written reasons why he does not approve the draft.

(8) Where a draft is laid before Parliament under subsection (7)(a)(ii), if neither House passes a resolution disapproving the draft within 40 days—

    (a) the Commission may issue the code in the form of the draft, and

    (b) it shall come into force in accordance with provision made by the Secretary of State by order.

(9) If, or in so far as, a code relates to a duty imposed by or under section 149, 153 or 154 of the Equality Act 2010 (public sector equality duty) the Secretary of State shall consult the Scottish Ministers and the Welsh Ministers before—

    (a) approving a draft under subsection (7)(a) above, or

    (b) making an order under subsection (8)(b) above.

(10) In relation to a code of practice under subsection (4), the Secretary of State shall consult the Scottish Ministers before—

    (a) approving a draft under subsection (7)(a) above, or

    (b) making an order under subsection (8)(b) above.

## 15 Codes of practice: supplemental

(1) The Commission may revise a code issued under section 14; and a reference in this section or in that section to the issue of a code shall be treated as including a reference to the revision of a code.

(2) The 40 day period specified in section 14(8)—

    (a) shall begin with the date on which the draft is laid before both Houses (or, if laid before each House on a different date, with the later date), and

    (b) shall be taken not to include a period during which—

        (i) Parliament is prorogued or dissolved, or

        (ii) both Houses are adjourned for more than four days.

(3) A code issued under section 14 may be revoked by the Secretary of State, at the request of the Commission, by order.

(4) A failure to comply with a provision of a code shall not of itself make a person liable to criminal or civil proceedings; but a code—

    (a) shall be admissible in evidence in criminal or civil proceedings, and

    (b) shall be taken into account by a court or tribunal in any case in which it appears to the court or tribunal to be relevant.

(5) Subsection (4)(b) does not apply in relation to a code issued under section 14(4).

(6) The Secretary of State may by order amend section 14 so as to vary the range of matters that codes of practice under that section may address.

## 16 Inquiries

(1) The Commission may conduct an inquiry into a matter relating to any of the Commission's duties under sections 8, 9 and 10.

(2) If in the course of an inquiry the Commission begins to suspect that a person may have committed an unlawful act—

    (a) in continuing the inquiry the Commission shall, so far as possible, avoid further consideration of whether or not the person has committed an unlawful act,

    (b) the Commission may commence an investigation into that question under section 20,

    (c) the Commission may use information or evidence acquired in the course of the inquiry for the purpose of the investigation, and

    (d) the Commission shall so far as possible ensure (whether by aborting or suspending the inquiry or otherwise) that any aspects of the inquiry which concern the person investigated, or may require his involvement, are not pursued while the investigation is in progress.

(3) The report of an inquiry—

    (a) may not state (whether expressly or by necessary implication) that a specified or identifiable person has committed an unlawful act, and

    (b) shall not otherwise refer to the activities of a specified or identifiable person unless the Commission thinks that the reference—

        (i) will not harm the person, or

        (ii) is necessary in order for the report adequately to reflect the results of the inquiry.

(4) Subsections (2) and (3) shall not prevent an inquiry from considering or reporting a matter relating to human rights (whether or not a necessary implication arises in relation to the Equality Act 2010).

(5) Before settling a report of an inquiry which records findings which in the Commission's opinion are of an adverse nature and relate (whether expressly or by necessary implication) to a specified or identifiable person the Commission shall—

    (a) send a draft of the report to the person,

    (b) specify a period of at least 28 days during which he may make written representations about the draft, and

    (c) consider any representations made.

(6) Schedule 2 makes supplemental provision about inquiries

## 17 Grants

(1) In pursuance of any of its duties under sections 8 and 9 the Commission may make grants to another person.

(2) A grant under subsection (1) may be made subject to conditions (which may, in particular, include conditions as to repayment).

(3) A power under this Part to co-operate with or assist a person may not be exercised by the provision of financial assistance otherwise than in accordance with this section.

## 18 Human rights

In pursuance of its duties under section 9 the Commission may (without prejudice to the generality of section 13) co-operate with persons interested in human rights within the United Kingdom or elsewhere.

## 20 Investigations

(1) The Commission may investigate whether or not a person—

    (a) has committed an unlawful act,

    (b) has complied with a requirement imposed by an unlawful act notice under section 21, or

    (c) has complied with an undertaking given under section 23.

(2) The Commission may conduct an investigation under subsection (1)(a) only if it suspects that the person concerned may have committed an unlawful act.

(3) A suspicion for the purposes of subsection (2) may (but need not) be based on the results of, or a matter arising during the course of, an inquiry under section 16.

(4) Before settling a report of an investigation recording a finding that a person has committed an unlawful act or has failed to comply with a requirement or undertaking the Commission shall—

    (a) send a draft of the report to the person,

    (b) specify a period of at least 28 days during which he may make written representations about the draft, and

    (c) consider any representations made.

(5) Schedule 2 makes supplemental provision about investigations.

## 21 Unlawful act notice

(1) The Commission may give a person a notice under this section (an 'unlawful act notice') if—

    (a) he is or has been the subject of an investigation under section 20(1)(a), and

    (b) the Commission is satisfied that he has committed an unlawful act.

(2) A notice must specify—
   (a)   the unlawful act, and
   (b)   the provision of the Equality Act 2010 by virtue of which the act is unlawful.
(3) A notice must inform the recipient of the effect of—
   (a)   subsections (5) to (7),
   (b)   section 20(1)(b), and
   (c)   section 24(1).
(4) A notice may—
   (a)   require the person to whom the notice is given to prepare an action plan for the purpose of avoiding repetition or continuation of the unlawful act;
   (b)   recommend action to be taken by the person for that purpose.
(5) A person who is given a notice may, within the period of six weeks beginning with the day on which the notice is given, appeal to the appropriate court or tribunal on the grounds—
   (a)   that he has not committed the unlawful act specified in the notice, or
   (b)   that a requirement for the preparation of an action plan imposed under subsection (4)(a) is unreasonable.
(6) On an appeal under subsection (5) the court or tribunal may—
   (a)   affirm a notice;
   (b)   annul a notice;
   (c)   vary a notice;
   (d)   affirm a requirement;
   (e)   annul a requirement;
   (f)   vary a requirement;
   (g)   make an order for costs or expenses.
(7) In subsection (5) 'the appropriate court or tribunal' means—
   (a)   an employment tribunal, if a claim in respect of the alleged unlawful act could be made to it, or
   (b)   the county court (in England and Wales) or the sheriff (in Scotland), if a claim in respect of the alleged unlawful act could be made to it or to him.

## 22   Action plans
(1) This section applies where a person has been given a notice under section 21 which requires him (under section 21(4)(a)) to prepare an action plan.
(2) The notice must specify a time by which the person must give the Commission a first draft plan.
(3) After receiving a first draft plan from a person the Commission shall—
   (a)   approve it, or
   (b)   give the person a notice which—
      (i)    states that the draft is not adequate,
      (ii)   requires the person to give the Commission a revised draft by a specified time, and
      (iii)  may make recommendations about the content of the revised draft.
(4) Subsection (3) shall apply in relation to a revised draft plan as it applies in relation to a first draft plan.
(5) An action plan comes into force—
   (a)   if the period of six weeks beginning with the date on which a first draft or revised draft is given to the Commission expires without the Commission—
      (i)    giving a notice under subsection (3)(b), or
      (ii)   applying for an order under subsection (6)(b), or
   (b)   upon a court's declining to make an order under subsection (6)(b) in relation to a revised draft of the plan.
(6) The Commission may apply to the county court (in England and Wales) or to the sheriff (in Scotland)—
   (a)   for an order requiring a person to give the Commission a first draft plan by a time specified in the order,
   (b)   for an order requiring a person who has given the Commission a revised draft plan to prepare and give to the Commission a further revised draft plan—

(i)    by a time specified in the order, and

(ii)   in accordance with any directions about the plan's content specified in the order, or

(c)   during the period of five years beginning with the date on which an action plan prepared by a person comes into force, for an order requiring the person—

(i)    to act in accordance with the action plan, or

(ii)   to take specified action for a similar purpose.

(7) An action plan may be varied by agreement between the Commission and the person who prepared it.

(8) Paragraphs 10 to 14 of Schedule 2 apply (but omitting references to oral evidence) in relation to consideration by the Commission of the adequacy of a draft action plan as they apply in relation to the conduct of an inquiry.

(9) A person commits an offence if without reasonable excuse he fails to comply with an order under subsection (6); and a person guilty of an offence under this subsection shall be liable on summary conviction to a fine not exceeding level 5 on the standard scale.

## 23 Agreements

(1) The Commission may enter into an agreement with a person under which—

(a) the person undertakes—

(i)    not to commit an unlawful act of a specified kind, and

(ii)   to take, or refrain from taking, other specified action (which may include the preparation of a plan for the purpose of avoiding an unlawful act), and

(b) the Commission undertakes not to proceed against the person under section 20 or 21 in respect of any unlawful act of the kind specified under paragraph (a)(i).

(2) The Commission may enter into an agreement with a person under this section only if it thinks that the person has committed an unlawful act.

(3) But a person shall not be taken to admit to the commission of an unlawful act by reason only of entering into an agreement under this section.

(4) An agreement under this section—

(a) may be entered into whether or not the person is or has been the subject of an investigation under section 20,

(b) may include incidental or supplemental provision (which may include provision for termination in specified circumstances), and

(c) may be varied or terminated by agreement of the parties.

(5) This section shall apply in relation to the breach of a duty specified in section 34(2) as it applies in relation to the commission of an unlawful act; and for that purpose the reference in subsection (1)(b) above to section 20 or 21 shall be taken as a reference to section 32.

## 24 Applications to court

(1) If the Commission thinks that a person is likely to commit an unlawful act, it may apply—

(a) in England and Wales, to the county court for an injunction restraining the person from committing the act, or

(b) in Scotland, to the sheriff for an interdict prohibiting the person from committing the act.

(2) Subsection (3) applies if the Commission thinks that a party to an agreement under section 23 has failed to comply, or is likely not to comply, with an undertaking under the agreement.

(3) The Commission may apply to the county court (in England and Wales) or to the sheriff (in Scotland) for an order requiring the person—

(a) to comply with his undertaking, and

(b) to take such other action as the court or the sheriff may specify.

## 24A Enforcement powers: supplemental

(1) This section has effect in relation to—

(a) an act which is unlawful because, by virtue of any of sections 13 to 18 of the Equality Act 2010, it amounts to a contravention of any of Parts 3, 4, 5, 6 or 7 of that Act,

(b)    an act which is unlawful because it amounts to a contravention of section 60(1) of that Act (or to a contravention of section 111 or 112 of that Act that relates to a contravention of section 60(1) of that Act) (enquiries about disability and health),

(c)    an act which is unlawful because it amounts to a contravention of section 106 of that Act (information about diversity in range of election candidates etc.),

(d)    an act which is unlawful because, by virtue of section 108(1) of that Act, it amounts to a contravention of any of Parts 3, 4, 5, 6 or 7 of that Act, or

(e)    the application of a provision, criterion or practice which, by virtue of section 19 of that Act, amounts to a contravention of that Act.

(2)    For the purposes of sections 20 to 24 of this Act, it is immaterial whether the Commission knows or suspects that a person has been or may be affected by the unlawful act or application.

(3)    For those purposes, an unlawful act includes making arrangements to act in a particular way which would, if applied to an individual, amount to a contravention mentioned in subsection (1)(a).

(4)    Nothing in this Act affects the entitlement of a person to bring proceedings under the Equality Act 2010 in respect of a contravention mentioned in subsection (1).

## 28    Legal assistance

(1)    The Commission may assist an individual who is or may become party to legal proceedings if—

(a)    the proceedings relate or may relate (wholly or partly) to a provision of the Equality Act 2010, and

(b)    the individual alleges that he has been the victim of behaviour contrary to a provision of the Act.

(2)    The Commission may assist an individual who is or may become party to legal proceedings in England and Wales if and in so far as the proceedings concern or may concern the question of a landlord's reasonableness in relation to consent to the making of an improvement to a dwelling where the improvement would be likely to facilitate the enjoyment of the premises by the tenant or another lawful occupier having regard to a disability.

(3)    The Commission may assist an individual who is or may become a party to legal proceedings in Scotland if and in so far as the proceedings concern or may concern the question whether—

(a)    it is unreasonable for a landlord to withhold consent to the carrying out of work in relation to a house (within the meaning of the Housing (Scotland) Act 2006) for the purpose of making the house suitable for the accommodation, welfare or employment of any disabled person who occupies, or intends to occupy, the house as a sole or main residence, or

(b)    any condition imposed by a landlord on consenting to the carrying out of such work is unreasonable.

(4)    In giving assistance under this section the Commission may provide or arrange for the provision of—

(a)    legal advice;

(b)    legal representation;

(c)    facilities for the settlement of a dispute;

(d)    any other form of assistance.

(5)    Assistance may not be given under subsection (1) in relation to alleged behaviour contrary to a provision of Part 12 of the Equality Act 2010 (disabled person; transport).

(6)    Where proceedings relate or may relate partly to a provision of the Equality Act 2010 and partly to other matters—

(a)    assistance may be given under subsection (1) in respect of any aspect of the proceedings while they relate to a provision of the Act, but

(b)    if the proceedings cease to relate to a provision of the Act, assistance may not be continued under subsection (1) in respect of the proceedings (except in so far as it is permitted by virtue of subsection (7) or (8)).

(7)    The Lord Chancellor may by order disapply subsection (6)(b), and enable the Commission to give assistance under subsection (1), in respect of legal proceedings which—

(a)    when instituted, related (wholly or partly) to a provision of the Equality Act 2010,

(b)    have ceased to relate to the provision of the Act, and

(c)    relate (wholly or partly) to any of the Convention rights within the meaning given by section 1 of the Human Rights Act 1998.

(8)    The Secretary of State may by order enable the Commission to give assistance under this section in respect of legal proceedings in the course of which an individual who is or has been a disabled person relies or proposes to rely on a matter relating to his disability; but

an order under this subsection may not permit assistance in relation to alleged behaviour contrary to a provision of Part 12 of the Equality Act 2010.

(9)    An order under subsection (7) or (8) may make provision generally or only in relation to proceedings of a specified kind or description (which in the case of an order under subsection (7) may, in particular, refer to specified provisions of the Equality Act 2010) or in relation to specified circumstances.

(10)    This section is without prejudice to the effect of any restriction imposed, in respect of representation—

(a)    by virtue of an enactment (including an enactment in or under an Act of the Scottish Parliament), or

(b)    in accordance with the practice of a court.

(11)    A legislative provision which requires insurance or an indemnity in respect of advice given in connection with a compromise contract or agreement shall not apply to advice provided by the Commission under this section.

(12)    This section applies to a provision of Community law which—

(a)    relates to discrimination on grounds of sex (including reassignment of gender), racial origin, ethnic origin, religion, belief, disability, age or sexual orientation, and

(b)    confers rights on individuals as it applies to the Equality Act 2010.

(15)    In its application by virtue of subsection (12), subsection (1)(b) shall have effect as if it referred to an allegation by an individual that he is disadvantaged by—

(a)    an enactment (including an enactment in or under an Act of the Scottish Parliament) which is contrary to a provision of Community law, or

(b)    a failure by the United Kingdom to implement a right as required by Community law.

## 30    Judicial review and other legal proceedings

(1)    The Commission shall have capacity to institute or intervene in legal proceedings, whether for judicial review or otherwise, if it appears to the Commission that the proceedings are relevant to a matter in connection with which the Commission has a function.

(2)    The Commission shall be taken to have title and interest in relation to the subject matter of any legal proceedings in Scotland which it has capacity to institute, or in which it has capacity to intervene, by virtue of subsection (1).

(3)    The Commission may, in the course of legal proceedings for judicial review which it institutes (or in which it intervenes), rely on section 7(1)(b) of the Human Rights Act 1998 (breach of Convention rights); and for that purpose—

(a)    the Commission need not be a victim or potential victim of the unlawful act to which the proceedings relate,

(b)    the Commission may act only if there is or would be one or more victims of the unlawful act,

(c)    section 7(3) and (4) of that Act shall not apply, and

(d)    no award of damages may be made to the Commission (whether or not the exception in section 8(3) of that Act applies);

and an expression used in this subsection and in section 7 of the Human Rights Act 1998 has the same meaning in this subsection as in that section.

(4)    Subsections (1) and (2)—

(a)    do not create a cause of action, and

(b)    are, except as provided by subsection (3), subject to any limitation or restriction imposed by virtue of an enactment (including an enactment in or under an Act of the Scottish Parliament) or in accordance with the practice of a court.

*Interpretation*

## 34   Unlawful

(1)   In this Part (except section 30(3)) 'unlawful' means contrary to a provision of the Equality Act 2010.

(2)   But action is not unlawful for the purposes of this Part by reason only of the fact that it contravenes a duty under or by virtue of any of the following provisions of the Equality Act 2010—

    (a)   section 1 (public sector duty regarding socio-economic inequalities),

    (b)   section 149, 153 or 154 (public sector equality duty),

    (c)   Part 12 (disabled persons: transport), or

    (d)   section 190 (disability: improvements to let dwelling houses).

## 35   General

In this Part—

    'act' includes deliberate omission,

    'groups' has the meaning given by section 10,

    'the Commission' means the Commission for Equality and Human Rights,

    'disabled person' has the meaning given by section 8,

    'human rights' has the meaning given by section 9,

    ...

    'race' includes colour, nationality, ethnic origin and national origin,

    'religion or belief' has the same meaning as in section 10 of the Equality Act 2010, and

    'sexual orientation' has the same meaning as in section 12 of the Equality Act 2010.


# CORPORATE MANSLAUGHTER AND CORPORATE HOMICIDE ACT 2007
# (2007, c. 19)

*Corporate manslaughter and corporate homicide*

## 1   The offence

(1)   An organisation to which this section applies is guilty of an offence if the way in which its activities are managed or organised—

    (a)   causes a person's death, and

    (b)   amounts to a gross breach of a relevant duty of care owed by the organisation to the deceased.

(2)   The organisations to which this section applies are—

    (a)   a corporation;

    (b)   a department or other body listed in Schedule 1;

    (c)   a police force;

    (d)   a partnership, or a trade union or employers' association, that is an employer.

(3)   An organisation is guilty of an offence under this section only if the way in which its activities are managed or organised by its senior management is a substantial element in the breach referred to in subsection (1).

(4)   For the purposes of this Act—

    (a)   'relevant duty of care' has the meaning given by section 2, read with sections 3 to 7;

    (b)   a breach of a duty of care by an organisation is a 'gross' breach if the conduct alleged to amount to a breach of that duty falls far below what can reasonably be expected of the organisation in the circumstances;

    (c)   'senior management', in relation to an organisation, means the persons who play significant roles in—

        (i)   the making of decisions about how the whole or a substantial part of its activities are to be managed or organised, or

        (ii)   the actual managing or organising of the whole or a substantial part of those activities.

(5)   The offence under this section is called—
  (a)   corporate manslaughter, in so far as it is an offence under the law of England and Wales or Northern Ireland;
  (b)   corporate homicide, in so far as it is an offence under the law of Scotland.
(6)   An organisation that is guilty of corporate manslaughter or corporate homicide is liable on conviction on indictment to a fine.
(7)   The offence of corporate homicide is indictable only in the High Court of Justiciary.

2     **Meaning of 'relevant duty of care'**
(1)   A 'relevant duty of care', in relation to an organisation, means any of the following duties owed by it under the law of negligence—
  (a)   a duty owed to its employees or to other persons working for the organisation or performing services for it;
  (b)   a duty owed as occupier of premises;
  ...
(2)   A reference in subsection (1) to a duty owed under the law of negligence includes a reference to a duty that would be owed under the law of negligence but for any statutory provision under which liability is imposed in place of liability under that law.
(3)   For the purposes of this Act, whether a particular organisation owes a duty of care to a particular individual is a question of law.
      The judge must make any findings of fact necessary to decide that question.
(4)   For the purposes of this Act there is to be disregarded—
  (a)   any rule of the common law that has the effect of preventing a duty of care from being owed by one person to another by reason of the fact that they are jointly engaged in unlawful conduct;
  (b)   any such rule that has the effect of preventing a duty of care from being owed to a person by reason of his acceptance of a risk of harm.
  ...

8     **Factors for jury**
(1)   This section applies where—
  (a)   it is established that an organisation owed a relevant duty of care to a person, and
  (b)   it falls to the jury to decide whether there was a gross breach of that duty.
(2)   The jury must consider whether the evidence shows that the organisation failed to comply with any health and safety legislation that relates to the alleged breach, and if so—
  (a)   how serious that failure was;
  (b)   how much of a risk of death it posed.
(3)   The jury may also—
  (a)   consider the extent to which the evidence shows that there were attitudes, policies, systems or accepted practices within the organisation that were likely to have encouraged any such failure as is mentioned in subsection (2), or to have produced tolerance of it;
  (b)   have regard to any health and safety guidance that relates to the alleged breach.
(4)   This section does not prevent the jury from having regard to any other matters they consider relevant.
(5)   In this section 'health and safety guidance' means any code, guidance, manual or similar publication that is concerned with health and safety matters and is made or issued (under a statutory provision or otherwise) by an authority responsible for the enforcement of any health and safety legislation.

9     **Power to order breach etc. to be remedied**
(1)   A court before which an organisation is convicted of corporate manslaughter or corporate homicide may make an order (a 'remedial order') requiring the organisation to take specified steps to remedy—
  (a)   the breach mentioned in section 1(1) ('the relevant breach');
  (b)   any matter that appears to the court to have resulted from the relevant breach and to have been a cause of the death;

(c) any deficiency, as regards health and safety matters, in the organisation's policies, systems or practices of which the relevant breach appears to the court to be an indication.

(2) A remedial order may be made only on an application by the prosecution specifying the terms of the proposed order.

Any such order must be on such terms (whether those proposed or others) as the court considers appropriate having regard to any representations made, and any evidence adduced, in relation to that matter by the prosecution or on behalf of the organisation.

(3) Before making an application for a remedial order the prosecution must consult such enforcement authority or authorities as it considers appropriate having regard to the nature of the relevant breach.

(4) A remedial order—

(a) must specify a period within which the steps referred to in subsection (1) are to be taken;

(b) may require the organisation to supply to an enforcement authority consulted under subsection (3), within a specified period, evidence that those steps have been taken.

A period specified under this subsection may be extended or further extended by order of the court on an application made before the end of that period or extended period.

(5) An organisation that fails to comply with a remedial order is guilty of an offence, and liable on conviction on indictment to a fine.

## 10 Power to order conviction etc. to be publicised

(1) A court before which an organisation is convicted of corporate manslaughter or corporate homicide may make an order (a 'publicity order') requiring the organisation to publicise in a specified manner—

(a) the fact that it has been convicted of the offence;

(b) specified particulars of the offence;

(c) the amount of any fine imposed;

(d) the terms of any remedial order made.

(2) In deciding on the terms of a publicity order that it is proposing to make, the court must—

(a) ascertain the views of such enforcement authority or authorities (if any) as it considers appropriate, and

(b) have regard to any representations made by the prosecution or on behalf of the organisation.

(3) A publicity order—

(a) must specify a period within which the requirements referred to in subsection (1) are to be complied with;

(b) may require the organisation to supply to any enforcement authority whose views have been ascertained under subsection (2), within a specified period, evidence that those requirements have been complied with.

(4) An organisation that fails to comply with a publicity order is guilty of an offence, and liable on conviction on indictment to a fine.

## 17 DPP's consent required for proceedings

Proceedings for an offence of corporate manslaughter—

(a) may not be instituted in England and Wales without the consent of the Director of Public Prosecutions;

(b) may not be instituted in Northern Ireland without the consent of the Director of Public Prosecutions for Northern Ireland.

## 18 No individual liability

(1) An individual cannot be guilty of aiding, abetting, counselling or procuring the commission of an offence of corporate manslaughter.

(1A) An individual cannot be guilty of an offence under Part 2 of the Serious Crime Act 2007 (encouraging or assisting crime) by reference to an offence of corporate manslaughter.

(2) An individual cannot be guilty of aiding, abetting, counselling or procuring, or being art and part in, the commission of an offence of corporate homicide.

**19    Convictions under this Act and under health and safety legislation**

(1)    Where in the same proceedings there is—

(a)    a charge of corporate manslaughter or corporate homicide arising out of a particular set of circumstances, and

(b)    a charge against the same defendant of a health and safety offence arising out of some or all of those circumstances,

the jury may, if the interests of justice so require, be invited to return a verdict on each charge.

(2)    An organisation that has been convicted of corporate manslaughter or corporate homicide arising out of a particular set of circumstances may, if the interests of justice so require, be charged with a health and safety offence arising out of some or all of those circumstances.

(3)    In this section 'health and safety offence' means an offence under any health and safety legislation.

**20    Abolition of liability of corporations for manslaughter at common law**

The common law offence of manslaughter by gross negligence is abolished in its application to corporations, and in any application it has to other organisations to which section 1 applies.

## EQUALITY ACT 2010
## (2010, c. 15)

PART 2
EQUALITY: KEY CONCEPTS

CHAPTER 1
PROTECTED CHARTERISTICS

**4    The protected characteristics**

The following characteristics are protected characteristics—

age;
disability;
gender reassignment;
marriage and civil partnership;
pregnancy and maternity;
race;
religion or belief;
sex;
sexual orientation.

**5    Age**

(1)    In relation to the protected characteristic of age—

(a)    a reference to a person who has a particular protected characteristic is a reference to a person of a particular age group;

(b)    a reference to persons who share a protected characteristic is a reference to persons of the same age group.

(2)    A reference to an age group is a reference to a group of persons defined by reference to age, whether by reference to a particular age or to a range of ages.

**6    Disability**

(1)    A person (P) has a disability if—

(a)    P has a physical or mental impairment, and

(b)    the impairment has a substantial and long-term adverse effect on P's ability to carry out normal day-to-day activities.

(2)    A reference to a disabled person is a reference to a person who has a disability.

(3)    In relation to the protected characteristic of disability—

(a)  a reference to a person who has a particular protected characteristic is a reference to a person who has a particular disability;

(b)  a reference to persons who share a protected characteristic is a reference to persons who have the same disability.

(4)  This Act (except Part 12 and section 190) applies in relation to a person who has had a disability as it applies in relation to a person who has the disability; accordingly (except in that Part and that section)—

(a)  a reference (however expressed) to a person who has a disability includes a reference to a person who has had the disability, and

(b)  a reference (however expressed) to a person who does not have a disability includes a reference to a person who has not had the disability.

(5)  A Minister of the Crown may issue guidance about matters to be taken into account in deciding any question for the purposes of subsection (1).

(6)  Schedule 1 (disability: supplementary provision) has effect.

## 7    Gender reassignment

(1)  A person has the protected characteristic of gender reassignment if the person is proposing to undergo, is undergoing or has undergone a process (or part of a process) for the purpose of reassigning the person's sex by changing physiological or other attributes of sex.

(2)  A reference to a transsexual person is a reference to a person who has the protected characteristic of gender reassignment.

(3)  In relation to the protected characteristic of gender reassignment—

(a)  a reference to a person who has a particular protected characteristic is a reference to a transsexual person;

(b)  a reference to persons who share a protected characteristic is a reference to transsexual persons.

## 8    Marriage and civil partnership

(1)  A person has the protected characteristic of marriage and civil partnership if the person is married or is a civil partner.

(2)  In relation to the protected characteristic of marriage and civil partnership—

(a)  a reference to a person who has a particular protected characteristic is a reference to a person who is married or is a civil partner;

(b)  a reference to persons who share a protected characteristic is a reference to persons who are married or are civil partners.

## 9    Race

(1)  Race includes—

(a)  colour;

(b)  nationality;

(c)  ethnic or national origins.

(2)  In relation to the protected characteristic of race—

(a)  a reference to a person who has a particular protected characteristic is a reference to a person of a particular racial group;

(b)  a reference to persons who share a protected characteristic is a reference to persons of the same racial group.

(3)  A racial group is a group of persons defined by reference to race; and a reference to a person's racial group is a reference to a racial group into which the person falls.

(4)  The fact that a racial group comprises two or more distinct racial groups does not prevent it from constituting a particular racial group.

(5)  A Minister of the Crown—

(a)  must by order amend this section so as to provide for caste to be an aspect of race;

(b)  may by order amend this Act so as to provide for an exception to a provision of this Act to apply, or not to apply, to caste or to apply, or not to apply, to caste in specified circumstances.

(6)  The power under section 207(4)(b), in its application to subsection (5), includes power to amend this Act.

## 10    Religion or belief

(1)   Religion means any religion and a reference to religion includes a reference to a lack of religion.

(2)   Belief means any religious or philosophical belief and a reference to belief includes a reference to a lack of belief.

(3)   In relation to the protected characteristic of religion or belief—

     (a)   a reference to a person who has a particular protected characteristic is a reference to a person of a particular religion or belief;

     (b)   a reference to persons who share a protected characteristic is a reference to persons who are of the same religion or belief.

## 11    Sex

In relation to the protected characteristic of sex—

     (a)   a reference to a person who has a particular protected characteristic is a reference to a man or to a woman;

     (b)   a reference to persons who share a protected characteristic is a reference to persons of the same sex.

## 12    Sexual orientation

(1)   Sexual orientation means a person's sexual orientation towards—

     (a)   persons of the same sex,

     (b)   persons of the opposite sex, or

     (c)   persons of either sex.

(2)   In relation to the protected characteristic of sexual orientation—

     (a)   a reference to a person who has a particular protected characteristic is a reference to a person who is of a particular sexual orientation;

     (b)   a reference to persons who share a protected characteristic is a reference to persons who are of the same sexual orientation.

CHAPTER 2
PROHIBITED CONDUCT

*Discrimination*

## 13    Direct discrimination

(1)   A person (A) discriminates against another (B) if, because of a protected characteristic, A treats B less favourably than A treats or would treat others.

(2)   If the protected characteristic is age, A does not discriminate against B if A can show A's treatment of B to be a proportionate means of achieving a legitimate aim.

(3)   If the protected characteristic is disability, and B is not a disabled person, A does not discriminate against B only because A treats or would treat disabled persons more favourably than A treats B.

(4)   If the protected characteristic is marriage and civil partnership, this section applies to a contravention of Part 5 (work) only if the treatment is because it is B who is married or a civil partner.

(5)   If the protected characteristic is race, less favourable treatment includes segregating B from others.

(6)   If the protected characteristic is sex—

     (a)   less favourable treatment of a woman includes less favourable treatment of her because she is breast-feeding;

     (b)   in a case where B is a man, no account is to be taken of special treatment afforded to a woman in connection with pregnancy or childbirth.

(7)   Subsection (6)(a) does not apply for the purposes of Part 5 (work).

(8)   This section is subject to sections 17(6) and 18(7).

## 14    Combined discrimination: dual characteristics

(1)   A person (A) discriminates against another (B) if, because of a combination of two relevant protected characteristics, A treats B less favourably than A treats or would treat a person who does not share either of those characteristics.

(2)   The relevant protected characteristics are—

(a)    age;
(b)    disability;
(c)    gender reassignment;
(d)    race;
(e)    religion or belief;
(f)     sex;
(g)    sexual orientation.

(3)    For the purposes of establishing a contravention of this Act by virtue of subsection (1), B need not show that A's treatment of B is direct discrimination because of each of the characteristics in the combination (taken separately).

(4)    But B cannot establish a contravention of this Act by virtue of subsection (1) if, in reliance on another provision of this Act or any other enactment, A shows that A's treatment of B is not direct discrimination because of either or both of the characteristics in the combination.

(5)    Subsection (1) does not apply to a combination of characteristics that includes disability in circumstances where, if a claim of direct discrimination because of disability were to be brought, it would come within section 116 (special educational needs).

(6)    A Minister of the Crown may by order amend this section so as to—
(a)    make further provision about circumstances in which B can, or in which B cannot, establish a contravention of this Act by virtue of subsection (1);
(b)    specify other circumstances in which subsection (1) does not apply.

(7)    The references to direct discrimination are to a contravention of this Act by virtue of section 13.

## 15    Discrimination arising from disability

(1)    A person (A) discriminates against a disabled person (B) if—
(a)    A treats B unfavourably because of something arising in consequence of B's disability, and
(b)    A cannot show that the treatment is a proportionate means of achieving a legitimate aim.

(2)    Subsection (1) does not apply if A shows that A did not know, and could not reasonably have been expected to know, that B had the disability.

## 16    Gender reassignment discrimination: cases of absence from work

(1)    This section has effect for the purposes of the application of Part 5 (work) to the protected characteristic of gender reassignment.

(2)    A person (A) discriminates against a transsexual person (B) if, in relation to an absence of B's that is because of gender reassignment, A treats B less favourably than A would treat B if—
(a)    B's absence was because of sickness or injury, or
(b)    B's absence was for some other reason and it is not reasonable for B to be treated less favourably.

(3)    A person's absence is because of gender reassignment if it is because the person is proposing to undergo, is undergoing or has undergone the process (or part of the process) mentioned in section 7(1).

## 17    Pregnancy and maternity discrimination: non-work cases

(1)    This section has effect for the purposes of the application to the protected characteristic of pregnancy and maternity of—
(a)    Part 3 (services and public functions);
(b)    Part 4 (premises);
(c)    Part 6 (education);
(d)    Part 7 (associations).

(2)    A person (A) discriminates against a woman if A treats her unfavourably because of a pregnancy of hers.

(3)    A person (A) discriminates against a woman if, in the period of 26 weeks beginning with the day on which she gives birth, A treats her unfavourably because she has given birth.

(4)    The reference in subsection (3) to treating a woman unfavourably because she has given birth includes, in particular, a reference to treating her unfavourably because she is breast-feeding.

(5)   For the purposes of this section, the day on which a woman gives birth is the day on which—

(a)   she gives birth to a living child, or

(b)   she gives birth to a dead child (more than 24 weeks of the pregnancy having passed).

(6)   Section 13, so far as relating to sex discrimination, does not apply to anything done in relation to a woman in so far as—

(a)   it is for the reason mentioned in subsection (2), or

(b)   it is in the period, and for the reason, mentioned in subsection (3).

## 18   Pregnancy and maternity discrimination: work cases

(1)   This section has effect for the purposes of the application of Part 5 (work) to the protected characteristic of pregnancy and maternity.

(2)   A person (A) discriminates against a woman if, in the protected period in relation to a pregnancy of hers, A treats her unfavourably—

(a)   because of the pregnancy, or

(b)   because of illness suffered by her as a result of it.

(3)   A person (A) discriminates against a woman if A treats her unfavourably because she is on compulsory maternity leave.

(4)   A person (A) discriminates against a woman if A treats her unfavourably because she is exercising or seeking to exercise, or has exercised or sought to exercise, the right to ordinary or additional maternity leave.

(5)   For the purposes of subsection (2), if the treatment of a woman is in implementation of a decision taken in the protected period, the treatment is to be regarded as occurring in that period (even if the implementation is not until after the end of that period).

(6)   The protected period, in relation to a woman's pregnancy, begins when the pregnancy begins, and ends—

(a)   if she has the right to ordinary and additional maternity leave, at the end of the additional maternity leave period or (if earlier) when she returns to work after the pregnancy;

(b)   if she does not have that right, at the end of the period of 2 weeks beginning with the end of the pregnancy.

(7)   Section 13, so far as relating to sex discrimination, does not apply to treatment of a woman in so far as—

(a)   it is in the protected period in relation to her and is for a reason mentioned in paragraph (a) or (b) of subsection (2), or

(b)   it is for a reason mentioned in subsection (3) or (4).

## 19   Indirect discrimination

(1)   A person (A) discriminates against another (B) if A applies to B a provision, criterion or practice which is discriminatory in relation to a relevant protected characteristic of B's.

(2)   For the purposes of subsection (1), a provision, criterion or practice is discriminatory in relation to a relevant protected characteristic of B's if—

(a)   A applies, or would apply, it to persons with whom B does not share the characteristic,

(b)   it puts, or would put, persons with whom B shares the characteristic at a particular disadvantage when compared with persons with whom B does not share it,

(c)   it puts, or would put, B at that disadvantage, and

(d)   A cannot show it to be a proportionate means of achieving a legitimate aim.

(3)   The relevant protected characteristics are—

age;

disability;

gender reassignment;

marriage and civil partnership;

race;

religion or belief;

sex;

sexual orientation.

*Adjustments for disabled persons*

## 20    Duty to make adjustments

(1)    Where this Act imposes a duty to make reasonable adjustments on a person, this section, sections 21 and 22 and the applicable Schedule apply; and for those purposes, a person on whom the duty is imposed is referred to as A.

(2)    The duty comprises the following three requirements.

(3)    The first requirement is a requirement, where a provision, criterion or practice of A's puts a disabled person at a substantial disadvantage in relation to a relevant matter in comparison with persons who are not disabled, to take such steps as it is reasonable to have to take to avoid the disadvantage.

(4)    The second requirement is a requirement, where a physical feature puts a disabled person at a substantial disadvantage in relation to a relevant matter in comparison with persons who are not disabled, to take such steps as it is reasonable to have to take to avoid the disadvantage.

(5)    The third requirement is a requirement, where a disabled person would, but for the provision of an auxiliary aid, be put at a substantial disadvantage in relation to a relevant matter in comparison with persons who are not disabled, to take such steps as it is reasonable to have to take to provide the auxiliary aid.

(6)    Where the first or third requirement relates to the provision of information, the steps which it is reasonable for A to have to take include steps for ensuring that in the circumstances concerned the information is provided in an accessible format.

(7)    A person (A) who is subject to a duty to make reasonable adjustments is not (subject to express provision to the contrary) entitled to require a disabled person, in relation to whom A is required to comply with the duty, to pay to any extent A's costs of complying with the duty.

(8)    A reference in section 21 or 22 or an applicable Schedule to the first, second or third requirement is to be construed in accordance with this section.

(9)    In relation to the second requirement, a reference in this section or an applicable Schedule to avoiding a substantial disadvantage includes a reference to—

   (a)    removing the physical feature in question,

   (b)    altering it, or

   (c)    providing a reasonable means of avoiding it.

(10)   A reference in this section, section 21 or 22 or an applicable Schedule (apart from paragraphs 2 to 4 of Schedule 4) to a physical feature is a reference to—

   (a)    a feature arising from the design or construction of a building,

   (b)    a feature of an approach to, exit from or access to a building,

   (c)    a fixture or fitting, or furniture, furnishings, materials, equipment or other chattels, in or on premises, or

   (d)    any other physical element or quality.

(11)   A reference in this section, section 21 or 22 or an applicable Schedule to an auxiliary aid includes a reference to an auxiliary service.

(12)   A reference in this section or an applicable Schedule to chattels is to be read, in relation to Scotland, as a reference to moveable property.

(13)   The applicable Schedule is, in relation to the Part of this Act specified in the first column of the Table, the Schedule specified in the second column.

| Part of this Act | Applicable Schedule |
| --- | --- |
| Part 3 (services and public functions) | Schedule 2 |
| Part 4 (premises) | Schedule 4 |
| Part 5 (work) | Schedule 8 |
| Part 6 (education) | Schedule 13 |
| Part 7 (associations) | Schedule 15 |
| Each of the Parts mentioned above | Schedule 15 |

## 21 Failure to comply with duty

(1) A failure to comply with the first, second or third requirement is a failure to comply with a duty to make reasonable adjustments.

(2) A discriminates against a disabled person if A fails to comply with that duty in relation to that person.

(3) A provision of an applicable Schedule which imposes a duty to comply with the first, second or third requirement applies only for the purpose of establishing whether A has contravened this Act by virtue of subsection (2); a failure to comply is, accordingly, not actionable by virtue of another provision of this Act or otherwise.

## 22 Regulations

(1) Regulations may prescribe—

 (a) matters to be taken into account in deciding whether it is reasonable for A to take a step for the purposes of a prescribed provision of an applicable Schedule;

 (b) descriptions of persons to whom the first, second or third requirement does not apply.

(2) Regulations may make provision as to—

 (a) circumstances in which it is, or in which it is not, reasonable for a person of a prescribed description to have to take steps of a prescribed description;

 (b) what is, or what is not, a provision, criterion or practice;

 (c) things which are, or which are not, to be treated as physical features;

 (d) things which are, or which are not, to be treated as alterations of physical features;

 (e) things which are, or which are not, to be treated as auxiliary aids.

(3) Provision made by virtue of this section may amend an applicable Schedule.

*Discrimination: supplementary*

## 23 Comparison by reference to circumstances

(1) On a comparison of cases for the purposes of section 13, 14, or 19 there must be no material difference between the circumstances relating to each case.

(2) The circumstances relating to a case include a person's abilities if—

 (a) on a comparison for the purposes of section 13, the protected characteristic is disability;

 (b) on a comparison for the purposes of section 14, one of the protected characteristics in the combination is disability.

(3) If the protected characteristic is sexual orientation, the fact that one person (whether or not the person referred to as B) is a civil partner while another is married is not a material difference between the circumstances relating to each case.

(4) If the protected characteristic is sexual orientation, the fact that one person (whether or not the person referred to as B) is married to or the civil partner of a person of the same sex while another is married to or the civil partner of a person of the opposite sex is not a material difference between the circumstances relating to each case.

## 24 Irrelevance of alleged discriminator's characteristics

(1) For the purpose of establishing a contravention of this Act by virtue of section 13(1), it does not matter whether A has the protected characteristic.

(2) For the purpose of establishing a contravention of this Act by virtue of section 14(1), it does not matter—

 (a) whether A has one of the protected characteristics in the combination;

 (b) whether A has both.

## 25 References to particular strands of discrimination

(1) Age discrimination is—

 (a) discrimination within section 13 because of age;

 (b) discrimination within section 19 where the relevant protected characteristic is age.

(2) Disability discrimination is—

 (a) discrimination within section 13 because of disability;

 (b) discrimination within section 15;

     (c)    discrimination within section 19 where the relevant protected characteristic is disability;

     (d)    discrimination within section 21.

(3)   Gender reassignment discrimination is—

     (a)    discrimination within section 13 because of gender reassignment;

     (b)    discrimination within section 16;

     (c)    discrimination within section 19 where the relevant protected characteristic is gender reassignment.

(4)   Marriage and civil partnership discrimination is—

     (a)    discrimination within section 13 because of marriage and civil partnership;

     (b)    discrimination within section 19 where the relevant protected characteristic is marriage and civil partnership.

(5)   Pregnancy and maternity discrimination is discrimination within section 17 or 18.

(6)   Race discrimination is—

     (a)    discrimination within section 13 because of race;

     (b)    discrimination within section 19 where the relevant protected characteristic is race.

(7)   Religious or belief-related discrimination is—

     (a)    discrimination within section 13 because of religion or belief;

     (b)    discrimination within section 19 where the relevant protected characteristic is religion or belief.

(8)   Sex discrimination is—

     (a)    discrimination within section 13 because of sex;

     (b)    discrimination within section 19 where the relevant protected characteristic is sex.

(9)   Sexual orientation discrimination is—

     (a)    discrimination within section 13 because of sexual orientation;

     (b)    discrimination within section 19 where the relevant protected characteristic is sexual orientation.

*Other prohibited conduct*

## 26    Harassment

(1)   A person (A) harasses another (B) if—

     (a)    A engages in unwanted conduct related to a relevant protected characteristic, and

     (b)    the conduct has the purpose or effect of—

          (i)    violating B's dignity, or

          (ii)   creating an intimidating, hostile, degrading, humiliating or offensive environment for B.

(2)   A also harasses B if—

     (a)    A engages in unwanted conduct of a sexual nature, and

     (b)    the conduct has the purpose or effect referred to in subsection (1)(b).

(3)   A also harasses B if—

     (a)    A or another person engages in unwanted conduct of a sexual nature or that is related to gender reassignment or sex,

     (b)    the conduct has the purpose or effect referred to in subsection (1)(b), and

     (c)    because of B's rejection of or submission to the conduct, A treats B less favourably than A would treat B if B had not rejected or submitted to the conduct.

(4)   In deciding whether conduct has the effect referred to in subsection (1)(b), each of the following must be taken into account—

     (a)    the perception of B;

     (b)    the other circumstances of the case;

     (c)    whether it is reasonable for the conduct to have that effect.

(5)   The relevant protected characteristics are—

     age;

     disability;

     gender reassignment;

     race;

        religion or belief;

        sex;

        sexual orientation.

## 27   Victimisation

(1)   A person (A) victimises another person (B) if A subjects B to a detriment because—

    (a)   B does a protected act, or

    (b)   A believes that B has done, or may do, a protected act.

(2)   Each of the following is a protected act—

    (a)   bringing proceedings under this Act;

    (b)   giving evidence or information in connection with proceedings under this Act;

    (c)   doing any other thing for the purposes of or in connection with this Act;

    (d)   making an allegation (whether or not express) that A or another person has contravened this Act.

(3)   Giving false evidence or information, or making a false allegation, is not a protected act if the evidence or information is given, or the allegation is made, in bad faith.

(4)   This section applies only where the person subjected to a detriment is an individual.

(5)   The reference to contravening this Act includes a reference to committing a breach of an equality clause or rule.

PART 5
WORK

CHAPTER 1
EMPLOYMENT, ETC.

*Employees*

## 39   Employees and applicants

(1)   An employer (A) must not discriminate against a person (B)—

    (a)   in the arrangements A makes for deciding to whom to offer employment;

    (b)   as to the terms on which A offers B employment;

    (c)   by not offering B employment.

(2)   An employer (A) must not discriminate against an employee of A's (B)—

    (a)   as to B's terms of employment;

    (b)   in the way A affords B access, or by not affording B access, to opportunities for promotion, transfer or training or for receiving any other benefit, facility or service;

    (c)   by dismissing B;

    (d)   by subjecting B to any other detriment.

(3)   An employer (A) must not victimise a person (B)—

    (a)   in the arrangements A makes for deciding to whom to offer employment;

    (b)   as to the terms on which A offers B employment;

    (c)   by not offering B employment.

(4)   An employer (A) must not victimise an employee of A's (B)—

    (a)   as to B's terms of employment;

    (b)   in the way A affords B access, or by not affording B access, to opportunities for promotion, transfer or training or for any other benefit, facility or service;

    (c)   by dismissing B;

    (d)   by subjecting B to any other detriment.

(5)   A duty to make reasonable adjustments applies to an employer.

(6)   Subsection (1)(b), so far as relating to sex or pregnancy and maternity, does not apply to a term that relates to pay—

    (a)   unless, were B to accept the offer, an equality clause or rule would have effect in relation to the term, or

    (b)   if paragraph (a) does not apply, except in so far as making an offer on terms including that term amounts to a contravention of subsection (1)(b) by virtue of section 13, 14 or 18.

(7)   In subsections (2)(c) and (4)(c), the reference to dismissing B includes a reference to the termination of B's employment—

    (a)   by the expiry of a period (including a period expiring by reference to an event or circumstance);

    (b)   by an act of B's (including giving notice) in circumstances such that B is entitled, because of A's conduct, to terminate the employment without notice.

(8)   Subsection (7)(a) does not apply if, immediately after the termination, the employment is renewed on the same terms.

## 40   Employees and applicants: harassment

(1)   An employer (A) must not, in relation to employment by A, harass a person (B)—

    (a)   who is an employee of A's;

    (b)   who has applied to A for employment.

## 41   Contract workers

(1)   A principal must not discriminate against a contract worker—

    (a)   as to the terms on which the principal allows the worker to do the work;

    (b)   by not allowing the worker to do, or to continue to do, the work;

    (c)   in the way the principal affords the worker access, or by not affording the worker access, to opportunities for receiving a benefit, facility or service;

    (d)   by subjecting the worker to any other detriment.

(2)   A principal must not, in relation to contract work, harass a contract worker.

(3)   A principal must not victimise a contract worker—

    (a)   as to the terms on which the principal allows the worker to do the work;

    (b)   by not allowing the worker to do, or to continue to do, the work;

    (c)   in the way the principal affords the worker access, or by not affording the worker access, to opportunities for receiving a benefit, facility or service;

    (d)   by subjecting the worker to any other detriment.

(4)   A duty to make reasonable adjustments applies to a principal (as well as to the employer of a contract worker).

(5)   A 'principal' is a person who makes work available for an individual who is—

    (a)   employed by another person, and

    (b)   supplied by that other person in furtherance of a contract to which the principal is a party (whether or not that other person is a party to it).

(6)   'Contract work' is work such as is mentioned in subsection (5).

(7)   A 'contract worker' is an individual supplied to a principal in furtherance of a contract such as is mentioned in subsection (5)(b).

*Employment services*

## 55   Employment service-providers

(1)   A person (an 'employment service-provider') concerned with the provision of an employment service must not discriminate against a person—

    (a)   in the arrangements the service-provider makes for selecting persons to whom to provide, or to whom to offer to provide, the service;

    (b)   as to the terms on which the service-provider offers to provide the service to the person;

    (c)   by not offering to provide the service to the person.

(2)   An employment service-provider (A) must not, in relation to the provision of an employment service, discriminate against a person (B)—

    (a)   as to the terms on which A provides the service to B;

    (b)   by not providing the service to B;

    (c)   by terminating the provision of the service to B;

    (d)   by subjecting B to any other detriment.

(3)   An employment service-provider must not, in relation to the provision of an employment service, harass—

    (a)   a person who asks the service-provider to provide the service;

    (b)   a person for whom the service-provider provides the service.

(4)  An employment service-provider (A) must not victimise a person (B)—
    (a)  in the arrangements A makes for selecting persons to whom to provide, or to whom to offer to provide, the service;
    (b)  as to the terms on which A offers to provide the service to B;
    (c)  by not offering to provide the service to B.
(5)  An employment service-provider (A) must not, in relation to the provision of an employment service, victimise a person (B)—
    (a)  as to the terms on which A provides the service to B;
    (b)  by not providing the service to B;
    (c)  by terminating the provision of the service to B;
    (d)  by subjecting B to any other detriment.
(6)  A duty to make reasonable adjustments applies to an employment service-provider, except in relation to the provision of a vocational service.
(7)  The duty imposed by section 29(7)(a) applies to a person concerned with the provision of a vocational service; but a failure to comply with that duty in relation to the provision of a vocational service is a contravention of this Part for the purposes of Part 9 (enforcement).

## 56  Interpretation

(1)  This section applies for the purposes of section 55.
(2)  The provision of an employment service includes—
    (a)  the provision of vocational training;
    (b)  the provision of vocational guidance;
    (c)  making arrangements for the provision of vocational training or vocational guidance;
    (d)  the provision of a service for finding employment for persons;
    (e)  the provision of a service for supplying employers with persons to do work;
    (f)  the provision of a service in pursuance of arrangements made under section 2 of the Employment and Training Act 1973 (functions of the Secretary of State relating to employment);
    (g)  the provision of a service in pursuance of arrangements made or a direction given under section 10 of that Act (careers services);
    (h)  the exercise of a function in pursuance of arrangements made under section 2(3) of the Enterprise and New Towns (Scotland) Act 1990 (functions of Scottish Enterprise, etc. relating to employment);
    (i)  an assessment related to the conferment of a relevant qualification within the meaning of section 53 above (except in so far as the assessment is by the qualifications body which confers the qualification).
(3)  This section does not apply in relation to training or guidance in so far as it is training or guidance in relation to which another provision of this Part applies.
(4)  This section does not apply in relation to training or guidance for pupils of a school to which section 85 applies in so far as it is training or guidance to which the responsible body of the school has power to afford access (whether as the responsible body of that school or as the responsible body of any other school at which the training or guidance is provided).
(5)  This section does not apply in relation to training or guidance for students of an institution to which section 91 applies in so far as it is training or guidance to which the governing body of the institution has power to afford access.
(6)  'Vocational training' means—
    (a)  training for employment, or
    (b)  work experience (including work experience the duration of which is not agreed until after it begins).
(7)  A reference to the provision of a vocational service is a reference to the provision of an employment service within subsection (2)(a) to (d) (or an employment service within subsection (2)(f) or (g) in so far as it is also an employment service within subsection (2)(a) to (d)); and for that purpose—
    (a)  the references to an employment service within subsection (2)(a) do not include a reference to vocational training within the meaning given by subsection (6)(b), and

(b)    the references to an employment service within subsection (2)(d) also include a reference to a service for assisting persons to retain employment.

(8)    A reference to training includes a reference to facilities for training.

*Recruitment*

## 60   Enquiries about disability and health

(1)    A person (A) to whom an application for work is made must not ask about the health of the applicant (B)—

    (a)    before offering work to B, or

    (b)    where A is not in a position to offer work to B, before including B in a pool of applicants from whom A intends (when in a position to do so) to select a person to whom to offer work.

(2)    A contravention of subsection (1) (or a contravention of section 111 or 112 that relates to a contravention of subsection (1)) is enforceable as an unlawful act under Part 1 of the Equality Act 2006 (and, by virtue of section 120(8), is enforceable only by the Commission under that Part).

(3)    A does not contravene a relevant disability provision merely by asking about B's health; but A's conduct in reliance on information given in response may be a contravention of a relevant disability provision.

(4)    Subsection (5) applies if B brings proceedings before an employment tribunal on a complaint that A's conduct in reliance on information given in response to a question about B's health is a contravention of a relevant disability provision.

(5)    In the application of section 136 to the proceedings, the particulars of the complaint are to be treated for the purposes of subsection (2) of that section as facts from which the tribunal could decide that A contravened the provision.

(6)    This section does not apply to a question that A asks in so far as asking the question is necessary for the purpose of—

    (a)    establishing whether B will be able to comply with a requirement to undergo an assessment or establishing whether a duty to make reasonable adjustments is or will be imposed on A in relation to B in connection with a requirement to undergo an assessment,

    (b)    establishing whether B will be able to carry out a function that is intrinsic to the work concerned,

    (c)    monitoring diversity in the range of persons applying to A for work,

    (d)    taking action to which section 158 would apply if references in that section to persons who share (or do not share) a protected characteristic were references to disabled persons (or persons who are not disabled) and the reference to the characteristic were a reference to disability, or

    (e)    if A applies in relation to the work a requirement to have a particular disability, establishing whether B has that disability.

(7)    If the effect of a relevant matter on a person (A) differs according to the effect it has on a person of the same sex as A, according to whether A is married, in a civil partnership, or for some other reason due to A's family status, a comparison for the purposes of this section of the effect of that matter on persons of the opposite sex must be with a person of the opposite sex to A who is in the same position as A and in particular—

    (a)    where A is married to someone of the opposite sex, A is to be compared to a person of the opposite sex to A ('B') where B is married to someone of the opposite sex to B;

    (b)    where A is married to someone of the same sex as A or is in a civil partnership, A is to be compared to B where B is married to someone of the same sex as B or is in a civil partnership.

(8)    Subsection (6)(e) applies only if A shows that, having regard to the nature or context of the work—

    (a)    the requirement is an occupational requirement, and

    (b)    the application of the requirement is a proportionate means of achieving a legitimate aim.

(9)   'Work' means employment, contract work, a position as a partner, a position as a member of an LLP, a pupillage or tenancy, being taken as a devil, membership of a stable, an appointment to a personal or public office, or the provision of an employment service; and the references in subsection (1) to offering a person work are, in relation to contract work, to be read as references to allowing a person to do the work.

(10)  A reference to offering work is a reference to making a conditional or unconditional offer of work (and, in relation to contract work, is a reference to allowing a person to do the work subject to fulfilment of one or more conditions).

(11)  The following, so far as relating to discrimination within section 13 because of disability, are relevant disability provisions—

(a)   section 39(1)(a) or (c);
(b)   section 41(1)(b);
(c)   section 44(1)(a) or (c);
(d)   section 45(1)(a) or (c);
(e)   section 47(1)(a) or (c);
(f)   section 48(1)(a) or (c);
(g)   section 49(3)(a) or (c);
(h)   section 50(3)(a) or (c);
(i)   section 51(1);
(j)   section 55(1)(a) or (c).

(12)  An assessment is an interview or other process designed to give an indication of a person's suitability for the work concerned.

(13)  For the purposes of this section, whether or not a person has a disability is to be regarded as an aspect of that person's health.

(14)  This section does not apply to anything done for the purpose of vetting applicants for work for reasons of national security.

## CHAPTER 3
## EQUALITY OF TERMS

### *Sex equality*

## 64   Relevant types of work

(1)   Sections 66 to 70 apply where—

(a)   a person (A) is employed on work that is equal to the work that a comparator of the opposite sex (B) does;
(b)   a person (A) holding a personal or public office does work that is equal to the work that a comparator of the opposite sex (B) does.

(2)   The references in subsection (1) to the work that B does are not restricted to work done contemporaneously with the work done by A.

## 65   Equal work

(1)   For the purposes of this Chapter, A's work is equal to that of B if it is—

(a)   like B's work,
(b)   rated as equivalent to B's work, or
(c)   of equal value to B's work.

(2)   A's work is like B's work if—

(a)   A's work and B's work are the same or broadly similar, and
(b)   such differences as there are between their work are not of practical importance in relation to the terms of their work.

(3)   So on a comparison of one person's work with another's for the purposes of subsection (2), it is necessary to have regard to—

(a)   the frequency with which differences between their work occur in practice, and
(b)   the nature and extent of the differences.

(4)   A's work is rated as equivalent to B's work if a job evaluation study—

(a)   gives an equal value to A's job and B's job in terms of the demands made on a worker, or

      (b)    would give an equal value to A's job and B's job in those terms were the evaluation not made on a sex-specific system.

(5)    A system is sex-specific if, for the purposes of one or more of the demands made on a worker, it sets values for men different from those it sets for women.

(6)    A's work is of equal value to B's work if it is—

      (a)    neither like B's work nor rated as equivalent to B's work, but

      (b)    nevertheless equal to B's work in terms of the demands made on A by reference to factors such as effort, skill and decision-making.

## 66    Sex equality clause

(1)    If the terms of A's work do not (by whatever means) include a sex equality clause, they are to be treated as including one.

(2)    A sex equality clause is a provision that has the following effect—

      (a)    if a term of A's is less favourable to A than a corresponding term of B's is to B, A's term is modified so as not to be less favourable;

      (b)    if A does not have a term which corresponds to a term of B's that benefits B, A's terms are modified so as to include such a term.

(3)    Subsection (2)(a) applies to a term of A's relating to membership of or rights under an occupational pension scheme only in so far as a sex equality rule would have effect in relation to the term.

(4)    In the case of work within section 65(1)(b), a reference in subsection (2) above to a term includes a reference to such terms (if any) as have not been determined by the rating of the work (as well as those that have).

## 67    Sex equality rule

(1)    If an occupational pension scheme does not include a sex equality rule, it is to be treated as including one.

(2)    A sex equality rule is a provision that has the following effect—

      (a)    if a relevant term is less favourable to A than it is to B, the term is modified so as not to be less favourable;

      (b)    if a term confers a relevant discretion capable of being exercised in a way that would be less favourable to A than to B, the term is modified so as to prevent the exercise of the discretion in that way.

(3)    A term is relevant if it is—

      (a)    a term on which persons become members of the scheme, or

      (b)    a term on which members of the scheme are treated.

(4)    A discretion is relevant if its exercise in relation to the scheme is capable of affecting—

      (a)    the way in which persons become members of the scheme, or

      (b)    the way in which members of the scheme are treated.

(5)    The reference in subsection (3)(b) to a term on which members of a scheme are treated includes a reference to the term as it has effect for the benefit of dependants of members.

(6)    The reference in subsection (4)(b) to the way in which members of a scheme are treated includes a reference to the way in which they are treated as the scheme has effect for the benefit of dependants of members.

(7)    If the effect of a relevant matter on a person (A) differs according to the effect it has on a person of the same sex as A, according to whether A is married, in a civil partnership, or for some other reason due to A's family status, a comparison for the purposes of this section of the effect of that matter on persons of the opposite sex must be with a person of the opposite sex to A who is in the same position as A and in particular—

      (a)    where A is married to, or the civil partner of, someone of the opposite sex, A is to be compared to a person of the opposite sex to A ('B') where B is married to or (as the case may be) the civil partner of someone of the opposite sex to B;

      (b)    where A is married to, or the civil partner of, someone of the same sex, A is to be compared to B where B is married to or (as the case may be) the civil partner of someone of the same sex as B.

(8)    A relevant matter is—

      (a)    a relevant term;

      (b)    a term conferring a relevant discretion;

      (c)    the exercise of a relevant discretion in relation to an occupational pension scheme.

(9)   This section, so far as relating to the terms on which persons become members of an occupational pension scheme, does not have effect in relation to pensionable service before 8 April 1976.

(10)  This section, so far as relating to the terms on which members of an occupational pension scheme are treated, does not have effect in relation to pensionable service before 17 May 1990.

## 68   Sex equality rule: consequential alteration of schemes

(1)   This section applies if the trustees or managers of an occupational pension scheme do not have power to make sex equality alterations to the scheme.

(2)   This section also applies if the trustees or managers of an occupational pension scheme have power to make sex equality alterations to the scheme but the procedure for doing so—
       (a)   is liable to be unduly complex or protracted, or
       (b)   involves obtaining consents which cannot be obtained or which can be obtained only with undue delay or difficulty.

(3)   The trustees or managers may by resolution make sex equality alterations to the scheme.

(4)   Sex equality alterations may have effect in relation to a period before the date on which they are made.

(5)   Sex equality alterations to an occupational pension scheme are such alterations to the scheme as may be required to secure conformity with a sex equality rule.

## 69   Defence of material factor

(1)   The sex equality clause in A's terms has no effect in relation to a difference between A's terms and B's terms if the responsible person shows that the difference is because of a material factor reliance on which—
       (a)   does not involve treating A less favourably because of A's sex than the responsible person treats B, and
       (b)   if the factor is within subsection (2), is a proportionate means of achieving a legitimate aim.

(2)   A factor is within this subsection if A shows that, as a result of the factor, A and persons of the same sex doing work equal to A's are put at a particular disadvantage when compared with persons of the opposite sex doing work equal to A's.

(3)   For the purposes of subsection (1), the long-term objective of reducing inequality between men's and women's terms of work is always to be regarded as a legitimate aim.

(4)   A sex equality rule has no effect in relation to a difference between A and B in the effect of a relevant matter if the trustees or managers of the scheme in question show that the difference is because of a material factor which is not the difference of sex.

(5)   'Relevant matter' has the meaning given in section 67.

(6)   For the purposes of this section, a factor is not material unless it is a material difference between A's case and B's.

## 70   Exclusion of sex discrimination provisions

(1)   The relevant sex discrimination provision has no effect in relation to a term of A's that—
       (a)   is modified by, or included by virtue of, a sex equality clause or rule, or
       (b)   would be so modified or included but for section 69 or Part 2 of Schedule 7.

(2)   Neither of the following is sex discrimination for the purposes of the relevant sex discrimination provision—
       (a)   the inclusion in A's terms of a term that is less favourable as referred to in section 66(2)(a);
       (b)   the failure to include in A's terms a corresponding term as referred to in section 66(2)(b).

(3)   The relevant sex discrimination provision is, in relation to work of a description given in the first column of the table, the provision referred to in the second column so far as relating to sex.

| Description of work | Provision |
| --- | --- |
| Employment | Section 39(2) |
| Appointment to a personal office | Section 49(6) |
| Appointment to a public office | Section 50(6) |

## 71 Sex discrimination in relation to contractual pay

(1) This section applies in relation to a term of a person's work—
   (a) that relates to pay, but
   (b) in relation to which a sex equality clause or rule has no effect.

(2) The relevant sex discrimination provision (as defined by section 70) has no effect in relation to the term except in so far as treatment of the person amounts to a contravention of the provision by virtue of section 13 or 14.

*Pregnancy and maternity equality*

## 72 Relevant types of work

Sections 73 to 76 apply where a woman—
   (a) is employed, or
   (b) holds a personal or public office.

## 73 Maternity equality clause

(1) If the terms of the woman's work do not (by whatever means) include a maternity equality clause, they are to be treated as including one.

(2) A maternity equality clause is a provision that, in relation to the terms of the woman's work, has the effect referred to in section 74(1), (6) and (8).

(3) In the case of a term relating to membership of or rights under an occupational pension scheme, a maternity equality clause has only such effect as a maternity equality rule would have.

## 74 Maternity equality clause: pay

(1) A term of the woman's work that provides for maternity-related pay to be calculated by reference to her pay at a particular time is, if each of the following three conditions is satisfied, modified as mentioned in subsection (5).

(2) The first condition is that, after the time referred to in subsection (1) but before the end of the protected period—
   (a) her pay increases, or
   (b) it would have increased had she not been on maternity leave.

(3) The second condition is that the maternity-related pay is not—
   (a) what her pay would have been had she not been on maternity leave, or
   (b) the difference between the amount of statutory maternity pay to which she is entitled and what her pay would have been had she not been on maternity leave.

(4) The third condition is that the terms of her work do not provide for the maternity-related pay to be subject to—
   (a) an increase as mentioned in subsection (2)(a), or
   (b) an increase that would have occurred as mentioned in subsection (2)(b).

(5) The modification referred to in subsection (1) is a modification to provide for the maternity-related pay to be subject to—
   (a) any increase as mentioned in subsection (2)(a), or
   (b) any increase that would have occurred as mentioned in subsection (2)(b).

(6) A term of her work that—
   (a) provides for pay within subsection (7), but
   (b) does not provide for her to be given the pay in circumstances in which she would have been given it had she not been on maternity leave,
is modified so as to provide for her to be given it in circumstances in which it would normally be given.

(7)   Pay is within this subsection if it is—
   (a)   pay (including pay by way of bonus) in respect of times before the woman is on maternity leave,
   (b)   pay by way of bonus in respect of times when she is on compulsory maternity leave, or
   (c)   pay by way of bonus in respect of times after the end of the protected period.
(8)   A term of the woman's work that—
   (a)   provides for pay after the end of the protected period, but
   (b)   does not provide for it to be subject to an increase to which it would have been subject had she not been on maternity leave,
   is modified so as to provide for it to be subject to the increase.
(9)   Maternity-related pay is pay (other than statutory maternity pay) to which a woman is entitled—
   (a)   as a result of being pregnant, or
   (b)   in respect of times when she is on maternity leave.
(10)  A reference to the protected period is to be construed in accordance with section 18.

## 75   Maternity equality rule

(1)   If an occupational pension scheme does not include a maternity equality rule, it is to be treated as including one.
(2)   A maternity equality rule is a provision that has the effect set out in subsections (3) and (4).
(3)   If a relevant term does not treat time when the woman is on maternity leave as it treats time when she is not, the term is modified so as to treat time when she is on maternity leave as time when she is not.
(4)   If a term confers a relevant discretion capable of being exercised so that time when she is on maternity leave is treated differently from time when she is not, the term is modified so as not to allow the discretion to be exercised in that way.
(5)   A term is relevant if it is—
   (a)   a term relating to membership of the scheme,
   (b)   a term relating to the accrual of rights under the scheme, or
   (c)   a term providing for the determination of the amount of a benefit payable under the scheme.
(6)   A discretion is relevant if its exercise is capable of affecting—
   (a)   membership of the scheme,
   (b)   the accrual of rights under the scheme, or
   (c)   the determination of the amount of a benefit payable under the scheme.
(7)   This section does not require the woman's contributions to the scheme in respect of time when she is on maternity leave to be determined otherwise than by reference to the amount she is paid in respect of that time.
(8)   This section, so far as relating to time when she is on ordinary maternity leave but is not being paid by her employer, applies only in a case where the expected week of childbirth began on or after 6 April 2003.
(9)   This section, so far as relating to time when she is on additional maternity leave but is not being paid by her employer—
   (a)   does not apply to the accrual of rights under the scheme in any case;
   (b)   applies for other purposes only in a case where the expected week of childbirth began on or after 5 October 2008.
(10)  In this section—
   (a)   a reference to being on maternity leave includes a reference to having been on maternity leave, and
   (b)   a reference to being paid by the employer includes a reference to receiving statutory maternity pay from the employer.

## 76   Exclusion of pregnancy and maternity discrimination provisions

(1)   The relevant pregnancy and maternity discrimination provision has no effect in relation to a term of the woman's work that is modified by a maternity equality clause or rule.

(1A) The relevant pregnancy and maternity discrimination provision has no effect in relation to a term of the woman's work—

    (a)    that relates to pay, but

    (b)    in relation to which a maternity equality clause or rule has no effect.

(2) The inclusion in the woman's terms of a term that requires modification by virtue of section 73(2) or (3) is not pregnancy and maternity discrimination for the purposes of the relevant pregnancy and maternity discrimination provision.

(3) The relevant pregnancy and maternity discrimination provision is, in relation to a description of work given in the first column of the table, the provision referred to in the second column so far as relating to pregnancy and maternity.

| Description of work | Provision |
| --- | --- |
| Employment | Section 39(2) |
| Appointment to a personal office | Section 49(6) |
| Appointment to a public office | Section 50(6) |

*Disclosure of information*

## 77 Discussions about pay

(1) A term of a person's work that purports to prevent or restrict the person (P) from disclosing or seeking to disclose information about the terms of P's work is unenforceable against P in so far as P makes or seeks to make a relevant pay disclosure.

(2) A term of a person's work that purports to prevent or restrict the person (P) from seeking disclosure of information from a colleague about the terms of the colleague's work is unenforceable against P in so far as P seeks a relevant pay disclosure from the colleague; and 'colleague' includes a former colleague in relation to the work in question.

(3) A disclosure is a relevant pay disclosure if made for the purpose of enabling the person who makes it, or the person to whom it is made, to find out whether or to what extent there is, in relation to the work in question, a connection between pay and having (or not having) a particular protected characteristic.

(4) The following are to be treated as protected acts for the purposes of the relevant victimisation provision—

    (a)    seeking a disclosure that would be a relevant pay disclosure;

    (b)    making or seeking to make a relevant pay disclosure;

    (c)    receiving information disclosed in a relevant pay disclosure.

(5) The relevant victimisation provision is, in relation to a description of work specified in the first column of the table, section 27 so far as it applies for the purposes of a provision mentioned in the second column.

| Description of work | Provision by virtue of which section 27 has effect |
| --- | --- |
| Employment | Section 39(3) or (4) |
| Appointment to a personal office | Section 49(5) or (8) |
| Appointment to a public office | Section 50(5) or (9) |

## 78 Gender pay gap information

(1) Regulations may require employers to publish information relating to the pay of employees for the purpose of showing whether, by reference to factors of such description as is prescribed, there are differences in the pay of male and female employees.

(2) This section does not apply to—

        (a)    an employer who has fewer than 250 employees;

        (b)    a person specified in Schedule 19;

        (c)    a government department or part of the armed forces not specified in that Schedule.

  (3)  The regulations may prescribe—

        (a)    descriptions of employer;

        (b)    descriptions of employee;

        (c)    how to calculate the number of employees that an employer has;

        (d)    descriptions of information;

        (e)    the time at which information is to be published;

        (f)    the form and manner in which it is to be published.

  (4)  Regulations under subsection (3)(e) may not require an employer, after the first publication of information, to publish information more frequently than at intervals of 12 months.

  (5)  The regulations may make provision for a failure to comply with the regulations—

        (a)    to be an offence punishable on summary conviction by a fine not exceeding level 5 on the standard scale;

        (b)    to be enforced, otherwise than as an offence, by such means as are prescribed.

  (6)  The reference to a failure to comply with the regulations includes a reference to a failure by a person acting on behalf of an employer.

*Supplementary*

## 79    Comparators

  (1)  This section applies for the purposes of this Chapter.

  (2)  If A is employed, B is a comparator if subsection (3) or (4) applies.

  (3)  This subsection applies if—

        (a)    B is employed by A's employer or by an associate of A's employer, and

        (b)    A and B work at the same establishment.

  (4)  This subsection applies if—

        (a)    B is employed by A's employer or an associate of A's employer,

        (b)    B works at an establishment other than the one at which A works, and

        (c)    common terms apply at the establishments (either generally or as between A and B).

  (5)  If A holds a personal or public office, B is a comparator if—

        (a)    B holds a personal or public office, and

        (b)    the person responsible for paying A is also responsible for paying B.

  (6)  If A is a relevant member of the House of Commons staff, B is a comparator if—

        (a)    B is employed by the person who is A's employer under subsection (6) of section 195 of the Employment Rights Act 1996, or

        (b)    if subsection (7) of that section applies in A's case, B is employed by the person who is A's employer under that subsection.

  (7)  If A is a relevant member of the House of Lords staff, B is a comparator if B is also a relevant member of the House of Lords staff.

  (8)  Section 42 does not apply to this Chapter; accordingly, for the purposes of this Chapter only, holding the office of constable is to be treated as holding a personal office.

  (9)  For the purposes of this section, employers are associated if—

        (a)    one is a company of which the other (directly or indirectly) has control, or

        (b)    both are companies of which a third person (directly or indirectly) has control.

## 80    Interpretation and exceptions

  (1)  This section applies for the purposes of this Chapter.

  (2)  The terms of a person's work are—

        (a)    if the person is employed, the terms of the person's employment that are in the person's contract of employment, contract of apprenticeship or contract to do work personally;

        (b)    if the person holds a personal or public office, the terms of the person's appointment to the office.

(3)   If work is not done at an establishment, it is to be treated as done at the establishment with which it has the closest connection.

(4)   A person (P) is the responsible person in relation to another person if—
   (a)   P is the other's employer;
   (b)   P is responsible for paying remuneration in respect of a personal or public office that the other holds.

(5)   A job evaluation study is a study undertaken with a view to evaluating, in terms of the demands made on a person by reference to factors such as effort, skill and decision-making, the jobs to be done—
   (a)   by some or all of the workers in an undertaking or group of undertakings, or
   (b)   in the case of the armed forces, by some or all of the members of the armed forces.

(6)   In the case of Crown employment, the reference in subsection (5)(a) to an undertaking is to be construed in accordance with section 191(4) of the Employment Rights Act 1996.

(7)   ...

(8)   Schedule 7 (exceptions) has effect.

## PART 8
## PROHIBITED CONDUCT: ANCILLARY

### 108  Relationships that have ended

(1)   A person (A) must not discriminate against another (B) if—
   (a)   the discrimination arises out of and is closely connected to a relationship which used to exist between them, and
   (b)   conduct of a description constituting the discrimination would, if it occurred during the relationship, contravene this Act.

(2)   A person (A) must not harass another (B) if—
   (a)   the harassment arises out of and is closely connected to a relationship which used to exist between them, and
   (b)   conduct of a description constituting the harassment would, if it occurred during the relationship, contravene this Act.

(3)   It does not matter whether the relationship ends before or after the commencement of this section.

(4)   A duty to make reasonable adjustments applies to A if B is placed at a substantial disadvantage as mentioned in section 20.

(5)   For the purposes of subsection (4), sections 20, 21 and 22 and the applicable Schedules are to be construed as if the relationship had not ended.

(6)   For the purposes of Part 9 (enforcement), a contravention of this section relates to the Part of this Act that would have been contravened if the relationship had not ended.

(7)   But conduct is not a contravention of this section in so far as it also amounts to victimisation of B by A.

### 109  Liability of employers and principals

(1)   Anything done by a person (A) in the course of A's employment must be treated as also done by the employer.

(2)   Anything done by an agent for a principal, with the authority of the principal, must be treated as also done by the principal.

(3)   It does not matter whether that thing is done with the employer's or principal's knowledge or approval.

(4)   In proceedings against A's employer (B) in respect of anything alleged to have been done by A in the course of A's employment it is a defence for B to show that B took all reasonable steps to prevent A—
   (a)   from doing that thing, or
   (b)   from doing anything of that description.

(5)   This section does not apply to offences under this Act (other than offences under Part 12 (disabled persons: transport)).

## 110   Liability of employees and agents

(1)   A person (A) contravenes this section if—
    (a)   A is an employee or agent,
    (b)   A does something which, by virtue of section 109(1) or (2), is treated as having been done by A's employer or principal (as the case may be), and
    (c)   the doing of that thing by A amounts to a contravention of this Act by the employer or principal (as the case may be).

(2)   It does not matter whether, in any proceedings, the employer is found not to have contravened this Act by virtue of section 109(4).

(3)   A does not contravene this section if—
    (a)   A relies on a statement by the employer or principal that doing that thing is not a contravention of this Act, and
    (b)   it is reasonable for A to do so.

(4)   A person (B) commits an offence if B knowingly or recklessly makes a statement mentioned in subsection (3)(a) which is false or misleading in a material respect.

(5)   A person guilty of an offence under subsection (4) is liable on summary conviction to a fine not exceeding level 5 on the standard scale.

(5A)   A does not contravene this section if A—
    (a)   does not conduct a relevant marriage,
    (b)   is not present at, does not carry out, or does not otherwise participate in, a relevant marriage, or
    (c)   does not consent to a relevant marriage being conducted,
for the reason that the marriage is the marriage of a same sex couple.

(5B)   Subsection (5A) applies to A only if A is within the meaning of 'person' for the purposes of section 2 of the Marriage (Same Sex Couples) Act 2013; and other expressions used in subsection (5A) and section 2 of that Act have the same meanings in that subsection as in that section

(5BA)   If A is a protected person, A does not contravene this section if A—
    (a)   does not allow religious premises to be used as the place at which two people register as civil partners of each other under Part 2 of the Civil Partnership Act 2004 ('the 2004 Act'), or
    (b)   does not provide, arrange, facilitate or participate in, or is not present at—
        (i)   an occasion during which two people register as civil partners of each other on religious premises under Part 2 of the 2004 Act, or
        (ii)   a ceremony or event in England or Wales to mark the formation of a civil partnership,
for the reason that the person does not wish to do things of that sort in relation to civil partnerships generally, or those between two people of the same sex, or those between two people of the opposite sex.

(5BB)   In subsection (5BA)—
    'protected person' has the meaning given by section 30ZA(2) of the 2004 Act;
    'religious premises' has the meaning given by section 6A(3C) of the 2004 Act.

(5C)   A does not contravene this section by refusing to solemnise a relevant Scottish marriage for the reason that the marriage is the marriage of two persons of the same sex.

(5D)   A does not contravene this section by refusing to register a relevant Scottish civil partnership for the reason that the civil partnership is between two persons of the same sex.

(5E)   Subsections (5C) and (5D) apply only if A is an approved celebrant.

(5F)   Expressions used in subsections (5C) to (5E) have the same meaning as in paragraph 25B of Schedule 3.

(5G)   A chaplain does not contravene this section by refusing to solemnise a relevant Scottish forces marriage for the reason that the marriage is the marriage of two persons of the same sex.

(5H)   Expressions used in subsection (5G) have the same meaning as in paragraph 25C of Schedule 3.

(6)   Part 9 (enforcement) applies to a contravention of this section by A as if it were the contravention mentioned in subsection (1)(c).

(7)   The reference in subsection (1)(c) to a contravention of this Act does not include a reference to disability discrimination in contravention of Chapter 1 of Part 6 (schools).

## 111   Instructing, causing or inducing contraventions

(1)   A person (A) must not instruct another (B) to do in relation to a third person (C) anything which contravenes Part 3, 4, 5, 6 or 7 or section 108(1) or (2) or 112(1) (a basic contravention).

(2)   A person (A) must not cause another (B) to do in relation to a third person (C) anything which is a basic contravention.

(3)   A person (A) must not induce another (B) to do in relation to a third person (C) anything which is a basic contravention.

(4)   For the purposes of subsection (3), inducement may be direct or indirect.

(5)   Proceedings for a contravention of this section may be brought—

   (a)   by B, if B is subjected to a detriment as a result of A's conduct;

   (b)   by C, if C is subjected to a detriment as a result of A's conduct;

   (c)   by the Commission.

(6)   For the purposes of subsection (5), it does not matter whether—

   (a)   the basic contravention occurs;

   (b)   any other proceedings are, or may be, brought in relation to A's conduct.

(7)   This section does not apply unless the relationship between A and B is such that A is in a position to commit a basic contravention in relation to B.

(8)   A reference in this section to causing or inducing a person to do something includes a reference to attempting to cause or induce the person to do it.

(9)   For the purposes of Part 9 (enforcement), a contravention of this section is to be treated as relating—

   (a)   in a case within subsection (5)(a), to the Part of this Act which, because of the relationship between A and B, A is in a position to contravene in relation to B;

   (b)   in a case within subsection (5)(b), to the Part of this Act which, because of the relationship between B and C, B is in a position to contravene in relation to C.

## 112   Aiding contraventions

(1)   A person (A) must not knowingly help another (B) to do anything which contravenes Part 3, 4, 5, 6 or 7 or section 108(1) or (2) or 111 (a basic contravention).

(2)   It is not a contravention of subsection (1) if—

   (a)   A relies on a statement by B that the act for which the help is given does not contravene this Act, and

   (b)   it is reasonable for A to do so.

(3)   B commits an offence if B knowingly or recklessly makes a statement mentioned in subsection (2)(a) which is false or misleading in a material respect.

(4)   A person guilty of an offence under subsection (3) is liable on summary conviction to a fine not exceeding level 5 on the standard scale.

(5)   For the purposes of Part 9 (enforcement), a contravention of this section is to be treated as relating to the provision of this Act to which the basic contravention relates.

(6)   The reference in subsection (1) to a basic contravention does not include a reference to disability discrimination in contravention of Chapter 1 of Part 6 (schools).

PART 9
ENFORCEMENT

CHAPTER 1
INTRODUCTORY

## 113   Proceedings

(1)   Proceedings relating to a contravention of this Act must be brought in accordance with this Part.

...

## CHAPTER 3
## EMPLOYMENT TRIBUNALS

### 120 Jurisdiction

(1) An employment tribunal has, subject to section 121, jurisdiction to determine a complaint relating to—
   (a)   a contravention of Part 5 (work);
   (b)   a contravention of section 108, 111 or 112 that relates to Part 5.
(2) An employment tribunal has jurisdiction to determine an application by a responsible person (as defined by section 61) for a declaration as to the rights of that person and a worker in relation to a dispute about the effect of a non-discrimination rule.
(3) An employment tribunal also has jurisdiction to determine an application by the trustees or managers of an occupational pension scheme for a declaration as to their rights and those of a member in relation to a dispute about the effect of a non-discrimination rule.
(4) An employment tribunal also has jurisdiction to determine a question that—
   (a)   relates to a non-discrimination rule, and
   (b)   is referred to the tribunal by virtue of section 122.
(5) In proceedings before an employment tribunal on a complaint relating to a breach of a non-discrimination rule, the employer—
   (a)   is to be treated as a party, and
   (b)   is accordingly entitled to appear and be heard.
(6) Nothing in this section affects such jurisdiction as the High Court, the county court, the Court of Session or the sheriff has in relation to a non-discrimination rule.
(7) Subsection (1)(a) does not apply to a contravention of section 53 in so far as the act complained of may, by virtue of an enactment, be subject to an appeal or proceedings in the nature of an appeal.
(8) In subsection (1), the references to Part 5 do not include a reference to section 60(1).

### 123 Time limits

(1) Subject to section 140B, proceedings on a complaint within section 120 may not be brought after the end of—
   (a)   the period of 3 months starting with the date of the act to which the complaint relates, or
   (b)   such other period as the employment tribunal thinks just and equitable.
(2) Proceedings may not be brought in reliance on section 121(1) after the end of—
   (a)   the period of 6 months starting with the date of the act to which the proceedings relate, or
   (b)   such other period as the employment tribunal thinks just and equitable.
(3) For the purposes of this section—
   (a)   conduct extending over a period is to be treated as done at the end of the period;
   (b)   failure to do something is to be treated as occurring when the person in question decided on it.
(4) In the absence of evidence to the contrary, a person (P) is to be taken to decide on failure to do something—
   (a)   when P does an act inconsistent with doing it, or
   (b)   if P does no inconsistent act, on the expiry of the period in which P might reasonably have been expected to do it.

### 124 Remedies: general

(1) This section applies if an employment tribunal finds that there has been a contravention of a provision referred to in section 120(1).
(2) The tribunal may—
   (a)   make a declaration as to the rights of the complainant and the respondent in relation to the matters to which the proceedings relate;
   (b)   order the respondent to pay compensation to the complainant;
   (c)   make an appropriate recommendation.

(3)	An appropriate recommendation is a recommendation that within a specified period the respondent takes specified steps for the purpose of obviating or reducing the adverse effect on the complainant of any matter to which the proceedings relate.

(4)	Subsection (5) applies if the tribunal—
	(a)	finds that a contravention is established by virtue of section 19, but
	(b)	is satisfied that the provision, criterion or practice was not applied with the intention of discriminating against the complainant.

(5)	It must not make an order under subsection (2)(b) unless it first considers whether to act under subsection (2)(a) or (c).

(6)	The amount of compensation which may be awarded under subsection (2)(b) corresponds to the amount which could be awarded by the county court or the sheriff under section 119.

(7)	If a respondent fails, without reasonable excuse, to comply with an appropriate recommendation, the tribunal may—
	(a)	if an order was made under subsection (2)(b), increase the amount of compensation to be paid;
	(b)	if no such order was made, make one.

CHAPTER 4<br>EQUALITY OF TERMS

## 127	Jurisdiction

(1)	An employment tribunal has, subject to subsection (6), jurisdiction to determine a complaint relating to a breach of an equality clause or rule.

(2)	The jurisdiction conferred by subsection (1) includes jurisdiction to determine a complaint arising out of a breach of an equality clause or rule; and a reference in this Chapter to a complaint relating to such a breach is to be read accordingly.

(3)	An employment tribunal also has jurisdiction to determine an application by a responsible person for a declaration as to the rights of that person and a worker in relation to a dispute about the effect of an equality clause or rule.

(4)	An employment tribunal also has jurisdiction to determine an application by the trustees or managers of an occupational pension scheme for a declaration as to their rights and those of a member in relation to a dispute about the effect of an equality rule.

(5)	An employment tribunal also has jurisdiction to determine a question that—
	(a)	relates to an equality clause or rule, and
	(b)	is referred to the tribunal by virtue of section 128(2).

(6)	This section does not apply to a complaint relating to an act done when the complainant was serving as a member of the armed forces unless—
	(a)	the complainant has made a service complaint about the matter, and
	(b)	the complaint has not been withdrawn.

(7)	Subsections (2) to (6) of section 121 apply for the purposes of subsection (6) of this section as they apply for the purposes of subsection (1) of that section.

(8)	In proceedings before an employment tribunal on a complaint relating to a breach of an equality rule, the employer—
	(a)	is to be treated as a party, and
	(b)	is accordingly entitled to appear and be heard.

(9)	Nothing in this section affects such jurisdiction as the High Court, the county court, the Court of Session or the sheriff has in relation to an equality clause or rule.

## 129	Time limits

(1)	This section applies to—
	(a)	a complaint relating to a breach of an equality clause or rule;
	(b)	an application for a declaration referred to in section 127(3) or (4).

(2)	Proceedings on the complaint or application may not be brought in an employment tribunal after the end of the qualifying period.

(3)	If the complaint or application relates to terms of work other than terms of service in the armed forces, the qualifying period is, in a case mentioned in the first column of the table, the period mentioned in the second column, subject to section 140B.

| Case | Qualifying period |
|------|-------------------|
| A standard case | The period of 6 months beginning with the last day of the employment or appointment. |
| A concealment case (but not if it is also a concealment or incapacity case (or both)) | The period of 6 months beginning with the day on which the stable working relationship ended. |
| A concealment case (but not if it is also an incapacity case) | The period of 6 months beginning with the day on which the worker discovered (or could with reasonable diligence have discovered) the qualifying fact. |
| An incapacity case (but not if it is also a concealment case) | The period of 6 months beginning with the day on which the worker ceased to have the incapacity. |
| A case which is a concealment case and an incapacity case | The period of 6 months beginning with the later of the days on which the period would begin if the case were merely a concealment or incapacity case. |

(4)    If the complaint or application relates to terms of service in the armed forces, the qualifying period is, in a case mentioned in the first column of the table, the period mentioned in the second column, subject to section 140B.

| Case | Qualifying period |
|------|-------------------|
| A standard case | The period of 9 months beginning with the last day of the period of service during which the complaint arose. |
| A concealment case (but not if it is also an incapacity case) | The period of 9 months beginning with the day on which the worker discovered (or could with reasonable diligence have discovered) the qualifying fact. |
| An incapacity case (but not if it is also a concealment case) | The period of 9 months beginning with the day on which the worker ceased to have the incapacity. |
| A case which is a concealment case and an incapacity case | The period of 9 months beginning with the later of the days on which the period would begin if the case were merely a concealment or incapacity case. |

**130    Section 129: supplementary**

(1)    This section applies for the purposes of section 129.

(2)    A standard case is a case which is not—

    (a)    a stable work case,

    (b)    a concealment case,

    (c)    an incapacity case, or

    (d)    a concealment case and an incapacity case.

(3)    A stable work case is a case where the proceedings relate to a period during which there was a stable working relationship between the worker and the responsible person (including any time after the terms of work had expired).

(4)    A concealment case in proceedings relating to an equality clause is a case where— an incapacity case.

    (a)    the responsible person deliberately concealed a qualifying fact from the worker, and

    (b)    the worker did not discover (or could not with reasonable diligence have discovered) the qualifying fact until after the relevant day.

(5) A concealment case in proceedings relating to an equality rule is a case where—
    (a) the employer or the trustees or managers of the occupational pension scheme in question deliberately concealed a qualifying fact from the member, and
    (b) the member did not discover (or could not with reasonable diligence have discovered) the qualifying fact until after the relevant day.

(6) A qualifying fact for the purposes of subsection (4) or (5) is a fact—
    (a) which is relevant to the complaint, and
    (b) without knowledge of which the worker or member could not reasonably have been expected to bring the proceedings.

(7) An incapacity case in proceedings relating to an equality clause with respect to terms of work other than terms of service in the armed forces is a case where the worker had an incapacity during the period of 6 months beginning with the later of—
    (a) the relevant day, or
    (b) the day on which the worker discovered (or could with reasonable diligence have discovered) the qualifying fact deliberately concealed from the worker by the responsible person.

(8) An incapacity case in proceedings relating to an equality clause with respect to terms of service in the armed forces is a case where the worker had an incapacity during the period of 9 months beginning with the later of—
    (a) the last day of the period of service during which the complaint arose, or
    (b) the day on which the worker discovered (or could with reasonable diligence have discovered) the qualifying fact deliberately concealed from the worker by the responsible person.

(9) An incapacity case in proceedings relating to an equality rule is a case where the member of the occupational pension scheme in question had an incapacity during the period of 6 months beginning with the later of—
    (a) the relevant day, or
    (b) the day on which the member discovered (or could with reasonable diligence have discovered) the qualifying fact deliberately concealed from the member by the employer or the trustees or managers of the scheme.

(10) The relevant day for the purposes of this section is—
    (a) the last day of the employment or appointment, or
    (b) the day on which the stable working relationship between the worker and the responsible person ended.

## 131 Assessment of whether work is of equal value

(1) This section applies to proceedings before an employment tribunal on—
    (a) a complaint relating to a breach of an equality clause or rule, or
    (b) a question referred to the tribunal by virtue of section 128(2).

(2) Where a question arises in the proceedings as to whether one person's work is of equal value to another's, the tribunal may, before determining the question, require a member of the panel of independent experts to prepare a report on the question.

(3) The tribunal may withdraw a requirement that it makes under subsection (2); and, if it does so, it may—
    (a) request the panel member to provide it with specified documentation;
    (b) make such other requests to that member as are connected with the withdrawal of the requirement.

(4) If the tribunal requires the preparation of a report under subsection (2) (and does not withdraw the requirement), it must not determine the question unless it has received the report.

(5) Subsection (6) applies where—
    (a) a question arises in the proceedings as to whether the work of one person (A) is of equal value to the work of another (B), and
    (b) A's work and B's work have been given different values by a job evaluation study.

(6) The tribunal must determine that A's work is not of equal value to B's work unless it has reasonable grounds for suspecting that the evaluation contained in the study—
    (a) was based on a system that discriminates because of sex, or
    (b) is otherwise unreliable.

(7)    For the purposes of subsection (6)(a), a system discriminates because of sex if a difference (or coincidence) between values that the system sets on different demands is not justifiable regardless of the sex of the person on whom the demands are made.

(8)    A reference to a member of the panel of independent experts is a reference to a person—
   (a)    who is for the time being designated as such by the Advisory, Conciliation and Arbitration Service (ACAS) for the purposes of this section, and
   (b)    who is neither a member of the Council of ACAS nor one of its officers or members of staff.

(9)    'Job evaluation study' has the meaning given in section 80(5).

## 132    Remedies in non-pensions cases

(1)    This section applies to proceedings before a court or employment tribunal on a complaint relating to a breach of an equality clause, other than a breach with respect to membership of or rights under an occupational pension scheme.

(2)    If the court or tribunal finds that there has been a breach of the equality clause, it may—
   (a)    make a declaration as to the rights of the parties in relation to the matters to which the proceedings relate;
   (b)    order an award by way of arrears of pay or damages in relation to the complainant.

(3)    The court or tribunal may not order a payment under subsection (2)(b) in respect of a time before the arrears day.

(4)    In relation to proceedings in England and Wales, the arrears day is, in a case mentioned in the first column of the table, the day mentioned in the second column.

| Case | Arrears day |
|------|-------------|
| A standard case | The day falling 6 years before the day on which the proceedings were instituted. |
| A concealment case or an incapacity case (or a case which is both). | The day on which the breach first occurred. |

(5)    In relation to proceedings in Scotland, the arrears day is the first day of—
   (a)    the period of 5 years ending with the day on which the proceedings were commenced, or
   (b)    if the case involves a relevant incapacity, or a relevant fraud or error, the period determined in accordance with section 135(6) and (7).

CHAPTER 5

MISCELLANEOUS

## 136    Burden of proof

(1)    This section applies to any proceedings relating to a contravention of this Act.

(2)    If there are facts from which the court could decide, in the absence of any other explanation, that a person (A) contravened the provision concerned, the court must hold that the contravention occurred.

(3)    But subsection (2) does not apply if A shows that A did not contravene the provision.

(4)    The reference to a contravention of this Act includes a reference to a breach of an equality clause or rule.

(5)    This section does not apply to proceedings for an offence under this Act.

(6)    A reference to the court includes a reference to—
   (a)    an employment tribunal;
   (b)    the Asylum and Immigration Tribunal;
   (c)    the Special Immigration Appeals Commission;
   (d)    the First-tier Tribunal;
   (e)    the Special Educational Needs Tribunal for Wales;
   (f)    the First-tier Tribunal for Scotland Health and Education Chamber.

PART 11
ADVANCEMENT OF EQUALITY

CHAPTER 2
POSITIVE ACTION

**158    Positive action: general**

(1)    This section applies if a person (P) reasonably thinks that—

  (a)    persons who share a protected characteristic suffer a disadvantage connected to the characteristic,

  (b)    persons who share a protected characteristic have needs that are different from the needs of persons who do not share it, or

  (c)    participation in an activity by persons who share a protected characteristic is disproportionately low.

(2)    This Act does not prohibit P from taking any action which is a proportionate means of achieving the aim of—

  (a)    enabling or encouraging persons who share the protected characteristic to overcome or minimise that disadvantage,

  (b)    meeting those needs, or

  (c)    enabling or encouraging persons who share the protected characteristic to participate in that activity.

(3)    Regulations may specify action, or descriptions of action, to which subsection (2) does not apply.

(4)    This section does not apply to—

  (a)    action within section 159(3), or

  (b)    anything that is permitted by virtue of section 104.

(5)    If section 104(7) is repealed by virtue of section 105, this section will not apply to anything that would have been so permitted but for the repeal.

(6)    This section does not enable P to do anything that is prohibited by or under an enactment other than this Act.

**159    Positive action: recruitment and promotion**

(1)    This section applies if a person (P) reasonably thinks that—

  (a)    persons who share a protected characteristic suffer a disadvantage connected to the characteristic, or

  (b)    participation in an activity by persons who share a protected characteristic is disproportionately low.

(2)    Part 5 (work) does not prohibit P from taking action within subsection (3) with the aim of enabling or encouraging persons who share the protected characteristic to—

  (a)    overcome or minimise that disadvantage, or

  (b)    participate in that activity.

(3)    That action is treating a person (A) more favourably in connection with recruitment or promotion than another person (B) because A has the protected characteristic but B does not.

(4)    But subsection (2) applies only if—

  (a)    A is as qualified as B to be recruited or promoted,

  (b)    P does not have a policy of treating persons who share the protected characteristic more favourably in connection with recruitment or promotion than persons who do not share it, and

  (c)    taking the action in question is a proportionate means of achieving the aim referred to in subsection (2).

(5)    'Recruitment' means a process for deciding whether to—

  (a)    offer employment to a person,

  (b)    make contract work available to a contract worker,

  (c)    offer a person a position as a partner in a firm or proposed firm,

  (d)    offer a person a position as a member of an LLP or proposed LLP,

  (e)    offer a person a pupillage or tenancy in barristers' chambers,

(f)    take a person as an advocate's devil or offer a person membership of an advocate's stable,

(g)    offer a person an appointment to a personal office,

(h)    offer a person an appointment to a public office, recommend a person for such an appointment or approve a person's appointment to a public office, or

(i)    offer a person a service for finding employment.

(6)    This section does not enable P to do anything that is prohibited by or under an enactment other than this Act.

## SCHEDULE 1
## DISABILITY: SUPPLEMENTARY PROVISION 1      **Section 6**

### PART 1
### DETERMINATION OF DISABILITY

#### *Impairment*

1.    Regulations may make provision for a condition of a prescribed description to be, or not to be, an impairment.

#### *Long-term effects*

2.    (1)    The effect of an impairment is long-term if—

    (a)    it has lasted for at least 12 months,

    (b)    it is likely to last for at least 12 months, or

    (c)    it is likely to last for the rest of the life of the person affected.

(2)    If an impairment ceases to have a substantial adverse effect on a person's ability to carry out normal day-to-day activities, it is to be treated as continuing to have that effect if that effect is likely to recur.

(3)    For the purposes of sub-paragraph (2), the likelihood of an effect recurring is to be disregarded in such circumstances as may be prescribed.

(4)    Regulations may prescribe circumstances in which, despite sub-paragraph (1), an effect is to be treated as being, or as not being, long-term.

#### *Severe disfigurement*

3.    (1)    An impairment which consists of a severe disfigurement is to be treated as having a substantial adverse effect on the ability of the person concerned to carry out normal day-to-day activities.

(2)    Regulations may provide that in prescribed circumstances a severe disfigurement is not to be treated as having that effect.

(3)    The regulations may, in particular, make provision in relation to deliberately acquired disfigurement.

#### *Substantial adverse effects*

4.    Regulations may make provision for an effect of a prescribed description on the ability of a person to carry out normal day-to-day activities to be treated as being, or as not being, a substantial adverse effect.

#### *Effect of medical treatment*

5.    (1)    An impairment is to be treated as having a substantial adverse effect on the ability of the person concerned to carry out normal day-to-day activities if—

    (a)    measures are being taken to treat or correct it, and

    (b)    but for that, it would be likely to have that effect.

(2)    'Measures' includes, in particular, medical treatment and the use of a prosthesis or other aid.

(3)    Sub-paragraph (1) does not apply—

    (a)   in relation to the impairment of a person's sight, to the extent that the impairment is, in the person's case, correctable by spectacles or contact lenses or in such other ways as may be prescribed;

    (b)   in relation to such other impairments as may be prescribed, in such circumstances as are prescribed.

### *Certain medical conditions*

6.    (1)   Cancer, HIV infection and multiple sclerosis are each a disability.

    (2)   HIV infection is infection by a virus capable of causing the Acquired Immune Deficiency Syndrome

### *Deemed disability*

7.    (1)   Regulations may provide for persons of prescribed descriptions to be treated as having disabilities.

    (2)   The regulations may prescribe circumstances in which a person who has a disability is to be treated as no longer having the disability.

    (3)   This paragraph does not affect the other provisions of this Schedule.

### *Progressive conditions*

8.    (1)   This paragraph applies to a person (P) if—

    (a)   P has a progressive condition,

    (b)   as a result of that condition P has an impairment which has (or had) an effect on P's ability to carry out normal day-to-day activities, but

    (c)   the effect is not (or was not) a substantial adverse effect.

    (2)   P is to be taken to have an impairment which has a substantial adverse effect if the condition is likely to result in P having such an impairment.

    (3)   Regulations may make provision for a condition of a prescribed description to be treated as being, or as not being, progressive.

### *Past disabilities*

9.    (1)   A question as to whether a person had a disability at a particular time ('the relevant time') is to be determined, for the purposes of section 6, as if the provisions of, or made under, this Act were in force when the act complained of was done had been in force at the relevant time.

    (2)   The relevant time may be a time before the coming into force of the provision of this Act to which the question relates.

SCHEDULE 7

| EQUALITY OF TERMS: EXCEPTIONS | **Section 80** |
|---|---|

PART 1

TERMS OF WORK

### *Compliance with laws regulating employment of women, etc.*

1.    Neither a sex equality clause nor a maternity equality clause has effect in relation to terms of work affected by compliance with laws regulating—

    (a)   the employment of women;

    (b)   the appointment of women to personal or public offices.

### *Pregnancy, etc.*

2.    A sex equality clause does not have effect in relation to terms of work affording special treatment to women in connection with pregnancy or childbirth.

SCHEDULE 8
WORK: REASONABLE ADJUSTMENTS                    **Section 83**

PART 1
INTRODUCTORY

*Preliminary*

1.      This Schedule applies where a duty to make reasonable adjustments is imposed on A by this Part of this Act.

*The duty*

2.      (1)   A must comply with the first, second and third requirements.

(2)   For the purposes of this paragraph—

(a)   the reference in section 20(3) to a provision, criterion or practice is a reference to a provision, criterion or practice applied by or on behalf of A;

(b)   the reference in section 20(4) to a physical feature is a reference to a physical feature of premises occupied by A;

(c)   the reference in section 20(3), (4) or (5) to a disabled person is to an interested disabled person.

(3)   In relation to the first and third requirements, a relevant matter is any matter specified in the first column of the applicable table in Part 2 of this Schedule.

(4)   In relation to the second requirement, a relevant matter is—

(a)   a matter specified in the second entry of the first column of the applicable table in Part 2 of this Schedule, or

(b)   where there is only one entry in a column, a matter specified there.

(5)   If two or more persons are subject to a duty to make reasonable adjustments in relation to the same interested disabled person, each of them must comply with the duty so far as it is reasonable for each of them to do so.

3.      (1)   This paragraph applies if a duty to make reasonable adjustments is imposed on A by section 55 (except where the employment service which A provides is the provision of vocational training within the meaning given by section 56(6)(b)).

(2)   The reference in section 20(3), (4) and (5) to a disabled person is a reference to an interested disabled person.

(3)   In relation to each requirement, the relevant matter is the employment service which A provides.

(4)   Sub-paragraph (5) of paragraph 2 applies for the purposes of this paragraph as it applies for the purposes of that paragraph.

PART 2
INTERESTED DISABLED PERSON

*Preliminary*

4.      An interested disabled person is a disabled person who, in relation to a relevant matter, is of a description specified in the second column of the applicable table in this Part of this Schedule.

*Employers (see section 39)*

5.      (1)   This paragraph applies where A is an employer.

| *Relevant matter* | *Description of disabled person* |
| --- | --- |
| Deciding to whom to offer employment. | A person who is, or has notified A that the person may be, an applicant for the employment. |
| Employment by A. | An applicant for employment by A. An employee of A's. |

(2)  Where A is the employer of a disabled contract worker (B), A must comply with the first, second and third requirements on each occasion when B is supplied to a principal to do contract work.

(3)  In relation to the first requirement (as it applies for the purposes of sub-paragraph (2))—

(a)  the reference in section 20(3) to a provision, criterion or practice is a reference to a provision, criterion or practice applied by or on behalf of all or most of the principals to whom B is or might be supplied,

(b)  the reference to being put at a substantial disadvantage is a reference to being likely to be put at a substantial disadvantage that is the same or similar in the case of each of the principals referred to in paragraph (a), and

(c)  the requirement imposed on A is a requirement to take such steps as it would be reasonable for A to have to take if the provision, criterion or practice were applied by or on behalf of A.

(4)  In relation to the second requirement (as it applies for the purposes of sub-paragraph (2))—

(a)  the reference in section 20(4) to a physical feature is a reference to a physical feature of premises occupied by each of the principals referred to in sub-paragraph (3)(a),

(b)  the reference to being put at a substantial disadvantage is a reference to being likely to be put at a substantial disadvantage that is the same or similar in the case of each of those principals, and

(c)  the requirement imposed on A is a requirement to take such steps as it would be reasonable for A to have to take if the premises were occupied by A.

(5)  In relation to the third requirement (as it applies for the purposes of sub-paragraph (2))—

(a)  the reference in section 20(5) to being put at a substantial disadvantage is a reference to being likely to be put at a substantial disadvantage that is the same or similar in the case of each of the principals referred to in sub-paragraph (3)(a), and

(b)  the requirement imposed on A is a requirement to take such steps as it would be reasonable for A to have to take if A were the person to whom B was supplied.

*Principals in contract work (see section 41)*

6.      (1)  This paragraph applies where A is a principal.

| Relevant matter | Description of disabled person |
| --- | --- |
| Contract work that A may make available. | A person who is, or has notified A that the person may be, an applicant to do the work. |
| Contract work that A makes available. | A person who is supplied to do the work. |

(2)  A is not required to do anything that a disabled person's employer is required to do by virtue of paragraph 5.

*Employment service-providers (see section 55)*

16.     This paragraph applies where—
         (a)    A is an employment service-provider, and
         (b)    the employment service which A provides is vocational training within the
                meaning given by section 56(6)(b).

| Relevant matter | Description of disabled person |
| --- | --- |
| Deciding to whom to offer to provide the service. | A person who is, or has notified A that the person may be, an applicant for the provision of the service. |
| Provision by A of the service. | A person who applies to A for the provision of the service. |
|  | A person to whom A provides the service. |

*Trade organisations (see section 57)*

17.     This paragraph applies where A is a trade organisation.

| Relevant matter | Description of disabled person |
| --- | --- |
| Deciding to whom to offer membership of the organisation. | A person who is, or has notified A that the person may be, an applicant for membership. |
| Membership of the organisation. | An applicant for membership. A member. |

*Local authorities (see section 58)*

18.     (1)    This paragraph applies where A is a local authority.

| Relevant matter | Description of disabled person |
| --- | --- |
| A member's carrying-out of official business. | The member. |

        (2)    Regulations may, for the purposes of a case within this paragraph, make provision—
               (a)    as to circumstances in which a provision, criterion or practice is, or is not, to
                      be taken to put a disabled person at the disadvantage referred to in the first
                      requirement;
               (b)    as to circumstances in which a physical feature is, or is not, to be taken to put
                      a disabled person at the disadvantage referred to in the second requirement;
               (c)    as to circumstances in which it is, or in which it is not, reasonable for a local
                      authority to be required to take steps of a prescribed description;
               (d)    as to steps which it is always, or which it is never, reasonable for a local authority
                      to take.

*Occupational pensions (see section 61)*

19. This paragraph applies where A is, in relation to an occupational pension scheme, a responsible person within the meaning of section 61.

| Relevant matter | Description of disabled person |
| --- | --- |
| Carrying out A's functions in relation to the scheme. | A person who is or may be a member of the scheme. |

## PART 3
## LIMITATION ON THE DUTY

*Lack of knowledge of disability, etc.*

20. (1) A is not subject to a duty to make reasonable adjustments if A does not know, and could not reasonably be expected to know—
    (a) in the case of an applicant or potential applicant, that an interested disabled person is or may be an applicant for the work in question;
    (b) in any case referred to in Part 2 of this schedule, that an interested disabled person has a disability and is likely to be placed at the disadvantage referred to in the first, second or third requirement.
   (2) An applicant is, in relation to the description of A specified in the first column of the table, a person of a description specified in the second column (and the reference to a potential applicant is to be construed accordingly)

| Description of A | Applicant |
| --- | --- |
| An employer | An applicant for employment |
| A firm or proposed firm | A candidate for a position as a partner |
| An LLP or proposed LLP | A candidate for a position as a member |
| A barrister or barrister's clerk | An applicant for a pupillage or tenancy |
| An advocate or advocate's clerk | An applicant for being taken as an advocate's devil or for becoming a member of a stable |
| A relevant person in relation to a personal or public office | A person who is seeking appointment to, or recommendation or approval for appointment to, the office |
| A qualifications body | An applicant for the conferment of a relevant qualification |
| An employment service-provider | An applicant for the provision of an employment service |
| A trade organisation | An applicant for membership |

   (3) If the duty to make reasonable adjustments is imposed on A by section 55, this paragraph applies only in so far as the employment service which A provides is vocational training within the meaning given by section 56(6)(b).

## SCHEDULE 9
## WORK: EXCEPTIONS                                                    **Section 83**
## PART 1
## OCCUPATIONAL REQUIREMENTS

*General*

1. (1) A person (A) does not contravene a provision mentioned in sub-paragraph (2) by applying in relation to work a requirement to have a particular protected characteristic, if A shows that, having regard to the nature or context of the work—
    (a) it is an occupational requirement,
    (b) the application of the requirement is a proportionate means of achieving a legitimate aim, and

(c)     the person to whom A applies the requirement does not meet it (or A has reasonable grounds for not being satisfied that the person meets it).

(2)     The provisions are—
        (a)     section 39(1)(a) or (c) or (2)(b) or (c);
        (b)     section 41(1)(b);
        (c)     section 44(1)(a) or (c) or (2)(b) or (c);
        (d)     section 45(1)(a) or (c) or (2)(b) or (c);
        (e)     section 49(3)(a) or (c) or (6)(b) or (c);
        (f)     section 50(3)(a) or (c) or (6)(b) or (c);
        (g)     section 51(1).

(3)     The references in sub-paragraph (1) to a requirement to have a protected characteristic are to be read—
        (a)     in the case of gender reassignment, as references to a requirement not to be a transsexual person (and section 7(3) is accordingly to be ignored);
        (b)     in the case of marriage and civil partnership, as references to a requirement not to be married or a civil partner (and section 8(2) is accordingly to be ignored).

(4)     In the case of a requirement to be of a particular sex, sub-paragraph (1) has effect as if in paragraph (c), the words from '(or' to the end were omitted.

*Religious requirements relating to sex, marriage etc., sexual orientation*

2.      (1)     A person (A) does not contravene a provision mentioned in sub-paragraph (2) by applying in relation to employment a requirement to which sub-paragraph (4) applies if A shows that—
        (a)     the employment is for the purposes of an organised religion,
        (b)     the application of the requirement engages the compliance or non-conflict principle, and
        (c)     the person to whom A applies the requirement does not meet it (or A has reasonable grounds for not being satisfied that the person meets it).

        (2)     The provisions are—
        (a)     section 39(1)(a) or (c) or (2)(b) or (c);
        (b)     section 49(3)(a) or (c) or (6)(b) or (c);
        (c)     section 50(3)(a) or (c) or (6)(b) or (c);
        (d)     section 51(1).

        (3)     A person does not contravene section 53(1) or (2)(a) or (b) by applying in relation to a relevant qualification (within the meaning of that section) a requirement to which sub-paragraph (4) applies if the person shows that—
        (a)     the qualification is for the purposes of employment mentioned in sub-paragraph (1)(a), and
        (b)     the application of the requirement engages the compliance or non-conflict principle.

        (4)     This sub-paragraph applies to—
        (a)     a requirement to be of a particular sex;
        (b)     a requirement not to be a transsexual person;
        (c)     a requirement not to be married or a civil partner;
        (ca)    a requirement not to be married to or the civil partner of a person of the same sex;
        (cb)    a requirement not to be the civil partner of a person of the opposite sex;
        (d)     a requirement not to be married to, or the civil partner of, a person who has a living former spouse or civil partner;
        (e)     a requirement relating to circumstances in which a marriage or civil partnership came to an end;
        (f)     a requirement related to sexual orientation.

        (5)     The application of a requirement engages the compliance principle if the requirement is applied so as to comply with the doctrines of the religion.

        (6)     The application of a requirement engages the non-conflict principle if, because of the nature or context of the employment, the requirement is applied so as to avoid conflicting with the strongly held religious convictions of a significant number of the religion's followers.

(7)   A reference to employment includes a reference to an appointment to a personal or public office.

(8)   In the case of a requirement within sub-paragraph (4)(a), sub-paragraph (1) has effect as if in paragraph (c) the words from '(or' to the end were omitted.

### *Other requirements relating to religion or belief*

3.     A person (A) with an ethos based on religion or belief does not contravene a provision mentioned in paragraph 1(2) by applying in relation to work a requirement to be of a particular religion or belief if A shows that, having regard to that ethos and to the nature or context of the work—

     (a)   it is an occupational requirement,

     (b)   the application of the requirement is a proportionate means of achieving a legitimate aim, and

     (c)   the person to whom A applies the requirement does not meet it (or A has reasonable grounds for not being satisfied that the person meets it).

### *Armed forces*

4.    (1)   A person does not contravene section 39(1)(a) or (c) or (2)(b) by applying in relation to service in the armed forces a relevant requirement if the person shows that the application is a proportionate means of ensuring the combat effectiveness of the armed forces.

    (2)   A relevant requirement is—

     (a)   a requirement to be a man;

     (b)   a requirement not to be a transsexual person.

    (3)   This Part of this Act, so far as relating to age or disability, does not apply to service in the armed forces; and section 55, so far as relating to disability, does not apply to work experience in the armed forces.

### *Employment services*

5.    (1)   A person (A) does not contravene section 55(1) or (2) if A shows that A's treatment of another person relates only to work the offer of which could be refused to that other person in reliance on paragraph 1, 2, 3 or 4.

    (2)   A person (A) does not contravene section 55(1) or (2) if A shows that A's treatment of another person relates only to training for work of a description mentioned in sub-paragraph (1).

    (3)   A person (A) does not contravene section 55(1) or (2) if A shows that—

     (a)   A acted in reliance on a statement made to A by a person with the power to offer the work in question to the effect that, by virtue of sub-paragraph (1) or (2), A's action would be lawful, and

     (b)   it was reasonable for A to rely on the statement.

    (4)   A person commits an offence by knowingly or recklessly making a statement such as is mentioned in sub-paragraph (3)(a) which in a material respect is false or misleading.

    (5)   A person guilty of an offence under sub-paragraph (4) is liable on summary conviction to a fine not exceeding level 5 on the standard scale.

### *Interpretation*

6.    (1)   This paragraph applies for the purposes of this Part of this Schedule.

    (2)   A reference to contravening a provision of this Act is a reference to contravening that provision by virtue of section 13.

    (3)   A reference to work is a reference to employment, contract work, a position as a partner or as a member of an LLP, or an appointment to a personal or public office.

    (4)   A reference to a person includes a reference to an organisation.

    (5)   A reference to section 39(2)(b), 44(2)(b), 45(2)(b), 49(6)(b) or 50(6)(b) is to be read as a reference to that provision with the omission of the words 'or for receiving any other benefit, facility or service'.

    (6)   A reference to section 39(2)(c), 44(2)(c), 45(2)(c), 49(6)(c), 50(6)(c), 53(2)(a) or 55(2)(c) (dismissal, etc.) does not include a reference to that provision so far as relating to sex.

(7) The reference to paragraph (b) of section 41(1), so far as relating to sex, is to be read as if that paragraph read—

    '(b) by not allowing the worker to do the work.'

## PART 2
## EXCEPTIONS RELATING TO AGE

### Preliminary

7.    For the purposes of this Part of this Schedule, a reference to an age contravention is a reference to a contravention of this Part of this Act, so far as relating to age.

### Benefits based on length of service

10. (1) It is not an age contravention for a person (A) to put a person (B) at a disadvantage when compared with another (C), in relation to the provision of a benefit, facility or service in so far as the disadvantage is because B has a shorter period of service than C.

(2) If B's period of service exceeds 5 years, A may rely on sub-paragraph (1) only if A reasonably believes that doing so fulfils a business need.

(3) A person's period of service is whichever of the following A chooses—

  (a) the period for which the person has been working for A at or above a level (assessed by reference to the demands made on the person) that A reasonably regards as appropriate for the purposes of this paragraph, or

  (b) the period for which the person has been working for A at any level.

(4) The period for which a person has been working for A must be based on the number of weeks during the whole or part of which the person has worked for A.

(5) But for that purpose A may, so far as is reasonable, discount—

  (a) periods of absence;

  (b) periods that A reasonably regards as related to periods of absence.

(6) For the purposes of sub-paragraph (3)(b), a person is to be treated as having worked for A during any period in which the person worked for a person other than A if—

  (a) that period counts as a period of employment with A as a result of section 218 of the Employment Rights Act 1996, or

  (b) if sub-paragraph (a) does not apply, that period is treated as a period of employment by an enactment pursuant to which the person's employment was transferred to A.

(7) For the purposes of this paragraph, the reference to a benefit, facility or service does not include a reference to a benefit, facility or service which may be provided only by virtue of a person's ceasing to work.

### The national minimum wage: young workers

11. (1) It is not an age contravention for a person to pay a young worker (A) at a lower rate than that at which the person pays an older worker (B) if—

  (a) the hourly rate for the national minimum wage for a person of A's age is lower than that for a person of B's age, and

  (b) the rate at which A is paid is below the single hourly rate.

(2) A young worker is a person who qualifies for the national minimum wage at a lower rate than the single hourly rate; and an older worker is a person who qualifies for the national minimum wage at a higher rate than that at which the young worker qualifies for it.

(3) The single hourly rate is the rate prescribed under section 1(3) of the National Minimum Wage Act 1998.

### The national minimum wage: apprentices

12. (1) It is not an age contravention for a person to pay an apprentice who does not qualify for the national minimum wage at a lower rate than the person pays an apprentice who does.

(2) An apprentice is a person who—

  (a) is employed under a contract of apprenticeship, or

(b)   as a result of provision made by virtue of section 3(2)(a) of the National Minimum Wage Act 1998 (persons not qualifying), is treated as employed under a contract of apprenticeship.

## Redundancy

13.  (1)   It is not an age contravention for a person to give a qualifying employee an enhanced redundancy payment of an amount less than that of an enhanced redundancy payment which the person gives to another qualifying employee, if each amount is calculated on the same basis.

   (2)   It is not an age contravention to give enhanced redundancy payments only to those who are qualifying employees by virtue of sub-paragraph (3)(a) or (b).

   (3)   A person is a qualifying employee if the person—
      (a)   is entitled to a redundancy payment as a result of section 135 of the Employment Rights Act 1996,
      (b)   agrees to the termination of the employment in circumstances where the person would, if dismissed, have been so entitled,
      (c)   would have been so entitled but for section 155 of that Act (requirement for two years' continuous employment), or
      (d)   agrees to the termination of the employment in circumstances where the person would, if dismissed, have been so entitled but for that section.

   (4)   An enhanced redundancy payment is a payment the amount of which is, subject to sub-paragraphs (5) and (6), calculated in accordance with section 162(1) to (3) of the Employment Rights Act 1996.

   (5)   A person making a calculation for the purposes of sub-paragraph (4)—
      (a)   may treat a week's pay as not being subject to a maximum amount;
      (b)   may treat a week's pay as being subject to a maximum amount above that for the time being specified in section 227(1) of the Employment Rights Act 1996;
      (c)   may multiply the appropriate amount for each year of employment by a figure of more than one.

   (6)   Having made a calculation for the purposes of sub-paragraph (4) (whether or not in reliance on sub-paragraph (5)), a person may multiply the amount calculated by a figure of more than one.

   (7)   In sub-paragraph (5), 'the appropriate amount' has the meaning given in section 162 of the Employment Rights Act 1996, and 'a week's pay' is to be read with Chapter 2 of Part 14 of that Act.

   (8)   For the purposes of sub-paragraphs (4) to (6), the reference to 'the relevant date' in subsection (1)(a) of section 162 of that Act is, in the case of a person who is a qualifying employee by virtue of sub-paragraph (3)(b) or (d), to be read as reference to the date of the termination of the employment.

## Insurance etc.

14.  (1)   It is not an age contravention for an employer to make arrangements for, or afford access to, the provision of insurance or a related financial service to or in respect of an employee for a period ending when the employee attains whichever is the greater of—
      (a)   the age of 65, and
      (b)   the state pensionable age.

   (2)   It is not an age contravention for an employer to make arrangements for, or afford access to, the provision of insurance or a related financial service to or in respect of only such employees as have not attained whichever is the greater of—
      (a)   the age of 65, and
      (b)   the state pensionable age.

   (3)   Sub-paragraphs (1) and (2) apply only where the insurance or related financial service is, or is to be, provided to the employer's employees or a class of those employees—
      (a)   in pursuance of an arrangement between the employer and another person, or
      (b)   where the employer's business includes the provision of insurance or financial services of the description in question, by the employer.

   (4)   The state pensionable age is the pensionable age determined in accordance with the rules in paragraph 1 of Schedule 4 to the Pensions Act 1995.

*Child care*

15. (1) A person does not contravene a relevant provision, so far as relating to age, only by providing, or making arrangements for or facilitating the provision of, care for children of a particular age group.

    (2) The relevant provisions are—

        (a) section 39(2)(b);

        (b) section 41(1)(c);

        (c) section 44(2)(b);

        (d) section 45(2)(b);

        (e) section 47(2)(b);

        (f) section 48(2)(b);

        (g) section 49(6)(b);

        (h) section 50(6)(b);

        (i) section 57(2)(a);

        (j) section 58(3)(a).

    (3) Facilitating the provision of care for a child includes—

        (a) paying for some or all of the cost of the provision;

        (b) helping a parent of the child to find a suitable person to provide care for the child;

        (c) enabling a parent of the child to spend more time providing care for the child or otherwise assisting the parent with respect to the care that the parent provides for the child.

    (4) A child is a person who has not attained the age of 17.

    (5) A reference to care includes a reference to supervision.

*Contributions to personal pension schemes*

16. (1) A Minister of the Crown may by order provide that it is not an age contravention for an employer to maintain or use, with respect to contributions to personal pension schemes, practices, actions or decisions relating to age which are of a specified description.

    (2) An order authorising the use of practices, actions or decisions which are not in use before the order comes into force must not be made unless the Minister consults such persons as the Minister thinks appropriate.

    (3) 'Personal pension scheme' has the meaning given in section 1 of the Pension Schemes Act 1993; and 'employer', in relation to a personal pension scheme, has the meaning given in section 318(1) of the Pensions Act 2004.

## PART 3
## OTHER EXCEPTIONS

*Non-contractual payments to women on maternity leave*

17. (1) A person does not contravene section 39(1)(b) or (2), so far as relating to pregnancy and maternity, by depriving a woman who is on maternity leave of any benefit from the terms of her employment relating to pay.

    (2) The reference in sub-paragraph (1) to benefit from the terms of a woman's employment relating to pay does not include a reference to—

        (a) maternity-related pay (including maternity-related pay that is increase-related),

        (b) pay (including increase-related pay) in respect of times when she is not on maternity leave, or

        (c) pay by way of bonus in respect of times when she is on compulsory maternity leave.

    (3) For the purposes of sub-paragraph (2), pay is increase-related in so far as it is to be calculated by reference to increases in pay that the woman would have received had she not been on maternity leave.

    (4) A reference to terms of her employment is a reference to terms of her employment that are not in her contract of employment, her contract of apprenticeship or her contract to do work personally.

    (5) 'Pay' means benefits—

        (a) that consist of the payment of money to an employee by way of wages or salary, and

    (b)    that are not benefits whose provision is regulated by the contract referred to in sub-paragraph (4).

(6)   'Maternity-related pay' means pay to which a woman is entitled—
    (a)    as a result of being pregnant, or
    (b)    in respect of times when she is on maternity leave.

*Benefits dependent on marital status, etc.*

18.   (1)   A person does not contravene this Part of this Act, so far as relating to sexual orientation, by doing anything which prevents or restricts a person who is not married from having access to a benefit, facility or service—
    (a)    the right to which accrued before 5 December 2005 (the day on which section 1 of the Civil Partnership Act 2004 came into force), or
    (b)    which is payable in respect of periods of service before that date.

(2)   A person does not contravene this Part of this Act, so far as relating to sexual orientation, by providing married persons and civil partners (to the exclusion of all other persons) with access to a benefit, facility or service.

# MODERN SLAVERY ACT 2015
## (2015, c. 30)

## 1   Slavery, servitude and forced or compulsory labour

(1)   A person commits an offence if—
    (a)    the person holds another person in slavery or servitude and the circumstances are such that the person knows or ought to know that the other person is held in slavery or servitude, or
    (b)    the person requires another person to perform forced or compulsory labour and the circumstances are such that the person knows or ought to know that the other person is being required to perform forced or compulsory labour.

(2)   In subsection (1) the references to holding a person in slavery or servitude or requiring a person to perform forced or compulsory labour are to be construed in accordance with Article 4 of the Human Rights Convention.

(3)   In determining whether a person is being held in slavery or servitude or required to perform forced or compulsory labour, regard may be had to all the circumstances.

(4)   For example, regard may be had—
    (a)    to any of the person's personal circumstances (such as the person being a child, the person's family relationships, and any mental or physical illness) which may make the person more vulnerable than other persons;
    (b)    to any work or services provided by the person, including work or services provided in circumstances which constitute exploitation within section 3(3) to (6).

(5)   The consent of a person (whether an adult or a child) to any of the acts alleged to constitute holding the person in slavery or servitude, or requiring the person to perform forced or compulsory labour, does not preclude a determination that the person is being held in slavery or servitude, or required to perform forced or compulsory labour.

# EUROPEAN UNION (WITHDRAWAL) ACT 2018
## (2018, c. 16)

## 1   Repeal of the European Communities Act 1972

The European Communities Act 1972 is repealed on exit day.

## 2   Saving for EU-derived domestic legislation

(1)   EU-derived domestic legislation, as it has effect in domestic law immediately before IP completion day, continues to have effect in domestic law on and after IP completion day.

(2)   ...

(3)    This section is subject to section 5 and Schedule 1 (exceptions to savings and incorporation) and section 5A (savings and incorporation: supplementary).

## 3    Incorporation of direct EU legislation

(1)    Direct EU legislation, so far as operative immediately before IP completion day, forms part of domestic law on and after IP completion day.

(2)    In this Act "direct EU legislation" means—

    (a)    any EU regulation, EU decision or EU tertiary legislation, as it has effect in EU law immediately before IP completion day and so far as—

        (ai)    it is applicable to and in the United Kingdom by virtue of Part 4 of the withdrawal agreement,

        (bi)    it neither has effect nor is to have effect by virtue of section 7A or 7B,

        (i)    it is not an exempt EU instrument (for which see section 20(1) and Schedule 6), and

        (ii)    ...

        (iii)    its effect is not reproduced in an enactment to which section 2(1) applies,

    (b)    any Annex to the EEA agreement, as it has effect in EU law immediately before IP completion day and so far as—

        (ai)    it is applicable to and in the United Kingdom by virtue of Part 4 of the withdrawal agreement,

        (bi)    it neither has effect nor is to have effect by virtue of section 7A or 7B,

        (i)    it refers to, or contains adaptations of, anything falling within paragraph (a), and

        (ii)    its effect is not reproduced in an enactment to which section 2(1) applies, or

    (c)    Protocol 1 to the EEA agreement (which contains horizontal adaptations that apply in relation to EU instruments referred to in the Annexes to that agreement), as it has effect in EU law immediately before IP completion day and so far as—

        (i)    it is applicable to and in the United Kingdom by virtue of Part 4 of the withdrawal agreement, and

        (ii)    it neither has effect nor is to have effect by virtue of section 7A or 7B.

(3)    For the purposes of this Act, any direct EU legislation is operative immediately before exit day if—

    (a)    in the case of anything which comes into force at a particular time and is stated to apply from a later time, it is in force and applies immediately before IP completion day,

    (b)    in the case of a decision which specifies to whom it is addressed, it has been notified to that person before IP completion day, and

    (c)    in any other case, it is in force immediately before exit day.

(4)    This section—

    (a)    brings into domestic law any direct EU legislation only in the form of the English language version of that legislation, and

    (b)    does not apply to any such legislation for which there is no such version,

but paragraph (a) does not affect the use of the other language versions of that legislation for the purposes of interpreting it.

(5)    This section is subject to section 5 and Schedule 1 (exceptions to savings and incorporation) and section 5A (savings and incorporation: supplementary).

## 4    Saving for rights etc. under section 2(1) of the ECA

(1)    Any rights, powers, liabilities, obligations, restrictions, remedies and procedures which, immediately before IP completion day—

    (a)    are recognised and available in domestic law by virtue of section 2(1) of the European Communities Act 1972, and

    (b)    are enforced, allowed and followed accordingly,

continue on and after IP completion day to be recognised and available in domestic law (and to be enforced, allowed and followed accordingly).

(2)    Subsection (1) does not apply to any rights, powers, liabilities, obligations, restrictions, remedies or procedures so far as they—

    (a)    form part of domestic law by virtue of section 3,

    (aa)    are, or are to be, recognised and available in domestic law (and enforced, allowed and followed accordingly) by virtue of section 7A or 7B, or

      (b)    arise under an EU directive (including as applied by the EEA agreement) and are not of a kind recognised by the European Court or any court or tribunal in the United Kingdom in a case decided before exit day (whether or not as an essential part of the decision in the case).

(3) This section is subject to section 5 and Schedule 1 (exceptions to savings and incorporation) and section 5A (savings and incorporation: supplementary).

## 5     Exceptions to savings and incorporation

(1) The principle of the supremacy of EU law does not apply to any enactment or rule of law passed or made on or after IP completion day.

(2) Accordingly, the principle of the supremacy of EU law continues to apply on or after IP completion day so far as relevant to the interpretation, disapplication or quashing of any enactment or rule of law passed or made before IP completion day.

(3) Subsection (1) does not prevent the principle of the supremacy of EU law from applying to a modification made on or after IP completion day of any enactment or rule of law passed or made before IP completion day if the application of the principle is consistent with the intention of the modification.

(4) The Charter of Fundamental Rights is not part of domestic law on or after IP completion day.

(5) Subsection (4) does not affect the retention in domestic law on or after IP completion day in accordance with this Act of any fundamental rights or principles which exist irrespective of the Charter (and references to the Charter in any case law are, so far as necessary for this purpose, to be read as if they were references to any corresponding retained fundamental rights or principles).

(6) Schedule 1 (which makes further provision about exceptions to savings and incorporation) has effect.

(7) Subsections (1) to (6) and Schedule 1 are subject to relevant separation agreement law (for which see section 7C).

## 6     Interpretation of retained EU law

(1) A court or tribunal—

      (a)    is not bound by any principles laid down, or any decisions made, on or after IP completion day by the European Court, and

      (b)    cannot refer any matter to the European Court on or after IP completion day.

(2) Subject to this and subsections (3) to (6), a court or tribunal may have regard to anything done on or after IP completion day by the European Court, another EU entity or the EU so far as it is relevant to any matter before the court or tribunal.

(3) Any question as to the validity, meaning or effect of any retained EU law is to be decided, so far as that law is unmodified on or after IP completion day and so far as they are relevant to it—

      (a)    in accordance with any retained case law and any retained general principles of EU law, and

      (b)    having regard (among other things) to the limits, immediately before IP completion day, of EU competences.

(4) But—

      (a)    the Supreme Court is not bound by any retained EU case law,

      (b)    the High Court of Justiciary is not bound by any retained EU case law when—

           (i)    sitting as a court of appeal otherwise than in relation to a compatibility issue (within the meaning given by section 288ZA(2) of the Criminal Procedure (Scotland) Act 1995) or a devolution issue (within the meaning given by paragraph 1 of Schedule 6 to the Scotland Act 1998), or

           (ii)    sitting on a reference under section 123(1) of the Criminal Procedure (Scotland) Act 1995, and

      (ba)    a relevant court or relevant tribunal is not bound by any retained EU case law so far as is provided for by regulations under subsection (5A),

      (c)    no court or tribunal is bound by any retained domestic case law that it would not otherwise be bound by.

(5) In deciding whether to depart from any retained EU case law by virtue of subsection (4)(a) or (b), the Supreme Court or the High Court of Justiciary must apply the same test as it would apply in deciding whether to depart from its own case law.

    ...

(6)    Subsection (3) does not prevent the validity, meaning or effect of any retained EU law which has been modified on or after IP completion day from being decided as provided for in that subsection if doing so is consistent with the intention of the modifications.

(6A) Subsections (1) to (6) are subject to relevant separation agreement law (for which see section 7C).

(7)    In this Act—

"retained case law" means—

(a)      retained domestic case law, and

(b)      retained EU case law;

"retained domestic case law" means any principles laid down by, and any decisions of, a court or tribunal in the United Kingdom, as they have effect immediately before IP completion day and so far as they—

(a)      relate to anything to which section 2, 3 or 4 applies, and

(b)      are not excluded by section 5 or Schedule 1,

(as those principles and decisions are modified by or under this Act or by other domestic law from time to time);

"retained EU case law" means any principles laid down by, and any decisions of, the European Court, as they have effect in EU law immediately before IP completion day and so far as they—

(a)      relate to anything to which section 2, 3 or 4 applies, and

(b)      are not excluded by section 5 or Schedule 1,

(as those principles and decisions are modified by or under this Act or by other domestic law from time to time);

"retained EU law" means anything which, on or after IP completion day, continues to be, or forms part of, domestic law by virtue of section 2, 3 or 4 or subsection (3) or (6) above (as that body of law is added to or otherwise modified by or under this Act or by other domestic law from time to time);

"retained general principles of EU law" means the general principles of EU law, as they have effect in EU law immediately before IP completion day and so far as they—

(a)      relate to anything to which section 2, 3 or 4 applies, and

(b)      are not excluded by section 5 or Schedule 1,

(as those principles are modified by or under this Act or by other domestic law from time to time).

## 7    Status of retained EU law

(1)    Anything which—

(a)      was, immediately before exit day, primary legislation of a particular kind, subordinate legislation of a particular kind or another enactment of a particular kind, and

(b)      continues to be domestic law on and after exit day by virtue of section 1A(2) or 1B(2),

continues to be domestic law as an enactment of the same kind.

(1A) Anything which—

(a)      was, immediately before IP completion day, primary legislation of a particular kind, subordinate legislation of a particular kind or another enactment of a particular kind, and

(b)      continues to be domestic law on and after IP completion day by virtue of section 2,

continues to be domestic law as an enactment of the same kind.

(2)    Retained direct principal EU legislation cannot be modified by any primary or subordinate legislation other than—

(a)      an Act of Parliament,

(b)      any other primary legislation (so far as it has the power to make such a modification), or

(c)      any subordinate legislation so far as it is made under a power which permits such a modification by virtue of—

(i)      paragraph 3, 5(3)(a) or (4)(a), 8(3), 10(3)(a) or (4)(a), 11(2)(a) or 12(3) of Schedule 8,

(ii)      any other provision made by or under this Act,

        (iii)    any provision made by or under an Act of Parliament passed before, and in the same Session as, this Act, or

        (iv)    any provision made on or after the passing of this Act by or under primary legislation.

(3)    Retained direct minor EU legislation cannot be modified by any primary or subordinate legislation other than—

    (a)    an Act of Parliament,

    (b)    any other primary legislation (so far as it has the power to make such a modification), or

    (c)    any subordinate legislation so far as it is made under a power which permits such a modification by virtue of—

        (i)    paragraph 3, 5(2) or (4)(a), 8(3), 10(2) or (4)(a) or 12(3) of Schedule 8,

        (ii)    any other provision made by or under this Act,

        (iii)    any provision made by or under an Act of Parliament passed before, and in the same Session as, this Act, or

        (iv)    any provision made on or after the passing of this Act by or under primary legislation.

(4)    Anything which is retained EU law by virtue of section 4 cannot be modified by any primary or subordinate legislation other than—

    (a)    an Act of Parliament,

    (b)    any other primary legislation (so far as it has the power to make such a modification), or

    (c)    any subordinate legislation so far as it is made under a power which permits such a modification by virtue of—

        (i)    paragraph 3, 5(3)(b) or (4)(b), 8(3), 10(3)(b) or (4)(b), 11(2)(b) or 12(3) of Schedule 8,

        (ii)    any other provision made by or under this Act,

        (iii)    any provision made by or under an Act of Parliament passed before, and in the same Session as, this Act, or

        (iv)    any provision made on or after the passing of this Act by or under primary legislation.

(5)    For other provisions about the status of retained EU law, see—

    (a)    section 5(1) to (3) and (7) (status of retained EU law in relation to other enactments or rules of law),

    (b)    section 6 (status of retained case law and retained general principles of EU law),

    (ba)    section 7C (status of case law of European Court etc. in relation to retained EU law which is relevant separation agreement law),

    (c)    section 15(2) and Part 2 of Schedule 5 (status of retained EU law for the purposes of the rules of evidence),

    (d)    paragraphs 13 to 16 of Schedule 8 (affirmative and enhanced scrutiny procedure for, and information about, instruments which amend or revoke subordinate legislation under section 2(2) of the European Communities Act 1972 including subordinate legislation implementing EU directives),

    (e)    paragraphs 19 and 20 of that Schedule (status of certain retained direct EU legislation for the purposes of the Interpretation Act 1978), and

    (f)    paragraph 30 of that Schedule (status of retained direct EU legislation for the purposes of the Human Rights Act 1998).

(6)    In this Act—

"retained direct minor EU legislation" means any retained direct EU legislation which is not retained direct principal EU legislation;

"retained direct principal EU legislation" means—

    (a)    any EU regulation so far as it—

        (i)    forms part of domestic law on and after IP completion day by virtue of section 3, and

        (ii)    was not EU tertiary legislation immediately before IP completion day, or

    (b)    any Annex to the EEA agreement so far as it—

        (i)    forms part of domestic law on and after IP completion day by virtue of section 3, and

        (ii)    refers to, or contains adaptations of, any EU regulation so far as it falls within paragraph (a),

(as modified by or under this Act or by other domestic law from time to time).

# STATUTORY INSTRUMENTS

## EMPLOYMENT PROTECTION (CONTINUITY OF EMPLOYMENT) REGULATIONS 1996
## (SI 1996 No. 3147)

**2    Application**

These Regulations apply to any action taken in relation to the dismissal of an employee which consists of—

    (a)    his making a claim in accordance with a dismissal procedures agreement designated by an order under section 110 of the Employment Rights Act 1996,

    (b)    the presentation by him of a relevant complaint of dismissal,

    (c)    any action taken by a conciliation officer under section 18 of the Employment Tribunals Act 1996,

    (d)    the making of a relevant settlement agreement,

    (e)    the making of an agreement to submit a dispute to arbitration in accordance with a scheme having effect by virtue of an order under section 212A of the Trade Union and Labour Relations (Consolidation) Act 1992,

    (f)    a decision taken arising out of the use of a statutory dispute resolution procedure contained in Schedule 2 to the Employment Act 2002 (Dispute Resolution) Regulations 2004, such a procedure applies, or

    (g)    a decision taken arising out of the use of the statutory duty to consider procedure contained in Schedule 6 of the Employment Equality (Age) Regulations 2006.

**3    Continuity of employment where employee re-engaged**

(1)   The provisions of this regulation shall have effect to preserve the continuity of a person's period of employment for the purposes of—

    (a)    Chapter I of Part XIV of the Employment Rights Act 1996 (continuous employment), and

    (b)    that Chapter as applied by subsection (2) of section 282 of the Trade Union and Labour Relations (Consolidation) Act 1992 for the purposes of that section.

(2)   If in consequence of any action to which these Regulations apply a dismissed employee is reinstated or re-employed by his employer or by a successor or associated employer of the employer—

    (a)    the continuity of that employee's period of employment shall be preserved, and

    (b)    the period beginning with the date on which the dismissal takes effect and ending with the date of reinstatement or re-engagement shall count in the computation of the employee's period of continuous employment.

**4    Exclusion of operation of section 214 of the Employment Rights Act 1996 where redundancy or equivalent payment repaid**

(1)   Section 214 of the Employment Rights Act 1996 (continuity broken where employee re-employed after the making of a redundancy payment or equivalent payment) shall not apply where—

    (a)    in consequence of any action to which these Regulations apply a dismissed employee is reinstated or re-employed by his employer or by a successor or associated employer of the employer,

    (b)    the terms upon which he is so reinstated or re-engaged include provision for him to repay the amount of a redundancy payment or an equivalent payment paid in respect of the relevant dismissal, and

    (c)    that provision is complied with.

(2)   For the purposes of this regulation the cases in which a redundancy payment shall be treated as having been paid are the cases mentioned in section 214(5) of the Employment Rights Act 1996.

# WORKING TIME REGULATIONS 1998
# (SI 1998 No. 1833)

PART II

RIGHTS AND OBLIGATIONS CONCERNING WORKING TIME

## 3  General

(1)  The provisions of this Part have effect subject to the exceptions provided for in Part III of these Regulations.

(2)  Where, in this Part, separate provision is made as respects the same matter in relation to workers generally and to young workers, the provision relating to workers generally applies only to adult workers and those young workers to whom, by virtue of any exception in Part 3, the provision relating to young workers does not apply.

## 4  Maximum weekly working time

(1)  Unless his employer has first obtained the worker's agreement in writing to perform such work a worker's working time, including overtime, in any reference period which is applicable in his case shall not exceed an average of 48 hours for each seven days.

(2)  An employer shall take all reasonable steps, in keeping with the need to protect the health and safety of workers, to ensure that the limit specified in paragraph (1) is complied with in the case of each worker employed by him in relation to whom it applies and shall keep up-to-date records of all workers who carry out work to which it does not apply by reason of the fact that the employer has obtained the worker's agreement as mentioned in paragraph (1).

(3)  Subject to paragraphs (4) and (5) and any agreement under regulation 23(b), the reference periods which apply in the case of a worker are—

(a)  where a relevant agreement provides for the application of this regulation in relation to successive periods of 17 weeks, each such period, or

(b)  in any other case, any period of 17 weeks in the course of his employment.

(4)  Where a worker has worked for his employer for less than 17 weeks, the reference period applicable in his case is the period that has elapsed since he started work for his employer.

(5)  Paragraphs (3) and (4) shall apply to a worker who is excluded from the scope of certain provisions of these Regulations by regulation 21 as if for each reference to 17 weeks there were substituted a reference to 26 weeks.

(6)  For the purposes of this regulation, a worker's average working time for each seven days during a reference period shall be determined according to the formula—

$$\frac{A + B}{C}$$

where—

A is the aggregate number of hours comprised in the worker's working time during the course of the reference period;

B is the aggregate number of hours comprised in his working time during the course of the period beginning immediately after the end of the reference period and ending when the number of days in that subsequent period on which he has worked equals the number of excluded days during the reference period; and

C is the number of weeks in the reference period.

(7)  In paragraph (6), 'excluded days' means days comprised in—

(a)  any period of annual leave taken by the worker in exercise of his entitlement under regulation 13;

(b)  any period of sick leave taken by the worker;

(c)    any period of maternity, paternity, adoption or parental leave taken by the worker; and

(d)    any period in respect of which the limit specified in paragraph (1) did not apply in relation to the worker by reason of the fact that the employer has obtained the worker's agreement as mentioned in paragraph (1).

## 5    Agreement to exclude the maximum

(1)    ...

(2)    An agreement for the purposes of regulation 4—

(a)    may either relate to a specified period or apply indefinitely; and

(b)    subject to any provision in the agreement for a different period of notice, shall be terminable by the worker by giving not less than seven days' notice to his employer in writing.

(3)    Where an agreement for the purposes of regulation 4 makes provision for the termination of the agreement after a period of notice, the notice period provided for shall not exceed three months.

(4)    ...

## 5A    Maximum working time for young workers

(1)    A young worker's working time shall not exceed—

(a)    eight hours a day, or

(b)    40 hours a week.

(2)    If, on any day, or, as the case may be, during any week, a young worker is employed by more than one employer, his working time shall be determined for the purpose of paragraph (1) by aggregating the number of hours worked by him for each employer.

(3)    For the purposes of paragraphs (1) and (2), a week starts at midnight between Sunday and Monday.

(4)    An employer shall take all reasonable steps, in keeping with the need to protect the health and safety of workers, to ensure that the limits specified in paragraph (1) are complied with in the case of each worker employed by him in relation to whom they apply.

## 6    Length of night work

(1)    A night worker's normal hours of work in any reference period which is applicable in his case shall not exceed an average of eight hours for each 24 hours.

(2)    An employer shall take all reasonable steps, in keeping with the need to protect the health and safety of workers, to ensure that the limit specified in paragraph (1) is complied with in the case of each night worker employed by him.

(3)    The reference periods which apply in the case of a night worker are—

(a)    where a relevant agreement provides for the application of this regulation in relation to successive periods of 17 weeks, each such period, or

(b)    in any other case, any period of 17 weeks in the course of his employment.

(4)    Where a worker has worked for his employer for less than 17 weeks, the reference period applicable in his case is the period that has elapsed since he started work for his employer.

(5)    For the purposes of this regulation, a night worker's average normal hours of work for each 24 hours during a reference period shall be determined according to the formula—

$$\frac{A}{B - C}$$

where—

**A** is the number of hours during the reference period which are normal working hours for that worker;

**B** is the number of days during the reference period; and

**C** is the total number of hours during the reference period comprised in rest periods spent by the worker in pursuance of his entitlement under regulation 11, divided by 24.

...

(6)    An employer shall ensure that no night worker employed by him whose work involves special hazards or heavy physical or mental strain works for more than eight hours in any 24-hour period during which the night worker performs night work.

(7) For the purposes of paragraph (7), the work of a night worker shall be regarded as involving special hazards or heavy physical or mental strain if—

    (a) it is identified as such in—

        (i) a collective agreement, or

        (ii) a workforce agreement,

    which takes account of the specific effects and hazards of night work, or

    (b) it is recognised in a risk assessment made by the employer under regulation 3 of the Management of Health and Safety at Work Regulations 1992 as involving a significant risk to the health or safety of workers employed by him.

## 6A Night work by young workers

An employer shall ensure that no young worker employed by him works during the restricted period.

## 7 Health assessment and transfer of night workers to day work

(1) An employer—

    (a) shall not assign an adult worker to work which is to be undertaken during periods such that the worker will become a night worker unless—

        (i) the employer has ensured that the worker will have the opportunity of a free health assessment before he takes up the assignment; or

        (ii) the worker had a health assessment before being assigned to work to be undertaken during such periods on an earlier occasion, and the employer has no reason to believe that that assessment is no longer valid, and

    (b) shall ensure that each night worker employed by him has the opportunity of a free health assessment at regular intervals of whatever duration may be appropriate in his case.

(2) Subject to paragraph (4), an employer—

    (a) shall not assign a young worker to work during the restricted period unless—

        (i) the employer has ensured that the young worker will have the opportunity of a free assessment of his health and capacities before he takes up the assignment; or

        (ii) the young worker had an assessment of his health and capacities before being assigned to work during the restricted period on an earlier occasion, and the employer has no reason to believe that that assessment is no longer valid; and

    (b) shall ensure that each young worker employed by him and assigned to work during the restricted period has the opportunity of a free assessment of his health and capacities at regular intervals of whatever duration may be appropriate in his case.

(3) For the purposes of paragraphs (1) and (2), an assessment is free if it is at no cost to the worker to whom it relates.

(4) The requirements in paragraph (2) do not apply in a case where the work a young worker is assigned to do is of an exceptional nature.

(5) No person shall disclose an assessment made for the purposes of this regulation to any person other than the worker to whom it relates, unless—

    (a) the worker has given his consent in writing to the disclosure, or

    (b) the disclosure is confined to a statement that the assessment shows the worker to be fit—

        (i) in a case where paragraph (1)(a)(i) or (2)(a)(i) applies, to take up an assignment, or

        (ii) in a case where paragraph (1)(b) or (2)(b) applies, to continue to undertake an assignment.

(6) Where—

    (a) a registered medical practitioner has advised an employer that a worker employed by the employer is suffering from health problems which the practitioner considers to be connected with the fact that the worker performs night work, and

    (b) it is possible for the employer to transfer the worker to work—

        (i) to which the worker is suited, and

       (ii)    which is to be undertaken during periods such that the worker will cease to be a night worker,

the employer shall transfer the worker accordingly.

## 8    Pattern of work

Where the pattern according to which an employer organises work is such as to put the health and safety of a worker employed by him at risk, in particular because the work is monotonous or the work-rate is predetermined, the employer shall ensure that the worker is given adequate rest breaks.

## 9    Records

An employer shall—

(a)    keep records which are adequate to show whether the limits specified in regulations 4(1), 5A(1) and 6(1) and (7) and the requirements in regulations 6A and 7(1) and (2) are being complied with in the case of each worker employed by him in relation to whom they apply; and

(b)    retain such records for two years from the date on which they were made.

## 10    Daily rest

(1)    A worker is entitled to a rest period of not less than eleven consecutive hours in each 24-hour period during which he works for his employer.

(2)    Subject to paragraph (3), a young worker is entitled to a rest period of not less than twelve consecutive hours in each 24-hour period during which he works for his employer.

(3)    The minimum rest period provided for in paragraph (2) may be interrupted in the case of activities involving periods of work that are split up over the day or of short duration.

## 11    Weekly rest period

(1)    Subject to paragraph (2), a worker is entitled to an uninterrupted rest period of not less than 24 hours in each seven-day period during which he works for his employer.

(2)    If his employer so determines, a worker shall be entitled to either—

(a)    two uninterrupted rest periods each of not less than 24 hours in each 14-day period during which he works for his employer; or

(b)    one uninterrupted rest period of not less than 48 hours in each such 14-day period, in place of the entitlement provided for in paragraph (1).

(3)    Subject to paragraph (8), a young worker is entitled to a rest period of not less than 48 hours in each seven-day period during which he works for his employer.

(4)    For the purpose of paragraphs (1) to (3), a seven-day period or (as the case may be) 14-day period shall be taken to begin—

(a)    at such times on such days as may be provided for for the purposes of this regulation in a relevant agreement; or

(b)    where there are no provisions of a relevant agreement which apply, at the start of each week or (as the case may be) every other week.

(5)    In a case where, in accordance with paragraph (4), 14-day periods are to be taken to begin at the start of every other week, the first such period applicable in the case of a particular worker shall be taken to begin—

(a)    if the worker's employment began on or before the date on which these Regulations come into force, on 5 October 1998; or

(b)    if the worker's employment begins after the date on which these Regulations come into force, at the start of the week in which that employment begins.

(6)    For the purposes of paragraphs (4) and (5), a week starts at midnight between Sunday and Monday.

(7)    The minimum rest period to which a worker is entitled under paragraph (1) or (2) shall not include any part of a rest period to which the worker is entitled under regulation 10(1), except where this is justified by objective or technical reasons or reasons concerning the organisation of work.

(8)    The minimum rest period to which a young worker is entitled under paragraph (3)—

(a)    may be interrupted in the case of activities involving periods of work that are split up over the day or are of short duration; and

(b)    may be reduced where this is justified by technical or organisation reasons, but not to less than 36 consecutive hours.

## 12 Rest breaks

(1) Where a worker's daily working time is more than six hours, he is entitled to a rest break.

(2) The details of the rest break to which a worker is entitled under paragraph (1), including its duration and the terms on which it is granted, shall be in accordance with any provisions for the purposes of this regulation which are contained in a collective agreement or a workforce agreement.

(3) Subject to the provisions of any applicable collective agreement or workforce agreement, the rest break provided for in paragraph (1) is an uninterrupted period of not less than 20 minutes, and the worker is entitled to spend it away from his workstation if he has one.

(4) Where a young worker's daily working time is more than four and a half hours, he is entitled to a rest break of at least 30 minutes, which shall be consecutive if possible, and he is entitled to spend it away from his workstation if he has one.

(5) If, on any day, a young worker is employed by more than one employer, his daily working time shall be determined for the purpose of paragraph (4) by aggregating the number of hours worked by him for each employer.

## 13 Entitlement to annual leave

(1) Subject to paragraph (5), a worker is entitled to four weeks' annual leave in each leave year.

(2) ...

(3) A worker's leave year, for the purposes of this regulation, begins—

    (a) on such date during the calendar year as may be provided for in a relevant agreement; or

    (b) where there are no provisions of a relevant agreement which apply—

        (i) if the worker's employment began on or before 1 October 1998, on that date and each subsequent anniversary of that date; or

        (ii) if the worker's employment begins after 1 October 1998, on the date on which that employment begins and each subsequent anniversary of that date.

(4) Paragraph (3) does not apply to a worker to whom Schedule 2 applies (workers employed in agriculture) in Wales or Scotland except where, in the case of a worker partly employed in agriculture, a relevant agreement so provides.

(5) Where the date on which a worker's employment begins is later than the date on which (by virtue of a relevant agreement) his first leave year begins, the leave to which he is entitled in that leave year is a proportion of the period applicable under paragraph (2) equal to the proportion of that leave year remaining on the date on which his employment begins.

(6)–(8) ...

(9) Leave to which a worker is entitled under this regulation may be taken in instalments, but—

    (a) it may only be taken in the leave year in respect of which it is due, and

    (b) it may not be replaced by a payment in lieu except where the worker's employment is terminated.

## 13A Entitlement to additional annual leave

(1) Subject to regulation 26A and paragraphs (3) and (5), a worker is entitled in each leave year to a period of additional leave determined in accordance with paragraph (2).

(2) The period of additional leave to which a worker is entitled under paragraph (1) is—

    (a) in any leave year beginning on or after 1st October 2007 but before 1st April 2008, 0.8 weeks;

    (b) in any leave year beginning before 1st October 2007, a proportion of 0.8 weeks equivalent to the proportion of the year beginning on 1st October 2007 which would have elapsed at the end of that leave year;

    (c) in any leave year beginning on 1st April 2008, 0.8 weeks;

    (d) in any leave year beginning after 1st April 2008 but before 1st April 2009, 0.8 weeks and a proportion of another 0.8 weeks equivalent to the proportion of the year beginning on 1st April 2009 which would have elapsed at the end of that leave year;

    (e) in any leave year beginning on or after 1st April 2009, 1.6 weeks.

(3)    The aggregate entitlement provided for in paragraph (2) and regulation 13(1) is subject to a maximum of 28 days.

(4)    A worker's leave year begins for the purposes of this regulation on the same date as the worker's leave year begins for the purposes of regulation 13.

(5)    Where the date on which a worker's employment begins is later than the date on which his first leave year begins, the additional leave to which he is entitled in that leave year is a proportion of the period applicable under paragraph (2) equal to the proportion of that leave year remaining on the date on which his employment begins.

(6)    Leave to which a worker is entitled under this regulation may be taken in instalments, but it may not be replaced by a payment in lieu except where—

(a)    the worker's employment is terminated; or

(b)    the leave is an entitlement that arises under paragraph (2)(a), (b) or (c); or

(c)    the leave is an entitlement to 0.8 weeks that arises under paragraph (2)(d) in respect of that part of the leave year which would have elapsed before 1 April 2009.

(7)    A relevant agreement may provide for any leave to which a worker is entitled under this regulation to be carried forward into the leave year immediately following the leave year in respect of which it is due.

(8)    This regulation does not apply to workers to whom the Agricultural Wages (Scotland) Act 1949 applies (as that Act had effect on 1 July 1999).

## 14    Compensation related to entitlement to leave

(1)    Paragraphs (1) to (4) of this regulation apply where—

(a)    a worker's employment is terminated during the course of his leave year, and

(b)    on the date on which the termination takes effect ('the termination date'), the proportion he has taken of the leave to which he is entitled in the leave year under regulation 13 and regulation 13A differs from the proportion of the leave year which has expired.

(2)    Where the proportion of leave taken by the worker is less than the proportion of the leave year which has expired, his employer shall make him a payment in lieu of leave in accordance with paragraph (3).

(3)    The payment due under paragraph (2) shall be—

(a)    such sum as may be provided for for the purposes of this regulation in a relevant agreement, or

(b)    where there are no provisions of a relevant agreement which apply, a sum equal to the amount that would be due to the worker under regulation 16 in respect of a period of leave determined according to the formula—

$$(A \times B) - C$$

where—

**A** is the period of leave to which the worker is entitled under regulation 13 and regulation 13A;

**B** is the proportion of the worker's leave year which expired before the termination date, and

**C** is the period of leave taken by the worker between the start of the leave year and the termination date.

(4)    A relevant agreement may provide that, where the proportion of leave taken by the worker exceeds the proportion of the leave year which has expired, he shall compensate his employer, whether by a payment, by undertaking additional work or otherwise.

## 15    Dates on which leave is taken

(1)    A worker may take leave to which he is entitled under regulation 13 and regulation 13A on such days as he may elect by giving notice to his employer in accordance with paragraph (3), subject to any requirement imposed on him by his employer under paragraph (2).

(2)    A worker's employer may require the worker—

(a)    to take leave to which the worker is entitled under regulation 13 or regulation 13A; or

      (b)    not to take such leave (subject, where it applies, to the requirement in regulation 13(12)),

on particular days, by giving notice to the worker in accordance with paragraph (3).

(3)    A notice under paragraph (1) or (2)—

      (a)    may relate to all or part of the leave to which a worker is entitled in a leave year;

      (b)    shall specify the days on which leave is or (as the case may be) is not to be taken and, where the leave on a particular day is to be in respect of only part of the day, its duration; and

      (c)    shall be given to the employer or, as the case may be, the worker before the relevant date.

(4)    The relevant date, for the purposes of paragraph (3), is the date—

      (a)    in the case of a notice under paragraph (1) or (2)(a), twice as many days in advance of the earliest day specified in the notice as the number of days or part-days to which the notice relates, and

      (b)    in the case of a notice under paragraph (2)(b), as many days in advance of the earliest day so specified as the number of days or part-days to which the notice relates.

(5)    Any right or obligation under paragraphs (1) to (4) may be varied or excluded by a relevant agreement.

(6)    This regulation does not apply to a worker to whom Schedule 2 applies (workers employed in agriculture) in Wales or Scotland except where, in the case of a worker partly employed in agriculture, a relevant agreement so provides.

## 15A    Leave during the first year of employment

(1)    During the first year of his employment, the amount of leave a worker may take at any time in exercise of his entitlement under regulation 13 or regulation 13A is limited to the amount which is deemed to have accrued in his case at that time under paragraph (2) or (2A), as modified under paragraph (3) in a case where that paragraph applies, less the amount of leave (if any) that he has already taken during that year.

(2)    For the purposes of paragraph (1), in the case of workers to whom the Agricultural Wages (Scotland) Act 1949 applies, leave is deemed to accrue over the course of the worker's first year of employment, at the rate of one-twelfth of the amount specified in regulation 13(1) on the first day of each month of that year.

(2A) Except where paragraph (2) applies, for the purposes of paragraph (1), leave is deemed to accrue over the course of the worker's first year of employment, at the rate of one-twelfth of the amount specified in regulation 13(1) and regulation 13A(2), subject to the limit contained in regulation 13A(3), on the first day of each month of that year.

(3)    Where the amount of leave that has accrued in a particular case includes a fraction of a day other than a half-day, the fraction shall be treated as a half-day if it is less than a half-day and as a whole day if it is more than a half-day.

(4)    This regulation does not apply to a worker whose employment began on or before 25th October 2001.

## 16    Payment in respect of periods of leave

(1)    A worker is entitled to be paid in respect of any period of annual leave to which he is entitled under regulation 13 and regulation 13A, at the rate of a week's pay in respect of each week of leave.

(2)    Sections 221 to 224 of the 1996 Act shall apply for the purpose of determining the amount of a week's pay for the purposes of this regulation, subject to the modifications set out in paragraph (3).

(3)    The provisions referred to in paragraph (2) shall apply—

      (a)    as if references to the employee were references to the worker;

      (b)    as if references to the employee's contract of employment were references to the worker's contract;

      (c)    as if the calculation date were the first day of the period of leave in question; and

      (d)    as if the references to sections 227 and 228 did not apply.

(4)    A right to payment under paragraph (1) does not affect any right of a worker to remuneration under his contract ('contractual remuneration'), and paragraph (1) does not confer a right under that contract.

(5)    Any contractual remuneration paid to a worker in respect of a period of leave goes towards discharging any liability of the employer to make payments under this

regulation in respect of that period; and, conversely, any payment of remuneration under this regulation in respect of a period goes towards discharging any liability of the employer to pay contractual remuneration in respect of that period.

## 17    Entitlements under other provisions

Where during any period a worker is entitled to a rest period, rest break or annual leave both under a provision of these Regulations and under a separate provision (including a provision of his contract), he may not exercise the two rights separately, but may, in taking a rest period, break or leave during that period, take advantage of whichever right is, in any particular respect, the more favourable.

PART III
EXCEPTIONS

## 18    Excluded sectors

(1)   These Regulations do not apply—
    (a)   to workers to whom the Merchant Shipping (Maritime Labour Convention) (Hours of Work) Regulations 2018 apply;
    (b)   to workers to whom the Fishing Vessels (Working Time: Sea-fishermen) Regulations 2004 apply; or
    (c)   to workers to whom the Merchant Shipping (Working Time: Inland Waterways) Regulations 2003 apply

(2)   Regulations 4(1) and (2), 6(1), (2) and (7), 7(1) and (6), 8, 10(1), 11(1) and (2), 12(1), 13, 13A and 16 do not apply—
    (a)   where characteristics peculiar to certain specific services such as the armed forces or the police, or to certain specific activities in the civil protection services, inevitably conflict with the provisions of these Regulations;
    (aa)  to workers to whom the Civil Aviation (Working Time) Regulations 2004 apply;
    (c)   to the activities of workers who are doctors in training.

(3)   Paragraph (2)(c) has effect only until 31st July 2004.

(4)   Regulations 4(1) and (2), 6(1), (2) and (7), 8, 10(1), 11(1) and (2) and 12(1) do not apply to workers to whom the Road Transport (Working Time) Regulations 2005 apply.

(5)   Regulation 24 does not apply to workers to whom the Cross-border Railway Services (Working Time) Regulations 2008 apply.

## 19    Domestic service

Regulations 4(1) and (2), 5A(1) and (4), 6(1), (2) and (7), 6A, 7(1), (2) and (6) and 8 do not apply in relation to a worker employed as a domestic servant in a private household.

## 20    Unmeasured working time

(1)   Regulations 4(1) and (2), 6(1), (2) and (7), 10(1), 11(1) and (2) and 12(1) do not apply in relation to a worker where, on account of the specific characteristics of the activity in which he is engaged, the duration of his working time is not measured or predetermined or can be determined by the worker himself, as may be the case for—
    (a)   managing executives or other persons with autonomous decision-taking powers;
    (b)   family workers; or
    (c)   workers officiating at religious ceremonies in churches and religious communities.

(2)   ...

## 21    Other special cases

Subject to regulation 24, regulations 6(1), (2) and (7), 10(1), 11(1) and (2) and 12(1) do not apply in relation to a worker—
    (a)   where the worker's activities are such that his place of work and place of residence are distant from one another, including cases where the worker is employed in offshore work, or his different places of work are distant from one another;
    (b)   where the worker is engaged in security and surveillance activities requiring a permanent presence in order to protect property and persons, as may be the case for security guards and caretakers or security firms;

(c)    where the worker's activities involve the need for continuity of service or production, as may be the case in relation to—
    (i)    services relating to the reception, treatment or care provided by hospitals or similar establishments (including the activities of doctors in training), residential institutions and prisons;
    (ii)   work at docks or airports;
    (iii)  press, radio, television, cinematographic production, postal and tele-communications services and civil protection services;
    (iv)   gas, water and electricity production, transmission and distribution, house-hold refuse collection and incineration;
    (v)    industries in which work cannot be interrupted on technical grounds;
    (vi)   research and development activities;
    (vii)  agriculture;
    (viii) the carriage of passengers on regular urban transport services;
(d)    where there is a foreseeable surge of activity, as may be the case in relation to—
    (i)    agriculture;
    (ii)   tourism; and
    (iii)  postal services;
(e)    where the worker's activities are affected by—
    (i)    an occurrence due to unusual and unforeseeable circumstances, beyond the control of the worker's employer;
    (ii)   exceptional events, the consequences of which could not have been avoided despite the exercise of all due care by the employer; or
    (iii)  an accident or the imminent risk of an accident;
(f)    where the worker works in railway transport and—
    (i)    his activities are intermittent;
    (ii)   he spends his working time on board trains; or
    (iii)  his activities are linked to transport timetables and to ensuring the continuity and regularity of traffic.

## 22   Shift workers

(1)  Subject to regulation 24—
    (a)    regulation 10(1) does not apply in relation to a shift worker when he changes shift and cannot take a daily rest period between the end of one shift and the start of the next one;
    (b)    paragraphs (1) and (2) of regulation 11 do not apply in relation to a shift worker when he changes shift and cannot take a weekly rest period between the end of one shift and the start of the next one; and
    (c)    neither regulation 10(1) nor paragraphs (1) and (2) of regulation 11 apply to workers engaged in activities involving periods of work split up over the day, as may be the case for cleaning staff.
(2)  For the purposes of this regulation—
    'shift worker' means any worker whose work schedule is part of shift work; and
    'shift work' means any method of organising work in shifts whereby workers succeed each other at the same workstations according to a certain pattern, including a rotating pattern, and which may be continuous or discontinuous, entailing the need for workers to work at different times over a given period of days or weeks.

## 23   Collective and workforce agreements

A collective agreement or a workforce agreement may—
    (a)    modify or exclude the application of regulations 6(1) to (3) and (7), 10(1), 11(1) and (2) and 12(1), and
    (b)    for objective or technical reasons or reasons concerning the organisation of work, modify the application of regulation 4(3) and (4) by the substitution, for each reference to 17 weeks, of a different period, being a period not exceeding 52 weeks,
in relation to particular workers or groups of workers.

## 24   Compensatory rest

Where the application of any provision of these Regulations is excluded by regulation 21 or 22, or is modified or excluded by means of a collective agreement or a workforce agreement under regulation 23(a), and a worker is accordingly required by his employer to work during a period which would otherwise be a rest period or rest break—

    (a)    his employer shall wherever possible allow him to take an equivalent period of compensatory rest, and

    (b)    in exceptional cases in which it is not possible, for objective reasons, to grant such a period of rest, his employer shall afford him such protection as may be appropriate in order to safeguard the worker's health and safety.

## 24A   Mobile workers

(1)    Regulations 6(1), (2) and (7), 10(1), 11(1) and (2) and 12(1) do not apply to a mobile worker in relation to whom the application of those regulations is not excluded by any provision of regulation 18.

(2)    A mobile worker, to whom paragraph (1) applies, is entitled to adequate rest, except where the worker's activities are affected by any of the matters referred to in regulation 21(e).

(3)    For the purposes of this regulation, 'adequate rest' means that a worker has regular rest periods, the duration of which are expressed in units of time and which are sufficiently long and continuous to ensure that, as a result of fatigue or other irregular working patterns, he does not cause injury to himself, to fellow workers or to others and that he does not damage his health, either in the short term or in the longer term.

## 25   Workers in the armed forces

(1)    Regulation 9 does not apply in relation to a worker serving as a member of the armed forces.

(2)    Regulations 5A, 6A, 10(2) and 11(3) do not apply in relation to a young worker serving as a member of the armed forces.

(3)    In a case where a young worker is accordingly required to work during the restricted period or is not permitted the minimum rest period provided for in regulation 10(2) or 11(3) he shall be allowed an appropriate period of compensatory rest.

## 25A   Doctors in training

(1)    Paragraph (1) of regulation 4 is modified in its application to workers who are doctors in training as follows—

    (a)    for the reference to 48 hours there is substituted a reference to 58 hours with effect from 1st August 2004 until 31st July 2007;

    (b)    for the reference to 48 hours there is substituted a reference to 56 hours with effect from 1st August 2007 until 31st July 2009.

(2)    In the case of workers who are doctors in training, paragraphs (3)-(5) of regulation 4 shall not apply and paragraphs (3) and (4) of this regulation shall apply in their place.

(3)    Subject to paragraph (4), the reference period which applies in the case of a worker who is a doctor in training is, with effect from 1st August 2004—

    (a)    where a relevant agreement provides for the application of this regulation in relation to successive periods of 26 weeks, each such period; and

    (b)    in any other case, any period of 26 weeks in the course of his employment.

(4)    Where a doctor in training has worked for his employer for less than 26 weeks, the reference period applicable in his case is the period that has elapsed since he started work for his employer.

## 26A   Entitlement to additional annual leave under a relevant agreement

(1)    Regulation 13A does not apply in relation to a worker whose employer, as at 1st October 2007 and by virtue of a relevant agreement, provides each worker employed by him with an annual leave entitlement of 1.6 weeks or 8 days (whichever is the lesser) in addition to each worker's entitlement under regulation 13, provided that such additional annual leave—

    (a)    may not be replaced by a payment in lieu except in relation to a worker whose employment is terminated;

      (b)    may not be carried forward into a leave year other than that which immediately follows the leave year in respect of which the leave is due; and

      (c)    is leave for which the worker is entitled to be paid at not less than the rate of a week's pay in respect of each week of leave, calculated in accordance with sections 221 to 224 of the 1996 Act, modified such that—

          (i)    references to the employee are references to the worker;

          (ii)   references to the employee's contract of employment are references to the worker's contract;

          (iii)  the calculation date is the first day of the period of leave in question; and

          (iv)  the references to sections 227 and 228 do not apply.

(2)    Notwithstanding paragraph (1), any additional annual leave in excess of 1.6 weeks or 8 days (whichever is the lesser) to which a worker is entitled, shall not be subject to the conditions of that paragraph.

(3)    This regulation shall cease to apply to a worker from the day when an employer ceases to provide additional annual leave in accordance with the conditions in paragraph (1).

(4)    This regulation does not apply to workers to whom the Agricultural Wages (Scotland) Act 1949 applies (as that Act had effect on 1 July 1999).

## 27    Young workers: *force majeure*

(1)    Regulations 5A, 6A, 10(2) and 12(4) do not apply in relation to a young worker where his employer requires him to undertake work which no adult worker is available to perform and which—

      (a)    is occasioned by either—

          (i)    an occurrence due to unusual and unforeseeable circumstances, beyond the employer's control, or

          (ii)   exceptional events, the consequences of which could not have been avoided despite the exercise of all due care by the employer;

      (b)    is of a temporary nature; and

      (c)    must be performed immediately.

(2)    Where the application of regulation 5A, 6A, 10(2) or 12(4) is excluded by paragraph (1), and a young worker is accordingly required to work during a period which would otherwise be a rest period or rest break, his employer shall allow him to take an equivalent period of compensatory rest within the following three weeks.

## 27A   Other exceptions relating to young workers

(1)    Regulation 5A does not apply in relation to a young worker where—

      (a)    the young worker's employer requires him to undertake work which is necessary either to maintain continuity of service or production or to respond to a surge in demand for a service or product;

      (b)    no adult worker is available to perform the work, and

      (c)    performing the work would not adversely affect the young worker's education or training.

(2)    Regulation 6A does not apply in relation to a young worker employed—

      (a)    in a hospital or similar establishment, or

      (b)    in connection with cultural, artistic, sporting or advertising activities, in the circumstances referred to in paragraph (1).

(3)    Regulation 6A does not apply, except in so far as it prohibits work between midnight and 4 a.m., in relation to a young worker employed in—

      (a)    agriculture;

      (b)    retail trading;

      (c)    postal or newspaper deliveries;

      (d)    a catering business;

      (e)    a hotel, public house, restaurant, bar or similar establishment, or

      (f)    a bakery,

in the circumstances referred to in paragraph (1).

(4)   Where the application of regulation 6A is excluded by paragraph (2) or (3), and a young worker is accordingly required to work during a period which would otherwise be a rest period or rest break—

   (a)   he shall be supervised by an adult worker where such supervision is necessary for the young worker's protection, and

   (b)   he shall be allowed an equivalent period of compensatory rest.

## PART IV
## MISCELLANEOUS

## 29     Offences

(1)   An employer who fails to comply with any of the relevant requirements shall be guilty of an offence.

(2)   The provisions of paragraph (3) shall apply where an inspector is exercising or has exercised any power conferred by Schedule 3.

(3)   It is an offence for a person—

   (a)   to contravene any requirement imposed by the inspector under paragraph 2 of Schedule 3;

   (b)   to prevent or attempt to prevent any other person from appearing before the inspector or from answering any question to which the inspector may by virtue of paragraph 2(2)(e) of Schedule 3 require an answer;

   (c)   to contravene any requirement or prohibition imposed by an improvement notice or a prohibition notice (including any such notice as is modified on appeal);

   (d)   intentionally to obstruct the inspector in the exercise or performance of his powers or duties;

   (e)   to use or disclose any information in contravention of paragraph 8 of Schedule 3;

   (f)   to make a statement which he knows to be false or recklessly to make a statement which is false, where the statement is made in purported compliance with a requirement to furnish any information imposed by or under these Regulations.

(4)   An employer guilty of an offence under paragraph (1) shall be liable—

   (a)   on summary conviction, to a fine not exceeding the statutory maximum;

   (b)   on conviction on indictment, to a fine.

(5)   A person guilty of an offence under paragraph (3) shall be liable to the penalty prescribed in relation to that provision by paragraphs (6), (7) or (8) as the case may be.

(6)   A person guilty of an offence under sub-paragraph (3)(a), (b) or (d) shall be liable on summary conviction to a fine not exceeding level 5 on the standard scale.

(7)   A person guilty of an offence under sub-paragraph (3)(c) shall be liable—

   (a)   on summary conviction, to imprisonment for a term not exceeding three months, or a fine not exceeding the statutory maximum;

   (b)   on conviction on indictment, to imprisonment for a term not exceeding two years, or a fine, or both.

(8)   A person guilty of an offence under any of the sub-paragraphs of paragraph (3) not falling within paragraphs (6) or (7) above, shall be liable—

   (a)   on summary conviction, to a fine not exceeding the statutory maximum;

   (b)   on conviction on indictment—

      (i)   if the offence is under sub-paragraph (3)(e), to imprisonment for a term not exceeding two years or a fine or both;

      (ii)   if the offence is not one to which the preceding sub-paragraph applies, to a fine.

(9)   The provisions set out in regulations 29A–29E below shall apply in relation to the offences provided for in paragraphs (1) and (3).

## 29A    Offences due to fault of other person

Where the commission by any person of an offence is due to the act or default of some other person, that other person shall be guilty of the offence, and a person may be charged with and convicted of the offence by virtue of this paragraph whether or not proceedings are taken against the first-mentioned person.

**30    Remedies**

(1)    A worker may present a complaint to an employment tribunal that his employer—

    (a)    has refused to permit him to exercise any right he has under—

        (i)    regulation 10(1) or (2), 11(1), (2) or (3), 12(1) or (4), 13 or 13A;

        (ii)    regulation 24, in so far as it applies where regulation 10(1), 11(1) or (2) or 12(1) is modified or excluded;

        (iii)    regulation 24A, in so far as it applies where regulation 10(1), 11(1) or (2) or 12(1) is excluded; or

        (iv)    regulation 25(3), 27A(4)(b) or 27(2); or

    (b)    has failed to pay him the whole or any part of any amount due to him under regulation 14(2) or 16(1).

(2)    Subject to regulation 30B, an employment tribunal shall not consider a complaint under this regulation unless it is presented—

    (a)    before the end of the period of three months (or, in a case to which regulation 38(2) applies, six months) beginning with the date on which it is alleged that the exercise of the right should have been permitted (or in the case of a rest period or leave extending over more than one day, the date on which it should have been permitted to begin) or, as the case may be, the payment should have been made;

    (b)    within such further period as the tribunal considers reasonable in a case where it is satisfied that it was not reasonably practicable for the complaint to be presented before the end of that period of three or, as the case may be, six months.

(2A)    Where the period within which a complaint must be presented in accordance with paragraph (2) is extended by regulation 15 of the Employment Act 2002 (Dispute Resolution) Regulations 2004, the period within which the complaint must be presented shall be the extended period rather than the period in paragraph (2).

(3)    Where an employment tribunal finds a complaint under paragraph (1)(a) well-founded, the tribunal—

    (a)    shall make a declaration to that effect, and

    (b)    may make an award of compensation to be paid by the employer to the worker.

(4)    The amount of the compensation shall be such as the tribunal considers just and equitable in all the circumstances having regard to—

    (a)    the employer's default in refusing to permit the worker to exercise his right, and

    (b)    any loss sustained by the worker which is attributable to the matters complained of.

(5)    Where on a complaint under paragraph (1)(b) an employment tribunal finds that an employer has failed to pay a worker in accordance with regulation 14(2) or 16(1), it shall order the employer to pay to the worker the amount which it finds to be due to him.

**30B    Extension of time limit to facilitate conciliation before institution of proceedings**

(1)    In this regulation—

    (a)    Day A is the day on which the worker concerned complies with the requirement in subsection (1) of section 18A of the Employment Tribunals Act 1996 (requirement to contact ACAS before instituting proceedings) in relation to the matter in respect of which the proceedings are brought, and

    (b)    Day B is the day on which the worker concerned receives or, if earlier, is treated as receiving (by virtue of regulations made under subsection (11) of that section) the certificate issued under subsection (4) of that section.

(2)    In working out when the time limit set by regulation 30(2)(a) expires the period beginning with the day after Day A and ending with Day B is not to be counted.

(3)    If the time limit set by regulation 30(2)(a) would (if not extended by this paragraph) expire during the period beginning with Day A and ending one month after Day B, the time limit expires instead at the end of that period.

(4)    The power conferred on the employment tribunal by regulation 30(2)(b) to extend the time limit set by paragraph (2)(a) of that regulation is exercisable in relation to that time limit as extended by this regulation.

## 35    Restrictions on contracting out

(1)    Any provision in an agreement (whether a contract of employment or not) is void in so far as it purports—

    (a)    to exclude or limit the operation of any provision of these Regulations, save in so far as these Regulations provide for an agreement to have that effect, or

    (b)    to preclude a person from bringing proceedings under these Regulations before an employment tribunal.

(2)    Paragraph (1) does not apply to—

    (a)    any agreement to refrain from instituting or continuing proceedings where a conciliation officer has taken action under any of sections 18A–18C of the Employment Tribunals Act 1996 (conciliation); or

    (b)    any agreement to refrain from instituting or continuing proceedings within section 18(1)(j) of the Employment Tribunals Act 1996 (proceedings under these Regulations where conciliation is available), if the conditions regulating compromise agreements under these Regulations are satisfied in relation to the agreement.

(3)    For the purposes of paragraph (2)(b) the conditions regulating settlement agreements under these Regulations are that—

    (a)    the agreement must be in writing,

    (b)    the agreement must relate to the particular complaint,

    (c)    the worker must have received advice from a relevant independent adviser as to the terms and effect of the proposed agreement and, in particular, its effect on his ability to pursue his rights before an employment tribunal,

    (d)    there must be in force, when the adviser gives the advice, a contract of insurance, or an indemnity provided for members of a profession or professional body, covering the risk of a claim by the worker in respect of loss arising in consequence of the advice,

    (e)    the agreement must identify the adviser, and

    (f)    the agreement must state that the conditions regulating settlement agreements under these Regulations are satisfied.

(4)    A person is a relevant independent adviser for the purposes of paragraph (3)(c)—

    (a)    if he is a qualified lawyer,

    (b)    if he is an officer, official, employee or member of an independent trade union who has been certified in writing by the trade union as competent to give advice and as authorised to do so on behalf of the trade union, or

    (c)    if he works at an advice centre (whether as an employee or as a volunteer) and has been certified in writing by the centre as competent to give advice and as authorised to do so on behalf of the centre.

(5)    But a person is not a relevant independent adviser for the purposes of paragraph (3) (c) in relation to the worker—

    (a)    if he is, is employed by or is acting in the matter for the employer or an associated employer,

    (b)    in the case of a person within paragraph (4)(b) or (c), if the trade union or advice centre is the employer or an associated employer, or

    (c)    in the case of a person within paragraph (4)(c), if the worker makes a payment for the advice received from him.

(6)    In paragraph (4)(a), 'qualified lawyer' means—

    (a)    as respects England and Wales, a person who, for the purposes of the Legal Services Act 2007), is an authorised person in relation to an activity which constitutes the exercise of a right of audience or the conduct of litigation (within the meaning of that Act); and

    (b)    as respects Scotland, an advocate (whether in practice as such or employed to give legal advice), or a solicitor who holds a practising certificate.

(6A)    A person shall be treated as being a qualified lawyer within paragraph 6(a) if he is a Fellow of the Institute of Legal Executives employed by a solicitors' practice.

(7)    For the purposes of paragraph (5) any two employers shall be treated as associated if

    (a)    one is a company of which the other (directly or indirectly) has control; or

    (b)    both are companies of which a third person (directly or indirectly) has control; and 'associated employer' shall be construed accordingly.

PART V
SPECIAL CLASSES OF PERSON

## 36 Agency workers not otherwise 'workers'

(1) This regulation applies in any case where an individual ('the agency worker')—

    (a) is supplied by a person ('the agent') to do work for another ('the principal') under a contract or other arrangements made between the agent and the principal; but

    (b) is not, as respects that work, a worker, because of the absence of a worker's contract between the individual and the agent or the principal; and

    (c) is not a party to a contract under which he undertakes to do the work for another party to the contract whose status is, by virtue of the contract, that of a client or customer of any profession or business undertaking carried on by the individual.

(2) In a case where this regulation applies, the other provisions of these Regulations shall have effect as if there were a worker's contract for the doing of the work by the agency worker made between the agency worker and—

    (a) whichever of the agent and the principal is responsible for paying the agency worker in respect of the work; or

    (b) if neither the agent nor the principal is so responsible, whichever of them pays the agency worker in respect of the work,

and as if that person were the agency worker's employer.

## 37 Crown employment

(1) Subject to paragraph (4) and regulation 38, these Regulations have effect in relation to Crown employment and persons in Crown employment as they have effect in relation to other employment and other workers.

(2) In paragraph (1) 'Crown employment' means employment under or for the purposes of a government department or any officer or body exercising on behalf of the Crown functions conferred by a statutory provision.

(3) For the purposes of the application of the provisions of these Regulations in relation to Crown employment in accordance with paragraph (1)—

    (a) references to a worker shall be construed as references to a person in Crown employment; and

    (b) references to a worker's contract shall be construed as references to the terms of employment of a person in Crown employment.

(4) No act or omission by the Crown which is an offence under regulation 29 shall make the Crown criminally liable, but the High Court or, in Scotland, the Court of Session may, on the application of a person appearing to the Court to have an interest, declare any such act or omission unlawful.

## 42 Non-employed trainees

For the purposes of these Regulations, a person receiving relevant training, otherwise than under a contract of employment, shall be regarded as a worker, and the person whose undertaking is providing the training shall be regarded as his employer.

SCHEDULE 1
WORKFORCE AGREEMENTS

1. An agreement is a workforce agreement for the purposes of these Regulations if the following conditions are satisfied—

    (a) the agreement is in writing;

    (b) it has effect for a specified period not exceeding five years;

    (c) it applies either—

        (i) to all of the relevant members of the workforce, or

        (ii) to all of the relevant members of the workforce who belong to a particular group;

    (d) the agreement is signed—

        (i) in the case of an agreement of the kind referred to in sub-paragraph (c)(i), by the representatives of the workforce, and in the case of an agreement of the kind referred to in sub-paragraph (c)(ii) by the representatives of the group to which the agreement applies (excluding, in either case, any representative not a relevant member of the workforce on the date on which the agreement was first made available for signature), or

    (ii)    if the employer employed 20 or fewer workers on the date referred to in sub-paragraph (d)(i), either by the appropriate representatives in accordance with that sub-paragraph or by the majority of the workers employed by him;

  (e)    before the agreement was made available for signature, the employer provided all the workers to whom it was intended to apply on the date on which it came into effect

with copies of the text of the agreement and such guidance as those workers might reasonably require in order to understand it fully.

2.    For the purposes of this Schedule—

'a particular group' is a group of the relevant members of a workforce who undertake a particular function, work at a particular workplace or belong to a particular department or unit within their employer's business;

'relevant members of the workforce' are all of the workers employed by a particular employer, excluding any worker whose terms and conditions of employment are provided for, wholly or in part, in a collective agreement;

'representatives of the workforce' are workers duly elected to represent the relevant members of the workforce, 'representatives of the group' are workers duly elected to represent the members of a particular group, and representatives are 'duly elected' if the election at which they were elected satisfied the requirements of paragraph 3 of this Schedule.

3.    The requirements concerning elections referred to in paragraph 2 are that—

  (a)    the number of representatives to be elected is determined by the employer;

  (b)    the candidates for election as representatives of the workforce are relevant members of the workforce, and the candidates for election as representatives of a group are members of the group;

  (c)    no worker who is eligible to be a candidate is unreasonably excluded from standing for election;

  (d)    all the relevant members of the workforce are entitled to vote for representatives of the workforce, and all the members of a particular group are entitled to vote for representatives of the group;

  (e)    the workers entitled to vote may vote for as many candidates as there are representatives to be elected;

  (f)    the election is conducted so as to secure that—

    (i)    so far as is reasonably practicable, those voting do so in secret, and

    (ii)    the votes given at the election are fairly and accurately counted.

# MATERNITY AND PARENTAL LEAVE ETC. REGULATIONS 1999
## (SI 1999 No. 3312)

### PART II
### MATERNITY LEAVE

**4    Entitlement to ordinary maternity leave and to additional maternity leave**

(1)    An employee is entitled to ordinary maternity leave and to additional maternity leave provided that she satisfies the following conditions—

  (a)    no later than the end of the fifteenth week before her expected week of childbirth, or, if that is not reasonably practicable, as soon as is reasonably practicable, she notifies her employer of—

    (i)    her pregnancy;

    (ii)    the expected week of childbirth, and

    (iii)    the date on which she intends her ordinary maternity leave period to start,

  and

      (b)   if requested to do so by her employer, she produces for his inspection a certificate from—
         (i)    a registered medical practitioner, or
         (ii)   a registered midwife,
      stating the expected week of childbirth.

(1A) An employee who has notified her employer under paragraph (1)(a)(iii) of the date on which she intends her ordinary maternity leave period to start may subsequently vary that date, provided that she notifies her employer of the variation at least—
      (a)   28 days before the date varied, or
      (b)   28 days before the new date,
whichever is the earlier, or, if that is not reasonably practicable, as soon as is reasonably practicable.

(2)   Notification under paragraph (1)(a)(iii) or (1A)—
      (a)   shall be given in writing, if the employer so requests, and
      (b)   shall not specify a date earlier than the beginning of the eleventh week before the expected week of childbirth.

(3)   Where, by virtue of regulation 6(1)(b), an employee's ordinary maternity leave period commences with the day which follows the first day after the beginning of the fourth week before the expected week of childbirth on which she is absent from work wholly or partly because of pregnancy—
      (a)   paragraph (1) does not require her to notify her employer of the date specified in that paragraph, but
      (b)   (whether or not she has notified him of that date) she is not entitled to ordinary maternity leave or to additional maternity leave unless she notifies him as soon as is reasonably practicable that she is absent from work wholly or partly because of pregnancy and of the date on which her absence on that account began.

(4)   Where, by virtue of regulation 6(2), an employee's ordinary maternity leave period commences on the day which follows the day on which childbirth occurs—
      (a)   paragraph (1) does not require her to notify her employer of the date specified in that paragraph, but
      (b)   (whether or not she has notified him of that date) she is not entitled to ordinary maternity leave or to additional maternity leave unless she notifies him as soon as is reasonably practicable after the birth that she has given birth and of the date on which the birth occurred.

(5)   The notification provided for in paragraphs (3)(b) and (4)(b) shall be given in writing, if the employer so requests.

## 6    Commencement of maternity leave periods

(1)   Subject to paragraph (2), an employee's ordinary maternity leave period commences with the earlier of—
      (a)   the date which she notifies to her employer, in accordance with regulation 4, as the date on which she intends her ordinary maternity leave period to start, or, if by virtue of the provision for variation in that regulation she has notified more than one such date, the last date she notifies, and
      (b)   the day which follows the first day after the beginning of the fourth week before the expected week of childbirth on which she is absent from work wholly or partly because of pregnancy.

(2)   Where the employee's ordinary maternity leave period has not commenced by virtue of paragraph (1) when childbirth occurs, her ordinary maternity leave period commences on the day which follows the day on which childbirth occurs.

(3)   An employee's additional maternity leave period commences on the day after the last day of her ordinary maternity leave period.

## 7    Duration of maternity leave periods

(1)   Subject to paragraphs (2) and (5), an employee's ordinary maternity leave period continues for the period of twenty six weeks from its commencement, or until the end of the compulsory maternity leave period provided for in regulation 8 if later.

(2)   Subject to paragraph (5), where any requirement imposed by or under any relevant statutory provision prohibits the employee from working for any period after the end

of the period determined under paragraph (1) by reason of her having recently given birth, her ordinary maternity leave period continues until the end of that later period.

(3)   In paragraph (2), 'relevant statutory provision' means a provision of—
    (a)   an enactment, or
    (b)   an instrument under an enactment,
    other than a provision for the time being specified in an order under section 66(2) of the 1996 Act.

(4)   Subject to paragraph (5), where an employee is entitled to additional maternity leave her additional maternity leave period continues until the end of the period of 26 weeks from the day on which it commenced.

(5)   Where the employee is dismissed after the commencement of an ordinary or additional maternity leave period but before the time when (apart from this paragraph) that period would end, the period ends at the time of the dismissal.

(6)   An employer who is notified under any provision of regulation 4 of the date on which, by virtue of any provision of regulation 6, an employee's ordinary maternity leave period will commence or has commenced shall notify the employee of the date on which her additional maternity leave period shall end.

(7)   The notification provided for in paragraph (6) shall be given to the employee—
    (a)   where the employer is notified under regulation 4(1)(a)(iii), (3)(b) or (4)(b), within 28 days of the date on which he received the notification;
    (b)   where the employer is notified under regulation 4(1A), within 28 days of the date on which the employee's ordinary maternity leave period commenced.

## 8   Compulsory maternity leave

The prohibition in section 72 of the 1996 Act, against permitting an employee who satisfies prescribed conditions to work during a particular period (referred to as a 'compulsory maternity leave period'), applies—
    (a)   in relation to an employee who is entitled to ordinary maternity leave, and
    (b)   in respect of the period of two weeks which commences with the day on which childbirth occurs.

## 9   Application of terms and conditions during ordinary maternity leave and additional maternity leave

(1)   An employee who takes ordinary maternity leave or additional maternity leave—
    (a)   is entitled, during the period of leave, to the benefit of all of the terms and conditions of employment which would have applied if she had not been absent, and
    (b)   is bound, during that period, by any obligations arising under those terms and conditions, subject only to the exceptions in sections 71(4)(b) and 73(4)(b) of the 1996 Act.

(2)   In paragraph (1)(a), 'terms and conditions' has the meaning given by sections 71(5) and 73(5) of the 1996 Act, and accordingly does not include terms and conditions about remuneration.

(3)   For the purposes of sections 71 and 73 of the 1996 Act, only sums payable to an employee by way of wages or salary are to be treated as remuneration.

(4)   In the case of accrual of rights under an employment-related benefit scheme within the meaning given by Schedule 5 to the Social Security Act 1989, nothing in paragraph (1)(a) concerning the treatment of additional maternity leave shall be taken to impose a requirement which exceeds the requirements of paragraph 5 of that Schedule.

## 10   Redundancy during maternity leave

(1)   This regulation applies where, during an employee's ordinary or additional maternity leave period, it is not practicable by reason of redundancy for her employer to continue to employ her under her existing contract of employment.

(2)   Where there is a suitable available vacancy, the employee is entitled to be offered (before the end of her employment under her existing contract) alternative employment with her employer or his successor, or an associated employer, under a new contract of employment which complies with paragraph (3) (and takes effect immediately on the ending of her employment under the previous contract).

(3)   The new contract of employment must be such that—
   (a)   the work to be done under it is of a kind which is both suitable in relation to the employee and appropriate for her to do in the circumstances, and
   (b)   its provisions as to the capacity and place in which she is to be employed, and as to the other terms and conditions of her employment, are not substantially less favourable to her than if she had continued to be employed under the previous contract.

## 11   Requirement to notify intention to return during a maternity leave period

(1)   An employee who intends to return to work earlier than the end of her additional maternity leave period shall give to her employer not less than 8 weeks' notice of the date on which she intends to return.

(2)   If an employee attempts to return to work earlier than the end of her additional maternity leave period without complying with paragraph (1), her employer is entitled to postpone her return to a date such as will secure, subject to paragraph (3), that he has 8 weeks' notice of her return.

(2A)   An employee who complies with her obligations in paragraph (1) or whose employer has postponed her return in the circumstances described in paragraph (2), and who then decides to return to work—
   (a)   earlier than the original return date, must give her employer not less than 8 weeks' notice of the date on which she now intends to return;
   (b)   later than the original return date, must give her employer not less than 8 weeks' notice ending with the original return date.

(2B)   In paragraph (2A) the 'original return date' means the date which the employee notified to her employer as the date of her return to work under paragraph (1), or the date to which her return was postponed by her employer under paragraph (2).

(3)   An employer is not entitled under paragraph (2) to postpone an employee's return to work to a date after the end of the relevant maternity leave period.

(4)   If an employee whose return to work has been postponed under paragraph (2) has been notified that she is not to return to work before the date to which her return was postponed, the employer is under no contractual obligation to pay her remuneration until the date to which her return was postponed if she returns to work before that date.

(5)   This regulation does not apply in a case where the employer did not notify the employee in accordance with regulation 7(6) and (7) of the date on which her additional maternity leave period would end.

## 12A   Work during maternity leave period

(1)   Subject to paragraph (5), an employee may carry out up to 10 days' work for her employer during her statutory maternity leave period without bringing her maternity leave to an end.

(2)   For the purposes of this regulation, any work carried out on any day shall constitute a day's work.

(3)   Subject to paragraph (4), for the purposes of this regulation, work means any work done under the contract of employment and may include training or any activity undertaken for the purposes of keeping in touch with the workplace.

(4)   Reasonable contact from time to time between an employee and her employer which either party is entitled to make during a maternity leave period (for example to discuss an employee's return to work) shall not bring that period to an end.

(5)   Paragraph (1) shall not apply in relation to any work carried out by the employee at any time from childbirth to the end of the period of two weeks which commences with the day on which childbirth occurs.

(6)   This regulation does not confer any right on an employer to require that any work be carried out during the statutory maternity leave period, nor any right on an employee to work during the statutory maternity leave period.

(7)   Any days' work carried out under this regulation shall not have the effect of extending the total duration of the statutory maternity leave period.

PART III
PARENTAL LEAVE

## 13    Entitlement to parental leave

(1)    An employee who—

(a)    has been continuously employed for a period of not less than a year [or is to be treated as having been so employed by virtue of paragraph (1A)]; and

(b)    has, or expects to have, responsibility for a child,

is entitled, in accordance with these Regulations, to be absent from work on parental leave for the purpose of caring for that child.

(1A)    ...

(2)    An employee has responsibility for a child, for the purposes of paragraph (1), if—

(a)    he has parental responsibility or, in Scotland, parental responsibilities for the child; or

(b)    he has been registered as the child's father under any provision of section 10(1) or 10A(1) of the Births and Deaths Registration Act 1953 or of section 18(1) or (2) of the Registration of Births, Deaths and Marriages (Scotland) Act 1965.

(3)    ...

## 14    Extent of entitlement

(1)    An employee is entitled to eighteen weeks' leave in respect of any individual child.

(1A)    ...

(2)    Where the period for which an employee is normally required, under his contract of employment, to work in the course of a week does not vary, a week's leave for the employee is a period of absence from work which is equal in duration to the period for which he is normally required to work.

(3)    Where the period for which an employee is normally required, under his contract of employment, to work in the course of a week varies from week to week or over a longer period, or where he is normally required under his contract to work in some weeks but not in others a week's leave for the employee is a period of absence from work which is equal in duration to the period calculated by dividing the total of the periods for which he is normally required to work in a year by 52.

(4)    Where an employee takes leave in periods shorter than the period which constitutes, for him, a week's leave under whichever of paragraphs (2) and (3) is applicable in his case, he completes a week's leave when the aggregate of the periods of leave he has taken equals the period constituting a week's leave for him under the applicable paragraph.

## 15    When parental leave may be taken

An employee may not exercise any entitlement to parental leave in respect of a child after the date of the child's eighteenth birthday.

## 16    Default provisions in respect of parental leave

The provisions set out in Schedule 2 apply in relation to parental leave in the case of an employee whose contract of employment does not include a provision which—

(a)    confers an entitlement to absence from work for the purpose of caring for a child, and

(b)    incorporates or operates by reference to all or part of a collective agreement or workforce agreement.

## 16A    Review

(1)    The Secretary of State must from time to time—

(a)    carry out a review of regulations 13 to 16 and Schedule 2,

(b)    set out the conclusions of the review in a report, and

(c)    publish the report.

(2)    In carrying out the review the Secretary of State must, so far as is reasonable, have regard to how Council Directive 2010/18/EU of 8 March 2010 implementing the revised framework agreement on parental leave (which is implemented by means of regulations 13 to 16 and Schedule 2) is implemented in other member States.

(3) The report must in particular—
    (a) set out the objectives intended to be achieved by the regulatory system established by those regulations,
    (b) assess the extent to which those objectives are achieved, and
    (c) assess whether those objectives remain appropriate and, if so, the extent to which they could be achieved with a system that imposes less regulation.

(4) The first report under this regulation must be published before the end of the period of five years beginning with the day on which this regulation comes into force.

(5) Reports under this regulation are afterwards to be published at intervals not exceeding five years.

PART IV
PROVISIONS APPLICABLE IN RELATION TO MORE THAN ONE KIND
OF ABSENCE

## 17 Application of terms and conditions during periods of leave

An employee who takes parental leave—
    (a) is entitled, during the period of leave, to the benefit of her employer's implied obligation to her of trust and confidence and any terms and conditions of her employment relating to—
        (i) notice of the termination of the employment contract by her employer;
        (ii) compensation in the event of redundancy, or
        (iii) disciplinary or grievance procedures;
    (b) is bound, during that period, by her implied obligation to her employer of good faith and any terms and conditions of her employment relating to—
        (i) notice of the termination of the employment contract by her;
        (ii) the disclosure of confidential information;
        (iii) the acceptance of gifts or other benefits, or
        (iv) the employee's participation in any other business.

## 18 Right to return after maternity or parental leave

(1) An employee who returns to work after a period of ordinary maternity leave, or a period of parental leave of four weeks or less, which was—
    (a) an isolated period of leave, or
    (b) the last of two or more consecutive periods of statutory leave which did not include—
        (i) any period of parental leave of more than four weeks; or
        (ii) any period of statutory leave which when added to any other period of statutory leave (excluding parental leave) taken in relation to the same child means that the total amount of statutory leave taken in relation to that child totals more than 26 weeks,

(2) An employee who returns to work after—
    (a) a period of additional maternity leave, or a period of parental leave of more than four weeks, whether or not preceded by another period of statutory leave, or
    (b) a period of ordinary maternity leave, or a period of parental leave of four weeks or less, not falling within the description in paragraph (1)(a) or (b) above,
is entitled to return from leave to the job in which she was employed before her absence or, if it is not reasonably practicable for the employer to permit her to return to that job, to another job which is both suitable for her and appropriate for her to do in the circumstances.

(3) The reference in paragraphs (1) and (2) to the job in which an employee was employed before her absence is a reference to the job in which she was employed—
    (a) if her return is from an isolated period of statutory leave, immediately before that period began;
    (b) if her return is from consecutive periods of statutory leave, immediately before the first such period.

(4) This regulation does not apply where regulation 10 applies.

**18A   Incidents of the right to return**

(1)   An employee's right to return under regulation 18(1) or (2) is a right to return—

    (a)   with her seniority, pension rights and similar rights as they would have been if she had not been absent, and

    (b)   on terms and conditions not less favourable than those which would have applied if she had not been absent.

(2)   In the case of accrual of rights under an employment-related benefit scheme within the meaning given by Schedule 5 to the Social Security Act 1989, nothing in paragraph (1)(a) concerning the treatment of additional maternity leave shall be taken to impose a requirement which exceeds the requirements of paragraphs 5 and 6 of that Schedule.

(3)   The provisions in paragraph (1) for an employee to be treated as if she had not been absent refer to her absence—

    (a)   if her return is from an isolated period of statutory leave, since the beginning of that period;

    (b)   if her return is from consecutive periods of statutory leave, since the beginning of the first such period.

**19   Protection from detriment**

(1)   An employee is entitled under section 47C of the 1996 Act not to be subjected to any detriment by any act, or any deliberate failure to act, by her employer done for any of the reasons specified in paragraph (2).

(2)   The reasons referred to in paragraph (1) are that the employee—

    (a)   is pregnant;

    (b)   has given birth to a child;

    (c)   is the subject of a relevant requirement, or a relevant recommendation, as defined by section 66(2) of the 1996 Act;

    (d)   took, sought to take or availed herself of the benefits of, ordinary maternity leave or additional maternity leave;

    (e)   took or sought to take—

        (i)   …

        (ii)   parental leave, or

        (iii)   time off under section 57A of the 1996 Act;

    (ee)   failed to return after a period of ordinary or additional maternity leave in a case where—

        (i)   the employer did not notify her, in accordance with regulation 7(6) and (7) or otherwise, of the date on which the period in question would end, and she reasonably believed that that period had not ended, or

        (ii)   the employer gave her less than 28 days' notice of the date on which the period in question would end, and it was not reasonably practicable for her to return on that date;

    (eee)   undertook, considered undertaking or refused to undertake work in accordance with regulation 12A;

    (f)   declined to sign a workforce agreement for the purpose of these Regulations, or

    (g)   being—

        (i)   a representative of members of the workforce for the purposes of Schedule 1, or

        (ii)   a candidate in an election in which any person elected will, on being elected, become such a representative,

        performed (or proposed to perform) any functions or activities as such a representative or candidate.

(3)   For the purposes of paragraph (2)(d), a woman avails herself of the benefits of ordinary maternity leave if, during her ordinary maternity leave period, she avails herself of the benefit of any of the terms and conditions of her employment preserved by section 71 of the 1996 Act and regulation 9 during that period.

(3A)   For the purposes of paragraph (2)(d), a woman avails herself of the benefits of additional maternity leave if, during her additional maternity leave period, she avails herself of the benefit of any of the terms and conditions of her employment preserved by section 73 of the 1996 Act and regulation 9 during that period.

(4)   Paragraph (1) does not apply in a case where the detriment in question amounts to dismissal within the meaning of Part X of the 1996 Act.

(5)   Paragraph (2)(b) only applies where the act or failure to act takes place during the employee's ordinary or additional maternity leave period.

(6)   For the purposes of paragraph (5)—
   (a)   where an act extends over a period, the reference to the date of the act is a reference to the last day of that period, and
   (b)   a failure to act is to be treated as done when it was decided on.

(7)   For the purposes of paragraph (6), in the absence of evidence establishing the contrary an employer shall be taken to decide on a failure to act—
   (a)   when he does an act inconsistent with doing the failed act, or
   (b)   if he has done no such inconsistent act, when the period expires within which he might reasonably have been expected to do the failed act if it were to be done.

## 20   Unfair dismissal

(1)   An employee who is dismissed is entitled under section 99 of the 1996 Act to be regarded for the purposes of Part X of that Act as unfairly dismissed if—
   (a)   the reason or principal reason for the dismissal is of a kind specified in paragraph (3), or
   (b)   the reason or principal reason for the dismissal is that the employee is redundant, and regulation 10 has not been complied with.

(2)   An employee who is dismissed shall also be regarded for the purposes of Part X of the 1996 Act as unfairly dismissed if—
   (a)   the reason (or, if more than one, the principal reason) for the dismissal is that the employee was redundant;
   (b)   it is shown that the circumstances constituting the redundancy applied equally to one or more employees in the same undertaking who held positions similar to that held by the employee and who have not been dismissed by the employer, and
   (c)   it is shown that the reason (or, if more than one, the principal reason) for which the employee was selected for dismissal was a reason of a kind specified in paragraph (3).

(3)   The kinds of reason referred to in paragraphs (1) and (2) are reasons connected with—
   (a)   the pregnancy of the employee;
   (b)   the fact that the employee has given birth to a child;
   (c)   the application of a relevant requirement, or a relevant recommendation, as defined by section 66(2) of the 1996 Act;
   (d)   the fact that she took, sought to take or availed herself of the benefits of, ordinary maternity leave or additional maternity leave;
   (e)   the fact that she took or sought to take—
      (i)   ...
      (ii)   parental leave, or
      (iii)   time off under section 57A of the 1996 Act;
   (ee)   the fact that she failed to return after a period of ordinary or additional maternity leave in a case where—
      (i)   the employer did not notify her, in accordance with regulation 7(6) and (7) or otherwise, of the date on which the period in question would end, and she reasonably believed that that period had not ended, or
      (ii)   the employer gave her less than 28 days' notice of the date on which the period in question would end, and it was not reasonably practicable for her to return on that date;
   (eee)   the fact that she undertook, considered undertaking or refused to undertake work in accordance with regulation 12A;
   (f)   the fact that she declined to sign a workforce agreement for the purposes of these Regulations, or
   (g)   the fact that the employee, being—
      (i)   a representative of members of the workforce for the purposes of Schedule 1, or

   (ii) a candidate in an election in which any person elected will, on being elected, become such a representative,

performed (or proposed to perform) any functions or activities as such a representative or candidate.

(4) Paragraphs (1)(b) and (3)(b) only apply where the dismissal ends the employee's ordinary or additional maternity leave period.

(5) Paragraphs (3) and (3A) of regulation 19 apply for the purposes of paragraph (3)(d) as they apply for the purposes of paragraph (2)(d) of that regulation.

(6) ...

(7) Paragraph (1) does not apply in relation to an employee if—

  (a) it is not reasonably practicable for a reason other than redundancy for the employer (who may be the same employer or a successor of his) to permit her to return to a job which is both suitable for her and appropriate for her to do in the circumstances;

  (b) an associated employer offers her a job of that kind, and

  (c) she accepts or unreasonably refuses that offer.

(8) Where on a complaint of unfair dismissal any question arises as to whether the operation of paragraph (1) is excluded by the provisions of paragraph ... (7), it is for the employer to show that the provisions in question were satisfied in relation to the complainant.

## 21 Contractual rights to maternity or parental leave

(1) This regulation applies where an employee is entitled to—

  (a) ordinary maternity leave;

  (b) additional maternity leave, or

  (c) parental leave,

(referred to in paragraph (2) as a 'statutory right') and also to a right which corresponds to that right and which arises under the employee's contract of employment or otherwise.

(2) In a case where this regulation applies—

  (a) the employee may not exercise the statutory right and the corresponding right separately but may, in taking the leave for which the two rights provide, take advantage of whichever right is, in any particular respect, the more favourable, and

  (b) the provisions of the 1996 Act and of these Regulations relating to the statutory right apply, subject to any modifications necessary to give effect to any more favourable contractual terms, to the exercise of the composite right described in sub-paragraph

  (a) as they apply to the exercise of the statutory right.

### SCHEDULE 1
### WORKFORCE AGREEMENTS

1. An agreement is a workforce agreement for the purposes of these Regulations if the following conditions are satisfied—

  (a) the agreement is in writing;

  (b) it has effect for a specified period not exceeding five years;

  (c) it applies either—

   (i) to all of the relevant members of the workforce, or

   (ii) to all of the relevant members of the workforce who belong to a particular group;

  (d) the agreement is signed—

   (i) in the case of an agreement of the kind referred to in sub-paragraph (c)(i), by the representatives of the workforce, and in the case of an agreement of the kind referred to in sub-paragraph (c)(ii), by the representatives of the group to which the agreement applies (excluding, in either case, any representative not a relevant member of the workforce on the date on which the agreement was first made available for signature), or

       (ii)    if the employer employed 20 or fewer employees on the date referred to in sub-paragraph (d)(i), either by the appropriate representatives in accordance with that sub-paragraph or by the majority of the employees employed by him; and

    (e)    before the agreement was made available for signature, the employer provided all the employees to whom it was intended to apply on the date on which it came into effect with copies of the text of the agreement and such guidance as those employees might reasonably require in order to understand it in full.

2.      For the purposes of this Schedule—

'a particular group' is a group of the relevant members of a workforce who undertake a particular function, work at a particular workplace or belong to a particular department or unit within their employer's business;

'relevant members of the workforce' are all of the employees employed by a particular employer, excluding any employee whose terms and conditions of employment are provided for, wholly or in part, in a collective agreement;

'representatives of the workforce' are employees duly elected to represent the relevant members of the workforce, 'representatives of the group' are employees duly elected to represent the members of a particular group, and representatives are 'duly elected' if the election at which they were elected satisfied the requirements of paragraph 3 of this Schedule.

3.      The requirements concerning elections referred to in paragraph 2 are that—

    (a)    the number of representatives to be elected is determined by the employer;

    (b)    the candidates for election as representatives of the workforce are relevant members of the workforce, and the candidates for election as representatives of a group are members of the group;

    (c)    no employee who is eligible to be a candidate is unreasonably excluded from standing for election;

    (d)    all the relevant members of the workforce are entitled to vote for representatives of the workforce, and all the members of a particular group are entitled to vote for representatives of the group;

    (e)    the employees entitled to vote may vote for as many candidates as there are representatives to be elected, and

    (f)    the election is conducted so as to secure that—

       (i)    so far as is reasonably practicable, those voting do so in secret, and

       (ii)    the votes given at the election are fairly and accurately counted.

## SCHEDULE 2
## DEFAULT PROVISIONS IN RESPECT OF PARENTAL LEAVE

### *Conditions of entitlement*

1.      An employee may not exercise any entitlement to parental leave unless—

    (a)    he has complied with any request made by his employer to produce for the employer's inspection evidence of his entitlement, of the kind described in paragraph 2;

    (b)    he has given his employer notice, in accordance with whichever of paragraphs 3 to 5 is applicable, of the period of leave he proposes to take, and

    (c)    in a case where paragraph 6 applies, his employer has not postponed the period of leave in accordance with that paragraph.

2.      The evidence to be produced for the purpose of paragraph 1(a) is such evidence as may reasonably be required of—

    (a)    the employee's responsibility or expected responsibility for the child in respect of whom the employee proposes to take parental leave;

    (b)    the child's date of birth or, in the case of a child who was placed with the employee for adoption, the date on which the placement began.

*Notice to be given to employer*

3.  Except in a case where paragraph 4 or 5 applies, the notice required for the purpose of paragraph 1(b) is notice which—
    (a)  specifies the dates on which the period of leave is to begin and end, and
    (b)  is given to the employer at least 21 days before the date on which that period is to begin.

4.  Where the employee is the father of the child in respect of whom the leave is to be taken, and the period of leave is to begin on the date on which the child is born, the notice required for the purpose of paragraph 1(b) is notice which—
    (a)  specifies the expected week of childbirth and the duration of the period of leave, and
    (b)  is given to the employer at least 21 days before the beginning of the expected week of childbirth.

5.  Where the child in respect of whom the leave is to be taken is to be placed with the employee for adoption by him and the leave is to begin on the date of the placement, the notice required for the purpose of paragraph 1(b) is notice which—
    (a)  specifies the week in which the placement is expected to occur and the duration of the period of leave, and
    (b)  is given to the employer at least 21 days before the beginning of that week, or, if that is not reasonably practicable, as soon as is reasonably practicable.

*Postponement of leave*

6.  An employer may postpone a period of parental leave where—
    (a)  neither paragraph 4 nor paragraph 5 applies, and the employee has accordingly given the employer notice in accordance with paragraph 3;
    (b)  the employer considers that the operation of his business would be unduly disrupted if the employee took leave during the period identified in his notice;
    (c)  the employer agrees to permit the employee to take a period of leave—
        (i)   of the same duration as the period identified in the employee's notice, and
        (ii)  beginning on a date determined by the employer after consulting the employee, which is no later than six months after the commencement of that period;
    (d)  the employer gives the employee notice in writing of the postponement which—
        (i)   states the reason for it, and
        (ii)  specifies the dates on which the period of leave the employer agrees to permit the employee to take will begin and end, and
    (e)  that notice is given to the employee not more than seven days after the employee's notice was given to the employer.

*Minimum periods of leave*

7.  An employee may not take parental leave in a period other than the period which constitutes a week's leave for him under regulation 14 or a multiple of that period, except in a case where the child in respect of whom leave is taken is entitled to a disability living allowance, armed forces independent payment or parental independence payment.

*Maximum annual leave allowance*

8.  An employee may not take more than four weeks' leave in respect of any individual child during a particular year.

9.  For the purposes of paragraph 8, a year is the period of twelve months beginning—
    (a)  except where sub-paragraph (b) applies, on the date on which the employee first became entitled to take parental leave in respect of the child in question, or
    (b)  in a case where the employee's entitlement has been interrupted at the end of a period of continuous employment, on the date on which the employee most recently became entitled to take parental leave in respect of that child,
    and each successive period of twelve months beginning on the anniversary of that date.

# PART-TIME WORKERS (PREVENTION OF LESS FAVOURABLE TREATMENT) REGULATIONS 2000
## (SI 2000 No. 1551)

PART I
GENERAL AND INTERPRETATION

## 1    Citation, commencement and interpretation

(1)    These Regulations may be cited as the Part-time Workers (Prevention of Less Favourable Treatment) Regulations 2000 and shall come into force on 1 July 2000.

(2)    In these Regulations—

'the 1996 Act' means the Employment Rights Act 1996;

'contract of employment' means a contract of service or of apprenticeship, whether express or implied, and (if it is express) whether oral or in writing;

'employee' means an individual who has entered into or works under or (except where a provision of these Regulations otherwise requires) where the employment has ceased, worked under a contract of employment;

'employer', in relation to any employee or worker, means the person by whom the employee or worker is or (except where a provision of these Regulations otherwise requires) where the employment has ceased, was employed;

'pro rata principle' means that where a comparable full-time worker receives or is entitled to receive pay or any other benefit, a part-time worker is to receive or be entitled to receive not less than the proportion of that pay or other benefit that the number of his weekly hours bears to the number of weekly hours of the comparable full-time worker;

'worker' means an individual who has entered into or works under or (except where a provision of these Regulations otherwise requires) where the employment has ceased, worked under—

(a)    a contract of employment; or

(b)    any other contract, whether express or implied and (if it is express) whether oral or in writing, whereby the individual undertakes to do or perform personally any work or services for another party to the contract whose status is not by virtue of the contract that of a client or customer of any profession or business undertaking carried on by the individual.

(3)    In the definition of the pro rata principle and in regulations 3 and 4 'weekly hours' means the number of hours a worker is required to work under his contract of employment in a week in which he has no absences from work and does not work any overtime or, where the number of such hours varies according to a cycle, the average number of such hours.

## 2    Meaning of full-time worker, part-time worker and comparable full-time worker

(1)    A worker is a full-time worker for the purpose of these Regulations if he is paid wholly or in part by reference to the time he works and, having regard to the custom and practice of the employer in relation to workers employed by the worker's employer under the same type of contract, is identifiable as a full-time worker.

(2)    A worker is a part-time worker for the purpose of these Regulations if he is paid wholly or in part by reference to the time he works and, having regard to the custom and practice of the employer in relation to workers employed by the worker's employer under the same type of contract, is not identifiable as a full-time worker.

(3)    For the purposes of paragraphs (1), (2) and (4), the following shall be regarded as being employed under different types of contract—

(a)    employees employed under a contract that is not a contract of apprenticeship;

(b)    employees employed under a contract of apprenticeship;

(c)    workers who are not employees;

(d)    any other description of worker that it is reasonable for the employer to treat differently from other workers on the ground that workers of that description have a different type of contract.

(4)    A full-time worker is a comparable full-time worker in relation to a part-time worker if, at the time when the treatment that is alleged to be less favourable to the part-time worker takes place—

(a)    both workers are—

(i)    employed by the same employer under the same type of contract, and

(ii)    engaged in the same or broadly similar work having regard, where relevant, to whether they have a similar level of qualification, skills and experience; and

(b)    the full-time worker works or is based at the same establishment as the part-time worker or, where there is no full-time worker working or based at that establishment who satisfies the requirements of sub-paragraph (a), works or is based at a different establishment and satisfies those requirements.

## 3    Workers becoming part-time

(1)    This regulation applies to a worker who—

(a)    was identifiable as a full-time worker in accordance with regulation 2(1); and

(b)    following a termination or variation of his contract, continues to work under a new or varied contract, whether of the same type or not, that requires him to work for a number of weekly hours that is lower than the number he was required to work immediately before the termination or variation.

(2)    Notwithstanding regulation 2(4), regulation 5 shall apply to a worker to whom this regulation applies as if he were a part-time worker and as if there were a comparable full-time worker employed under the terms that applied to him immediately before the variation or termination.

(3)    The fact that this regulation applies to a worker does not affect any right he may have under these Regulations by virtue of regulation 2(4).

## 4    Workers returning part-time after absence

(1)    This regulation applies to a worker who—

(a)    was identifiable as a full-time worker in accordance with regulation 2(1) immediately before a period of absence (whether the absence followed a termination of the worker's contract or not);

(b)    returns to work for the same employer within a period of less than twelve months beginning with the day on which the period of absence started;

(c)    returns to the same job or to a job at the same level under a contract, whether it is a different contract or a varied contract and regardless of whether it is of the same type, under which he is required to work for a number of weekly hours that is lower than the number he was required to work immediately before the period of absence.

(2)    Notwithstanding regulation 2(4), regulation 5 shall apply to a worker to whom this regulation applies ('the returning worker') as if he were a part-time worker and as if there were a comparable full-time worker employed under—

(a)    the contract under which the returning worker was employed immediately before the period of absence; or

(b)    where it is shown that, had the returning worker continued to work under the contract mentioned in sub-paragraph (a) a variation would have been made to its term during the period of absence, the contract mentioned in that sub-paragraph including that variation.

(3)    The fact that this regulation applies to a worker does not affect any right he may have under these Regulations by virtue of regulation 2(4).

PART II
RIGHTS AND REMEDIES

## 5    Less favourable treatment of part-time workers

(1)    A part-time worker has the right not to be treated by his employer less favourably than the employer treats a comparable full-time worker—

(a)    as regards the terms of his contract; or

    (b)   by being subjected to any other detriment by any act, or deliberate failure to act, of his employer.

(2)   The right conferred by paragraph (1) applies only if—
    (a)   the treatment is on the ground that the worker is a part-time worker, and
    (b)   the treatment is not justified on objective grounds.

(3)   In determining whether a part-time worker has been treated less favourably than a comparable full-time worker the pro rata principle shall be applied unless it is inappropriate.

(4)   A part-time worker paid at a lower rate for overtime worked by him in a period than a comparable full-time worker is or would be paid for overtime worked by him in the same period shall not, for that reason, be regarded as treated less favourably than the comparable full-time worker where, or to the extent that, the total number of hours worked by the part-time worker in the period, including overtime, does not exceed the number of hours the comparable full-time worker is required to work in the period, disregarding absences from work and overtime.

## 6 Right to receive a written statement of reasons for less favourable treatment

(1)   If a worker who considers that his employer may have treated him in a manner which infringes a right conferred on him by regulation 5 requests in writing from his employer a written statement giving particulars of the reasons for the treatment, the worker is entitled to be provided with such a statement within twenty-one days of his request.

(2)   A written statement under this regulation is admissible as evidence in any proceedings under these Regulations.

(3)   If it appears to the tribunal in any proceedings under these Regulations—
    (a)   that the employer deliberately, and without reasonable excuse, omitted to provide a written statement, or
    (b)   that the written statement is evasive or equivocal,
it may draw any inference which it considers it just and equitable to draw, including an inference that the employer has infringed the right in question.

(4)   This regulation does not apply where the treatment in question consists of the dismissal of an employee, and the employee is entitled to a written statement of reasons for his dismissal under section 92 of the 1996 Act.

## 7 Unfair dismissal and the right not to be subjected to detriment

(1)   An employee who is dismissed shall be regarded as unfairly dismissed for the purposes of Part X of the 1996 Act if the reason (or, if more than one, the principal reason) for the dismissal is a reason specified in paragraph (3).

(2)   A worker has the right not to be subjected to any detriment by any act, or any deliberate failure to act, by his employer done on a ground specified in paragraph (3).

(3)   The reasons or, as the case may be, grounds are—
    (a)   that the worker has—
        (i)   brought proceedings against the employer under these Regulations;
        (ii)   requested from his employer a written statement of reasons under regulation 6;
        (iii)   given evidence or information in connection with such proceedings brought by any worker;
        (iv)   otherwise done anything under these Regulations in relation to the employer or any other person;
        (v)   alleged that the employer had infringed these Regulations; or
        (vi)   refused (or proposed to refuse) to forgo a right conferred on him by these Regulations, or
    (b)   that the employer believes or suspects that the worker has done or intends to do any of the things mentioned in sub-paragraph (a).

(4)   Where the reason or principal reason for dismissal or, as the case may be, ground for subjection to any act or deliberate failure to act, is that mentioned in paragraph (3)(a) (v), or (b) so far as it relates thereto, neither paragraph (1) nor paragraph (2) applies if the allegation made by the worker is false and not made in good faith.

(5)   Paragraph (2) does not apply where the detriment in question amounts to the dismissal of an employee within the meaning of Part X of the 1996 Act.

## 8   Complaints to employment tribunals etc.

(1)   Subject to regulation 7(5), a worker may present a complaint to an employment tribunal that his employer has infringed a right conferred on him by regulation 5 or 7(2).

(2)   Subject to paragraph (3), an employment tribunal shall not consider a complaint under this regulation unless it is presented before the end of the period of three months (or, in a case to which regulation 13 applies, six months) beginning with the date of the less favourable treatment or detriment to which the complaint relates or, where an act or failure to act is part of a series of similar acts or failures comprising the less favourable treatment or detriment, the last of them.

(2A)   Regulation 8A (extension of time limits to facilitate conciliation before institution of proceedings) applies for the purposes of paragraph (2).

(3)   A tribunal may consider any such complaint which is out of time if, in all the circumstances of the case, it considers that it is just and equitable to do so.

(4)   For the purposes of calculating the date of the less favourable treatment or detriment under paragraph (2)—

   (a)   where a term in a contract is less favourable, that treatment shall be treated, subject to paragraph (b), as taking place on each day of the period during which the term is less favourable;

   (b)   where an application relies on regulation 3 or 4 the less favourable treatment shall be treated as occurring on, and only on, in the case of regulation 3, the first day on which the applicant worked under the new or varied contract and, in the case of regulation 4, the day on which the applicant returned; and

   (c)   a deliberate failure to act contrary to regulation 5 or 7(2) shall be treated as done when it was decided on.

(5)   In the absence of evidence establishing the contrary, a person shall be taken for the purposes of paragraph (4)(c) to decide not to act—

   (a)   when he does an act inconsistent with doing the failed act; or

   (b)   if he has done no such inconsistent act, when the period expires within which he might reasonably have been expected to have done the failed act if it was to be done.

(6)   Where a worker presents a complaint under this regulation it is for the employer to identify the ground for the less favourable treatment or detriment.

(7)   Where an employment tribunal finds that a complaint presented to it under this regulation is well founded, it shall take such of the following steps as it considers just and equitable—

   (a)   making a declaration as to the rights of the complainant and the employer in relation to the matters to which the complaint relates;

   (b)   ordering the employer to pay compensation to the complainant;

   (c)   recommending that the employer take, within a specified period, action appearing to the tribunal to be reasonable, in all the circumstances of the case, for the purpose of obviating or reducing the adverse effect on the complainant of any matter to which the complaint relates.

(8)   …

(9)   Where a tribunal orders compensation under paragraph (7)(b), the amount of the compensation awarded shall be such as the tribunal considers just and equitable in all the circumstances having regard to—

   (a)   the infringement to which the complaint relates, and

   (b)   any loss which is attributable to the infringement having regard, in the case of an infringement of the right conferred by regulation 5, to the pro rata principle except where it is inappropriate to do so.

(10)   The loss shall be taken to include—

   (a)   any expenses reasonably incurred by the complainant in consequence of the infringement, and

   (b)   loss of any benefit which he might reasonably be expected to have had but for the infringement.

(11) Compensation in respect of treating a worker in a manner which infringes the right conferred on him by regulation 5 shall not include compensation for injury to feelings.

(12) In ascertaining the loss the tribunal shall apply the same rule concerning the duty of a person to mitigate his loss as applies to damages recoverable under the common law of England and Wales or (as the case may be) Scotland.

(13) Where the tribunal finds that the act, or failure to act, to which the complaint relates was to any extent caused or contributed to by action of the complainant, it shall reduce the amount of the compensation by such proportion as it considers just and equitable having regard to that finding.

(14) If the employer fails, without reasonable justification, to comply with a recommendation made by an employment tribunal under paragraph (7)(c) the tribunal may, if it thinks it just and equitable to do so—

    (a) increase the amount of compensation required to be paid to the complainant in respect of the complaint, where an order was made under paragraph (7)(b); or

    (b) make an order under paragraph (7)(b).

## 8A Extension of time limit to facilitate conciliation before institution of proceedings

(1) In this regulation—

    (a) Day A is the day on which the worker concerned complies with the requirement in subsection (1) of section 18A of the Employment Tribunals Act 1996 (requirement to contact ACAS before instituting proceedings) in relation to the matter in respect of which the proceedings are brought, and

    (b) Day B is the day on which the worker concerned receives or, if earlier, is treated as receiving (by virtue of regulations made under subsection (11) of that section) the certificate issued under subsection (4) of that section.

(2) In working out when the time limit set by regulation 8(2) expires the period beginning with the day after Day A and ending with Day B is not to be counted.

(3) If the time limit set by regulation 8(2) would (if not extended by this paragraph) expire during the period beginning with Day A and ending one month after Day B, the time limit expires instead at the end of that period.

(4) The power conferred on the employment tribunal by regulation 8(3) to extend the time limit set by paragraph (2) of that regulation is exercisable in relation to that time limit as extended by this regulation.

## 9 Restrictions on contracting out

Section 203 of the 1996 Act (restrictions on contracting out) shall apply in relation to these Regulations as if they were contained in that Act.

PART III

MISCELLANEOUS

## 11 Liability of employers and principals

(1) Anything done by a person in the course of his employment shall be treated for the purposes of these Regulations as also done by his employer, whether or not it was done with the employer's knowledge or approval.

(2) Anything done by a person as agent for the employer with the authority of the employer shall be treated for the purposes of these Regulations as also done by the employer.

(3) In proceedings under these Regulations against any person in respect of an act alleged to have been done by a worker of his, it shall be a defence for that person to prove that he took such steps as were reasonably practicable to prevent the worker from—

    (a) doing that act; or

    (b) doing, in the course of his employment, acts of that description.

# TRADE UNION RECOGNITION (METHOD OF COLLECTIVE BARGAINING) ORDER 2000
## (SI 2000 No. 1300)

**2    Specification of method**

The method specified for the purposes of paragraphs 31(3) and 63(2) of Schedule A1 to the Trade Union and Labour Relations (Consolidation) Act 1992 is the method set out under the heading 'the specified method' in the Schedule to this Order.

THE SCHEDULE
PREAMBLE

The method specified below ('the specified method') is one by which collective bargaining might be conducted in the particular, and possibly rare, circumstances discussed in the following paragraph. The specified method is not designed to be applied as a model for voluntary procedural agreements between employers and unions.

Because most voluntary agreements are not legally binding and are usually concluded in a climate of trust and co-operation, they do not need to be as prescriptive as the specified method. However, the Central Arbitration Committee ('CAC') must take the specified method into account when exercising its powers to impose a method of collective bargaining under paragraphs 31(3) and 63(2) of Schedule A1 to the Trade Union and Labour Relations (Consolidation) Act 1992. In exercising those powers the CAC may depart from the specified method to such extent as it thinks appropriate in the circumstances of individual cases. Paragraph 31(3) provides for the CAC to impose a method of collective bargaining in cases where a union (or unions, where two or more unions act jointly) has been recognised by an employer by means of an award of the CAC under Part 1 of Schedule A1, but the employer and union(s) have been unable to agree a method of bargaining between themselves, or have failed to follow an agreed method. Paragraph 63(2) provides for the CAC to impose a bargaining method in cases where an employer and a union (or unions) have entered an agreement for recognition, as defined by paragraph 52 of Part II of Schedule A1, but cannot agree a method of bargaining, or have failed to follow the agreed method.

The bargaining method imposed by the CAC has effect as if it were a legally binding contract between the employer and the union(s). If one party believes the other is failing to respect the method, the first party may apply to the court for an order of specific performance, ordering the other party to comply with the method. Failure to comply with such an order could constitute contempt of court.

Once the CAC has imposed a bargaining method, the parties can vary it, including the fact that it is legally binding, by agreement provided that they do so in writing.

The fact that the CAC has imposed a method does not affect the rights of individual workers under either statute or their contracts of employment. For example, it does not prevent or limit the rights of individual workers to discuss, negotiate or agree with their employer terms of their contract of employment, which differ from the terms of any collective agreement into which the employer and the union may enter as a result of collective bargaining conducted by this method. Nor does the imposed method affect an individual's statutory entitlement to time off for trade union activities or duties.

In cases where the CAC imposes a bargaining method on the parties, the employer is separately obliged, in accordance with Section 70B of the Trade Union and Labour Relations (Consolidation) Act 1992 (as inserted by section 5 of the Employment Relations Act 1999), to consult union representatives periodically on his policy, actions and plans on training. The specified method does not discuss how such consultations should be organised.

The law confers certain entitlements on independent trade unions which are recognised for collective bargaining purposes. For example, employers must disclose, on request, certain types of information to the representatives of the recognised unions. The fact that the CAC has imposed a bargaining method does not affect these existing statutory entitlements.

## THE SPECIFIED METHOD

### The Parties

1.  The method shall apply in each case to two parties, who are referred to here as the 'employer' and the 'union'. Unless the text specifies otherwise, the term 'union' should be read to mean 'unions' in cases where two or more unions are jointly recognised.

### The Purpose

2.  The purpose is to specify a method by which the employer and the union conduct collective bargaining concerning the pay, hours and holidays of the workers comprising the bargaining unit.

3.  The employer shall not grant the right to negotiate pay, hours and holidays to any other union in respect of the workers covered by this method.

### The Joint Negotiating Body

4.  The employer and the union shall establish a Joint Negotiating Body (JNB) to discuss and negotiate the pay, hours and holidays of the workers comprising the bargaining unit. No other body or group shall undertake collective bargaining on the pay, hours and holidays of these workers, unless the employer and the union so agree.

### JNB Membership

5.  The membership of the JNB shall usually comprise three employer representatives (who together shall constitute the Employer Side of the JNB) and three union representatives (who together shall constitute the Union Side of the JNB). Each union recognised by the employer in respect of the bargaining unit shall be entitled to one seat at least. To meet this requirement, the Union Side may need to be larger than three and in this eventuality the employer shall be entitled to increase his representation on the JNB by the same number, if he wishes.

6.  The employer shall select those individuals who comprise the Employer Side. The individuals must either be those who take the final decisions within the employer's organisation in respect of the pay, hours and holidays of the workers in the bargaining unit or who are expressly authorised by the employer to make recommendations directly to those who take such final decisions. Unless it would be unreasonable to do so, the employer shall select as a representative the most senior person responsible for employment relations in the bargaining unit.

7.  The union shall select those individuals who comprise the Union Side in accordance with its own rules and procedures. The representatives must either be individuals employed by the employer or individuals employed by the union who are officials of the union within the meaning of sections 1 and 119 of the Trade Union and Labour Relations (Consolidation) Act 1992 ('the 1992 Act').

8.  The JNB shall determine their own rules in respect of the attendance at JNB meetings of observers and substitutes who deputise for JNB members.

### Officers

9.  The Employer Side shall select one of its members to act as its Chairman and one to act as its Secretary. The Union Side shall select one of its members to act as its Chairman and one to act as its Secretary. The same person may perform the roles of Chairman and Secretary of a Side.

10. For the twelve months from the date of the JNB's first meeting, meetings of the JNB shall be chaired by the Chairman of the Employer Side. The Chairman of the Union Side shall chair the JNB's meetings for the following twelve months. The chairmanship of JNB meetings will alternate in the same way thereafter at intervals of twelve months. In the absence of the person who should chair JNB meetings, a JNB meeting shall be chaired by another member of that person's Side.

**11.** The Secretary of the Employer Side shall act as Secretary to the JNB. He shall circulate documentation and agendas in advance of JNB meetings, arrange suitable accommodation for meetings, notify members of meetings and draft the written record of JNB meetings. The Secretary of the Employer Side shall work closely with the Secretary of the Union Side in the discharge of these duties, disclosing full information about his performance of these tasks.

## JNB Organisation

**12.** Draft agendas shall be circulated at least three working days in advance of JNB meetings. The draft record of JNB meetings shall be circulated within ten working days of the holding of meetings for approval at the next JNB meeting. The record does not need to be a verbatim account, but should fully describe the conclusions reached and the actions to be taken.

**13.** Subject to the timetable of meetings stipulated in paragraphs 15, 17, 20 and 28 below, the date, timing and location of meetings shall be arranged by the JNB's Secretary, in full consultation with the Secretary of the Union Side, to ensure maximum attendance at meetings. A meeting of the JNB shall be quorate if 50% or more of each Side's members (or, where applicable, their substitutes) are in attendance.

## Bargaining Procedure

**14.** The union's proposals for adjustments to pay, hours and holidays shall be dealt with on an annual basis, unless the two Sides agree a different bargaining period.

**15.** The JNB shall conduct these negotiations for each bargaining round according to the following staged procedure.

*Step 1* — The union shall set out in writing, and send to the employer, its proposals (the 'claim') to vary the pay, hours and holidays, specifying which aspects it wants to change. In its claim, the union shall set out the reasons for its proposals, together with the main supporting evidence at its disposal at the time. In cases where there is no established annual date when the employer reviews the pay, hours and holidays of all the workers in the bargaining unit, the union shall put forward its first claim within three months of this method being imposed (and by the same date in subsequent rounds). Where such a common review date is established, the union shall submit its first claim at least a month in advance of that date (and by the same date in subsequent rounds). In either case, the employer and the union may agree a different date by which the claim should be submitted each year. If the union fails to submit its claim by this date, then the procedure shall be ended for the bargaining round in question. Exceptionally, the union may submit a late claim without this penalty if its work on the claim was delayed while the Central Arbitration Committee considered a relevant complaint by the union of failure by the employer to disclose information for collective bargaining purposes.

*Step 2* — Within ten working days of the Employer Side's receipt of the union's letter, a quorate meeting of the JNB shall be held to discuss the claim. At this meeting, the Union Side shall explain its claim and answer any reasonable questions arising to the best of its ability.

*Step 3* —

(a)     Within fifteen working days immediately following the Step 2 meeting, the employer shall either accept the claim in full or write to the union responding to its claim. If the Employer Side requests it, a quorate meeting of the JNB shall be held within the fifteen day period to enable the employer to present this written response directly to the Union Side. In explaining the basis of his response, the employer shall set out in this written communication all relevant information in his possession. In particular, the written communication shall contain information costing each element of the claim and describing the business consequences, particularly any staffing implications, unless the employer is not required to disclose such information for any of the reasons specified in section 182(1) of the 1992 Act. The basis of these estimated costs and effects, including the main assumptions that the employer has used, shall be set out in the communication. In determining what information is disclosed as relevant, the employer shall be under no greater obligation that he is under the general duty imposed on him by sections 181 and 182 of the 1992 Act to disclose information for the purposes of collective bargaining.

(b)     If the response contains any counter-proposals, the written communication shall set out the reasons for making them, together with the supporting evidence. The letter shall provide information estimating the costs and staffing consequences of implementing each element of the counter proposals, unless the employer is not required to disclose such information for any of the reasons specified in section 182(1) of the 1992 Act.

*Step 4* — Within ten working days of the Union Side's receipt of the employer's written communication, a further quorate meeting of the JNB shall be held to discuss the employer's response. At this meeting, the Employer Side shall explain its response and answer any reasonable questions arising to the best of its ability.

*Step 5* — If no agreement is reached at the Step 4 meeting (or the last of such meetings if more than one is held at that stage in the procedure), another quorate meeting of the JNB shall be held within ten working days. The union may bring to this meeting a maximum of two other individuals employed by the union who are officials within the meaning of the sections 1 and 119 of the 1992 Act. The employer may bring to the meeting a maximum of two other individuals who are employees or officials of an employer's organisation to which the employer belongs. These additional persons shall be allowed to contribute to the meeting, as if they were JNB members.

*Step 6* — If no agreement is reached at the Step 5 meeting (or the last of such meetings if more than one meeting is held at that stage in the procedure), within five working days the employer and the union shall consider, separately or jointly, consulting ACAS about the prospect of ACAS helping them to find a settlement of their differences through conciliation. In the event that both parties agree to invite ACAS to conciliate, both parties shall give such assistance to ACAS as is necessary to enable it to carry out the conciliation efficiently and effectively.

16.    The parties shall set aside half a working day for each JNB meeting, unless the Employer Side Chairman and the Union Side Chairman agree a different length of time for the meeting. Unless it is essential to do otherwise, meetings shall be held during the normal working time of most union members of the JNB. Meetings may be adjourned, if both Sides agree. Additional meetings at any point in the procedure may be arranged, if both Sides agree. In addition, if the Employer Side requests it, a meeting of the JNB shall be held before the union has submitted its claim or before the employer is required to respond, enabling the Employer Side to explain the business context within which the employer shall assess the claim.

17.    The employer shall not vary the contractual terms affecting the pay, hours or holidays of workers in the bargaining unit, unless he has first discussed his proposals with the union. Such proposals shall normally be made by the employer in the context of his consideration of the union's claim at Steps 3 or 4. If, however, the employer has not tabled his proposals during that process and he wishes to make proposals before the next bargaining round commences, he must write to the union setting out his proposals and the reasons for making them, together with the supporting evidence. The letter shall provide information estimating the costs and staffing consequences of implementing each element of the proposals, unless the employer is not required to disclose such information for any of the reasons specified in section 182(1) of the 1992 Act. A quorate meeting of the JNB shall be held within five working days of the Union Side's receipt of the letter. If there is a failure to resolve the issue at that meeting, then meetings shall be arranged, and steps shall be taken, in accordance with Steps 5 and 6 of the above procedure.

18.    Paragraph 17 does not apply to terms in the contract of an individual worker where that worker has agreed that the terms may be altered only by direct negotiation between the worker and the employer.

## Collective Agreements

19.    Any agreements affecting the pay, hours and holidays of workers in the bargaining unit, which the employer and the union enter following negotiations, shall be set down in writing and signed by the Chairman of the Employer Side and by the Chairman of the Union Side or, in their absence, by another JNB member on their respective Sides.

20.    If either the employer or union consider that there has been a failure to implement the agreement, then that party can request in writing a meeting of the JNB to discuss the alleged failure. A quorate meeting shall be held within five working days of the receipt of the request by the JNB Secretary. If there is a failure to resolve the issue at that meeting, then meetings shall be arranged, and steps shall be taken, in accordance with Steps 5 and 6 of the above procedure.

## Facilities and Time Off

21.    If they are employed by the employer, union members of the JNB:
      — shall be given paid time off by the employer to attend JNB meetings;
      — shall be given paid time off by the employer to attend a two hour pre-meeting of the Union Side before each JNB meeting; and shall be given paid time off by the employer to hold a day-long meeting to prepare the claim at Step 1 in the bargaining procedure.
The union members of the JNB shall schedule such meetings at times which minimise the effect on production and services. In arranging these meetings, the union members of the JNB shall provide the employer and their line management with as much notice as possible and give details of the purpose of the time off, the intended location of the meeting and the timing and duration of the time off. The employer shall provide adequate heating and lighting for these meetings, and ensure that they are held in private.

22.    If they are not employed by the employer, union members of the JNB or other union officials attending JNB meetings shall be given sufficient access to the employer's premises to allow them to attend Union Side pre-meetings, JNB meetings and meetings of the bargaining unit as specified in paragraph 23.

23.    The employer shall agree to the union's reasonable request to hold meetings with members of the bargaining unit on company premises to discuss the Step 1 claim, the employer's offer or revisions to either. The request shall be made at least three working days in advance of the proposed meeting. However, the employer is not required to provide such facilities, if the employer does not possess available premises which can be used for meetings on the scale suggested by the union. The employer shall provide adequate heating and lighting for meetings, and ensure that the meeting is held in private. Where such meetings are held in working time, the employer is under no obligation to pay individuals for the time off. Where meetings take place outside normal working hours, they should be arranged at a time which is otherwise convenient for the workers.

24.    Where resources permit, the employer shall make available to the Union Side of the JNB such typing, copying and word-processing facilities as it needs to conduct its business in private.

25.    Where resources permit, the employer shall set aside a room for the exclusive use of the Union Side of the JNB. The room shall possess a secure cabinet and a telephone.

26.    In respect of issues which are not otherwise specified in this method, the employer and the union shall have regard to the guidance issued in the ACAS Code of Practice on Time Off for Trade Union Duties and Activities and ensure that there is no unwarranted or unjustified failure to abide by it.

## Disclosure of Information

27.  The employer and the union shall have regard to the ACAS Code of Practice on the Disclosure of Information to Trade Unions for Collective Bargaining Purposes and ensure that there is no unwarranted or unjustified failure to abide by it in relation to the bargaining arrangements specified by this method.

## Revision of the Method

28.  The employer or the union may request in writing a meeting of the JNB to discuss revising any element of this method, including its status as a legally binding contract. A quorate meeting of the JNB shall be held within ten working days of the receipt of the request by the JNB Secretary. This meeting shall be held in accordance with the same arrangements for the holding of other JNB meetings.

## General

29.  The employer and the union shall take all reasonable steps to ensure that this method to conduct collective bargaining is applied efficiently and effectively.

30.  The definition of a 'working day' used in this method is any day other than a Saturday or a Sunday, Christmas Day or Good Friday, or a day which is a bank holiday.

31.  All time limits mentioned in this method may be varied on any occasion, if both the employer and the union agree.

# TELECOMMUNICATIONS (LAWFUL BUSINESS PRACTICE) (INTERCEPTION OF COMMUNICATIONS) REGULATIONS 2000 (SI 2000 No. 2699)

## 2  Interpretation

In these Regulations—

   (a)  references to a business include references to activities of a government department, of any public authority or of any person or office holder on whom functions are conferred by or under any enactment;

   (b)  a reference to a communication as relevant to a business is a reference to—
      (i)  a communication—
         (aa)  by means of which a transaction is entered into in the course of that business, or
         (bb)  which otherwise relates to that business, or
      (ii)  a communication which otherwise takes place in the course of the carrying on of that business;

   (c)  'regulatory or self-regulatory practices or procedures' means practices or procedures—
      (i)  compliance with which is required or recommended by, under or by virtue of—
         (aa)  any provision of the law of a member state or other state within the European Economic Area, or
         (bb)  any standard or code of practice published by or on behalf of a body established in a member state or other state within the European Economic Area which includes amongst its objectives the publication of standards or codes of practice for the conduct of business, or
      (ii)  which are otherwise applied for the purpose of ensuring compliance with anything so required or recommended;

   (d)  'system controller' means, in relation to a particular telecommunication system, a person with a right to control its operation or use.

## 3    Lawful interception of a communication

(1)   For the purpose of section 1(5)(a) of the Act, conduct is authorised, subject to paragraphs (2) and (3) below, if it consists of interception of a communication, in the course of its transmission by means of a telecommunication system, which is effected by or with the express consent of the system controller for the purpose of—

   (a)   monitoring or keeping a record of communications—
      (i)   in order to—
         (aa)   establish the existence of facts, or
         (bb)   ascertain compliance with regulatory or self-regulatory practices or procedures which are—
               applicable to the system controller in the carrying on of his business or applicable to another person in the carrying on of his business where that person is supervised by the system controller in respect of those practices or procedures, or
         (cc)   ascertain or demonstrate the standards which are achieved or ought to be achieved by persons using the system in the course of their duties, or
      (ii)   in the interests of national security, or
      (iii)   for the purpose of preventing or detecting crime, or
      (iv)   for the purpose of investigating or detecting the unauthorised use of that or any other telecommunication system, or
      (v)   where that is undertaken—
         (aa)   in order to secure, or
         (bb)   as an inherent part of,
            the effective operation of the system (including any monitoring or keeping of a record which would be authorised by section 3(3) of the Act if the conditions in paragraphs (a) and (b) thereof were satisfied); or
   (b)   monitoring communications for the purpose of determining whether they are communications relevant to the system controller's business which fall within regulation 2(b)(i) above; or
   (c)   monitoring communications made to a confidential voice-telephony counselling or support service which is free of charge (other than the cost, if any, of making a telephone call) and operated in such a way that users may remain anonymous if they so choose.

(2)   Conduct is authorised by paragraph (1) of this regulation only if—
   (a)   the interception in question is effected solely for the purpose of monitoring or (where appropriate) keeping a record of communications relevant to the system controller's business;
   (b)   the telecommunication system in question is provided for use wholly or partly in connection with that business;
   (c)   the system controller has made all reasonable efforts to inform every person who may use the telecommunication system in question that communications transmitted by means thereof may be intercepted; and
   (d)   in a case falling within—
      (i)   paragraph (1)(a)(ii) above, the person by or on whose behalf the interception is effected is a person specified in section 6(2)(a) to (i) of the Act;
      (ii)   paragraph (1)(b) above, the communication is one which is intended to be received (whether or not it has been actually received) by a person using the telecommunication system in question.

(3)   Conduct falling within paragraph (1)(a)(i) above is authorised only to the extent that Article 5 of Directive 97/66/EC of the European Parliament and of the Council of 15 December 1997 concerning the processing of personal data and the protection of privacy in the telecommunications sector so permits as amended by Directive 2009/136/EC of the European Parliament and of the Council of 25 November 2009 amending Directive 2002/22/EC on universal service and users' rights relating to electronic communications networks and services, Directive 2002/58/EC concerning the processing of personal data and the protection of privacy in the electronic communications sector and Regulation (EC) No. 2006/2004 on co-operation between national authorities responsible for the enforcement of consumer protection laws.

# FIXED-TERM EMPLOYEES (PREVENTION OF LESS FAVOURABLE TREATMENT) REGULATIONS 2002 (SI 2002 No. 2034)

PART 1
GENERAL AND INTERPRETATION

**1　Citation, commencement and interpretation**

(1)　These Regulations may be cited as the Fixed-term Employees (Prevention of Less Favourable Treatment) Regulations 2002 and shall come into force on 1st October 2002.

(2)　In these Regulations—

'the 1996 Act' means the Employment Rights Act 1996;

'collective agreement' means a collective agreement within the meaning of section 178 of the Trade Union and Labour Relations (Consolidation) Act 1992; the trade union parties to which are independent trade unions within the meaning of section 5 of that Act;

'employer', in relation to any employee, means the person by whom the employee is (or, where the employment has ceased, was) employed;

'fixed-term contract' means a contract of employment that, under its provisions determining how it will terminate in the normal course, will terminate—

(a)　on the expiry of a specific term,

(b)　on the completion of a particular task, or

(c)　on the occurrence or non-occurrence of any other specific event other than the attainment by the employee of any normal and bona fide retiring age in the establishment for an employee holding the position held by him,

and any reference to 'fixed-term' shall be construed accordingly;

'fixed-term employee' means an employee who is employed under a fixed-term contract;

'permanent employee' means an employee who is not employed under a fixed-term contract, and any reference to 'permanent employment' shall be construed accordingly;

'pro rata principle' means that where a comparable permanent employee receives or is entitled to pay or any other benefit, a fixed-term employee is to receive or be entitled to such proportion of that pay or other benefit as is reasonable in the circumstances having regard to the length of his contract of employment and to the terms on which the pay or other benefit is offered;

'renewal' includes extension and references to renewing a contract shall be construed accordingly;

'workforce agreement' means an agreement between an employer and his employees or their representatives in respect of which the conditions set out in Schedule 1 to these Regulations are satisfied.

**2　Comparable employees**

(1)　For the purposes of these Regulations, an employee is a comparable permanent employee in relation to a fixed-term employee if, at the time when the treatment that is alleged to be less favourable to the fixed-term employee takes place,

(a)　both employees are—

(i)　employed by the same employer, and

(ii)　engaged in the same or broadly similar work having regard, where relevant, to whether they have a similar level of qualification and skills; and

(b)　the permanent employee works or is based at the same establishment as the fixed-term employee or, where there is no comparable permanent employee working or based at that establishment who satisfies the requirements of sub-paragraph (a), works or is based at a different establishment and satisfies those requirements.

(2)　For the purposes of paragraph (1), an employee is not a comparable permanent employee if his employment has ceased.

PART 2
RIGHTS AND REMEDIES

## 3     Less favourable treatment of fixed-term employees

(1)   A fixed-term employee has the right not to be treated by his employer less favourably than the employer treats a comparable permanent employee—

    (a)   as regards the terms of his contract; or

    (b)   by being subjected to any other detriment by any act, or deliberate failure to act, of his employer.

(2)   Subject to paragraphs (3) and (4), the right conferred by paragraph (1) includes in particular the right of the fixed-term employee in question not to be treated less favourably than the employer treats a comparable permanent employee in relation to—

    (a)   any period of service qualification relating to any particular condition of service,

    (b)   the opportunity to receive training, or

    (c)   the opportunity to secure any permanent position in the establishment.

(3)   The right conferred by paragraph (1) applies only if—

    (a)   the treatment is on the ground that the employee is a fixed-term employee, and

    (b)   the treatment is not justified on objective grounds.

(4)   Paragraph (3)(b) is subject to regulation 4.

(5)   In determining whether a fixed-term employee has been treated less favourably than a comparable permanent employee, the pro rata principle shall be applied unless it is inappropriate.

(6)   In order to ensure that an employee is able to exercise the right conferred by paragraph (1) as described in paragraph (2)(c) the employee has the right to be informed by his employer of available vacancies in the establishment.

(7)   For the purposes of paragraph (6) an employee is 'informed by his employer' only if the vacancy is contained in an advertisement which the employee has a reasonable opportunity of reading in the course of his employment or the employee is given reasonable notification of the vacancy in some other way.

## 4     Objective justification

(1)   Where a fixed-term employee is treated by his employer less favourably than the employer treats a comparable permanent employee as regards any term of his contract, the treatment in question shall be regarded for the purposes of regulation 3(3)(b) as justified on objective grounds if the terms of the fixed-term employee's contract of employment, taken as a whole, are at least as favourable as the terms of the comparable permanent employee's contract of employment.

(2)   Paragraph (1) is without prejudice to the generality of regulation 3(3)(b).

## 5     Right to receive a written statement of reasons for less favourable treatment

(1)   If an employee who considers that his employer may have treated him in a manner which infringes a right conferred on him by regulation 3 requests in writing from his employer a written statement giving particulars of the reasons for the treatment, the employee is entitled to be provided with such a statement within twenty-one days of his request.

(2)   A written statement under this regulation is admissible as evidence in any proceedings under these Regulations.

(3)   If it appears to the tribunal in any proceedings under these Regulations—

    (a)   that the employer deliberately, and without reasonable excuse, omitted to provide a written statement, or

    (b)   that the written statement is evasive or equivocal,

it may draw any inference which it considers it just and equitable to draw, including an inference that the employer has infringed the right in question.

(4)   This regulation does not apply where the treatment in question consists of the dismissal of an employee, and the employee is entitled to a written statement of reasons for his dismissal under section 92 of the 1996 Act.

**6      Unfair dismissal and the right not to be subjected to detriment**

(1)    An employee who is dismissed shall be regarded as unfairly dismissed for the purposes of Part 10 of the 1996 Act if the reason (or, if more than one, the principal reason) for the dismissal is a reason specified in paragraph (3).

(2)    An employee has the right not to be subjected to any detriment by any act, or any deliberate failure to act, of his employer done on a ground specified in paragraph (3).

(3)    The reasons or, as the case may be, grounds are—

(a)    that the employee—

(i)     brought proceedings against the employer under these Regulations;

(ii)    requested from his employer a written statement under regulation 5 or regulation 9;

(iii)   gave evidence or information in connection with such proceedings brought by any employee;

(iv)   otherwise did anything under these Regulations in relation to the employer or any other person;

(v)    alleged that the employer had infringed these Regulations;

(vi)   refused (or proposed to refuse) to forgo a right conferred on him by these Regulations;

(vii)  declined to sign a workforce agreement for the purposes of these Regulations, or

(viii) being—

(aa)   a representative of members of the workforce for the purposes of Schedule 1, or

(bb)   a candidate in an election in which any person elected will, on being elected,

become such a representative,

performed (or proposed to perform) any functions or activities as such a representative or candidate, or

(b)    that the employer believes or suspects that the employee has done or intends to do any of the things mentioned in sub-paragraph (a).

(4)    Where the reason or principal reason for dismissal or, as the case may be, ground for subjection to any act or deliberate failure to act, is that mentioned in paragraph (3)(a) (v), or (b) so far as it relates thereto, neither paragraph (1) nor paragraph (2) applies if the allegation made by the employee is false and not made in good faith.

(5)    Paragraph (2) does not apply where the detriment in question amounts to dismissal within the meaning of Part 10 of the 1996 Act.

**7      Complaints to employment tribunals etc.**

(1)    An employee may present a complaint to an employment tribunal that his employer has infringed a right conferred on him by regulation 3, or (subject to regulation 6(5)), regulation 6(2).

(2)    Subject to paragraph (3), an employment tribunal shall not consider a complaint under this regulation unless it is presented before the end of the period of three months beginning—

(a)    in the case of an alleged infringement of a right conferred by regulation 3(1) or 6(2), with the date of the less favourable treatment or detriment to which the complaint relates or, where an act or failure to act is part of a series of similar acts or failures comprising the less favourable treatment or detriment, the last of them;

(b)    in the case of an alleged infringement of the right conferred by regulation 3(6), with the date, or if more than one the last date, on which other individuals, whether or not employees of the employer, were informed of the vacancy.

(2A)   Regulation 7A (extension of time limits to facilitate conciliation before institution of proceedings) applies for the purposes of paragraph (2).

(3)    A tribunal may consider any such complaint which is out of time if, in all the circumstances of the case, it considers that it is just and equitable to do so.

(4) For the purposes of calculating the date of the less favourable treatment or detriment under paragraph (2)(a)—

    (a) where a term in a contract is less favourable, that treatment shall be treated, subject to paragraph (b), as taking place on each day of the period during which the term is less favourable;

    (b) a deliberate failure to act contrary to regulation 3 or 6(2) shall be treated as done when it was decided on.

(5) In the absence of evidence establishing the contrary, a person shall be taken for the purposes of paragraph (4)(b) to decide not to act—

    (a) when he does an act inconsistent with doing the failed act; or

    (b) if he has done no such inconsistent act, when the period expires within which he might reasonably have been expected to have done the failed act if it was to be done.

(6) Where an employee presents a complaint under this regulation in relation to a right conferred on him by regulation 3 or 6(2) it is for the employer to identify the ground for the less favourable treatment or detriment.

(7) Where an employment tribunal finds that a complaint presented to it under this regulation is well founded, it shall take such of the following steps as it considers just and equitable—

    (a) making a declaration as to the rights of the complainant and the employer in relation to the matters to which the complaint relates;

    (b) ordering the employer to pay compensation to the complainant;

    (c) recommending that the employer take, within a specified period, action appearing to the tribunal to be reasonable, in all the circumstances of the case, for the purpose of obviating or reducing the adverse effect on the complainant of any matter to which the complaint relates.

(8) Where a tribunal orders compensation under paragraph (7)(b), the amount of the compensation awarded shall be such as the tribunal considers just and equitable in all the circumstances having regard to—

    (a) the infringement to which the complaint relates, and

    (b) any loss which is attributable to the infringement.

(9) The loss shall be taken to include—

    (a) any expenses reasonably incurred by the complainant in consequence of the infringement, and

    (b) loss of any benefit which he might reasonably be expected to have had but for the infringement.

(10) Compensation in respect of treating an employee is a manner which infringes the right conferred on him by regulation 3 shall not include compensation for injury to feelings.

(11) In ascertaining the loss the tribunal shall apply the same rule concerning the duty of a person to mitigate his loss as applies to damages recoverable under the common law of England and Wales or (as the case may be) the law of Scotland.

(12) Where the tribunal finds that the act, or failure to act, to which the complaint relates was to any extent caused or contributed to by action of the complainant, it shall reduce the amount of the compensation by such proportion as it considers just and equitable having regard to that finding.

(13) If the employer fails, without reasonable justification, to comply with a recommendation made by an employment tribunal under paragraph (7)(c) the tribunal may, if it thinks it just and equitable to do so—

    (a) increase the amount of compensation required to be paid to the complainant in respect of the complaint, where an order was made under paragraph (7)(b); or

    (b) make an order under paragraph (7)(b).

## 8    Successive fixed-term contracts

(1) This regulation applies where—

    (a) an employee is employed under a contract purporting to be a fixed-term contract, and

    (b) the contract mentioned in sub-paragraph (a) has previously been renewed, or the employee has previously been employed on a fixed-term contract before the start of the contract mentioned in sub-paragraph (a).

(2)    Where this regulation applies then, with effect from the date specified in paragraph (3), the provision of the contract mentioned in paragraph (1)(a) that restricts the duration of the contract shall be of no effect, and the employee shall be a permanent employee, if—

(a)    the employee has been continuously employed under the contract mentioned in paragraph 1 (a), or under that contract taken with a previous fixed-term contract, for a period of four years or more, and

(b)    the employment of the employee under a fixed-term contract was not justified on objective grounds—

(i)    where the contract mentioned in paragraph (1)(a) has been renewed, at the time when it was last renewed;

(ii)    where that contract has not been renewed, at the time when it was entered into.

(3)    The date referred to in paragraph (2) is whichever is the later of—

(a)    the date on which the contract mentioned in paragraph (1)(a) was entered into or last renewed, and

(b)    the date on which the employee acquired four years' continuous employment.

(4)    For the purposes of this regulation Chapter 1 of Part 14 of the 1996 Act shall apply in determining whether an employee has been continuously employed, and any period of continuous employment falling before the 10th July 2002 shall be disregarded.

(5)    A collective agreement or a workforce agreement may modify the application of paragraphs (1) to (3) of this regulation in relation to any employee or specified description of employees, by substituting for the provisions of paragraph (2) or paragraph (3), or for the provisions of both of those paragraphs, one or more different provisions which, in order to prevent abuse arising from the use of successive fixed-term contracts, specify one or more of the following—

(a)    the maximum total period for which the employee or employees of that description may be continuously employed on a fixed-term contract or on successive fixed-term contracts;

(b)    the maximum number of successive fixed-term contracts and renewals of such contracts under which the employee or employees of that description may be employed; or

(c)    objective grounds justifying the renewal of fixed-term contracts, or the engagement of the employee or employees of that description under successive fixed-term contracts,

and those provisions shall have effect in relation to that employee or an employee of that description as if they were contained in paragraphs (2) and (3).

## 9    Right to receive written statement of variation

(1)    If an employee who considers that, by virtue of regulation 8, he is a permanent employee requests in writing from his employer a written statement confirming that his contract is no longer fixed-term or that he is now a permanent employee, he is entitled to be provided, within twenty-one days of his request, with either—

(a)    such a statement, or

(b)    a statement giving reasons why his contract remains fixed-term.

(2)    If the reasons stated under paragraph (1)(b) include an assertion that there were objective grounds for the engagement of the employee under a fixed-term contract, or the renewal of such a contract, the statement shall include a statement of those grounds.

(3)    A written statement under this regulation is admissible as evidence in any proceedings before a court, an employment tribunal and the Commissioners of the Inland Revenue.

(4)    If it appears to the court or tribunal in any proceedings—

(a)    that the employer deliberately, and without reasonable excuse, omitted to provide a written statement, or

(b)    that the written statement is evasive or equivocal,

it may draw any inference which it considers it just and equitable to draw.

(5)    An employee who considers that, by virtue of regulation 8, he is a permanent employee may present an application to an employment tribunal for a declaration to that effect.

(6) No application may be made under paragraph (5) unless—

    (a)   the employee in question has previously requested a statement under paragraph (1) and the employer has either failed to provide a statement or given a statement of reasons under paragraph (1)(b), and

    (b)   the employee is at the time the application is made employed by the employer.

## PART 3
## MISCELLANEOUS

## 10   Restrictions on contracting out

Section 203 of the 1996 Act (restrictions on contracting out) shall apply in relation to these Regulations as if they were contained in that Act.

## 12   Liability of employers and principals

(1) Anything done by a person in the course of his employment shall be treated for the purposes of these Regulations as also done by his employer, whether or not it was done with the employer's knowledge or approval.

(2) Anything done by a person as agent for the employer with the authority of the employer shall be treated for the purposes of these Regulations as also done by the employer.

(3) In proceedings under these Regulations against any person in respect of an act alleged to have been done by an employee of his, it shall be a defence for that person to prove that he took such steps as were reasonably practicable to prevent the employee from—

    (a)   doing that act, or

    (b)   doing, in the course of his employment, acts of that description.

## PART 5
## EXCLUSIONS

## 18   Government training schemes etc.

(1) These Regulations shall not have effect in relation to a fixed-term employee who is employed on a scheme, designed to provide him with training or work experience for the purpose of assisting him to seek or obtain work, which is either—

    (a)   provided to him under arrangements made by the Government, or

    (b)   funded in whole or part by an Institution of the European Community.

(2) These Regulations shall not have effect in relation to a fixed-term employee whose employment consists in attending a period of work experience not exceeding one year that he is required to attend as part of a higher education course.

(3) For the purpose of paragraph (2) 'a higher education course' means—

    (a)   in England and Wales, a course of a description referred to in Schedule 6 to the Education Reform Act 1988;

    (b)   in Scotland, a course of a description falling within section 38 of the Further and Higher Education (Scotland) Act 1992; and

    (c)   in Northern Ireland, a course of a description referred to in Schedule 1 to the Further Education (Northern Ireland) Order 1997.

## 19   Agency workers

(1) Save in respect of paragraph 1 of Part 1 of Schedule 2, these Regulations shall not have effect in relation to employment under a fixed-term contract where the employee is an agency worker.

(2) In this regulation 'agency worker' means any person who is supplied by an employment business to do work for another person under a contract or other arrangements made between the employment business and the other person.

(3) In this regulation 'employment business' means the business (whether or not carried on with a view to profit and whether or not carried on in conjunction with any other business) of supplying persons in the employment of the person carrying on the business, to act for, and under the control of, other persons in any capacity.

## 20    Apprentices

These Regulations shall not have effect in relation to employment under a fixed-term contract where the contract is a contract of apprenticeship, an apprenticeship agreement (within the meaning of section 32 of the Apprenticeships, Skills, Children and Learning Act 2009) or approved English apprenticeship agreement (within the meaning of section A1(3) of the Apprenticeships, Skills, Children and Learning Act 2009).

## SCHEDULE 1
## WORKFORCE AGREEMENTS

1. An agreement is a workforce agreement for the purposes of these Regulations if the following conditions are satisfied—
    (a) the agreement is in writing;
    (b) it has effect for a specified period not exceeding five years;
    (c) it applies either—
        (i) to all of the relevant members of the workforce, or
        (ii) to all of the relevant members of the workforce who belong to a particular group;
    (d) the agreement is signed—
        (i) in the case of an agreement of the kind referred to in subparagraph (c)(i), by the representatives of the workforce, and in the case of an agreement of the kind referred to in sub-paragraph (c)(ii) by the representatives of the group to which the agreement applies (excluding, in either case, any representative not a relevant member of the workforce on the date on which the agreement was first made available for signature), or
        (ii) if the employer employed 20 or fewer employees on the date referred to in sub-paragraph (d)(i), either by the appropriate representatives in accordance with that sub-paragraph or by the majority of the employees employed by him;
    (e) before the agreement was made available for signature, the employer provided all the employees to whom it was intended to apply on the date on which it came into effect with copies of the text of the agreement and such guidance as those employees might reasonably require in order to understand it fully.
2. For the purposes of this Schedule—
    'a particular group' is a group of the relevant members of a workforce who undertake a particular function, work at a particular workplace or belong to a particular department or unit within their employer's business;
    'relevant members of the workforce' are all of the employees employed by a particular employer, excluding any employee whose terms and conditions of employment are provided for, wholly or in part, in a collective agreement;
    'representatives of the workforce' are employees duly elected to represent the relevant members of the workforce, 'representatives of the group' are employees duly elected to represent the members of a particular group, and representatives are 'duly elected' if the election at which they were elected satisfied the requirements of paragraph 3 of this Schedule.
3. The requirements concerning elections referred to in paragraph 2 are that—
    (a) the number of representatives to be elected is determined by the employer;
    (b) the candidates for election as representatives of the workforce are relevant members of the workforce, and the candidates for election as representatives of a group are members of that group;
    (c) no employee who is eligible to be a candidate is unreasonably excluded from standing for election;
    (d) all the relevant members of the workforce are entitled to vote for representatives of the workforce, and all the members of a particular group are entitled to vote for representatives of the group;
    (e) the employees entitled to vote may vote for as many candidates as there are representatives to be elected;

  (f)     the election is conducted so as to secure that—
      (i)     so far as is reasonably practicable, those voting do so in secret, and
      (ii)     the votes given at the election are fairly and accurately counted.

# PATERNITY AND ADOPTION LEAVE REGULATIONS 2002
## (SI 2002 No. 2788)

PART I
GENERAL

## 3   Application

(1)    The provisions relating to paternity leave under regulation 4 below have effect only in relation to children—
  (a)     born on or after 6th April 2003, or
  (b)     whose expected week of birth begins on or after that date.

(2)    The provisions relating to paternity leave under regulation 8 and adoption leave under regulation 15 below have effect only in relation to children—
  (a)     matched with a person who is notified of having been matched on or after 6th April 2003, or
  (b)     placed for adoption on or after that date.

(3)    Regulation 28 (protection from detriment) has effect only in relation to an act or failure to act which takes place on or after 8th December 2002.

(4)    For the purposes of paragraph (3)—
  (a)     where an act extends over a period, the reference to the date of the act is a reference to the last day of that period, and
  (b)     a failure to act is to be treated as done when it was decided on.

(5)    For the purposes of paragraph (4), in the absence of evidence establishing the contrary an employer shall be taken to decide on a failure to act—
  (a)     when he does an act inconsistent with doing the failed act, or
  (b)     if he has done no such inconsistent act, when the period expires within which he might reasonably have been expected to do the failed act if it was to be done.

(6)    Regulation 29 (unfair dismissal) has effect only in relation to dismissals where the effective date of termination (within the meaning of section 97 of the 1996 Act) falls on or after 8th December 2002.

PART 2
PATERNITY LEAVE

## 4   Entitlement to paternity leave: birth

(1)    Subject to paragraph (1A), an employee is entitled to be absent from work for the purpose of caring for a child or supporting the child's mother if he—
  (a)     satisfies the conditions specified in paragraph (2), and
  (b)     has complied with the notice requirements in regulation 6 and, where applicable, the evidential requirements in that regulation.

(1A) An employee is not entitled to be absent from work under paragraph (1) if the employee has taken any shared parental leave in respect of the child.

(2)    The conditions referred to in paragraph (1) are that the employee—
  (a)     has been continuously employed for a period of not less than 26 weeks ending with the week immediately preceding the 14th week before the expected week of the child's birth;
  (b)     is either—
      (i)     the father of the child or;
      (ii)     married to [the civil partner] or the partner of the child's mother, but not the child's father;

(c)  has, or expects to have—
  (i)  if he is the child's father, responsibility for the upbringing of the child;
  (ii)  if he is the mother's husband[, civil partner] or partner but not the child's father, the main responsibility (apart from any responsibility of the mother) for the upbringing of the child.

(3)  An employee shall be treated as having satisfied the condition in paragraph (2)(a) on the date of the child's birth notwithstanding the fact that he has not then been continuously employed for a period of not less than 26 weeks, where—
  (a)  the date on which the child is born is earlier than the 14th week before the week in which its birth is expected, and
  (b)  the employee would have been continuously employed for such a period if his employment had continued until that 14th week.

(4)  An employee shall be treated as having satisfied the condition in paragraph (2)(b)(ii) if he would have satisfied it but for the fact that the child's mother has died.

(5)  An employee shall be treated as having satisfied the condition in paragraph (2)(c) if he would have satisfied it but for the fact that the child was stillborn after 24 weeks of pregnancy or has died.

(6)  An employee's entitlement to leave under this regulation shall not be affected by the birth, or expected birth, of more than one child as a result of the same pregnancy.

## 5  Options in respect of leave under regulation 4

(1)  An employee may choose to take either one week's leave or two consecutive weeks' leave in respect of a child under regulation 4.

(2)  The leave may only be taken during the period which begins with the date on which the child is born and ends—
  (a)  except in the case referred to in sub-paragraph (b), 56 days after that date;
  (b)  in a case where the child is born before the first day of the expected week of its birth, 56 days after that day.

(3)  Subject to paragraph (2) and, where applicable, paragraph (4), an employee may choose to begin his period of leave on—
  (a)  the date on which the child is born;
  (b)  the date falling such number of days after the date on which the child is born as the employee may specify in a notice under regulation 6, or
  (c)  a predetermined date, specified in a notice under that regulation, which is later than the first day of the expected week of the child's birth.

(4)  In a case where the leave is in respect of a child whose expected week of birth begins before 6th April 2003, an employee may choose to begin a period of leave only on a predetermined date, specified in a notice under regulation 6, which is at least 28 days after the date on which that notice is given.

## 6  Notice and evidential requirements for leave under regulation 4

(1)  An employee must give his employer notice of his intention to take leave in respect of a child under regulation 4, specifying—
  (a)  the expected week of the child's birth;
  (b)  the length of the period of leave that, in accordance with regulation 5(1), the employee has chosen to take, and
  (c)  the date on which, in accordance with regulation 5(3) or (4), the employee has chosen that his period of leave should begin.

(2)  The notice provided for in paragraph (1) must be given to the employer—
  (a)  in or before the 15th week before the expected week of the child's birth, or
  (b)  in a case where it was not reasonably practicable for the employee to give the notice in accordance with sub-paragraph (a), as soon as is reasonably practicable.

(3)  Where the employer requests it, an employee must also give his employer a declaration, signed by the employee, to the effect that the purpose of his absence from work will be that specified in regulation 4(1) and that he satisfies the conditions of entitlement in regulation 4(2)(b) and (c).

(4) An employee who has given notice under paragraph (1) may vary the date he has chosen as the date on which his period of leave will begin, subject to paragraph (5) and provided that he gives his employer notice of the variation—

(a) where the variation is to provide for the employee's period of leave to begin on the date on which the child is born, at least 28 days before the first day of the expected week of the child's birth;

(b) where the variation is to provide for the employee's period of leave to begin on a date that is a specified number of days (or a different specified number of days) after the date on which the child is born, at least 28 days before the date falling that number of days after the first day of the expected week of the child's birth;

(c) where the variation is to provide for the employee's period of leave to begin on a predetermined date (or a different predetermined date), at least 28 days before that date,

or, if it is not reasonably practicable to give the notice at least 28 days before whichever day or date is relevant, as soon as is reasonably practicable.

(5) In a case where regulation 5(4) applies, an employee may only vary the date which he has chosen as the date on which his period of leave will begin by substituting a different predetermined date.

(6) In a case where—

(a) the employee has chosen to begin his period of leave on a particular predetermined date, and

(b) the child is not born on or before that date,

the employee must vary his choice of date, by substituting a later predetermined date or (except in a case where regulation 5(4) applies) exercising an alternative option under regulation 5(3), and give his employer notice of the variation as soon as is reasonably practicable.

(7) An employee must give his employer a further notice, as soon as is reasonably practicable after the child's birth, of the date on which the child was born.

(8) Notice under paragraph (1), (4), (6) or (7) shall be given in writing, if the employer so requests.

## 7    Commencement of leave under regulation 4

(1) Except in the case referred to in paragraph (2), an employee's period of paternity leave under regulation 4 begins on the date specified in his notice under regulation 6(1), or, where he has varied his choice of date under regulation 6(4) or (6), on the date specified in his notice under that provision (or the last such notice if he has varied his choice more than once).

(2) In a case where—

(a) the employee has chosen to begin his period of leave on the date on which the child is born, and

(b) he is at work on that date,

the employee's period of leave begins on the day after that date.

## 8    Entitlement to paternity leave: adoption

(1) Subject to paragraph (1A), an employee is entitled to be absent from work for the purpose of caring for a child or supporting the child's adopter if he—

(a) satisfies the conditions specified in paragraph (2), and

(b) has complied with the notice requirements in regulation 10 and, where applicable, the evidential requirements in that regulation.

(1A) An employee is not entitled to be absent from work under paragraph (1) if the employee—

(a) has taken any shared parental leave in respect of the child; ...

(b) has exercised a right to take time off under section 57ZJ of the 1996 Act in respect of the child; or

(c) has already taken paternity leave in relation to the child as a result of the child being placed with a prospective adopter who is at the time of the placement the employee's spouse, civil partner or partner.

(2)    The conditions referred to in paragraph (1) are that the employee—
    (a)    has been continuously employed for a period of not less than 26 weeks ending with the week in which the child's adopter is notified of having been matched with the child;
    (b)    is either married to[, the civil partner] or the partner of the child's adopter, and
    (c)    has, or expects to have, the main responsibility (apart from the responsibility of the adopter) for the upbringing of the child.

(3)    In paragraph (2)(a), 'week' means the period of seven days beginning with Sunday.

(4)    An employee shall be treated as having satisfied the condition in paragraph (2)(b) if he would have satisfied it but for the fact that the child's adopter died during the child's placement.

(5)    An employee shall be treated as having satisfied the condition in paragraph (2)(c) if he would have satisfied it but for the fact that the child's placement with the adopter has ended.

(6)    An employee's entitlement to leave under this regulation shall not be affected by the placement for adoption of more than one child as part of the same arrangement.

## 9    Options in respect of leave under regulation 8

(1)    An employee may choose to take either one week's leave or two consecutive weeks' leave in respect of a child under regulation 8.

(2)    The leave may only be taken during the period of 56 days beginning with the date on which the child is placed with the adopter.

(3)    Subject to paragraph (2) and, where applicable, paragraph (4), an employee may choose to begin a period of leave under regulation 8 on—
    (a)    the date on which the child is placed with the adopter;
    (b)    the date falling such number of days after the date on which the child is placed with the adopter as the employee may specify in a notice under regulation 10, or
    (c)    a predetermined date, specified in a notice under that regulation, which is later than the date on which the child is expected to be placed with the adopter.

(4)    In a case where the adopter was notified of having been matched with the child before 6th April 2003, the employee may choose to begin a period of leave only on a predetermined date, specified in a notice under regulation 10, which is at least 28 days after the date on which that notice is given.

## 10    Notice and evidential requirements for leave under regulation 8

(1)    An employee must give his employer notice of his intention to take leave in respect of a child under regulation 8, specifying—
    (a)    the date on which the adopter was notified of having been matched with the child;
    (b)    the date on which the child is expected to be placed with the adopter;
    (c)    the length of the period of leave that, in accordance with regulation 9(1), the employee has chosen to take, and
    (d)    the date on which, in accordance with regulation 9(3) or (4), the employee has chosen that his period of leave should begin.

(2)    The notice provided for in paragraph (1) must be given to the employer—
    (a)    no more than seven days after the date on which the adopter is notified of having been matched with the child, or
    (b)    in a case where it was not reasonably practicable for the employee to give notice in accordance with sub-paragraph (a), as soon as is reasonably practicable.

(3)    Where the employer requests it, an employee must also give his employer a declaration, signed by the employee, to the effect that the purpose of his absence from work will be that specified in regulation 8(1) and that he satisfies the conditions of entitlement in regulation 8(2)(b) and (c).

(4)    An employee who has given notice under paragraph (1) may vary the date he has chosen as the date on which his period of leave will begin, subject to paragraph (5) and provided that he gives his employer notice of the variation—
    (a)    where the variation is to provide for the employee's period of leave to begin on the date on which the child is placed with the adopter, at least 28 days before the date specified in the employee's notice under paragraph (1) as the date on which the child is expected to be placed with the adopter;

       (b)     where the variation is to provide for the employee's period of leave to begin on a date that is a specified number of days (or a different specified number of days) after the date on which the child is placed with the adopter, at least 28 days before the date falling that number of days after the date specified in the employee's notice under paragraph (1) as the date on which the child is expected to be placed with the adopter;

       (c)     where the variation is to provide for the employee's period of leave to begin on a predetermined date, at least 28 days before that date,

or, if it is not reasonably practicable to give the notice at least 28 days before whichever date is relevant, as soon as is reasonably practicable.

(5)    In a case where regulation 9(4) applies, an employee may only vary the date which he has chosen as the date on which his period of leave will begin by substituting a different predetermined date.

(6)    In a case where—

       (a)     the employee has chosen to begin his period of leave on a particular predetermined date, and

       (b)     the child is not placed with the adopter on or before that date,

the employee must vary his choice of date, by substituting a later predetermined date or (except in a case where regulation 9(4) applies) exercising an alternative option under regulation 9(3), and give his employer notice of the variation as soon as is reasonably practicable.

(7)    An employee must give his employer a further notice, as soon as is reasonably practicable after the child's placement, of the date on which the child was placed.

(8)    Notice under paragraph (1), (4), (6) or (7) shall be given in writing, if the employer so requests.

## 11    Commencement of leave under regulation 8

(1)    Except in the case referred to in paragraph (2), an employee's period of paternity leave under regulation 8 begins on the date specified in his notice under regulation 10(1), or, where he has varied his choice of date under regulation 10(4) or (6), on the date specified in his notice under that provision (or the last such date if he has varied his choice more than once).

(2)    In a case where—

       (a)     the employee has chosen to begin his period of leave on the date on which the child is placed with the adopter, and

       (b)     he is at work on that date,

the employee's period of leave begins on the day after that date.

## 12    Application of terms and conditions during paternity leave

(1)    An employee who takes paternity leave—

       (a)     is entitled, during the period of leave, to the benefit of all of the terms and conditions of employment which would have applied if he had not been absent, and

       (b)     is bound, during that period, by any obligations arising under those terms and conditions, subject only to the exception in section 80C(1)(b) of the 1996 Act.

(2)    In paragraph (1)(a), 'terms and conditions of employment' has the meaning given by section 80C(5) of the 1996 Act, and accordingly does not include terms and conditions about remuneration.

(3)    For the purposes of section 80C of the 1996 Act, only sums payable to an employee by way of wages or salary are to be treated as remuneration.

## 13    Right to return after paternity leave

(1)    An employee who returns to work after a period of paternity leave which was—

       (a)     an isolated period of leave, or

       (b)     the last of two or more consecutive periods of statutory leave which did not include any—

           (i)     period of parental leave of more than four weeks; or

     (ii)    period of statutory leave which when added to any other periods of statutory leave (excluding parental leave) taken in relation to the same child means that the total amount of statutory leave taken in relation to that child totals more than 26 weeks,

(2)    An employee who returns to work after a period of paternity leave not falling within the description in paragraph (1)(a) or (b) above is entitled to return from leave to the job in which he was employed before his absence, or, if it is not reasonably practicable for the employer to permit him to return to that job, to another job which is both suitable for him and appropriate for him to do in the circumstances.

(3)    The reference in paragraphs (1) and (2) to the job in which an employee was employed before his absence is a reference to the job in which he was employed—

    (a)    if his return is from an isolated period of paternity leave, immediately before that period began;

    (b)    if his return is from consecutive periods of statutory leave, immediately before the first such period.

## 14    Incidents of the right to return after paternity leave

(1)    An employee's right to return under regulation 13 is a right to return—

    (a)    with his seniority, pension rights and similar rights—

        (i)    in a case where the employee is returning from consecutive periods of statutory leave which included a period of additional adoption leave or additional maternity leave, as they would have been if the period or periods of his employment prior to the additional adoption leave or (as the case may be) additional maternity leave were continuous with the period of employment following it;

        (ii)    in any other case, as they would have been if he had not been absent, and (b) on terms and conditions not less favourable than those which would have applied if he had not been absent.

(2)    The provision in paragraph (1)(a)(i) concerning the treatment of periods of additional maternity leave or additional adoption leave is subject to the requirements of paragraphs 5, 5B and 6 of Schedule 5 to the Social Security Act 1989 (equal treatment under pension schemes: maternity absence, adoption leave and family leave).

(3)    The provisions in paragraph (1)(a)(ii) and (b) for an employee to be treated as if he had not been absent refer to his absence—

    (a)    if his return is from an isolated period of paternity leave, since the beginning of that period;

    (b)    if his return is from consecutive periods of statutory leave, since the beginning of the first such period.

PART III

ADOPTION LEAVE

## 15    Entitlement to ordinary adoption leave

(1)    Subject to paragraph (1A), an employee is entitled to ordinary adoption leave in respect of a child if he—

    (a)    satisfies the conditions specified in paragraph (2), and

    (b)    has complied with the notice requirements in regulation 17 and, where applicable, the evidential requirements in that regulation.

(1A) An employee is not entitled to be absent from work under paragraph (1) in relation to a child if the employee has already taken ordinary adoption leave as a result of that child being placed, or expected to be placed, with the employee under section 22C of the Children Act 1989.

(2)    The conditions referred to in paragraph (1) are that the employee—

    (a)    is the child's adopter; [and]

    (b)    ...

    (c)    has notified the agency that he agrees that the child should be placed with him and on the date of placement.

(3)    ...

(4)  An employee's entitlement to leave under this regulation shall not be affected by the placement for adoption of more than one child as part of the same arrangement.

## 16  Options in respect of ordinary adoption leave

(1)  Except in the case referred to in paragraph (2), an employee may choose to begin a period of ordinary adoption leave on—
  (a)  the date on which the child is placed with him for adoption, or
  (b)  a predetermined date, specified in a notice under regulation 17, which is no more than 14 days before the date on which the child is expected to be placed with the employee and no later than that date.
(2)  In a case where the employee was notified of having been matched with the child before 6th April 2003, the employee may choose to begin a period of leave only on a predetermined date, specified in a notice under regulation 17, which is after 6th April 2003 and at least 28 days after the date on which that notice is given.

## 17  Notice and evidential requirements for ordinary adoption leave

(1)  An employee must give his employer notice of his intention to take ordinary adoption leave in respect of a child, specifying—
  (a)  the date on which the child is expected to be placed with him for adoption, and
  (b)  the date on which, in accordance with regulation 16(1) or (2), the employee has chosen that his period of leave should begin.
(2)  The notice provided for in paragraph (1) must be given to the employer—
  (a)  no more than seven days after the date on which the employee is notified of having been matched with the child for the purposes of adoption, or
  (b)  in a case where it was not reasonably practicable for the employee to give notice in accordance with sub-paragraph (a), as soon as is reasonably practicable.
(3)  Where the employer requests it, an employee must also provide his employer with evidence, in the form of one or more documents issued by the adoption agency that matched the employee with the child, of—
  (a)  the name and address of the agency;
  (b)  ...
  (c)  the date on which the employee was notified that he had been matched with the child, and
  (d)  the date on which the agency expects to place the child with the employee.
(4)  An employee who has given notice under paragraph (1) may vary the date he has chosen as the date on which his period of leave will begin, subject to paragraph (5) and provided that he gives his employer notice of the variation—
  (a)  where the variation is to provide for the employee's period of leave to begin on the date on which the child is placed with him for adoption, at least 28 days before the date specified in his notice under paragraph (1) as the date on which the child is expected to be placed with him;
  (b)  where the variation is to provide for the employee's period of leave to begin on a predetermined date (or a different predetermined date), at least 28 days before that date,
  or, if it is not reasonably practicable to give the notice 28 days before whichever date is relevant, as soon as is reasonably practicable.
(5)  In a case where regulation 16(2) applies, an employee may only vary the date which he has chosen as the date on which his period of leave will begin by substituting a different predetermined date.
(6)  Notice under paragraph (1) or (4) shall be given in writing, if the employer so requests.
(7)  An employer who is given notice under paragraph (1) or (4) of the date on which an employee has chosen that his period of ordinary adoption leave should begin shall notify the employee, within 28 days of his receipt of the notice, of the date on which the period of additional adoption leave to which the employee will be entitled (if he satisfies the conditions in regulation 20(1)) after his period of ordinary adoption leave ends.
(8)  The notification provided for in paragraph (7) shall be given to the employee—
  (a)  where the employer is given notice under paragraph (1), within 28 days of the date on which he received that notice;

(b)    where the employer is given notice under paragraph (4), within 28 days of the date on which the employee's ordinary adoption leave period began.

## 18    Duration and commencement of ordinary adoption leave

(1)    Subject to regulations 22 and 24, an employee's ordinary adoption leave period is a period of 26 weeks

(2)    Except in the case referred to in paragraph (3), an employee's ordinary adoption leave period begins on the date specified in his notice under regulation 17(1), or, where he has varied his choice of date under regulation 17 (4), on the date specified in his notice under that provision (or the last such date if he has varied his choice more than once).

(3)    In a case where—

    (a)    the employee has chosen to begin his period of leave on the date on which the child is placed with him, and

    (b)    he is at work on that date,

    the employee's period of leave begins on the day after that date.

## 19    Application of terms and conditions during ordinary adoption leave and additional adoption leave

(1)    An employee who takes ordinary adoption leave or additional adoption leave—

    (a)    is entitled, during the period of leave, to the benefit of all of the terms and conditions of employment which would have applied if he had not been absent, and

    (b)    is bound, during that period, by any obligations arising under those terms and conditions, subject only to the exception in sections 75A(3)(b) and 75B(4)(b) of the 1996 Act.

(2)    In paragraph (1)(a), 'terms and conditions of employment' has the meaning given by sections 75A(4) and 75B(5) of the 1996 Act, and accordingly does not include terms and conditions about remuneration.

(3)    For the purposes of sections 75A(4) and 75B(5) of the 1996 Act, only sums payable to an employee by way of wages or salary are to be treated as remuneration.

## 20    Additional adoption leave: entitlement, duration and commencement

(1)    An employee is entitled to additional adoption leave in respect of a child if—

    (a)    the child was placed with him for adoption,

    (b)    he took ordinary adoption leave in respect of the child, and

    (c)    his ordinary adoption leave period did not end prematurely under regulation 22(2)(a) or 24.

(2)    Subject to regulations 22 and 24, an employee's additional adoption leave period is a period of 26 weeks beginning on the day after the last day of his ordinary adoption leave period.

## 21A    Work during adoption leave period

(1)    An employee may carry out up to 10 days' work for his employer during his statutory adoption leave period without bringing his statutory adoption leave to an end.

(2)    For the purposes of this regulation, any work carried out on any day shall constitute a day's work.

(3)    Subject to paragraph (4), for the purposes of this regulation, work means any work done under the contract of employment and may include training or any activity undertaken for the purposes of keeping in touch with the workplace.

(4)    Reasonable contact from time to time between an employee and his employer which either party is entitled to make during an adoption leave period (for example to discuss an employee's return to work) shall not bring that period to an end.

(5)    This regulation does not confer any right on an employer to require that any work be carried out during the statutory adoption leave period, nor any right on an employee to work during the statutory adoption leave period.

(6)    Any days' work carried out under this regulation shall not have the effect of extending the total duration of the statutory adoption leave period.

## 22    Disrupted placement in the course of adoption leave

(1) This regulation applies where—

    (a) an employee has begun a period of adoption leave in respect of a child before the placement of the child with him, and the employee is subsequently notified that the placement will not be made, or

    (b) during an employee's period of adoption leave in respect of a child placed with him—

        (i) the child dies, or

        (ii) the child is returned after being placed for adoption.

(2) Subject to regulation 24, in a case where this regulation applies—

    (a) except in the circumstances referred to in sub-paragraphs (b) and (c), the employee's adoption leave period ends eight weeks after the end of the relevant week specified in paragraph (3);

    (b) where the employee is taking ordinary adoption leave and the period of 26 weeks provided for in regulation 18 ends within eight weeks of the end of the relevant week—

        (i) the employee's ordinary adoption leave period ends on the expiry of the 26-week period;

        (ii) the employee is entitled to additional adoption leave, and (iii) the employee's additional adoption leave period ends eight weeks after the end of the relevant week;

        (iii) where the employee is taking additional adoption leave and the period of 26 weeks provided for in regulation 20 ends within eight weeks of the end of the relevant week, the employee's additional adoption leave period ends on the expiry of the 26-week period.

(3) The relevant week referred to in paragraph (2) is—

    (a) in a case falling within paragraph (1)(a), the week during which the person with whom the child was to be placed for adoption is notified that the placement will not be made;

    (b) in a case falling within paragraph (1)(b)(i), the week during which the child dies;

    (c) in a case falling within paragraph (1)(b)(ii), the week during which the child is returned.

(3A) In paragraph (1) 'returned after being placed for adoption' means—

    (a) returned under sections 31 to 35 of the Adoption and Children Act 2002;

    (b) in Scotland, returned to the adoption agency, adoption society or nominated person in accordance with section 25(6) of the Adoption and Children (Scotland) Act 2007; or

    (c) where the child is placed in accordance with section 22C of the Children Act 1989, returned to the adoption agency following a termination of the placement.

(4) where the child is placed in accordance with section 22C of the Children Act 1989, returned to the adoption agency following a termination of the placement. In paragraph (3), 'week' means the period of seven days beginning with Sunday.

## 23    Redundancy during adoption leave

(1) This regulation applies where, during an employee's ordinary or additional adoption leave period, it is not practicable by reason of redundancy for his employer to continue to employ him under his existing contract of employment.

(2) Where there is a suitable available vacancy, the employee is entitled to be offered (before the end of his employment under his existing contract) alternative employment with his employer or his employer's successor, or an associated employer, under a new contract of employment which complies with paragraph (3) and takes effect immediately on the ending of his employment under the previous contract.

(3) The new contract of employment must be such that—

    (a) the work to be done under it is of a kind which is both suitable in relation to the employee and appropriate for him to do in the circumstances, and

    (b) its provisions as to the capacity and place in which he is to be employed, and as to the other terms and conditions of his employment, are not substantially less favourable to him than if he had continued to be employed under the previous contract.

## 24 Dismissal during adoption leave

Where an employee is dismissed after an ordinary or additional adoption leave period has begun but before the time when (apart from this regulation) that period would end, the period ends at the time of the dismissal.

## 25 Requirement to notify intention to return during adoption leave period

(1) An employee who intends to return to work earlier than the end of his additional adoption leave period must give his employer at least 8 weeks' notice of the date on which he intends to return.

(2) If an employee attempts to return to work earlier than the end of his additional adoption leave period without complying with paragraph (1), his employer is entitled to postpone his return to a date such as will secure, subject to paragraph (3), that he has at least 8 weeks' notice of the employee's return.

(2A) An employee who complies with his obligations in paragraph (1) or whose employer has postponed his return in the circumstances described in paragraph (2), and who then decides to return to work—

    (a) earlier than the original return date, must give his employer not less than 8 weeks' notice of the date on which he now intends to return;

    (b) later than the original return date, must give his employer not less than 8 weeks' notice ending with the original return date.

(2B) In paragraph (2A) the 'original return date' means the date which the employee notified to his employer as the date of his return to work under paragraph (1), or the date to which his return was postponed by his employer under paragraph (2).

(3) An employer is not entitled under paragraph (2) to postpone an employee's return to work to a date after the end of the employee's additional adoption leave period.

(4) If an employee whose return has been postponed under paragraph (2) has been notified that he is not to return to work before the date to which his return was postponed, the employer is under no contractual obligation to pay him remuneration until the date to which his return was postponed if he returns to work before that date.

(5) This regulation does not apply in a case where the employer did not notify the employee in accordance with regulation 17(7) and (8) of the date on which the employee's additional adoption leave period would end.

(6) In a case where an employee's adoption leave is curtailed because regulation 22 applies, the references in this regulation to the end of an employee's additional adoption leave period are references to the date on which that period would have ended had that regulation not applied, irrespective of whether it was the employee's ordinary adoption leave period or his additional adoption leave period that was curtailed.

## 26 Right to return after adoption leave

(1) An employee who returns to work after a period of ordinary adoption leave which was—

    (a) an isolated period of leave, or

    (b) the last of two or more consecutive periods of statutory leave which did not include any—

        (i) period of parental leave of more than four weeks; or

        (ii) period of statutory leave which when added to any other periods of statutory leave (excluding parental leave) taken in relation to the same child means that the total amount of statutory leave taken in relation to that child totals more than 26 weeks,

(2) An employee who returns to work after—

    (a) a period of additional adoption leave, whether or not preceded by another period of statutory leave, or

    (b) a period of ordinary adoption leave not falling within the description in paragraph (1)(a) or (b) above,

is entitled to return from leave to the job in which he was employed before his absence, or, if it is not reasonably practicable for the employer to permit him to return to that job, to another job which is both suitable for him and appropriate for him to do in the circumstances.

(3)   The reference in paragraphs (1) and (2) to the job in which an employee was employed before his absence is a reference to the job in which he was employed—
 (a)   if his return is from an isolated period of adoption leave, immediately before that period began;
 (b)   if his return is from consecutive periods of statutory leave, immediately before the first such period.

(4)   This regulation does not apply where regulation 23 applies.

## 27    Incidents of the right to return from adoption leave

(1)   An employee's right to return under regulation 26 is to return—
 (a)   with his seniority, pension rights and similar rights as they would have been if he had not been absent, and
 (b)   on terms and conditions … not less favourable than those which would have been applied to him if he had not been absent.

(2)   In the case of accrual of rights under an employment-related benefit scheme within the meaning given by Schedule 5 to the Social Security Act 1989, nothing in paragraph (1)(a) concerning the treatment of additional adoption leave shall be taken to impose a requirement which exceeds the requirements of paragraphs 5, 5B and 6 of that Schedule.

(3)   The provisions in paragraph (1) for an employee to be treated as if he had not been absent refer to his absence—
 (a)   if his return is from an isolated period of ordinary adoption leave, since the beginning of that period;
 (b)   if his return is from consecutive periods of statutory leave, since the beginning of the first such period.

PART 4

PROVISIONS APPLICABLE IN RELATION TO BOTH PATERNITY AND
ADOPTION LEAVE

## 28    Protection from detriment

(1)   An employee is entitled under section 47C of the 1996 Act not to be subjected to any detriment by any act, or any deliberate failure to act, by his employer because—
 (a)   the employee took or sought to take paternity leave or ordinary or additional adoption leave;
 (za)  the employee took or sought to take time off under section 57ZE of the 1996 Act;
 (zb)  the employer believed that the employee was likely to take time off under section 57ZE of the 1996 Act;
 (zc)  the employee took or sought to take time off under section 57ZJ or 57ZL of the 1996 Act;
 (zd)  the employer believed that the employee was likely to take time off under section 57ZJ or 57ZL of the 1996 Act;
 (b)   the employer believed that the employee was likely to take ordinary or additional adoption leave, …
 (bb)  the employee undertook, considered undertaking or refused to undertake work in accordance with regulation 21A; or
 (c)   the employee failed to return after a period of additional adoption leave in a case where—
   (i)    the employer did not notify him, in accordance with regulation 17(7) and (8) or otherwise, of the date on which that period ended, and he reasonably believed that the period had not ended, or
   (ii)   the employer gave him less than 28 days' notice of the date on which the period would end, and it was not reasonably practicable for him to return on that date.

(2)   Paragraph (1) does not apply where the detriment in question amounts to dismissal within the meaning of Part 10 of the 1996 Act.

## 29    Unfair dismissal

(1)    An employee who is dismissed is entitled under section 99 of the 1996 Act to be regarded for the purpose of Part 10 of that Act as unfairly dismissed if—

(a)    the reason or principal reason for the dismissal is of a kind specified in paragraph (3), or

(b)    the reason or principal reason for the dismissal is that the employee is redundant, and regulation 23 has not been complied with.

(2)    An employee who is dismissed shall also be regarded for the purposes of Part 10 of the 1996 Act as unfairly dismissed if—

(a)    the reason (or, if more than one, the principal reason) for the dismissal is that the employee was redundant;

(b)    it is shown that the circumstances constituting the redundancy applied equally to one or more employees in the same undertaking who had positions similar to that held by the employee and who have not been dismissed by the employer, and

(c)    it is shown that the reason (or, if more than one, the principal reason) for which the employee was selected for dismissal was a reason of a kind specified in paragraph (3).

(3)    The kinds of reason referred to in paragraph (1) and (2) are reasons connected with the fact that—

(za)    the employee took or sought to take time off under section 57ZE of the 1996 Act;

(zb)    the employer believed that the employee was likely to take time off under section 57ZE of the 1996 Act;

(zc)    the employee took or sought to take time off under section 57ZJ or 57ZL of the 1996 Act;

(zd)    the employer believed that the employee was likely to take time off under section 57ZJ or 57ZL of the 1996 Act;

(a)    the employee took, or sought to take, paternity or adoption leave;

(b)    the employer believed that the employee was likely to take ordinary or additional adoption leave,

(bb)    the employee undertook, considered undertaking or refused to undertake work in accordance with regulation 21A; or

(c)    the employee failed to return after a period of additional adoption leave in a case where—

(i)    the employer did not notify him, in accordance with regulation 17(7) and (8) or otherwise, of the date on which that period would end, and he reasonably believed that the period had not ended, or

(ii)    the employer gave him less than 28 days' notice of the date on which the period would end, and it was not reasonably practicable for him to return on that date.

(4)    Paragraph (1) does not apply in relation to an employee who took adoption leave if—

(a)    immediately before the end of his additional adoption leave period (or, if it ends by reason of dismissal, immediately before the dismissal) the number of employees employed by his employer, added to the number employed by any associated employer of his employer, did not exceed five, and

(b)    it is not reasonably practicable for the employer (who may be the same employer or a successor of his) to permit the employee to return to a job which is both suitable for the employee and appropriate for him to do in the circumstances or for an associated employer to offer the employee a job of that kind.

(5)    Paragraph (1) does not apply in relation to an employee if—

(a)    it is not reasonably practicable for a reason other than redundancy for the employer (who may be the same employer or a successor of his) to permit the employee to return to a job which is both suitable for the employee and appropriate for him to do in the circumstances;

(b)    an associated employer offers the employee a job of that kind, and

(c)    the employee accepts or unreasonably refuses that offer.

(6)    Where, on a complaint of unfair dismissal, any question arises as to whether the operation of paragraph (1) is excluded by the provisions of paragraph (4) or (5), it is for the employer to show that the provisions in question were satisfied in relation to the complainant.

## 30    Contractual rights to paternity or adoption leave

(1)  This regulation applies where an employee is entitled to —
  (a)    paternity leave,
  (b)    ordinary adoption leave, or
  (c)    additional adoption leave,

(referred to in paragraph (2) as a 'statutory right') and also to a right which corresponds to that right and which arises under the employee's contract of employment or otherwise.

(2)  In a case where this regulation applies —
  (a)    the employee may not exercise the statutory right and the corresponding right separately but may, in taking the leave for which the two rights provide, take advantage of whichever right is, in any particular respect, the more favourable, and
  (b)    the provisions of the 1996 Act and of these Regulations relating to the statutory right apply, subject to any modifications necessary to give effect to any more favourable contractual terms, to the exercise of the composite right described in sub-paragraph (a) as they apply to the exercise of the statutory right.

# AGENCY WORKERS REGULATIONS 2010
# (SI 2010 No. 93)

PART 1
GENERAL AND INTERPRETATION

## 2    Interpretation

In these Regulations —

'the 1996 Act' means the Employment Rights Act 1996;

'assignment' means a period of time during which an agency worker is supplied by one or more temporary work agencies to a hirer to work temporarily for and under the supervision and direction of the hirer;

'contract of employment' means a contract of service or of apprenticeship, whether express or implied, and (if it is express) whether oral or in writing;

'employee' means an individual who has entered into or works under or, where the employment has ceased, worked under a contract of employment;

'employer', in relation to an employee or worker, means the person by whom the employee or worker is (or where the employment has ceased, was) employed;

'employment' —
  (a)    in relation to an employee, means employment under a contract of employment, and
  (b)    in relation to a worker, means employment under that worker's contract,
and 'employed' shall be construed accordingly;

'hirer' means a person engaged in economic activity, public or private, whether or not operating for profit, to whom individuals are supplied, to work temporarily for and under the supervision and direction of that person; and

'worker' means an individual who is not an agency worker but who has entered into or works under (or where the employment has ceased, worked under) —
  (a)    a contract of employment, or
  (b)    any other contract, whether express or implied and (if it is express) whether oral or in writing, whereby the individual undertakes to do or perform personally any work or services for another party to the contract whose status is not by virtue of the contract that of a client or customer of any profession or business undertaking carried on by the individual,
and any reference to a worker's contract shall be construed accordingly.

## 3    The meaning of agency worker

(1)  In these Regulations 'agency worker' means an individual who —
  (a)    is supplied by a temporary work agency to work temporarily for and under the supervision and direction of a hirer; and

(b) has a contract with the temporary work agency which is—
    (i) a contract of employment with the agency, or
    (ii) any other contract with the agency to perform work or services personally.

(2) But an individual is not an agency worker if—
  (a) the contract the individual has with the temporary work agency has the effect that the status of the agency is that of a client or customer of a profession or business undertaking carried on by the individual; or
  (b) there is a contract, by virtue of which the individual is available to work for the hirer, having the effect that the status of the hirer is that of a client or customer of a profession or business undertaking carried on by the individual.

(3) For the purposes of paragraph (1)(a) an individual shall be treated as having been supplied by a temporary work agency to work temporarily for and under the supervision and direction of a hirer if—
  (a) the temporary work agency initiates or is involved as an intermediary in the making of the arrangements that lead to the individual being supplied to work temporarily for and under the supervision and direction of the hirer, and
  (b) the individual is supplied by an intermediary, or one of a number of intermediaries, to work temporarily for and under the supervision and direction of the hirer.

(4) An individual treated by virtue of paragraph (3) as having been supplied by a temporary work agency, shall be treated, for the purposes of paragraph (1)(b), as having a contract with the temporary work agency.

(5) An individual is not prevented from being an agency worker—
  (a) because the temporary work agency supplies the individual through one or more intermediaries;
  (b) because one or more intermediaries supply that individual;
  (c) because the individual is supplied pursuant to any contract or other arrangement between the temporary work agency, one or more intermediaries and the hirer;
  (d) because the temporary work agency pays for the services of the individual through one or more intermediaries; or
  (e) because the individual is employed by or otherwise has a contract with one or more intermediaries.

(6) Paragraph (5) does not prejudice the generality of paragraphs (1) to (4).

## 4 The meaning of temporary work agency

(1) In these Regulations 'temporary work agency' means a person engaged in the economic activity, public or private, whether or not operating for profit, and whether or not carrying on such activity in conjunction with others, of—
  (a) supplying individuals to work temporarily for and under the supervision and direction of hirers; or
  (b) paying for, or receiving or forwarding payment for, the services of individuals who are supplied to work temporarily for and under the supervision and direction of hirers.

(2) Notwithstanding paragraph (1)(b) a person is not a temporary work agency if the person is engaged in the economic activity of paying for, or receiving or forwarding payments for, the services of individuals regardless of whether the individuals are supplied to work for hirers.

PART 2
RIGHTS

## 5 Rights of agency workers in relation to the basic working and employment conditions

(1) Subject to regulation 7, an agency worker (A) shall be entitled to the same basic working and employment conditions as A would be entitled to for doing the same job had A been recruited by the hirer—
  (a) other than by using the services of a temporary work agency; and
  (b) at the time the qualifying period commenced.

(2) For the purposes of paragraph (1), the basic working and employment conditions are
  (a) where A would have been recruited as an employee, the relevant terms and conditions that are ordinarily included in the contracts of employees of the hirer;

       (b)    where A would have been recruited as a worker, the relevant terms and conditions that are ordinarily included in the contracts of workers of the hirer, whether by collective agreement or otherwise, including any variations in those relevant terms and conditions made at any time after the qualifying period commenced.

(3)   Paragraph (1) shall be deemed to have been complied with where—

       (a)    an agency worker is working under the same relevant terms and conditions as an employee who is a comparable employee, and

       (b)    the relevant terms and conditions of that comparable employee are terms and conditions ordinarily included in the contracts of employees, who are comparable employees of the hirer, whether by collective agreement or otherwise.

(4)   For the purposes of paragraph (3) an employee is a comparable employee in relation to an agency worker if at the time when the breach of paragraph (1) is alleged to take place—

       (a)    both that employee and the agency worker are—

            (i)    working for and under the supervision and direction of the hirer, and

            (ii)   engaged in the same or broadly similar work having regard, where relevant, to whether they have a similar level of qualification and skills; and

       (b)    the employee works or is based at the same establishment as the agency worker or, where there is no comparable employee working or based at that establishment who satisfies the requirements of sub-paragraph (a), works or is based at a different establishment and satisfies those requirements.

(5)   An employee is not a comparable employee if that employee's employment has ceased.

## 6    Relevant terms and conditions

(1)   In regulation 5(2) and (3) 'relevant terms and conditions' means terms and conditions relating to—

       (a)    pay;

       (b)    the duration of working time;

       (c)    night work;

       (d)    rest periods;

       (e)    rest breaks; and

       (f)    annual leave.

(2)   For the purposes of paragraph (1)(a), 'pay' means any sums payable to a worker of the hirer in connection with the worker's employment, including any fee, bonus, commission, holiday pay or other emolument referable to the employment, whether payable under contract or otherwise, but excluding any payments or rewards within paragraph (3).

(3)   Those payments or rewards are—

       (a)    any payment by way of occupational sick pay;

       (b)    any payment by way of a pension, allowance or gratuity in connection with the worker's retirement or as compensation for loss of office;

       (c)    any payment in respect of maternity, paternity, parental bereavement or adoption leave;

       (d)    any payment referable to the worker's redundancy;

       (e)    any payment or reward made pursuant to a financial participation scheme;

       (f)    any bonus, incentive payment or reward which is not directly attributable to the amount or quality of the work done by a worker, and which is given to a worker for a reason other than the amount or quality of work done such as to encourage the worker's loyalty or to reward the worker's long-term service;

       (g)    any payment for time off under Part 6 of the 1996 Act or section 169 of the Trade Union and Labour Relations (Consolidation) Act 1992 (payment for time off for carrying out trade union duties etc.);

       (h)    a guarantee payment under section 28 of the 1996 Act;

       (i)    any payment by way of an advance under an agreement for a loan or by way of an advance of pay (but without prejudice to the application of section 13 of the 1996 Act to any deduction made from the worker's wages in respect of any such advance);

       (j)    any payment in respect of expenses incurred by the worker in carrying out the employment; and

(k)    any payment to the worker otherwise than in that person's capacity as a worker.

(4)    For the purposes of paragraphs (2) and (3) any monetary value attaching to any payment or benefit in kind furnished to a worker by the hirer shall not be treated as pay of the worker except any voucher or stamp which is—

(a)    of fixed value expressed in monetary terms, and

(b)    capable of being exchanged (whether on its own or together with other vouchers, stamps or documents, and whether immediately or only after a time) for money, goods or services (or for any combination of two or more of those things).

(5)    In this regulation—

'financial participation scheme' means any scheme that offers workers of the hirer—

(a)    a distribution of shares or options, or

(b)    a share of profits in cash or in shares;

'night time', in relation to an individual, means—

(a)    a period—

(i)    the duration of which is not less than seven hours, and

(ii)    which includes the period between midnight and 5 a.m.,

which is determined for the purposes of these Regulations by a working time agreement, or

(b)    in default of such a determination, the period between 11 p.m. and 6 a.m.;

'night work' means work during night time;

'relevant training' means work experience provided pursuant to a training course or programme, training for employment, or both, other than work experience or training—

(a)    the immediate provider of which is an educational institution or a person whose main business is the provision of training, and

(b)    which is provided on a course run by that institution or person;

'rest period', in relation to an individual, means a period which is not working time, other than a rest break or leave to which that individual is entitled either under the Working Time Regulations 1998 or under the contract between that individual and the employer of that individual;

'working time', in relation to an individual means—

(a)    any period during which that individual is working, at the disposal of the employer of that individual and carrying out the activity or duties of that individual,

(b)    any period during which that individual is receiving relevant training, and

(c)    any additional period which is to be treated as working time for the purposes of the Working Time Regulations 1998 under a working time agreement; and

'working time agreement', in relation to an individual, means a workforce agreement within the meaning of regulation 2(1) of the Working Time Regulations 1998, which applies to the individual any provision of—

(a)    a collective agreement which forms part of a contract between that individual and the employer of that individual, or

(b)    any other agreement in writing which is legally enforceable as between the individual and the employer of that individual.

# 7    Qualifying period

(1)    Regulation 5 does not apply unless an agency worker has completed the qualifying period.

(2)    To complete the qualifying period the agency worker must work in the same role with the same hirer for 12 continuous calendar weeks, during one or more assignments.

(3)    For the purposes of this regulation and regulations 8 and 9, the agency worker works in 'the same role' unless—

(a)    the agency worker has started a new role with the same hirer, whether supplied by the same or by a different temporary work agency;

(b)    the work or duties that make up the whole or the main part of that new role are substantively different from the work or duties that made up the whole or the main part of the previous role; and

(c)    the temporary work agency has informed the agency worker in writing of the type of work the agency worker will be required to do in the new role.

(4)    For the purposes of this regulation, any week during the whole or part of which an agency worker works during an assignment is counted as a calendar week.

(5)   For the purposes of this regulation and regulations 8 and 9, when calculating whether any weeks completed with a particular hirer are continuous, where—
- (a)   the agency worker has started working during an assignment, and there is a break, either between assignments or during an assignment, when the agency worker is not working,
- (b)   paragraph (8) applies to that break, and
- (c)   the agency worker returns to work in the same role with the same hirer,

any continuous weeks during which the agency worker worked for that hirer before the break shall be carried forward and treated as continuous with any weeks during which the agency worker works for that hirer after the break.

(6)   For the purposes of this regulation and regulation 8, when calculating the number of weeks during which the agency worker has worked, where the agency worker has—
- (a)   started working in a role during an assignment, and
- (b)   is unable to continue working for a reason described in paragraph (8)(c) or (8)(d)(i), (ii) or (iii),

for the period that is covered by one or more such reasons, that agency worker shall be deemed to be working in that role with the hirer, for the original intended duration, or likely duration of the assignment, whichever is the longer.

(7)   Where—
- (a)   an assignment ends on grounds which are maternity grounds within the meaning of section 68A of the 1996 Act, and
- (b)   the agency worker is deemed to be working in that role in accordance with paragraph (6),

the fact that an agency worker is actually working in another role, whether for the same or a different hirer during the period mentioned in paragraph (6) or any part of that period, does not affect the operation of that paragraph.

(8)   This paragraph applies where there is a break between assignments, or during an assignment, when the agency worker is not working, and the break is—
- (a)   for any reason and the break is not more than six calendar weeks;
- (b)   wholly due to the fact that the agency worker is incapable of working in consequence of sickness or injury, and the requirements of paragraph (9) are satisfied;
- (c)   related to pregnancy, childbirth or maternity and is at a time in a protected period;
- (d)   wholly for the purpose of taking time off or leave, whether statutory or contractual, to which the agency worker is otherwise entitled which is—
  - (i)   ordinary, compulsory or additional maternity leave;
  - (ii)   ordinary or additional adoption leave;
  - (iii)   paternity leave;
  - (iv)   time off or other leave not listed in sub-paragraph (d)(i), (ii) or (iii); or
  - (v)   for more than one of the reasons listed in sub-paragraph (d)(i) to (iv);
- (e)   wholly due to the fact that the agency worker is required to attend at any place in pursuance of being summoned for service as a juror under the Juries Act 1974, the Coroners Act 1988, the Court of Session Act 1988 or the Criminal Procedure (Scotland) Act 1995, and the break is 28 calendar weeks or less;
- (f)   wholly due to a temporary cessation in the hirer's requirement for any worker to be present at the establishment and work in a particular role, for a pre-determined period of time according to the established custom and practices of the hirer; or
- (g)   wholly due to a strike, lock-out or other industrial action at the hirer's establishment; or
- (h)   wholly due to more than one of the reasons listed in sub-paragraphs (b), (c), (d), (e), (f) or (g).

(9)   Paragraph (8)(b) only applies where—
- (a)   the break is 28 calendar weeks or less;
- (b)   paragraph (8)(c) does not apply; and
- (c)   if required to do so by the temporary work agency, the agency worker has provided such written medical evidence as may reasonably be required.

(10) For the purposes of paragraph (8)(c), a protected period begins at the start of the pregnancy, and the protected period associated with any particular pregnancy ends at

the end of the 26 weeks beginning with childbirth or, if earlier, when the agency worker returns to work.

(11) For the purposes of paragraph (10) 'childbirth' means the birth of a living child or the birth of a child whether living or dead after 24 weeks of pregnancy.

(12) Time spent by an agency worker working during an assignment before 1st October 2011 does not count for the purposes of this regulation.

## 8    Completion of the qualifying period and continuation of the regulation 5 rights

Where an agency worker has completed the qualifying period with a particular hirer, the rights conferred by regulation 5 shall apply and shall continue to apply to that agency worker in relation to that particular hirer unless—

(a)    that agency worker is no longer working in the same role, within the meaning of regulation 7(3), with that hirer; or

(b)    there is a break between assignments, or during an assignment, when the agency worker is not working, to which regulation 7(8) does not apply.

## 9    Structure of assignments

(1)    Notwithstanding paragraphs (1) and (2) of regulation 7, and regulation 8, if paragraphs (3) and (4) apply an agency worker shall be treated as having completed the qualifying period from the time at which the agency worker would have completed the qualifying period but for the structure of the assignment or assignments mentioned in paragraph (3).

(2)    Notwithstanding paragraphs (1) and (2) of regulation 7, and regulation 8, if paragraphs (3) and (4) apply an agency worker who has completed the qualifying period and—

(a)    is no longer entitled to the rights conferred by regulation 5, but

(b)    would be so entitled but for the structure of the assignment or assignments mentioned in paragraph (3),

shall be treated as continuing to be entitled to those rights from the time at which the agency worker completed that period.

(3)    This paragraph applies when an agency worker has—

(a)    completed two or more assignments with a hirer (H),

(b)    completed at least one assignment with H and one or more earlier assignments with hirers connected to H, or

(c)    worked in more than two roles during an assignment with H, and on at least two occasions has worked in a role that was not the 'same role' as the previous role within the meaning of regulation 7(3).

(4)    This paragraph applies where—

(a)    the most likely explanation for the structure of the assignment, or assignments, mentioned in paragraph (3) is that H, or the temporary work agency supplying the agency worker to H, or, where applicable, H and one or more hirers connected to H, intended to prevent the agency worker from being entitled to, or from continuing to be entitled to, the rights conferred by regulation 5; and

(b)    the agency worker would be entitled to, or would continue to be entitled to, the rights conferred by regulation 5 in relation to H, but for that structure.

(5)    The following matters in particular shall be taken into account in determining whether the structure of the assignment or assignments mentioned in paragraph (3) shows that the most likely explanation for it is that mentioned in paragraph (4)(a)—

(a)    the length of the assignments;

(b)    the number of assignments with H and, where applicable, hirers connected to H;

(c)    the number of times the agency worker has worked in a new role with H and, where applicable, hirers connected to H, and that new role is not the 'same role' within the meaning of regulation 7(3);

(d)    the number of times the agency worker has returned to work in the same role within the meaning of regulation 7(3) with H and, where applicable, hirers connected to H;

(e)    the period of any break between assignments with H and, where applicable, hirers connected to H.

(6) For the purposes of this regulation hirers are connected to a hirer if one hirer (directly or indirectly) has control of the other hirer or a third person (directly or indirectly) has control of both hirers.

## 12 Rights of agency workers in relation to access to collective facilities and amenities

(1) An agency worker has during an assignment the right to be treated no less favourably than a comparable worker in relation to the collective facilities and amenities provided by the hirer.

(2) The rights conferred by paragraph (1) apply only if the less favourable treatment is not justified on objective grounds.

(3) 'Collective facilities and amenities' includes, in particular—
   (a)   canteen or other similar facilities;
   (b)   child care facilities; and
   (c)   transport services.

(4) For the purposes of paragraph (1) an individual is a comparable worker in relation to an agency worker if at the time when the breach of paragraph (1) is alleged to take place—
   (a)   both that individual and the agency worker are—
      (i)   working for and under the supervision and direction of the hirer, and
      (ii)   engaged in the same or broadly similar work having regard, where relevant, to whether they have a similar level of qualification and skills;
   (b)   that individual works or is based at the same establishment as the agency worker or, where there is no comparable worker working or based at that establishment who satisfies the requirements of sub-paragraph (a), works or is based at a different establishment and satisfies those requirements; and
   (c)   that individual is an employee of the hirer or, where there is no employee satisfying the requirements of sub-paragraphs (a) and (b), is a worker of the hirer and satisfies those requirements.

## 13 Rights of agency workers in relation to access to employment

(1) An agency worker has during an assignment the right to be informed by the hirer of any relevant vacant posts with the hirer, to give that agency worker the same opportunity as a comparable worker to find permanent employment with the hirer.

(2) For the purposes of paragraph (1) an individual is a comparable worker in relation to an agency worker if at the time when the breach of paragraph (1) is alleged to take place—
   (a)   both that individual and the agency worker are—
      (i)   working for and under the supervision and direction of the hirer, and
      (ii)   engaged in the same or broadly similar work having regard, where relevant, to whether they have a similar level of qualification and skills;
   (b)   that individual works or is based at the same establishment as the agency worker; and
   (c)   that individual is an employee of the hirer or, where there is no employee satisfying the requirements of sub-paragraphs (a) and (b), is a worker of the hirer and satisfies those requirements.

(3) For the purposes of paragraph (1), an individual is not a comparable worker if that individual's employment with the hirer has ceased.

(4) For the purposes of paragraph (1) the hirer may inform the agency worker by a general announcement in a suitable place in the hirer's establishment.

PART 3
LIABILITY, PROTECTIONS AND REMEDIES

## 14 Liability of temporary work agency and hirer

(1) Subject to paragraph (3)(a) a temporary work agency shall be liable for any breach of regulation 5, to the extent that it is responsible for that breach.

(2) The hirer shall be liable for any breach of regulation 5, to the extent that it is responsible for that breach.

(3)  A temporary work agency shall not be liable for a breach of regulation 5 where it is established that the temporary work agency—

    (a)  obtained, or has taken reasonable steps to obtain, relevant information from the hirer—

        (i)  about the basic working and employment conditions in force in the hirer;

        (ii)  if needed to assess compliance with regulation 5, about the relevant terms and conditions under which an employee of the hirer is working where—

        (aa)  that employee is considered to be a comparable employee in relation to that agency worker for the purposes of regulation 5(4), and

        (bb)  those terms and conditions are ordinarily included in the contract of such a comparable employee;

        and

        (iii)  which explains the basis on which it is considered that the employee referred to in sub-paragraph (ii)(aa) is a comparable employee;

    (b)  where it has received such information, has acted reasonably in determining what the agency worker's basic working and employment conditions should be at the end of the qualifying period and during the period after that until, in accordance with regulation 8, the agency worker ceases to be entitled to the rights conferred by regulation 5; and

    (c)  ensured that where it has responsibility for applying those basic working and employment conditions to the agency worker, that agency worker has been treated in accordance with the determination described in sub-paragraph (b),

and to the extent that the temporary work agency is not liable under this provision, the hirer shall be liable.

(4)  ...

(5)  Where more than one temporary work agency is a party to the proceedings, when deciding whether or not each temporary work agency is responsible in full or in part, the employment tribunal shall have regard to the extent to which each agency was responsible for the determination, or application, of any of the agency worker's basic working and employment conditions.

(6)  The hirer shall be liable for any breach of regulation 12 or 13.

(7)  In relation to the rights conferred by regulation 17—

    (a)  a temporary work agency shall be liable for any act, or any deliberate failure to act, of that temporary work agency; and

    (b)  the hirer shall be liable for any act, or any deliberate failure to act, of the hirer.

## 15   Restrictions on contracting out

Section 203 of the 1996 Act (restrictions on contracting out) shall apply in relation to these Regulations as if they were contained in that Act.

## 16   Right to receive information

(1)  An agency worker who considers that the hirer or a temporary work agency may have treated that agency worker in a manner which infringes a right conferred by regulation 5, may make a written request to the temporary work agency for a written statement containing information relating to the treatment in question.

(2)  A temporary work agency that receives such a request from an agency worker shall, within 28 days of receiving it, provide the agency worker with a written statement setting out—

    (a)  relevant information relating to the basic working and employment conditions of the workers of the hirer,

    (b)  the factors the temporary work agency considered when determining the basic working and employment conditions which applied to the agency worker at the time when the breach of regulation 5 is alleged to have taken place, and

    (c)  where the temporary work agency seeks to rely on regulation 5(3), relevant information which—

        (i)  explains the basis on which it is considered that an individual is a comparable employee, and

        (ii)  describes the relevant terms and conditions, which apply to that employee.

(3) If an agency worker has made a request under paragraph (1) and has not been provided with such a statement within 30 days of making that request, the agency worker may make a written request to the hirer for a written statement containing information relating to the relevant basic working and employment conditions of the workers of the hirer.

(4) A hirer that receives a request made in accordance with paragraph (3) shall, within 28 days of receiving it, provide the agency worker with such a statement.

(5) An agency worker who considers that the hirer may have treated that agency worker in a manner which infringes a right conferred by regulation 12 or 13, may make a written request to the hirer for a written statement containing information relating to the treatment in question.

(6) A hirer that receives such a request from an agency worker shall, within 28 days of receiving it, provide the agency worker with a written statement setting out—

(a) all relevant information relating to the rights of a comparable worker in relation to the rights mentioned in regulation 12 or, as the case may be, regulation 13, and

(b) the particulars of the reasons for the treatment of the agency worker in respect of the right conferred by regulation 12 or, as the case may be, regulation 13.

(7) Paragraphs (1) and (3) apply only to an agency worker who at the time that worker makes such a request is entitled to the right conferred by regulation 5.

(8) Information provided under this regulation, whether in the form of a written statement or otherwise, is admissible as evidence in any proceedings under these Regulations.

(9) If it appears to the tribunal in any proceedings under these Regulations—

(a) that a temporary work agency or the hirer (as the case may be) deliberately, and without reasonable excuse, failed to provide information, whether in the form of a written statement or otherwise, or

(b) that any written statement supplied is evasive or equivocal,

it may draw any inference which it considers it just and equitable to draw, including an inference that that temporary work agency or hirer (as the case may be) has infringed the right in question.

## 17   Unfair dismissal and the right not to be subjected to detriment

(1) An agency worker who is an employee and is dismissed shall be regarded as unfairly dismissed for the purposes of Part 10 of the 1996 Act if the reason (or, if more than one, the principal reason) for the dismissal is a reason specified in paragraph (3).

(2) An agency worker has the right not to be subjected to any detriment by, or as a result of, any act, or any deliberate failure to act, of a temporary work agency or the hirer, done on a ground specified in paragraph (3).

(3) The reasons or, as the case may be, grounds are—

(a) that the agency worker—

(i) brought proceedings under these Regulations;

(ii) gave evidence or information in connection with such proceedings brought by any agency worker;

(iii) made a request under regulation 16 for a written statement;

(iv) otherwise did anything under these Regulations in relation to a temporary work agency, hirer, or any other person;

(v) alleged that a temporary work agency or hirer has breached these Regulations;

(vi) refused (or proposed to refuse) to forgo a right conferred by these Regulations; or

(b) that the hirer or a temporary work agency believes or suspects that the agency worker has done or intends to do any of the things mentioned in sub-paragraph (a).

(4) Where the reason or principal reason for subjection to any act or deliberate failure to act is that mentioned in paragraph (3)(a)(v), or paragraph 3(b) so far as it relates to paragraph (3)(a)(v), neither paragraph (1) nor paragraph (2) applies if the allegation made by the agency worker is false and not made in good faith.

(5) Paragraph (2) does not apply where the detriment in question amounts to a dismissal of an employee within the meaning of Part 10 of the 1996 Act.

## 18 Complaints to employment tribunals etc.

(1) In this regulation 'respondent' includes the hirer and any temporary work agency.

(2) Subject to regulation 17(5), an agency worker may present a complaint to an employment tribunal that a temporary work agency or the hirer has infringed a right conferred on the agency worker by regulation 5, 12, 13 or 17 (2).

(4) Subject to paragraph (5), an employment tribunal shall not consider a complaint under this regulation unless it is presented before the end of the period of three months beginning—

    (a) in the case of an alleged infringement of a right conferred by regulation 5, 12 or 17(2), with the date of the infringement, detriment or breach to which the complaint relates or, where an act or failure to act is part of a series of similar acts or failures comprising the infringement, detriment or breach, the last of them;

    (b) in the case of an alleged infringement of the right conferred by regulation 13, with the date, or if more than one the last date, on which other individuals, whether or not employed by the hirer, were informed of the vacancy.

(4A) Regulation 18A (extension of time limits to facilitate conciliation before institution of proceedings) applies for the purposes of paragraph (4).

(5) A tribunal may consider any such complaint which is out of time if, in all the circumstances of the case, it considers that it is just and equitable to do so.

(6) For the purposes of calculating the date of the infringement, detriment or breach, under paragraph (4)(a)—

    (a) where a term in a contract infringes a right conferred by regulation 5, 12 or 17(2), that infringement or breach shall be treated, subject to subparagraph (b), as taking place on each day of the period during which the term infringes that right or breaches that duty;

    (b) a deliberate failure to act that is contrary to regulation 5, 12 or 17(2) shall be treated as done when it was decided on.

(7) In the absence of evidence establishing the contrary, a person (P) shall be taken for the purposes of paragraph (6)(b) to decide not to act—

    (a) when P does an act inconsistent with doing the failed act; or

    (b) if P has done no such inconsistent act, when the period expires within which P might reasonably have been expected to have done the failed act if it was to be done.

(8) Where an employment tribunal finds that a complaint presented to it under this regulation is well founded, it shall take such of the following steps as it considers just and equitable—

    (a) making a declaration as to the rights of the complainant in relation to the matters to which the complaint relates;

    (b) ordering the respondent to pay compensation to the complainant;

    (c) recommending that the respondent take, within a specified period, action appearing to the tribunal to be reasonable, in all the circumstances of the case, for the purpose of obviating or reducing the adverse effect on the complainant of any matter to which the complaint relates.

(9) Where a tribunal orders compensation under paragraph (8)(b), and there is more than one respondent, the amount of compensation payable by each or any respondent shall be such as may be found by the tribunal to be just and equitable having regard to the extent of each respondent's responsibility for the infringement to which the complaint relates.

(10) Subject to paragraphs (12) and (13), where a tribunal orders compensation under paragraph (8)(b), the amount of the compensation awarded shall be such as the tribunal considers just and equitable in all the circumstances having regard to—

    (a) the infringement or breach to which the complaint relates; and

    (b) any loss which is attributable to the infringement.

(11) The loss shall be taken to include—

    (a) any expenses reasonably incurred by the complainant in consequence of the infringement or breach; and

    (b)    loss of any benefit which the complainant might reasonably be expected to have had but for the infringement or breach.

(12)  Subject to paragraph (13), where a tribunal orders compensation under paragraph (8)(b), any compensation which relates to an infringement or breach of the rights—

    (a)    conferred by regulation 5; or

    (b)    conferred by regulation 17(2) to the extent that the infringement or breach relates to regulation 5,

shall not be less than two weeks' pay, calculated in accordance with regulation 19.

(13)  Paragraph (12) does not apply where the tribunal considers that in all the circumstances of the case, taking into account the conduct of the claimant and respondent, two weeks' pay is not a just and equitable amount of compensation, and the amount shall be reduced as the tribunal consider appropriate.

(14)  Where a tribunal finds that regulation 9(4) applies and orders compensation under paragraph (8)(b), the tribunal may make an additional award of compensation under paragraph 8(b), which shall not be more than £5,000, and where there is more than one respondent the proportion of any additional compensation awarded that is payable by each of them shall be such as the tribunal considers just and equitable having regard to the extent to which it considers each to have been responsible for the fact that regulation 9(4)(a) applies.

(14A)  In relation to an infringement or breach for which a tribunal orders a respondent to pay compensation under paragraph (8)(b), the tribunal may order the respondent also to pay a penalty under section 12A of the Employment Tribunals Act 1996 only if the tribunal decides not to exercise the power under paragraph (14) to make an additional award of compensation against the respondent.

(15)  Compensation in respect of treating an agency worker in a manner which infringes the right conferred by regulation 5, 12 or 13, shall not include compensation for injury to feelings.

(16)  In ascertaining the loss the tribunal shall apply the same rule concerning the duty of a person to mitigate loss as applies to damages recoverable under the common law of England and Wales or (as the case may be) the law of Scotland.

(17)  Where the tribunal finds that the act, or failure to act, to which the complaint relates was to any extent caused or contributed to by action of the complainant, it shall reduce the amount of the compensation by such proportion as it considers just and equitable having regard to that finding.

(18)  If a temporary work agency or the hirer fails, without reasonable justification, to comply with a recommendation made by an employment tribunal under paragraph (8)(c) the tribunal may, if it thinks it just and equitable to do so—

    (a)    increase the amount of compensation required to be paid to the complainant in respect of the complaint, where an order was made under paragraph (8)(b); or

    (b)    make an order under paragraph (8)(b).

## 18A  Extension of time limit to facilitate conciliation before institution of proceedings

(1)  In this regulation—

    (a)    Day A is the day on which the worker concerned complies with the requirement in subsection (1) of section 18A of the Employment Tribunals Act 1996 (requirement to contact ACAS before instituting proceedings) in relation to the matter in respect of which the proceedings are brought, and

    (b)    Day B is the day on which the worker concerned receives or, if earlier, is treated as receiving (by virtue of regulations made under subsection (11) of that section) the certificate issued under subsection (4) of that section.

(2)  In working out when the time limit set by regulation 18(4) expires the period beginning with the day after Day A and ending with Day B is not to be counted.

(3)  If the time limit set by regulation 18(4) would (if not extended by this paragraph) expire during the period beginning with Day A and ending one month after Day B, the time limit expires instead at the end of that period.

(4)  The power conferred on the employment tribunal by regulation 18(5) to extend the time limit set by paragraph (4) of that regulation is exercisable in relation to that time limit as extended by this regulation.

## 19    Calculating a week's pay

(1)    For the purposes of regulation 18(12)—

    (a)    a week's pay shall be the higher of—

        (i)    the average weekly pay received by the agency worker, in relation to the assignment to which the claim relates, in the relevant period; and

        (ii)    the average weekly pay the agency worker should have been receiving by virtue of regulation 5, in relation to the assignment to which the claim relates, in the relevant period; and

    (b)    for the purposes of this paragraph, only payments in respect of basic pay whether by way of annual salary, payments for actual time worked or by reference to output or otherwise shall be taken into account.

(2)    The relevant period is—

    (a)    where the assignment has ended on or before the date the complaint was presented to the tribunal under regulation 18(2), the four week period (or in a case where the assignment was shorter than four weeks, that period) ending with the last day of the assignment to which the claim relates; or

    (b)    where the assignment has not so ended the four week period (or in the case where that assignment was shorter than four weeks, that period) ending with the date of the complaint.

## 20    Liability of employers and principals

(1)    Anything done by a person in the course of employment shall be treated for the purposes of these Regulations as also done by their employer, whether or not it was done with that employer's knowledge or approval.

(2)    Anything done by a person as agent for the employer with the authority of the employer shall be treated for the purposes of these Regulations as also done by the employer.

(3)    In proceedings under these Regulations against any person in respect of an act alleged to have been done by an employee of that person, it shall be a defence for that person to prove that he or she took such steps as were reasonably practicable to prevent the employee from—

    (a)    doing that act; or

    (b)    doing, in the course of his or her employment, acts of that description.

# EXCLUSIVITY TERMS IN ZERO HOURS CONTRACTS (REDRESS) REGULATIONS 2015
# (SI 2015 No. 2021)

## 2    Unfair dismissal and the right not to be subjected to detriment

(1)    An employee who works under a zero hours contract is to be regarded for the purposes of Part 10 of the 1996 Act as unfairly dismissed if the reason (or, if more than one, the principal reason) for the dismissal is the reason specified in paragraph (3).

(2)    A worker who works under a zero hours contract has the right not to be subjected to any detriment by, or as a result of, any act, or any deliberate failure to act, of an employer done for the reason specified in paragraph (3).

(3)    The reason is that the worker breached a provision or purported provision of the zero hours contract to which section 27A(3)(1) of the 1996 Act applies.

(4)    Paragraph (2) does not apply where the detriment in question amounts to a dismissal of an employee within the meaning of Part 10 of the 1996 Act.

(5)    Section 108 of the 1996 Act (qualifying period of employment) does not apply in relation to a dismissal to which paragraph (1) applies.

## 3    Complaints to employment tribunals

(1)    Subject to regulation 2(4), a worker may present a complaint to an employment tribunal that an employer has infringed the right conferred on the worker by regulation 2(2).

(2)    Subject to paragraph (3), an employment tribunal must not consider a complaint under this regulation unless it is presented before the end of the period of three months

beginning with the date of the act or failure to act to which the complaint relates or, where that act or failure is part of a series of similar acts or failures, the last of them.

(3) A tribunal may consider any such complaint which is out of time if, in all the circumstances of the case, it considers that it is just and equitable to do so.

(4) For the purposes of paragraph (2)—

    (a) where an act extends over a period, the 'date of the act' means the last day of that period; and

    (b) failure to do something is to be treated as occurring when the person in question decided on it.

(5) In the absence of evidence to the contrary, a person (P) is to be taken to decide on failure to do something—

    (a) when P does an act inconsistent with doing it, or

    (b) if P does no inconsistent act, on the expiry of the period in which P might reasonably have been expected to do it.

(6) Where a worker presents a complaint under this regulation it is for the employer to identify the ground on which any act, or deliberate failure to act, was done.

## 4     Remedies

(1) Where an employment tribunal finds that a complaint presented to it under regulation 3 is well founded, it must take such of the following steps as it considers just and equitable—

    (a) making a declaration as to the rights of the complainant and the employer in relation to the matters to which the complaint relates; and

    (b) ordering the employer to pay compensation to the complainant.

(2) Subject to paragraphs (5) and (6), where a tribunal orders compensation under paragraph (1)(b), the amount of the compensation awarded must be such as the tribunal considers just and equitable in all the circumstances having regard to—

    (a) the infringement to which the complaint relates; and

    (b) any loss which is attributable to the act, or failure to act, which infringed the complainant's right.

(3) The loss must be taken to include—

    (a) any expenses reasonably incurred by the complainant in consequence of the act, or failure to act, to which the complaint relates; and

    (b) loss of any benefit which the complainant might reasonably be expected to have had but for that act or failure to act.

(4) In ascertaining the loss the tribunal must apply the same rule concerning the duty of a person to mitigate loss as applies to damages recoverable under the common law of England and Wales or (as the case may be) the law of Scotland.

(5) Where—

    (a) the detriment to which the worker is subjected is the termination of the worker's contract, but

    (b) that contract is not a contract of employment,

any compensation awarded under paragraph (1)(b) must not exceed the limit specified in paragraph (6).

(6) The limit is the total of—

    (a) the sum which would be the basic award for unfair dismissal, calculated in accordance with section 119 of the 1996 Act, if the worker had been an employee and the contract terminated had been a contract of employment; and

    (b) the sum for the time being specified in section 124(1ZA)(1) of the 1996 Act which is the limit for a compensatory award to a person calculated in accordance with section 123 of the 1996 Act.

(7) Where the tribunal finds that the act, or failure to act, to which the complaint relates was to any extent caused or contributed to by action of the complainant, it must reduce the amount of the compensation by such proportion as it considers just and equitable having regard to that finding.

# EQUALITY ACT 2010 (GENDER PAY GAP INFORMATION) REGULATIONS 2017
## (SI 2017 No. 172)

**2    Duty to publish annual information relating to pay**

(1)    A relevant employer must publish, for 2017 and each subsequent year, the following information—

    (a)    the difference between the mean hourly rate of pay of male full-pay relevant employees and that of female full-pay relevant employees (see regulation 8);

    (b)    the difference between the median hourly rate of pay of male full-pay relevant employees and that of female full-pay relevant employees (see regulation 9);

    (c)    the difference between the mean bonus pay paid to male relevant employees and that paid to female relevant employees (see regulation 10);

    (d)    the difference between the median bonus pay paid to male relevant employees and that paid to female relevant employees (see regulation 11);

    (e)    the proportions of male and female relevant employees who were paid bonus pay (see regulation 12); and

    (f)    the proportions of male and female full-pay relevant employees in the lower, lower middle, upper middle and upper quartile pay bands (see regulation 13).

(2)    The relevant employer must publish the information required by paragraph (1) within the period of 12 months beginning with the snapshot date.

(3)    In compiling the information required by paragraph (1), the relevant employer is not required to include data relating to a relevant employee if—

    (a)    the employee is employed under a contract personally to do work, and

    (b)    the employer does not have, and it is not reasonably practicable for the employer to obtain, the data.

**14    Information to be accompanied by signed statement**

(1)    The information published under regulation 2 must be accompanied by a written statement which—

    (a)    confirms that the information is accurate; and

    (b)    is signed in accordance with paragraph (2).

(2)    Where the relevant employer is—

    (a)    a body corporate other than a limited liability partnership within the meaning of the Limited Liability Partnerships Act 2000, the written statement must be signed by a director (or equivalent);

    (b)    a limited liability partnership, the written statement must be signed by a designated member (see section 8 of that Act);

    (c)    the partners in a limited partnership registered under the Limited Partnerships Act 1907, the written statement must be signed by a general partner (see section 3 of that Act);

    (d)    the partners in any other kind of partnership, the written statement must be signed by a partner;

    (e)    the members or officers of an unincorporated body of persons other than a partnership, the written statement must be signed by a member of the governing body or a senior officer;

    (f)    any other type of body, the written statement must be signed by the most senior employee.

(3)    In this regulation, 'partnership' means—

    (a)    a partnership within the Partnership Act 1890;

    (b)    a limited partnership registered under the Limited Partnerships Act 1907; or

    (c)    a firm, or an entity of a similar character, formed under the law of a country outside the United Kingdom.

**15    Form and manner of publication**

(1)    The requirement in regulation 2 to publish information, and the requirement in regulation 14 for the information to be accompanied by a written statement, are requirements that that information and statement be published on the employer's website—

    (a)    in a manner that is accessible to all its employees and to the public; and

    (b)    for a period of at least three years beginning with the date of publication.

(2)   A relevant employer must also publish on a website designated for that purpose by the Secretary of State—

    (a)    the information required by regulation 2, and

    (b)    the name and job title of the person who signed the statement required by regulation 14.

# PARENTAL BEREAVEMENT LEAVE REGULATIONS 2020
## (SI 2020 No. 249)

**4     Entitlement to parental bereavement leave**

(1)   An employee is entitled to be absent from work to take parental bereavement leave if he or she—

    (a)    satisfies one of the conditions specified in paragraph (2), and

    (b)    complies with the notice requirements in regulation 6.

(2)   The conditions referred to in paragraph (1) are that, at the date of C's death, the employee is—

    (a)    C's parent;

    (b)    C's natural parent and named in an order made pursuant to section 51A(2)(a) of the Adoption and Children Act 2002 or section 11(3)(aa) of the Children (Scotland) Act 1995, provided that such an order has not subsequently been revoked or discharged;

    (c)    a person with whom C has been placed for adoption, for so long as that placement has not been disrupted, as mentioned in paragraph (3);

    (d)    an adopter—

        (i)    with whom C was living, following C's entry into Great Britain from outside the United Kingdom in connection with or for the purposes of adoption which does not involve the placement of C for adoption under the law of any part of the United Kingdom, and

        (ii)   who has received official notification in respect of C;

    (e)    an intended parent of C;

    (f)    C's parent in fact; or

    (g)    the partner of P.

(3)   For the purposes of paragraph (2)(c), a placement has been disrupted—

    (a)    when C has been returned under sections 31 to 35 of the Adoption and Children Act 2002,

    (b)    in Scotland, when C has been returned to the adoption agency, adoption society or nominated person in accordance with section 25(6) of the Adoption and Children (Scotland) Act 2007, or

    (c)    when C's placement—

        (i)    with a local authority foster parent who is also a prospective adopter in accordance with section 22C of the Children Act 1989 following consideration in accordance with subsection (9B)(c) of that section, or

        (ii)   with a prospective adopter in accordance with section 81 of the Social Services and Well-being (Wales) Act 2014, has been terminated.

(4)   Subject to paragraph (6), a person is C's parent in fact if that person, for a continuous period of at least four weeks ending with the day on which C dies—

    (a)    lived with C in the person's own home, and

    (b)    had day to day responsibility for C's care.

(5)   For the purposes of the continuous period mentioned in paragraph (4), no account is to be taken of any absences of a temporary or intermittent nature.

(6)   A person is not to be regarded as C's parent in fact if—

    (a)    C is in the care of that person in premises in which any parent of C's, or any person who is not a parent of C's but who has responsibility for C, is living, or

    (b)    that person was or is entitled to receive remuneration, whether by way of wages or otherwise, in respect of the care of C.

(7)   A person has responsibility for C, for the purposes of paragraph (6)(a), if the person—
  (a)   has parental responsibility, within the meaning of section 3 of the Children Act 1989, or
  (b)   in Scotland, has parental responsibilities or parental rights, within the meaning of sections 1 and 2 of the Children (Scotland) Act 1995.
(8)   For the purposes of paragraph (6)(b), the following payments are not to be regarded as remuneration—
  (a)   any fee or allowance paid by a local authority to a foster parent;
  (b)   payments wholly or mainly intended to reimburse the person for expenses which arise from, or are expected to arise from, the person's care of C;
  (c)   amounts received pursuant to the terms of a will, trust or similar instrument which makes provision in respect of C's care.
(9)   In this regulation—
  (a)   'P' means any person who satisfies one of the conditions in paragraph (2)(a) to (f);
  (b)   'partner' means a person (whether of a different sex or the same sex) who lives with C and P in an enduring family relationship but is not a relative of P of a kind specified in sub-paragraph (c);
  (c)   the relatives of P referred to in sub-paragraph (b) are P's parent, grandparent, sister, brother, aunt or uncle;
  (d)   references to relationships in sub-paragraph (c)—
    (i)   are to relationships of the full blood or half blood or, in the case of an adopted person, such of those relationships as would exist but for the adoption, and
    (ii)   include the relationship of a child with his adoptive, or former adoptive, parents,
    but do not include any other adoptive relationships.
(10)   Where an employee is eligible to take parental bereavement leave under this regulation as a result of the death of more than one child, the employee is entitled to parental bereavement leave in respect of each child.

**5      Options in respect of parental bereavement leave**
(1)   The minimum period of parental bereavement leave which may be taken by an employee is one week.
(2)   An employee may choose to take either one or two weeks' parental bereavement leave.
(3)   Where an employee chooses to take two weeks' parental bereavement leave, the weeks need not be consecutive.
(4)   Parental bereavement leave may be taken at any time within the period of 56 weeks beginning with the date of C's death.
(5)   Paragraphs (1), (2) and (3) of this regulation are subject to regulation 8.

# CODE OF PRACTICE

## ACAS — DISCIPLINARY AND GRIEVANCE PROCEDURES – CODE OF PRACTICE 1

### Introduction

1.      This Code is designed to help employers, employees and their representatives deal with disciplinary and grievance situations in the workplace.

- Disciplinary situations include misconduct and/or poor performance. If employers have a separate capability procedure they may prefer to address performance issues under this procedure. If so, however, the basic principles of fairness set out in this Code should still be followed, albeit that they may need to be adapted.
- Grievances are concerns, problems or complaints that employees raise with their employers.

The Code does not apply to redundancy dismissals or the non renewal of fixed term contracts on their expiry.

2.      Fairness and transparency are promoted by developing and using rules and procedures for handling disciplinary and grievance situations. These should be set down in writing, be specific and clear. Employees and, where appropriate, their representatives should be involved in the development of rules and procedures. It is also important to help employees and managers understand what the rules and procedures are, where they can be found and how they are to be used.

3.      Where some form of formal action is needed, what action is reasonable or justified will depend on all the circumstances of the particular case. Employment tribunals will take the size and resources of an employer into account when deciding on relevant cases and it may sometimes not be practicable for all employers to take all of the steps set out in this Code.

4.      That said, whenever a disciplinary or grievance process is being followed it is important to deal with issues fairly. There are a number of elements to this:

- Employers and employees should raise and deal with issues **promptly** and should not unreasonably delay meetings, decisions or confirmation of those decisions.
- Employers and employees should act **consistently**.
- Employers should carry out any necessary **investigations**, to establish the facts of the case.
- Employers should **inform** employees of the basis of the problem and give them an opportunity to **put their case** in response before any decisions are made.
- Employers should allow employees to be **accompanied** at any formal disciplinary or grievance meeting.
- Employers should allow an employee to **appeal** against any formal decision made.

DISCIPLINE

*Keys to handling disciplinary issues in the workplace*

### Establish the facts of each case

5.      It is important to carry out necessary investigations of potential disciplinary matters without unreasonable delay to establish the facts of the case. In some cases this will require the holding of an investigatory meeting with the employee before proceeding to any disciplinary hearing. In others, the investigatory stage will be the collation of evidence by the employer for use at any disciplinary hearing.

6.      In misconduct cases, where practicable, different people should carry out the investigation and disciplinary hearing.

7.      If there is an investigatory meeting this should not by itself result in any disciplinary action. Although there is no statutory right for an employee to be accompanied at a formal investigatory meeting, such a right may be allowed under an employer's own procedure.

8.      In cases where a period of suspension with pay is considered necessary, this period should be as brief as possible, should be kept under review and it should be made clear that this suspension is not considered a disciplinary action.

## Inform the employee of the problem

9.      If it is decided that there is a disciplinary case to answer, the employee should be notified of this in writing. This notification should contain sufficient information about the alleged misconduct or poor performance and its possible consequences to enable the employee to prepare to answer the case at a disciplinary meeting. It would normally be appropriate to provide copies of any written evidence, which may include any witness statements, with the notification.

10.     The notification should also give details of the time and venue for the disciplinary meeting and advise the employee of their right to be accompanied at the meeting.

## Hold a meeting with the employee to discuss the problem

11.     The meeting should be held without unreasonable delay whilst allowing the employee reasonable time to prepare their case.

12.     Employers and employees (and their companions) should make every effort to attend the meeting. At the meeting the employer should explain the complaint against the employee and go through the evidence that has been gathered. The employee should be allowed to set out their case and answer any allegations that have been made. The employee should also be given a reasonable opportunity to ask questions, present evidence and call relevant witnesses. They should also be given an opportunity to raise points about any information provided by witnesses. Where an employer or employee intends to call relevant witnesses they should give advance notice that they intend to do this.

## Allow the employee to be accompanied at the meeting

13.     Workers have a statutory right to be accompanied by a companion where the disciplinary meeting could result in:
   • a formal warning being issued; or
   • the taking of some other disciplinary action; or
   • the confirmation of a warning or some other disciplinary action (appeal hearings).

14.     The chosen companion may be a fellow worker, a trade union representative, or an official employed by a trade union. A trade union representative who is not an employed official must have been certified by their union as being competent to accompany a worker.

15.     To exercise the statutory right to be accompanied workers must make a reasonable request. What is reasonable will depend on the circumstances of each individual case. However, it would not normally be reasonable for workers to insist on being accompanied by a companion whose presence would prejudice the hearing nor would it be reasonable for a worker to ask to be accompanied by a companion from a remote geographical location if someone suitable and willing was available on site.

16.     The companion should be allowed to address the hearing to put and sum up the worker's case, respond on behalf of the worker to any views expressed at the meeting and confer with the worker during the hearing. The companion does not, however, have the right to answer questions on the worker's behalf, address the hearing if the worker does not wish it or prevent the employer from explaining their case.

## Decide on appropriate action

17.     After the meeting decide whether or not disciplinary or any other action is justified and inform the employee accordingly in writing.

18.     Where misconduct is confirmed or the employee is found to be performing unsatisfactorily it is usual to give the employee a written warning. A further act of misconduct or failure to improve performance within a set period would normally result in a final written warning.

19.     If an employee's first misconduct or unsatisfactory performance is sufficiently serious, it may be appropriate to move directly to a final written warning. This might occur where the employee's actions have had, or are liable to have, a serious or harmful impact on the organisation.

20.     A first or final written warning should set out the nature of the misconduct or poor performance and the change in behaviour or improvement in performance required (with timescale). The employee should be told how long the warning will remain current. The

employee should be informed of the consequences of further misconduct, or failure to improve performance, within the set period following a final warning. For instance that it may result in dismissal or some other contractual penalty such as demotion or loss of seniority.

21.     A decision to dismiss should only be taken by a manager who has the authority to do so. The employee should be informed as soon as possible of the reasons for the dismissal, the date on which the employment contract will end, the appropriate period of notice and their right of appeal.

22.     Some acts, termed gross misconduct, are so serious in themselves or have such serious consequences that they may call for dismissal without notice for a first offence. But a fair disciplinary process should always be followed, before dismissing for gross misconduct.

23.     Disciplinary rules should give examples of acts which the employer regards as acts of gross misconduct. These may vary according to the nature of the organisation and what it does, but might include things such as theft or fraud, physical violence, gross negligence or serious insubordination.

24.     Where an employee is persistently unable or unwilling to attend a disciplinary meeting without good cause the employer should make a decision on the evidence available.

## Provide employees with an opportunity to appeal

25.     Where an employee feels that disciplinary action taken against them is wrong or unjust they should appeal against the decision. Appeals should be heard without unreasonable delay and ideally at an agreed time and place. Employees should let employers know the grounds for their appeal in writing.

26.     The appeal should be dealt with impartially and wherever possible, by a manager who has not previously been involved in the case.

27.     Workers have a statutory right to be accompanied at appeal hearings.

28.     Employees should be informed in writing of the results of the appeal hearing as soon as possible.

## Special cases

29.     Where disciplinary action is being considered against an employee who is a trade union representative the normal disciplinary procedure should be followed. Depending on the circumstances, however, it is advisable to discuss the matter at an early stage with an official employed by the union, after obtaining the employee's agreement.

30.     If an employee is charged with, or convicted of a criminal offence this is not normally in itself reason for disciplinary action. Consideration needs to be given to what effect the charge or conviction has on the employee's suitability to do the job and their relationship with their employer, work colleagues and customers.

GRIEVANCE

*Keys to handling grievances in the workplace*

## Let the employer know the nature of the grievance

31.     If it is not possible to resolve a grievance informally employees should raise the matter formally and without unreasonable delay with a manager who is not the subject of the grievance. This should be done in writing and should set out the nature of the grievance.

## Hold a meeting with the employee to discuss the grievance

32.     Employers should arrange for a formal meeting to be held without unreasonable delay after a grievance is received.

33.     Employers, employees and their companions should make every effort to attend the meeting. Employees should be allowed to explain their grievance and how they think it should be resolved. Consideration should be given to adjourning the meeting for any investigation that may be necessary.

## Allow the employee to be accompanied at the meeting

34.     Workers have a statutory right to be accompanied by a companion at a grievance meeting which deals with a complaint about a duty owed by the employer to the worker. So this would apply where the complaint is, for example, that the employer is not honouring the worker's contract, or is in breach of legislation.

35.    The chosen companion may be a fellow worker, a trade union representative or an official employed by a trade union. A trade union representative who is not an employed official must have been certified by their union as being competent to accompany a worker.

36.    To exercise the right to be accompanied a worker must first make a reasonable request. What is reasonable will depend on the circumstances of each individual case. However it would not normally be reasonable for workers to insist on being accompanied by a companion whose presence would prejudice the hearing nor would it be reasonable for a worker to ask to be accompanied by a companion from a remote geographical location if someone suitable and willing was available on site.

37.    The companion should be allowed to address the hearing to put and sum up the worker's case, respond on behalf of the worker to any views expressed at the meeting and confer with the worker during the hearing. The companion does not however, have the right to answer questions on the worker's behalf, address the hearing if the worker does not wish it or prevent the employer from explaining their case.

## Decide on appropriate action

38.    Following the meeting decide on what action, if any, to take. Decisions should be communicated to the employee, in writing, without unreasonable delay and, where appropriate, should set out what action the employer intends to take to resolve the grievance. The employee should be informed that they can appeal if they are not content with the action taken.

## Allow the employee to take the grievance further if not resolved

39.    Where an employee feels that their grievance has not been satisfactorily resolved they should appeal. They should let their employer know the grounds for their appeal without unreasonable delay and in writing.

40.    Appeals should be heard without unreasonable delay and at a time and place which should be notified to the employee in advance.

41.    The appeal should be dealt with impartially and wherever possible by a manager who has not previously been involved in the case.

42.    Workers have a statutory right to be accompanied at any such appeal hearing.

43.    The outcome of the appeal should be communicated to the employee in writing without unreasonable delay.

## Overlapping grievance and disciplinary cases

44.    Where an employee raises a grievance during a disciplinary process the disciplinary process may be temporarily suspended in order to deal with the grievance. Where the grievance and disciplinary cases are related it may be appropriate to deal with both issues concurrently.

## Collective grievances

45.    The provisions of this code do not apply to grievances raised on behalf of two or more employees by a representative of a recognised trade union or other appropriate workplace representative. These grievances should be handled in accordance with the organisation's collective grievance process.

# INDEX

Printed in the USA
CPSIA information can be obtained
at www.ICGtesting.com
LVHW080835171024
794056LV00006B/1354